'I know of no *Letters* which capture so movingly the arc of a man's life: the book is like a prose version of a medieval wheel-of-fortune tragedy. Yet even to the end there remains a residual belief in grace and gaiety.'

Michael Billington, *Guardian*

'He had been the wittiest, the most feared theatre critic of his generation. He had been a stylish polemicist, with a devastating line in relaxed insolence. He had insisted with passion on the importance of high definition performance ... He himself was rebel, clown and loner to the last.'

Ian McIntyre, *The Times*

'This huge collection of Tynan's letters, edited with love and care by his widow, contains a few examples of that ability to get things wrong, but many more examples of his intellectual energy and his enthusiasm for the theatre ... They make lively reading.'

Charles Osborne, *Sunday Telegraph*

'What was brilliant about him is that no subject on earth was out of bounds. Not despair, not desire, not hope, not life between the sheets. He chose the life of the intellectual and he was prepared to go all the way.'

Neroli Lawson, *Evening Standard*

'Kathleen Tynan has made Herculean efforts in editing her late husband's correspondence, and on the evidence of the *Kenneth Tynan Letters* it was time well spent.'

Anthony Quinn, *Independent*

'The elegant style and sheer width of Kenneth Tynan permeates every single [letter]: the entire collection is a total delight.'

Joseph Connolly, *Hampstead & Highgate Express*

KENNETH TYNAN
LETTERS

Kathleen Tynan, novelist, journalist
and screenwriter, was the author of
The Summer Aeroplane and *Agatha*.
Her biography of her husband,
The Life of Kenneth Tynan,
was published to great acclaim in 1987.
Kathleen Tynan died in 1995.

KENNETH TYNAN
LETTERS

EDITED BY

Kathleen Tynan

Minerva

A Minerva Paperback
KENNETH TYNAN LETTERS

First published in Great Britain 1994
by Weidenfeld & Nicolson
This Minerva edition published 1995
by Mandarin Paperbacks
an imprint of Reed International Books Ltd
Michelin House, 81 Fulham Road, London sw3 6rb
and Auckland, Melbourne, Singapore and Toronto

Reprinted 1995

Copyright © 1994 by Kathleen Tynan
The author has asserted her moral rights

A CIP catalogue record for this title
is available from the British Library
ISBN 0 7493 9586 9

Printed and bound in Great Britain
by Clays Ltd, St Ives plc

CONTENTS

ILLUSTRATIONS

Frontispiece: Kenneth Tynan *(Observer)*

Between pages 144 and 145

The first letter from Orson Welles, 1943 (Estate of Orson Welles)
Julian Holland, 1943
Ken as Hamlet, Birmingham, 1945 (Logan, Birmingham)
Ken with Pauline Whittle in Bournemouth, 1945
Ken while at Oxford (H.J. Whitlock & Sons Ltd)
A doodle from Ken's Oxford notebook
Ken as Judge Gaunt in his production of Maxwell Anderson's *Winterset*, 1948 (Kenneth Parker)
The ad for Ken's production of *Samson Agonistes*, Oxford, 1947
Ken at Cheltenham, 1948 (Hugo van Wadenoyen)
Ken's eighteenth-century designs for his Oxford production of *Hamlet* at Cheltenham, 1948
Ken's twenty-first birthday party, April 1948 (Mirror Syndication International)
Ken with Pat Brewer at Lichfield, 1949 (London Casino Photo Service)
Ken directing *The Beaux' Stratagem* at Lichfield, 1949 (*The Illustrated*)
Ken directing Diana Dors and Roger Livesey in *Man of the World* by C.E. Webber, 1950 (Estate of Angus McBean)
Ken in London, 1950 (Daniel Farson)
The wedding of Ken and Elaine Dundy, London, 25 January 1951 (The Source/Solo)
Ken with Cecil Beaton, 1952 (National Portrait Gallery/Estate of Paul Tanqueray)
The critic Tynan joins the *Daily Sketch*, 1953
Ken with his daughter Tracy, 1953
Learning to fight bulls, 1952 (Peter Buckley)
Ken with Tennessee Williams, Valencia, 1955 (Duncan Melvin)
Ken at El Vino's, 1958 (Susan Greenberg)
Gore Vidal, Truman Capote and James Jones, 1957
Elaine and Ken, c. 1956
Ken and the committee, 1960 (*New York Post*/Joseph Wershba)
Ken with Lawrence Ferlinghetti, San Francisco, 1959 (Harry Redl)
Antonio Ordóñez with Ernest Hemingway, Spain, 1959 (Lara, Madrid)
Ken's farewell party at the Forum of the Twelve Caesars, New York, May 1960

For Tracy, Roxana and Matthew Tynan

PREFACE

Writers hate to write, almost all of them, certainly Ken. But he was a natural with words, with what he called the 'magic innovation of our species'. If blocked in the main endeavour of delivering a book or an article, he would turn to off-duty writing: to his journal, begun late in life, where he might deliver himself of a self-punishing complaint about his own indolent and hateful character; or more often, and from childhood until a few months before he died, to the pleasurable business of writing letters. Here he could perform as if on holiday, lying abed in the mornings, scribbling a clerihew or a bit of pastiche for a letter to a friend, or dictating to his secretary – a process begun in his middle years, one he enjoyed and took trouble over. (I recall a pretty young secretary who worked for Ken in Los Angeles complaining to me that he would worry over the choice and placement of an adjective in a letter to his accountant or his doctor. What a waste of time, she felt, when he could be out in the sun.)

Impassioned political letters to the press he would usually write on his own, setting down, with four fingers on his electric typewriter, his thoughts on censorship, the crimes of capitalism and the Common Market, or some abuse of human rights. Love letters or letters to close friends, either typewritten or in his elegant hand, were as impeccably constructed as everything else he wrote, but with an added lightness and ease of expression that made them as much a pleasure to read as they were to write.

Ken kept other people's letters if they were particularly amusing, or if he thought he might refer to them in a profile. As for his own letters, carbons were kept by various secretaries on an irregular basis. A sturdy archive from his decade as dramaturg at the National Theatre, however, survives, since Ken kept it for a book he planned to write on that period. On one occasion in the late 1970s he shipped it – without making copies – to Los Angeles and then back to Europe, where at one point the whole precious thing landed up by error in Warsaw.

After his death in 1980 a few unpublished oddities turned up in Ken's souvenir file – a tearful love letter, a long account of his chastening two years as script advisor at Ealing Studios, two letters to his first wife Elaine Dundy (no doubt returned to him by request so that he could use their contents in an article) and drafts of angry letters to newspapers. Though he believed it was the critic's job to write for posterity, Ken had no thought to preserve the ticking evidence of his life beyond the grave.

Much of the correspondence in this book – representing a little over half of the total – was solicited from friends and lovers who generously turned over letters to me for use in my 1987 biography of my husband; and many were gathered for this collection. Julian Holland, Ken's Birmingham schoolfriend, produced a cornucopia of letters written between 1943 and 1948: not merely performances on Ken's part but epistolary explorations of his ideas, style, love life and intellectual development. In one of these letters he suggests that he and Holland should keep and even privately publish their correspondence. But Ken failed to keep Holland's, forgot about his own letters and set out for London on a stellar trail.

A number of the letters I include come from individual archives – such as those of Cyril Connolly, Cecil Beaton and Louise Brooks. Many come from institutional archives, those of magazines ranging from *Playboy* to the *New Yorker*, from universities, and from agents, editors and publishers. Our children kept his letters, poems and drawings, as I kept every letter he sent to me.

I have taken the liberty of including quite a few memoranda of the National Theatre period, and some to the directors and producers of the erotic revues *Oh! Calcutta!* and *Carte Blanche* – all from carbon copies and therefore not necessarily exactly what was despatched. In the last section of the book I have included, in the absence of carbons, half a dozen letters taken from secretarial notebooks.

To benefit from a fresh, unbiassed eye, I asked the writer Garry O'Connor to make a preliminary selection. From there my aim was to choose the finest, most entertaining or most quirky letters, rather than those which chart Ken's life. To redress the balance I have prefaced each chapter with a short biographical introduction, and added further interludes to clarify, for example, the complex altercation arising from Ken's attack on Truman Capote's *In Cold Blood*, or the battles and feuds at the National Theatre provoked by Ken's championing of Rolf Hochhuth's play *Soldiers*. Much of this material, I should add, is appropriated from my biography of Ken.

I have made cuts within letters mainly because of excessive length, and hardly ever to censor. Individuals are usually given a note only on their first appearance in the letters, but the index will point the reader to other references. Some readers may feel that I have annotated too heavily. In mitigation I can only plead that I have tried to provide for both British and American readers; the former may find redundant notes that are essential to the latter, and vice versa. Ken's range of reference was immense, and most readers will want to skim over, or ignore, some of this information.

A list of Ken's published books is included, though all but *Profiles* (1989) are out of print. Largely due to Random House (US), Ken's writing will now be brought back – and under editorial hands other than my own (I shall remain merely cheerleader, and possibly martinet).

I had wonderful help in the preparation of this book. First my thanks to my brilliant, knowledgeable and hardworking editor, Allegra Huston, at Weidenfeld and Nicolson. Thanks to Garry O'Connor for his contribution; and to my scholarly and entertaining researcher Andrew Weale. To Colleen Collier who worked devotedly and effectively on every aspect of the book. To Peggy Laurel who helped in New York. To Lesley Baxter, who typed the manuscript and organized the notes. And to various itinerant helpmeets: Julie Barber, Kate Kelly, Glen Kidston, Edward Chancellor and Hamish Robinson.

I would particularly like to thank my editor at Random House, Sharon Delano, and Ion Trewin at Weidenfeld and Nicolson.

Finally my deep and loving thanks to Ken for his company then, and the pleasure of his words now.

ACKNOWLEDGEMENTS

The editor and publishers would like to express their thanks to the following individuals, estates and institutions:

Rozina Adler; Betty Angel; Lord Annan; Peter Ashmore; The Hon. David Astor; K. K. Auchincloss; Frith Banbury; Charles Barr; Freddie Bass; Hercules Bellville; The Rt. Hon. Tony Benn; Eric Bentley; Simon Michael Bessie; Robert Bingham; Boaty Boatwright; Sir Dirk Bogarde; Andrew Bolton; John Bomhoff; Arthur Boyars; Stefan Brecht; Alan Brien; Patricia Burke; D. J. Buttress; Simon Callow; Professor John Carey; Humphrey Carpenter; Jeffrey Carrier; Johnny Carson; Tsai Chin; Barnaby Conrad; Dr Jane Cottis; Geoffrey Darby; Michael Davie; James Dawson; Allan Delynn; Robert Dennis; Eric Diesel; William Donaldson; J. P. Donleavy; Ernie Eban; Hillard Elkins; Patricia Brewer Feeney; Jules Feiffer; Lawrence Ferlinghetti; Michael Fitzgerald; The Rt. Hon. Michael Foot; Philip French; Christopher Fry; William Gaskill; Edward Goldsmith; Beryl Graves; Jerome Greenfield; John Gross; Edith Haggard; Jean Halton; The Earl of Harewood; Elizabeth Zaiman Harris; Václav Havel; Joseph Heller; Clive E. Hereward; Michael Herr; Professor E. J. Hobsbawm; Rolf Hochhuth; Anthony Holden; Julian Holland; Hazel Young Holt; Emilie Jacobson; Henry L. James; Lt-Col. Sir John Johnston; Lord Kennet; Mary King; Chris Knutsen; Barbara Leaming; Hermione Lee; Bernard Levin; Professor Robert W. Lewis; Antonin J. Liehm; Paul McCartney; Robert David MacDonald; P. S. McLean; Susan Macready; Conroy Maddox; Hugh Manning; Charles Marowitz; John P. Marquand Jr; George Melly; Elly Horovitz Miller; Adrian Mitchell; Celia Mitchell; Sheridan Morley; John Mortimer; Phyllis Newman; Edna O'Brien; Lady Olivier; C. A. Parker; Randolph Patilos; George Plimpton; Eileen Rabbinowitz; Nick Rampulla; David R. Richards; David Riva; Maria Riva; James Roose-Evans; Barbara Brecht Schaal; Peter Shaffer; Frank Shelley; Ned Sherrin; David Shipman; Pauline Whittle Siff; Barbara Siggs Simon; Yolande Sonnabend; Daniel Topolski; Wendy Trewin; Grant Ujifusa; Hugo Vickers; Vanessa Vreeland; Peter Vukasin; Alexander Walker; Irving Wardle; Leon Wieseltier; Michael Weller; Beatrice Welles; John Wells; Michael White; Michael Wigram; Clifford Williams; Sandy Wilson; Dr Colin Woolf; B. A. Young.

The estates of: James Agate; Lord Beaverbrook; Louise Brooks; Sir Hugh Carleton Greene; Viscount Chandos; Bill and Annie Davis; George Devine; John Dexter; Marlene Dietrich; Lord Fisher of Lambeth; Aaron A. Frosch; Robert Graves; Sir Harold Hobson; Terence Kilmartin; David Lean; John Lennon; Joan Miller; Lord Olivier; Terence Rattigan; Sir Ralph Richardson; Irwin Shaw; William Shawn; A. C. Spectorsky; James Thurber; Thornton Wilder.

The BBC; The Bentley Library, Columbia University; The Bentley Historical Library, University of Michigan; The Berliner Ensemble; Birmingham Central Library; Birmingham University; Boston University Library; The British Council; The British Film

Institute; The British Library; The British Newspaper Library; The Central Library, Bromley; Central Office of Information; Chelsea Library; Churchill College, Cambridge; Curtis Brown Ltd; Equity; *Esquire* magazine; The *Evening Standard*; French Embassy, London, cultural office; The *Guardian*, archive; The Goethe Institute; Hammersmith and Fulham Library; The Harry Ransom Humanities Research Center, University of Texas at Austin; The Imperial War Museum; International Creative Management; King Edward's School, Birmingham; The Law Society; Irving P. Lazar Agency; The Lord Chamberlain's Office; Magdalen College, Oxford; Mander and Mitchenson Theatre Collection; Marylebone Cricket Club; Max Ascoli College, Boston University; Merton College, Oxford; The National Museum of Photography; National Sound Archive; New York Public Library, Berg Collection; New York Public Library, mid-Manhattan branch; New York Public Library for the Performing Arts, Billy Rose Theatre Collection; *New Yorker*; *New Yorker*, library and archive; News International; The *Observer*; Ohio Wesleyan University; Oxford University; Bernard Quaritch Ltd; *Playboy* magazine; The Press Association; The Royal National Theatre; St Andrew's Hospital, Northampton; John Sandoe Books; Sotheby's, London (The Cecil Beaton Estate); State University of New York at Newpaltz; The *Sunday Telegraph*; Swedish Embassy, cultural office; The Theatre Museum, London; University of North Dakota; University of Tulsa; University of Wisconsin at Madison; Vassar College Library (The Mary McCarthy Archive); Wisconsin Center for Film and Theater Research; Yale University Library.

CHAPTER ONE

The School Years

Kenneth Peacock Tynan was born on the morning of 2 April 1927 in Birmingham, England. The birth certificate lists the parents as Peter Tynan – occupation 'draper (shopkeeper)' – and Rose Tynan. The certificate is not devoutly accurate, for Peter Tynan was in fact Sir Peter Peacock, a fifty-four-year-old justice of the peace and civic dignitary, six times mayor of the north-country town of Warrington, and a successful businessman.

The mother was a thirty-eight-year-old unmarried Lancashire woman of Irish origin. About the birth there was nothing hasty, for the parents had been living together as man and wife for some years.

Peter Peacock had abandoned a wife – who would not divorce him – and five children, in favour of the plain but loving Rose. To protect his secret he arranged a carefully orchestrated double life: in Birmingham he was Peter Tynan, in Warrington Sir Peter Peacock. When Kenneth asked his father what he had done before he ran Peacock Stores, the answer was, 'I worked in a broken biscuit factory.' No response could have been more provocative or enraging to his son than Sir Peter's amiable refusal to engage, inform, or explain who he was. With the coming and going of cousins and hangers-on, the whispering and conniving, the intrusiveness of the lie, it was astonishing that Ken did not discover his illegitimacy until his father's death in 1948. Perhaps, as his cousins suggest, he merely buried the knowledge of it.

From an early age his parents were in awe of this astonishingly intelligent child. Realizing how unusual he was, they not so much spoiled him, as encouraged him to satisfy his huge curiosity. They gave him money to buy books, records and subscriptions to magazines; money to go to the movies several times a week (he worshipped American film), and money to buy, on one occasion, a monocle.

On 3 September 1939, while playing with his cousins on a windy bluff near the seaside town of Bournemouth, he heard on the coastguard's radio Chamberlain's declaration of war. Though the city of Birmingham endured severe air raids and the deaths of thousands of its citizens, Ken's war was relatively unfearsome.

His diaries of the period, begun at the age of six (of which only 1939 and

1941 exist) are full of mouth-watering descriptions of his mother's cooking; accounts of his father's practical jokes; and his comments on films (the test for which was 'Can you remember that you enjoyed them?'), visits to the pantomime, to see The Man Who Came to Dinner *('The greatest play ever written'), and to see John Gielgud in* Dear Brutus *for which Ken awarded the actor 96 points out of 100. But it was Donald Wolfit's performance in* Macbeth *in 1938 that left the indelible impression.*

The young Birmingham critic was a born fan. Between 1939 and 1941, he managed to collect the signatures of Winston Churchill and the whole of the War Cabinet, H.G. Wells, Lady Astor, Joseph Kennedy, a fistful of famous actors and almost every comic and vaudevillian at work. But he was not merely a fan: in his 141 letters to his friend Julian Holland between 1943 and 1948, the schoolboy and undergraduate chronicled his experiments: as actor, director, academic, seducer, sportsman, gamesman, dandy, lover of jazz, politician, debater, comedian, showman, and explorer in 'the great cause of words' – as playwright, novelist, journalist and overridingly, as theatre critic. The vanity and the boastful bravura are mitigated by flashes of self-doubt, for with Holland he could unbutton without fear of humiliation.

Though he never announced he would make reviewing a career, he precociously and brilliantly recorded his playgoing: he seemed to know himself in an uncannily sure way. He caught the great performances of Wolfit, Olivier, Richardson and Gielgud and pinned them to paper in reviews, many of which he polished up for his first book, He That Plays the King, *published in 1950.*

With Holland, Ken could test out new political hats. Was he a high Tory, an anarchist or a Fabian Socialist? Without doubt, he was a libertarian (demanding the repeal of the punitive laws governing divorce, homosexuality and abortion); glorying in 'sensual pleasure' and 'contemplative leisure'. Most important, Julian shared his great passion for Citizen Kane, *which Ken sat through five times (once with eyes shut to savour the sound track) the first week it opened in Birmingham. From thenceforward – an enduring passion which lasted to the end of Tynan's life – Welles was the great man, and the substitute father figure.*

The powerhouse for this provincial overreacher was the ancient grammar school King Edward's, which he entered as a scholar in 1938 and left in 1945 with two further scholarships to Oxford. While at King Edward's he won twelve major school prizes, was secretary to the debating and literary societies, editor of the school magazine, member of the first eleven cricket team. In his Higher School Certificate he received distinctions in English, history and in two scholarship papers.

'His style of living was a premeditated one', a contemporary whom Tynan, aged eleven, had asked to be his Boswell, recalled. 'His was a very adult

mentality, and one that wanted to make an impact.' 'I stake all my hopes on him becoming a great literary character', this friend recorded in his diary of 1944. 'For his is the stuff geniuses are made of.'

'As long as I'm not ignored,' Ken wrote to Holland. His was the classic aesthete's reponse to a philistine background – to make an impression and to escape. There is little in the correspondence about his kindly working-class mother or his elderly, self-made father. Only at the end of his life did he look back at the comfortable ordinariness of his childhood with wistful nostalgia.

To the Editor, *Film Weekly*[1]

'Wicken'[2]
229, Portland Road,
Edgbaston,
Birmingham 17[3]
[Published 12 February 1938]

[Dear Sir]

If it is actually true that Warner Brothers intend to put Humphrey Bogart in a series of 'B' pictures, they will be making the greatest mistake of their lives. His gangster in <u>Dead End</u>,[4] the 'D.A.' in <u>Marked Woman</u>[5] and the producer in <u>Stand-In</u>[6] were great pieces of acting, and show Bogart to be a grand character actor who needs real recognition.[7]

K. Tynan

[1] The eleven-year-old Kenneth Peacock Tynan wrote in response to an article headed 'Bogart Demoted' in *Film Weekly* on 29 January 1938. In an article on Bogart, 'The Man and the Myth' (*Playboy*, June 1966), he referred to this letter as his 'debut in print'.

[2] The house was named after the village of Wicken north of Buckingham, birthplace of Rose Tynan's mother, Rebecca Mitchell.

[3] All addresses are given in full on their first mention, and thereafter abbreviated to the street address, unless abbreviated otherwise by KPT.

[4] First of the Dead End Kids films adapted by Lillian Hellman from Sidney Kingsley's play and directed by William Wyler (US, 1937).

[5] Gangster melodrama directed by Lloyd Bacon starring Bette Davis in which Bogart played the District Attorney (US, 1937).

[6] Lighthearted Hollywood satire directed by Tay Garnett, starring Leslie Howard and Joan Blondell (US, 1937).

[7] Humphrey Bogart (1899–1957) did not disappoint his young fan, going on to star in *The Maltese Falcon* (US, 1941), *Casablanca* (US, 1943), *In a Lonely Place* (US, 1950) and *The African Queen* (US/UK, 1951), for which he won an Academy Award. In his 1966 homage KPT described Bogart as an exemplar of stoicism, quoting Seneca: '"Death is master of all the years that are behind us" – and Bogart's voice told us as much.'

To Henry Hall[1]

229, Portland Road
[1939]

Dear Mr. Hall,

After such a long while of listening to you on the wireless, I feel that I must write to tell you how much I used to enjoy your programmes. They included all the latest songs sung as only your band can sing them.

I am only twelve, and a very keen autograph hunter, so I would think it a very great honour if you could just autograph this letter at the end, and perhaps ask some of the other members of the band to do the same. It would be an additional honour if you could ask some of the other players on the Hippodrome bill to sign it, such as Lucan & McShane,[2] and the other famous artistes.

I enclose a stamped addressed envelope.

Thanking you once again for the many hours of happy listening, and fervently waiting for '... the next time ...' I hear you over the air.

Your faithful fan,
K.P. Tynan

[1] Henry Hall (1898–1989), English dance band leader who had a long-running radio programme, *Henry Hall's Guest Night*.
[2] Arthur Lucan (1887–1954), music-hall comedian and creator of 'Old Mother Riley'; his wife, Kitty McShane (1898–1964), played opposite him as Old Mother Riley's daughter.

To Arthur Askey[1]

'Kenrose',[2]
9 Brightlands Avenue,
Southbourne,
Bournemouth,
12 March 1940

Dear Mr. Askey,

This is the third time I have written to you, and on each of the previous occasions, I have been sent a photo with a PRINT of your autograph on it. Please, this time, could you oblige me by sending me your personal autograph? I know you must get many requests for it, but couldn't you just do it this once, personally? I could not consider my collection complete without your autograph (personal!) in it.

Third time lucky?

(Still) Your faithful 'fan',
(Master) Kenneth Tynan

P.S. I will subscribe to any charity fund you name if I can have your signature.[3]

[1] Arthur Askey (1900–82), diminutive English comedian of radio, film and music hall.
[2] The Tynans' holiday house, named for KPT and his mother Rose.
[3] Askey replied, 'Here you are, playmate. Yours "Big-Heartedly" Arthur Askey.'

To the *Melody Maker and Rhythm*[1]

229, Portland Road
[Published 20 September 1941]

Visiting a news theatre in Birmingham, I saw a film entitled 'Beat Me Daddy 8 to the Bar'.[2] I expected something blatantly commercial and got – Wingy Mannone[3] [*sic*] and his Orchestra.

Although there was a certain amount of corny close harmony, Wingy and his boys (as far as I could see there were six in the band – trumpet, trombone, clarinet, piano, bass, and guitar) played two numbers, the first a medium-fast of great improvisation, which opens the film; and the second, a blues, which ends it.

This latter is super stuff: Wingy's vocal particularly intrigued me, and the clarinettist (who sounds something like Joe Marsala[4]) and the trombonist are both swell improvisers. I earnestly advise your readers to see this film.

Kenneth P. Tynan[5]

[1] KPT had corresponded with the *Melody Maker and Rhythm* for several years.
[2] Directed by Larry Caballos, featuring music by 'Wingy' Manone (US, 1941).
[3] Joseph 'Wingy' Manone (1904–82), master of the jazz trumpet who became a popular radio and film personality.
[4] Joe Marsala (1907–78), self-taught jazz clarinettist who worked for Manone.
[5] KPT recorded in his diary (16 November 1941): 'On the bus, on the way home, a chap sat down next to me, asked if I was Kenneth Tynan, and said he had read a letter of mine in the MM. Was delighted to hear that he is a fan.'

To Julian Holland[1]

K.E.S. Camp,[2]
Newnham Bridge,
Worcs.
Sunday [13 September 1943]

Dear Jules:

Here, at last, is a letter. I am so very sorry to have neglected you, but I am on the Brains Trust here, and I work 11 hours a day. That, plus such extraneous amusements as hop-pickers, land girls,[3] and local pubs, has filled up my time effectively, obliviously, and unseen. I had not noticed my appalling omission until this pissing morn; hence my incoherent dismay.

Afterthought: I prepared a list of things that might have interested you, but the call of nature, heralded by a loud phart at 3 a.m., saw otherwise, and it had to be sacrificed.

First, then, a critique of your letter:

p.1: Have I read 'Preludes & Studies'?[4]

Yes, yes, yes. Excellent. Especially the one on Paganini. And the one on Webster. Excellent. [...]

p.3: Apropos of Pat Martin.[5] She has just written to tell me that her parents twigged our last meeting, and have not only closed the matter, but also sat on the lid. In short, all is over. Sad. Very.

p.4: Re Joy,[6] and my 'abominable behaviour'. <u>And</u> your statement that man is a social animal. Dear Jules, if there had never been outlandish hermits, the very word 'society' would never have existed. I, in short, am the exception that breaks the rule. 'You are young at present' ... PHOOEY. I had a damn good time, and neither girl was offended.

p.6: List of guests.[7] Apropos of your mention of BES: he joined the navy yesterday. BHM[8] followed him. A gloomy blow to the Brains Trust. [...]

I have sent my list to Joy, but here it is again, impromptu:

ORSON WELLES[9]
ALEXANDER WOOLLCOTT[10]
JESUS CHRIST
D.H. LAWRENCE
PABLO PICASSO
THEOPHILE GAUTIER[11]
LEO PAVIA[12]
JAMES JOYCE

PAUL CEZANNE
JAMES THURBER
A.N. OTHER

A.N.O.=[DUKE] ELLINGTON, G.B.S., SWINBURNE, JEAN COCTEAU, SHAKESPEARE, BAUDELAIRE, JOHNSON, VIRGINIA WOOLF, DISNEY, GAUGUIN, BOB HOPE, GEORGE JEAN NATHAN,[13] or God knows who else; or God. Or Jack Benny.[14] [...]

'Casablanca'.[15] What did I like about it.

(a) NOT the photography, which was pitiable
(b) Bogart
(c) Rains
(d) The brief interlude with the two immigrants who are obtaining nationalisation. They have, they say, mastered the language. Then

1st: What watch is it, dear?
2nd: Five watch.
1st: Dear me; such watch?

(e) The glimpse of Greenstreet[16]
(f) Peter Lorre[17]
(g) Paul Henreid[18]
(h) Bogart
(i) Bogart
(j) NOT the fact that John Huston[19] did not direct it. [...]

Now what may I say of myself? One: I have been correspondingly [sic] warmly with Joy. Two: I have received a naïve but superbly encouraging letter from Patsy.[20] Three: Enid Hammerton and Ruby Wagstaff living up to early promise. Four: Betty Wyer, Joyce Phillips, Betty Hill, Nancy & Bridget Hartshorn, Clarice Maynard and Norma Pullen are all excellent local pieces. The second was unfortunately hauled from my toils after no more than a couple of kisses by a sad apple named Peter Laister.[21] To coin a phrase, chagrin besets. [...] Smoking is getting a hold; I AM VICE-RADDLED. [...]

Getting very intimate with Johnny Ounsted,[22] who runs the 'Brains Trust'. [...] Told me dozens of foul stories, including one about a girl with hay fever who was invited to dinner. She secreted a couple of minute handkerchiefs in her bosom, but was unfortunately caught by a paroxysm of sneezing halfway through the entrée. She fumbled about her breasts until someone saw fit to ask her what was the matter. She replied: 'nothing – but – but I could have sworn I had two when I started.'

J.O. liked your gag of the two pederasts. He made an amazing remark to me: 'To carry your character to its logical conclusion, Ken, you ought to be rabidly homosexual.' [...]

What more? There is a mad cow in the barn, a bull that brays in the next field, and a lovely girl in the cottage over the way. What more may I ask? Only comfort, and chain to pull. And a wondering why I am ever possessed to piss at 6 a.m., a strange lust which has overcome me since I came here.

So I close in haste with a <u>magnificent</u> anecdote, maybe the best I have heard. It is a true story of Orson Welles. The master was due to lecture at a small midwestern town; the audience was small, & there was no one to introduce him. He undertook to do it himself.

'Ladies & gentlemen,' he said, 'I will tell you the highlights of my life. I am a director of plays, a producer of plays, & an actor on the legitimate stage. I am a writer, a producer, and an actor in motion pictures. I write, direct, and act on the radio. I am a magician. I also paint and sketch, and I am a book-publisher. I am a violinist, and I am a pianist.' Here he leaned forward: 'Isn't it a pity there are so many of me and so few of you?' [...]

Love and kisses.
Love to KMH.
KTCM[23] just pharted in my face. DANG!
Ken.

---

[1] Julian Holland (b. 1925), the highly intelligent son of a printer, Hoover salesman and local supporter of the Tory party. Despite a two-year age gap, Holland and KPT had become firm friends – obsessed in their search for culture – during the KES (King Edward's School) school year of 1942. In 1943 Holland joined the BBC in London as a recorded programme assistant. In 1946 he became a producer for *Radio Newsreel*, and edited *World at One* and *Today* 1981–6. (See PS to letter of 4 March 1944.)

[2] This was the third year that KES (which KPT had entered in 1938) had pitched a school farm camp at Newnham Bridge, Worcestershire, to serve the annual brigade of voluntary hop-pickers as part of the war effort. A 'Brains Trust' (so called after the popular BBC panel discussion programme) was formed from a nucleus of Sixth Formers to assist the local Ministry of Food. The boys would collect the hop-pickers' ration books along with their orders for food, pick up the supplies and deliver them to the fields. KPT shared a tent pitched in an apple orchard. One night during a fierce storm he played King Lear to an attentive audience of schoolboys.

[3] The hop-pickers were traditionally from working-class Midlands families; 'land girls' – voluntary members of the Women's Land Army – were recruited for farm work in the wartime absence of male labourers.

[4] Alan Dent, *Preludes and Studies* (1942).

[5] Pat Martin attended King Edward's High School for Girls. She was probably the first of many to whom KPT proposed marriage.

[6] Joy Matthews, a vivacious, auburn-haired Birmingham girl. See letter of 29 January 1944.

[7] Possibly the guest list for an ideal dinner party.

[8] Brian Swingler (BES) left KES in 1943 and Bruce McGowen (BHM) in 1942.

[9] Orson Welles (1915–85). The director-writer-performer-impresario stunned and seduced KPT with *Citizen Kane*, which he saw on 4 March 1942, the day it opened in Birmingham. He was 'dazzled by its narrative virtuosity' and 'its shocking but always relevant cuts' (Holland had managed to get hold of the script). In the KES *Chronicle* of December 1943 Ken wrote of Welles: 'He is a writer of the most brittle poetry ... a wit as only Americans can be wits ... a producer of plays in kingly fashion, independent as a signpost in all he does. He is a gross and glorious director of motion pictures, the like of which we have not seen since the great days of the German cinema; he reproduces life as it is sometimes seen in winged dreams. Watch him well, for he is a major prophet, with the hopes of a generation clinging to his heels.'

[10] Alexander Woollcott (1887–1943). An obituary by KPT of the flamboyant New York drama critic had appeared in the KES *Chronicle* in July 1943 mourning the loss of 'an all-embracing, non-respecting, joy-loving genius; a great dramatic critic, a brilliant wit'.

[11] Théophile Gautier (1811–72), French Romantic poet, novelist, journalist and travel writer.

[12] Leo Pavia (1875–1945), child prodigy at the piano, who disliked performing in public and gave it up, though he remained famous for his impromptu pastiche. He translated Oscar Wilde into German and became the companion to the drama critic James Agate.

[13] George Jean Nathan (1882–1958), American drama critic and essayist who introduced contemporary European plays to the US, and proselytized for Eugene O'Neill.

[14] Jack Benny (1894–1974), American radio, television and film comedian.

[15] Directed by Michael Curtiz, starring Humphrey Bogart and Ingrid Bergman (US, 1942).

[16] Sidney Greenstreet (1879–1954), corpulent English actor whose films include *The Maltese Falcon* (US, 1941) and *The Woman in White* (US, 1948).

[17] Peter Lorre (1904–64), Hungarian-born actor who appeared in films including *M* (Germany, 1931) and *The Maltese Falcon* (US, 1941).

[18] Paul Henreid (1907–92, born Paul von Henreid), Austrian actor who fled to Britain, then the US, before the war; his films include *Night Train to Munich* (US, 1940) and *Now, Voyager* (US, 1942).

[19] John Huston (1906–87) had so far directed only two films: *The Maltese Falcon* (US, 1941; which shared many actors with *Casablanca*) and *In This Our Life* (US, 1942). He would go on to make *The Treasure of the Sierra Madre* (US, 1948) for which he won Academy Awards for direction and screenplay, *The African Queen* (US/UK, 1951) and *The Dead* (UK, 1987).

[20] Possibly Pat Martin.

[21] KES scientist.

[22] A young KES mathematics master. See letter of 29 January 1944.

[23] K.M. Hewitt (KMH) and K.T.C. McKenzie (KTCM) both left KES in 1943.

To Julian Holland

229, Portland Road
9th Oct. [1943]

Dear J.:

Reading Rotha,[1] Nilsen,[2] Pudovkin[3] – have been moved to make a list of the most significant films in the history of the cinema. Herewith the result – in no particular order. Agree?

> 'The Street' (Karl Grune)
> 'Zvenigora' (Dovjenko)
> 'La Passion de Jeanne d'Arc' (Dreyer)
> 'The Battleship Potemkin' (Eisenstein)
> 'Alexander Nevsky' (Eisenstein)
> 'Therèse Racquin' [*sic*] (Jacques Feyder)
> 'The Last Laugh' (Murnau)
> 'M' (Lang)
> 'Siegfried' (Lang)
> 'New Babylon' (Kozintsev & Trauberg)
> 'Mother' (Pudovkin)
> 'Cabinet of Dr Caligari' (Wiene)
> 'The Joyless Street' (Pabst)
> 'Kameradschaft' (Pabst)
> 'Citizen Kane' (Welles)[4]

N.B. Ask Joy to show you the 'Quiz for Intellectuals'[5] I sent her in my last letter. I composed it; and it's pretty stiff. Have a try. Make it a real rouser. Why I wrote that I don't know. Maybe it's association of ideas; most things are.

Thursday, 6.0, Gaumont.[6]

Till then ...

K.P.T.

---

[1] Paul Rotha (1907–84), leading British documentary filmmaker of the 1930s and 1940s and author of books on film, such as *The Film Till Now* (1930).

[2] Probably Vladimir Nilsen, cinematographer and author of *The Cinema as a Graphic Art* (1940).

[3] Vsevolod Pudovkin (1893–1953), Russian film director and theorist, whose books include *Film Technique* (1933) and *Film-Acting* (1935).

[4] *The Street* (Germany, 1923), dir. Karl Grune (1890–1962), silent; *Zvenigora* (USSR, 1928), dir. Alexander Dovzhenko (1894–1956), silent; *La Passion de Jeanne d'Arc* (France, 1928), dir. Carl Dreyer (1889–1968), silent; *The Battleship Potemkin* (USSR, 1925), dir. Sergei Eisenstein (1898–1948), silent; *Alexander Nevsky* (USSR, 1938), dir. Eisenstein, sound; *Thérèse Raquin* (Germany, 1928), dir. Jacques Feyder (1885–1948), silent; *The Last Laugh* (Germany, 1924), dir. F.W. Murnau (1888–1931), silent; *M* (Germany, 1931), dir. Fritz Lang (1890–1976), sound; *Siegfried* (Germany, 1924), dir. Lang, silent; *New Babylon* (USSR, 1929), dir. Grigori Kozintsev (1905–73) and Leonid Trauberg (b. 1902), silent; *Mother* (Russia, 1905), dir. Pudovkin, silent; *The Cabinet of Dr Caligari* (Germany, 1919), dir. Robert Wiene (1881–1938), silent; *The Joyless Street* (Germany, 1925), dir. Georg Pabst (1885–1967), silent; *Kameradschaft* (Germany/France, 1931), dir. Pabst, sound; *Citizen Kane* (US, 1941), dir. Welles, sound.

[5] KPT set his friends complicated cultural puzzles. On one he wrote, '10 out of the total of 50

would be bloody good from anyone, and I'll bet no one could get more than 40.' He sent Holland 15 literary quotes on such subjects as Pope, the nineteenth-century Parnassian poet Le Conte de Lisle and the Jesuits, and asked him to identify the author – who in each case was KPT.
[6] The Gaumont cinema in Scarlet Street, Birmingham.

To Julian Holland

229, Portland Road
10th Oct. [1943]

Dearest Jules:

Forgive me, forgive me, forgive; I am in a trance. In one of our larger public parks tonight I met the Girl of a Lifetime. She is intensely mystic, considers me a 'brilliant creature', and is lovelier than twice lovely. Her only free evening next week is Thursday so I have booked her. Our date, I fear, must lapse; but I still love you. In my present condition, however, I love her kisses more; I have only had one at the time of writing, but that was enough. We were closer together than good and evil. [...]

Miss you.
K.P.T.

To Julian Holland

229, Portland Rd
[29 October 1943]

Dear [Julian]:

Thanks for a honey of a letter. I'm terrific; I have made the supreme conquest of my life and believe me mister it aint hay. Met her at busstop in paradise street and have taken her out twice; says she wants to marry me, have two-three kids, and will let me next june before hsc[1] YUM; first time in reprobate life i ever used word love to a woman query am i slipping. she isnt intelligent but neither is she dumb as her conversation shows; our first cosy little chat and brother was it cosy was on the subject of sex relations before marriage. Says she wants to go to the ends of the earth with me little does she guess that what i want from her i can get at the top of the road. the old poetical advance simply shattered her she loves to have verses quoted at her apropos of her. laps it up and you know i can dish it out. saw joy [Matthews] last week, told her all, and bade fond farewell. she is in dunstable comma beds[2] for her health which is suffering from tonsilitis.

bought magnifique book last week quote new yorker[3] wartime album unqu a selection of cartoons from wartime n y. is wonderful, i paid zany sum of fifteen (15) bobs[4] for it and still fondle it with reverence as the bishop said to the actress. [...]

stole wonderful book from sellyoak library quote complete works of baudelaire in translation by a j symons unqu. eat this letter it is evidence.

saw laughton in rembrandt[5] at local cinema last night. his masterstroke. lovely comment by him quote i dont see you as other people do i see [you] as the air around you, as the water you wash in, as the light that falls on you see you. i see you as if i were not here at all unqu. [...]

wonderful moderndress production of quote taming of shrew unqu at rep. Ayliff[6] again. car, flashlight camera, kodak, box with cema on it, exits through audience, etc, etc. a wonderful as i say bit of trickery. margaret leightons[7] katherina is perfectly spoken but poor girl she is so angular.

further sex. i am going to fully explore gwen (thats her name) on sunday yes i know ive split an infinitive but she split my world from top to bottom just by winking back.

what im reading now tchehov [*sic*] hauptmann[8] strindberg ibsen gorki andreyev[9] and a gloomier lot of bastards ive never tripped over. [...]

facts abt woollcott culled from readers digest:

george jean nathan called him the times square seidlitz powder[10]

when he was slashing at all as dramatic critic of n y times, bloke a said: i see where woollcott has dropped fifty pounds. bloke b asked: on whom.

when alec saw thornton wilders moving little epic quote our town unqu,[11] he was discovered after the second interval sitting on the fire escape weeping. the stage manager asked him: are you going to support the play mr woollcott. he replied: support it? id as soon think of supporting the twenty-third psalm.

he was once addressing a meeting in the very mid west. at the end a proud little man stood up and boasted that when they were young he used to ride on woollcotts sled. alec glared, then said: i never had a sled and if i had, you couldnt BUY a ride.

[...] i am now doing a superb thing. i am typing this on a bus yes i said a bus. gwen just phoned and said she dreamt about me last night. we were married and were sitting in a bedroom, me in a black and red dressing gown and she in a green one. she lay on the bed all night but i just smoked. maybe its symbolical, but anyway she does not know me very well does she. [...]

So youre at elstree.[12] how wonderful. if you go to ealing studios[13] and mention my name theyll show you round the place; ask for Miss Doris Douet of the publicity dept and say you have 'studied film technique here and on the continent but have never seen filmmaking in practice'. thats what i said and she spent a whole afternoon showing me round, makeup room, moviola, teknikolor apparatus, sets, still room, cameras, etc, etc. try it.

other errands:

1) scour the continental bookstalls in leicester sq for american and french mag.s
2) try the pam-pam restaurant opp. the Empire leic sq.
3) try the threepenny slotmachines (i mean slotmachines) in the amusement arcades (or as i call them, sex tunnels) on the strand if you feel that old urge.
4) go to the windmill[14] and give my regards to huia cooper.[15] that girls got skin like velvety copper
5) write to your mp and get into a debate some afternoon. can be fun.
6) spend an evening at hydeparkcorner listening to the low buzz of the traffic and the americans snatching prostitutes from right under your aquiline nose.
7) go to the alex reid and lefevre galleries, quartermile from Picc Circ, theres generally something worthwhile hung there [...]

New vulgarism ex RE Kirby:[16]

Re the woman who was divorced four times. First husband was Donald Budge;[17] she divorced him cos he was all balls and bounce; second was Don Bradman;[18] he went because once you got him in you couldnt get him out; third was Gordon Richards;[19] he needed four mounts a day. Number four was Father Christmas; he came only once a year; and that was down the chimney.

Godbewithyou, ye devils spawn.
K.P.T.

[1] Higher School Certificate, the equivalent then of Advanced Level examinations.

[2] Dunstable, near Luton, Bedfordshire.

[3] KPT and Holland planned, but failed, to produce their own version of the *New Yorker*, to be called the *Midlander*. Julian Holland recalls that they wanted to translate the New York scene to Birmingham: 'Just about the daftest thing you can imagine.'

[4] A bob – slang for a shilling – would be worth about £1 today.

[5] Film biography of the artist (UK, 1936) directed by Alexander Korda, with Charles Laughton (1899–1962) and Laughton's wife, Elsa Lanchester.

[6] Henry K. Ayliff (1871–1949), South African-born actor and director who mounted celebrated productions at the Birmingham Repertory Theatre 1922–44. This intimate theatre, founded by Sir Barry Jackson in 1913, became the training ground for actors such as Ralph Richardson, Laurence Olivier, Paul Scofield and, in the 1950s, Albert Finney.

[7] Margaret Leighton (1922–76) joined the Old Vic in 1944, made her New York debut in 1946 and won Tony Awards for *Separate Tables* (1956) and *The Night of the Iguana* (1962).

[8] Gerhart Hauptmann (1862–1946), German Nobel Prize-winning novelist and playwright in the tradition of Ibsen and Strindberg.

[9] Leonid Nicolaievich Andreyev (1871–1919), Russian playwright and novelist.

[10] A laxative.

[11] Thornton Wilder (1897–1976), American novelist and playwright, was awarded the Pulitzer Prize for *Our Town* (1938) and *The Skin of Our Teeth* (1942).

[12] Village in Hertfordshire north of London, where MGM set up a studio in 1938.

[13] In 1929 the director Basil Dean formed Associated Talking Pictures and in 1931 built a studio at Ealing Green. From 1938 to 1958 Ealing Studios was run by Michael Balcon.

[14] Variety theatre in Great Windmill Street, London, famous for its statuesque nudes, and for staying open throughout World War II. It closed in 1964 and is now a cinema.

[15] A petite, dark-haired dancer.

[16] KES contemporary.

[17] Don Budge (b. 1915), American tennis player who won the men's singles, men's doubles (with Gene Mako) and mixed doubles (with Alice Marble) at Wimbledon two years running (1937, 1938).

[18] Sir Donald Bradman (b. 1908); he holds the record for the highest Australian Test score against England as well as making the highest batting average and number of centuries in Test history.

[19] Sir Gordon Richards (1904–86), English jockey. Between 1921 and 1954 he was champion jockey 26 times and rode 4870 winners.

To Julian Holland

229 portland rd

4 11 43

dear [Julian]

thanks for a swell writeup vacant mon next and onwards for masonic ladies nights[1]/ newfound love as you call it little do you guess is now transformed into a listless diddering wreck by fervent attentions of kpt she still loves me though and i fool that i am lap it up and let me tell you that in this case it is practically what you think it is / bleak yet sightly, bleak yet sightly is probably what i shall think of quote journey into f unqu[2] incidentally welles himself is almost up his own pipe with anger over the cutting and editing which was not done by him it seems that twentiethcenturyfox did the job as it were behind his back whilst he was in s america getting localcolor for his next film whose title i forget[3] on his return quote who the hell cut it the janitor unquote was welles comment however it may still be a trim piece of work [...]

as you have seen quote ambersons unqu[4] didnt you retch at the scene where dolores costello claps tim holts head to her breast i thought it terrible by the bye anne baxters good isnt she particularly the scene where she takes her leave of holt and goes into the chemists shop the opening sequences are good with their jangled odds of conversation winging out of the highly atmospheric gloom did you notice how the earlier sequences were shot with the edge of the film faded to suggest age i think the best scene is that in which richard bennett hes grandpa loses his reason you remember all about the earth and the sun i like the ending too the mike swinging up and into a ray of light and orson welles out of the void the acting throughout is exqu but of course the real star is agnes moorhead[5] [*sic*] that performance is the finest i have ever seen particularly when she sits down and laughs at tim holt and the scene where he taunts her for being in love with cotten and she screams at him from behind her bedroom door her entire performance was logical hysteria which is rare very rare [...]

your mention of joy prompts me to tell you that the girl made a rash promise to me she offered to firewatch[6] at school until ten p m if i could work up a substantial bet which she could share brash little filly isnt she gwens breasts are as firm as belltents in a light breeze incidentally she is masochistic she likes to have her breasts squeezed quote until it hurts unqu i am still faintly chagrined at having to reach her clitoris by way of her buttocks a case of after the dustcart comes the lord mayors show dont you think she always wears pure silk underclothes as i found out last week when we had an evening together alone in my house she is really most obliging in this matter of undressing incidentally destroy this page eat it if necessary my imagination is running away with me migod if youre sexless im more than making up the discrepancy dripdripdrip [...]

kpt x his mark

---

[1] There were many Masonic lodges in Birmingham. No doubt their ladies' nights would have been KPT's idea of hell.

[2] *Journey Into Fear* (US, 1942). Orson Welles adapted this film melodrama with Joseph Cotten, and co-directed with Norman Foster. It starred Cotten, Welles, Dolores Del Rio and Agnes Moorehead. KPT had not yet seen the film (it opened on 19 March at the Gaumont). On 29 April 1943 Welles had written to thank KPT for a letter and to complain that the studio (RKO, not Fox as KPT reports) had re-edited his previous film, *The Magnificent Ambersons*, without his knowledge. He added, 'The picture suffered from all this meddling, but your letter makes me feel the result perhaps wasn't as disastrous as I'd feared.' KPT also had the temerity to correspond with the distinguished film critic of the *Observer*, C.A. Lejeune, about *Journey Into Fear*.
[3] Eventually released as *It's All True* (US, 1942).
[4] *The Magnificent Ambersons* (US, 1942), Orson Welles' account of the decline of an established family, starred Joseph Cotten (1905–94), Agnes Moorehead, Anne Baxter (1923–85), Dolores Costello (1905–79, mother of John Barrymore) and Tim Holt (1918–73, also known for John Huston's 1948 *The Treasure of the Sierra Madre*).
[5] Agnes Moorehead (1906–74), American actress who joined Welles' Mercury Theater Company in 1940, played Kane's mother in *Citizen Kane*, and was nominated for the Best Supporting Actress Academy Award for her performance in *The Magnificent Ambersons*.
[6] Birmingham endured 77 air raids during World War II; the Germans would drop incendiary bombs as markers for the high explosive bombs. Three boys and two masters were deputed to stay overnight at the school to guard against fire. The girls' school had a similar arrangement. Pocket money per night came to 3s.6d. KPT discovered underground access to the girls' school, or 'Janery' as he called it, after Jane the sexy *Daily Mirror* cartoon heroine.

To Julian Holland

229 portland rd
30 11 43

dear [Julian]

[...] A few wild things about jimmy durante.[1] it seems that whilst walking down fifth avenue one day he was overtaken by a vast lumpy woman and a diminutive bedraggled husband with a tiny feather in his hat. shrieked schnozzola:

'Lookit! Lookit! A Mountaineer! A Mountaineer! Intrepid! Intrepid!'

And another:

'I caint even go buy myself a cup of coffee. Theyd mob me. Id be reckognised. I caint disguise my probiscuity. Jimmy the Man! Jimmy the Human Being!'

———

When (if they let me) I edit the Chronicle,[2] I shall of course write all the original contributions myself. and i have found the perfect quotation for the editorial to that chronicle. Its from Webster:

'You are your own chronicle too much, and grossly flatter yourself'[3]

———

djr now joined cff[4] fighting for bumbledom.[5] chances are 2–1 i shall be made a praefectus.[6] others (prob) geoff darby, pat welch and/or geoff

hackett. if derek allcott[7] would comb his hair they might consider him
.... give me a silent prayer (to my god not yours) ...

have i ever told you about double-talk? its the american talk by which
you listen, hear something that sounds perfectly logical, and when its
over you realise you havent understood a word of it. heres a wonderful
example. try it on someone next time you go to a restaurant; i have and
the girl says 'Oh, yes', begins to walk off and then, generally, faints.
    'Well, take now youre in a restaurant. So you say to the waiter:
"Gimme the chicken and vegetables but portostat with the chicken
with the fustatis on it." So he says, "What!" And you say, "You know,
the portostat and moonsign the savina on the top, with the vegetables"'
    The guy responsible for that is a mr whitey bimstein.[8] [...]
    i am coming to london on thursday december 30 and shall return to
bham [Birmingham] about wednesday or thursday of the next week. i
hear the hotels are full but i am writing to the strand palace[9] my old
joint to attempt a booking. now my questions to you are
(a) when will you have a holiday?
(b) if i cant make the strand p, how is the rooming situation in palmers
lodge[10] or whatever the bloody place is called?
(c) could you book for a few shows for me? details later.
write soon plus fornicating report. [...]
WRITE BACK TIME IS FUCK PRECIOUS

KPT

[1] Jimmy ('Schnozzle') Durante (1893–1980), radio, film and stage comedian and songwriter who
began on the vaudeville circuit.
[2] The KES magazine to which KPT contributed.
[3] John Webster, *The Duchess of Malfi*, Act III, Sc. i.

⁴D.J. Reese was Captain of the School XV rugby team; (Sir) Colin Figures, who left KES in 1943, entered the Diplomatic Service and was Deputy Secretary of the Cabinet Office 1985–9.
⁵'Officiousness', from Mr Bumble, the beadle in Charles Dickens' *Oliver Twist* (1837–8).
⁶KPT was made prefect in the spring term of 1944.
⁷Geoffrey Darby, a close friend of KPT's (see letter of 29 January 1944); after Cambridge, he went into advertising and worked for Schweppes. Pat Welch, a KES contemporary who became a Methodist lay preacher, recalled that KPT gave his schoolfriends an idea of potential freedom. Geoffrey Hackett, KPT's best friend at Birmingham's Elementary School and a contemporary at KES where he excelled as a sportsman, went to Cambridge and then into advertising. Derek Allcott left KES in 1943.
⁸Morris 'Whitey' Bimstein (1897–1969), American boxing trainer, so called because of his white eyelashes.
⁹KPT had previously stayed at this hotel in the Strand, London WC2, on visits with his mother.
¹⁰Holland's address was Palmer's Lodge, Alum Lane, Elstree, Hertfordshire.

To Julian Holland

229, Portland Road
8th Dec AT[1] 16 [1943]

Mr Holland sɪʀ!
  [. . .] Now for the Play.[2] I am sending you a summary of the Acts that I brushed off last night before receiving you. Anything omitted I'll discuss here. Yes, I am keeping your play letters.
  Now to the character of Satan. I like the idea of Bogart's dry wit – but are we witty enough to keep it up? I suggest a more bombastic character, with a penchant to sly asides – in short – yes, you've guessed it – ORSON WELLES, with a soupçon of Monty Woolley?[3] A sort of celestial wcfields?[4] He is not, surely, horrified by God's goodness – nothing horrifies him. He is merely irritated and amused, and later merely irritated. Nothing CAN terrify him for he fears nothing. I agree that we can have no ethical values – we might point the moral that the characterising feature of hell is not that it is immoral, but THAT IT HAS NO STANDARDS AT ALL. It cannot criticise or judge, it can merely like or dislike, be repelled by or attracted to – all a matter of the SENSES.
  I like the idea of no curtains in Act ɪɪ and the musical background – though I should select some of Alban Berg's Violin Concerto, some recent Schonberg,[5] and (later) some of the first 3 movements of Walton's Symphony.[6] The birth of Christ could be heralded with some of the 'Ronde du Sabbat' from Berlioz' Fantastic Symphony.[7]
  The madman I think is a little ᴛᴏᴏ stagey; think how it would look. It's one of those cases where the idea's good but won't stand translation.

Re Christ: I INSIST! It's the climax!! Perlease!

Re Hitler: clarified and modified in new draft. [...]

Re writing it: let's spend that Sunday in very hard writing – I'll bring my typewriter. We'll get a full idea of the sort of style – is it to be childsimple or chestertonepigrammatic?[8] We mus [*sic*] think, too, of some sceptical lines, and some subsidiary characters for hell – look up Milton for the minor fallen angels.

Suggestion: let's keep ALL our letters – if youve got any old ones of mine send them along some time and I'll document them for private publication ....

Lunch with Joy tomorrow. Then 'King's Row'.[9] Think she should take a shot of me every so often, just for the hell of it ... [...]

Back to correcting chronicle proofs ....

Back to Latin unseen ....

KPT

Back to back to baku bakus bacchus bacchae euripides euripides oh the hell with it back to methuselah.

Back soon.

STOP! Mother found your last but one letter in a coat that was going to be cleaned and there was an almighty fuss. She threatened to stop my allowance 'if this was what I spent it on', and made me promise I hadnt had intercourse with Freda.[10] So WATCHITWILLYA?

Sayonara! (Jap farewell: 'since it must be')

kptjjh:

title for play: 'the work of a moment': or, some abstruse quotation (always a good thing).

ACT I: Scene: Hell

A brothel is the temple, with prostitutes as priestesses and the bar as the altar. Devil is playing ginrummy; the world has not yet been created. God is a doddering old man with some fantastic liberal ideas; he has some 'immoral' ideas about morality.

Excuse for creation of world: Devil wants to get rid of a troublemaking God, and says he may have control of the world he (Satan) is about to create. The real reason is that the Devil's power of creation has been questioned; he SAYS he created himself but some of his followers refuse to accept that. His speech, in which he describes how he created himself, might be worked up into something good. So he creates Earth, and Man, and Woman.

ACT II: Earth

Adam and Eve are bored: God is afflicting them just as he afflicted

Satan. Then Satan gives them Sex and appears to them in the person of a Snake. He has pitied their Ennui. Then he gives them further pleasure by (a) intro of wife-beating (b) of murder (Cain and Abel). Then he gets tired, and dislikes the hold that God's 'immoral' hints of Xtianity are achieving. So he creates an evasive hypocrite, J.C., who will show by his example the worthlessness of Xtianity. But the people of Earth are such fools that they worship what they should have scorned. Then Renaissance (ex God), countered by Reformation (ex Satan). Then Reason (ex Satan) to counter faith (ex God). Could be brought up to date with present war. Satan, by the way, is puzzled at God's threats of fiery hell after death. He likes Hell fine.

ACT III: Postcreation

Satan, seeing God making Hitler into a comic caricature of himself, is enraged, and seeks to destroy the world. God refuses to do it, and becomes engaged in an almighty struggle with the devil – at least, to him it is almighty, and he strikes heroic attitudes. But Satan just takes him figuratively by the seat of the pants and brings him to order by showing him a woman. This unsettles God's Xtianity and brings him back to Satan by having intercourse.

Then Judgment Day, with Satan presiding. He only forgives those who have created beauty – as he has a flair for art. This might mean

(a) that Hell is a place of beautiful godlessness or

(b) that artists are the devil's spawn.

A nice choice.

The piece ends with our being informed that the world was only created the previous evening. For ... a thousand ages in thy sight are like an evening gone[11] ....

(what about evolution)

a few characteristics in men which Satan could claim as his own:

intuition

conventionality

not immorality, but amorality

add some – this is last minute

1) God = W E Gladstone[12]

2) Satan: Orson Welles

A Message to YOU from the Portuguese National
Union of Grass-cutters. Come along –
and bring a friend ....

[1] Anno Tynani.

[2] KPT's first letter about this arcane amorality play was of 24 November: 'The whole point of it, I feel, is that the Devil is horrified by the goodness of God and considers him immoral.' In a letter of 27 December he wrote, 'We are preaching the case of scepticism and the senses.'

[3] Monty Woolley (1888–1963), American actor famous for his film portrayal of Alexander Woollcott (thinly disguised as 'Sheridan Whiteside') in *The Man Who Came to Dinner* (US, 1942).

[4] W. C. Fields (1879–1946), bulbous-nosed comic actor of stage and screen; KPT wrote of him in *Sight and Sound*, February 1951: 'He would screw up his lips to one side and purse his eyes before committing himself to speech; and then he would roll vowels around his palate as if it were a sieve with which he was prospecting for nuggets.'

[5] Arnold Schönberg (1874–1951), Austrian composer, developed 12-note composition and was the teacher of Alban Berg (1885–1935).

[6] Sir William Turner Walton (1902–83), English composer of works such as *Façade* (modelled on Schönberg's *Pierrot lunaire*), and the music to Olivier's films *Henry V* (1944) and *Hamlet* (1948).

[7] Composed in 1830. The correct title is 'Songe d'une nuit de sabbat'.

[8] G. K. Chesterton (1874–1936), English poet and author of works including the Father Brown stories.

[9] The story of three children growing up in a small town, directed by Sam Wood, starring among others the young Ronald Reagan (US, 1941).

[10] Another local girl.

[11] From a hymn by Isaac Watts in the *Psalms of David Imitated* (1719).

[12] William Ewart Gladstone (1809–98), Liberal Prime Minister 1868–74 and 1880–85, responsible for educational and electoral reforms.

To Julian Holland

229 Pupuportland Rd
16th Dec, 16 A.T. [1943]

Dear [Julian]:

Reply to letter of Tuesday.

First, a smattering of odd facts. First, this is being typed on the orderly room[1] typewriter. Second, I have bought two excellent books, 'Just Another Word' by Ivor Brown,[2] and 'The Theatre in Soviet

Russia' by Andre van Gyseghem.[3] Third, I saw a much smoother and clearer version of 'Potemkin' at the Overseas Club[4] last night with Freda, who enjoyed it enormously and whom I have definitely HOOKEDISAIDHOOKED. I read the first hundred pages of 'Ulysses' in the reflib[5] the other day; it is prob the finest comic classic of our time. There is one glorious chapter in which he parodies EVERY English prose style from Malory to Shaw – and does it superbly. Just an exercise in virtuosity but what a master. Last, I have formulated my credo, taken largely from D H Lawrence:

I BELIEVE

(1) That sex is the supreme mystical emotion
(2) That Natural Man should indulge his appetites completely amorally
(3) That Good and Evil are words, meaningless in the presence of the Ideal, which is beauty (note: this comes from Mallarmé)[6]
(4) That the world is the symbol of life and should be worshipped
(5) That Christianity has emphasised the Light Gods too much; and that the Dark Gods should be stressed to restore the balance
(6) That Evil is something distinct from both the Light and the Dark Gods, and is a negation of both
(7) Part, at least, of the creation is to be attributed to the Dark Gods
(8) That this belief should not be accepted without consideration of the others (this cuts out the petty sensualist) [...]

'DU BARRY WAS A LADY'[7] drags – but I hate Skelton.[8] Good moments: Virginia O'Brien's song about striptease called 'Slice it where you like, its still Salome'; ALL the other songs, esp Skelton's 'If you don't love an Esquire girl'; AAANNNDDD

ZZEERROO MMOOSSTTEELL

Zero Mostel Zero Mostel[9] does a wonder but marve lus burlesque not burlesque tour de bloody force of imitation of the balding Boyer[10] in a recent lovescene. All the old traits – inability to smoke, difficulty with hair and false teeth are all here, with the brisk viciousness of the cartoonist's art. The voice, the gesture is exquisite all in all the best five minutes for many many months many many. [...]

goodbye my friends the TYPEwriter is a real b7_½ard and DO y thoitaay BEITHINK "I%d bettttttter wring ghgoff before L becom. incoh¼r@nt. bHle£s ttonyb 3tts wiCh the ?acred?eak of mammon and %oloch. see you soon – ah, got the = 6 = working again ...

K.P.T.

(¼£85) – thats shit in hieroglyphics .....

[1] Reserved for officers in the wartime Junior Training Corps.

[2] Ivor Brown (1891–1974), drama critic of the *Observer* (1929–54) and during the war its editor. In 1954 he was ousted as drama critic and replaced by the youthful upstart KPT.

[3] André van Gyseghem, *The Theatre in Soviet Russia* (1943).

[4] A social club for members of the Allied forces from overseas and students of Birmingham University.

[5] The Birmingham Reference Library.

[6] Stéphane Mallarmé (1842–98), French poet and founder with Verlaine of the Symbolist Movement.

[7] Film adaptation of Broadway musical comedy directed by Roy del Ruth, with Gene Kelly and Lucille Ball (US, 1943).

[8] Richard 'Red' Skelton (b. 1913), burlesque and vaudeville actor who starred in many MGM musicals with the singing comedienne Virginia O'Brien (b. 1921).

[9] Zero Mostel (1915–77), actor and stand-up comic. In his profile of Mel Brooks (*Show People*, 1980) with whom Mostel worked on *The Producers* (1967), KPT quoted Brooks as saying: 'It was like working in the middle of a thunderstorm. Bolts of Zero – blinding flashes of Zero – were all around you.'

[10] Charles Boyer (1897–1978), French actor who became one of Hollywood's most successful romantic leading men.

To Julian Holland

229, Portland Rd.
27.12.43

Dear Yules

[...] Now to Chaos. My parents have chosen to take my going to London as a matter for a vote of confidence. They say I have no right to go against their wishes at sixteen; and my mother has threatened (quite seriously) to disinherit me if I go. My father has become extremely traditional about it; he chooses to see a sinister design behind your taking a flat just before I arrive, and I think he thinks you are homosexual. My visiting aunts, uncles, and firemen have been enlisted to help her plead. I have had to insult them all, severally; to one weeping relation I actually said, 'Get the hell out of here, you bore me.' A family split is imminent; my mother feels the rest of the gang are laughing at her lack of control over me.

Why does she object to my going? Simply and solely because of That Letter, about you and Tony[1] getting drunk and being stroked by whores. Mother is determined to believe that you are the incarnation of Carnal Temptation; and your damning remark about your flat ('what a brothel it will be!') has finally decided the matter. I have argued with her that you don't mean it seriously, that you forgot it the second you wrote it, but she will not accept this. She regards your mind as Carlyle regarded Swinburne's – as a cesspool in which you sit and piss filth.[2]

That is the outline – everyone is emoting but me.

What do I want? I want you – but I'd better break it gently.

I have tried to get references for you from outsiders – but Mother is sure that I have bought them into it. What I want is for you to write to her, and explain how foolish her doubts and fears are. Be stolid, sober, and sincere, and she'll lap it up. Tell her what a good, restrained chap you are, and make her laugh at her qualms.

This is just a suggestion; if you don't want to do it, by all means don't – it's a lot to ask. But if you have a few minutes to spare, it might ease things here a little.

I have written a song to Gerard Manley Hopkins 'When will you, peace'; I have bought Paparelli's book[3] on playing the blues and can now play them; I have been overwhelmed by the art of Meyerhold.[4] [...]

write to mrs t

bye

kpt

HOLD THIS. MY NEXT TO BE WRITTEN ENTIRELY IN JOYCE'S
STREAM-OF-CONSCIOUSNESS METHOD.

[1] Anthony Betts, ex-KES boy and one-time scientist who shared a flat with Holland in London. See letter of 29 January 1944.

[2] An apocryphal story credited to the nineteenth-century illustrator Andrew Lang, who reported a dinner-party remark by the historian Thomas Carlyle about the poet Algernon Charles Swinburne: 'He sits in a cesspool and adds to it.'

[3] Frank Paparelli, *The Blues and How to Play 'Em* (1942).

[4] Vsevolod Emillevich Meyerhold (1874–c.1940), Russian actor and director opposed to the naturalistic theatre of Stanislavsky; he was given his own theatre in Moscow in 1920 but fell out of favour and was imprisoned in the 1930s.

To Julian Holland

229, Portland Rd.,

22nd January, 17 A.T. [1944]

Dear Julian:

[...] Time's been full: Journal[1] (abbreviated) follows:

Tues. Jan 11th

School back. B. H. Williams[2] 'was again the knife of the party, bursting with brutal conviviality.' Launched onto the French Revolution with May.[3] Head Master[4] talked learnedly about how the war has affected the Balance of Power. Saw 'Holy Matrimony'[5] in the afternoon, and was considerably amused by one stroke of genius, viz.:

'American claims mole record: has 105!'

Then went round to my new plump Kathleen.[6] She peeked round the door gingerly and said: 'I'm in isolation', which I took to mean 'I'm alone.' It was only after necking frantically with her for about 10 minutes that I discovered that she was in isolation for scarlet fever ....

Dreamt of 'a KPT clad in insecure porridge-stained pyjamas insulting Ivor Novello[7] and Noel Coward[8] simultaneously and undefeatedly, and finally beating Dame Lillian Braithwaite[9] with a metaphorical umbrella. I know it was metaphorical because there was a large card attached to it reading:

"This umbrella is metaphorical. By Order." '

Wed, Jan 12

Mr Sheldon's[10] teeth have arrived; his face is at least three inches longer. Read A.J.A. Symons exciting biography of the greatest literary figure and stylist of the last century, the ornate and homosexual Frederick Rolfe, Baron Corvo.[11] Also picked up a 'Lilliput'[12] containing a remarkable picture of Orson Welles. He follows me around.

Went to Overseas Club, and with Dave at my right foot, Charles at my left, Sam on my left arm, Geoff on my right, and M.F.M. Jones havering around.[13] A clique which exceeded that of our lounging effeminate, Neville Hill.[14] We saw Jean Gabin in 'Quai des Brumes'.[15] Gabin is solid and Spencer Tracyish; Michèle Morgan smoulders most enticingly; but the direction is unnoticeable, apart from a murder in a cellar with a wireless playing a Bach Mass upstairs.

Read Stephen Crane's poetical 'Bowery Tales'[16] as nightcap.

Thur, Jan 13th

'Woke up realising that from my point of view this war should end in defeat for the Allies. Victory will be an anti-climax which my dramatic sense instantly rejects. Defeat alone will satisfy my grasp for things to FEEL.'

'Frederick Rolfe, heralded by the dark, moulting flutterings of the raven on his crest, is a beautifully recondite figure.' (All quotations from ME)

Have a new pose: arrogance, bass voice, hanging lower lip. Which reads O-R-S-O-N.

Suggested to REG[17] an intimate revue with the girls school. [...]

Saturday, January 15th
PETER CRESSWELL[18] KNOWS ORSON WELLES
I now carry a black silk umbrella with a red silk ribbon wound <u>spirally</u> round it.

Peter Cresswell talked brilliantly on the Drama at the Youth Forum.[19] He described the Stratford Memorial Theatre[20] as 'definitely a white elephant, though it is painted strawberry pink.' But he saw little in films, disliked exhibitionist producers; and didn't mention Orson.

With a vibrant umbrella, I sprang up. I said my name was K P Tynan, and that I was angry. I told Cresswell all about the Soviet producers; hinted that he ought to learn something about continental films; and told him that he ought to worship Orson Welles – if he had ever heard of him.

He rose, this crabby, wizened, young-old man, and said he had spent two years in Russia studying drama under Stanislavsky;[21] he had travelled through Germany & France studying film technique: and he was a personal friend of Orson Welles!

I had a good chat with Cresswell afterwards. I asked him about Welles – was he great? Cresswell said: 'He is the greatest man I have ever known. He is a very great genius – perverse and difficult, but there's something very terrific there.'

He extended His hand to me, and He said: 'I (this I) am very glad to have known you, Mr Tynan.' And I (this I) said: 'Thanks ... thanks ...' [...]

Wrote Chapter 1 of a novel I am planning about a paranoic, called 'A Child is Born'. Chap. 1 is all about his birth; there is a dingy cat which excretes whenever the action flags. [...]

Tues. Jan 18th
Read Stekel on 'Sexual Aberrations'[22] and brooded all day. [...]

Friday, Jan 21st
Gave a perfectly timed selection of pictures (all color) on the Epidiascope,[23] & talked successfully on the Impressionists, Post-Impressionists, and Picasso. Showed <u>60</u> pictures in <u>60</u> minutes. Took as my text Manet's 'The most important person in any picture is the light.' [...]

Saturday, Jan 22nd
Saw 'SALUDOS AMIGOS'[24] and thought it the next best Disney to 'Fantasia'. Goofy's Gaucho scene v.g.; the Donald Duck-llama scene

excellent; the Pedro sequence amusing & well observed – <u>BUT</u> the Rio scenes, and 'Brasie' – ooh lovely.

The warm white sand the surf – and Disney's soul satisfying and exotic colors – the flowers with red lips; the tropical vegetation which is transformed into animal life; the bananas which become toucans; the red drips of paint which become the legs of flamingos; the blue waterfall – and behind it all the compelling samba rhythm. I samba'd all the way home.

———

Surely Disney loves color more than any man since Cézanne? Well!

Write soon. Sorry if the style is flat; I write at breakneck speed . . . All love from P. S. McLean, K. S. Makin[25] and the

Arts Society [26]

and its patron

K.P.T.

[1] The Holland correspondence is the only direct source for excerpts from KPT's journals, from which he worked up some of his theatre reviews for his first book *He That Plays the King* (1950)

[2] Barry Williams, a KES contemporary. See letter of 29 January 1944.

[3] A KES History master.

[4] Charles Richard Morris (1898–1990), later Lord Morris of Grasmere, a distinguished academic, was headmaster 1943–8 (KPT told Holland that he was the 'best headman any village ever had'). Morris ran the Sixth Form History class to which KPT belonged, on the Oxbridge tutorial system. In *Reputations* (1981), a BBC programme about KPT, Morris said of him, 'It always seemed to me ... even when he was using very striking sentences, striking words ... he meant exactly what he said.'

[5] Nunnally Johnson's film version of Arnold Bennett's novel *Buried Alive*, with Monty Woolley and Gracie Fields (US, 1943).

[6] Kathleen Richmond. KPT had described her to Holland as 'a gorgeous young light-heavyweight ... who kisses like a kick from Whirlaway' (26 December 1943). (Whirlaway has been variously explained as: a fairground ride, a whirling water spray, a small vortex-shaped confection, a douche bag, or the racehorse who won the Kentucky Derby in 1941.)

[7] Ivor Novello (1893–1951), British stage matinée idol, author and composer whose plays include *Careless Rapture* (1936) and *The Dancing Years* (1939).

[8] Sir Noël Coward (1899–1973) wrote of KPT in his diary on 20 September 1951, 'A curious young man, very intelligent and with a certain integrity'. KPT described Coward's performance at the Café de Paris in 1951 as 'exuberant, replete to the brim with a burning, bright *nostalgie de la boo-hoo*, taut, facially, as an appalled monolith' (*Panorama*, 1952).

[9] Dame Lillian Braithwaite (1873–1948), English actress who played many Shakespearean parts in Sir Frank Benson's company, then became a star of West End comedies.

[10] G. A. Sheldon, a KES English master. See letter of 29 January 1944.

[11] A. J. A. Symons (1900–41), bibliographer, dandy and authority on the literature of the 1890s. Author of *The Quest for Corvo*, a biography of Frederick Rolfe (1860–1913), known as Baron Corvo, the English novelist and essayist whose rejection of the Roman Catholic Church inspired his most famous novel, *Hadrian VII* (1904).

[12] *Lilliput* (founded 1937), 'The Pocket Magazine for Everyone', contained photographs, articles and short stories.

[13] Probably David Bench, Charles Parker, Geoff Darby and Sam Drinkwater; along with M. F. M. Jones, all KES boys. See letter of 29 January 1944.

[14] Neville Hill, Holland's cultural companion, succeeded by KPT.

[15] *Quai des Brumes* (France, 1938; *Port of Shadows* in US), classic melodrama directed by Marcel Carné, starring Jean Gabin (1904–76) and Michèle Morgan (b. 1920).

[16] Stephen Crane (1871–1900), American novelist known for *The Red Badge of Courage* (1895). *Bowery Tales* was published in 1900.

[17] R. E. Greenway, KES Geography master in charge of the school Dramatic Society. See letter of 29 January 1944.

[18] Untraced.

[19] A monthly seminar started in 1939 and held at Birmingham University for young people to discuss current questions such as 'Youth and War'.

[20] The Shakespeare Memorial Theatre, Stratford, built in 1879, burnt down 1926, re-opened 1932, now houses the Royal Shakespeare Company.

[21] Konstantin Sergeievich Stanislavsky (1863–1938), Russian actor, director and teacher who founded the Moscow Arts Theatre in 1898. The author of several books on acting, he was an important influence on the American 'Method' school.

[22] Wilhelm Stekel, *Sexual Aberrations: The Phenomena of Fetishism in Relation to Sex* (1930).

[23] A projector for slides.

[24] Disney's film of Donald Duck and friends in South America (US, 1943).

[25] P. S. McLean, a close friend of KPT's, left KES in 1944 and later joined the Foreign Office; K. S. Makin, another close KES friend and fellow prankster. See letter of 29 January 1944.

[26] KPT wanted to rename the school Literary Society the Four Arts Society, which would explore 1) painting, sculpture, architecture; 2) music and ballet; 3) film, drama and radio; 4) literature.

To Julian Holland

229, Portland Rd.
26th January; 1944

My dear boy:

It is with some diffidence and not a little timerity [*sic*] that I take up my pen to extend my thoughts to you: but there is an abundance of news, one piece of which is so startling and satisfying in itself that none shall keep me from transmitting it posthaste to you. Before growing to a point, and revealing to you that which has caused me such unwonted excitement, it were pleasant for me, and, I trust, for you, to set down two odd pieces I have transcribed from a new word-monger in 'Punch'. He writes a weekly entertainment under the heading of 'Table-talk of Amos Intolerable':[1] and I admit to submitting to no little measure of risibility at my first reading these gems. The first is a suggestion made by Amos for a title of a biography of an eminent but discredited peer:

'Noblesse Oblique'

And the second is the name he has adopted for a biography upon which he is working of the justly renowned fabulist:

'Aesop's Foibles'

But this, I conceive, is inchoate chitchat; I had best release the cat from the bag. This morning, whilst enjoying a warming sip of a popular milk beverage, there was thrust upon me a letter from an Organisation, ostensibly calling itself the Workers' Film Association.[2] In a pet (for it much displeases me to be disturbed as I eat) I brusquely ripped open the envelope, and extracted the smoothly folded missive. It was written by a gentleman whose prose style was by no means equal to the information he educed. For the merely nominal fee of £1–5–0 each he will lend me Sergei Eisenstein's 'Potemkin' and 'The General Line'.[3]

Not unnaturally, I abandoned my warm drink and fled to school. An immediate conference with Mr Ounsted and our egregious head master was productive of these conclusions:

1. That he (Mr Morris) was unwilling lightly to provoke a Communist outbreak in the school so early in his administration.

2. That therefore he would suggest that we project 'Potemkin' on March 13th, and reserve 'The General Line' for the succeeding term.

Hence my eagerness to communicate to you. Nothing, dear boy, would occasion me more urgent pleasure than to enable you to be present at the showing of 'The General Line', which will be in May. May I, therefore, ask you whether you are like to be free in May: and require of you to send me a date or dates when I may wait on you in Birmingham? ...

Maybe I've quit thinking and maybe not, but you know how it is, you want to get away and first thing you know you're in a picture show and staring at some fool film.[4] Well, that's the way it was with me. I was there and I was smoking quite some and Leslie Howard and Bette Davis were out there playing around. I thought it was crazy and it was a darned good cigarette. Maybe I'm crazy, I don't know. I'm from Missouri. Leslie Howard, he was there and a round little guy named Eric or something, Eric Blore. I looked hard and I laughed a lot but all I could see when I looked at Leslie Howard playing a ham actor was soft bones rolling around on the bed of the Atlantic and I felt plenty for Leslie Howard. Then suddenly I was roaring and I was remembering something Eric Blore said. He said:

'If I weren't a gentleman's gentleman, I could be such a cad's cad!' [. . .]

Mene, mene, tekel upharsin,[5] which simply means that in his new book Mr Jack Iams[6] has bitten off considerably more than he can comfortably chew. That is not to say, however, that 'Prophet by Experience' is a bad book. On the contrary, it is not a bad book. But whereas a bad book may amuse and still be a bad book, a good book need not amuse and still be a good book. Which proves nothing, except perhaps the truth of Flaubert's dictum: chacun a son gout, which was nothing more nor less than his way of saying 'One man's meat is another man's spam.' Though of course he would never have been so crude about it. Flaubert once defined the qualities requisite in a judge; a judge, he says, must be leisurely, sweet-spoken, and wrong. I translate because I am writing for the people. But to return. Flaubert's judge is quite unlike me, who am rapid, rude, and right. As Ivor Brown so wittily quoted from 'Othello' in his eulogy of 'The Man Who Came to Dinner': 'Rude am I in my speech.' Ivor and I have had our quarrels, notably over the Bergner,[7] who took all the critics in beautifully. I don't recall that he objected at the time. My divining rod, on the other hand, just took one look and said 'NO'.

'Prophet by Experience' is all about two reporters who try to lure an old réclus out of his cave. He greets them with these words, which immediately bring to mind Pater[8] at his most lyrical or Shelley at his silliest: 'No fancy pants, I.' You will say this is bottom-drawer humor, that it is what Henry James would have called 'a leetle bit off the top'. To which I reply: yes, but so is most of Massinger's[9] humour, not to mention Mark Twain. Or Bret Harte.[10] [. . .]

There is a phrase from Pierre Louys[11] which would describe this book perfectly, but unfortunately I have lent my copy to the milkman. It's no use you moderns saying that I've no need to quote, you know the one I mean. Because you DON'T. No one ever reads Pierre Louÿs nowadays. Lying perdu in my memory is something that Baudelaire said of Walter Pater that would apply perfectly to modern prose-writers. Unfortunately I can't remember it for the life of me. Sarah[12] would have known it.

And that's about enough pastiche for one letter. Hope you recognised imitations of Lord Chesterfield,[13] Hemingway,[14] and Agate,[15] in that order. Only other news is my purchase of 'Heritage of Symbolism'[16] and a one-vol complete edition of Boswell; my first dip produced this:

'Jones loved beer, and did not get very forward in the church.'

But this MUST do.

Was given a threepage essay for caplessness by one of the Shock Troops.[17] Young whippersnapper. Young belly-acher. Did it, however, and handed it in deprecatingly. Like Max[18] in his cartoon of himself.

Bye.

K. P. T.

[...]

---

[1] *Punch*, a satirical magazine started in 1841, which folded in 1992. Richard Mallett wrote 'Table Talk of Amos Intolerable'.

[2] Amateur filmmaking unit belonging to the Communist Party, founded in the early 1930s by Ralph Bond.

[3] Silent Communist propaganda film by Sergei Eisenstein (USSR, 1929).

[4] *It's Love I'm After* (US, 1937), comedy about the backstage fighting of a stage star couple, directed by Archie Mayo, starring Leslie Howard (1893–1943; best known as Ashley Wilkes in *Gone With the Wind*), Bette Davis (1908–89) and the English actor Eric Blore (1887–1959).

[5] The Book of Daniel, 5.25.

[6] 1943 book by Samuel Harrey 'Jack' Iams, American crime fiction writer.

[7] The Viennese actress Elisabeth Bergner (1897–1986) had moved to England in 1933.

[8] Walter Pater (1839–94), English critic and essayist influenced by the aesthetics of the Pre-Raphaelite movement; author of *Appreciations: with an Essay on Style* (1889).

[9] Philip Massinger (1583–1640), English dramatist famous for *A New Way to Pay Old Debts* (printed 1633).

[10] Bret Harte (1836–1902), American essayist and short story writer, spent his last years in England.

[11] Pierre Louÿs (1870–1925), French author of poems including *Chansons de Bilitis*, the subject of one of the most successful literary hoaxes of the nineteenth century, and novels such as *Aphrodite: moeurs antiques* (1876) and *La Femme et le Pantin* (1898).

[12] Sarah Bernhardt (1844–1923), legendary French actress.

[13] Lord Chesterfield (1694–1773), English statesman, orator and wit, author of *Letters* to his natural son Philip Stanhope (published 1774).

[14] Ernest Hemingway (1899–1961), American novelist and short story writer. In 'Papa and the Playwright' (*Playboy*, May 1964), KPT described their first meeting, in Madrid in the mid-1950s: 'Expecting a booming titan, I had been amazed to shake hands with a gruff, gigantic boy, shy and reticent in manner despite the heroic head.'

[15] James Agate (1877–1947), dramatic critic of the *Sunday Times* 1923–47.

[16] C. M. Bowra, *The Heritage of Symbolism* (1943).

[17] Maurice 'Willie' Shock was made head boy of KES in 1943; no doubt the 'Shock Troops' were the prefects under his command. See letter of 29 January 1944. Vice-Chancellor of the University of Leicester (1977–87), he was knighted in 1988.

[18]Max Beerbohm (1872–1956), celebrated English satirist, cartoonist and novelist, replaced George Bernard Shaw as drama critic of the *Saturday Review*.

To Julian Holland

229, Portland Rd.
29.1.44

Dear J:

[...] Extracts from Journal: [...]

Mon, Jan 24: Impromptu Debate.[1] Me on the futility of clothes ('Rousseau and I want you to go back to 'le noble sauvage'. Frankly, we're pretty sauvage ourselves .....'
and 'Our clothes are bad; they keep man from brother man ... and incidentally from sister woman') wrote up some BRILLIANT minutes which Geoff Darby will never dare to read. (EG: 'A T Tolley,[2] briefly accusing the Acting Secretary of homosexuality whilst firewatching ...')

Saw Leslie Howard – but this I've told you before. I've probably repeated myself dreadfully in this letter, if so, sorry, but my time's so full I really cannot remember anything ....

Tues, Jan 25: [Dr] Johnson is marvellous. He delves into the obvious and brings forth truth; your modern writer delves into the subtle and brings forth the super-subtle.

[...]

Sat, Jan 29: Lacked 'that lift'. Dennis Reese at school. Saw 'Bachelor Mother'[3] which I thought delightful and beautifully handled. Ginger Rogers plays this sort of light stuff better than anyone.

Then went to Hall Green[4] with Kathleen. I had been told all week that there was a version of Our Show to be put on at Club; and that It was Tewnite, and called 'Hellzasockin'.[5] I went. It was not on. There had been a hoax a gigantesque conspiracy. I. soon. found. out. why. I had been at the place half an hour, selling dance tickets, and oiling around indiscrimately [*sic*], when my coat was ceremoniously presented to me by a Gink,[6] and I was shown the door. I asked Pete Mac what was up. He said that there were five Ginks who ran a Fascist League[7] in Hall Green and that they had taken exception to my remarks about being a Tory Imperialist[8] at the Youth Forum. So they had got me there just for the pleasure of chastening me and seeing me go.

Little, ufcawss, did they guess. They (Christopher Busby,[9] Bulgin,[10] and a spotty bespekked fellow I instantly christened Jukes) were rather underestimating me, I feel. I had them brought to me. I quietly placed my coatandhat on the floor, and, taking a deepish breath, I went into the most exquisite flow of mordant sarcasm I have ever administered – at each Fascist, one, of course, following another. They stammered. They were baffled. And, though I seemed unconcerned, I despised them with that indigenous spite which I reserve for political fanatics. Behind their eyes, I said, I saw the whole grisly chronicle of political assassinations since Machiavelli; I began by telling them I did not give autographs on Saturdays, and from there on I was intarissable. I relished every rolling syllable; and when one of them dared to be petty and lowlife about Kathleen's morals, I nearly showed wrath. Selfcontrol and my whipwords triumphed; occasionally a little guttery ('You remind me, my friend, of a turkey I once ate … but don't be insulted – the turkey looked very much like Humphrey Bogart …') sometimes extremely foxy ('You amuse me; you are so drool'); and mostly just blinding. I might depart with some gain of face – but I fear they'll never love me there.

By the way, if you hear distorted versions of this, try to be impartial. My conduct made Kathleen agree to marry me in three years time when dv[11] I shall be an undergrad. Breach of Promise. And I don't really want to have It with her. And anyway she suggested it so I'm All Right.

A few extracts from the 'Characters' in my Index: [...]

Mick Banton:[12] a keen, spruce, nose-projecting hound. Under my influence; he tries to see thru me, but the more he tries, the deeper he becomes entangled. Has intelligence but scoffs at subtlety.

JDC:[13] Neardeaf mountebank, with a sound knowledge of History, a rocky basis of Communism, and an inexorable flow of words. Has presented so effective a mask to the world that he has forgotten his inner self, which has withered.

RCD:[14] Bulky Daily-Express addict. Bristling black moustache and brusquely intimate method of teaching. Classical brain, but the lips of a professional toper.

Geoff Darby: Roundfaced, pushful, amiable. Vast propensity for looking distrait. Has the best type of self-confidence – sunny and avowed.

Joyce Griffiths: Colorless but naively attractive girl, with no personality and a wideyed retinue. What is known as a physical success.

Ken Hudson: Hall Green lurker. Associates indiscriminately with JJH.

Ambles, not walks; brown with tobacco; lacks willpower and loathes effort. The makings of a monumental drug addict.

Neville Hill: Lounging and gruffly effeminate egoist, with an eye cocked to fashionable literary taste among the unfashionable, and to unfashionable literary taste among the fashionable. Makes his own secondhand remarks seem original by affecting to deliver them 'aside'.

W Hall: A bland, offhand paranoiac with a delight in quietly inflicting himself on everyone. Sets physics prep like an introspective executioner.

Joy Matthews: Redhaired and staid: shallow – but a good background for Me. Splashes about in life's waters, never bothering to take off her clothes and dive into it.

Gillian Key: Not a flame, because she never sparked. Just calf-love – but what calves!

F L Kay:[15] Small, dapper, shiny-suited, scanty-haired bourgeois with ideas about everything, and 'idees fixes' about most things. A wit, but diffident enough to respect those less intelligent than himself. [...]

K S Makin: Delightful KEHS zany, with an ebullient and impish diffidence. [...]

Pete McLean: A quiet, flatfaced artist; perceptive and receptive, both of me and of new ideas. Tolerant and trustworthy. DIRTY laugh he has though very dirty. [...]

J O[unsted]: Devotee of T S Eliot, liver with Ballet Girls whose grandfathers are Protestant Archdeacons, and possessor of very low mind; chairman of lit soc. His youth is his passport to our confidence.

Ernest Price: Ex-Jamaican schoolmaster, aesthetically blind, childish and disgusting by turn in conversation. Suspected of not only being a Schoolmaster for Schoolmastering's Sake.[16] Bears resemblance to an owl – a stuffed owl. In Gorki's phrase: 'He is like mush, to those who can't chew.' [...]

GAS[heldon]: Aged and tottering opium addict, with a precise and unimpassioned knowledge of English Literature. Hater of extremism.

M Shock: A tidy mind with some dark and dirty corners. Tendency to condescend; love of authority; and little enough else.

Joe Simon: a bland and licentious Jew; intelligence and a certain low and incisive wit. [...]

B H Williams: A bombastic, oily rascal with dirty humours and foul connexions. The only lout I allow to address me by my Christian name.

ARE THEY <u>TEREW</u>? FOR IT IS (ISN'T IT?) THE <u>TEREWTH</u> THAT REALLY MATTERS, AFTER ALL.

That is all. That is all. Just saw dreadful film about American airman (George Montgomery[17]) saving Mr Churchill. Am writing to him:

Dr. Mr Montgomery:

Thank you for saving my life. I consider you a Bum. Also what a Ham!

(signed) Winston Churchill.

1.20 a.m. Judas priest I'm tired
'Yuhnight.

KPT

---

[1] KPT had now commandeered the school Debating Society (of which he was acting secretary) where he would break down those 'inhibitions of speech', as one master tactfully recalls, 'which led to his later verbal sensationalism'.
[2] KES contemporary who shared a love of jazz with KPT and who 'defended sensuality to the last ditch' at the Impromptu Debate. He later became Professor of English at Carlton University, Ottawa.
[3] Comedy directed by Garson Kanin, starring Ginger Rogers and David Niven (US, 1939)
[4] The Youth Club in Hall Green (a district of Birmingham) was run by a liberal-minded Reverend Percy Chatterton. Dances were held on Saturday night.
[5] KPT and Holland's summer 1943 version of Ole Olsen and Chic Johnson's anarchic film *Hellzapoppin* (US, 1942) was reviewed in the school magazine: 'Messrs Tynan and Holland appeared to have had the bewilderment of the audience as their principal aim.' When a dummy cat fell from the flies, the exchange went: 'Where did that cat come from?' 'The catwalk, of course.'
[6] Local slang for 'man'.
[7] KPT's invention.
[8] By the end of 1944 KPT had abandoned Tory Imperialism and was momentarily seduced by Shaw's Fabian Socialism, 'which does not mean the mobocracy I had feared'. Two weeks later he joined an anarchist group.
[9] Head boy of Camp Hill Grammar School, one of the seven schools that formed the KE foundation.
[10] KES contemporary.
[11] deus volens, 'God willing'.
[12] Michael P. Banton (b. 1926), KES contemporary who became Professor of Sociology at Bristol University 1965–92.
[13] J. D. Copeland, History master.
[14] R. C. 'Daddy' Dunt, Classics master.
[15] Latin master.

[16] KPT said of him, 'Of few others can one truly say, "Ecce homo".'
[17] George Montgomery (b. 1916), star of westerns in the 1940s and 1950s.

To Julian Holland

229, Portland Rd.
9th February, 16 AT [1944]

Dear J;
    [...] Feb 4: Saw 'Demi-paradise'[1] with Kathleen. Found it really
excellent, with an almost Gallic wit. Laurence Olivier[2] is both stolid
and brilliantly subtle; one of the nicest (in the true sense) performances
I remember. Anatol [*sic*] de Grunwald[3] deserves great credit especially
for the first half-hour. Felix Aylmer[4] is first-rate as a wealthy ship-
owner who takes snuff and knows Bradshaw backwards – a French
character, if ever I saw one. Touches of genius in Olivier's introduction
to an English village. He walks down the high street with Penelope
Dudley Ward,[5] and a woman whizzes past on a bike. All we hear from
her (and we never see her again) is ' . . . don't forget . . 7–30 . . the
Bishop . . what is truth . .'. Anthony Asquith[6] directed deftly. [...]

Your letter: [...]

5. Re Novel and Play. Sorry if I've offended you, but
    (a) We cannot write in collaboration by post. Corvo tried it and
        failed miserably. So did Thackeray. And so shall not we. When
        you have a week, we will spend day and night together on it. But
        you cannot create masterpieces by remote control.
    (b) Au contraire, my novel is here to hand, to be touched up as I am
        moved.
    (c) Don't worry; I'm quite determined to get this play done. [...]

I am wondering whether I am really a repulsive character – whether
my pose is exorcising the real Me. Hope not. But I wonder, nevertheless, wish I could be sure. The President of the Overseas Club said
balls to me . . . .
    Fucking lyrical tonight, aren't I?
    Bye now – I'm going to indulge one of my less lovable aberrations
. . .

                                                                    KPT
[...]

[1] *The Demi-Paradise* (UK, 1943) was, according to Olivier's biographer Anthony Holden, 'an Anthony Asquith exercise to help the British people warm to their new Russian allies', inspired by Churchill's Information Officer in charge of 'showbiz propaganda work'.
[2] Laurence Olivier (1907–89), knighted in 1947 and created a life peer in 1970. In *The Demi-Paradise* he played a Russian engineer posted to an English village packed with the national virtues, eccentricities and vices.
[3] Anatole de Grunwald (1910–67), Russian-born producer and screenwriter working in Britain.
[4] Sir Felix Aylmer (1899–1979), English actor who appeared in both British and American films, including *Henry V* (UK, 1944) and *Quo Vadis* (US, 1951).
[5] Penelope Dudley Ward (1914–82), English stage and film actress.
[6] Anthony Asquith (1902–68), English director and son of the Liberal Prime Minister. Also directed *The Winslow Boy* (UK, 1948) and *The Browning Version* (UK, 1951).

To Julian Holland

Edgbaston
19 February [1944]

Dear Jules
 [...] Fri, Feb 18:
 Am playing Shylock in Dramsoc production at end of term of last acts of the Merchant in mod dress. I should be brilliant. Read through the play whilst firewatching and decided to make him a young man, prematurely aged through persecution and hardened in [sic] a cold-blooded Harpagon.[1]
 Reread 'The Waste Land' and found it marvellous. Eliot says more for belief in this poem than the Archbishop of Canterbury ever did. It is, I conceive, the most important poem of this century, and, with Wilf Owen's[2] 'Strange Meeting', the best.
 Reread Thurber's fables,[3] from which I gleaned the word 'mouse' for woman, which I am busy making fashionable. [...]
 Remark on the Ten Commandments: 'Number 7 should be attempted and at least four others'. Definition of a he-man: 'A man who can't cross his legs for nuts'.

Ooh.   G'by.
KPT.

[1] Protagonist of Molière's *L'Avare* (The Miser, 1668).
[2] Wilfred Owen (1893–1918), English poet killed in action in the last week of the First World War. 'Strange Meeting' was written between November 1917 and February 1918.
[3] James Thurber's *Fables of Our Times* and *Famous Poems Illustrated* (1940).

To Julian Holland

229, Portland Rd.
29.2.44

Dear Jules:

[...] The Civics Society[1] have began a Bye-Election for the KES Division of Birmingham, with four candidates: Rawll[2] (Cons), Darby (Lib), Makin (Soc), Self (Ind. Confucian[3]). Willie Shock is said to be running the thing: and from hour to hour he makes bland and shocking additions to the rules, each one negating the next and generally creating a situation of hopeless disorder, conducive of mob chaos in the hands of such as the quite untrustworthy B H Williams. I have evolved a Fourteen-point Charter for Rationalists,[4] and 5 General Principles – involved the abolition of Political Organisations, of Legislative Government, of Organised Religion, of Conventional Morality – and the introduction of Contemplative Leisure[5] as the highest aim of man. The 14 points are superb, and include the repeal of laws against divorce, unnatural vice, and abortion. I have sent myself telegrams from Gandhi and Chiang Kai-Chek and held my first meeting today in the bogs. More later.

Debate on Socialism. I spoke of course against it, but there were those in the audience who disagreed, and the principles of socialism were made safe by those for democracy.

I have lately read Agate's 'Here's Richness!'[6] Do grab this: you can spend few hours better than with it.

I don't mind being considered a lunatic, but to be considered a harmless lunatic is too much. Yet that is my woeful situation at school. And your suggestive pen-portrait is all too nearly true.

In tears, I am,
    perhaps too insincerely,
        the boy upon whom
          so little depends
          and so much is
            weighing

AND now there's no blarsted ink _nd the Tyypewriter iiiis going al, to ell

ohgod
bbbbye
kpt

[1] The Civics Society was run by R. A. Greenway.
[2] Peter Rawll left KES in 1945.
[3] 'Confucianism stood for a sense of freedom and the joy of living,' KPT had argued in a debate on 27 March proposing that 'This House considers Happiness to be the Supreme Aim of Life'.
[4] So called in honour of Woodrow Wilson's 'Fourteen Point Charter', included in a speech of 8 January 1918 envisaging ways of ensuring the peace after the ending of World War I. Point 14 proposed the formation of a League of Nations.
[5] In a letter to Richard Crossman, Minister of Housing and Local Government in 1963, Ken proposed a Ministry of Leisure.
[6] *Here's Richness*, an anthology with a foreword by Osbert Sitwell (1942).

To Julian Holland

229, Portland Rd.
[4 March 1944]

Dear Jules:

Thanks for your very interesting review of Wolfit's Richard.[1] Agate always regarded this as one of his best: though, as Wolfit would be the first to admit, the moon-like face he possesses, shroud it though he may in whiskers and bedizen it with lines, is, like Garrick's,[2] essentially a comic face, a comic mask, perhaps (witness his garrulous Bottom, which he plays like Leonard Henry[3]). Richard III is a Renaissance villain, a wonderful development of Iago, and, to me at least, one of the most fascinating in a wonderful gallery of rogues.

I agree with you about Wolfit's women players; they succeeded in wrecking his Lear. Agate's theory of the great actor dominating all rather falls through in practice, for even a Gielgud[4] could not overawe such flimsy baggages as Wolfit is provided with.

Hope you like 'As You Like It'; apart from Act I, which is ridiculous and full of textual inconsistencies, this play is a joy, full of the country beyond Stratford and the gentlest of ironic commentaries on life. Touchstone and Jaques would be ideal travelling companions, except that Jaques would probably grow into a crashing bore and T. into a hairsplitting logic-chopper. [...]

The election:

On Thursday morn JDC[opeland] spotted my fourteen points, and immediately violated all privilege as well as all courtesy by tearing them down. I learnt of this, and became involved in an argument with him over the principle of the thing. He said they were disgusting and a mockery; I offered him the chance of taking up the challenge which I had issued the previous day to convince any member of the school or staff of their reasonableness within thirty minutes. He replied by taking the matter to REG (chairman, Civics Society). REG agreed with JDC, and asked me to retract the points or withdraw. I was proudly forced to withdraw. As I emerged from REG, I bumped into Charles and Gentle,[5] who were both enthusiastic about my program (especially the telegrams from Chiang Kai-Chek and Gandhi), and offered to speak in my support. I returned to tell REG I was back, but he had gone to offer the vacancy to Parker.

1. Censored as obscene
2. Censored as parochial
3. Censored as obscene
4.   „   „   „
5.   „   „   „
6.   „   „   „

and so on. I left it at that. Next morning Shock told me that REG was refusing to let me re-enter the lists, since that would mean his having to admit that he had CHANGED HIS MIND, and this would be infra dig. I hurtled to REG and argued vehemently with him for an hour. He remained calm and quite firm, so I acted – quite unscrupulously, I fear, but another great journalist once did it: I published a vast denunciation in green ink on our noticeboard headed:

'J'ACCUSE ...'

I accused the Lord Mayor of the Borough (REG) of refusing to allow me free speech: of refusing even to allow me to explain and apologise to my supporters for withdrawing; of ignoring the fact that I had spent a considerable sum on telegrams, etc, and that Gentle and Charles had prepared speeches and were coming to support me: all of which was true.

And now the entire business is off, because the other three candidates, Darby, Keith, and Pete Rawll, all withdrew in sympathy.

Another spanner into the works – quite unintentionally. [...]

Entered Gaumont Cinema, and found confronting me a vast picture of a Man, in a tall coat, with a floppy fur hat enveloping his head. His hands were clasped behind his back, and he regarded me. Brilliantly to parody a line of Victor Hugo (how brilliantly you'll never know):

'L'oeil était dans la caverne, et regardait Ken'[6]

I sank to my knees and salaamed, saying 'O Thou, My Infinite Lord and Master, in league and solemn covenant with Moloch and Mammon[7] I pray you to open forth your lips to shew forth Thy praise, for Thou art Eminently Worshipful, and I humble Myself before Thee, Pappy'

But He replied nothing, but continued to stand with his feet on the announcement: 'March 19th and Week: "Journey Into Fear"'

Nice phrase of Father Joseph's[8] for erection:
  'My concupiscences took fright.'
  Charles and Gentle send love, so do Pete McLean and Barry Williams.
  And now, goodnight.
  (The original of that Hugo line ends 'Cain')
  bhdkryusjwusyhrug758jgu jgly:[9]

KPT

JJH[olland]: Pseudo-worldly lover of compromise with mammon, with an annoying manner of cockiness and a pernicious habit of giving advice to genius. Great affection for the Large Vistas of Abstraction and few practical abilities save a certain suave and grinning charm.

'Not the Terewth, but do the Masses know the Terewth?'

---

[1] Sir Donald Wolfit (1902–68), last of the great touring actor/managers. KPT first saw Wolfit play Macbeth in November 1938, and was 'scared to death for days afterwards'.
[2] David Garrick (1717–79), the foremost English actor of his generation.
[3] Leonard Henry (1891–73), English actor and popular radio comedian.
[4] Sir (Arthur) John Gielgud (b. 1904), English actor and director. He had just directed *The Cradle Song* at the Apollo and was about to star in a repertory season at the Theatre Royal, Haymarket.
[5] Possibly C.A. Parker; 'Gentle' was possibly the nickname of D.J. Reuss.
[6] 'La Conscience', in *La Légende des Siècles* (1859).
[7] From Milton's *Paradise Lost*. Moloch was a Canaanite idol to whom children were sacrificed; Mammon, 'the least erected spirit that fell from heaven', symbolized wealth and greed.
[8] Possibly a nickname for a KES boy.
[9] Random typing.

To Julian Holland

King Edward's School
13 March [1944]

Dear Jules:
  I have seen Wolfit four times:[1]
  (1) 'Macbeth': wild, rasping, and gory. Well in tradition, with the witches' scenes receiving their usual dreadful handling.

(2) 'Lear': probably his best performance. Full of dignity, and with a grand entrance. Lear should be a mighty oak of man, like the Ancient of Days, yet 'blasted with ecstasy'. Wolfit combines power with pathos to a remarkable degree.

(3) 'Twelfth Night': a nicely lugubrious Malvolio.

(4) 'Midsummer Night's Dream': Bottom with great gusto; he has a clown's mask.

[...] You say that Hamlet should be undecided in his actions. As a Hamlet student, I can of course refute this. Only in his actions is he decisive. It is when he calls into play that awful intelligence of his, and begins arguing with himself (as when he fails to kill the praying King) that he lapses into dubiety. Remember that his indecision is not an integral part of his character; cut it out, and the prince is still a great creation. But the play is two hours shorter ...

He suffers from splenetic fits of melancholy, as when he insults Ophelia and browbeats Gertrude; then he is the jerky neurotic once more. Each actor will create a new Hamlet; and if you can see the play without noticing inconsistency between what he says and the way he says it, then the new creation is a triumph. Any sexual pervert could make a roaring success of Hamlet.

[...] I am bursting with the Big News:

On Friday night Joe Simon and I picked up two chorus girls from the Alex.[2] pantomime. One (mine) is called Jean Stringer. She is black-haired, petite, & intelligent. Likes Orson Welles & revels in Benny's Boyer.[3] And she is without exception the prettiest girl I have ever seen. If you want proof of my love:

1) I ate almost nothing on Saturday & Sunday.

2) I wrote her three postcards on Sunday.

On her invitation I am taking Joe & three others to the stage-door tonight; we are going to take Jean and four other lovely chorines to supper. I never want to pick up another girl; she is the sort of mouse you could have intercourse with and never feel ashamed. Her ambition is ballet, she adores Helpmann,[4] she is 16, & this is her first show. She has three other boyfriends about whom I am not giving a solitary damn. Let her '... loose now & then, A scatter'd smile; and that I'll live upon.'[5]

More later.

Other news fades [...]

I am having a black silk coat as Shylock.

That is All. Over to You.

Over.

KPT

[1] Wolfit's company played at the Theatre Royal, Birmingham 1943–5. KPT would usually sit 'on the shelf' for 9d. He wrote of Wolfit, all of whose performances of the Shakespearean repertory he saw in Birmingham in 1944: 'There has never been an actor of greater gusto than Wolfit: he has dynamism, energy, bulk and stature, and he joins these together with a sheer relish for resonant words which splits small theatres as Caruso shattered wine-glasses.' KPT argued he was no ham: 'On the contrary, he moves very slowly and predatorily, with immense finesse, and rises to his climaxes in clear and cogent steps' (*He That Plays the King*, 1950).

[2] Alexandra Theatre, Station Street, Birmingham, a repertory and touring company theatre.
[3] Jack Benny's imitation of Charles Boyer, probably on *The Jack Benny Programme*, broadcast on radio in the US 1932–50, and periodically in Britain.
[4] Sir Robert Helpmann (1909–86), Australian-born dancer, actor and director. Principal dancer at the Sadler's Wells Ballet 1933–50. Played Hamlet at the Old Vic in 1944, followed by other leading Shakespearean roles.
[5] *As You Like It*, Act III, Sc.v.

To Julian Holland

King Edward's School
Wednesday [5 April 1944]

Dear Jules:

Abysmally sorry about failing to write, but life has been very full. Don't remember when I last wrote, but will carry on from March 20th. [...]

Tues, March 21st

[...] Met a very attractive A.T.S.[1] friend; she is connected with blood transfusion and left me with the words: 'Cheer-Ho! I'm just going out on a Bleed!'

Wed, Mar 22

Saw 'Journey into Fear' again. The impression of fear emerges more clearly at a second visit, when one can overlook the ramifications of plot. The ending I conceive to be definitive: anything else would have been anti-climax.

Picked up an overwhelming and ebullient mouse named Patricia Evelyn Parkes.[2] She is fearfully affected, horribly emotional, and sensationally erotic; she told me three vile limericks. Her personality has as much vehemence as mine. [...]

Fri, Mar 24

[...] Gave a deliberately underplayed performance as Shylock for the Dramatic Society; the rest of the cast was meagre, and gave me little or no support. My restraint, I am told, has been regarded as part of a 'new conception' of the part; in fact, it was nothing of the sort – rather a scorn of the mouthing and ranting usually accorded to the part. Try to see Wolfit's Jew and tell me about it. [...]

Mon, Mar 27

Joint Debate: 'Happiness is the highest aim of man'.[3] I received a great and quite unexpected ovation on entering the Girls School

Lecture Theatre (audience abt. 200); it seems they knew me of old. I made certainly the best speech of my life, and dominated the debate like a patriarch.[4] The rest of the affair was merely a series of comments on & addenda to my effort; and my summing-up, daringly concessive to Shock (who opposed me), resulted in a small personal triumph, victory by 90 votes to 60. [...]

Wed, Mar 29th
   [...] C. R. Morris had a long talk to me about prefectship & coop-eration with the school. It seems that, if I am to be made a prefect, which he desires, and I misbehave myself or indulge any of my pro-vocative habits, he will waste very little time over expelling me; on the other hand, if I remain a free-lance, he is prepared to make allowance for me. He asks me to think it over.
   Now here is my great dilemma: shall I shackle myself, become continent, self-disciplined, and virtuous? or shall I carry freely on, and let the prefects go hang? Your advice, please – and bloody well not fatherly, please! [...]
   Bye for now; am off to play ping-pong with Willie S[hock].

[Ken]

[1] Auxiliary Territorial Service.
[2] A Birmingham actress.
[3] The Annual Joint Debate with the girls' school was held on 27 March 1944. KPT, proposing the motion, claimed that he revelled in the luxury of sensual pleasure, and concluded that it was better to have loafed and lost, than never to have loafed at all. Geoffrey Darby's minutes record that Maurice Shock said the proposer stood or fell by selfish pleasure, to which KPT replied that he was there to make the House *think*. James Dawson (see letter of 20 June 1945) noted in his diary: 'Tynan was at his very best today; brilliantly wrong.'
[4] For the rest of KPT's life, 'dominating any situation like a "patriarch"' was precisely what he felt he could never achieve.

To Julian Holland

Edgbaston
15 April [1944]

Dear Jules

   Tues Apr 11
   [...] Council for Education in World Citizenship opened.[1] About

600 dull young people, including 70% of women. Mostly the type that wears sweaters to keep warm. Made several pickups – but all the vigour of a pick-up lies in the fact that you don't know your victim. At the Conference you do – everyone wears a little label with name and school on it. Some idiot emblazoned mine with 'Good Old Peacock' in bright red ink. The process is: 10 a.m.: a lecture and questions/ 11.30–12.45 we split up into twentyfive discussion groups, each with an adult leader, and a chairman and secretary elected by the group – under five headings: USA, British Empire, USSR, World Economic Policy, and Political Cooperation/ 2.0 – another lecture 3.30–4.30 – more discussion. I was in a group consisting of 25 girls and five boys – all drab and wordless. Was immediately elected chairman. Our subject was USSR so I talked for half an hour about China. Our group leader is an earnest, energetic, ruddy young bitch named Jones who is vibrantly Communist. No one else said a ruddy word. [. . .]

Thurs, Apr 13
[. . .] First net practice of the year. Tiger Smith[2] immediately spotted my salient fault and put it right. I am now an erratic and aggressive batsman. Smith is very sound. [. . .]
    Was taken to the Crescent and introduced to Lionel Dunn.[3]
    Mr Dunn
    Is such fun.
    A word from Lionel
    Is fionel.
    I outwitted him in conversation; he has homosexual designs on me and expressed his intention of frequenting the Kardomah[4] in the future. I shall encourage him just out of pure puck. My occasional flash of phrase bewildered him; he calls me sweet kate.[5] Best remark was from Hugh;[6] Lionel said that Hugh was the caterpillar type – an excellent Rosencrantz. No, said Hugh – gilded-stern!

Friday, Apr 14:
    A good day – talk by a likeable Communist named Osyakovsky.[7] If anyone could convert me to Socialism, at least, he would have done so. But I remained firm, and asked him whether he had come to England expressly to incite the people to revolution. He shook me with his brief answer – YES.
    The afternoon's talk was wonderful – a reasonable, and perfect American named Newell talked about Anglo-American relations. With perfect intonation and timing he debunked the habit of the upper classes of rhapsodising about hands-across-the-sea, etc. He was scep-

tical of extremes, ironically tolerant of ideals, and all in all completely captivating. Thirty-eight people besieged him for an autograph. The most satisfying American I can remember.

Then to the flicks with two Coventry girls I met at the conference. Necked with both – both have filthy minds but are pretty and well-spoken. We therefore got on excellently. It's the unemotional and statuesque daughters of the nouveau riche who can't get along with me: the lower orders lap me up. [. . .]

Regards to Tony and to yourself

KPT

[1] A London-based organization founded by the classicist Gilbert Murray; it was an educational offshoot of the League of Nations Union.
[2] The KES cricket coach.
[3] Leading actor of the amateur Crescent Theatre, Birmingham, he later turned professional.
[4] A first-floor coffee shop in New Street in the centre of Birmingham, frequented by young people of panache. KPT used to take his typewriter there and work when not 'imposing myself very happily' on a bevy of regulars.
[5] *The Taming of the Shrew*, Act IV Sc. i.
[6] In April 1944 the burly twenty-three-year-old Manning (b. 1920) was approached in the Kardomah by 'a lank young man with hair like flax on a distaff' (as Manning described him), who knelt before him, kissed his hand, and said, 'You're talking about Ibsen. You're talking about my god.' Through Manning, who was established in amateur dramatic companies, KPT entered a new world of theatre. Manning later became a professional actor and in 1975 president of British Actors Equity.
[7] One of a group of lecturers associated with the Russia Today Society.

To Julian Holland

Birmingham
26 April [1944]

Dear Jules,

I have volumes to tell you, but not now; I have a damnable apology.

Your last letter, which arrived last Saturday, was received in my absence, and much amused the postman by its designation of me. My mother was very obtusely annoyed, resented being laughed at by a menial, and had the cheek to <u>burn</u> the letter unopened.

I can only offer my apologies, and ask you to write again; I have already rebuked my mother for her highhandedness.

Once more: regrets.

I have <u>so</u> much to tell –

Ken

P.S. To pile on the agony, I told her that your letter contained Act I of The Play.

P.P.S. Incidentally, plays about ideas are no good without genius. Let's write a closet tragedy first.

P.P.P.S. To give you a foretaste of the magnitude of my next letter:
    Within the last week I have seen 'As You Like It', 'Taming of the Shrew', 'Macbeth', and 'Hamlet';¹ and have written since Sunday 7500 words in essays or criticism!

P.P.P.P.S. Love to Tony and more apologies to you. Love to you, too. Ultimum Scriptum: have heard from Charles: HE IS IN LOVE!!

---

¹ *The Taming of the Shrew, Macbeth* and *Hamlet* were directed at the Shakespeare Memorial Theatre, Stratford, by Robert Atkins. George Hayes, according to KPT, was a 'stagey' Macbeth; John Byron played Hamlet.

To Julian Holland

Edgbaston
14 May [1944]

Dear Jules:
    [...]
Tues, 2nd May: H.M. [head master] talked about the Sermon on the Mount. I cannot agree with this very superficial and wrong-headed bit of rhetoric. Especially do I revolt from:
    'Take no heed of thy body ...'
    C.I.¹ with Barbara in the Gt Western arcade. My first.
Thurs, May 4: Prefected. Presented P.R.² with a Van Gogh self-portrait and a miniature Rembrandt. Also began extensive plans, with enthusiastic support, for a Prefects' Room Revue at the end of term, with Willie doing a cancan. QUERY: WILL YOU HELP ME WORK OUT A SHOW ON YOUR NEXT LEAVE? YOU WILL NOT GO UNSUNG. [...]
Thurs, 11:
    [...] Indulged my aberration with Babs in the GT W arcade. Then

(at 10-30) went home to write a seven page essay on 'Should a critic of poetry be himself a poet?' Decided no: since the critical and poetic temperament are poles apart, and each is a fulltime job. And to assert that the critic needs the discipline of creative writing is just balls, because at present criticism is the only remaining form of creative writing which demands any discipline at all.

Fri, May 12: Read Verlaine's 'Art poètique'.[3] Lovely and sonorous.

Cricket at Harborne[4] – by Monday I shall have played cricket for seven days without a break.[5]

Remark of mine about [Jane]:[6] 'She's climbing the social ladder – lad by lad.'

Sat, May 13:

[...] Read Edmund Blunden's 'Cricket Country'[7] and learn to love my game, thou infamous numskull!

In a week of pr-f-ctsh'p, I have given twelve essays. [...]

TRY AND BE HOME FOR JUNE 9th. I am lecturing to the Literary Society on 'ART AND I'[8] – an autobiography of an eclectic. My publicity campaign has already begun; there are to be three posters on the societies' notice-board; every essay I give is on 'KP Tynan'; the HM is to announce it in prayers; and two notices are to be sent round the school about it. If possible, too, a broadsheet will go round, so that I may ascertain whether the audience will have to be accommodated in Big School, or whether I shall have to address them from the balcony of the pavilion. Anyhowsobeit, it will be a grand affair – a history of the Influences that have Gone to the Making of KPT.

Prediction: that I shall get the Bunce essay[9] if GAS[heldon] does the selection. If CRM[orris] does it, I may flop; he dislikes Romanticism in essays.

The hour has begun to witch, so I'd best away.
Write back.
Les sanglots longs
de l'automne[10]
will be falling
when I am myself
  again.

Love from
and his aberration (still flourishing)
K.P.T.
[...]

To Julian Holland

Edgbaston
19 May [1944]

Dear Dewstrump[1] (vide Marlowe)

Dear J:
   Typewriter is on loan to the P.R., so I must use my hands.
   'The Bee, a busy little soul,
   Has never heard of birth control;
   And that is why, in days like these,
   We see so many sons of B's.' [...]

Tues, 16th
   My bedroom is now embellished with photographs of the following:
   Orson Welles, Peggy Cummins,[2] Teresa Wright,[3] Katherine [*sic*] Cornell,[4] Geo. S. Kaufman, Maxwell Anderson,[5] Salvador Dali, Jean Cocteau, Max Ernst, Picasso, Baudelaire, Irving,[6] and Whitman (as untidy and bighearted as Hampstead Heath).
   C.R. Morris said a good thing without realising it: 'It is an established fact that to a listener three miles from Hampstead Heath on a Bank Holiday the buzz of the crowd at 10 p.m. is higher than that at 5 p.m. by almost an octave.'
   Read the new 'Cornhill':[7] excellent article by Clive Bell[8] on Sickert; good article by Robin Ironside[9] on Pater; and poorish article by someone on Delacroix. Ironside quotes Henry James on Pater ('a deep

purple man') and George Moore[10] ('In the pages of Pater, the English language lies in state.') But best of all is Osbert Lancaster[11] on the architecture of Dublin, a mixture of 'ferro-concrete, fortresses of high finance' and 'olde-worlde Cotswold revivalism'.

Restarted 'Pickwick'. What a grand book this is! There is something gorgeous on every page, whether it be a delicious turn of phrase or a new hint of caricature.

Advice: read Longinus. The best of the ancient Greek literary critics; on the advice of Saintsbury's 'Hist. of Criticism',[12] I read a bit and was amazed. [...]

Thu, 18th
Designed and executed the most egotistical poster this school has seen: It is headed with a painted reproduction of my red and yellow scarf; there follows an announcement that KPT will talk to the Litsoc [Literary Society], and will also sing (unaccompanied) his own setting of Verlaine's 'Chanson d'Automne' (this is true!); and then a series of my gods, each illustrated with a suitable symbol. E.g. D. H. Lawrence: a pool of blood and two testicles.

Stravinsky: a musical stave, inverted, with 8 flats and 6 sharps.

Max Beerbohm: a monocle and a wispy moustache.

Van Gogh like this:

Welles by a pair of eyes.

And so on; a dozen more. Best is Baudelaire: a black nude [...]

Fri, 19th
Went to Town Hall and heard and saw Smuts'[13] speech on receiving the freedom of the city. This put my mind at rest; I was wondering what <u>had</u> happened to the freedom of this city, – and now I know he's got it.

He is a short, hard, red man, with a snowy goat-beard and busy eyes; surrounded by circumambient wisps of white hair. He speaks like a man of thirty.

My own heartiest applause came when he told us to look for Russia in the pages of Tolstoy rather than Marx; Marx was a German to the last.

Before he arrived at the Town Hall, Willie Shock & I gatecrashed the Council House in an effort to sign the attendance book for the day. We were foiled; but not until we had burst thru a door marked 'PRI-VATE' into a long corridor lined with khaki. When we did this, the officer in charge gave the order to 'Present Arms'; we looked up the corridor, and retired hurriedly on discovering that Smuts was about ten yards away, coming in our direction. It seems that not only am I caviare to the general, I am also caviare to the fieldmarshal. [...]

    ... when men and women agree,
    it is only in their conclusions; their
    reasons are always different. (Santayana)[14]

Well, Julian,
I am
still in
  love

← This is a mistake.

— He in love.

You'll find that sort of thing through life.

She is beautiful like flocks of washed sheep: newly washed and pristine. Like white clouds that pass eternally, the wonderful clouds. She blossoms about me as I write yes here and here yes here she seems with and of me. This is tangible ecstasy and this is infatuation and life and all sorts of big abstracts but it is more much more please God it is much more

                        farewell
                        KPT

[1] There is no 'Dewstrump' in the works of Christopher Marlowe.
[2] Peggy Cummins (b. 1925), Welsh-born stage actress who played leading roles in several British and American films of the 1940s and 1950s, including *Green Grass of Wyoming* (US, 1948) and *To Dorothy a Son* (UK, 1954).
[3] Teresa Wright (b. 1918), American actress who made her film debut in 1941 as Bette Davis's daughter in *The Little Foxes*, and won the Best Supporting Actress Academy Award for *Mrs Miniver* (US, 1942).
[4] Katharine Cornell (1898–1974), American stage actress. Her most memorable parts include Juliet, Elizabeth in *The Barretts of Wimpole Street* and the title role in Anouilh's *Antigone*.
[5] Maxwell Anderson (1888–1959), American playwright (*Winterset*, 1935), he also wrote the screenplay of John Huston's *Key Largo* (US, 1948).
[6] Sir Henry Irving (1838–1905), Shakespearean actor long associated with the Lyceum Theatre, London, where he partnered Ellen Terry in plays including Goethe's *Faust* (1885) and Tennyson's *Becket* (1893). He was the first actor to be knighted (in 1895).

[7] A literary magazine founded in January 1860 by George Smith, of which Thackeray was the first editor.
[8] Clive Bell (1881–1964), English art and literary critic; he married Virginia Woolf's sister Vanessa.
[9] Robin Ironside (1912–65), English painter and author of books including *British Painting Since 1939* (1948).
[10] George Moore (1852–1933), Anglo-Irish novelist (*Esther Waters*, 1894) who helped launch Dublin's Abbey Theatre in 1904.
[11] Sir Osbert Lancaster (1908–86), English artist famous for his *Daily Express* pocket cartoons. He also designed sets and costumes for ballet and opera, particularly at Glyndebourne.
[12] *The History of Criticism and Literary Taste in Europe (1900–1904)* by George Saintsbury (1845–1933), for twenty years Professor of English Literature and Rhetoric at Edinburgh.
[13] Jan Christian Smuts (1870–1950), South African statesman. After serving as Minister of Justice, he became Prime Minister in 1939, a post he held until 1948. During World War II he became a close adviser to Winston Churchill, having been appointed a field marshal in the British Army in 1941.
[14] George Santayana (1863–1952), Spanish American philosopher, poet and novelist.

To Julian Holland

Edgbaston
[15 August 1944]

Dear j

[...] as you may have guessed my life has been cricket for the last week – watching r i scorers cricket festival[1] at the county ground and composing lovely clerihews about the players. e-frightfully-g: (when l j Todd took six for forty-four):

l j todd
should not be confused with god.
todd bowls at the festival;
god bowls at mephistofel.

------

i have seen the scrubby frank lee score an alert 98; and i have seen denis brookes of northants compile a leisurely hundred. twice i have seen frank woolley, that model of elegance, go in to bat. i have watched the negligent mastery of w r hammond, standing easily at first slip, or roaming predatory, unconscious of his own grace. he made seventy on sunday, and left the field blowing its hand after contact with his coverdrives.

but my chiefest thrill of the week was an opening stand of 171, followed by another of 148, between c s dempster and r t simpson.[2] dempsters power and timing we knew of old, but simpson was gloriously new. he is an introspective almost australian batsman in method; apart from occasional hints of fallibility when he nears his century, [...] he hits with incredible ease and strength. his drives ripple over the ground in outward manifestation of an inner energy a dynamic quiddity which possesses him. he is only twenty-two; and before long australian fields will know his worth. in one week (last week) his scores in successive innings were: 79, 99, 86, 47, 71 – 382 runs in one week! [...]

Well goodbye thou good old man[3]

K.

[1] Lt-Col. R.I. ('Rusty') Scorer (1892–1976). He played cricket for Warwickshire in the 1930s, and during the war he organized cricket festivals at the County Ground in Edgbaston, close to KES. This third festival drew a crowd of 40,000.

[2] L.J. Todd (Kent), Frank Lee (Somerset), Denis Brookes (Northamptonshire), Frank Woolley (Kent), W.R. Hammond (Gloucestershire), C.S. Dempster (New Zealand), R.T. Simpson (Nottinghamshire).

[3] *As You Like It*, Act II Sc. iii.

To Julian Holland

edgbaston
9 December 1944

dear julian,

   i write sans capitals because this wretched machine prints them below the line like ⊤his which destroys the symmetry.

   so to your letter. a night at the opera with grouchochicoharpo[1] sounds fine, but a night at the opera with gianni schicchi and il tabarro[2] [*sic*] strikes few chords. you know my views about opera being little more than a sentimentally amusing bastard. [...]

   i consider your supposition about Kane the merest flimflam. the fact of the matter is, of course, that kane was the nearest welles could get to kubla kahn [*sic*].[3]

   and let me hear no more foolery about not paying high prices. for once youll pay them and love it. please.

   from me there is much.

   my intention for the next few months is to read novels; hence i have read em forsters lovely and intimate howards end; turgenevs wonderful fathers and sons; and shall read madame bovary, bros karamazov, and best of all mrs woolfs to the lighthouse.

i have bought a pipe. [...]

my week

it was a week, take it for all in all,
i shall not look upon its like again.[4]

monday

the gods go abegging.[5]

i must say i liked beechams manhandling of handel. and the spry young muscular swain rassine[6] is a perpetual joy. but the ballet lacks form and line; it is curiously uninteresting to the critical eye.

miracle in the gorbals.[7]

this, to me, was a cataclysm. i found to my dismay afterwards that i had sweated away four pounds whilst watching its electric motion. to watch it is not to enjoy recreation, but to take part in what seems almost physical procreation. celia franca proudly lustful pas seul; the attitudinising david paltenghi as bedogcollared officialdom; david [*sic*] hamilton,[8] uncannily making one despise and despise him; and the soft, stern agony of helpmann.

nowhere have i seen such gigantic power in choreography. helpmanns is a gaunt, ascetic genius; and i am tingling still with the ecstasy he evoked. [...]

tuesday

volpone, or the fox[9]

hazlitt[10] would have loved this performance. almost lovingly wolfit savoured every syllable; and in the colossal 'milk of unicorns and panther's breath' speech the house was burdened with verbal perfume. how he impressed too with the hissing delivery of his triumphant 'I am volpone, and thisssss my sssslave'

the prowl which this great actor affects, the splayed-out hands and muscular solidity were terribly effective i bravoed at the last curtain – the first time i have ever done so. i would as happily see wolfit do this splendid comedy as see ellen terry[11] in any of shakespeares.

joan greenwood[12] was very bad.

wednesday

hamlet[13]

gertrude may call him pursy, but i cannot reconcile myself to a stubby dane. of course the performance spoke throughout of wonderfully accurate forethought, and the delivery was impeccable; but one felt that here was comprehension rather than concentration. the actor tried to limn in all the traits of hamlets complexity, and failed to weld them into a living whole. all of hamlet was there, but not a whole hamlet. how all occasions was beautifully spoken, and (as on the previous night) climax came with the line of completest egotism: 'this is i, hamlet the dane', with a whirl of the cloak and a dashing bestrid the coffin.

miss greenwood was a tolerable ophelia; but the best touches in her madness came, i suspect, from wolfits direction rather than herself. and will someone tell her that blank verse is not always 1–2–1–2, but sometimes 1–2–2–1?

wolfits curtains were, as ever, gorgeously theatrical.[14] irvings cannot have been far different.

thursday
macbeth

after much thought i find my ultimate opinion coincides with my original, spontaneous impression. this is the greatest piece of shake-spearean acting i have ever seen.

i may make a reservation for wolfits lear; but his macbeth hit me with such tremendous impact that i hesitate to do so. the correct note was struck from the outset; macbeths utter dependence upon his wife (finely played, apart from some unfortunate slips during the sleepwalking, by dorothy black[15]), which dependence is beautifully inverted in the duologue after the vision of bloodboltered banquo at the feast. the change was astoundingly done. the remorseful murderer was henceforth proud of his misdeeds, and went to a greyhaired death with his crimes on his brow like a halo. as malcolm beautifully says: 'angels are bright still, though the brightest fell'.

there was another directly significant touch later. when macduff announces that he was 'untimely ripped', wolfit let fall his sword; and instantly the clang of battle outside ceased, and all became a pregnant hush. again, my heart all but stopped when wolfit bellowed at macduff: 'my names macbeeeeeettthh ...' tomorrowandtomorrow i cannot imagine better spoken; what a violent, extravagant, peerless man of men! all must bow to him. his mastery of macbeth is absolute.

friday
merchant of venice

miss idens[16] portia suffers badly by comparison with joan millers[17] at the alex. miss miller was sunny, but sophisticated and alert; the iden was merely any musical-comedy ingenue dressing up for a cheap lark. an atrociously plump jessica, too, all but marred lorenzos glorious speech-song at the end; agate is right; ones stature can make or destroy drama. following the traditional irvingesque interpretation, wolfit made the jew a tragic figure, dignified and undismayed. but so great was his power that we never laughed at the 'my daughter & my ducats' speech, as shakespeare intended us to. wolfit so irreparably joined the jews fear for his daughter and his pelf into a common anxiety for 'his house' that he made us weep; and thus over toppled the whole balance of the play, which is too slight to bear the weight of tragedy. instance: after wolfits spitting had ended the trial scene, a great many people got up to go, thinking the play was over. thus did a great actor by his very greatness succeed in ruining what is otherwise a wellmade piece enough.

saturday
comus[18]

quite patently a first effort in choreography. it is really no more than a series of breathlessly lovely tableaux. helpmanns exquisite tempting of the lady was the cream of miming; but the nature of miltons poem is to render it episodic and something hackneyed – the whole, i mean. the decor again was eloquent and opulent; and helpmanns dexterous fingers leave an indelible mark on the mind. i loved purcells music.

giselle.[19]

this seems to elude helpmann. for the first time he truly danced – and marvellously. dancing is poetry with arms and legs; and helpmann is dancing incarnate. but he seems happier out of classical ballet. here he was over-shadowed by margot fonteyns giselle, the most moving piece of feminine art i have encountered. she is, i imagine, a more reliable person than her erratic, statuesque partner. his is the creative genius; and hers the interpretors. [...]

ever,
k.

(sorrynoink)

[1] The Marx Brothers, *A Night at the Opera* (US, 1937).

[2] Two one-act operas in Puccini's *Trittico*, premiered at the Metropolitan, New York, 14 December 1918.

[3] 'Kubla Khan' (1797–8), visionary poem by Samuel Taylor Coleridge (1772–1834). Kane's mansion was called 'Xanadu'.

[4] 'He was a man, take him for all in all . . .': *Hamlet*, Act I Sc. ii.

[5] Ballet choreographed by Ninette de Valois (1936) for the Vic Wells, with music by Handel arranged by Sir Thomas Beecham (1879–1961), the long-time resident conductor of the London Philharmonic Orchestra.

[6] Alexis Rassine, principal dancer at Sadler's Wells.

[7] Ballet choreographed by Robert Helpmann (1944) at Sadler's Wells, with music by Arthur Bliss and designed by Edward Burra.

[8] Celia Franca, David Paltenghi, Gordon Hamilton, Sadler's Wells dancers on tour at the Birmingham Alexandra Theatre.

[9] Ben Jonson, *Volpone*, first performed 1605–6.

[10] William Hazlitt (1778–1830), English essayist, journalist and drama critic. *The Spirit of the Age* (1825) was a critical assessment of many of his contemporaries, including Coleridge, Wordsworth and Lamb.

[11] Dame Ellen Terry (1848–1928), English actress, mother of the designer Edward Gordon Craig and great-aunt of Sir John Gielgud.

[12] Joan Greenwood (1921–87), leading lady of British stage and film remarkable for the velvety quality of her voice.

[13] With Wolfit in the lead.

[14] Wolfit's curtain calls were celebrated: at the end of a performance a hand would draw the curtain apart and the actor would appear to make a speech.

[15] Dorothy Black (1899–1985), South African-born actress who played leading roles in London and Stratford before joining Wolfit's touring company in 1944 to play Lady Macbeth and the Queen in *Hamlet*.

[16] Rosalind Iden (1911–90), third wife of Sir Donald Wolfit, who often played opposite him.

[17] Joan Miller (1910–88), Canadian actress who appeared at the Alexandra Theatre, Birmingham, in the 1942–3 season. She made her New York debut in 1953 in *A Pin to See the Peepshow*; KPT writes of the London production in letter of 10 June 1951.

[18] Ballet choreographed by Helpmann with music by Purcell arranged by Constant Lambert, first performed on 14 January 1942.

[19] Ballet in two acts by Théophile Gautier and the Chevalier de Saint-Georges, choreographed by Jean Coralli, with music by Adolph Adam (1841).

To Julian Holland

Edgbaston
14 December 1944

Dear J:

Magdalen College, Oxford, is a strange and lovable place. Stern and aloof, it offers no scholarships; it calls them demyships. Like scholarships (as offered by the younger colleges), they are worth from £30–£100. And as a result of an interview with me last Monday (a half-hour of controversy with the benign C. S. Lewis[1]), they have awarded me their solitary Open Demyship in Modern Subjects. And my scholarship worries[2] are over.

'Abraham Lincoln'[3] on Thursday was a tumultuous success. Kemp[4] gave us a whole column on the following day which was almost ecstatic. What he said about me was particularly pleasing. He predicts great things for me in o.u.d.s.[5]

> So, in lazy joy;
> Ken
> [. . .]

[1] C. S. Lewis (1898–1963), English critic and academic, novelist (*The Chronicles of Narnia*, 1950–56) and Christian apologist (*The Screwtape Letters*, 1942); Fellow of Magdalen College, Oxford 1925–54.
[2] In November KPT had sat a scholarship examination at Balliol College, Oxford. While awaiting the results, he sat for a demyship at Magdalen. The demyship provided £50 a year which, with his City of Birmingham and state scholarships, more than covered his tuition.
[3] By John Drinkwater (1918). The play was performed by the KES Drama Society on the school's new stage. The *Chronicle* reported that KPT played the part of Lincoln 'with remarkable command and technique . . . Tynan rightly dominated'.
[4] Thomas Charles Kemp (1891–1955), drama critic who, from 1935 until his death, was on the *Birmingham Post*. For some time Chairman of the Crescent Theatre, he described KPT as an actor of 'unusual promise'.
[5] Oxford University Dramatic Society, founded 1885.

To Julian Holland

> Edgbaston
> 9 January 1945

Dear J:

Herewith postal orders for my debts, with a little extra to cover the cost of heating your flat. And don't argue.

The outlook for 'Hamlet'[1] (that is, an immediate Hamlet) is bleak. The New Dramatic Co.[2] were, as you know, offended from the start by our presumption in seizing Pauline;[3] and their committee seems to feel that something lighter (such as 'Dover Road'[4]) would be better to follow the heavier exertions of 'Berkeley Square'.[5] I am doing my best to get into their good books; I even accepted a 'bit' part in 'B. S.' to sweeten them. But they all (the Committee, I mean) seem scared of 'Hamlet', especially since they know next to nothing of the proposed protagonist. Still, we must hope. I am myself feeling extremely downcast.

The Birmingham Film Club is showing the new Disney, 'Symphony

Hour',[6] on Thursday. It is, I believe, the sequel to 'Fantasia', and is not to be generally released.

> And that is all from
> H.T.T. K.T.[7]

[1] KPT and Holland had worked on a cut version of *Hamlet* (using the G. B. Harrison Penguin edition), excising Rosencrantz and Guildenstern. 'To be or not to be' became the prologue, and the play moved fast and furiously. They hoped Hugh Manning would direct it for the recently formed New Dramatic Company. KPT promised to bring enough young men from KES to fill the minor parts of the company's first major productions if he were allowed to play Hamlet.

[2] The New Dramatic Company was an offshoot of the Crescent Theatre, an amateur company which performed revues in parks and local halls as part of wartime entertainment called 'Holidays at Home'. The players would rehearse at all hours, live on bread, jam and tea and crawl home in the pitch dark, for there were still blackouts.

[3] Pauline Whittle, the lead actress of the New Dramatic Company, a dark-haired, white-skinned beauty with the modest manner of a D. W. Griffith heroine. KPT wanted her for Ophelia and engineered a reading of the play at his house. She recalls that first meeting with KPT: 'Aesthetic, tall, appealing. I was riveted, because you simply didn't see people like that in Birmingham.'

[4] Comedy by A. A. Milne, first performed 7 June 1922.

[5] A fantasy by John A. Balderston with J. C. Squire, first performed 6 October 1926; KPT played Lord Stanley.

[6] A fifteen-minute Disney short in which Mickey Mouse conducts the orchestra.

[7] 'He that thou knowest thine': *Hamlet*, Act IV, Sc. vi.

To Julian Holland

> edgbaston.
> [22 January 1945]

dear j:

harry james[1] and i are getting encouragingly friendly, and he tells me the prospects for hamlet are moderately bright, and almost blindingly so if we leave it until after the next production (probably the dover road)

i gave a brilliant lecture to the lit soc on 'towards a new hamlet'. hugh and the newdramsoc stage manageress, joan cutler came along to help me out in reading extracts. i began with a survey of all the critical opinions on the play, from richardson[2] through goethe[3] and bradley[4] right up to dover wilson[5] and the best of them all, e e stoll.[6] i gave masterly summaries of more than twenty such critics; then discussed the great hamlets of the british stage (from kemble[7] to gielgud[8]), using the prompt copy of kemble's drury lane hamlet (which is, by the way, almost as subtly cut as our own, and in places much more). i went on to productions of hamlet outside england, laying stress on akimovs[9]

1932 production at the vakhtangov theatre in moscow, where ophelia was not mad but drunk, and hamlet a stubby ambitious little mountebank. then i used your synopsis of helpmann's[10] hamlet (with additions; you miss a great deal out, notably the ophelia-gertrude duplication, the laertes-ophelia incest, and the coffin scene with gertrude inside) and the tchaikovsky[11] music to illustrate the psychoanalytical view of hamlet. i pointed out my main theme, that shakespeare was neither psychologist nor psycho-analyst; he was not concerned with making appearances seem real; and his greatest strength lies in that 'willing suspension of disbelief' which we call dramatic illusion.

next i gave my own opinion of the play and how it should be cut (mentioning your name), and finally delivered the soliloquies and a few scenes from the play with the assistance of hugh and joan. [...]

but enough of this. once more: hamlet is completely cast and planned (hugh playing polonius); all that is needed is the o.k. of the committee; if this is not forthcoming, hugh is going to battle with his conscience and i think hamlet will tip the balance.

---

other news: [...]

The youth forum presented its reconstruction report last saturday. this is a vast affair (weighing much as largish sprat) and it was compiled by the reconstruction committee of the youth forum. last weeks meeting was to receive amendments and vote on the report. now i read the thing, saw how hideously written it was, overgrown with jungle english, journalese and (worse) official jargon, so i rose on saturday to intervene in the great cause of words, with 88 ungrammatical and syntactical amendments, excising unnecessary verbiage and pompous periphrasis wherever they were flourishing. i have now been invited to correct the final draft and rephrase it. we do not fight in vain. worry about words; they are the only consistent elements in your life. as remy de gourmont[12] said 'ideas are well enough until you are twenty; after that only words will do' [...]

he that thou knowest thayn,
kaypeetee

[1] Henry L. James (b. 1919), a founder member of the New Dramatic Company who became a senior civil servant in the Ministry of Information.
[2] William Richardson (1743–1814), Scottish author of essays on Shakespeare, including *Philosophical Analysis and Illustration of Some of Shakespeare's Remarkable Characters*, which includes a study of Hamlet.

[3]Johann Wolfgang von Goethe (1749–1832) wrote several essays/reviews on *Hamlet*, including *The Story of Hamlet* (1797) and *Review of the Tragedy of Hamlet* (1827).

[4]A. C. Bradley (1851–1935), Professor of Poetry at Oxford 1901–6 and author of *Shakespearian Tragedy* (1904).

[5]John Dover Wilson (1881–1969), author of *The Essential Shakespeare* (1932), *What Happens in Hamlet* (1935) and *The Fortunes of Falstaff* (1943).

[6]E. E. Stoll (1874–1959), American scholar who argued that Shakespeare should be understood within the conventions of Elizabethan drama. His works include *Hamlet* (1919) and *Shakespeare Studies* (1927).

[7]John Philip Kemble (1757–1823) made his London debut in 1783 as Hamlet. Hazlitt wrote of his performance: 'Later actors have played the part with more energy ... but Kemble's sensible, lonely Hamlet has not been surpassed.'

[8]Gielgud had first played Hamlet in 1930 at the Old Vic, and achieved record runs in London and New York. Hailed by the critics as the greatest Shakespearean actor of his generation, he played the part frequently in the 1930s, and in 1944 included the play in his repertory season at the Theatre Royal, Haymarket.

[9]Nikolai Pavlovich Akimov (1901–68), Russian set designer and director whose 1932 production of *Hamlet* in Moscow had to be taken off due to public outrage.

[10]Robert Helpmann played Hamlet with the Old Vic Company in 1944 (co-directed by Michael Benthall and Tyrone Guthrie) and again in 1948 during the Stratford-upon-Avon season. KPT heard him as Hamlet in a radio version and wrote to Holland on 9 March 1944 to tell him how good the performance had been: 'Great neurotic tension. And after all Hamlet is the reductio ad absurdum of neurotics.'

[11]Tchaikovsky's overture-fantasia 'Hamlet' (1888) was used by Helpmann for his 1942 ballet, designed by Leslie Hurry.

[12]Rémy de Gourmont (1858–1915), French Symbolist novelist, critic and essayist.

To Julian Holland

King Edwards School,
31 January 1945

dear jayjayaitch:

your first letter was nice. but i dont trust george jean [nathan] any more. rereading –the critic and the drama– i conclude that though his critical foundation rings true, he is too lavish with both praise and blame, and lets that gilding pen of his run into ecstasies in either direction on the least provocation. [...]

your dream-girl has the most beautiful name i have ever heard. that is sufficient recommendation to a soft old word-fancier like myself. but probably the reiteration of your phrase –dreamgirl– will make you feel faintly sick, so i will leave you to stew in your mess of lurve.

incidentally, what happened to the other ballet-and-wolfit fan you contacted? felicity somethingorother. perhaps you have absented yourself from felicity awhile?[1] or what?

february tenth sounds sexy. [. . .]

now for –henry v–.[2]

i must demur over your use of the word –impure–. you remind me of those absurd patriotic fanatics who have spent so much time and energy over what they call –purifying the language–. they would exclude from their several tongues all words of foreign derivation or origin, and close the door firmly against any further usurpers; forgetting as they do so that language is a common global heritage, springing from one source, responsible to no man for its endless developments into new magic and finer gossamer, into subtler interminglings and closer analysis. so is it with art. art springs from that glorious thing, the human (and divine) attribute of seeing beyond appearances; in brief, from imagination. imaginative power has been split up, and directed into divers channels – the chisel, the brush, the pen, and the camera, to name a few. you would keep each compartment of art watertight; would keep stage and screen rigorously apart and aloof from each other, forgetting that both are different versions of the same thing, the drama of motion. –henry v– is not overwhelmingly filmic, self-consciously filmic; i agree. why should it be? the film of –the man who came to dinner– was almost literally a photographed play; the camera never moved. yet the result was uproarious; because nothing the camera could do could add to the irresistible fun provided by the acid pens of messrs kaufman and hart. similarly with –henry v–. even in the charge, the camera is not used imaginatively; it moves almost parallel to the ground, and no more. but it is in harmony with the film as a whole and that sequence in particular; it is filmically apt, and a success. the fade-across from the globe to the battlefields and back is the only really empirical leap that the film makes, cinematically. it is the music, and not the camera that binds the film together; but you do not talk of impurity when music and the film are intermingled into a fire-new creation, a tapestry. the unrealistic sets are a mere quibble on your part; you say the audience accepts them because it knows it is looking at a photographed play. but surely the play above all things has aimed at realism; mr gielgud's edwardian interior[3] is just as accurate a representation as mr welles' in –magnificent ambersons–. my view veers: i take my mind to the formalised sets of the german expressionist cinema, to the first filmic film, with its hideously and patently unreal exteriors –the cabinet of dr caligari–. mr sherriff[4] [*sic*] has merely civilised the gloomy longings of the 1923 epic[5] into perfect formal aptness, which would be equally effective on stage or screen,

and which could not be made more effective by becoming –filmic–.
their very essence on the screen is that they are new, easy to look
at, and hence easily forgettable; which as mr agate insists, is what a
set ought to be. [...]

look out for another item of hollywood news: orson welles has
announced that he will henceforth make only one film per annum,
and will devote the rest of his time to politics, and his new column
in the 'NY Post'.[6] current reports on this column are unfavorable.
it is slashed as being 'too clever, unfunny, no originality, no inside
information, too condescending, too pompous'. a pity.

re h g-b's[7] lengthy exposition of the necessity of retaining
'tobeornottobe': one of the chief vices of shakespeare critics has
been to gloss over their idol's most glaring errors and lapses of
taste by finding in them new subtleties and double ententes. that
is what harley is doing. balls to him.

---

the new dramco had a committee meeting last sunday, a stormy
committee meeting. it was decided that harry james should produce
the next play, to be presented in march, and probably used in the
late summer for 'brighterbirmingham'[8] shows. meanwhile it was
decided (by a narrow but perceptible majority) that 'hamlet', produced
by h g manning, will follow in late may or early june. we have their
full financial support, and all goes well; harry has shown his good
taste by choosing –you cant take it with you–[9] as his interim play,
and has cast me for the plum comic part, played for three years on
broadway by mischa auer.[10] you must know the play; the first and
best of kaufman-harts lunatic farces. [...]

bad news. pauline whittle (remember) has for a considerable time
been the acknowledged girl-friend of bill moore,[11] producer and
leading man of 'Berkeley sq.' but she is very young, very impression-
able, and she likes people who have preserved their poetic souls in
the industrial heart of an empire. e.g. me.

[...] nothing else of new. joy is on the evening despatch,[12] i lym-
phatically note. no more. all is dun and umber.

> het ha ttho uknowes tthine.
> kahay pehee tahee

---

[1] *Hamlet*, Act V Sc. ii.

[2] *Henry V* (UK, 1944), Laurence Olivier's film version of the Shakespeare play, with music by William Walton.

[3] Probably a reference to *The Circle*, Somerset Maugham's comedy of 1920s' manners, performed in an Edwardian setting during Gielgud's season at the Theatre Royal, Haymarket.

[4] Paul Sheriff (1903–65), Olivier's production designer for *Hamlet* and *Henry V*. Though he based his designs for *Henry V* on *Les Très Riches Heures du Duc du Berry*, they were, according to the film historian David Shipman, as striking in their time as German Expressionist design was in the 1920s.

[5] I.e. *The Cabinet of Doctor Caligari*, in fact made in 1919. See also letter of 9 October 1943.

[6] Welles's column in the *New York Post* ran January–November 1945.

[7] Harley Granville-Barker (1877–1946), English playwright, actor and director who campaigned for a national theatre. He edited, with G. B. Harrison, *A Companion to Shakespearean Studies* (1934) and wrote prefaces to the plays.

[8] Part of a Government wartime scheme set up in 1942 to encourage local authorities to organize holiday entertainment.

[9] *You Can't Take It With You*, play by George Kaufman and Moss Hart (1936). Performed 5, 6, 7 July 1945 by the New Dramatic Company, directed by Harry James. KPT played Kolenkov, the ballet master.

[10] Mischa Auer (1905–67), Russian-born actor who specialized in comic character roles.

[11] William Moore, an actor with the New Dramatic Company, later became a professional.

[12] The *Evening Despatch*, a Birmingham newspaper.

To Hugh Manning

Edgbaston
[? February 1945]

Dear Hugh:

I have received an urgent letter from Julian. I quote:

'I am fully determined that this production shall come off. Bugger anyone who steps in the way. Fight them. The New Dramatic Co – what of it? If Pauline desires to play Ophelia – what the hell – persuade her! All this false loyalty of Hugh's is bunk – bourgeois bunk at that. I'm all for social loyalty but it's incompatible with art and art comes first . . . Make offers to such of their members as you desire and present the thing yourself. You can worry about the hall in two months.'

I make no comment.

Now Julian has been contacting Helpmann and Wolfit about the new 'Hamlet' through a friend of both. He has received from Helpmann a complete synopsis of his 'Hamlet' and has, all in all, been going to one hell of a lot of trouble. I leave the rest to you and your conscience. And remember that I have a very high opinion of both.

He That Thou Knowest Thine,
K.P.T.

To Julian Holland

Edgbaston
17 February 1945

Dear J:

Thank you for an adult letter. I hate to see your whimsy leaving you, but leaving you it is; you are maturing, become more profound in emotion, less draped with illusions.

I was surprised to stumble over that word 'love'. The very existence of such a word in your mind proves that your imagination has obscured common-sense. Reason tells us, in that thin (but so direct) voice of his, that love is the imaginary amalgamation of two very different things: the physical needs of the body, and the mental need for sympathetic companionship. Love occurs when a passionate belief in either of these needs causes the boundaries between them to break, and the red flush of one is allowed to spread across and permeate the other. Obviously in your case, [you] have saturated your need for companionship, and now that you have realised she is human and has a body, you wildly transcribe what you feel as love. But good luck to you ...

My love life has undergone one startling volte face. Irene[1] is Out. She was too deeply entangled, and was (I knew) preparing to wait for my return both from the Army and the University. Knowing her determination, I judged that she would and could do it. But I knew I couldn't.

I am now within a pebble's flip of a sordid physical affair with petite, enigmatic, intellectual, 24-year-old Enid[2] (whose bright yellow hair, and bitchy sarcasm you may have observed in the Kardomah). What gives me added zest is the fact that Enid is also Lionel Dunn's mistress. Yes, Lionel is bisexual, with a slight preference for homo. What an imbroglio! Enid playing second fiddle to dozens of fiancés! I am taking her to the Molière play at the Rep (a new translation of 'Le Malade Imaginaire'). And (at last) she bites when she kisses. Hard. And I love it.

Now back to you. Stop saying 'It can never be.' Of course it can. Don't soliloquise in romantic self-pity all the days of your life – go in and get her if she's willing ... The husband will almost certainly never know, and (if he is a man with any consideration for his wife's needs), he will never mind. And if he does, kill him. [...]

I am sorry to confess that I now have proof of my egotism. I am terribly bad at remembering faces, dates, names, and opinions; I have immensely [*sic*] difficulty in recalling anything not directly concerned with myself. In short, I am so occupied with analysing my own reactions and studying my own attitude that I hear, and see – but do not absorb what goes on about me. All that I observe rebounds quickly off the resilient core of ego within. That is also my reason for being unwilling to express definite opinions on morals, politics, ethics, economics, people, etc: because I can[not] interest myself enough in them to arrive at decisions. Only in the things that concern <u>me</u> intimately do I dare to propound judgment.

'Hamlet':
re the 'Swear'.[3] I cut that myself and omitted to mention it. I think that whole scene is laughable in the extreme with the ghost there at all. Hence I very cleverly cut him. If you remember, we spent a long while trying to discover how we could cut the ghost out of the scene, but finally decided it was impossible. I got the hint that it was possible from Dover Wilson, who notes that, on the three occasions when Hamlet proposes the oath, he is NOT repeating himself. [...]

Hugh is bringing a Hamlet party up to see Gielgud[4] on March 31st, of which I shall be one. More details later.

I have fallen again since my earlier pages. This time for Eleana,[5] who is playing Gertrude. But this too must wait.

Ever
Ken.

[1] Irene informed KPT he was a miserable sinner and added, 'If only *you'd be* miserable.'
[2] Surname deleted. A thin, blonde and blue-eyed girl, accused of being a robber of virginity, and described by contemporaries as intense and analytical.
[3] In Act I, Sc.v, Hamlet makes Horatio and Marcellus swear they will 'never make known what you have seen tonight'.
[4] Gielgud's repertory season at the Theatre Royal, Haymarket, October 1944 to May 1945.
[5] Eleana Fraser, a member of the NDC, played Gertrude to KPT's Hamlet.

To Julian Holland

Edgbaston
3 March 1945

Dear J:
In reply to yours of 18 ult.:

You say of 'Emma' that 'It is a tale to be read alone.' But there lies the point. None of Jane [Austen]'s works has a plot. They are all ludicrously plotless, and situationless. I suspect that much of our pleasure in reading her comes from the smug critic in all of us who can sit back and say 'Of course, this is childish; only a woman could get away with it.' But of course nowadays no one reads her except intimate friends of G.B. Stern[1] and Sheila Kaye-Smith;[2] everyone else is much too busy talking about her.

You suggest that the time and money spent on filming 'The Man Who Came to Dinner' would have been better spent on something 'essentially filmic' (what is essentially filmic, by the way). To this I raise two objections, one practical and one theoretical. The first is that probably the money spent on 'The Man' would have been spent on a technicolor Western. And the second is that it is abominably easy to be pretentiously effective with Film. It is as easy to use as it is easy to abuse, and only the most delicately attuned aesthetic sense (whatever that is) can distinguish chaff from grain. Any Hollywood director, including Mr. Welles, could produce a chunk of arty Film by a few monstrous foreshortenings and a little discreet gloom. I am prepared to accept Cinema as a fascinating and intensely dramatic and unusually diverting flame; but not as an art. I think that is final. [...]

Re Enid Julian, this is the big news, this week's psychological headline, this week's burn-this-immediately – I have slept in the same bed as Lionel Dunn. Last Wednesday. I went round to her flat, played around with her awhile, and playfully desired her to undress. She did, instantly – stripped stark naked and leapt and lunged at me. God, what could I do? It was coitus interruptus at its juiciest. I have no illusions: she is a ruinous cobra and a despicable hoyden; but she fascinates. I have not yet decided whether I am the fly and she the flypaper, or I the fly and she the ointment. [...]

Incidentally, I wrote a poem about my Enid experience. You see I had to try twice; the first time, vibrate as she might, I was impotent. It is a delightful poem and most subtly pornographic.

I am reading 'Vision and Design' by Roger Fry.[3] It contains the most coherent aesthetic theory I know, the most commonsensical and lucid, too. Read it please. PLEASE.

Also reread Max's[4] 'Christmas Garland'. What a feast-day of smiling satire!

I have begun Locke's 'Essay on Human Understanding'.[5] Fine and direct; prose as tight and pedestrian as good prose should be.

'You Can't Take It With You' is coming along fine. I shall be a riot as Kolenkhov. Read the play and send me some opinions of it.

I had to register today. And in a few careless minutes my future was decided. I 'expressed a preference' for the mines.[6] Everyone in the place stopped dead and just looked at me. The man behind the counter said it was the first time that had happened in his entire experience. Perhaps I was foolish. Tell me.

***

'Hamlet' rehearsals are shaping well. [...] Hugh and I have, by the way, been making one or two minor extra cuts; but Hugh insists on over-dramatising and over-posing the whole thing. I shall of course play it down tremendously on the stage. Incidentally, theatrical circles in Birmingham are buzzing with it. Even Norman Painting of B.U.D.S.[7] (whose 'King Lear' has received only tepid applause) has been heard to mention it.

One important thing: the 'To be or not to be' soliloquy is <u>impossible</u> as a prologue. In the first place, it is too alive and alertly meditative to be spoken by Hamlet, dead; that is to say, its turns of speech are too questing and sincere in their appraisal of suicide to be spoken by one already passed over. And in the second place, if we are to have it as a prologue-explanation (which is the function of a prologue) it is equally useless, because it explains nothing about the play at all. 'Hamlet' is not a play about suicide. [...] Act II Sc i is Polonius and Ophelia; but between this scene and the 'pity 'tis 'tis true' scene we are inserting the 'to be or not to be'. I think it's glorious and ideal; how about you?

***

Remark by Professor Lowes Dickinson[8] on Joad[9] which so far holds my Riband for the wittiest remark of the year: 'I hear Joad has redis-covered God. I imagine he pronounces it with a soft G and a long O ...'

***

I like this, culled from the 'New Yorker': 'We have just received a request from the Writers' War Board in Washington for a definition of Democracy. Democracy is the line which forms on the right. It is the sawdust which trickles slowly from a hole in the stuffed shirt, it is the dent in the high hat. Democracy is the recurrent suspicion that more than half the people will be right more than half the time. Democracy is a letter to the editor. Democracy is the request, on a morning in the fifth year of war, from a Writers' War Board for a definition of Democracy.'

***

POULENC[10] visits B'ham on March 14th and I am going. With Enid. I am her pet.

[...] 'Voir ...
KPT
[...]

[1] G. B. (Gladys Bertha) Stern (1890–1973), romantic English novelist.
[2] Sheila Kaye-Smith (1887–1956), popular English novelist.
[3] Roger Fry (1866–1934), Cambridge-educated art critic and painter, associated with the Bloomsbury set: *Vision and Design* (1920).
[4] Beerbohm.
[5] John Locke (1632–1704), English philosopher: *An Essay Concerning Human Understanding* (1690).
[6] For compulsory national service. Ten per cent of boys reaching military service age were chosen, by ballot, to work in the mines (and were known as the 'Bevin Boys').
[7] Norman Painting acted with the Birmingham University Dramatic Society, and later became famous as Phil Archer on the BBC radio serial *The Archers*.
[8] Goldsworthy Lowes Dickinson (1862–1932), English historian and philosopher.
[9] C. E. M. Joad (1891–1953), English philosopher who took part in the BBC 'Brains Trust'.
[10] Francis Poulenc (1899–1963), French composer (one of Les Six) of chamber and choral music, songs, ballet and opera.

To Julian Holland

Kardomah Café,
New St.
[17 March 1945]

Dear Jules:
I am beset with difficulties of a most complex nature. To solve them it is essential that Enid should come to London on March 31st with us. Can you accommodate her and me at no. 225? Please, my ever so angel, don't refuse. My private life hangs in the balance.

Ever,
Ken

To Julian Holland

Edgbaston
19 March 1945

Dear J:

[...]

1. Enid is <u>not</u> coming to London. I can't stand her.
2. We are doing a performance of 'Hamlet' at <u>Hall Green</u>!
3. Where have you heard 'ill reports' of Enid?
4. I am reading Lamb's 'Specimens from the Dramatists about the time of Shakespeare'.[1] M-m-m. I have found that a man I always suspected of being a great poet, George Peele,[2] <u>is</u> a great poet.
5. This is Big. This is me, Julian, me grown sentimental and drooling. Me relinquishing the old past of feckless confidant and Good Friend for that of Lovah! This is me writing in all solemnity to tell you that <u>I am in love with Joy</u>. There can be no mistake, Jules. Only she can give me that salmon-spawning leap in the belly, that sudden uprushing exhilaration <u>on sight</u>. To meet her accidentally in the street pleases me a thousand times more than sleeping with Enid. I spent a weekend in Stratford with this wideyed marigold. Jules, write and TELL HER TO LOVE ME, PLEASE. This is real O Christ Jules believe and stop grinning you great black black-hearted otter!

I mean, really do mean all this, I'm hysterically in love with Joy. I love Joy. I love Joy. I love Joy. Yes Joy Matthews. Yes, Joy, Joy.

God!

Write to her and help me.

Ken

P.S. I am in love with Joy Matthews. You remember Joy, Julian, she is not in love with me how could she be, she who has adored Reg Paveley. She should love me, for I am good and clever.

---

[1] By Charles Lamb (1775–1834), published in 1808.
[2] George Peele (1556–96), author of plays, pageants and verse on courtly and patriotic themes.

To the Secretary of the Tutorial Board

King Edward's School.
4 May 1945

Dear Sir,

A casual word dropped by Mr. Bevin[1] in the House of Commons yesterday has prompted me to write to you. He stated that a limited number of scholarship-holders will be indefinitely deferred from military service in the near future, and permitted to take up residence at their Universities.

Last November I was awarded an Open Demyship to Magdalen. I have not yet been called up (I was eighteen in April), and I am naturally very anxious to know whether I may be affected by this new loop-hole. Could you possibly let me know the machinery by which the 'limited number' will be selected?

Very sincerely,
Kenneth P. Tynan

P.S. My home address is:
229, Portland Rd.,
Edgbaston,
Birmingham, 17.

---

[1] Ernest Bevin (1881–1951), Labour MP who served in Churchill's War Cabinet as Minister of Labour and National Service, later Foreign Secretary in Attlee's Labour government, 1945–51.

To Julian Holland

Edgbaston
10 May 1945

Dear J:

This is about the end. I cannot go on very much longer.

To explain: VE night[1] and VE + 1 – night might have been the most terrible of my life. On Monday all was well. Geoff Darby, his girlfriend, myself and Joy had a select binge, which did no harm to anyone and pleased us all immensely. On Tuesday night the party was larger. We met at the St. James,[2] and had an uproarious evening, Hugh acting as M.C. and sending us out into the streets for more and different branches of the Allied Services he could buy drinks for. There were Stuart, Cecilia, Pat Evans, Pat Anderson, Tay Lippitt, Bill Moore, Pauline, Pat Brewer, David Bird, Joan Cutler, Aura Dennis, Norman Banford, Joy, myself, Hugh – and dozens more.[3] We then conga'ed up and down and around town until about 1 a.m., full of cherry brandy and champagne.

So far so very good. You note from the list I give that the undesirables had begun to appear. I had noticed with increasing distress Joy's habit of going out of the St. James for periods of 10 minutes or so with David Bird; but now it was worse. Without saying goodnight, the girl whom I had dated and fêted walked off home with this Bird creature. I followed, fighting drunk, with Pat Brewer, and we almost came to blows. I suddenly realised that he was stronger than I and left it at that. He had to leave her in Moseley,[4] and I walked the rest of the [way] with her, and stopped at her house.

Now all this I could reasonably understand. David was a good deal more sober than I was, and probably Joy felt safer with him. And he wasn't necking with her.

But Wednesday night capped everything. I have never felt nearer to murder than I did then and do now. As before we met at the St. James – the same party augmented by Harry James, Derek Allcott, Leila Chambers,[5] and others. At 7 o'clock we went to a Midland Jazz Jamboree at the Midland Institute, but came out at 8.30 because of its unutterable corniness. Walking back to the St. James, we bumped into Keith Makin and Bernard Owen. I spotted them. I introduced them to the party and asked them to join it, though they knew hardly any of the others. I introduced Bernard Owen to Joy.

Then we decided to commandeer a tram and break into the Union.[6] The party was now about 50 strong, and it did break into the Union, augmented by Birmingham University Students, girl-less and eager.

Then I noticed something. Joy, who would never let me kiss her in public, was kissing Bernard Owen all over the place in public. As on the previous night, she had arranged to meet me, and without a word disappeared with somebody else.

At first I didn't mind. I told myself that, as before, everyone was kissing everyone else. I went around and kissed everyone else just to demonstrate the point to myself.

Then we left the Union – about 100 strong – and made for Moseley, led by Hugh. The horrible rasping sore throat I had was getting rapidly worse. And so far as I could see the only two honourable girls in the party were Pat Evans & Pat Brewer. We walked along in a colossal line spread out across Bristol Rd – all except Joy and Bernard, who walked ecstatically in front, embracing each other every few yards. Then I got mad. I went completely berserk and walked bang into the headlights of a car approaching along Priory Rd. I was utterly, utterly despondent, and I ran wildly towards them. Hugh brought me down into the gutter by a flying tackle as the car passed. I dashed off after Joy, croaking in a reedy hoarse treble that I was taking her home and that I would slit both their throats if they didn't stop. Of course, they didn't. They stopped, <u>laughed at me</u> (O Christ) and proceeded to neck in front of me in the middle of the road.

It took eight of them to stop me from strangling the filthy bitch and that low bastard.

Finally Hugh (who was perfectly <u>wonderful</u> to me all evening, suggested that we go to Moseley Park. Joy and Bernard had to go. I ran up to Joy and croaked goodnight. She laughed and walked on. I didn't see her again. That night I invited Pat Brewer to stop the night with me, as Hugh was running me home in the car anyway. She came. But mother <u>refused</u> to entertain her, and made her leave to walk 8 miles home. I was completely humiliated, and had to drag her back in tears. Mother was still nagging and shouting, and swearing not to give her any breakfast. I managed to smuggle her into a bed at about 3.30 a.m., but she had gone by 7. Julian, I just can't stand any more humiliation. I want to kill Joy, and to kill my mother. I write in the warm light of midmorning. This is not madness that I have uttered.

Ken

[1] 8 May 1945.

[2] A cellar bar in New Street, popular with American Services personnel.

[3] Stuart Johnson, NDC actor and director; Cecilia Barnes, Pat Anderson, Pat Evans, William Moore, Pauline Whittle and Aura Dennis were NDC actors – Barnes and Anderson played Court ladies in *Hamlet*; A.J. Lippitt, a demon fast-bowler whom KPT described as 'perpetually deprecating', left KES in 1945 and went into the Civil Service; Pat Brewer, KE Girls' School and Kardomah friend, later became a professional actress and worked for KPT at the Lichfield Repertory; David Bird, KES prefect, played the Player King in *Hamlet*; Joan Cutler (stage manager of the NDC who also worked on the *Evening Despatch*) and Norman Banford (an Egyptian doctor) were Kardomah friends.

[4] A district of Birmingham.

[5] A KES friend.

[6] Birmingham University Students' Union.

To Pauline Whittle

King Edward's School
25 May 1945 3.10 p.m.

Dear Pauline:

I am approaching the end of what has been the happiest twenty-four hours to date of my life. Not just relative happiness, but pure, exuberant bliss, quite absolute. I am so instinct with joy that I could wish life to cease. Sweet Christ, spew up from Hell some Baudelaire to sing this ecstasy. And you ... thank you.

Ken

To Julian Holland

King Edward's School
2 June 1945

This is a VERY PRIVATE letter which MAY BE USED as Toilet Paper

Dear J:

A deal of unimportant news, and one colossal surprise. [...]

Now to my news – staggering, ironic news. Pauline and I are in love and intend to become engaged as soon as possible. After Whit Monday at my house I rang her up, having kissed her for the first time and revelled in it, and asked her to lunch with me later in the week. She was dubious and hesitant, and when I accordingly kept the date she stood me up. I rang up again; she was ill; I protested my affection; and she said, in tones of utter sincerity which gave me a thrill of pure bliss: 'Ken, for the last six months I've been worshipping the ground you walked on.'[1] So we have gone on seeing each other and are helplessly in love:

The Pauline Stakes are over; a noncombatant saw the dogs snapping and walked off with the bone.

Hugh is incredulous, and tends to scoff at me as an upstart stripling who doesn't know what love is. But he is not broody about it, as I feared he might be.

Incidentally, an amazing thing occurred at the Joint Hop at school on May 25th. We put over a very witty 'I Want to Be An Actor'[2] that

Harry James wrote, and it was a hit. Afterwards I was accosted by a
fast, loose, sophisticated bitch named [Claire][3] who confessed that it
was she who had been sending me Valentines and Xmas Cards. I took
her quietly aside and told her I was going to undress her. She pinned
me to the wall, stroked my hair tigerishly and kissed me with these
words 'O how loathsome and unapproachable you are.' I escorted her
to Commander Langley's[4] room and proceeded to play the beast with
two backs. And – here's the odd thing – I discovered that she enjoys
being spanked!

Incredible luck! But it was strictly a one-night stand. She's an apostle
of Culchah[5] with a capital Robert Helpmann.

And she couldn't approach Pauline, unspankable tho' the latter innocent is.

Believe me, J, this Pauline episode is going to grow into a common
autobiography. I think I mean it this time. Reciprocity from the desirable is now my recipe for love.

Quand même,[6]
K.

P.S. Can you manage to see 'Hamlet' June 13th?
P.P.S. If we are engaged before June 25th I shall congratulate myself
on it in the 'Chronicle'![7]
P.P.P.S. Doubtless Joe would send love if he were here. So love from
Joe.
P.P.P.P.S. Yes, K.P.T. is in love. England must be a land fit for Eros
to live in.[8]

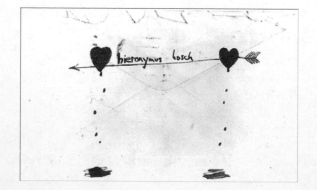

[1] Pauline Whittle wrote to KPT on 5 January 1980 that when they lunched at the Lantern restaurant in Corporation Street, 'I was so overcome by an overwhelming passion for you. I could not lift the soup-spoon to my lips. My hand was shaking so much ... You were a thrilling young man, tall and elegant ... original in thought and deed, full of charm.'

[2] A mock Victorian melodrama written in rhyming couplets involving four characters played by members of the audience selected by the master of ceremonies (KPT in this case) on the merits of their reading of specimen couplets. The chosen were given costumes and scripts. The audience meanwhile were given balls of newspaper to throw at bad actors, and encouraged to hiss and boo. According to Harry James this popular event played about a hundred times in the area.

[3] Name changed.

[4] Deputy head of KES known as 'Second Master'.

[5] Presumably 'Claire' assumed an upper-class accent. KPT's slight Birmingham accent had disappeared by the time he left Oxford.

[6] For a year or more, KPT signed off with Sarah Bernhardt's motto. Dared to jump a ditch, aged nine, she did so, and badly hurt herself. As she was carried away, she cried out in fury, 'I should do it again, *quand même* [in spite of everything], if they dared me again! I shall always do what I want to do!'

[7] KPT edited the school magazine for the summer edition of 1945.

[8] From Lloyd George's speech at Wolverhampton, 23 November 1918: 'What is our task? To make Britain a fit country for heroes to live in.'

To Julian Holland

Edgbaston
5 June 1945
10.20 p.m.

Dear J:

This must be brief, because I've just finished six adolescent pages to Pauline, who is Oban-bound.[1]

Your doubts about the quality of my passion are reasonable on the plane of pedestrian logic. But to me the position is perfectly explicable. On Thursday the 24th she told me that she loved me. And on Friday the 25th I am tearing off someone else's underwear. I did it, J, as a gesture. It was a Joint Hop; I had a reputation as a libertine to keep up; and I had to keep it up until I had <u>seen</u> Pauline to make quite sure it was not merely infatuation with my surface and my pose. I was not going to be hurt again as Joy so brilliantly hurt me. No more lacerations for me, I hope to Mammon. I had to assure myself in the ecstatic interval between her 'phone call and our meeting on Saturday that I still had the power of captivating and working my will on someone else. Once that was satisfactorily accomplished, I never wanted to see the atrocious slut again, and neither have I. Neither shall I. Believe this, J.

'Way of All Flesh'[2] is written with lovely solidity, but its rancour and malice at Victorianism are Stracheyesque[3] and démodé in the worst way. [...]

Incidentally, the new Woollcott 'Long Long Ago'[4] looks bad and awfully mannered. It includes [...] one good story.

Geo Gershwin: 'I wonder if my music will be played in a hundred years' time?'

Oscar Levant:[5] 'If you're still around, George, it will.' [...]

Next on my reading list is 'The Decline and Fall of the Roman Empire' and I intend to read it. That's a god-almighty resolution.

A few lines from Farjeon[6] to close:
'I MAY BE FAST, I MAY BE LOOSE,
I MAY BE EASY TO SEDUCE,
I MAY NOT BE PARTICULAR
TO KEEP THE PERPENDICULAR,
BUT ALL MY HORIZONTAL FRIENDS
ARE PRINCES, PEERS OR REVERENDS,
WHEN TOM OR DICK OR BERTIE CALL,
THEY LEAVE ME STRICTLY VERTICAL'

Quand même,
K.

---

[1] Pauline Whittle went to Oban, Scotland, on holiday with her mother.
[2] Novel by Samuel Butler (1835–1902), originally entitled *Ernest Pontifex*, published posthumously in 1903.
[3] Lytton Strachey (1880–1932), Cambridge-educated essayist and biographer, author of *Eminent Victorians* (1918), an attack on four pillars of the Victorian establishment.
[4] Part of *Selections* (1945).
[5] Oscar Levant (1906–72), American pianist, wit, performer and misanthrope.
[6] Herbert Farjeon (1887–1945), English playwright and dramatic critic; he owned and ran the 'Little Theatre' in London from 1938.

To Pauline Whittle

Edgbaston

5 June 1945 10.30 pm

Darling: God, that was a welcome card. Remote and very unrevealing; but it's contact, isn't it?

This must be a brave letter. No exotic quotations; no miserable, ignominious echoes of Swinburne, no trace of silvery, erotic decadence; no Musset; no motif of Delius – nothing but lucidity. For everything is clear now; suddenly crystal clear.

I had just returned from a very fine performance of 'The Light of Heart'[1] in the park when I knew that there was to be your card, that there was to be word from you. I hoped faintly yesterday, reckoning without the indubitable laxity of Scots postal services. Today after the play I <u>knew</u> you had written, and the tousled, haggard figure who dashed home in a series of jerky, rocket-like spurts would never have been recognised as the cultured 'petit maître' he aspires to be. Christ, I sweated home!

And there was a card.

I had to leave off 'The Way of All Flesh' to read Peter Quennell's 'Four Portraits'[2] – thumbnail (almost thumbnose) sketches of Boswell, Gibbon, Sterne, and John Wilkes – inhabitants all of that priceless century, the eighteenth. A period of cynical modishness, darling, – my exact spiritual atmosphere. I've since returned to Butler, but his spite is beginning to seem a little démodé. Rancour such as his doesn't live: I'm longing to get at the sublime, rotund sentences which Gibbon could mint. It is my intention to read 'The Decline and Fall of the Roman Empire'.

This is an almighty thought.

Yes, yes, in response to a question I hope to God you've asked yourself, I still love you incredibly. This is miraculous; because I love you so entirely that in forty-eight hours I can rehearse the emotions of a lifetime. Spiritually I have already loved you twenty times the length of my life.

(There's a programme of insouciant, lilting French cabaret songs on the radio as I write, and I have just lit a cigarette. Try and <u>see</u> me.)

It was announced officially by the Head Master this morning that Arts students at Universities born in 1927 have an all but certain chance of complete exemption from national service. So let's get engaged[3] and discover Oxford together.

Sorry to seem trite, but may I repeat some lines I hastily translated on the telephone to you: 'L'amour est l'art de conquérir, de posséder, et de retenir une âme. Si riche qu'elle nous soulève, et si pauvre qu'elle ait de nous le même besoin que nous avons d'elle.'[4]

I'm quoting this from memory. Since we loved, you've been holding the door of my memory wide open. And that is one sentence I shall not easily forget.

There's a poignant little first-love snatch of French song coming through now. I dare not write more; I weep readily these days.

Quand même
Ken
[...]

---

[1] By Welsh actor and playwright Emlyn Williams (1940).
[2] Sir Peter Quennell (1905–93), man of letters, poet and editor of the *Cornhill* magazine 1944–51; *Four Portraits* (1945). John Wilkes (1727–97) was an MP and essayist.
[3] KPT's engagement to Pauline Whittle lasted until March 1947.
[4] From *L'Amour* (1929) by the poet and playwright Paul Géraldy (pseud. of Paul Le Fèvre).

To Julian Holland

Edgbaston
20 June 1945

Dear J:

'Hamlet'[1] was a great success. Every seat at the Midland Institute was sold, and we had even to add an extra row of seats. This done, there were still people standing at the back of the hall. A very still and awed audience in every respect; the only centre of opposition being Lionel Dunn, who, like the parasite he is, came on someone else's complimentary ticket. His only comment on the show was: 'Thanks, I had a very comfortable seat.' He showed his pedantic disapproval of the cuts by refraining from applauding and walking straight out, talking loudly, at the final curtain.

Kemp[2] has begun to respect us. His crit., which I have not to hand but will try to enclose later, did us the signal honour of judging us by the standards of a professional company; that is, of assessing how muchwe fell short of the highest, & not by how much we excelled the lowest. He mentioned us as textual editors, and patently disapproved of the cutting of the advice to the players; and, in a moment of childish pedagoguery, put the word 'editors' in inverted commas.

Of my performance, he said that I tended to argue too much, and that I should learn to appeal to the heart instead of to the head. He just did not like our reading of the Nunnery scene; he thinks it should be all rant; and he holds it fit that he should be the final law on such matters of interpretation. He commends my forethought, but says uncompromisingly and flatly that my readings are 'often mistaken'. Nevertheless he insists that I always 'command attention'.

Pauline, he said, had a moment of supreme pathos, but failed to lead up to it. Hugh and Colin[3] were mentioned approvingly; Eleana could not assume Gertrude's years; but he concludes by saying that we have rendered the play 'vigorous and effective service'. A rather opinionated crit., but most encouraging and constructive. (Addendum: He thinks David Bird <u>the</u> best Player King he has ever seen.)

The Despatch crit. was pointless; very short, all praise and no blame. It applies the adjective 'neurotic' to my performance, however, which was what I was playing for.

Hall Green on Saturday enjoyed it immensely, and were quite wonderfully well-behaved with one significant exception: they laughed at the Ophelia mad scenes, for which I could have slaughtered them. They rocked, however, at the Hamlet–Polonius scenes (much more spontaneous glee than that at the Institute), and were suitably awestruck by the soliloquies and final curtain.

And now I am exhausted.

Thanks from the company for the telegram – we received, incidentally, about a dozen, including one from Joe Simon; who provided the skull for the grave scene, and demanded that there be a programme note to the effect that the part of Yorick was played by J.B. Simon.

Much of my enjoyment of the last week of 'Hamlet' was due to James Dawson,[4] who has lately been in terrific humorous form. Fate (and Astley's[5]) having provided him with a colossal sweep of red cloak and a helmet, he would be seen disappearing with a swirl and a glint around dark corners. We discovered him at the Dress Rehearsal sitting at the organ with a wild gleam in his eyes screaming 'Where's Lon Chaney[6] now?'

On Saturday we all signed each other's programmes, and it became

Jimmy's practice to append a quotation to each one he signed. His comment on that of Pat Anderson, a particularly repulsive maid-in-waiting, was typical:

'What, has this thing appeared again tonight?'

And on Hugh's:

'Pox, leave thy damnable faces, and begin!'

On Thursday evening, Hugh, David Bench[7] and I went unaccountably to Oxford for a couple of days. God, how magnificent and mellow it all is; the very stones seem lambent. We saw a goodish production of 'The Devil's Disciple'[8] at the Playhouse,[9] and bought books from the celebrated Blackwell (in The Broad[10]). I bought, read, and marvelled at Kafka's 'The Trial'; this is an experience you must on no account miss. It's a claustrophobic, earnestly surrealistic book – most eery – AND it has a meaning. It's the profoundest religious allegory of our times; possibly since Bunyan. But to understand it, I should read the chapter on Kafka in Norman Nicholson's 'Man and Literature'.[11]
[...]

At Oxford I made one of my best remarks for years. We went into a restaurant very late for supper; they had only something called 'brunch'. We asked what it contained, and were told: 'oh, carrots, sausage, cabbage, peas, some bacon, soya beans ...'

'And the rest, I suppose, is silage?'[12]

Woollcott's book contained one of the finest and subtlest anecdotes I know. A housemaster of an English public school was confronted by the mutilated corpse of a girl whose lover had battered her to death. He surveyed it awhile, then said: 'And what dangerous clown has done this?'

I have searched for the Kemp Krit, but it seems to have vanished. The Pauline hook-up still prospers. Next week, though, I start rehearsals of 'You Can't Take It With You' with Bill[13] present. That should be fairly sticky.

Next week I see 'Juno and the Paycock'[14] at the Rep. and Robert Morley[15] in 'The First Gentleman'[16] at the Royal.

When are you going to 'The Duchess of Malfi'?

Hugh and I are hoping to come to London in August – early August, with David Bench and possibly Pauline (though I don't think the latter would work, in Hugh's presence – he tends to become rather preoccupied and traditional about it). May I share 225? The others will hotel it.

Is July 19th possible? A chance of a chat with Jas. Aggot.[17]

Quand même,

k

P.S. The duel is tremendously good and <u>really</u> dangerous.
P.P.S. John Gielgud is taking a cut version of 'Hamlet' to Burma. I wrote to tell him of our cuts – at length. He wrote back to say that he had already chosen the version he was going to use, & that he had done a Certain Amount of That Sort of Thing in his Time Before.

---

[1] Frank Lister Kay, KES Latin master in charge of the Debating Society, recalled that KPT was carried off at the end of *Hamlet* 'horizontal and stiff (achieving, apparently, instant rigor mortis) over the heads of six bearers' – an idea KPT had no doubt borrowed from Helpmann's ballet of the play. Lord Morris, the Head Master, recalled that KPT's performance was much influenced by Gielgud's.
[2] The *Birmingham Post* drama critic.
[3] Colin Golby, KES contemporary, who played Horatio in *Hamlet*. Hugh Manning directed and played Claudius.
[4] KES contemporary who went into advertising. In 1940 KPT had asked Dawson to be his Boswell. Dawson recorded in his diary of January 1944 that his benefactor had now abandoned the idea: 'You may go now Dawson. I have done with you.' In December 1944 Dawson recorded that he had just left KPT 'picking up another girl ... when in their presence he becomes sticky, and can rarely emerge with less than two or three clinging to him. But one might as well expect humanity from him, as honey from a wasp.'
[5] Henry Astley had a theatrical costume shop in Broad Street, Birmingham.
[6] Lon Chaney Jr (1906–73) played the title role in *The Phantom of the Opera* (US, 1925).
[7] KES contemporary who became a pig farmer; he played Osric in *Hamlet*
[8] By George Bernard Shaw, first performed in New York in 1897, published in 1901.
[9] Oxford's repertory theatre, home of the Oxford University Dramatic Society.
[10] Broad Street, Oxford, commonly referred to as The Broad.
[11] Published 1943.
[12] 'The rest is silence': *Hamlet*, Act V Sc. ii.
[13] Bill Moore was Pauline Whittle's previous boyfriend.
[14] By the Irish playwright Sean O'Casey (1880–1964). First performed in 1924.
[15] Robert Morley (1908–92), English actor; played Sheridan Whiteside in *The Man Who Came to Dinner* (1941–3).
[16] Play by Norman Ginsbury (1945).
[17] James Agate.

During his last term at King Edward's School, Ken was made President of the Sixth Form Conference of the boys' and girls' school. To this event – at which he would perform Hamlet *and show* Citizen Kane *– he invited to talk the socialist editor of the* New Statesman and Nation, *Kingsley Martin*

*(1897–1968; his editorship ran 1932–62), who would speak on the Big Three
and the future of Europe, and the leading drama critic of the day, the* Sunday
Times's *James Agate. Ken admired the latter's robust and opinionated views,
and his style, which he later described as that of a 'butcher boy hypnotised by
Beerbohm'. Agate inspired him at this early age with 'an absolute conviction
that the purpose of life was to decide exactly when and why to use the adjective
"great" of an actor.'*

*On 19 July 1945, Ken met the critic at the station. He was wearing a
tropical suit and carrying a silver-knobbed cane, and in the taxi on the way
to the conference he placed a hand on his host's knee and asked, 'Are you a
homosexual, my boy?' 'I'm a-f-f-fraid not,' was the reply. 'Ah well,' Agate
said, 'I thought we'd get that out of the way.'*

Ken gave Agate a little poem in prose called 'L'Art pour L'Art', a perfumed
hommage *to Apollinaire ('Phoebus Apollinaire turned fasting friar'), Mallarmé and others. 'My Dear Hamlet', Agate wrote to him the next day, 'You
write better than I have ever attempted to write. The mistake you make is an
old one of trying to do too much ... Why, when you are in full spate of
discussion about Huysmans, lug in Voltaire? ... And I conjure you, now and
for ever, to put a stop to your punning.*

'Take my advice,' he concluded. 'Absent thee from quotation.'

*Ken wired back, 'I shall in all my best obey you, madam. Hamlet.' He then
defended himself by letter:*

To James Agate

Edgbaston
25 July 1945

Dear Mr Agate,
 You have dealt with me very temperately. But may I (it shall be for a
few moments only) have leave to quibble? My prose poem exudes
booksiness because the characters I limn in exude booksiness. Its atmosphere is their atmosphere; and its faults are their faults. My mistake, I
take it, is not that of trying to say too much, but of seeming to know
too much. I have, as you must know, never read de Sade[1] (the nearest
approach to him I have made is that best of bedside books, <u>Psychopathia
Sexualis</u>[2]); I have only seen the glow of Balzac refracted and dimmed
by upstart crows of critics; and of Meredith[3] I know only <u>The Egoist</u>.
My prose poem is impressionism at its worst – literary impressionism.
Its sufficient beauty is to conjure up by stealth from books an image of
the wordy marvels that were burgeoning in France after 1850. And if

I consider that a line of Marlowe may be perverted to apply to Mallarmé I unhesitatingly pervert it. The only connection between the two is: there is no connection. Just as my only rule is: there are no rules. Art laughs at locksmiths. My quid-pro-quem is irritatingly derivative and allusive because the Symbolists were; it is criticism in their own rarefied cloud-country.

I know what Rimbaud looked like; I don't think George Moore did.[4] The lines I quote, which he, impossibly, used to describe R.L.S., might easily represent his own over-idealised concept of the young jesting pilate. And as to the 'ponderous and marble jaws' of Proust: when I note that Shakespeare has coupled two words which by their pompous sonority suggest weight it is a sign of my own innate breeding and modesty that I prefer using his phrase to coining one of my own.

Like Sterne, 'I begin with writing the first sentence – and trusting to Almighty God for the second.' But my quotation-book never leaves my side. My principal fault (and it is quite unforgivable) is expounded by Nietzsche:

'What is the characteristic of all literary decadence? It is that life no longer resides in the whole. The word gets the upper hand and jumps out of the sentence, the sentence stretches too far and obscures the meaning of the page, the page acquires life at the expense of the whole – the whole is no longer a whole. The whole has ceased to live altogether; it is composite, summed-up, artificial, an unnatural product.'[5]

My work is a chain of soft phrases. I can only thank my Muses that it is a writer's privilege to have his chain tested by its strongest link.

Yours sincerely,
KENNETH P. TYNAN[6]

---

[1] The Marquis de Sade (1740–1814), French revolutionary and author of radical novels of sexual fantasy and perversion.
[2] Richard Krafft-Ebing (1840–1902), German psychiatrist: *Psychopathia Sexualis* (1876).
[3] George Meredith (1828–1909), English writer and journalist admired for his intricate narrative skill; *The Egoist* (1879) was his most famous novel.
[4] 'I think of Mr Stevenson as a consumptive youth wearing garlands of sad flowers with pale, weak hands, or leaning to a large plate-glass window, and scratching thereon exquisite profiles with a diamond pencil' (*The Confessions of a Young Man*, 1886).
[5] From Friedrich Nietzsche (1844–1900), 'The Case of Wagner', in *The Works of Friedrich Nietzsche* Vol. XI.

[6] Agate replied on 27 July warning KPT once more against using the quotation book, and again on 28 July, signing himself 'Polonius'. He quoted from four great dramatic critics: Shaw, Walkley, Beerbohm and Montague, 'master of all I mean by "quotation" instead of borrowers allowing quotation to be their master'. And he added that he did not want Tynan to write like any of them: 'I want you to make for yourself a style – which can be done only out of your own bowels and nobody else's – which will make people say, "That's Tynan", just as people say "That's Hazlitt" or "That's Lewes."'

To James Agate

Edgbaston
[30 July 1945]

DEAR MR AGATE,
    I believe in artifice for art's sake.
    I do not believe in sincerity or profundity.
    I believe in superficiality. I believe in shallowness.
    In fact, <u>quand même</u>, I believe in

KENNETH P. TYNAN

To James Agate[1]

[Telegram]

[July 1945]

POX DEVOUR ME FOR HAVING ALREADY ARRANGED TO BE IN LONDON
AUGUST 3RD TO 12TH WHAT NOW LETTER FOLLOWS HAMLET

[1] Agate had sent KPT a telegram announcing his arrival in Sutton Coldfield (a suburb of Birmingham) to judge a show. Would Tynan join him? Agate commented in his diaries *Ego 8* (from which this correspondence comes): 'The Post Office, staggered by the basic English of the first three words, repeats them to make sure.' On 5 August in London, he took KPT to lunch along with Hugh Manning, Julian Holland and David Bench, at the Imperial Hotel, Bloomsbury.

To Hazel Young and Barbara Siggs[1]

Edgbaston
3 August 1945

dear ladies

the tynans you mention at saltley[2] are none of me. my tynans spend their time and other people's money hectically profiteering in drapery.

the backstage s.w.[3] story is verbatim truth. so, probably, were the other stories you have heard. for example, it is a fact that i did make a speech to the assembled crowd at a british restaurant[4] on the subject of sterilisation of the german people.

i am going to –the duchess of malfi– tonight. webster and ford are my favourite elizabethan dramatists; i should say jacobean. i enjoy reading them more than i enjoy seeing shakespeare acted. [...]

elizabethan dramatists do not act better than they read. when one reads them one forgets the silly machinations of the plot and the transparency of the type-characters, and surrenders oneself to the crude, fortuitous wonders of the verse. on the stage they are frankly grand-guignol, and as such are not good drama. [...]

my views on modern dress shakespeare are traditionally agatian. the business of scenery is to be so in keeping with the atmosphere of the play that after a cursory glimpse it can fade into the plot and be forgotten. when modern dress and sets intervene in shakespeare, it is impossible to overlook them; they keep obtruding themselves and getting between the dramatist's purpose and his audience. as experiments they are vastly entertaining (in recent times, witness tyrone guthrie's[5] superb travesty of –the alchemist–, and sir barry's[6] –taming of the shrew–). but elizabethan cosmology, ideology, and social system are so far removed from ours that modern dress is in the last analysis a hopeless display of wrongheadedness. the restoration dramatists, i believe, would benefit from modern dress; the frills and flutters and fans in which we normally see them are encumbrances. the dialogue of wycherley, vanbrugh, and farquhar is an exact parallel to the clever dirt that young people were talking in the twenties. to dress congreve in the garb of 1925 bloomsbury would be the most rewarding of theatrical experiments. [...]

1) sports. i love cricket, rowing, fives, table-tennis; at all of which i am more than moderately good. i enjoy watching rugger, soccer, and tennis; and all forms of track athletics.

compulsory games are obviously idiotic. and it should be –viv<u>ent</u> les sitwells–.[7]

2) i have never written a book. i have begun many, and finished none. i write quickly, but polish slowly. i shall never write a sustained novel or critical essay; my collected works will bulk small but precious.

3) i enjoy –sylphides– almost as much as i hate –swan lake–. though at times it's perilously near cloud-cuckoo-land, and the fatal door to whimsey-whamsey, –sylphides– successfully treads the razor's edge and comes off triumphantly. –sylphides– is one of the few classical ballets i enjoy (–giselle– and –petrouchka– are the others). [...]

4) eccentricities: odd pets, to be toted around on pieces of string, such as mocking birds, grey rats, platypuses, dragonflies; cigarette-holders (if you smoke; which you should – every girl should have a vocation); large signet rings; eton crop à la ruth gipps[8] – elizabeth [*sic*] bergner; but eccentricity, like all forms of surreal art, must come from within, and must be creatively egoistic.

5) dark green with red spots, white with green and black circles – enough?[9]

oh well! is a slipshod translation of eh bien!, which means approximately what writers in –punch– mean when they say – however .... [...]

   i have no news on capital punishment, but my views on corporal punishment are pronounced. i believe, with mr coward, that –women should be beaten regularly, like gongs–.[10] i once mooted writing a curious little tome on the subject, called –like gongs–. your views?

[Ken]

---

[1] KES girls who knew KPT from a distance and decided to write a novel about him, undeterred by their History mistress who had warned them of his 'unsavoury reputation'. They finally met him at the Kardomah and he, in turn, decided to take their education in hand, setting them obscure intellectual quizzes and testing them with Consequences, or the Truth Game. In this letter KPT answered questions to help them with the proposed novel. Hazel Holt (her married name) later wrote a biography of Barbara Pym (1990) and Barbara Siggs married KPT's school friend Joe Simon.

[2] A district of Birmingham.

[3] Sadler's Wells; the story itself is now forgotten.

[4] Government-sponsored wartime canteens providing a healthy lunch. At one such restaurant KPT was challenged to make a speech. He jumped onto a table and proposed the sterilization of German men: 'We must cut them to the quick,' he told an audience of astounded blue-collar workers.

[5] Sir (William) Tyrone Guthrie (1900–71), English director notable for his productions of Shakespeare. Administrator of the Old Vic and Sadler's Wells 1939–45, he also founded the Stratford Ontario Festival, where he directed 1953–7.

[6] Sir Barry Jackson's production for the Birmingham Repertory Theatre.

[7] Edith, Osbert and Sacheverell Sitwell, the children of Sir George Sitwell, all became important literary figures in the 1920s.

[8] Ruth Gipps (b. 1921), composer, conductor and oboist.
[9] The question was what kind of ties KPT liked.
[10] Noël Coward, *Private Lives*, Act III.

To Julian Holland[1]

Edgbaston
8 October 1945.

Contrary to popular belief, my bright Bloomsburian, I had never read 'Crime and Punishment' until recently. What a stroke of pre-Jungian insight it was for Fyodor to give Raskolnikov a dream about the brutal mutilation of a donkey the day before he commits the murders. And what tension, what convulsive super-Chandlerian tension, in the chapter of the crime itself. The icy compactness of the book, Fyodor's sure mastery of the genre, place it planes above 'Karamazov', which is verbose and very diffuse.

I presume you heard Max last night. A beautifully precise elocution, combined with tolerant contempt for all that is and restrained rapture over all that was made it memorable. He has now said what I take to be the last word on The Film. He spoke of 'those performances – or rather those innumerable rehearsals – which Hollywood sends us'. His drinking-song for critics of the '90's was lilt and nonsense, but so unexpected; and it was oddly pleasurable to compare his carefully accurate pronunciation of 'Barr carr olle' with that of the BBC announcer who followed him: 'Barkroll'.[2]

Oxford welcomes me with ill-concealed loathing on Thursday of this week. They tell me I may have to do something else besides English Literature. The thought is painful.

Agate committed a Brownian error[3] yesterday. Complaining about George Relph's[4] lack of sonority, he said: 'This was a Pistol with a silencer.'

I am so happy to learn that you enjoyed 'Part II'.[5] May I nudge you in seemly fashion to spell Laurence Olivier correctly next time he crops up? And, toolian Julian of my very youth, eschew 'stink'. Please. Nicholas Hannen[6] did not 'stink'. And dear dazed vessel-of-emptiness Miles Malleson[7] was marvellous comick in Silence. What a stroke it was, having created an empty sapless reed in Shallow, for Shakespeare to set alongside him Silence, the mere echo of vacuity. Try reading their scenes together; there is no more naturalistic dialogue in our Theatre.

I refute your contention that Larrie out-acts Rafe.[8] The fact is that in the Shallow scenes Richardson is presenting us the easy, genial recruiting officer doing his duty as far as his penchant for graft will permit. He is always a knight, conscious – and conscious that others will be conscious – of his dignity. He is mind steadily outwitting overmuch matter, and signalling victories by what Ivor B. calls a 'crackling festival of wit'. A second and perhaps more relevant fact is that Falstaff has very few lines in the Shallow scenes.

I have perfected an impersonation – a voice impersonation – of Olivier delivering the 'Was ever woman in this humour woo'd?' soliloquy in 'R.III'.

Now I must pass on to you some news which may Turn Your Stomach. On the train back from London I discovered a seething turbulence of suppressed lust in Miss Whittle. [...] I found it passing fine myself. Her venery since then has been quite terrifying in its persistence. And I am a worn-out and prematurely ageing Gentle-man.

Oh, of course. You will despise Donald Wolfit for what I shall tell you of him. He has 'found it impossible to engage' Pauline. Apparently he only engaged her provisionally; he thought that a member of his company was leaving him. She has not left him; and he does not need Pauline. It is for this that Paul has got her release, refused an offer from the Alexandra; and, incidentally, put herself in a poor light with the Ministry of Labour. I am, you gather, incoherent with rage, and have written mordantly to the Great Hoary Old Ham. [...]

Saw 'The True Glory'.[9] The script is very brilliant, but the film is scrappy newsreel stuff, very noisy and very much in one key and devoid of contrast. Examples of script: 'When we got ter Berlin, I arsted our sargent: "Sarge", I said, " 'ow about a bit er leave?" "God blimey" he said, "we've got ter lick the Japs yet". Regular soldier. Keen.'

'Crarssing the Rhine was a helluva strain. In fact, it was just another D-day. (pause) Dangerous!'

Quand même,
Ken
[...]

---

[1] The last letter KPT wrote to Holland before going up to Oxford.

[2] Barcarolle, a type of song derived from songs of the Venetian gondoliers for voice or instrument, e.g. Chopin's Piano Barcarolle.

[3] A reference to the *Observer*'s drama critic Ivor Brown.

[4] George Relph (1888–1960), British character actor.

[5] *Henry IV, Part II*, performed by the Old Vic Company at the New Theatre, London.

[6] Nicholas Hannen (1881–1972) played Henry IV.

[7] Miles Malleson (1888–1969), English actor who specialized primarily in character roles and Restoration comedy in seasons with John Gielgud and at the Old Vic in the 1940s.

[8] Sir Ralph Richardson (1902–83), distinguished English actor; he was playing Falstaff to Olivier's Shallow.

[9] *The True Glory* (UK/US, 1945), Ministry of Information film about the last year of World War II through edited newsreels, directed by Carol Reed and Garson Kanin.

CHAPTER TWO

Oxford

Twenty years after Ken left Oxford, he wrote that he had spent most of his adult life 'trying to live with the knowledge that nothing can ever top the sense of privileged exhilaration I felt then'. He would say he was a creation of Oxford, but his contemporaries argue that he made Oxford in his own image. He set about imposing his own present tense, creating his own élite, repudiating nostalgia and pre-war upper-class values. And in so doing he became something of an intellectual pirate – unrationed, extravagant, funny, always intelligent, determined to introduce gaiety and release. He wore a purple doeskin suit with a gold satin shirt; as at King Edward's, he wanted to be noticed. The nineteen-year-old realized he had to be extremely professional if he were going to impress his contemporaries, who included future politicians like Tony Benn and Anthony Crosland, future journalists like Paul Johnson, William Rees-Mogg and Robin Day, the novelists Kingsley Amis and John Wain, the directors John Schlesinger, Lindsay Anderson and Tony Richardson; along with demobbed soldiers who had been through the Italian landings or D-Day. He couldn't just walk down the High Street with a lily in hand.

He assaulted university drama as director, actor and critic, arguing that 'this sad age needs to be dazzled, shaped and spurred by the spectacle of heroism'. He invaded university journalism and the Union debating society. In his maiden speech he opposed the motion 'that this House deplores the tyranny of convention' deploring extravagance in an extravagant way. So skilful was his manner of delivery that even his stammer seemed to be used with calculated effect. Thereafter this cadaverous stalking horse became the Union's entertainment, a 'licensed shocker'.

Behind the showman was a discreetly hard-working academic. Like Oscar Wilde, a predecessor at Magdalen, Ken was robustly effete. But unlike Wilde, he was exclusively heterosexual. Getting engaged to his many girlfriends seemed like a game that went deep into his unsure and unresolved past.

In July 1948 Sir Peter Peacock died and Ken learned for the first time that he was illegitimate. His friends reported that he expressed a lot of anger against his mother. He was shaken, but the more he considered his illegitimacy, the more he claimed to care for it. At last his childhood was interesting, confirmation that he was out of the ordinary, and quite soon he began to brag that his father had been financial adviser to Lloyd George. He liked the romantic notion that Sir Peter had sacrificed a larger career to run off with his mother. His old Birmingham friends remember that on his father's death he went 'dead' on them, closing his mind to Birmingham for good.

In the spring of 1948, in his last year at the university, he marked his twenty-first birthday by hiring a Thames river boat and celebrating with a hundred of his friends. He had now to face his Army medical examination and devised a stratagem of escape. He found a bizarre homosexual case history in Krafft-Ebing, covered himself with Yardley scent and presented himself at the office of the army psychiatrist. In a performance that went way overboard, he said he could not have sexual relations without the aid of spurs, and stammered outrageously. The doctor came to the conclusion that anyone who had taken so many pains to avoid serving his country should be excused.

In his farewell term Ken gave a party for the actress Gertrude Lawrence in November 1948. A week later he gave his last undergraduate performance at the Union in a debate which moved that 'this House would like to have it both ways'. He argued that there were at least forty or fifty ways of having it, and as the laughter became uncontrollable he added, glancing up towards the gallery which was packed with a posse of his girlfriends, 'not excluding the one on the grand piano', whereupon he was bombarded with violets and balloons.

The party was over and the famous undergraduate packed up his life and took it to London. A tearful Oxford muse mourned his departure in Isis:

> 'The Golden Age is finished, gone the grace,
> Who now so fit to fill KEN TYNAN's place.'

To Pauline Whittle

[Postcard][1]

[Oxford]
Sunday 10.30 am
[14 October 1945]

Paul darling:

How am I to compromise between my standards and normal undergraduate standards? That is only a secondary problem. The primary thing is to find out exactly what undergraduate standards are. And that is learnt painfully and with endless selfhatred: nevertheless I love you consumingly.

Quand même,
K.

[1] Of Gregorio Prieto's *The Kiss* (*c.* 1942–4).

To Julian Holland

[Postcard][1]

[Oxford]
Sunday 10.30 am
[14 October 1945]

Dear J:

The maze (or web) of profound sensations and self-analysis in which my first days here have involved me is almost impossible to describe in a letter. Your extroverted K.P.T. is become a morbid, Palinural[2] introvert. He is mentally in extreme anguish.

Quand même,
K.

[1] Of Gregorio Prieto's *Narcissus* (*c.* 1942–4).
[2] 'Palinurus' was the pseudonym under which Cyril Connolly (1903–74) wrote *The Unquiet Grave* (1944), a compilation of aphorisms, reflections and essays.

To Julian Holland

Magdalen College,
Oxford.
[30 October 1945]

Dear J;–

This Nan–Jean[1] hocus-pocus is unhealthy. I know several girls up here, but after three or four conversations they're almost as much in love with Pauline as they are with me. One girl at St. Anne's, Lucille Deny, has confessed to awful profundities of love for me; and she is a strange mixture of Catherine Morland and Miss Blandish[2] – part romantic, part sex – halfway between amoral and Balmoral. But I am giving her no encouragement. She has up to the moment bought me three lunches, two dinners, a theatre seat, upwards of 50 cigarettes, and three or four razor blades.[3]

I and my clique have invented and developed an entirely new game called 'Squolf' – played with golfclubs and a squash ball. Of this more when I see you.

Your survey of the theatre is welcome. But oh! those parties – with everything but champagne baths and lewd women lolling naked across magnificent white horses – those parties! Julian! You admit that your reading is dwindling; you are intellectually dilapidated. Oh!

I return the song without comment. May it prosper.

I saw 'The Italian Straw Hat'[4] last week. Told with great economy and swiftness; there are hardly any subtitles, and the film, long (2hrs) as it is, is miraculously deft. There is no slapstick in it; it is brittle farce told with tact and good taste, which are the qualities that would have made the German cinema the greatest of all.

Joad[5] and Kingsley Martin are speaking here this week; C.S. Lewis, my tutor, is terribly sound and sunny; the Film Club is showing 'Ivan the Terrible'[6] on Thursday; debates at the Union are only slightly higher quality than school debates; and when are you coming to visit me? Let me know and I'll book you a room at a moderate hotel. Any time will do. I (bad luck) cannot visit you in my first term. So Come. Soon.

Quand même,
K.

P.S. There are no such things as absolute values. (This is quite irrelevant, and not an obscure witticism)

---

[1] Jean Lumley supplanted Nan Long as Holland's girlfriend but the transition was not cleanly made.

[2] Heroines respectively of *Northanger Abbey* (Jane Austen, 1818) and *No Orchids for Miss Blandish* (James Hadley Chase, 1939).

[3] Razor blades were not officially rationed but apparently in short supply.

[4] Original title, *Un Chapeau de Paille d'Italie* (France, 1927), a silent adaptation by René Clair of the Labiche farce.

[5] Professor C.E.M. Joad (see letter of 3 March 1945).

[6] *Ivan the Terrible* (USSR, 1942–6) directed by Sergei Eisenstein, a three-part account of the life of the sixteenth-century tsar.

To Pauline Whittle

Magdalen College
Tuesday
[13 November 1945]

Paul darling;–

Geoffrey Wagner,[1] the minor poet who is playing Othello[2] to my Iago, has a friend named John Vere, a stage and screen actor now teaching at R.A.D.A.[3] He rehearsed for almost ten hours nonstop with unbelievable verve. His last film was the new Deborah Kerr opus, 'I see a Dark Stranger',[4] in which he plays a German spy. He told us a good thing about Agate. A very silly woman sitting opposite him had the temerity to say: 'Mr Agate, I'm putting my daughter on the stage, and I want you to help her.' Agate glowered awhile; then said:

'If you put her on the streets, I might.'

I have satisfied myself that I was <u>not</u> wrong about Basil.[5] The fact that he 'phoned whilst you were in sick bay, wants to go to R.A.D.A., and has a mother named (rather fancifully) Gwhwadwys Guy do nothing to allay my suspicions. Fascinating, no doubt, in the field of family gossip, such snippets of information have little part to play in the Search for Terewth. In which harness (I pray God) I wish to die. Basil (I can see) is an orchids-in-cellophane sort of man; a venez-garçon-deux-demitasses-du-café-noir sort of man; an emaciated, flamingo-like sort of man with a soft-ho!-my-pretty sort of gleam in his eye; a Mr-and-Mrs-Smith sort of man; a cold-hands-warm-heart sort of man; a don't-you-see-this-thing-is-bigger-than-either-of-us sort of man; a don't-let's-worry-too-much-about-<u>him</u> sort of man; a we've-all-got-our-little-repressions sort of man; a yes-darling-this-is-the-real-me-and-by-Christ-I'm-not-ashamed sort of man; a you-miss-whittle-are-a-woman-and-I-am-a-man sort of man; a he-need-never-know sort of man; a this-is-the-twentieth-century sort of man; a you-must-hate-me-now sort of man; an I-know-it's-unpleasant-but-better-safe-than-sorry-eh? sort of man; an I-never-went-to-a-University-but sort of man; an . . . .

Sorry.

I have bought Coward's own recording of 'Sigh No More'.[6] I weep over it hourly. That ginny, strained baritone is the dernier cri of pseudo-sophistication. And the song itself unquestionably belongs to us. I regard it as our personal property, and the thought of other people hearing it daily (sometimes twice daily) is terribly painful.

———————

[...] Now of London. I shall be in London for the first week of the vac; that is, roughly from the 14th of December to the 21st. When will you be there? I can alter my dates easily; and if you can let me know definitely I can ask Julian to book some theatre tickets.

Get Basil to whisk you over here in his helicopter (he <u>must</u> have a helicopter; isn't he known to half the secret services of Europe as 'The Black Arrow', including the Scandinavian?). Any afternoon will do.

I have never till recently known what <u>need</u> was.

AMAZING DRAMA MYSTERY SENSATION

WILDEYED STUDENT ASSAULTS 46-YEAR-OLD
R.A.D.A. OFFICE-BOY

BID TO KIDNAP FIANCEE FOILED

A prematurely senile undergraduate sat weeping tonight in a ☞ SEE P.8, COL. 4.

Quand même,
Ken

[1] A Christ Church undergraduate. On one occasion he invited KPT to his rooms in Peckwater quad to hear two dons, Gilbert Ryle and Hugh Trevor-Roper, debate 'Is Shee-ing better than Ski-ing?'
[2] Act III Sc. iii was performed in an acting contest for the Experimental Theatre Club.
[3] The Royal Academy of Dramatic Art, the London drama school.
[4] Comedy thriller directed by Frank Launder and co-starring Trevor Howard (UK, 1946).
[5] Basil (surname unknown) was about to become a mature student at RADA when Pauline met him on tour. She comments: 'We only met twice, both times accidentally.'
[6] The title song, written by Noël Coward, for a revue directed by Coward at the Piccadilly Theatre in 1945.

To Julian Holland

Magdalen College
Thursday[1]
[Postmark 21 November 1945]

Dear J;–

I have rediscovered Milton hand in hand with C. S. Lewis. God is my co-pilot.

Debate at the Union last week produced this:

'America, and the world in general, is suffering from delirium Trumans.'

My Iago won second prize out of twenty in the Experimental Theatre Club Acting Contests.[2] Next term the Magdalen Players are doing 'Winterset',[3] a pie into which my fingers will certainly probe.

Tonight I go to see Leslie Banks[4] and Hermione Baddeley[5] in a new play, 'Grand National Night';[6] tomorrow Marlene and Emil Jannings in 'The Blue Angel';[7] Friday to hear Alex Comfort[8] talking on 'The Ideology of the Romantics'; Saturday afternoon, to a Brains Trust including Lord David Cecil;[9] Saturday evening to see Jean-Jacques Bernard's 'Martine'.[10] As you will see, education here is purely sporadic and involuntary; education by accident.

I should like to come up to London from Saturday December 8th to Saturday December 15th. What is the position re flat? Is Berkeley[11] still in occupation? If so, and it is impossible for me to bed with you, could you, mon pigsmire, cope by letting me know? I am coming up with a friend at Worcester College, a [...] creature named Peter Symcox[12] (who will sleep alone whatever happens).

Now to shows. If I enclose a few quid in my next letter, could I ask you to prise us (and yourself, I hope) into 'Oedipus', 'The Rivals', 'Henry IV', 'Vanya', 'Sacred Flame',[13] and all the other beauties? Could I? Mmm?

Write back, pretious!

Quand même,
K.

P.S. Am reading Rilke!

<hr>

[1] A mistake: 21 November 1945 was a Wednesday.

[2] The undergraduate magazine *Isis* reported on 28 November 1945 that Kenneth Tynan was a good Iago, except for his voice, which 'seems to quiver unnaturally'.

[3] Play by Maxwell Anderson (1935).

[4] Leslie Banks (1890–1952), English actor famous for his portrayal of Mr Chips in the 1938 stage version of James Hilton's novella.

[5] Hermione Baddeley (1906–86), English actress and revue artiste.

[6] Mystery thriller written in 1946 by Dorothy and Campbell Christie.

[7] Film (Germany, 1930), directed by Josef Von Sternberg, starring Emil Jannings (1887–1950) as a professor who falls in love with a nightclub singer, played by Marlene Dietrich (1904–92) in the role that launched her international career.

[8] Alex Comfort (1920–74), physician, scientist, and later author of *The Joy of Sex* (1972). Though only 25, he had already written a number of novels and would publish these lectures as *Art and Social Responsibility: Lectures on the Ideology of Romanticism* (1947).

[9] Lord David Cecil (1902–86), Professor of English Literature at Oxford 1948–70; biographer of Jane Austen and Thomas Hardy.
[10] In May 1952 KPT directed the play (written 1922) for BBC Television, with Claire Bloom, Stanley Parker and Denholm Elliott.
[11] Berkeley Fase had written the words for Geoffrey Parsons's music for pantomimes in the 1930s. They lived in a flat on Southampton Row, London WC1, which Julian Holland briefly occupied when Parsons was called up.
[12] Close undergraduate friend who performed in KPT's ETC acting competition production of T. S. Eliot's *Sweeney Agonistes* (31 May 1946). Symcox became a theatre and opera producer/director for the Canadian Broadcasting Corporation.
[13] The Old Vic productions (1945–6) of *Oedipus*, *Henry IV* (Parts I and II) and Chekhov's *Uncle Vanya* with Olivier and Richardson; for *The Rivals* and *Sacred Flame*, see letter of 15 December 1945.

To Julian Holland

Collegium Beatae Sanctae
Mariae Magdalae
Saturdae
[1 December 1945]

Dear Old Julian;–

I don't know what you imagine you're apologising about. Quite sincerely, I see no cause.

I have received a rather clever letter from Harry [James]; very stinging, with a withering reference to 'plucked highbrows'. But I have sent him a beautifully modulated and ironic retort, containing a remark worthy of Oscar[1] at his worst. Harry complains that I cannot believe in modesty since I have none myself: 'My dear Harry, I can believe in anyone's modesty except my own; and I'm far too modest to believe in that.'

Here are £3, a first instalment. Peter will send you another £3 on Mondae.

Q.m.;–
Ken
[. . .]

[1] Wilde.

To Pauline Whittle

[Telegram]

11 December 1945

FOR CHRISTMAS DARLING I WANT EITHER LARGE AND ECSTATICALLY
INSCRIBED PORTRAIT OF YOU OR PROHIBITED EXPENSIVE CIGARETTE
LIGHTER OR BOTH = KEN

To Pauline Whittle

The Imperial Hotel
Russell Square
London, W.C.1
15/12/45

O my own darling;–

I was slightly drunk tonight. Peter, Julian, Jean and I went to see
Sonia Dresdel in 'The Sacred Flame',[1] which begins at 4.45 and ends
at the disgustingly thirsty hour of 7. I drank nine gins, two sherries,
and three ports.

At 11 the bars closed. It is now 12.35 and black spleen has spread
terribly around me as I open your lettercard – only just received.

At 10.10 on Friday Peter and I were in bed; and as I did not receive
the lettercard until to-(Saturday) night, I could not know that I should
be up at 10.30 to hear from you. I feel almost completely unhappy and
resentful of Fate. I must have had a premonition; because I have been
maundering to Jean about you all evening.

I must confess. So determined am I to have and to hold you that I
have asked Julian and Jean to look you up and keep a wary eye on you
while you are in London after Christmas. I will be frank; I asked him
to keep pretty strict tabs on your movements. Please forgive me; please.
Do look him up when you arrive; my peace of mind will be wonderfully
ensured.

———

I saw Danny Kaye in 'Wonder Man'[2] yesterday. Of 'Oedipus' & 'The
Critic'[3] I cannot speak briefly. Olivier was unspeakably poignant in the
former and abominably careless in the latter. [...]

———

To prove my quite tremendous devotion: this time by <u>law</u>.

I swear irrevocably that under any circumstances whatever I will goddamn well marry you before I am 25.

And there's a neat little breach of promise for you!

Quand même,
K.

P.S. RING ME 10.30 A.M. ON TUESDAY <u>PLEASE</u>!

[1] Play by Somerset Maugham (1928), performed at the St Martin's Theatre in November 1945, in which Sonia Dresdel (1909–76) played Nurse Wayland.

[2] Comedy-cum-gangster drama, directed by Bruce Humberstone, in which a student, played by Danny Kaye (1913–87), hunts for the killers of his twin brother (US, 1945).

[3] Sophocles' *Oedipus Rex* and Sheridan's *The Critic* made a famous Olivier double-bill in the second (1945–6) New Theatre season at the Old Vic.

To Pauline Whittle

229, Portland Road
21/12/45

Dear Paul;–

Out of a riot of turmoil and doubt I have snatched a few moments of composure. The dreadful riot is still there, but it is a background, a shadow; just as chaos is always brooding over cosmos. I have grasped serenity for an instant, I have stood outside myself to examine the part of me which demands your love. It is an imperious particle of my being; it loves anguish, and leaves the rack reluctantly; and it is fragile. The slightest wound turns it to hatred, and it is transfigured again by the merest touch of balm. Its agony is that it can never know indifference. It is a mercurial thing of wayward impulses which can die and be reborn a hundred times in a minute. Its native element is pain.

I am sure that I treat it cruelly and murderously from within; I infuse horrid doubts into it, and I awake whimpering and sweating from the dreams it forces upon me. Lately you have been flaying it from without.

I have said that this fiery particular spasmodic thing which is my love is imperious. It is also proud, almost tyrannous. Love, for it, is a state of mutual monopoly; the idea of sexual contact with any other than the beloved is quite unalterably foreign to it. Such contact would be boring and nauseating, even where it was not merely laughable. The only real emotion is love, and it is rich, singular, and complete. It is a constant victory without a vanquished; a mutual, incomparable triumph. It is helpless, furious, but quite irresistible. And it is impossible to imagine it separate from the reciprocal fire of the beloved. When that is exhausted it dies and all memory of it is obliterated. It is almost identification with the beloved; at least, it is an infinitely elastic umbilical cord which, though tenuous and excruciatingly tender, cannot be cut.

You, the concrete beloved, seem to have taken the shears in your own hands and cut the cord, in the secure hope that it can easily and unobtrusively be made whole again. In the cutting, you forgot that the sharp, blinding pain would be instantly communicated to me. When you admit that you have had an affair, however mild, with someone else, you injure me as surely as a strong, hobnailed kick in the pit of the stomach. The ineffable tautness, the ecstatic tension of our love is immediately slackened; the cord is hacked through and bruised irreparably. For it is as unthinkable for one in love to divide or split that love as it is for a man to separate his soul from his body. It is the complete denial, the absolute negation. It is as if you stood in the face of the sun and said, I see no light, or, what is heat?

This is the measure of my humility. I must seek humbly and unquestioningly to repair the damage. This thirsty, implacable need I feel forces me to rationalise the catastrophe and to go alone about the task of healing. For I know that unless the fissure is quite closed, it will tear jaggedly at the next parting, and this time there will be no healing, only the certain extinction of the core of my being and the appearance of a savage callous in your heart of hearts.

I could no more sleep with a woman other than you than I could sleep with a cow. There is no question of infidelity; there is faith, and there is death – there is no third alternative.

This is a bitter, ascetic conception of love, capable of great depths and great heights, quite incapable of compromise.

No one can have wished more passionately than I that it were laxer, that it could give respite even for an hour. But its roots are native within me, and I know that any looser love would be a pale, unsatisfactory thing. My soul dictates it and finds life through it. I must worship it, just as primitive men worshipped the earth which fed them. It is ageless, and has a new, vivid especial life every second. Its variety is endless. I ask no more.

This is not a jealous letter, an unwillingness to allow others to trespass on you. You are no more my property than The Bay of Naples. No; it is rather an agony of dissolution, a mute acceptance of the holy fact that when, even momentarily, you cease to love me, I cease to exist.

Because myself exists in you and through you, and dies in the awful moment when you become a part of someone else. We are each other; we have changed eyes and souls. And the horror is that chaos <u>can</u> return, – even in a moment.

Quand même,
Ken.

P.S. Phew!¹

¹ KPT wrote on the back of the envelope: '<u>a very moral exhortation!</u>'

To Pauline Whittle

229 Portland Rd.
[Postmark 6 January 1946]

Paul darling;–

Is this going to be a love letter? I don't know. That mighty moral instrument, the voice of Paul Robeson,¹ has been issuing gloriously from the radio, and I am knee-deep in its black, glutinous residue. A kind of pure, dishy sentimentality is clinging to the walls of the room – not a weak tearfulness, but a strong, wise regret of absence and a solid enjoyment of memory. Paul, I have to write to you now. It is midnight on Twelfth Night, and the crepuscular mushrooms are springing all about me. Tiny ectoplasmic waifs (whom I suspect to be fairies) are tripping in twilit ranks upon my shoulders. The lamps are out, and I want to be very still, I want no more to go a-roving in the light of the lunatic moon.² I want to be in earnest, silent and collected, while my mad thoughts shoot and soar towards you. This is Twelfth Night, lady,³ a peculiar feast,⁴ a pointless idiot festival which is the proper province of fools, wayward creatures and errant fanatics; whimseys and trifles and odd rites have their place on Twelfth Night – it is the time, above all, for doing unreasonable and mysterious things, for writing letters which ask nothing, desire nothing, tell nothing and require nothing. It is the at-random time for all things; the Lord Chief Justice may stand on his head and play a magnificent game of hopscotch with no man's censure, and lovers may leap into the young, bright air and care nothing for where they may fall. It is the moment for bouncing, it is the moment, the precise instant in the crazy old almanac, to be married and conceive and sleep and sleep. It is the time for the burning of the books and the polishing of the dancefloor; it is the time for slipping on ice and roars of irreverent laughter. It is the time when by unspoken consent we banish high seriousness, who else should be all divinity. And it is the time when Pan, that kindly, moral, fastidious old brute, nervously treads again the wanton paths that this clever century has so carelessly ploughed under. We smile (and do not jeer) when men hurt butterflies on Twelfth Night; on Twelfth Night men may seek Atlantis, may turn Yogi, squat on poles, turn to pillars of salt, be alchemists, spit flame or collect matches. It is the irregular hour, the time that no diary nor history will record; the off-duty period of all mankind. The lawgivers and makers of dates and names have cast off their pilgrim-grey robes, adorned with saturnine, sober embroideries of the zodiac. They called this day <u>Epiphany</u>. A name, you will agree, my own darling, of names! A mixture of titter and sneeze, an elephant with a stammer, an irresponsible fluke of jest! As eccentric a nonsense-word as Jabberwocky; and yet we tonight are the only ones perceptive enough to be laughing at it and with it. Epiphany is the carnival of self-confessed fools, who are all men; the fête of broken resolutions, wryly observed with a broadening smile; the saint's day of petty sinners, who attain to virtue not by hating, nor by fearing Sin, but by laughing at it; the indecipherable message of whose incomprehensible joy is, that before Life is complete, we must mingle Dreams with Reality, merge Reality into Dreams; and then laugh, loud and long, at the holy, indestructible mess which is the fated result.

What of us? What of us? How may we receive this foolish night's gifts? Let us, I say honestly, scoff gently at the idealism, the extremism, the hypocrisy, the shallowness of all we see about us. And then let us look, almost as an afterthought, at our love; and, when the first shock and thrill of joy is spent, let us laugh hysterically because we cannot pierce it, because it is inviolable; because it alone, of all our knowledge, returns smile for smile, confident, serene, supple; and permanent.

All which is but <u>one</u> of the many idiosyncrasies of,

quand même,
Ken.

P.S. 'This is Dillyrium, Ladie!' (See Actus I of the Graceful and thrice Worthie-to-be-Renowned dramatique poem of '12th-Night' by the Swan of poets, M. William Shaxper or Whom-You-Will)

---

[1] Paul Robeson (1898–1976), American singer and actor famous for his rendition of 'Ol' Man

River' in the film *Show Boat* (US, 1936) and his portrayal of Othello on stage, first in London in 1930, opposite Peggy Ashcroft, then in the US, including Broadway, 1943–5.
[2] Byron, 'So We'll Go No More A Roving' (1817).
[3] 'This is Illyria, lady': *Twelfth Night, or What You Will*, Act I Sc. ii.
[4] Festival on the twelfth day after Christmas, celebrating the manifestation of the infant Jesus to the Magi.

To Julian Holland

Magdalen College
Monday [4 February 1946]

Credit title: this is a <u>damned good</u> letter.

Dear J;–

The causes of my defection are numerous and nearly all of them are invalid. It were wasted labour for me to tell them over, as well as dry and salt reading for you. I may indicate with brave nonchalance one of the least pressing but most impressive: bronchial catarrh.

This past weekend has been quite impossible, because Paul was here. I had, on Sunday, the unusual excitement of sleeping with her in two different beds on the same day; one in Magdalen (to wit, my own) and one at her hôtel.

I have been elected to the Committee of the New Dramatic Company. An interesting and revolutionary volte face in company policy. not only, in the future, do committee members have to be able to <u>read</u>; they have to be able to read <u>plays</u>. Cecilia Barnes under this ruling is shaky but cheerful. I shall plug 'Alice'[1] for next Christmas. [...]

Recent reading:

'Arrival and Departure' (Old Koestler).[2] Very brilliant. Concludes that the raison d'être of most intellectual revolutionaries is a guilt complex. The nervous breakdown scenes are vivid and bright as naked electric bulbs.

'Decline & Fall of the': still plodding on; trying desperately to model my style on a blend between Jane's[3] masculine directness and Gibbon's effeminate fastidiousness. Opening sentence of my essay on Gibbon: 'The time has now come to take the snail by the horns.'

'Beowulf':[4] very much more than worth while. It should be read.

Most of Milton's prose: Arctic stuff, but good essay material. Lewis says that if Lamb and Gibbon had been the same person, mine are the

kind of essays they would have produced at prep school! He adds that
I have the makings either of a good First or an interesting Third.

'Collected Stories of Katherine Mansfield':⁵ How these women can
write! Where should we be without Jane, Emily, Virginia, and now
dear coughing Tabby Kitty. The oblique telling of a tale is at its finest
in her pages. There is no <u>objective</u> description of anything. We see
events, places, and people through fascinating opacities – the personality of the individual. A development, I suggest, of the first
storytelling methods our English novelists adopted – the epistolary
method, which obviously leaves no room for objectivity. My recent
reading in this field includes Choderlos de Laclos' 'Les Liaisons Dangereuses' – for which see last month's 'Horizon'.⁶

A thought: when did the worship of hairless, malodorous, kecking,
insanitary inarticulacy (i.e. babies) begin in Eng. Lit.? I trace it back to
Wordsworth's 'Ode';⁷ and no further. There are no wimpling, pink
babies in Shakespeare and Milton (at least, there is one, but it appears
in his only bad poem – 'On the Death of a Fair Infant'). This seems to
be another disgusting legacy of the Neo-romantics. Enthusiastic swine!
(I use the epithet with its correct 18th C. power of approbation.) The
Augustan attitude was much more sensible. A chap in close touch tells
me that when Chesterfield's first daughter was born, he merely said:
'Remove her. I shall take no further interest in her until she's got a
lover.'

Another thought: a fault of the naturalistic theatre. Its dependence
on the unrelieved meat of characterisation. It is, we may admit, interesting to watch the accumulation, as it were, of a man's habits, tricks,
and singularities. But (and this is the point) when the scene of choice,
the crux of the play arrives, we know the characters so well that we can
predict accurately exactly what they will do.

Heard [. . .] last week; [. . .] a very witty unrehearsed debate
between Shaw Desmond⁸ & C. S. Lewis (Desmond: You speak plainly,
Mr. Lewis, but your wisdom is cheaply got. C.S.L.: I am prepared to
admit, sir, that <u>my</u> part in this argument has been to propound the
penny-wise and the penny-plain.)

John Betjeman⁹ spoke on Thursday about Tennyson. He completely
succeeded in rehabilitating him as a man: he was apparently a great wit
and a humorist of boundless, spasmodic energy. In fact, Betjeman
suggests that the last lines of 'Enoch Arden'

('The villagers had never seen a costlier funeral')

may be intentionally amusing. Most Tennysonian anecdotes are of the
Victorian lavatory kind. Here is one of his favourites. Macready,¹⁰

playing Othello to a packed house, was horrified to notice that through-out the bedroom scene, there were incessant titters in the audience. Storming with rage, he went off; and as he did so, caught sight of a small white chamberpot under the bed. He rampaged across to the prop. man and in a voice strained with fury, said: 'What is the meaning of that white chamberpot?' With a look of abject apology the man replied: 'I'm terribly sorry, sir, but we couldn't get a flowered one.'

Another story of Tennyson: a female admirer requested a simile for a sheep on a hillside. He snarled: 'Lice on an old blanket.' [. . .]

The vesper bells are banging, which means dinner soon. Then off to a party of harlotry – undergraduettes, of whom three in fifty can be stared straight in the face without paralysis of the optic nerve. With them (in Lou Costello's[11] phrase) I shall 'trip a light fanatic'. Then home to my damp bed. Still, they're clever. You can't have everything, as a tall girl remarked to me yesterday.

Theological flash: I accept the story of the immaculate conception[12] because (a) it is a miracle of poetry even in the mind, and (b) the Jews are not poetic enough to have produced it if it hadn't really happened? But I do not approve of Christ's actions on this earth; I regard him as something of a criminal flop. Nevertheless, this does not affect my belief in his divine origin: why should the sins of the son be visited on the Father?

Now I must work. As I said to a bright chap the other day, it's a long way between the plough and the stars. In Oxford exams, at least.

Quand même,

K.

P.S. You have a 5-page deficit to make up before you even <u>begin</u> to reply.

---

[1] Lewis Carroll's *Alice in Wonderland* (1871), a Tynan/Holland adaptation, was eventually per-formed by the NDC at the Birmingham Midland Institute, February–April 1949, directed by Stuart Johnson.

[2] Arthur Koestler (1905–83), Hungarian-born British author of works including *Darkness at Noon* (1940); *Arrival and Departure* (1943) was his first novel in English.

[3] Austen.

[4] Heroic poem in Old English, dating from the eighth century.

[5] Katherine Mansfield (1888–1923), New Zealand short-story writer who lived in England; she died from tuberculosis.

[6] Monthly literary magazine founded in 1939 by Cyril Connolly, Stephen Spender and Peter Watson. *Les Liaisons Dangereuses* (1782) was discussed in an article (*Horizon*, January 1946) by Martin Turnell.

[7]'Ode: Intimations of Immortality' (1802–4): 'Behold the child among his new-born blisses, / A four years' darling of a pigmy size!'
[8]Shaw Desmond (1877–1960), Irish novelist and author of books on the afterlife.
[9]Sir John Betjeman (1906–84), English poet, an alumnus of Magdalen College, made Poet Laureate in 1974.
[10]William Charles Macready (1793–1873), English actor/manager rivalling Kean in his portrayal of the great Shakespearean tragic roles.
[11]Lou Costello (1906–59), American comic actor originally in burlesque, remembered for his partnership with Bud Abbott.
[12]Roman Catholic doctrine that from the moment of her conception, the Virgin Mary was unstained by original sin. KPT may be confusing this doctrine with that of the Virgin Birth.

To Julian Holland

Magdalen College
Tuesday [19 March 1946]

Dear J;–

Thank you for one of the most amusing envelopes of recent years. It repays an old debt with munificent interest. I weep to read of your being maimed.[1] Tell me, is it noticeable? are you obviously deformed? shall I have to make excuses for you amongst my friends? and if so, what kind of excuses? shall I say that Hermione Gingold[2] inflicted it on you with one of her curare-tipped talons after you mistook her for Walter Crisham[3] in Shaftesbury Avenue one night? or that it happened during a rehearsal of 'The Sleeping Beauty'? or simply that James (Dracula) Agate nipped it in an overflow of fraternal bliss?

In reply: I heard Koestler,[4] and, as usual, was much more impressed by his analogies and illustrations than by his real theme. [...] By the way, I have written a very mordant burlesque of the Koestler style which a glossy Oxford miscellany is printing at the beginning of next term.[5] Also an enlarged version of 'L'Art pour l'Art'.[6] I may as well retail the general Tynan gossip now. (a) Permanent new theatre drama crit. on 'Isis'[7] (b) one of the nucleus of six on the Editorial Staff of 'Cherwell',[8] the Oxford aesthetick mag., which will restart next term (c) permanent consort to the young and extremely lovely daughter of a Merton don[9] (a friend of Clunes,[10] Banks,[11] Gielgud, Rattigan,[12] Maugham ...) (d) prop and hysterical mainstay of Magdalen Players' Trinity production, Pat Hamilton's 'Rope'[13] (e) playing 'Avarice' in the Morality play at St. Mary's Church, 'The Castell of Perseveraunce', which, during the long vac., will tour the

Cathedral cities of S. & E. England in a caravan drawn by eight cream palfreys (vide 'Picture Post'[14]) (f) inconstant consort to a tired but brilliant sewing-circle of pseudo-débutantes (g) still personal adviser and philosopher to a Very Junior Member of the Wolfit Company (hereinafter to be referred to as 'darling girl'[15]) (h) woodcock-springe-setter in a Giant Literary Plot,[16] as to which he is Sworn to Blood-red Secrecy As Yet (i) and about seventeen other unremembered responsibilities.

I cannot write letters that hang together in this room. It is still sodden in cheap gin and hip deep in broken glass from a party I flung last Friday night. My scout said it was the worst mess he'd had to clean up since the Prince of Wales[17] had these rooms. He coped splendidly and still spits ground glass in every sentence he utters.

A few clerihews I composed at coffee today (I swear!):

> Arthur Koestler
> Said: 'First, le
> Petit bourgeois must go!'
> Well, he ought to know.

> . . .

> H.W. Fowler[18]
> Laughed out loud at the howler
> Of beginning a sentence
> With a nominativus Pendens

> . . .

> Edward Gibbon
> Wrote ad lib. on
> The bloody mystery
> Of later Roman history

> . . .

> 'Ho!' said Herodotus,[19]
> 'There's Aeschylus[20] throwing a sod at us.
> No matter: the "Persae"
> Is quite at my mercy'

[…] Come and see me <u>immediately</u> you have dropped this letter into the lavatory-pan.

Quand même,
Ken

[1] A heavy portable gas cooker had fallen on Holland's left index finger.
[2] Hermione Gingold (1897–1987), English actress and revue artiste whose shows include *Sweet and Low* (1943) and *Sweeter and Lower* (1944).
[3] Walter Crisham (b. 1906), American actor and dancer, who later played Valentin le Désossé in *Moulin Rouge* (US, 1952).
[4] Koestler was lecturing on BBC radio on 'What the Modern World is Doing to the Soul of Man'.
[5] KPT's article, 'Mr Koestler Takes It To Heart', was published in the May 1946 edition of the undergraduate magazine *Mandrake*.
[6] KPT's KES *Chronicle* article of July 1945. See letter of 25 July 1945.
[7] Undergraduate magazine, founded in 1892 and still in existence.
[8] Oxford magazine, founded in 1920 and still in existence.
[9] Geoffrey Mure was a Fellow of Merton, tutor in Philosophy 1920–47 and Warden of the college 1947–63. His daughter was called Janet.
[10] Alec Clunes (1912–70), English actor, noted for his work as Director of the Arts Theatre, London, 1942–54. His last important role was in Rolf Hochhuth's *Soldiers* (1968; see below, ch. 6).
[11] Leslie Banks. See letter of 21 November 1945.
[12] Sir Terence Rattigan (1911–77), popular English playwright; his works include *French Without Tears* (1936), *The Winslow Boy* (1946) and *The Browning Version* (1948).
[13] Psychological thriller by Patrick Hamilton (1929), filmed by Alfred Hitchcock (US, 1948).
[14] Weekly pictorial news magazine published 1938–57.
[15] Pauline Whittle.
[16] A plot by KPT's close friend Alan Beesley to commandeer *Cherwell*, make himself editor and KPT literary editor. KPT was addicted to the pungency and valour of Beesley's unmodish, extreme personality. Beesley had served in the RAF in Canada, attempted suicide and come up to the university in 1945. 'He is the disease of his generation in much the same sense as a pearl is a disease of the oyster,' wrote KPT of him in an *Isis* 'Idol' (12 February 1947).
[17] KPT's rooms in Cloister 5 had in fact been previously occupied by the bodyguard of the future King Edward VIII.
[18] Henry Watson Fowler (1858–1933), English lexicographer and compiler of the *Concise Oxford Dictionary* (1911), the *Pocket Oxford Dictionary* (1924) and *A Dictionary of Modern English Usage* (1926).
[19] Herodotus (*c*.485–*c*.425 BC), Greek historian.
[20] Aeschylus (*c*.525–*c*.456 BC), 'the father of Greek tragedy', author of *The Persae* and the *Oresteia*.

To Julian Holland

229 Portland Road
9/4/1946

Dear J;–
There is small reason for a letter: we have met, discoursed, and

rediscovered each other: there is, or should be, again that tacit gladness at contact which even street-drifting on chill afternoons could not dissipate. I have no news worth recording. The Ring[1] is collected, and glows with a kind of watery fire alone with itself in a snug, soft box: three bland opals, and half a dozen insistent chips of diamond. A strange girl, wearing a silken muff, boarded me in the Kardomah yesterday to tell me that she thought my Hamlet better than Wolfit's. I, it seems, was a great Dane; he but a Pekinese. I have acquired a K.E. cricket blazer (vive le sport) ideal for messing about in punts on snobbish rivers. A N.D.C. creature named Eryl[2] (a lovely bespectacled marvel with a smile of pure gum) told me that with it on I look thirty years younger.

I am reading Jeremy Taylor,[3] and I am aware that I am composed of dust and clay and that my life is a sad composition. He is of the gentler line of divineness – the breeding of St. Francis, of Fénelon,[4] of Melanchton;[5] not for him the stern, pietistic masculinity of a Luther, a Calvin, a Bossuet,[6] a Lancelot Andrewes.[7] Taylor is the last of the round, Ciceronian phrase-makers: flashes of him reappear in Landor[8] or in De Quincey,[9] and Ruskin[10] – but this artful gift of tricking out platitudes in such fashion that they appear gorgeously sensuous novelties died, for all purposes, with him.

Will you please present my humblest regrets to Hugo? I really wanted to see him, but impatience, impetuousness, and preoccupation sundered us. Tell him (if you will) that I think it hardly worth while to write a crit. of 'Romeo'[11] for him, but (a) if he really wishes it, and (b) if I can have his address, I'll do it for him.

I think I may now say: give my regards to that wise, nervous doxy of yours. (I thank God, by the way, that Pauline lacks Jean's firm intelligence and candid wit. It would shrivel me to a cinder.)

And, bien entendu, if you chance to run into Paul, poke her gently in the belly for me and tell her that I am surely laid waste with love of her.

Finally: Kardomah incident yesterday. I was sitting trying to cast the proposed production of 'Private Lives'[12] when I <u>saw</u> the perfect Amanda sitting across the room – a complete stranger, blonde, lazy, and wreathed in malicious smiles with serpents under 'em – with a strange man. Up I, and over to them. 'Excuse me, Madame', I said; 'would you please repeat this line: "How potent cheap music is"?' The man, scenting a pick-up, was enraged. Finally, Amanda consented to repeat the line: but a Tipton[13] accent betrayed her, and I regretfully returned to my table. But hardly had I seated myself, when the poor man leapt up, stormed across to me, and said, in a furious voice, 'Would you, sir, kindly repeat this: 'I'm subconsciously psychologically retarded; I'm producing a play called "A Fit Candidate for a Straight-Jacket". Good evening!' I was quite stunned.

My best remark for years. Bill Moore is probably going to India in the autumn, and displayed some doubts about the voyage which he refused to specify. Whereupon I: 'I know what it is, Bill: you're sicklied o'er with the pale thought of caste.'[14]

Quand même,
Ken.

P.S. Barry Morse[15] played Hamlet on Monday as if he had a code in the head. (World Copyright)

[1] A year later KPT claimed back the engagement ring and sold it.
[2] Eryl Smith played Barbara's sister in the company's production of Shaw's *Major Barbara* at the Midland Institute.
[3] Jeremy Taylor (1613–67), chaplain to Charles I and author of several religious manuals.
[4] François de Salignac de la Mothe Fénélon (1651–1715), French writer and ecclesiastic whose *Maximes des saints* (1695) was condemned by the Pope and whose *Télémaque* (1699) resulted in his banishment.
[5] Philip Melanchthon (1497–1560), German Protestant reformer and theologian who helped Martin Luther to prepare his German translation of the New Testament.
[6] Jacques Bénigne Bossuet (1627–1704), French theologian famous for his funeral orations and religious essays.
[7] Lancelot Andrewes (1555–1626), one of the English bishops commissioned to translate the Authorized Version of the Bible; famous also for his sermons.
[8] Walter Savage Landor (1775–1864), English poet and author whose works include *An Examination of Shakespeare* (1834).
[9] Thomas De Quincey (1785–1859), friend of Wordsworth and Coleridge, author of *Confessions of an English Opium-Eater* (1822).
[10] John Ruskin (1819–1900), art and social critic, champion of Turner and the Pre-Raphaelites.
[11] *Romeo and Juliet* opened on 1 March 1946 at the King's Theatre, Hammersmith, with Basil Langton and Renée Asherson in the title roles, and the young Eric Porter as the Page to Tybalt. Hugh Manning played a Page to the Prince.
[12] KPT planned to direct Coward's *Private Lives* for the NDC.
[13] Small town a few miles northwest of Birmingham.
[14] 'Sicklied o'er with the pale cast of thought': *Hamlet*, Act III Sc. i.
[15] Barry Morse (b. 1918), English actor who started his career in repertory and starred in television series such as *The Fugitive* and *Space 1999*.

To Hugh Manning

Magdalen College
[Postmark 17 April 1946]

Dear Hugh;–

Lately, Hugh, I've developed a positive <u>trend</u> for forgetting things. One of them was to reply to your letter. Forgive me.

I really can't think what to say. My life is very full; packed; stifling. I have got myself a sort of freelance job on the 'Isis'. I am acting furiously. [...]

Recent speakers at University Club have included J. Arthur Rank[1] – a tall man, resembling General de Gaulle in appearance and Sydney Howard[2] in voice. For Mr Rank, films are divided into two classes: popular and educational. He refuses to classify the Brilliant Others – 'The Southerners',[3] 'Lost Weekend',[4] etc, and now 'Scarlet Street'[5] (Fritz Lang); and intends to make a film life of the Virgin Mary with Ingrid Bergman.

Last night Dilys Powell[6] addressed the Film Society. A fascinating woman, as refreshing and sustaining as a douche of iced consommé.

Stephen Spender[7] talked on 'The Decline of the Symbol' to the English Club on Sunday – the most <u>brilliantly</u> informative talk I've yet heard up here. [...] I shall never disparage our Moderns again.

Basil Blackwell[8] talked last week on 'The Good Bookman' – a charming, serene old man with the natural pose of the genuine Augustan.

Next Tuesday I dine with Lord David Cecil at the Mitre by special invitation. I am a little shall we say trepidant, but think I can cope.

Incidentally, Spender is the Compleat Masculine Effeminate – lovely strong legs, which he draped in beautiful lines around each other; cavernous, witty eyes; a god-like profile; and a strong, sensual mouth and a most winning smile (they <u>all</u> have this). He reminded me of the title of Mr. Sinatra's newest song: 'My Nancy with the Laughing Face'. He also has the characteristic of vocalising the letters 't' and 'd'; that is to say, for 'Dante' he says 'Dantsi'; for 'reality' he says 'realitsy'. You'd be surprised how many of the Boys do that.

The Playhouse is doing 'The Ideal Husband'[9] [*sic*] this week and 'Playboy of the Western World'[10] next week. And you?

Look after Paul.

Quand même,
Ken

[1] J. Arthur Rank (1888–1972), later Lord Rank, heir to a flour and milling fortune who promoted

religious films in the early 1930s and became chairman of the Rank Organisation, for many years Britain's leading production and distribution company.
[2] Sydney Howard (1885–1946), Yorkshire-born comedian.
[3] Tale of a farmer struggling to survive in America's deep South, written and directed by Jean Renoir (US, 1945).
[4] Two days in the life of an alcoholic writer, written and directed by Billy Wilder (US, 1945).
[5] About a pimp wrongly accused of murdering a prostitute, directed by Fritz Lang (US, 1945).
[6] Dilys Powell, CBE (b. 1901), film critic of the *Sunday Times* 1939–79.
[7] Sir Stephen Spender (b. 1909), English poet, Professor of English at University College, London 1970–77, and friend of W.H. Auden and Christopher Isherwood.
[8] Sir Basil Blackwell (1889–1984), owner of the bookshop in Broad Street, Oxford (founded 1846).
[9] By Oscar Wilde (1895).
[10] By J.M. Synge, written and first performed in 1907 at the Abbey Theatre, Dublin.

To Julian Holland

Magdalen College
[Postmark 16 May 1946]

Mon cher;–

If you go (as you should) to the fathers of our criticism, you will find a puzzling admonition. They warn you to know, before you censure, exactly what a writer intended to set down and perfect. You must know what he wanted to create and whom he intended to read it. Unless you know this, your criticism may read fairly, but it will be almost completely irrelevant. You will find yourself condemning Kipling for not writing like Baudelaire; and, as in my case, Walter Winchell[1] for not being a G.H. Lewes.[2]

I specifically addressed my crit of 'Romeo' to one solitary and very disconsolate small-part actor at the King's, Hammersmith.[3] I wanted to make him laugh. I allowed myself to enter that class of writers which Desmond Macarthy[4] [*sic*] calls 'purveyors' for that particular purpose. You may justly say that 'le temps ne fait rien à l'affaire';[5] but that crit took me one half-hour to write. I wrote it because this depressed actor demanded it, and I took no pains save pains which might move him to chuckle and cheer.

In judging it by Olympian standards and slashing it with your scalpel, you are attacking a position which was never intended to be held. You are demolishing hack epistolary extravagance with a critical weapon which should be reserved for the most high.

You patronise me wickedly throughout your letter. I do not relish that smug, weary pseudo-friendliness which pours so intarissably out of you. You are unnecessarily hostile and laughably severe. 'Ken, it's very bad and you should know it.' Why try to soften your lapses into trite rudeness by introducing my name into them? It doesn't help, and you should know it. I will not have such pompous frankness lathered all over me. Who, dear putter-on of wax discs,[6] are you to make such injurious assertions? I think it's moderately comical but grossly over-written. Which is a much fairer (and clearer) estimate.

How nonsensical, by the way, to say that I rely 'on the reader's ignorance of the performance'! My crit was sent to be read by one who knew the performance backwards; and half its charm lies in the outrageous incongruity between what I say and what the TRT[7] really does.

In matters of style, you are still clinging to some journalistic ideal of lush extravagance which I thought you had abandoned these many months. You liked the style of that crit. A style which I deliberately contorted and exaggerated until it became a conscious burlesque of itself. I am horrified at your lack of discrimination. '. . . it has the good things of life in it . . .' what sentimental rot! you are thinking, though you don't know it and wouldn't like to admit it, of the cursing, whoring passages on Mercutio. They are suitably offensive and vulgar; but they are not 'the good things of life'.

Next, I must learn not to 'subject performances to the exigencies of my phrases.' Why in Heaven not? If an actor gives a thoroughly dull and unpleasing exhibition, may I not, in the interests of good reading, infuse a little energy and fascination into it? I would rather write amusingly and inaccurately than correctly and tediously.

Then comes your beautifully timed piece of impertinence: the digression on the history of dramatic criticism. So we all imitate Hazlitt, Leigh Hunt,[8] and Charles Lamb, do we? I should count him a poor soul who could not distinguish between Hazlitt and Lewes, Leigh Hunt and Max [Beerbohm], Lamb and Shaw; and even poorer who could not discern immediately that the later men were a vast improvement. And wherein, precisely, was Shaw not 'relative to his time'? And Archer?[9] And even Agate? I should have said that dramatic criticism was, if anything, too much a thing of its time, and therefore a transient and time-wasting business.

I am happy to think that my palpable nonsense reminded you of St John Ervine.[10] If I am, in latter years, anthologised as he has been, I shall be very well pleased. (I have never been to Chelsea, and therefore have full licence to say what I please about it. So dang and drat Chelsea, the miserable slime-pit!)

Now the set.[11] At which point I must come right out and say that I love and respect Hammersmith tube station. I cherish it as a lovely, functional thing. I wish more sets resembled it. It is charming. It has tunnels and balconies and steps, and the more tunnels and balconies and steps a set has, the better it will be for the future of our theatre. And if I ever see a set remotely like Rheims Cathedral, I shall malign it out of hand. I do not like Rheims Cathedral.

I thought the stools very funny, and quite original. It is 'metaphysical' wit, I agree, and may make you wonder, like Dr Johnson, 'not how you missed it, but by what perverseness of ingenuity it was ever found.' But it is a nice conceit, and I will not suffer it to be damned.

If I thought that Thurber had ever written a line on 'Romeo and Juliet', I should not presume to say anything about the play. The last and funniest word would have been said. But he hasn't, and the subject is still an open one.

Now to Basil C (smug name) Langton[12] and Gerald K (deed poll) Souper.[13] When writing to friends I am 'in a position to say' that George Bernard Shaw has the soul of an oyster and that the moon is made of pleistocene. Just how experienced does one have to be to perceive that Basil <u>is</u> a smug name, and Basil <u>C.</u> a degree smugger; and that Gerald K. Souper is not likely to be blazoned across the Haymarket in white lights unless he rubs off the corners of that awful 'K. Souper'?

Now Basil's Romeo. You have quite misunderstood what I said. I have forgotten my exact estimate, but I do know that it would take an avalanche and several bottles of whiskey to make me rate him a good verse-speaker. But I am a heretic about Romeo anyway. I don't think there are more than a dozen lines of poetry in the whole part. Similarly with Juliet, an even worse-written part to which perhaps only Shirley Temple could do full justice. Renee Asherson[14] did well to play an impossible part impossibly.

And wrought iron. I like wrought iron, and if there is a more innocuous thing to say I don't know of it. Leave me to my wrought iron and go thy ferro-concrete ways.

Now I have you on the old hip. You are quite speechless (certainly gasping and style-less) in amazement at the phrase 'lecherous as a monkey'. Just take down your volume of Shakespeare's History Plays (you know, like 'Henry v' and 'Richard iii') and turn to 'Henry iv' – Part ii, Act iii, Scene ii, l. 324, and you will find Falstaff referring to Shallow as being 'lecherous as a monkey'. Is that enough for you? And didn't you know? Because you should have. (By the way, my zoological friends tell me you're wrong about rabbits, who are much slandered little people.)

Here I must be a little more serious. You have never been to Oxford, and as far as I know, you have no close acquaintances amongst Oxford men. To talk of 'Oxford bawdry' to an Oxford man is in very bad taste, and incorrigibly vulgar. As well as being very inept. We [are] a well-bred University, and we do not habitually 'talk bawdy'. Any bawdiness in that crit was just original sin in me. But I don't think there was any. Juliet must look as if she wanted, above all sublunary things, to be Romeo's mistress. Otherwise the play is pointless. What I complained of was that I could not believe in that lovely creature's ever wanting Basil as a lover. Her excellent voluptuousness was wasted on him. The brute.

Of course you can make a 'cruel, fascinating vignette' of the Nurse. She is cruel (quite callous, in fact); and her babbling is fascinating. A vignette, or so I understand it, is a portrait in which certain violently salient points are emphasised, and others ignored. And that is precisely what I meant.

'Oh, Ken, it was a bad one'. Stop this nauseating pleading and cant. I might say with Max 'Let Mr Holland cease from crawling on his knees and shaking his fist.'

(Oh, I forgot. Touchstone's better moments plus a Faulconbridge retired and taken to drink equals Esmond Knight's Mercutio.[15] It is an unproven equation, but it works for me.)

And finally (your crowning garland of condescension) I will not write it over again in a fair copy. I will not stay in after school. Not until the school-master gets himself a degree.

Quand même,
Ken

P.S. Don't make irrelevant references to Pauline. I need her too much now to hear her inexplicably tagged on to a very rude letter and called 'my girl'.

---

[1] Walter Winchell (1897–1972), American journalist and drama critic.
[2] George Herbert Lewes (1817–78), English critic and author of works ranging from a popular history of philosophy to a novel in imitation of Goethe; he lived with George Eliot.
[3] KPT worked up the review he sent to Manning and included it in *He That Plays the King*: 'What a jelly among tragedies it is! How broken-backed a thing!' Of Langton's Romeo he wrote: 'His voice has but two notes, and he played a losing duet with himself all evening, rapt and repellent in self-love.'
[4] Sir Desmond MacCarthy (1878–1952), English writer and theatre critic for the *New Statesman*.

[5] Molière, *Le Misanthrope*, Act I Sc. ii.

[6] Julian Holland's first job at the BBC involved the editing and playing of material, recorded on acetate discs, for programmes such as *Radio Newsreel*.

[7] The Travelling Repertory Theatre, formed by Basil Langton in 1941.

[8] (James Henry) Leigh Hunt (1784–1859), English Romantic poet and essayist.

[9] William Archer (1856–1924), drama critic and theoretician responsible for the first English translations of Ibsen's plays.

[10] St John Ervine (1883–1971), Irish dramatist and critic whose early work was produced at the Abbey Theatre, Dublin.

[11] The designer was John Russell.

[12] Basil C. Langton (b. 1912), English actor, manager and director.

[13] Gerald Kay Souper played Friar Laurence.

[14] Renée Asherson (b. 1915), London-born actress who made her stage debut in John Gielgud's 1935 production of *Romeo and Juliet*; she married the actor Robert Donat.

[15] Esmond Knight (1906–87), English film and theatre actor who, though blinded while on active service with the Royal Navy in 1941, successfully continued his career after the war. Touchstone: the clown in *As You Like It*; Faulconbridge: the bastard in *King John*.

To Harry James

Magdalen College
[? May 1946]

Dear Harry;–

I have just received a most disquieting letter from Pauline. What is this dangerous nonsense she tells me about your abandoning Alice?[1] I feel at once horrified and desperately injured; a fierce sensation intensifies when she tells me that you are falling back on to that supporting crutch of mediocrity, 'Night Must Fall'.[2] If this brain-child of ours (of which I had the temerity to think very well) is still-born, the aspirations of the New Drama Company expire with it. What splendid irony there now is in that idealistic little blurb[3] which I have before me on the back of a 'Hamlet' programme! For the divine sake of moral integrity, cut it out of the next, and resign yourselves to the second-rate. Your dusty Olympus of the dramatic muse in James Watt St has by now, I doubt not, become what we should have guessed it would become – a blend of ping-pong club and matrimonial agency. Why not advertise for new members? Something like this:

'New Dramatic Company welcomes new members. Knowledge of house-painting and carpentry desirable; keenness at table-tennis, passion for washing-up and unenthusiasm for initiative essential. Awareness of dramatic art not necessarily a disqualification. Vocally recognisable natives of Birmingham preferred. Members will be required to answer questions on the works of Esther McCracken,[4] Emlyn Williams, Ben Travers,[5] Frederick Lonsdale[6] and other contemporary playwrights of European stature (if there <u>are</u> others)'

I am struggling to express my disgust. I have never suggested that the N.D.C. was capable in a moment of assuming the austere robes of drama's original newness and nobility without a little sheepishness and awkwardness; what I did insist was that the attempt to do so would be tremendously worth while. You observe how the Crescent have achieved gloriously something out of palpable nothing. You have dwindled visibly, abominably; and I am breathless with relief at not having been further deceived by your pretensions. If I see any suitable shockers or bedroom farces in the Oxford bookshops, I will send them on to you; meanwhile I am sure for the first time that Synge, O'Casey, Ibsen, Sheridan, Congreve, Webster, and their gigantic colleagues may sleep secure in their graves, without fear of further disturbance at your hands.

I can almost hear Lewis Carroll laughing at me from his vantage-point in limbo.

Quand même,
Ken

P.S. I am wishing for a letter to tell me I am mistaken.

[1] Harry James was on the managing committee of the NDC, but in fact had had nothing to do with the decision to postpone *Alice*.
[2] Popular thriller by Emlyn Williams, written in 1935.
[3] The blurb read, 'The aim of the company is the presentation of distinctive drama ...'
[4] Esther Helen McCracken (1902–71), English playwright and actress, author of *The Willing Spirit* (1936) and *Quiet Weekend* (1941).
[5] Ben Travers (1886–1980), author of 'Aldwych farces' including *A Cuckoo in the Nest* (1925) and *Thark* (1927).
[6] Frederick Lonsdale (1881–1954); plays include *The Last of Mrs Cheyney* (1925) and *Canaries Sometimes Sing* (1929).

To Pauline Whittle

Magdalen
Friday [? May/June 1946]

Dear Paul;

O MY GOD.

UNLESS YOU CAN ACQUIRE, VERY SOON, ONE PARTICULAR CHARACTERISTIC, I AM GOING TO PUSH MY WAY OUT OF YOUR LIFE. UNLESS

YOU CAN <u>KNOW</u>, EVERY INSTANT, THAT I LOVE YOU AND WOULD
RATHER BE WITH YOU THAN ANYWHERE, I SHALL HAVE TO THROW
IN THE SPONGE. IT IS VERY EASY TO SAY: 'WELL, YOU'VE GOT SO
MANY OTHER THINGS TO DO ...', OR 'YOU WOULDN'T WANT TO BE
WITH ME ...' AND SO FORTH: IT'S AN EASY EXCUSE FOR YOU. IT
PUTS A SPEAR THROUGH ME EVERY TIME YOU SAY IT. YOU <u>MUST</u>
ASSUME (PLEASE) THAT THE ONE INCONTROVERTIBLE FACT OF YOUR
EXISTENCE IS THAT I LOVE YOU; IF YOU CAN'T BELIEVE OR WON'T
BELIEVE THAT, THEN YOU MUST BE BLIND AND WE'RE QUITE
THROUGH.

I QUOTE: 'I HAVE DECIDED TO HITCH-HIKE TO THE LAKES IN JULY
OR AUGUST.' <u>WHY IN CHRIST'S NAME DIDN'T YOU TELL ME YOU</u>
<u>WERE GOING TO BE FREE IN JULY AND AUGUST?</u> IN ONE SENTENCE
YOU HAVE COMPLETELY WRECKED MY LONG VAC. WHEN EXACTLY
<u>ARE</u> YOU GOING TO BE FREE?

AGAIN, YOU SAY THAT YOU WILL GO TO THE LAKES 'AFTER <u>I</u> HAVE
BEEN TO STRATFORD'. WHEN THE HELL ARE YOU DOING <u>THAT</u>?
MAYN'T I KNOW? AND WOULD IT BE TOO MUCH FOR ME TO COME
OVER FROM BIRMINGHAM OCCASIONALLY TO SEE YOU? GOD, GOD,
GOD.

UNTIL SUNDAY;—

                                                                    Ken

P.S. Did you get my earlier letter?

To Elizabeth Zaiman[1]

Magdalen College
[24 May 1946]

Please, you woman.

I love you dearly ever dearly. Let that be a lesson to you. An object
lesson in don't-look-so-damn-lovely. If you come to rehearse tomorrow
I shall indisputably make immoral advances to you. Je ne puis plus, as
Molière would have said. There is very little more of my tether left.

May I quote from a letter Sarah wrote to 'Wonderful Boy' Sarcey:[2]

'Without you life is the face of a clock, bereft of its handle. My art
has been suckled and softled [*sic*] rocked by you in a tender cradle; you
are as necessary to me as sunlight and air. I am hungry for you as for
food, I am thirsty for you, and my thirst is overwhelming. Your words
are my food, your breath my wine. You are everything to me.'

After two hours in bed with you I promise to write and make famous prose thirty or forty times as good as that. And all of it about you.

I have tried to become distressed about your miseries. Un-, I may say, successfully. I am glad you have 'Good Intentions'. The natural sequel will take place on Friday afternoon: 'The Road to Hell' (in which we co-star). It rejoices me that you like my little Isis frolic.[3]

Did you know that all smooth things meet in you? that you are the cynosure of all light-curves? that you are a pure wave of limb? Of course you didn't. I can tell you of these things. Given half a chance. And half an hour.

Be passively loved, then. Hosts of great ladies made their reputation that way: the Dubarry,[4] for instance, and Caesar's Cleopatra.

A chap in close touch has just told me of Magdalen's bumps[5] today. And you, Velvet Paw, have vanished from my thoughts – pouf!

Quand même,
Ken

[1] An undergraduate reading medicine at St Hugh's College. Lively, quick-witted, and with dark curly hair, she became a close comrade of KPT's and worked with him as actress, wardrobe mistress and general factotum in seven plays and two revues.

[2] The influential French theatre critic Francisque Sarcey (1827–99), one of Sarah Bernhardt's greatest admirers.

[3] KPT's review (13 March 1946) of *Madame Louise*, a farce by Vernon Sylvaine at the New Theatre Oxford with Alfred Drayton and Robertson Hare. ('The one is Belch, the other beg-pardon.')

[4] Comtesse Marie Jean Du Barry (1741–93), daughter of a dressmaker who became the mistress of Louis XV and was guillotined during the French Revolution.

[5] Victories in the Oxford University summer eights rowing races.

To Elizabeth Zaiman

Collegium Beatae Sanctae
Mariae Magdalenae
Saturdae.
[27 May 1946]

Dear Lisbeth;–

All right. I cry off. Enough, enough! Let this unprogressive banter cease. I will strive to be content with a mere <u>liking</u> for you. And if I might (occasionally) escort you here and there, I should be so happy. Loose now and then a scattered smile, and that I'll live upon. (Ugh)

Don't (please) be bitch enough to take my earlier, pornographic letters seriously. I am feeling very temperate and continent, and I am studying hard to remain so.

Quand même,
Ken

To Julian Holland

Magdalen College
Friday [Postmark 8 June 1946]

Dearest J;–

My desk is piled high with interesting and very intelligent letters from you. It breaks my heart not to be able to answer them yet. In the last week I have: (a) produced and played the name part in 'Sweeney Agonistes'[1] (b) played Granillo[2] in 'Rope' – 4 performances (c) played Pelleas[3] – 3 performances (d) attended eight editorial conferences of the 'Cherwell'. I am quite eviscerated with toil. Please forgive me for a day or so: I dare not write now, so near is total lassitude.

Quand même,
Ken

[1] For which he won first prize in the acting competition.
[2] One of the main parts.
[3] *Pelléas et Mélisande* (1892) by the Belgian dramatist Maurice Maeterlinck, on which Debussy later based his opera of the same name.

To Hugh Manning

Magdalen College
Thursday
[Postmark 20 June 1946]

Dear Hugh;–

Before I answer your letter, some of my nicer exploits. I played Granillo in 'Rope' with great aplomb and received somewhat bemused critical plaudits.[1] My 'Pelleas' was under-rehearsed and was not a success: one of the critics said: 'Mr Tynan was acutely and understandably embarrassed by his part, and showed it by standing with one heel off the ground and clutching his abdomen.'[2] My production of 'Sweeney Agonistes' was a terrific success: after the very striking finish, my leading lady[3] had a heart attack. I still receive congratulations from all over Oxford on it, – and next term hope to produce Max Beerbohm's 'Savonarola Brown'.[4] Next term, too, I shall be playing Oswald in 'Ghosts'.[5] At last.

Finally, 'Isis' named me on its list of Oxford's six leading personalities: 'Oxford's best journalist, objectionable Kenneth Tynan.' I am well contented.

I shall be in Oxford until Monday, and in London for the Test[6] till Wednesday, so it seems unlikely that I shall see you. I received a copy of the Minutes of the last N.D.C. Committee Meeting, and they contained this ominous sentence: 'It was suggested that the Midland Institute Season in September should open with an <u>Intimate Revue</u>'. If this happens, I shall resign. I should very much like to do a production for the New: 'Winterset', 'The Critic', any Ibsen, any Thornton Wilder, any verse play; and I am having plenty of successful experience here, and there are several Oxford actors who would come to Birmingham to appear in anything I did.

Please let the Committee know that I am at their disposal; I have taken lessons in production from Michael Macowan[7] while I have been here, and from Peter Brook[8] (a Magdalen man). I could promise fairly startling results. When will the N.D.C. realise (as Nevill Coghill[9] is never tired of telling me) that amateurs cannot and must not do naturalistic plays; their sphere is unaffected rendering of verse drama, which they do better than anyone in the world.

Adios.

Quand même,
Ken

---

[1] 'Mr Kenneth Tynan, as the cowardly Granillo, is as good as the author allows him to be; for he contributes little to Act III.' (Review by R.M.C. in the *Oxford Magazine*, 6 June 1946.)
[2] The *Oxford Magazine*, 13 June 1946.
[3] Barbara Clegg, a Lady Margaret Hall undergraduate. Having seen her as Katharine in *Henry VIII* at Christ Church, KPT described her as 'the completest actress in Oxford'. She married the actor Michael Godley.
[4] This was never performed.
[5] KPT played Oswald in Ibsen's *Ghosts* in the ETC Acting Contest, 15 November 1946.
[6] Cricket: England versus India, played at Lord's on 22, 24, 25 June 1946. England won by ten wickets.

[7] Michael Macowan (1906–80), actor, director and head of the London Academy of Music and Dramatic Art 1954–66.

[8] Peter Brook (b. 1925), English theatre, opera, film and television director, his first production was *Dr Faustus* (Oxford, 1943). He joined Birmingham Rep., where he directed Paul Scofield in *King John* (1945), and was appointed co-director of the Royal Shakespeare Company in 1962, where his productions included *Marat/Sade* (1964). Since 1971 he has been Artistic Director of the Centre International de Recherche Théâtral which, in 1974, moved to Le Bouffe du Nord and became the Centre International de Créations Théâtrals. KPT wrote profiles of Brook in the arts magazine *Panorama* (Spring 1951) and *Harper's Bazaar* (April 1954).

[9] Nevill Coghill (1899–1980), Professor of English at Oxford, theatre director and senior member of OUDS.

To Elizabeth Zaiman

229 Portland Road
5/7/1946

Dearling Lisbeth;–

I know my guilt. I did not reply to your nice first letter. This is my crime and it is my sorrow. Take a huge handful of compassion and fling the flooding stuff into my face. I have been bad.

High finance[1] has almost succeeded in bamboozling me, but my return volley (which I patented last year, and which Geoff Brown[2] is doing nicely with on the Centre Court) shook them. The young foxes of the <u>Cherwell</u> (particularly Snake-Hips Harmer,[3] the Queen of Saudi Arabia) tried to buy me out. But Neville (Just Call Me Santa Claws) Labovitch[4] tipped me off, and I lashed out at them. Now all is well, and three men lie dead (one of them, regrettably, my uncle, who was staying with us at the time).

The 'thing I dreaded' on that distant Thursday did not happen. Now, as they are rather shame-facedly saying at Bikini,[5] it can be told. Vincent, the only Oxford printer who could handle <u>Cherwell</u>, had written to Barry saying he could no longer print us. It seems the dons wanted him to print exam. papers, and did not think it desirable that undergraduates should be for ever haunting his offices. We have talked things out with them since, and after much haggle and cudgel, all has been straightened out.

I have had a harrowing week (this in strictest confidence, to be read in a privy or any similar place of quiet communion): Pauline had a three-weeks delay which only broke yesterday evening. Was ever such drought? and I, worried to shatters about it, picturing headlines like 'BRILLIANT CAREER FRACTURED AS YOUNG POSEUR BECOMES

UNWILLING FATHER' and 'OXFORD AGHAST AT SHOCKING REV-
ELATIONS: Father at 19: "I didn't know", says pale youth' But this
horror is a gone thing.

We, my only apple, are staying at the High Ross,[6] where there are
very fine breakfasts, indeed. [...]

I should so genuinely adore to travel up via London that it's a shame
to see the red rims that are about my eyes as I tell you that with my
luggage and wardrobe it just wouldn't pay. I should collapse from over-
sweat and hernia inside ten yards. I live in Birmingham, remember?

(See Fig.1)

A ◉ BIRMINGHAM (pop.1,109,683)

    •

       •

          •

        B ◉ OXFORD (pop. about three million)

         •

           •

             C ◉ LONDON (pop pop pop pop)
(Fig.1)

ACB is greater than AB; therefore it would be one hell of a nuisance
and all very silly unless it were a very empty compartment with blinds
which they never are and you haven't got a compartmental sort of
mind.

Julian (to whom I gave your love) and I are [text missing] film notion[7]
we have been taken with. We are preparing a shooting script for a fairly
brilliant plot we have conceived, with what is possibly the most visually
startling ending any film ever had. Julian has just done a radio adaptation of 'Citizen Kane'.

Birmingham stands much where I left it. As it is the glorious summertime again, there is a greater variety of smells in the main streets;
but that is all. The New Dramatic Company prospers. I appeared in
some intimate revue for them last week; and our future plans include:

August production: S. N. Behrman's <u>Biography</u>

September production: My production of <u>Six Characters In Search
of an Author</u>

November production: <u>Johnson over Jordan</u>[8]

I saw Peterkyn's production of the Bros. Tarara[9] last week in Hammersmith. Visually brilliant, with Valk[10] huge and hirsute, bellowing
and pricking at folk with a big avalanche of beard and voice, swallowing

up Mr. Guinness"[11] heady nail-bitings at each bounding syllable. Valk is immense. But O God the bottomless tedium of Dostoevsky – victim of the masturbative itch, the persecution complex, the mob hysteria, the occupational neurosis, the bordello-revulsion complex, and all the most horrid and fashionable things that can afflict a writer – how I abominate his shrieking at me, his mad riots and shapelessness – and his Russian salad-ness, his Peter-the-Great-would-have-loved-it-ness, his Catherine-loved-being-whipped-why-shouldn't-you-ness, his lead-me-to-the-Urals-ness, his Hell's-eggs-why-aren't-you-terrified-ness – he is too interested in the reader to be a good writer.

'Frenzy'[12] (Academy) and 'Citizen Kane' are the two greatest films I have seen. Don't be repelled by the former: the critics are wrong; it's not about a sadist at all. (I was disappointed too, and Julian wept).

'Jour se Lève'[13] would go on to my list of the ten best films – which I compose herewith for you:

'Citizen Kane' (Orson Welles – American)
'Magnificent Ambersons' (Orson Welles – American)
'Frenzy' (Alf Sjoberg – Swedish)
'Jour se Lève' (Marcel Carné – French)
'Dernier Tournant' (– French)[14]
'Fury' (Fritz Lang – American)[15]
'M' (Fritz Lang – German)
'Strange Incident' (William Wyler – American)[16]
'Henry V' (Laurence Olivier – English)
'Lost Weekend' (Billy Wilder – American)

That's a very fugitive list, but it's how I feel now.
I must stop writing.
With honesty, I send you my love.
Pace Pauline.
(That word is Latin. But use the English word if you like. What a pace-maker you'd make!)

Quand même, dearling;
Ken

[1] Alan Beesley, KPT and Derek Lindsay (mysterious, saturnine and brilliant; he wrote one great novel, *The Rack* (1958) under the pseudonym A. E. Ellis) were the chief players in a successful coup to buy up the limited company which owned the moribund *Cherwell*. KPT was not able to buy shares since he was under age. On 18 October 1946, the first edition of the fortnightly magazine (with Alan Beesley editing, KPT as literary editor – soon to be co-editor) appeared.

There were contributions from John Wain and Robert Graves, and KPT's first published review of Laurence Olivier as King Lear.

[2] Geoff E. Brown reached the men's singles final at Wimbledon, where he was beaten by Y. Petra.

[3] Barry Harmer was a Wadham undergraduate and shareholder of *Cherwell*, ousted as literary editor by KPT, who found him antipathetic.

[4] An undergraduate at Brasenose reading History.

[5] Pacific island, the site of an atom bomb test in 1946.

[6] A cheap hotel with a café downstairs called the Ross, on the High Street in the centre of Oxford.

[7] A scenario written with Julian Holland which KPT described as 'a crisp, urgent crime film, with a taste for politics' called *The Eye is on this House*. The action was reflected in the eye of the murderer.

[8] 1932 play by S. N. Behrman (1893–1973); 1921 play by Luigi Pirandello (1867–1936); 1939 play by J. B. Priestley (1894–1984). None of these were produced.

[9] Peter Brook's production of Dostoevsky's *The Brothers Karamazov*.

[10] Frederick Valk (1901–56), German actor who made his first stage appearance in London in 1939 and subsequently worked with Donald Wolfit and the Old Vic Company.

[11] Sir Alec Guinness (b.1914) joined the Old Vic Company in 1936; his films include many Ealing comedies and an Oscar-winning performance in *The Bridge on the River Kwai* (UK, 1958). KPT's monograph *Alec Guinness* was first published in 1953.

[12] Directed by Alf Sjöberg (Sweden, 1944).

[13] *Le Jour se lève* (*Daybreak*), account of the final hours of a murderer, directed by Marcel Carné in collaboration with the poet/screenwriter Jacques Prévert (France, 1939).

[14] *Le Dernier Tournant*, French version of *The Postman Always Rings Twice* directed by Pierre Chenal (France, 1939).

[15] A traveller in a small town, nearly hanged for a murder he did not commit, decides to bring his persecutors to justice (US, 1936).

[16] Also known as *The Ox-Bow Incident*, western starring Henry Fonda, Dana Andrews and Anthony Quinn (US, 1943). It was in fact directed by William A. Wellman.

To Julian Holland

229 Portland Rd
12.8.46

Dear J:–

I think I can explain my laziness. Hugh sent me a telegram last Friday saying 'Unable to appear in "Six Characters" shall be in Czechoslovakia with Fay Compton.'[1] That just about settled that. I was nettled, but it was settled: no production for Pirandello at my hands. I cast about me for a new play, and settled on Rex Warner's translation of Euripides' 'Medea', which I am now in the throes of casting, staging, lighting and distorting. I shall play Chorus: and I am still searching for a 'Medea'.

Stratford last week was fine: best productions, easily, are Peter Brook's 'L.L.L.',[2] with Michael Macowan's Bloody Scot[3] just behind it. See both of these.

I like enormously your Eliot.[4] Of course the context is all wrong, and Eliot may object to our commercialising and distorting his lines. His 'Eye' is the black eye of the Furies; ours the bleared eye of a petty politician.

But – before we go any further – the other week I saw a film called 'The Spiral Staircase',[5] which makes all our eye tricks seem incredibly vieux jeu. In that film, a huge eye close-up is the symbol of death – and it's repeated almost ad nauseam. Much closer-up than even we dreamed of: right into the pupil, until the victim is seen reflected in it. Hunt the film down, and then consider whether we shall not be dubbed apes.

Did I return the Kuhlos–Peter[6] bit to you? Things have been so mixed up recently that I quite forget. I can't seem to find it here. Hope you have a copy. Let me know.

> Much love. And apologies.
>
> K.

[1] Fay Compton (1894–1978), English classical actress and member of the famous theatrical family, she also played in pantomime and variety.
[2] *Love's Labour's Lost*.
[3] *Macbeth*, with Robert Harris and Valerie Taylor.
[4] Lines borrowed from the final speech by Agatha in T. S. Eliot's *The Family Reunion* (1939), Part 1 Scene 3.
[5] Thriller directed by Robert Siodmak (US, 1945).
[6] Kuhlos and Peter were two characters in the KPT/Holland scenario, *The Eye is on this House*.

To Julian Holland

> 229 Portland Road
> 14/8/1946

Dear J:–

You need not fret. I have found the script – all of it – between pps. 261 and 262 of Boswell's 'Journal of a Tour to the Hebrides'. What possessed me to slip them there I cannot conceive.

Tut! Your rich beautiful prose is getting fragmentary and nervous. And there is no such word as ill-manners. There are <u>two</u> such words.

Thank you for the good wishes, both for 'Medea' and Stratford. Apart from the shows, Stratford provided me with a Thurberian mystery. I'll tell you. My fiancee and I were lunching at Marie Corelli's old house,[1] now taken over as a rest room for Shakespearean actors and other

Continental refugees by the British Council. We had eaten our watery pea soup, and were waiting for the serving-wench, a woman of about 38 with a strong resemblance to Virginia Woolf (or a depressed female turkey), to bring us our Hot Pot. She swept up with it very gracefully, and set it down before us. She was just leaving us, all was well, when she swung on her heel (the first time I've seen this difficult feat successfully performed), peered out of the window at the pavement, and said, very distinctly: 'The slug is come.' She was English, so there was no possibility of accent confusion. My fiancée, a fairly brittle girl of 21, nearly screamed, and tried to slip under the table, and it was only after a good deal of rough and tumble that I dissuaded her. The serving-wench looked on in some amusement. Then she said it again. 'The slug is come', she said gaily, and tramped off.

The Eliot. The old bird-watcher himself may not know, but the criticks will. They always have. They will say: 'By dragging in Mr Eliot's play,[2] these lewd-minded but invincible hoodlums have tried to attach to their disgusting little film a wholly spurious background of high tragedy and the Eumenides. It is, in fact, no more than a cheap commingling of 'The Spiral Staircase', 'Le Jour Se Lève', and Henri Barbusse's 'Le Feu'.[3] In the leading role (a drug addict and sadist!) Herbert Marshall[4] is not ideally cast, whilst Penelope Dudley Ward is rather too thin for the part of his idealistic mistress. As a coward, Mr Charles Laughton, now nearing his 88th birthday, has moments of great pathos: but it seems obvious that the part was rewritten to accommodate his great age. The direction is sketchy and the cutting bad and jagged; this may, however, be intentional. The music, specially written by Sir Edmundo Ros,[5] Governor-General of Haiti, is pleasing but quite irrelevant. All in all, you'll leave the cinema with your feet tapping.'

1000 words, hey?[6] You haven't a chance. Not a ghost. Producing a play[7] for the N.D.C. involves, not only casting, interpretation, and moves, and the actual direction of these at rehearsals, but also:

(a) designing the set
(b) building the set
(c) designing costumes
(d) obtaining costumes
(e) obtaining lighting
(f) painting set and backcloth
(g) getting tickets, and programmes printed
(h) looking after publicity
(i) rehearsing 7 nights and two afternoons per week

(j) transporting and erecting lights and set.

That's what I'm about now. So, if you ask me, I'll return the script I have, but I can't promise to do anything until term begins. I have to do Oxford work too – preparing another production ('Malfi'[8]) and writing for 'Cherwell'. [...]

Quand même, ma lovely.
K.

P.S. Textual criticism: p.3, l.8: 'little woman' probably refers to the accused's fiancée, Miss Pauline Shirley,[9] whom he later murdered in Bankok [*sic*]. The expression is jocular, for Miss Shirley was certainly not less than 5ft.7ins. in height at this period.

---

[1] Marie Corelli (1855–1924), real name Mary Mackay, writer of romantic melodramas, lived in Stratford from 1901. Her house, Masoncroft, is now part of Birmingham University.
[2] *The Family Reunion* (1939).
[3] Novel written during the Great War about life in the trenches.
[4] Herbert Marshall (1890–1966), English actor.
[5] Edmundo Ros (b.1910), Venezuelan bandleader/vocalist whose signature tune was 'Cuban Love Song'.
[6] Presumably work on the script.
[7] The play was Euripedes' *Medea*, performed at the Birmingham Midland Institute on 13 and 14 September 1946.
[8] *The Duchess of Malfi*, never produced.
[9] Pauline Whittle's stage name.

To Elizabeth Zaiman

229 Portland Road
26/8/1946

Dear Lisa;–

The new Priestley;[1] yes, please.

And you might ask about tickets for 'Love's Labours' and 'Faustus'. I've undertaken to cover the whole repertoire for 'Cherwell'.[2] I'll send the money as soon as you request it.

[...] You will understand why I had furious nightmares about [Hare[3]]: that quivering proboscis and snake-like leer terrify me beyond words. He is total reptile; voice, appearance, and manner of movement suggest some wandering anaconda turned from stalking pond animals and young antelopes to upright human prey. Sexually he is inexplicable in the good old Agatian manner. I particularly loathe and fear that strained, nonchalant, even blithe chuckle with which he tries to suggest that sex is no more than a matter of mild and passing interest to him. Actually it is more than half of his life. His relationship with me is tenuous in the extreme. I recall going into no forbidden tavern with him: and as to the night we spent together in Barnstaple, I can solemnly testify that he behaved perfectly and never even began to make advances to me. But – horrendum dictu – it is disquieting to reflect what obscene mental pictures of me fled through his dream that night. He slept fitfully, and his mind was in constant, turbulent motion.

> Quand même, darling.
> Ken

---

[1] *An Inspector Calls*, at the New Theatre with Ralph Richardson in the title role.
[2] If KPT did write reviews of these productions, they did not appear in the magazine.
[3] Name changed.

To Julian Holland

> 229 Portland Road
> 17/9/1946

Dear J;–

If this letter is a marathon limped, remember my disqualifications – 'Medea' still trailing on, book reviews and sly occasional 2000-word whimsies for 'Cherwell', degree work on 18th century, preparing productions of 'Song of Songs" and 'Ghosts' for next term, love-play with Plump False Face.[2]

There is so sprawling a conglomeration of opinions, new evidences of adulthood, things seen and digested, things read and relished, within me that I faint at the very thought of transcribing them. First I will answer your letter, and then impale on my keys anything I can remember of my recent life.

[...] let me assert in all confidence that 'Medea' was a brilliant, atmospherical production. It failed on Friday night because the lighting cues and music cues let me down; but for the two performances on Saturday it was astonishingly good. I played Chorus (acting as Prompter) in handcuffs and pink tights; and also, in a red cloak, played the Messenger who relates the news of Medea's slaughters as a thorough-going sadist, – to a background of the trumpet solos from 'Black and Tan Fantasy'[3] and 'Echoes of Harlem'.[4] Barbara Siggs thinks this is the best performance of a minor part she has ever seen; on Saturday I agreed with her. I used a balletic mime prologue (very dirty) to introduce the play (Ravel's 'La Valse') and elsewhere at crises I used 'The Mooche'[5] and the Sacred Dance of the Chosen Virgin from 'Sacre du Printemps'.[6] I designed the set and executed it myself: a pink palace, with an 18-ft silver sword draped across it: a wild, Blake-esque sky; two pillars on a rostrum; and a jet black house for Medea. The Despatch critic spoke of the production as having 'the genuine creative energy, the life force'; and compared me with Peter Brook.

That extravagant blurb is, I feel, more than necessary to swing you over from whatever opinionated stammering idiocy Hugh has been machine-gunning at you.

Of course our friendship isn't on the rocks; we are not emotionally mature enough for genuine situations like that. We merely know that occasionally we irritate each other, and occasionally enjoy different things for different reasons. I recall very distinctly sitting down and saying to Hugh [...]: 'Look, Smear, Smuggy Smear: you can't explain friendship by mutual respect. I think Julian, for instance, is incredibly pompous, boundlessly lewd, and at times unwarrantably priggish. Yet I would not resign or give up my title to his friendship for all the queers in Greenwich Village.' I had thought that you, Hugh, and I were intimate enough to expose each other freely and at no cost or rancour; I was going through one of those savage, bored, merciless moods which always seem to co-incide with Hugh's visits to Birmingham; I was tired; I was hungry. But I still defend my words; and I'll say the same of myself any time you care to hear me. I am lewd, I have pomp, I am prig. The trouble with us is that you are ethically finical and snobbish, and I am temperamentally finical and snobbish. [...]

The Rep is doing 'Our Town', which I see on Thursday. Sid Field's new show, 'Piccadilly Hayride',[7] has its premiere here next week; a large event. I have seen only one remarkable and one notable film in the last month: the remarkable film was 'The Dark Corner'.[8] This is, I think, the best of the tough black-and-white school: its every shot is pure big-city stuff; it recreates the hot, noisy, scuffling atmosphere of New York better than any film I have seen. It is laconic and very intelligently written; often witty ('I detest the dawn. The grass always looks as if it had been left out all night'). The newcomer Mark Stevens is very easy and amiable; and can act. Clifton Webb is of course quintessential serpent; Bendix, shambling bemusedly from assassination to Mr Edison's rockin'-chair, is first-rate; and Lucille Ball is beautiful. No, J, this has to be seen.

The notable film was a 'B' musical called 'Tars and Spars'[9] – notable (a) for two surrealist dances arranged and danced by Marc Platt[10] (b) for a young blonde boy called Sid Caesar[11] who out-Danny Kaye's Danny in a delirious burlesque of any aviation film. I go to the West End cinema every night this week at 8 p.m. to see this delicious monologue (it lasts 11 minutes) again. [. . .]

Now may I take you up on your giant heresy. I have deliberately scamped all else to fix my waning strength upon the unaccountable thin-skinned-ness and super-civilisation of that strange, sensitive band, the outlaws who cannot like Frederick Valk.

I do not know whether Valk's was a good Othello.[12] I do not know whether Valk's was a good stage performance. I cannot even be quite certain that it was a stage performance at all. Was it not rather some shaking of the earth's crust, some sudden, volcanic shudder which possessed the world and is now spent? I do not know. All I can say surely is that every time Valk plays Othello, there is an <u>event</u> happening of comparable magnitude to whatever may have gone on at Bikini. As a thing to have happened to one, as a thing to have witnessed and survived, Valk's Othello is unique. There can never have been so spectacular or so disquieting or so roughly daring or so wild a performance this century. Sure, there is not blood in his veins, but a slow corrosive venom, a sluggish black bile, inflammatory, perilous; for it explodes and careers insanely through his veins at the touch of fire; it is and he is electricity. If the earth's crust were to crack tonight and I to fall footlong into all Hell's flames, I should smile painfully but blandly, and say in Satan's face: 'I have seen it all before.' I have shared (almost agonisingly) the whole range of violent and pathetic emotion with a huge teddy-bear, uncannily able to radiate any of the emotions of the blood and infuse them into any person standing or sitting within two hundred yards of his voice. I write this hysterically because that is how I felt last Monday night. Enid Adams will tell you that I nearly had a heart attack during III.iii; my heart was leaping and thudding about as I have never known it before. I was breathless and beautifully exhausted at each curtain. I experienced full catharsis last Monday night.

Your criticism is angering and shallow. It is sarcastic-descriptive criticism, not interpretative criticism, 'Ranting, – mouth-foaming – hand-waving' – that is not criticism, it is embittered and uncritical cataloguing. Of course he spoke loud and foamed (have you ever seen any other Othello foam? and the text demands it) and moved his hands. He made a frontal assault on every emotion of pity and terror; and bludgeoned and coaxed out of one every lightest shade of all these emotions. His fantastic, irrational gusto perplexed me: it was this quality of unreason which makes me criticise his performance as an event and not as a theatrical achievement. I can still weep at the memory of his astonishing, piped 'the pity of eet, Yaggo, the pity of e-e-e-e-eet'.

Now to this question of poetry. I do not believe in music in verse; I believe that verse is either smooth and end-stopped or it is not. I do not go to the playhouse to hear poetry, particularly poetry as hackneyed as that of Othello. Mr Wolfit, on the other hand, worships poetry, and draws out every ounce of it. I seem to recall mentioning before his habit of giving 'Nature' its full six syllables. It embarrasses me to watch Wolfit when a line of exquisite poetry is put into his hands. Like a prize-fighter with a buttercup, like Lenny[13] with a puppy, he gently, caressingly, soothingly batters it to death; or, more often, regretfully strangles it by over-kindness. Valk, on the other hand, pierced to the core of poetry; mere tinkling words were too small and puny for him. He by his very presence <u>was</u> the incarnate spirit of emotional truth. There was no time for words in that great moment; no time for young striplings and RADA elocution and exquisite cadences; there was time for fire, rock, and air, and nothing less. The play and the words, all plays and words, were and are infinitely too small for the consummate genius of Frederick Valk.

After that I feel I can make one small amend. I speak personally. I know very well that Valk's performance would be useless and misleading to anyone who didn't know the lines. I did; and the impression was one of those transcendent, milestone experiences which must be recorded in personal terms or not at all.

Please, will that do?

Blessings;
K.

---

[1] KPT's stage adaptation of the Old Testament book, produced by the Experimental Theatre Club in November 1946.
[2] Possibly a reference to Hugh Manning, whom KPT believed had tried to wreck his production of *Medea*.
[3] Melody by James 'Bubber' Miley based on a spiritual, and one of the first successes of the Duke Ellington Band.
[4] Miniature jazz concerto written by Duke Ellington for the trumpeter 'Cootie' Williams.

[5] Written and recorded in 1928 by Duke Ellington.
[6] Ballet written in 1913 by the Russian composer Igor Stravinsky depicting the sacrifice of a young virgin at a pagan ceremony.
[7] Revue (1946) with music and lyrics by Dick Hurran and Phil Park.
[8] Thriller (US, 1946) directed by Henry Hathaway, starring Mark Stevens (b.1915), Clifton Webb (1891–1966), William Bendix (1906–64) and Lucille Ball (1911–89) who, before her 1950s comedy television series *I Love Lucy*, appeared in dozens of Hollywood films.
[9] Wartime musical directed by Alfred E. Green (US, 1945).
[10] Born Marcel le Platt (b. 1915), American dancer and choreographer of shows including *Ghost Town* (1939).
[11] Sid Caesar (b.1922), American comic actor who made his screen debut with *Tars and Spars*. As a TV star of the 1950s with *Your Show of Shows*, he influenced and launched a generation of comics, including Mel Brooks and Woody Allen.
[12] On 16 September 1946, KPT saw Frederick Valk play the Moor, opposite Wolfit's Iago, in Wolfit's production of *Othello*. He worked up this account of the performance, which he sent to Holland and also to James Agate. The critic published the review in *Ego 9* on 2 January 1947 and commented: 'Anybody reading this in a hundred years' time should know what these two actors had been like in these two great rôles . . . In other words, here is a great dramatic critic in the making.' On 30 May 1947 KPT published the piece in the undergraduate magazine *Oxford Viewpoint*.
[13] The gentle giant in John Steinbeck's *Of Mice and Men* (1937).

To Elizabeth Zaiman

Magdalen
Monday [28 October 1946]

Dear Liz;–

But I sent you a rehearsal list.[1] Rehearsals every Monday, Wednesday, + Friday at 5, <u>except</u> this Friday at 4.

And I do truly love you, my only, my precious – and I am not wicked & I have <u>such</u> a good heart.

Do, <u>do</u> come to rehearsals – 'twould be such fun.

C. S. Lewis now thinks I am the Wonder Boy again.[2]

<u>Such</u> love
Ken

[1] Rehearsals for *Ghosts*, produced for the ETC Acting Contest on 15 November 1946.
[2] According to KPT, Lewis was an 'incomparable' teacher, 'the most powerful and formative influence of my whole life up to that point'. Because of his stammer, the tutor would often read aloud his pupil's essays for him, then demonstrate how to argue in a vein of outrageous paradox. KPT wrote that he had the same swiftness as Dr Johnson 'to grasp the heart of a problem and the same sort of pouncing intelligence to follow it through to the conclusion' (*The Canadian C. S. Lewis Journal*, January 1979).

To Pauline Whittle

Magdalen College
Friday [29 November 1946]

Paul darling:–

[. . .] Why do you <u>suddenly</u> apologise about the Oxford train fares? I was only too happy to do it – particularly as I'd undertaken to do it before you came. You are positively crazy, darling, and please let's marry each other soon.

I'm going to Birmingham on Saturday December 15th (I <u>think</u> it's the 15th) – so send your next letter (and enclosure) to Portland Rd. I shall be in London in January, and I will come to Southport to see you. Pantomimes,¹ by the way, are dangerous: close proximity to strong, virile young men. Please, darling, don't fall in love with a broker's man,² a dame, or any part of a horse.

To my plans for next term you can add a <u>new Philosophy</u> we of the Cherwell have cooked up. It will be, we hope, as fashionable as Existentialism, and we shall publicise it every week in the paper, as well as making it the basis of our speeches when we invade the Union. It has no name as yet; vaguely we call it 'a Philosophy of Transience'.³ I'll tell you more later – it has quite set fire to me and my whole life will run accordingly. [. . .]

I am as well as this glacial weather will permit. Rehearsals are going with a zing – except that the man playing opposite me in 'The Pretenders'⁴ is the worst ham I have ever known. And the producer likes it, and is converting me into the same repulsive shape. But I shall refuse to be hamstrung.

By the way I love you, and being without you in this weather is like walking around in a bathing suit and no shoes. I want to wrap you round me almost all the time.

Aren't dance tunes of the early '30s wonderfully nostalgic? I have spent this morning weeping copiously over an Ambrose⁵ record of 'Smoke Gets In Your Eyes', with the gram. turned down very slow.

You remind me, darling, of a heroine of the silent screen, a maid of the D.W. Griffith school – surely the chastest, loveliest creatures in the history of art.

Goodnight, my lovely chaste one.

Love and be loved by
Ken

[1] Pauline's contract with Wolfit's company had ended and she joined the cast of *Cinderella* in Southport as a dancer.

[2] A stock character in *Aladdin* and other pantomimes: a bailiff.

[3] Cervillism, from the Latin for 'Cherwell', meant 'acquiescence in the fact of mortality, acceptance, and reconciliation with death,' wrote KPT, Beesley and co. in the magazine's editorial of 23 January 1947. They then proceeded to define this attitude as one which recognized death as 'the key to pleasure', cousin to Taoist detachment, favouring civilized organization in 'small groups ... the only indisputable facts are (a) the moment, and (b) our existence in it.'

[4] This production of Ibsen's play, produced under the auspices of the Friends of the Oxford University Dramatic Society, was first performed on 25 February 1947 in the Oxford Playhouse, directed by Glynne Wickham.

[5] Bert Ambrose (1897–1971), British bandleader of the 1930s and 1940s, whose signature tune was 'When Day is Done'.

To Elizabeth Zaiman

Edgbaston
End of December.
[28 December 1946]

Dear Old Year;–

Much too good. Thanks for a bad but big and bold book. Christmas was dull – family party – coagulation of the blood. I must buy you something – jewels, perhaps, or rich spices. Oh hell I'm tired of buying jewels. Cathay asked me how I knew ....

The point. Which is that I DON'T WANT to see the Master Builder[1] with a party. So I've written for two Press Tickets on Wednesday January 8th. For you and for me.

You can see the Alchemist[2] with me on January 15th or 16th Matinée, when I've been offered Press tickets.

Nice?

Love to hairbrush and your appealing self:

Ken

P.S. Have stumbled on a seventeen-year-old masochist. Now I have to keep stumbling on her.

[1] Ibsen's play (1892), directed by Peter Ashmore at the Arts Theatre, London, with Frederick Valk as Solness.

[2] By Ben Jonson (1610), directed by John Burrell at the New Theatre, London, with Ralph Richardson and Alec Guinness. KPT's reviews for both of the above productions are included in *He That Plays the King*.

To Pauline Whittle

229 Portland Rd.
[1 January 1947]

Darling Paul;–

An uninvited sickness of soul visited me this evening. Selfishly I feel I must share it with you; that is the only ultimate solace I know. The situation was this: I had a ticket for a party given at Bourneville[1] by the Prefects of K.E.S. It would admit me and 'friends'. About me I had Julian, Brian Wigmore,[2] Keith McGowan,[3] and David Bench. I had, you must understand, done no work at all during the day, and an appointment with the dentist awaited me in the morning. We had a very few, very dismal drinks in the St James; Brian was having his usual unconscious effect of making me feel (a) an unsuccessful poseur, and (b) that life was a frivolous waste (a word that scares me beyond all others). Keith was talking furtively & confidentially about sex, which was nearly intolerable. Then I opened a copy of Byron I had with me, & the following summary of all sublunary life shocked my sight: 'Eat, drink, toil, tremble, laugh, weep, sleep, & die.' I saw with terrific clarity that I had done all these things – except die. I suddenly knew that I would have to die soon; that slow wheels were coming full circle; that an old, fitful joy in life I once took was slipping irrevocably from me; and that, after a brief space, time would annihilate me in its brisk & heartless fashion. I was silent and desperate.

Then we moved on to the party in Bourneville Church Hall. It is a saddening place, bare & inhospitably hardseated. Its festoons of grinning rags chilled me. Bounding, thudding music shouted at me from a radiogram. Unbelievably young girls in long, dreamlike off-white gowns sang, clapped, loved & laughed, while piloting hordes of bright, horsy young men attended them. Brian dragged a painful chuckle from me with a monologue of appalling salacity. I was given cyder, cold and causing my stomach to swell. Julian was kind but as bored as I. He took us away and suggested a meal in town. In full ownership of my responsibilities & friendship, I refused. It was a maniacal gesture, but by now my mental tautness had communicated itself to my body. I felt deadened and inert (I was at no time even slightly tight; I had no wish or need to be). I travelled on the bus with Brian. He was quiet, yet obviously insensible to the magnitude of the experience I was conscious of. All the mocking arrows of rain-sleet and star-beams pointed to me and said: 'Waste! Waste! Waste!' Life became, after all, a monstrous and irksome procession of incidents acted in acute physical discomfort and uncongenial society.

When I arrived home (some fifty minutes ago) the first words I read were a hostile criticism of the <u>Cherwell</u> by S. P. B. Mais[4] in <u>The Queen</u>.[5]

I thought instinctively of you. And this mechanical tumult of words you have just borne the brunt of is the voice of my cramped spirit this first day of 1947. A day which I have thoroughly, almost systematically, done to death, & which almost killed me, in reciprocation.

My conscience tells me that that will do.

I know why I am suffering slight agonies of maladjustment so frequently these days. My attempt to live <u>in the moment</u>, looking neither forwards nor backwards, has led me to absorb myself too completely in the things going on immediately about me. I feel more poignantly the implications of circumstance because I have made it my creed to do so. And the implications of this dying evening were insipidity, sterility, unwantedness & despair.

The refuge from this, in which I coward-like, am for ever seeking shelter, is the certainty of your love. It is a sturdy & perennial thing, and it offers warmth & oblivion. Keep it airtight and watertight, darling. We both need it and the magic we can evoke within it. Behind the soft curtains of talk and flesh we are demi-gods in our own right.

That's all I had to say. I shall sleep tonight.

As ever, small angel:
Ken

P.S. I forgot the address of your digs. Please forgive me.

[1] A district of Birmingham.
[2] Member of the N.D.C.
[3] Son of the Archdeacon of Aston, a friend of KPT's from King Edward's School.
[4] S. P. B. Mais (1885–1975), author and broadcaster.
[5] *Queen* magazine, founded in 1861, merged with *Harper's Bazaar* in 1970 to become *Harper's and Queen*.

To Pauline Whittle[1]

[Telegram]

Oxford
3 February 1947

DEVASTATED BUT INEXPLICABLY ANGERED BY YOUR ILLNESS IT HAS DISLOCATED THE MAKINGS OF A WONDERFUL WEEK COME QUICKLY

I LOVE YOU VERY MUCH MEANWHILE MAKE DO WITH TEARS OF
SYMPATHY FROM BEYOND THE ANGELS — KEN[2]

[1] Addressed to Pauline Shirley, her stage name.
[2] Joe Simon, a KES contemporary, recalls KPT using the phrase 'Beyond the Angels Ken' two
years before while drinking champagne in a country pub. He often used it to sign off his letters.

To the Editor, the *Oxford Guardian*[1]

Magdalen College
[Published 25 April 1947]

Sir,—Your compact and often readable news-sheet was passed to me
to-day by a friend who told me I would find something actionable
inside it. I did. And I have to warn you that, should Miss Blumenthal
and Mr. Alan Clarke feel similarly offended, three very intricate libel
actions might face you for having described us as 'miscellaneous
morons.' Your Union Correspondent is neither wit, dramatic critic,
nor phrase-maker, and he is therefore particularly unsuited to speak
justly about my performance at the despatch box. I should like a discreet
retraction of the phrase, and a courteous one. Retractions do not *have*
to be funny.

I should, in conclusion, hate to think that I had made you at all ill at
ease or dumbfounded by writing a letter with no relevance at all to
politics. So I will tell you about my politics. A century ago I should
have been a feudal Tory; a century hence, an Anarchist. At the present
I am a Liberal, with Confucian leanings.

Yours, etc.,
KENNETH P. TYNAN

[1] Printed under the heading 'Tynan v. Skunk' in the Liberal Club's *Oxford Guardian* of 25 April
1947. In the 7 March issue 'Skunk' had attacked Tynan for his performance in the debate 'That
There is No Hope for the Modern Novel': 'Mr Tynan produced his effects by permutations of
four standard contortions. 1. The wild, appealing, distracted stare at the gallery. 2. The clutching
of the text of the speech (fully written out on mauve scented paper for subsequent publication) to
the heart with sinuously twisting fingers. 3. The body curved backwards like a bow ... convulsively
jerked into a vertical position for the ejection of a word ... 4. the palsy-twitching mandibles'.
KPT was thereafter referred to by Skunk (Anthony Walton) as 'Ken Ty Nan the Confucian
liberal'.

To Julian Holland[1]

8 Banbury Road
Oxford
[Postmark 1 July 1947]

Dear J;

I have flitted again as you see[2] – now to my thanks to you for 'Oklahoma'[3] – will do splendidly and I will send you the cash on Tuesday next – good.

Have been offered a permanent job at Windsor Rep on strength of my Holofernes[4] in OUDS – Coghill advises me not to take it, and the Windsor man in a kind letter agrees to hold the job till next year – there may be a Chair of Drama at Oxford in five years time and if I get a good degree Coghill says he will get me a lectureship – other things: I am negotiating with the lessee of the Scala, Charlotte St., to take it over next August as actor-manager of a permanent rep. for ex-undergraduates of Ox or Cam[5] – the profession would hate it but that's just the angle for publicity – closed shop etc. – the lessee has offered a very very reasonable price – £500 a month – Coghill is taking OUDS abroad to Berlin, Vienna, Paris, next summer in 'Romeo & Juliet' and wants me for Tybalt – I start work next week on an amateur film (running forty minutes) that we're making here – it's a study in claustrophobia called 'The Way Out'[6] – and I'm playing the menace, called 'The Invigilator' – I played cricket for Michael Barsley's BBC team[7] (Gilliam, Sp. Hughes, Belfrage, Reg Smith, etc) at Cassington Village[8] yesterday – scored one and took one for eleven – went to a party on Saturday with a stark naked syphilitic negress called Princess Tracy – C'est la Waugh but strictly true – am being pursued by a husband called Mitchell because I fucked his wife called Mitchell – am writing a play – Websterian tragedy in wellknown modern dress – Derek Patmore has offered me job (via James Pope-Hennessy) of dramatic critic on 'The Spectator' – even chance whether I take it.[9] For the rest, life is very dull. The rest of the world, I mean.

May come up for the Varsity match. May I call?

Ever, ever,
K.

---

[1] KPT's writing paper was now headed by his signature printed in red, green, or mauve.
[2] From digs at 31 Park Town to Banbury Road.

[3] Holland got tickets for the first London production of Rodgers and Hammerstein's musical (1943), which had opened in April.

[4] KPT played Holofernes in an OUDS production of *Love's Labour's Lost*, directed by Anthony Besch, in Merton College Garden 18–25 June 1947.

[5] KPT planned to run a 'New Commercial Theatre Club' and to lease a London theatre like the Scala for June 1950: 'the theatre to be dedicated to (a) versatility and shock (b) the exploration of new architectural forms for drama (c) the making of money (d) the revival of interest in heroic drama'. He proposed to produce plays for a permanent company to run in repertory, films (Lindsay Anderson to be in charge), and books and magazines (to be run by Alan Beesley).

[6] Apparently never made.

[7] The BBC's team, on which KPT was invited to play, included Laurence Gilliam (Radio Head of Features), Spike Hughes, who made music programmes and signed off with 'Bye for now', Bruce Belfrage a BBC announcer, and Reggie Smith, a producer in the Features Department, who married the novelist Olivia Manning.

[8] Village a few miles northwest of Oxford.

[9] KPT became second string to Peter Fleming as drama critic of the *Spectator* in 1951.

To Julian Holland

51 St John Street
Oxford
[Postmark 25 August 1947]

Dear J;

Thanks for two nearly identical letters. The Postal Order came safely through. [...]

I had a wonderful fortnight in Ireland, where you can walk into a shop and buy five dozen meringues at 3d each and sit in the orchestra stalls for 4/- and drink all day long. I saw Burgess Meredith & Paulette Goddard[1] in 'Winterset' at the Gaiety Theatre: the woman is the worst, most chirrupy-syrupy stage player I've seen, but Meredith is superb – the only convincing stage study in idealism I've seen.

Have you seen the 'Henry V' set of records on HMV? I bought them yesterday. God knows I'm no chauvinist, but each time I hear Olivier's wonderful guttural roar of 'Cry God for Harry, Engla-a-a-and & St. Ge-o-o-o-o-orge!' I would willingly go to the stake for Winston Churchill.

Adios!
K.

[1] Burgess Meredith (b.1908), American actor for whom *Winterset* was written. He married the actress Paulette Goddard (previously married to Charlie Chaplin) in 1944.

Early in the Hilary Term of 1947, outside the Playhouse Theatre, Ken met a tall girl with dark hair and an elegant face, called Gillian Rowe-Dutton. She was a medical student at St Anne's, the daughter of an Anglo-Irish civil servant, and much courted at the university. Jill Rowe-Dutton looked around Oxford and decided Ken was 'the mostest. He was startlingly funny, wonderful looking, unconscionably arrogant, and he could switch on intellectual brilliance like a floodlight.'

The two fell in love and Ken became a regular visitor to Jill's digs at 82A St Aldate's. In the vacation he took Pauline out to dinner on her birthday, 24 March, at the International restaurant in Birmingham, and broke off their engagement. He showed her a photograph of Jill and announced he had been living with her for a month. He wanted his letters back. Pauline was heartbroken.

Ken was soon engaged to his new love (announced in Isis *on 7 May) and persuaded his parents to sign a document consenting to the marriage of a minor to Miss Rowe-Dutton. But by September Jill returned to her former boyfriend, John Godley (later third Baron Kilbracken).*

As the following (undelivered) letter reveals, Ken was devastated. He had a great row with Jill, and slapped her face. In floods of tears she returned to her parents.

In the aftermath, during that autumn, Ken became engaged again and again: to Ruth Cropper, a Politics, Philosophy and Economics student, and to Gillian Staynes, a girl with Pre-Raphaelite hair and theatrical clothes. To his great friend Elizabeth Zaiman he would say, 'Let's get engaged', and she would answer, 'Yes, Ken, often.'

To Gillian Rowe-Dutton

[Oxford]
[September 1947]

Oh Chum—

This is IT IT IT IT IT IT. That is OUR ROOM – We furnished it, lived in it, sang in it, ate a hundred thousand meals in it, slept and fucked in it. I am not a VISITOR there: it is MINE. Please SEE me saying this with my face drenched with tears and my eyes red & nearly invisible. And see, too, my ANGUISH at your cool, bloody, hateful betrayal betrayal betrayal & lies lies lies.

This afternoon in bed you said 'JOHN & I ARE NOT GOING TO BE LOVERS'. And later: 'JOHN WANTS SOMEONE TO TALK TO.' O foul & not true! Why! Where O Chum is the vestige of CONSCIENCE? O chum chum chum. 'JOHN AND I ARE NOT GOING TO BE LOVERS' 'JOHN AND I ARE NOT GOING TO BE LOVERS' [...] O come & talk to me before I die.

Let me tell you again what you DID. I lay there silently, at rest, in peace. Entered you and a tall stooping STRANGER. I awoke and wondered what he was doing in our room. Then of course the sick horror & death of it returned to me. I realised you had lied & kidded & befooled me again. The stranger had won at the races & so you were going to celebrate [...]

And the first thing you did on entering the room was to make that quite clear by going straight to the shutters & LOCKING them – before my eyes, my dazed, poor, squeezed eyes. O you swine & he a swine, a callous, numb, self-engrossed swine! IT CANNOT BE GOOD IF IT MEANS THIS MAD SUFFERING. O God words are not strong or hurtful enough for your almighty crime. At that moment all the past loathing & despair & hate in me rose up & killed me again – for the hundredth time in 24 hours.

OUR ROOM – remember the Summer, and the gramophone & the fifty thousand scraps of life that made it OUR ROOM

I cannot hold the pen much longer.

O Swine

And the last killing blow (you were killing pretty surely then) was when I left. That I should leave! Next time I shall be there with barricades & bolts to keep you out. I will hold that room of ours & make it mine. You refused my dinner invitation as if it were a rather dull cup of coffee with a poor relation! DIDN'T YOU KNOW IT MEANT LIFE AND DEATH TO ME? Didn't you know I'd spent three hours in that room waiting for you to say yes, chum, yes, of course, yes.

And then – to return – when I left. How easily you could have said 'Sorry, chum' and squeezed my hand, & I should have been so happy & so grateful. But I got a curt, distant 'g-bye'. Because you were afraid. Because if you'd said 'Sorry, chum' John might have suspected that some tiny relic of sympathy & compassion still lived;

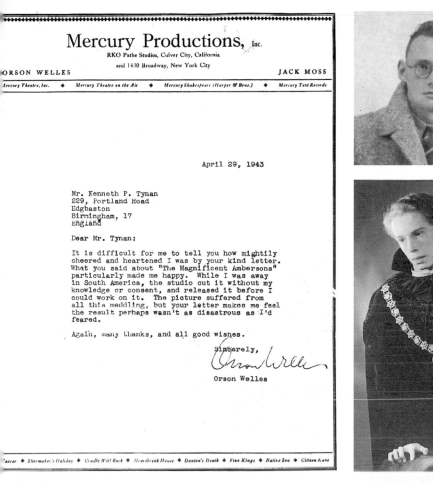

Mercury Productions, Inc.

RKO Pathe Studios, Culver City, California
and 1430 Broadway, New York City

ORSON WELLES   JACK MOSS

Mercury Theatre, Inc. ◆ Mercury Theatre on the Air ◆ Mercury Shakespeare (Harper & Bros.) ◆ Mercury Text Records

April 29, 1943

Mr. Kenneth P. Tynan
229, Portland Road
Edgbaston
Birmingham, 17
England

Dear Mr. Tynan:

It is difficult for me to tell you how mightily
cheered and heartened I was by your kind letter.
What you said about "The Magnificent Ambersons"
particularly made me happy. While I was away
in South America, the studio cut it without my
knowledge or consent, and released it before I
could work on it. The picture suffered from
all this meddling, but your letter makes me feel
the result perhaps wasn't as disastrous as I'd
feared.

Again, many thanks, and all good wishes.

Sincerely,

Orson Welles

Caesar ◆ Shoemaker's Holiday ◆ Cradle Will Rock ◆ Heartbreak House ◆ Danton's Death ◆ Five Kings ◆ Native Son ◆ Citizen Kane

The first letter from Orson Welles, 1943

right Julian Holland, 1943

ove right Ken as Hamlet in the New Dramatic Company
oduction in Birmingham, 1945

ght Ken with Pauline Whittle in Bournemouth, 1945

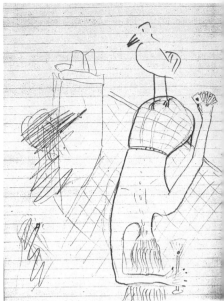

A doodle from Ken's Oxford notebook

Left Ken while at Oxford

Ken as Judge Gaunt in his production of Maxwell Anderson's *Winterset*, 1948

The ad for Ken's production of *Samson
Agonistes* in St Mary's Church, Oxford,
1947

Ken at Cheltenham, 1948

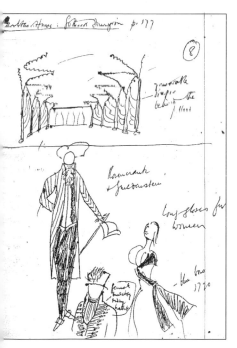

Ken's eighteenth-century designs for his
Oxford production of *Hamlet* at
Cheltenham, 1948

Ken's party on a Thames boat to celebrate his
twenty-first birthday, April 1948 (Hugh
Manning is second from left; Alan Beesley is
front row right)

Ken with Pat Brewer at Lichfield, 1949

Ken directing *The Beaux' Stratagem* at Lichfield, 1949

Ken directing Diana Dors and Roger Livesey in *Man of the World* by C. E. Webber, 1950

Ken in London, 1950

Ken with Cecil Beaton, 1952

Left The wedding of Ken and Elaine Dundy, London, 25 January 1951. Peter Wildeblood was the best man, Tessa Prendergast the maid of honour.

INTRODUCING KENNETH TYNAN
the liveliest writer of the day

DOWN WITH

scarecrows
snobs and
sniggers !

THE first thing any critic ought to make clear is his capacity for boredom. The man who never yawns in the theatre is a menace to it, as callow and gullible as he is insensitive. Only maniacs are never bored.

The extreme, total pleasure a critic gets out of a work of art is so elating that, in its absence, he resembles nothing so much as an addict who has lost his hypodermic.

disturbingly, and given us only one stage performance in the rough, grand manner he inherited from Edmund Kean.

That was "Antony and Cleopatra," two years ago. Since

operation on her eye kept her incommunicado.

Her presence in London would be a healthy distraction for our actresses. It might persuade some of them that

An odd, crippling snobbism seems to prevent our legitimate playwrights from linking their talents to music. It exists nowhere else, least of all in America, where good dramatists and novelists make a

'—Only maniacs are never bored . . .'

vues " which at present occ what ought to be an hone temple of carnality.

9 An announcement fro H. M. Tennents, the large and most influential manag ment in England, that the had decided to buy the A Theatre, which Alec Clunes about to relinquish after decade of non - commerci privateering.

And then, the presentation there of a season of plays Jean Giraudoux, the Fe French dramatist of his tir (he died in 1944), whose po sionate wit, hissing like red-h steel in ice-water, is still alm unknown in this country.

Adult

10 " Pal Joey," the most ad of the American music Written by Rodgers and Ha it tells the wry story of a you night-club M.C. and his dis trous affair with a million protectress; and it conta the original, unwholeso version of "Bewitch Bothered and Bewildered."

Its acrid, decayed - pes flavour, however, seems to c courage English producers as an alternative importa we are to get " Wish You W Here," which is as hear bracing as a year in a Bu camp.

Top The critic Tynan joins the *Daily Sketch*, 1953

Above left Ken with Tracy in the flat ir Hyde Park Gardens, 1953

Left Learning to fight bulls, c. 1954

Above Ken with Tennessee Williams, Valencia, 1955

en at El Vino's, 1958

ore Vidal (*top right*) Truman Capote (*middle*)
mes Jones (*right*) at Mount Street, 1957

aine and Ken, c. 1956

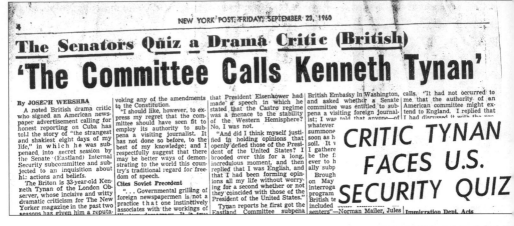

Ken and the committee, 1960

Ken with Lawrence Ferlinghetti at the City Lights
bookstore, San Francisco, 1959

Antonio Ordóñez with Ernest
Hemingway, Spain, 1959

Ken's farewell party
at the Forum of the
Twelve Caesars, Ne
York, May 1960
(seated, clockwise:
Ken, Vivien Leigh,
Arlene Francis,
James Thurber,
Helen Thurber,
Lillian Hellman)

that you still remembered me. He might have thought, for a moment, that you still considered me as a human being.

Oh how could you do it? You, chum. The you I <u>created</u> in February & shared through March, April, May, June, July, August – or are all these lovely months quite blotted out? You would do well to remember them. They are the months in which I gave you the rest of my life to keep & look after for me.

Chum, I'm 20 years old. John is much more. And after much less time with you, & with all his years of maturity, & with all the gap between his exit & my entrance to help him, he behaved like a hysterical child. HOW IN CHRIST'S NAME DO YOU THINK I SHALL BEHAVE?

Unless you come (you apart from John) – unless you can come to the conclusion we arrived at this afternoon – no strings – you will make all my hours blazing hell & my nights murderous & black, and I in turn will in self-defence have to <u>kill</u> as much of you as I can see

Chum, you know this isn't the real me talking when I say that. And you know you can so easily revive the real me and recreate him. And you know the real me is worth reviving.

In despair,
K.

<u>Lunch</u> please with me. Please <u>lunch</u>. Today.

To Julian Holland

51 St John St¹
having received
yours.
[Postmark 24 September 1947]

Dear Julian

Jill has left me. I thought several times of writing or coming to see you, because I think you know about that ache and that hunger and that waste and loss. I crumpled pretty completely. It was more complex than the wonted thing is, because Jill and her new lover are tangled up inextricably in the social life I have here, and the climate of embarrassment next term is going to be torrid. I had kept her for six months, and slept with her nightly. An Oedipus[2] had grown up which I can't yet dispel. Don't write and be nice, because you know as well as I do that you couldn't help. I am learning to aspire to that wonderful loneliness they talk about, and to solace myself with Shaw when he said: 'God is alone.'[3]

I had a letter from the copywright [*sic*] men saying that BBC records were copywright, so that was that.[4] I'm now doing 'Winterset'[5] instead, with incidental music from the Bartók 5th Quartet. <u>Love</u> that play.

Can't even tell you about Edinburgh, and Bruno Walter,[6] Szigeti,[7] Schnabel,[8] Jouvet,[9] and the rest, because I've just finished 4000 words on it for an Oxford magazine.[10] Some of the flashiest, sweetest journalism you'll ever read, but I wouldn't disgrace myself or you by rehashing it up like cold potatoes. Merely this of Jouvet's voice (from Virginia Woolf): 'His rough and hairy voice is like an unshaven chin.'[11]

Have been redoing the Elizabethans, and finding how pure an arrogant Bloomsburian Marlowe was; how voluminous and muscular Jonson was; how much I love Tourneur,[12] how much I loathe Spenser. And so forth. No fun yet.

I shall be in Birmingham on October 2nd to see 'King Lear',[13] and in London for the first night of Mae West[14] (when is that?) and the Redgrave 'Macbeth'[15] in November.

Spent Saturday night with Dylan Thomas,[16] a surly little pug but a master of pastiche and invective. Thinks himself the biggest and best phoney of all time, and may be right. Tried comforting myself with a weekend at Woodstock with my married lady, but erection just wouldn't explode. The way I felt wouldn't have raised the cock of a fly, much less taken the flies off a cock (This sounds funny when Dylan T. speaks it, but I see it's dead in print).

Would like to come and see '2d Coloured',[17] but the Lyric is too near to Jill's home for there to be any joy.

Dear J, come and see me some weekend.

Ever,

K.

[1] KPT's digs.

[2] Possibly a reference to the fact that Kilbracken was older than KPT.

[3] In the wake of Jill's departure, KPT told his tutor that he was going to commit suicide. C. S. Lewis reminded him that he had narrowly missed being killed by a land mine in Birmingham during the war, that he was as a result living on borrowed time. Ken promptly changed his plan.

[4] KPT had been planning a production of Karel Čapek's *The Insect Play* (1921) for the Experimental Theatre Club and wanted to use Alan Rawsthorne's recorded music.

[5] KPT's production of the play with the Experimental Theatre Club played 5–14 February at the Cowley Congregational Hall, Oxford.

[6] Bruno Walter (1876–1962), German-born conductor, associate of Gustav Mahler and renowned interpreter of music of the German Romantic tradition.

[7] Joseph Szigeti (1892–1973), Hungarian violinist who specialized in the work of contemporary composers.

[8] Artur Schnabel (1882–1951), American pianist and composer celebrated for his interpretation of the works of Beethoven.

[9] Louis Jouvet (1887–1951), French actor and director famous for his productions of Molière.

[10] *Oxford Viewpoint*: 'Edinburgh Diary' 31 October 1947.

[11] Untraced. Woolf makes no mention in her diary of seeing Jouvet in Paris; he never played in London.

[12] Meaning *The Revenger's Tragedy* (1607), now thought to be by Middleton.

[13] *King Lear* with John Phillips in the title role, directed by Willard Stoker, opened on 9 September 1947.

[14] Mae West's first appearance in London was on 24 January 1948, at the Prince of Wales Theatre as Diamond Lil, in her play of that name. KPT, with a group of friends, went backstage to pay homage.

[15] Sir Michael Redgrave (1908–85); in fact *Macbeth* opened in December 1947 at the Aldwych, transferred to Broadway in 1948.

[16] Dylan Thomas lived in or near Oxford between May 1946 and May 1949, commuting to London to seek work from the BBC. He lived with his wife Caitlin in a one-room studio cottage in the garden of the historian A.J.P. Taylor's house behind Magdalen. He later stayed at the Manor House, South Leigh, Witney.

[17] *Tuppence Coloured*, devised and directed by Laurier Lister (1947).

To Elizabeth Zaiman

[Postcard]

Magdalen College
[Postmark 20 October 1947]

Liz; Will you play a <u>whore</u>[1] for me, dear? and also supervise wardrobe? This is final.

Bestest love,
Ken
[...]

[1] She played the part of second street girl in *Winterset*.

To C. S. Lewis

51 St. John Street
Thursday [March 1948]

Dear Sir;
    You will recall that last term I missed a great many tutorials through bronchial trouble, and that I had a series of X-rays taken to ascertain the state of my chest. Happily I learnt during the vac that I need not worry immediately over my health, though I must be very watchful of the condition of my lungs in the future.
    The point is that last term my illness – and, even more, my anxiety – made it impossible, over long periods, for me to do any work, with the result that if I were to take Schools[1] in June I know I should do both myself and you less than justice.
    I wonder whether, on these grounds, you would be so kind as to ask the Tutorial Board for permission for me to stay up until December, and take Schools then.[2]
    I shall be most grateful and relieved.

Yours sincerely,
Kenneth P. Tynan

[1] Final examinations at Oxford, traditionally taken in the Examination Schools.
[2] C. S. Lewis wrote to W. J. M. McKenzie saying that since KPT's work the previous term had been 'very good', it was possible to argue both for and against his application. A meeting of the Tutorial Board on 12 March decided to allow KPT to postpone Schools till December.

To Dennis Mathew[1]

51 St. John Street
[March 1948]

Dear Dennis
    Final party arrangements, fixed yesterday:[2]
    Steamer leaves Westminster Pier (London) at 6 p.m. on Tuesday April 6th. It travels up-river to Eel Pie Island – there is a pause there for general promiscuity – and then returns to W'minster, arriving about 3 a.m.
    Your line-up sounds perfect.
    Yes, bring along your two alligators.[3]

£10–10–0,[4] though right when one thinks of trainfares to Oxford, might be wrong when one thinks of fares to London. However, I agree to it.

There will be a good piano laid on.

Yours,
Ken

[1] Mathew ran an Oxford jazz group called the Bandits
[2] KPT was twenty-one on 2 April 1948. The party followed on the 6th.
[3] Possibly two members of the band.
[4] The cost of the band.

Maxwell Anderson's 1935 play Winterset, *written in the wake of the Sacco–Vanzetti case, is a verse drama set in a tenement building centring on a miscarriage of justice. Ken loved everything American and particularly the gangster genre, which may explain why he fell upon this impenetrable moral tale, played the part of Judge Gaunt and turned the play into a successful piece of neo-Expressionistic theatre. (Many years later he argued that there were no good American plays written during the 1930s.)*

Halfway through the Oxford run, two rich French undergraduates saw the play and arranged for the whole production – with minor cast changes and under the banner of the Oxford University Players – to be shipped to Paris, to the Comédie des Champs Elysées, for one performance on 15 March. It was Ken's first trip abroad. Le Monde *reviewed the evening and described Ken as the latest disciple of Wilde and Ruskin.*

To Archie Campbell[1]

51 St. John Street
[22, March 1948]

Dear Mr Campbell;

I have just returned from Paris to find a letter waiting for me from my friend David Richards[2] of Lincoln College, explaining that you might be interested in arranging a broadcast or snippet about the recent visit of my company, the Oxford University Players, to Paris.

The trip was <u>sheer</u> fantasy from beginning to end – thirty-one undergraduates, tons of scenery were flown and shipped over to give one performance of an American play at the Comédie des Champs-Elysées. We were fêted – Jean-Louis Barrault[3] entertained us, Christian Dior invited us to his spring preview – and the play ('Winterset') was a huge success.

I could arrange to be in London at any time that would suit you, bringing programmes and newspaper cuttings to illustrate the story. I could also fix it so that one or two other members of the company were there too.

Let me know if and when and where we can meet.

Yours sincerely,
Kenneth P. Tynan[4]

[1] A drama producer on the BBC radio Third Programme.
[2] Undergraduate reading English.
[3] Jean-Louis Barrault (1910–94), mime and leading actor of the Comédie Française 1940–46; star of films including *Les Enfants du paradis* (1945).
[4] The broadcast was never made.

To the Editor, *Isis*

[51 St. John Street]
[Published 5 May 1948]

Dear Sir,—This is a reply to my newest traducer, Mr. Alan Brien,[1] who spread wickedness about me over a whole page of your issue of 5 May.

Mr. Brien is desperately mistaken, not only about what I represent but about what I am. He has taken the forgivably easy line of setting me amongst the *jeunesse dorée* whom, in your Editorial, you so roundly and rightly (though tritely) condemn. And he criticizes a piece of professional journalism I did for Vogue[2] because, he says, I have long hair, I support effeminacy, and I am 'fragile'. I admit the hair readily (and if Mr. Brien and I should ever meet, and his hair should be short-cropped, I assume I have reciprocal leave to gibe at his appearance); I should be a poor fool to deny my physical fragility; but the tough sinews of my mind and the nearly maniacal masculinity of my physical reflexes insist that I am very far from effeminacy. And it is surely hard, because I have a few friends with whom I work, laugh, write and act, that I should be accused of intellectual *dandyisme*. I am sure there must be *côteries* of the dull as well, with whose work and measure I should never dream of interfering. I am afraid I am genealogically unfitted to be a good snob; my private personality is that of an industrious Demy of Magdalen, forever embarrassed by his devotion to plays and books. And I must protest when this private personality is gratuitously misrepresented and involved in a criticism of an article written by my *professional* or *public* personality.

To please Vogue (who paid me well) I wrote a piece trying to prove that there was still some gaiety in Oxford, and that it was not wholly restricted to the rich. I wanted to show that one of the special joys of Oxford was that here intelligent people can, when they have worked enough, relax and be gay in their own uninhibited fashion, without the curb of intolerance; here gaiety is still *intelligent*, as well as heartfelt and fantastic. I prostituted myself, not without a little sly enjoyment, but securely hoping that I shall not need to do it too often. I assure Mr. Brien that my full-time private personality took that article very much less seriously than he did.

So – let's not be so grim and forbidding about things, shall we, Mr. Brien? Let's try not to glower so. After all, we're only here for three years.

Yours sincerely,
KEN PEACOCK TYNAN

[1] Alan Brien (b. 1925), a clever North Country undergraduate who had served as an air-gunner in the war, went on the attack in *Isis* of 5 May, accusing KPT of being a buffoon. It was the first piece Brien – who later became a well-known journalist and critic – had published. Years later he commented. 'If you couldn't be Ken Tynan you had to be Ken's enemy.' According to Brien KPT welcomed the attack: 'He knew that nothing so polishes up a star as an occasional vicious scratch on the chrome and he sought me out in my beer-drinking, hairy-jacketed, old sweats *New Statesman* reading lair: "Where have you been?" he said. "Everybody wants to meet you." '
[2] In March *Vogue* had published an article by KPT on Oxford, 'The Flair for Abandon', in which he wrote: 'What sets Oxford apart is ... a savour of gaiety ... a tang of flair ... a golden satin shirt.'

To Elly Horovitz[1]

51 St J St.
Oxford
Late Friday [June 1948]

Dear Ellington

Do you mind if we make this rather a longish one? because I have encountered this evening my old meddlesome bugbear, solitude. Oh,

I could, with such ease, rouse the old Eve in you by telling you I went out with Sylvie Rosenkavalier[2] and that it was the hugest and most relaxing fun – but I want you on other terms than plain man-versus-womanship; I want you on terms of heartsease and joy and mellowness and human comradeship, with a bonne bouche of sex when we were tired of the infinite world. I have been deeply, passionately miserable this evening; had a monastery been built I would have known something of what made St. John of the Cross a great as well as a good man. I should then have needed holy spring rain to make my roots live and flourish, where tonight I made do with beer.

I didn't get drunk, of course, and I didn't want to. Several Beesley's[3] [*sic*] invited me to Lincoln Commem, and Mike Murray-Leslie[4] wanted me for a party at the Doghouse; but I can no longer delight in things singly. I want to share – not on a fabulous scale, the scale of Timon of Athens – but frugally and meanly, with one other person. What distinguishes man from beast is, I am persuaded, the power of admiration – the power of spectatorship, of looking at things and doing so simply because he likes it; but man is herd-conscious enough not to be able to do it alone. I cannot again do it alone. I want a fellow-watcher, to keep with me my alert young vigil, my critical awareness of all that happens near me – plays, parties, tone poems, skirt-lengths, skies, flowers, flat-feet or frenzy. Sterne somewhere says, 'Let me have a companion of my way, were it but to remark how the shadows lengthen as the sun declines.'[5]

You remember our talk about how life was a series of predestinate, tangential beads threaded on a string – and how each bead was a mood, unsought but irresistible? This term has been bubbling with beads, but they have been threaded on a double string, our string and not merely mine. Weakened now and depleted, I can see a vast, cumbrous boulder of a bead rolling towards me; a mood of earsplitting self-pity and solitude, from which I can only cower, hide my head in bed, and sleep to be away from.

I can recall a time when any of twenty or thirty people could have cured and revived me. Now (and there has been no change in me) only you can do it. I feel sure enough of you to say that sanely and truly, with no fear that you might think I wanted only pity.

This is a cowardly letter, I know, and a very unstrategic one. I ought to write a gay and genial letter, a fireman-save-my-child sort of letter, a rippling and translucent letter, a happy letter, a me sort of letter, a you sort of letter. And God knows I will, but not now, not tonight; maybe next week, maybe for ages, but anyway, soon. Tonight is different.

If you were sad too, there'd be more excuse for all this. Sad people, by a sort of pride, tell each other of their sadness; just as rich people, by a sort of guilt, give their money away to each other.

This won't become a love-letter, my old perishable chum; it should rather be the tale of my love's ripening and blossoming into liking, and even into friendship. I like to think, when the hours telescope themselves away into everlastingness and it seems that time will never have a stop and that clocks are all chimeless, of the things in you and about you that I am so dearly and gaily loving; your memory is a big thing, its flair, its essential goodness, its sweetness – the way you jumble up in my mind things like the Grey Man[6] and sadisme and how are you and how is your sister and the gawdamn pussycat. Your chuckle is a pretty big thing, too; not Bach ever expressed contentment so fully. Better yet (things are crowding in now) your shrug, a bigger thing than all the duties and morals and manners of life – for it dismisses them all and makes them look foolish. And your firmness and directness and – but what a catalogue of abstractions! Stop it, Tynan, get wise, be the golden boy, get back to the wellknown surface where you belong, you tourist in the domains of philosophy.

I looked at a packet of Kensitas[7] this evening (a sorrowful man's eyes rarely leave the table-cloth, and this packet was lying on a table in the Taj[8]), and, reading the label, I discovered what I wished desperately to be. The label bore the manufacturer's name – 'J. Wix and Sons, Limited'. O to be J. Wix, or any of his myriad sons – for they are all limited! O to be limited, not to want to expand and embrace and belong to multitudes! to know one's sphere, and hold sway within it unmolested! How good that would be, how tranquil! For my world, the small soapy puffball I am at such pains to bear, needs another pair of hands to support it – it needs you, its joint Atlas.

Re-reading the last paragraph but one, I find it is bad – a phoney, too gushing exploration of things too real to me to be treated so tritely. Forgive it.

One's puniest enemies seem magnified when you are away – the tiniest slight or insult is enlarged into a vast challenge when our circle is broken. When you are here, I can say 'forgive us our trespasses, as we forgive them that trespass against us'; without you I say 'destroy them that trespass against me, and I will forgive my own trespasses.'

If all this isn't quite as important to you as it is to me, please tell me quickly and sternly.

Otherwise I shall derrop myself down the beeg sea.

Meanwhile
K.

I Love my Love with an L because she is Elly

---

[1] Elly Horovitz, daughter of an art publisher originally from Vienna, was reading PPE at Somerville College. Since term had ended Elly had returned to London.

[2] Sylvie Rosenfelder was reading Natural Science at St Anne's College.

[3] Alan Beesley was now married to Marie Woolf, the pretty Bohemian niece of Leonard Woolf, who was reading medicine at Somerville College.

[4] A medical student at the Radcliffe Infirmary.

[5] Possibly misquoted; the reference cannot be traced.

[6] Anthony Sylvester (now David), art critic, then a London suitor of Elly's.

[7] A brand of cigarettes.

[8] The Taj Mahal, at 16 Turl Street, opened in 1937 and is the second oldest Indian restaurant in Britain.

To Elly Horovitz

51 St. John Street
Oxf.
Wednesday
[? late June 1948]

Dear Elly;

You're quite right: you've never been to one of my parties. They're very good: packed and warm and infinitely relaxing; and I am a sober and diligent host, embarrassingly free with the drink: there is always my sort of music and never anyone else's – no Sambas, no Glenn Miller,[1] but records of the twenties and 'Ballin' the Jack'[2] and an occasional Al Jolson[3] to wake people up. There are never any gatecrashers and everyone except me is drunk ten minutes after they arrive. Sunday was good: I had been to Carol Mullen's[4] party the night before. It began at 10 and took place in a damp little cellar with a gas-stove in the corner. There was no drink: you had to bring your own so I cadged fluently the whole night. The place was full of Australians and Canadians and their wives: v.boring. It ended with breakfast at 6.30 – bacon and eggs and mushrooms and hot rolls. At 7.15 I left, slept till 10 and then got up to prepare for my own. We had fifteen bottles of gin and fifteen of white wine: it started at 2 and went on without a pause until 11.30. Michael Briggs[5] (who is nice but is <u>also</u> useless, which cancels <u>him</u> out) went to town with Sheila Zink.[6] Everyone discovered Ilsa <u>Echt</u>,[7] and Stanley[8] danced superbly with her. It got darker and mistier: lights trembling on the river: rows of people being <u>sick</u> into the river, especially George Babington,[9] who was sick three times. Beesley was hiding bottles of rum <u>everywhere</u>, and decided at 11 to climb into Somerville to sleep with Alison,[10] got spotted and had to fly for his life like a jackrabbit. Michael Murray-Leslie and Sheila K.[11] were so drunk that they danced with each other: Peebles[12] was so drunk that he <u>danced</u>. Seventeen gramophone records were broken, and my philology tutor[13] sang 'Yes sir that's my baby'. Stanley gave me a horrid tie hand-made by a Cornish navvy and Bidon[14] showed everyone the bites Peter King[15] had left on her shoulders (pretty husky stuff, this); and Ilsa was wonderful the whole time in hundreds of different ways – in French ways, in Italian ways, and for one wonderful moment, in Siamese ways. All v.gay, everyone said.

Still mad about you; still plotting like the entire Quai d'Orsay to carry you off somewhere soon, even if only to Shipton-under-Wychwood or Gravesend; still v.v. determined and with a lifetime to spare. Also, petite chum, increasingly serious: no time for comedy; I've got my teeth into your pants and I won't let go – that's a threat, or a promise, or a confirmation, or what you will. Don't even dare (will you) to go out of earshot again: put a telephone in the bathroom if there isn't one there already: and don't let's even talk about this again. César?[16]

Plans for 'Hamlet' move swiftly ahead – except that my second Gravedigger has just dropped out of the cast. Do you know any smallish, sleek, compact man who can do Cockney accents? Really urgent.

I'm writing this in bed too, stretching and yawning like a giant polecat and looking pretty silly. Soon I shall get up and have coffee with funny little Philip Warner[17] at the Playhouse, which is dull but vital. Then I shall lunch with Rees-Mogg:[18] dull but nice. Then I shall write about seventy letters about 'Hamlet': dull. But then: 'High Button Shoes'[19] and Oh! I wish you were here, just for general purposes.

Will you help me with 'Hamlet'? I mean, be around and contact people with me, and buy gin for me, and answer the telephone and be sweet? It's going to be indispensable: I like doing things together, especially things I like doing and <u>can</u> do. This could be fun, and more than fun.

I'll ring you on Friday evening, to arrange where to meet on

Saturday: I don't yet know what my timetable will be. Until then, go on thinking gay and hopeful thoughts about

Your astonishing
K

P.S. Erratum: p.1: for 'Dear Elly'
        <u>read</u> 'Darling Elly'
        (or 'Elly darling')

P.P.S. Damn well meet my train on Saturday. It's nice to be met: it gives <u>that lift</u>, and I need <u>that lift</u> and so do you. Purgatory must be much like Paddington: dim and enclosed, fuggy and full of people one's never met, waiting. Also sad.

[1] Glenn Miller (1904–44), American bandleader whose records included 'Moonlight Serenade', 'Little Brown Jug', and 'In the Mood'.

[2] Popular song written in 1913 by Chris Smith, lyrics by Jim Burris, first recorded in 1929 by the Louisiana Rhythm Kings.

[3] Al Jolson (1886–1950), Russian-born American singer and actor, star of early talking pictures such as *The Jazz Singer* (US, 1927).

[4] Mature undergraduate at Somerville College.

[5] Michael Briggs, an undergraduate at Merton College.

[6] Sheila Zinkin, an undergraduate at Somerville College.

[7] Undergraduate reading Modern Languages at St Hugh's College.

[8] Stanley Parker, a plump, epicene figure, the son of an Australian sheep farmer who lived on the fringe of university life and worked as a journalist and draughtsman. He had many contacts among the famous. KPT described him in *Cherwell* (14 June 1948), as 'an impulsive explorer of sunny moments', 'a Savoy Grill Falstaff', and later celebrated him in *He That Plays the King*.

[9] George Babington-Boselli was reading History at Wadham College.

[10] Alison Kershaw, an undergraduate at Somerville College.

[11] Sheila Kilner, not an undergraduate; she married Michael Murray-Leslie in 1950.

[12] The nickname of Baron Bernard von Friesen, a German undergraduate.

[13] J. A. W. Bennett was KPT's language tutor.

[14] The nickname of Corinne Hunt, not an undergraduate, who appeared in Sandy Wilson's three revues *High Broad and Corny* (June 1947), *Ritzy, Regal and Super* (February 1948), and *Oxford Circus* (September 1948), in all of which KPT appeared.

[15] Undergraduate at Oriel College whose father owned a chain of cinemas.

[16] César Cui (1835–1918), Russian composer of the opera *William Ratcliff* (1861), to whom Elly had introduced KPT.

[17] Undergraduate at Pembroke College studying French who had been a POW for three years.

[18] William Rees-Mogg (b.1928), undergraduate at Balliol College, later editor of *The Times* 1967–81, and created a life peer in 1988.

[19] 'Song and dandy show' (1947) by Stephen Longstreet, music by Jule Styne, lyrics by Sammy Cahn.

To Elly Horovitz

51 St J St
Oxford
Friday [? early July 1948]

Chère Ellington

Curious torpor has overcome me – but for a (to you) comperletely unexpected reason. A surfeit of partees, gay little partees. Ah you are I see jolly shaken. This is what has happened.

Last week, if you remember, twenty-three American girls pounced on Oxford like panthers. They are part of an experiment organised by a Philadelphia College to prove that travel broadens the mind, and instantly they return to N.Y. they are to be given an intelligence test for purposes of comparison with their previous rating. About Monday of this week they all decided to hero-worship me – I put on a little hysterical-youth act for them, which began it. They began buying back copies of Viewpoint[1] and Cherwell and Vogue and Ego 8, they visited me in dungareed battalions at the oddest times, and I replied by falling swoopstake and cropneck in love with them all, damn it, them <u>all</u>. They have wonderful names like Tresh and Paff and Smoke and Libby, and their libido is inexhaustible. There have been parties every night and most days since; on Wednesday Croucher[2] and I took some of them up for an aeroplane trip around Oxford, which cost the earth, but they loved it, and their quite spontaneous squeals, their wit, their clothes, their chocolate – and their cigarettes – made it quite de rigueur that we should give a party for them tonight, starting at midnight, in pyjamas. With twelve bottles of gin. For it is you see their last night in Oxford.

The one called Smoky (her picture was in the Mirror with Stanley [Parker]'s last week) wants me to go back to Connecticut with her.

Peebles is taking me to Portugal in his new Rolls-Royce in two weeks time – to live in a palace near Lisbon with Milo Cripps![3]

'Hamlet'[4] is moving along superbly. I am genuinely elated by it, and the constant presence of a dozen gaping American faces at every rehearsal spurred me on enormously. It now has glints, here and there, peeping through the text at roguish intervals, of a really spectacular brilliance, a true <u>shine</u>. And this leap ahead is due, I am sure, to the presence of an audience, and a sympathetic one at that.

Stratford. I have booked two seats for the performances on Monday 19th, Tuesday 20th, Wednesday 21st July. No Saturdays are possible (booked right up), and there are no seats anywhere before July 17th.

The plays are 'Troilus', 'Merchant of V' and 'Winter's Tale'. I now await your fiat about whether you want me to book two single rooms, two double rooms, or one double room at the Black Swan. Haste is of the utmost, for they book up v quickly.

By the way, try to see the Birmingham Rep modern dress version of 'The Rivals',[5] currently in London. I hear it really has that thing.

Elly.

Elly look.

Elly I.

Elly I want to marry you.

GOSH!

Quand même

K.

[1] *Oxford Viewpoint*, to which KPT had contributed in 1947 his reviews of Valk's *Othello*, Alec Guinness's *Richard II* and an 'Edinburgh Diary', along with two articles on tragedy called 'The Invincible Must' (all reprinted in edited form in *He That Plays the King*).

[2] Roger Croucher, a Magdalen undergraduate taken to court with KPT for letting off fireworks in St John's Street.

[3] An undergraduate at Corpus Christi reading Modern Languages, now Lord Parmoor.

[4] KPT's production for the Oxford University Players of the First Quarto text in eighteenth-century costume for the Cheltenham Festival (Civic Playhouse 7–14 August and in December at the Rudolf Steiner Hall in London). Peter Parker played Hamlet; Robert Hardy, Fortinbras; Lindsay Anderson, Horatio; and KPT, the Ghost.

[5] Sheridan's *The Rivals*, with Rosamond Burne and Ninian Brodie, directed by Willard Stoker, opened in London at the St James's in June 1948.

To Elly Horovitz

Betwn. Oxf. & Birmingham

About 10 p.m. Thursday [June/July 1948]

Elly Darling;

Sitting in a dirty train on a rainy track on a filthy night with dusty people, I write to you: it has been a long, shapeless day. I couldn't go home earlier, because I couldn't pay the train fare: I had to borrow it and that isn't easy after term. A big grey nostalgia crept over me: as Sheila or Denise[1] would understand, I felt a <u>stone</u>.

At lunch today I ran into Dylan Thomas, and Tony Schooling[2] took us back to his room and gave us Curaçao and gin, and Dylan talked disgustingly and grossly about tortures and hangings: and about a vile necrophilist mortuary attendant he had known called Jack Stiff. Then he became lyrical and spoke richly though thickly of his adolescence in Swansea: of a girl called Linda Slee whom he would caress in the Swansea sandpits: of how his mother suspected from the sand in his shoes and the sonnet in his pocket that he had been 'interfering' with some girl: and of how, for him, sand is now the symbol of guilt. All this was good. Then Alan Brien arrived, and the little Chinese Pim Sa'i, and Dylan said he would tell us an impromptu fable. 'Name any place in the world,' he said, 'and I will invent a tale to fit it.' 'Roumania' said Pim promptly. Dylan then told a tale of a peasant who had visions, which I have heard him tell of Moroccan peasants, of Spanish and of Finnish peasants. He is a great and moving mimic, especially talking about childhood; but he is too old, too disgustingly toadlike to be talking to undergraduates and toping in the middle of the afternoon. He depresses me beyond words. The man is a contented half-success and a disgruntled drunk at the same time. He is also very slow and inaudible.

(Ink run out: forgive the writing; it's the fault of this frightening train) [. . .]

(How I hate propelling pencils! little cracks come from inside, and the lead slides out, and you find yourself tearing the paper with the metal thing that pushes it up. I even prefer this awful stub.)

Opposite me is a picture of Tintern Abbey standing like a bay deer in the midst of a riverside meadow. In some such sequestered, forgiving place we must spend a delicious weekend v. soon: somewhere where we know we shan't meet anybody we know: somewhere where we cannot escape deciding that it's good to be together. I feel a sort of divine compassion for the whole human race when I'm with you – because they aren't with you.

Dilute all this by half if you like: it still means I'm pretty inescapably in love with you. Your move.

Ooh – we've stopped with a hell of a clanketty bonk. This seems to be Banbury: v.smelly (chicken & newspapers). Now there's no pencil left so [I'll] stop writing.

Love me a little in between times.

K.

[. . .][3]

---

[1] Denise Cremona, an undergraduate at Somerville College.
[2] Anthony Schooling, an older undergraduate at Pembroke.
[3] KPT saw less of Elly Horovitz during the vacation though they continued to be friends and met often in the Michaelmas term of 1948.

To Pauline Whittle

229 Portland Rd
July 22nd [1948]

Dear Paul,

Going briskly through an old cupboard yesterday, uprooting toy soldiers, contraceptives, evil-smelling sandwiches and bits of type-writers, I found a picture of a pouting plump thing with raving round calves and goodness if it wasn't you. So after a funny little p-ang I thought I'd better write and ask what you had been becoming in the last year. What brown and dingy digs house you now? And what are you having for breakfast? Yes, you'd better put Mrs Maconnachie's toast back in the rack and pay 'tention. (Just you put Mrs Maconnachie's toast down).

Now I've been thriving in strange, colourful ways – took a play of my own production to Paris, lived with Danny Kaye, written for 'Vogue', travelled with Duke Ellington, given parties in aeroplanes, married, divorced, drunk, sobered, laughed an awful lot, and wept twice. And now I'm doing a 'Hamlet' – read the hand-out I enclose – and think hard, little chum, whether you can't come and see it. (Write to me c/o Civic Playhouse, Cheltenham Spa). It promises to be gay-delightful, not to say big-powerful. And in September I'm doing a revue at the Playhouse, London.[1] At Christmas my Finals, and (I hope) a trip to California and Rio.

I wonder if you heard what happened to the Jill I deserted you for? We lived happily together until September, and then split disastrously and both nearly killed ourselves.[2] I then became engaged to a fashion model[3] – that ended in January. Now I'm taking a deep breath.

And how, after all, are you? I want to know. I want especially to know where you'll be between September 1st–10th; whether you're married; whether you like brilliant snobs with a vast breadth of human sym-pathies (that is what your bourgeois peacock has become); and whether you would be interested in corresponding with a young Englishman age 21 whose interests include reading, acting, talking, the Drama, the Film, cricket and can also speak colloquial French.

The people in Oxford who knew you still ask me urgently about you. There isn't a particle of you we don't know, remember, or want[4] – if you remember.

So write to me and let us meet and let us tell each other ripely and deliciously about all the good things that have happened to us since that meal in the International[5] sixteen months ago. (It was on the anniversary of that day that my production of 'Winterset' opened at the Comédie des Champs-Elysées).

At 10.45 a.m. this morning my father died.[6]

Ever

Ken

[1] *Oxford Circus*, produced by Sandy Wilson and performed on 26 September 1948. KPT's one-man 'Production Number', in which he played a camp director and parodied different acting styles, was deemed by the London critics the 'hit of the evening'.
[2] KPT may have thought of killing himself. Gillian Rowe-Dutton did not.
[3] Gillian Staynes, an undergraduate at St Anne's College. The engagement did not last long because Gillian 'couldn't marry a man who was first at a mirror before me'.
[4] 'There isn't a particle of you that I don't know, remember, and want': Noël Coward, *Private Lives*, Act I.
[5] The restaurant in Birmingham where KPT broke off his engagement to Pauline Whittle on 24 March 1947.
[6] Sir Peter Peacock died of uraemia, complicated by bronchitis, aged seventy-six. A few hours after his death his body was driven back to Warrington, to the family he had deserted a quarter of a century before. The town gave him a great civic funeral, but his wife buried him in the municipal cemetery without a headstone. Rose Tynan did not presume to attend the ceremony. For the first time KPT learnt that he was illegitimate. Thirty years later he told a journalist, 'I would have thought so much better of him if I had known.'

To Eileen Rabbinowitz[1]

229 Portland Road
[24 August 1948]

Dear Eileen,

Oh dear – you do take things so <u>spiritlessly</u>, so <u>seriously</u>. Learn to be dauntless, and to trample on the <u>minutiae</u> of deceit with a broad, arrogant grin, plus perhaps a slight wink. What the <u>hell</u> do they matter? If we're caught, I shall just giggle rather helplessly and that will be that. I shall then pose as the Shah of Persia for a whole glorious day and then flee for the coast, dragging my canoe behind me. I just haven't the time or the <u>ability</u> to take these things as solemnly as they ought to be taken. Nobody will make me believe that for a man and a maid to take a brief escape together is a business sombre enough to be worth one drop of sweat. So relax. [. . .]

Did you, by the way, receive an astonishingly sexy letter I wrote last Friday? Very long and self-absorbed it was. I <u>do</u> hope you got it. (You <u>did</u>, didn't you?)

How can I write as from Miss Hodges?[2] In the first place, she's dead drunk in the spare bedroom; in the second place, the postmark would be <u>Birmingham</u>. If you're sure this would pass unnoticed, I'll do it. Let me know by return.

I can of course meet the early train from London on Tuesday. It will involve you spending at least an hour or so unattended, because obviously I can't take you home to my place. But I'll be there; we'll lunch, we'll dine, & then I'll pop you into a cinema while I collect my luggage.

About the £5–5–0 (£6–15/-): I can lend it to you, but it will make life in Edinburgh difficult. I have no banking account,[3] you see, and it will have to come out of whatever I am allotted for Festival expenses. Anyway these expenses will be for one person only as far as my mother is concerned. So don't worry: you shall have it, no matter what.

About the rations problem.

There are two alternatives:

1) Either: we arrive at the Food Office[4] in Edinburgh telling them we've come for the Festival but don't yet know where we'll be staying – probably with friends. When we give them our ration books, yours has a big ink stain over the name, obliterating it completely. You give it as Tynan when asked. Difference in addresses is easy: we were separated, & have now come together.

2) Simpler still: we give our ration books to the Hotel with your name obliterated by ink.

Remember: they have no desire to throw us out on moral grounds. As long as we don't <u>advertise</u> our unmarriedness, they couldn't care less. The subterfuges of name-altering, etc, are just a polite fiction which has become a convention. The hotel isn't interested in our private affairs, it merely wants a show of decorum, to save its and our face. See? Bungler.

Ever,
K.

Write me a happy letter, blast you.

---

[1] A good-looking undergraduate reading French at St Anne's; the daughter of a rabbi.
[2] KPT's pseudonym, presumably used on envelopes for the benefit of Eileen's parents.
[3] KPT received £20 a fortnight in cash from his mother and extra on special demand.
[4] There were about 1,300 local food offices nationwide, responsible for the control of food rationing.

To Hugh Manning

229 Portland Rd
Monday [September 1948]

Dear Hugh,

What I meant about Alan Dent was that I had heard that you were suing him for using our 'Hamlet' text on the film. Seriously. Particularly the absence of Rosencrantz and Guildenstern.[1]

My Cheltenham Hamlet was a triumphant success. We played 9 performances to packed and roaring houses, & took more than twice as much money as any other company has made there. Donald Wolfit came up from town to the first night and wrote a review for the local press.[2] He thought me 'uncannily sensitive'. Paul Scofield[3] came on Monday; John Byron[4] and Frank Shelley[5] later in the week – Laurence Gilliam[6] was sent by Midland Regional to cover it – and the Third Programme[7] sent E.J. King-Bull.[8] I am satisfied that this is the most original production of 'Hamlet' ever performed, and easily the most mature work I have done. We were invited to take it on tour to Sweden during the Christmas vac, & have accepted.

All the stage people who came suggested constantly that we should try to put it on at the Fortune, the Lindsey or the Arts.[9] I have, however, very few contacts there. What is this you write about the New Lindsey? Of course I'd like to produce anywhere. But especially there: it is right in my territory, the province I know I can conquer.

I may be in London next weekend to see Harding of the Third Programme. When can I meet you? to talk, & go further?

Ever,
Ken

---

[1] Alan Holmes ('Jock') Dent (1905–78), author, critic and journalist, textual editor of Olivier's Shakespeare films. According to JH and KPT, he stole their idea of removing Rosencrantz and Guildenstern from the text of their 1945 *Hamlet* for Olivier's film (UK, 1948).
[2] In the *Cheltenham Echo*: 'Mr Tynan's production invites criticism on the highest level and should be judged as such, for it is a solid achievement.'
[3] Paul Scofield (b. 1922), English actor who had recently made his reputation at the Shakespeare Memorial Theatre, Stratford (1946–8). He won an Academy Award for his portrayal of Sir Thomas More in the film version of *A Man for All Seasons* (UK, 1966), and played Salieri in the original National Theatre production of Peter Shaffer's *Amadeus* (1979).
[4] Originally a ballet dancer, John Byron was an actor at the Oxford Playhouse 1941–5. He had played Hamlet at Stratford in 1944 (see letter of 26 April 1944).
[5] Leading actor and director at the Oxford Playhouse 1945–54.

[6] Nicknamed Lorenzo the Magnificent, he was BBC Radio Head of Features for 18 years until his death in 1964.

[7] Launched in 1946, the precursor of Radio 3.

[8] Edward King-Bull, a producer in the BBC Drama Department.

[9] London theatres.

CHAPTER THREE

The Boy Wonder

Now cast as the next *enfant terrible* of the English theatre Ken signed, in February 1949, a contract with Longman's for a book on drama. He then set off promptly for the provinces to run the David Garrick Theatre at Lichfield in Staffordshire.

In Lichfield Ken had an affair with a *Junoesque* actress called Patricia Brewer, to whom he proposed. Miss Brewer knew there was another woman, and that 'the moment you left him you were out of his mind'. Once returned to London, Ken sang and danced at an audition for the Windmill Theatre's semi-nude revue, and was told he was much too homosexual for their audience. He directed an Expressionist play called A Man of the World at the Lyric Hammersmith, with Roger Livesey and a seventeen-year-old J. Arthur Rank starlet called Diana Dors (Peter Brook described the production as 'a bit of Kafka, a shadow of Orson Welles, a flavour of French films'). He planned a production of Picasso's Desire Caught by the Tail, and a Macbeth with Peter Ustinov. He scripted a life of the jazz trumpeter Bix Beiderbecke for television, and co-adapted Antony and Cleopatra and Stella Gibbons' Cold Comfort Farm, and he frequented the little theatre clubs which were free of the censorship imposed by the Lord Chamberlain on the mainstream.

At the beautiful nineteenth-century Bedford theatre in Camden Town, north London, Ken directed the Victorian melodrama The Bells, with Frederick Valk playing the part Irving had made famous. In June of 1950, he joined a student festival at Salzburg to play the lead in e.e. cummings' him. Back in England he directed an Arts Council production of Othello and was complimented by Tyrone Guthrie for his 'technical and imaginative brilliance'.

In the autumn of that year, He That Plays the King, his collection of reviews and essays with an introduction by Orson Welles, was published, and reviewers pronounced the author comparable to Hazlitt and Shaw. Quite soon after, in a series of essays, speeches and radio broadcasts, Ken further explored his theory of dramatic aesthetics and the role of the critic. How did a particular entertainment strike a unique mind on one particular evening? A critic, he declared, should write for posterity. Powerfully affected by the plays of Arthur Miller and Tennessee Williams, which he saw in New York in the early 1950s, *this advocate of heroic acting and art for art's sake radically altered his position. The recipe for drama, he announced, was self-knowledge through desperation as practised by ordinary people, and not exclusively by heroes.*

Late in December of 1950 at a small theatre club called the Buckstone (the cockpit of the young theatre world), a petite American actress called Elaine Dundy, with round brown eyes and a pretty figure, had approached Ken to say she admired He That Plays the King. *He asked her out to lunch. They discovered that they both liked the Marx Brothers and W.C. Fields; they fell in love and took off together for Paris. Ken told her: 'I'm the illegitimate son of Sir Peter Peacock . . . I will either kill myself or die at the age of thirty, because I will have said everything there is to say. Will you marry me?' Married they were on 25 January 1951. But Ken's correspondence tells us little about the relationship.*

Nor do the letters tell us anything about the watershed in Ken's work life: he had been contracted to direct Cocteau's Les Parents Terribles *at the Arts Theatre, with the grande dame Fay Compton in the lead. After several rehearsals, Miss Compton announced that she had no confidence in her young director and had him fired. So humiliated was he that he felt he no longer had a future as a director. He claimed, years later, that this traumatic event changed the course of his life, and made him an observer rather than a participant. Yet on the evidence, he was already well established as a critic and journalist in 1950.*

Between the beginning of 1951 and the end of 1953, he wrote hundreds of thousands of words for magazines like the Spectator, Sight and Sound, Lilliput, Panorama, Bandwagon, Punch; *and the American* Harper's Bazaar, *the* New York Times *and* Mademoiselle.

During the early years of the 1950s this worshipper of talent formed friendships with Marlene Dietrich, Richard Burton, John Huston, Noël Coward, Laurence Olivier (a barbed friendship because Tynan had cruelly attacked the performances of Olivier's wife Vivien Leigh), Katharine Hepburn, Gene Kelly and Tennessee Williams.

The star trekker was now a star himself, dubbed in the press 'the new Bernard Shaw – albeit Shaw in fake leopard-skin trousers'. His reviews were read and quoted. 'They're wonderful,' John Gielgud would say, 'when it isn't you.' On 5 September Ken's first theatre review as resident critic of the Observer *appeared, and a golden period of brilliant writing ensued. As a critic Ken wrote about what was missing in the theatre and what was wrong with it, like the 'glibly codified fairytale world' of the country-house play, and of the cultural apathy of Britain – a country 'fearful of bad taste, obsessed by the monarchy and the past'.*

When the theatrical breakthrough did come in 1956, he championed the

English Stage Company, home of the new playwrights John Osborne, N. F. Simpson, Arnold Wesker and John Arden. In their work he found a mistrust of authority coupled with a 'passionate respect for the sanctity of the individual'.

He also wrote admiringly of Bertolt Brecht's craft, while he became a convert to Brecht's socialism. He defended the propaganda play – the theatre of 'parable, polemic and pamphlet'. Almost always he had a strong enough sense of the uniqueness of a theatrical experience not to overload it with ideology. He praised the work of Samuel Beckett and Eugene Ionesco (with reservations), and he wrote enthusiastically about Joan Littlewood's Theatre Workshop. He reserved his loudest cheers for the plays in which 'man among men, not man against man, is the well-spring of tragedy'.

The frenzied, fevered activity reflected in his letters gives no view of the inner life nor the self-doubts Ken confessed to his diary, and few revelations about the crises in his marriage. By 1953 he had begun the first of a number of affairs. In July 1957 he was in Spain with Carol Marcus Saroyan, a porcelain beauty and faux naif wit whom he particularly loved. One night as he and Carol lay talking in the dark, she said, 'Someone burly came in.' Ken shot up like a bolt, and the burly person said, 'I'm sorry, but I'm Mr Sullivan representing Mrs Tynan.' So ended the romance. Years later Tynan recorded the event in his journal and added, 'And so I went back to seven more years of the inferno with Elaine.'

To Elly Horovitz

62A Marlborough Place
NW8[1]
February 12th [1949]

Elly darling –

Thanks for the wire, which I've been living off since Thursday.

Here things are a bit melancholy; everything is grey-green, rain or fine, and Beate[2] has taken to giggling at the least little thing anybody says or does, and has almost become trying and dull. My odd little room is now fully furnished with Gothic bookcase, typewriter (new and smooth) and furry carpet; I have written a little, and seen one or two dull but important chaps. All else fails. Last night Cropper[3] gave a house-warming which was about as warm as yesterday's potatoes – no dancing, no sex, no noise, just a frigid, posed group of relatives and friends of the late Miss Cropper. I was screamingly bored and casual – the drink was cyder cup, and you know how near the sewer that can get – and at one stage I remember sidling up to one of the hostesses and saying very confidentially: 'If we sneak away now, my chicken, I know where there's a real party.' She will never speak to me again; I must have been a leetle beet tight to do that. Alan [Beesley] and Marie were there, the latter frailly beautiful in red and black and gold, Alan rampaging around full of impotent fury – he, by the way, has had the very good moneymaking idea of starting a nappy service in Oxford, where there isn't one. He has lately turned inventor: he has invented the mousetrap, the wheel, the hat for the head, a Perspex rain-deflector for small bicycles, and a sort of shootingstick that turns into an umbrella that turns into a harpoon. I can't imagine, off-hand, what sort of situation one would have to be in to want the last thing. A chap resting on a whale on a rainy day might conceivably need it, but not many other chaps. Tony Schooling, sniggering and shaking, coiled his neck around the door; Anne Davis bubbled over, the frothy thing; Peter Kneebone, very depressed and nervous at having lost Jill Williams,[4] rolled his eyes like Al Jolson and struck off into the night; a girl in a toga with at least seventeen breasts was punctured by a lovely Regency quill; and there were no queers present. I said get you queer[5] several times, but you must be right. It isn't very funny.

I went to Gainsborough Studios[6] the other day, and was shown over the place by Vivian Cox,[7] Associate Producer (so called because they're the only men who will associate with producers) and fat, limping Sidney Box.[8] I met Yolande Donlan,[9] blonde, shinylipped and vivacious as cornfield in April, Googie Withers,[10] a bit underbusted and over-bottomed but very nice, John McCallum,[11] Edward Rigby,[12] Petula Clarke[13] [*sic*] and Richard Hearne.[14] I also met The Man Who Gave You Madonna of the Seven Moons.[15] He looks ill. They were shooting 'Traveller's Joy', 'Don't Ever Leave Me', and 'Helter Skelter'.[16] I also met the chief Master Plasterer of the studios, who had just gone on strike, and had a drink with him and got masterly plastered. He said he thought MGM were wonderful because their figured scrollwork was so f—ing good. It's a new angle.

Apart from these things, nothing except books. Oh, and a film. Alan and I wanted to see 'The Street with no Name'[17] because Richard Widmark[18] is in it – the man with the hellbent snicker who was in 'Kiss of Death'. Apparently there's a scene in it where a machinegunned man literally flies to pieces in the street, like the aeroplane in the Battle of Britain film. There was a queue. We tried the Everyman Hampstead (nostalgia here: pause); where they were showing D W Griffith's astounding 'Intolerance',[19] which is silent, lasts three hours, and had a cast of twenty-two thousand. Queue. So we prowled back to Tottenham

Court Road and saw an old Bob Hope film. I should never have wasted time thus in Oxford. It is profoundly humiliating.

Which brings us I suppose to you.

Ah, hell. I love you, fat girl, forsaking all others. Dreaming last night, I was in America, stopping off at St. Louis, with ten thousand dollars, and a great deal of sunshine and happiness to plunge into. I went to a wonderful zany boardinghouse where they loved me and poured beer down my neck. I assisted ten thousand gallant negroes in hanging one murderous white man. I was shown the statue of Liberty, mysteriously moved from N.Y. to the Mississippi. It was, as I should have guessed, you. You were misty at the top, being so huge, you understand, and I could hardly make out what kind of torch you were bearing. For a moment the sun cut through, and foolishly I had a vision that it was a pingpong bat. I was probably mistaken.

So, after all, and all things considered, and bearing in mind the immense difficulties under which, and not forgetting the strain imposed by, and notwithstanding the – er – grimness of the – er – struggle, and with all thanks to Agents and Managers and God, and in spite of, and although, and albeit, – nevertheless, I love you now and for a century. Sexy pig.

I am coming up for the OUDS first-night. I am trying to get two seats, so be free, little one.

Quand même,
K.

A man at Ruth's party actually mentioned Cui.[20] I nearly wept.

---

[1] KPT had moved to 62A Marlborough Place, where he lived on and off for a year and a half.

[2] Beate von Schey, young Austrian landlady with whom KPT had a brief affair.

[3] Ruth Cropper, Oxford PPE graduate to whom KPT became briefly engaged in 1947.

[4] Anne Davis, Peter Kneebone, Jill Williams: Oxford friends and contemporaries of KPT. Kneebone was a cartoonist and illustrator with whom KPT collaborated on a book about Oxford, to be called 'Now At Last Demolished'. It was commissioned by Longman's but never written.

[5] A catchphrase of the time.

[6] Gainsborough Pictures, founded in 1928, was famous for its costume dramas.

[7] Vivian Cox (b. 1915), British producer, notably of *Father Brown* (UK, 1954) and *The Prisoner* (UK, 1954), both with Alec Guinness.

[8] Sidney Box (1907–83), British film producer and head of Gainsborough Pictures 1946–50; with his wife Muriel he won an Academy Award for the script of *The Seventh Veil* (UK, 1945).

[9] Yolande Donlan (b.1920), American actress and wife of the director Val Guest who starred in British films of the 1950s such as *Miss Pilgrim's Progress* (UK, 1950).

[10] Googie Withers (b.1917), English stage and film actress.

[11] John McCallum (b.1918), Australian actor and director; in 1948 he married Googie Withers,

with whom he starred in *It Always Rains on Sunday* (UK, 1947) and *The Loves of Joanna Godden* (UK, 1947).

[12] Edward Rigby (1879–1951), English character actor specializing in North Country parts.

[13] Petula Clark (b.1932), English child singing star who went on to play leading roles in musicals such as *Finian's Rainbow* (US, 1968) and *Goodbye Mr Chips* (UK, 1969).

[14] Richard Hearne (1909–79), English television and variety actor who created the character 'Mr Pastry'.

[15] English director Arthur Crabtree, whose film *Madonna of the Seven Moons* (UK, 1944) starred Stewart Granger and Phyllis Calvert.

[16] *Traveller's Joy* (UK, 1949), *Don't Ever Leave Me* (UK, 1949), *Helter Skelter* (UK, 1949): light comedies.

[17] *The Street with No Name* (US, 1948), thriller about an undercover FBI agent, directed by William Keighley.

[18] Richard Widmark (b.1914), American actor who made an Oscar-nominated film debut in Henry Hathaway's thriller *Kiss of Death* (US, 1947) and went on to star in many Hollywood Westerns of the 1950s and 1960s.

[19] US, 1916.

[20] The composer's name obviously reminded KPT of his romance with Elly Horovitz the previous year.

To Harry James

The David Garrick Theatre
Lichfield, Staffs.[1]
17th August 1949

Dear Harry;

I may be going to be very rude.

To begin with: I admit, buoyantly, to owing you £6–2–5d. But I will not honour the debt, though I can afford it, because I hold (and shall continue to hold in the courts) that you are not the same person who lent it to me. The style in which you write to me confounds and bemuses me. Arnold Bennett[2] called it the 'middle-aged cryptic', and wasn't really wrong. Instead of becoming a <u>nice</u> uncle (which was what I expected), you've become a <u>nasty</u> one. You see, I am now in a profession where one pays attention only to people with <u>proven skills</u>, with special, finely-trained talents and energies: I have been so busy trying to prove my own that I tend to be dilatory about replying to people whose skills I have either forgotten or not had recent proof of. This is all an oblique way of saying that I haven't time for what you said of 'Present Laughter',[3] and that when I pay you the £6–2–5 it will be in the form of a strange and possibly embarrassing present: if I can find an armadillo costing £6–2–5, it shall be yours. Or a rubber dinghy would do. Or some ashphalt.

In fact, I am refusing to pay you because you have been unpleasant to me: the Lichfield Khan is outraged, and has been pinked when he neither desired it nor was prepared for it, and this warrior child's wrath is torrid. If you'd like to take me to law (and it might be fun), I should do my utmost to savage you.

About 'P. Laughter'. In twenty weeks here I have been responsible for twenty productions: and that means engagement of artistes, publicity, lighting plots, property and costume plots, as well as direction of artistes, (I have no secretary). I soon realized that the only plan which would serve me would be to do two goodish productions, one bad production, and one good production each month (Next month we do 'Pygmalion',[4] 'The Taming of the Shrew', and 'Private Lives' in successive weeks, and the week before 'Pygmalion' comes 'Six Characters in Search of an Author'): you saw a bad production. This week we are rehearsing 'Portrait in Black'[5] in the morning, 'Six Characters' in the afternoon, and playing 'The Girl Who Couldn't Quite'[6] in the evening: we put on plays with an average of 18 hours rehearsal, and we nearly starve doing it.

The first thing one looks for in a weekly rep actor is his ability to learn lines quickly. That qualification romps away with the field: a photographic memory puts a man way ahead of his rivals: there is no photo-finish. My error has been engaging people who weren't accustomed to weekly; because I daren't admit to myself the over-riding importance of this knack: I now, with infinite regret and reluctance, turn away excellent players because they just cannot learn and remember – fine, flexible, versatile people who won't and can't stuff a part down their throats in five or six rehearsals.

'Present Laughter' was a fair example of a potentially fair cast who couldn't learn: and you must know (or remember) how easily a whole act can be wrecked by one hot neck under one sweaty collar because of one bad fluff. (Naturally the girl playing Joanna has been fired: she was intolerably bad.) Weekly rep is the Golgotha of drama, the final resting-place of those who have lost everything except their gift of memorising lines: and when we did 'P.L.' I had not yet reconciled myself to the graveyard. I have now. (Unless of course one can afford to pay one's actors up to £15–£20 a week, and we can't.)

If I can do one good or striking production every four weeks (and I have), I am deliriously happy. And any rep. producer will tell you the same, and be right where you are (I'm afraid) ignorantly wrong.

Finally: about the business in 'P. L.'. Coward insists, in the acting edition, that all business should be exactly as printed in the stage directions, without any additions or subtractions: and he must receive written notice of any proposed alterations. I was not merely using a hazy memory to mimic the Haymarket production, I was obeying instructions.

Why not stop over on the way to Edinburgh next week and see 'Six Characters'? [...]

If you buy your 'Illustrated'[7] you will see that I haven't kept my big mouth all that tightly shut.

Yours,
Ken

P.S. I am amusing myself by predicting the tone of your reply to this. I imagine it will be (a) super-elderly (b) flecked with amiable smiles (c) full of the nice things you're seeing in Edinburgh (it will take you some time to get round to it) and (d) with an AWFUL little nip in the last sentence – gnat-like.

Over to you.
K

---

[1] KPT's first production as resident director of the David Garrick Theatre at Lichfield in Staffordshire was J. B. Priestley's *The Linden Tree* (4 April 1949). After twenty-three further productions in twenty-three weeks, he announced: 'I now pretend to know only sixty per cent of what there is to know.'

[2] Arnold Bennett (1867–1931), popular English novelist of the late Victorian and Edwardian period.

[3] James had written in his letter of 16 June 1949 that the Tynan production of Noël Coward's 1942 play at Lichfield (which opened the week of 4 July) was 'the first piece of slipshod work I've ever seen from you in any sphere'.

[4] By George Bernard Shaw (1913); later the basis for the musical *My Fair Lady*.

[5] By Ivan Goff and Ben Roberts (1946).

[6] By Leo Marks (1947).

[7] In a short article about KPT's production of George Farquhar's *The Beaux' Stratagem* (1707), in which actors were dressed in costumes of different periods (Lichfield All-Sorts, the *Illustrated*, 9 July 1949), KPT was quoted as calling the concurrent West End production 'well-behaved'. In response, John Clements, its director and star, while admitting he had not seen the Lichfield production, wrote: 'If one gives a child a piece of Dresden china one must not be surprised if he covers it in garish paint' (*Illustrated*, 30 July 1949). Ken retaliated with a spirited defence of his own production (*Illustrated*, 20 August 1949).

To Pat Brewer[1]

as from
62A Marlborough Place
Wednesday [? October 1949]

Pat Darling;

I think we have been right all the time. This is very real and I am missing you very much: wee things like your snarl and the smell of your neck and your gurgle and the bat-eyed gleam behind the glasses. I am now formally and (I take it) irrevocably in love with you and in your power, and for this and a multitude more reasons, I should like to marry you as soon as it can decently be arranged.

Gosh.

Now to me: since I left you I have been to Bromley[2] (who want me to produce for them in 4 weeks' time, but their plays are chosen by a council of five, of whom I should <u>not</u> be one, and who have picked such gay little opuses as 'Devonshire Cream', 'September Tide', and 'It's a Boy!',[3] for me to do. <u>Not</u> so hot); I have been to Greenwich with Tom Latham[4] and in a very reserved and god-almighty manner I have <u>surveyed</u> a theatre. Tom investigated the gallery and put his foot through into the circle, so we left.[5] He took me to a display of fluorescent lighting at the Albert Hall, where I met an impudent small tart who turned out to be that nice Jean Kent[6] (v. rich). I have been invited to produce at the Tavistock Little Theatre by the Arts Council;[7] which is fine except that it's an amateur company; and best of all I have been <u>hotly pressed</u> to invest in and produce for the new company at the Royal Bedford Theatre, Camden Town.[8] (I have stipulated that I will only produce for them if I can have Karloff[9] & Peter Lorre in the same cast – AND they agreed, and are 'phoning Karloff's agents, M.C.A., tomorrow.) I dined with Jack Thursfield[10] & Hermione Baddeley on Monday: it was v. dull, Baddeley smoking huge cigars and bleating & moaning about [Hermione] Gingold the whole time. She calls her 'mother'. Jack happened to say that he liked Diana Allen's[11] toes, and Baddeley instantly whipped off shoes and stockings and yelled 'WHAT ABOUT THESE? They're the only things I've got that COULDN'T be false.' Finally, at lunch today my paranoiac 'Everybody's'[12] friend asked me to do a 2000 word article on Sharman Douglas.[13] I am ringing her tomorrow to ask her permission.

Tonight I went to the Palladium: Ink Spots dull:[14] <u>operatic</u> and not nearly as darkly intimate as one had supposed.

Florence Desmond[15] <u>really</u> tedious: haggard, hoarse, and finally reduced to impersonating Danny Kaye (so badly) and even Jane Wyman in 'Johnny Belinda'.[16] Two good things on the bill: Johnny Pules, the tiny aggressive clown in Borrah Minevitch's Harmonica Rascals,[17] and (best) a new comedian called Arthur English[18] (ARTHUR ENGLISH), who is the funniest thing I have seen since Sid Field.[19] He is as good as Field's Slasher Greene [*sic*] and Nigel Patrick's[20] Bar Gorman rolled into one, and more. He has my big eye on him.

Met a charming whore outside the Palladium. She asked me to come home with her to Holborn Viaduct; I rounded on her with 'What's your name, girl?' 'Shirley' she said with a big shy grin. 'How old are you?' 'Seventeen' 'Why are you in this business?' 'Well – it's my birthday in two weeks' time and I always do it just before my birthday so as to buy myself a present.'

This was too good, so I gave her ten bob, put her in a taxi and told it not to stop until it got to Holborn Viaduct. I walked home feeling jolly pleased.

Now – what about Oxford?

And – send my ration book to the address above: I'll be there on Friday. And could you forward any letters that come for me to the same address?

Kiss all of yourself that you can reach for me, and gently pat the rest.

Immediate: can you come to London this weekend arriving Sunday & leaving Tuesday morning?

Answer all these queries, do everything I say, and love me absolutely.

And so, dear heart–
Ken

[1] KPT's lead actress at Lichfield and girlfriend; she later married the actor Patrick Feeney.
[2] A south London suburb, home of the New Theatre. The original theatre (now replaced and renamed the Churchill) had previously been a swimming pool, and the white tiling was still visible in places.
[3] *Devonshire Cream* (1925), by Eden Phillpott. *September Tide* (1948), by Daphne du Maurier. *It's a Boy!* (1930), by Austin Melford.
[4] Untraced.
[5] A cinema, which at the time was being used as a warehouse.
[6] Jean Kent (b. 1921), British actress in films of the 1940s and 1950s such as *Fanny by Gaslight* (UK, 1944).
[7] In an annual Arts Council report for 1950–51, the Tavistock and District Society of Arts (Devon) is listed as providing venues for Arts Council managed tours and the Tavistock Little Theatre may well have been offered to KPT for his autumn 1950 tour of *Othello*.
[8] KPT invested with Pat Nye and John Penrose in the formation of a new theatre company at the Royal Bedford Theatre, Camden, north London. He was offered several plays in return for a huge investment of £2,000 provided by Rose Tynan and a male relative, most probably George

Peacock. There KPT directed *Craven House* by Diana Hamilton (adapted from the 1946 novel by Patrick Hamilton) in March 1950 and Leopold Lewis's *The Bells* (1872) with Frederick Valk in May 1950.

[9] Boris Karloff (1887–1969), English actor famous for horror movies such as *Frankenstein* (US, 1931).

[10] Untraced.

[11] An actress who appeared in two plays in London, *The Platinum Set* (1950) and *Who is Sylvia?* (1950).

[12] *Everybody's*, an illustrated weekly magazine, which would close in 1959.

[13] Socialite daughter of the then American Ambassador Lewis W. Douglas.

[14] American vocal group of the 1940s whose hits included 'If I Didn't Care' and 'Whispering Grass'.

[15] Florence Desmond (1905–93), English actress and impersonator.

[16] Jane Wyman (b.1914), American actress who won an Oscar for her performance in Jean Negulesco's *Johnny Belinda* (US, 1948); the first wife of Ronald Reagan.

[17] Borrah Minevitch (1904–55), Russian-American musician; the *Harmonica Rascals* featured in a number of 1930s' musicals including *One in a Million* (1936) and *Rascals* (1938).

[18] Arthur English (b. 1919), English comedian and ventriloquist.

[19] Sid Field (b. 1904), great English comic whose Slasher Green character KPT described in 'Five Eccentrics' (in *He That Plays the King*): the sketch 'involved his wearing a vastly beshouldered overcoat, a pencilled moustache and all the wily self-confidence of the local boy cutting a shady dash in the city'.

[20] Nigel Patrick (1913–81), English stage actor (*Present Laughter*, 1965, which he also directed); his films include *Spring in Park Lane* (UK, 1947) and *The League of Gentlemen* (UK, 1960).

'To Ronald Lewin'

62a Marlborough Place
[? May 1950]

Dear Mr Lewin;

I spoke to Frank Hauser' last week on the question of Third Programme talks, and he suggested I should write to you.

In the early autumn Longman's are publishing a book of mine on the theatre, called 'He That Plays the King':[3] it has to do with heroic acting and heroic plays. I wondered if there would be any possibility of my doing a Third Programme talk around the subject any time during the summer. I'm pretty consistently busy producing plays, and for the month of June I shall be in Salzburg,[4] but if you think it's worth talking about, please let us meet.

[...]

Yours sincerely,
Ken Tynan

[1] Ronald Lewin, organizer of talks for the Third Programme, and later a distinguished military historian. KPT subsequently met him and wrote a script, 'Styles and Producers', in which he argued that the English lacked a Diaghilev and Stanislavsky and proselytized for style nourished 'by absolute standards of aesthetics'. The talk was scheduled for 21 September but when KPT recorded with his pronounced stutter it was described in a BBC report as 'sometimes painful to listen to'. The talk was eventually read by Alvar Liddell.

[2] An Oxford contemporary who had become a BBC producer and theatre director.

[3] Published in October 1950.

[4] KPT was the lead in e.e. cummings' *him*, performed by an amateur company under the direction of the theatre critic Eric Bentley (b. 1916) at an eighteenth-century castle once owned by Max Reinhardt.

To the Editor, *Picture Post*[1]

[19] Upper Berkeley Street
London W.1[2]
[Published 16 December 1950]

Mr. Robert Kee's article ('Eternal Oxford', Nov. 25)[3] must surely have enraged a number of good people. Against their fury, I can only set my own reaction, one of opiate contentment. To begin with, he describes me as a legend, when I was beginning to think of myself as an exploded myth. The years between 1945 and 1948, which I spent at Oxford, were a superb parenthesis in my life and, like all the best parentheses, they mean more than all the rest of the sentence: e.g., 'Patriotism, social service, technological progress and godliness are (except for *living*) the most important activities of mankind.' Oxford, after the last war ended, was a mingling of two camps – bitter, excitable, buccaneering ex-Servicemen, and zany schoolboys like myself. Or, at least, my Oxford was: there were several thousand other people in the university whom I never met. Some of them, I believe, have since done quite good work.

But it was a trance – a full-time, high-pressure, blood-bustling trance: a drug that made you radiantly aware of everything except the laws of economics; an unpredictable anaesthetic under whose influence one made canoe-trips through sewers, overnight hops to Portugal, and friends. Oxford invites all kinds of excess, intellectual or sensual; yet it counters them with all kinds of reverend limitations. It welcomes the men who are willing to go to every extreme and make fools of themselves; but it tells them, with an asperity greater than they will ever find outside its walls, precisely how foolish they looked. Oxford has only to raise an eyebrow, a humane, witty, absurdly learned eyebrow, to puncture the hugest egotist. While you are there, you fear Oxford as much as you love it. In my three years (seventy-two weeks of term), I find that I was invited to just under three hundred parties: but against that, I had to write (apart from specialised research work and examinations) a six-thousand-word essay every week for my tutor; which means that I had written, after nine terms, the equivalent of five full-length books. (Some people were called upon to write twice as much.) Add to that the o.u.d.s., the Union, the theatre clubs, the political clubs, the magazines to be edited, the people to be met – and you have a rare and considerable maelstrom.

You can, of course, relax. It is easy to do that, because all one's friends are within a stone's-throw, and at Oxford no doors are ever locked (or *hardly* ever). But you relax guiltily, because there are always ninety other things, also within a stone's-throw, which you might be, and ought to be, doing. The keen east wind which blows across Siberia to Cambridge is unknown in Oxford – the wind which sharpens Cambridge wits, lowers Cambridge voices by an octave, and can change the Oxford stroll to the Cambridge stride, the Oxford giggle to the Cambridge belly-laugh, the Oxford flannel to the Cambridge tweed, the Oxford quiz to the Cambridge stare.

Oxford, since the last war, has been nothing like Beverley Nichols' Oxford[4] after the 1914–18 war, which hankered after vanished Edwardian dignity, laughed at Freud and Cubism, and got excited if a party went on after eleven o'clock. Oxford, in my time, was fast, piratical and quite clever, rarely reckless, drunk or heavily in debt. It was the safe place in which to put away my youth. I have not since been able to find it again; and it is a tribute to Oxford's maturing influences that I have not often wanted to look.

Ken Tynan

[1] Published under the headline 'One Man's Oxford: a letter from a legend'.
[2] KPT had moved in the late autumn.
[3] Robert Kee (b. 1919), English broadcaster and author of books including *The Green Flag* (1972) and *The World We Left Behind* (1984). In 'Eternal Oxford' Kee wrote: 'The only postwar name to have become a legend is Kenneth Tynan and he still dominates the scene today.'
[4] In *Patchwork* (1921), his second novel, a thinly veiled account of his time at Oxford, and *Twenty-Five* (1926), an early autobiography.

[Christmas 1950]

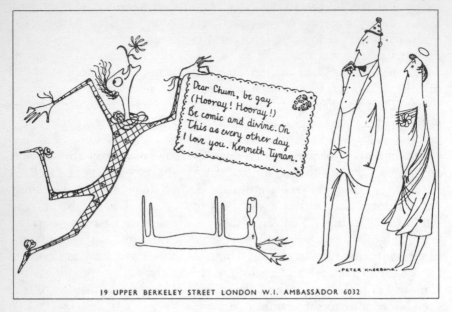

Dear Chum, be gay
(Hooray! Hooray!)
Be comic and divine. On
This as every other day
I love you. Kenneth Tynan.

19 UPPER BERKELEY STREET LONDON W.I. AMBASSADOR 6032

To the Editor, the *Evening Standard*

Upper Berkeley Street
[Published 22 May 1951]

Last week your Mr. Beverley Baxter[1] wrote gruffly of my brief appearance in Alec Guinness's Hamlet,[2] 'His performance is quite dreadful.'

Mr. Baxter had every excuse for feeling quarrelsome. That very morning he had received a new magazine called Panorama, more than half of which was taken up by a gigantic pseudonymous attack on almost every practising drama critic.[3] Of himself and a colleague he had read: 'They are the awful people one overhears in the interval, additionally sinister because one knows the commonplaces they utter will appear in print shortly in the — and Evening Standard.'

There was also a good deal about 'the Intimate Confessions style of their writing', and phrases like 'Mr Baxter's merciless volubility'.

Naturally he felt gloomy after all this. And, spotting that I am Panorama's dramatic critic, and recalling, perhaps, that I attacked contemporary criticism in a book published last year, he might have leapt to the conclusion that I wrote it.

I am afraid that I didn't. But I am quite a good enough critic to know that my performance in Hamlet is not 'quite dreadful': it is, in fact, only slightly less than mediocre. I do not actually exit through the scenery or wave at friends in the audience.

Ken Tynan

---

[1] Sir (Arthur) Beverley Baxter (1891–1964), drama critic of the London *Evening Standard* from 1943; also Conservative MP for Wood Green 1935–50.
[2] KPT played the Player King in the Alec Guinness Frank Hauser co-production which opened on 17 May 1951 at the New Theatre, London. The disastrous first night, in which the lighting system switched on and off as if handled by Frankenstein in an electrical storm, and KPT's giant phosphorescent ear glowed in the dark, has become part of theatre legend.
[3] By Gavin Lambert.

To Joan Miller[1]

19 Upper Berkeley St.
10th June, 1951

Dear Miss Miller,

Taking your first curtain call after the last performance of 'Peep-show' on Sunday night, you may have heard a pretty hysterical voice roaring 'Bravo!' I was finding it very difficult to applaud anyway; it seemed like the most callous kind of irreverence; but there was a tumult going on inside me which had to be let loose. So, in a strange, possessed way, I shouted my thanks.

No performance in my memory has broken down so many of the barriers that hide the last, deepest wrath of the human heart. Your incoherent battle with the hypodermic in the penultimate scene was not merely a sordid entreaty; it had the horrid anger of a child, awaking from its first nightmare, the rawness and the fright we feel when we see and <u>touch</u> inevitability. I have never been so appallingly convinced that the bottom of my stomach was going to drop out. The 'hospital' feeling, the 'first examination' feeling, that sense of the <u>unalterable</u> has never been so violently conveyed to me.

My wife and I, normally a gay enough pair of cynics, cried in the taxi home. It may be that the fact that 'Peepshow' is recent history made it seem more ominous and awful; as Brecht[2] has found in Germany, a lot of stories become more effective if the audience knows the ending, and becomes absorbed by <u>how</u> things happen, rather than by <u>what</u> things happen; whatever it was, we had seen the clearest, most moving piece of acting in London, and we both knew we would never have the courage to see it again.

I should be grateful if you could find a moment to tell your husband[3] what delight I took in his production – especially in the party scene (Scene 2) and the magnificently clumsy, casual, and coldblooded handling of the last scene of all.

In every generation there are about half a dozen actresses who are always better than their scripts: and actresses like this deserve and need plays to be written for them. Their skills demand vehicles. For me, at this moment, you are one of them; and, eliminating perhaps some of the over-florid and pompous gush in this letter, I intend to hang on to that opinion for at least twenty years.

Again, many thanks:

Yours sincerely
Ken Tynan

[1] Joan Miller was currently playing the condemned murderess Julia Almond in F. Tennyson Jesse's *A Pin to See the Peepshow* (1948, adapted from the 1934 novel).
[2] Bertolt Brecht (1898–1956), German radical playwright and in January 1949 founder of the Berliner Ensemble in East Berlin, devoted to the performance of his works. In notes begun in January 1950 KPT developed the notion that Brecht's style of acting would become a stylized shorthand. In *Theatre Newsletter* (17 February 1951) he recommended 'any of the writing of Bertold Brecht (not yet translated and published in book form over here).'
[3] Peter Cotes (b. 1912, brother of the film directors John and Roy Boulting), who was to direct the first production of Agatha Christie's long-running *The Mousetrap* the following year.

To Lord Beaverbrook[1]

19 Upper Berkeley Street
16 July [1951]

Dear Lord Beaverbrook;

My wife and I want to thank you for a fine evening. We felt – there isn't another word – privileged, and very grateful. I was duly tongue-tied, but that, I hope, will pass. Meanwhile, <u>gracias</u> for a rare glimpse.

I'll try, while in Spain, to string together something pungent about the bullfight[2] which you might like. I know I shall see things I shall want to tell you about.

Until then, I enclose a copy of my book.³ I still like parts of it; and the rest is, at worst, <u>characteristically</u> bad.

With renewed thanks –
Very sincerely,
Ken Tynan

---

¹ Lord Beaverbrook (1879–1964), Canadian-born Cabinet Minister in Churchill's Government and owner of the *Daily Express* and London *Evening Standard*. KPT had begun writing for the latter in May and became its drama critic in July.
² The idea of the bullfight had first attracted KPT at Oxford. (He wrote in *He That Plays the King* that the matador was the only symbol left in Europe that might compare to the exploits and deaths of Shakespeare's kings.) In March 1951 he had seen his first bullfights and wrote an article for the London *Evening Standard* (7 August 1951) on the matador Miguel Báez Litri. In *Bull Fever* (1955) he wrote that the bullfight was 'a logical extension of all the impulses my temperament holds – love of grace and valour, of poise and pride; and beyond these, the capacity to be exhilarated by mastery of technique'.
³ *He That Plays the King*.

To the Editor, *Theatre Weekly*¹

[The Irving Theatre²]
[London] W.C.2.
[Published 8 December 1951]

I've just read your review of our Grand Guignol season at the Irving, and since I vastly prefer the witness-box to the pillory, I thought you wouldn't mind if I tried to explain my motives in staging that amputated version of *Titus Andronicus*.

To begin with, I'd better make it clear that I've found more nobility, more grace, more passion and more exhilaration in the Spanish bullrings this year than I've seen on the English stage – except in a few performances by Olivier and Valk, and one of Wolfit's. And what's more, the same kind of nobility and exhilaration – a ritual, theatrical kind. Now a bullfight bears no emotional responses at all; with its splendours go its miseries, and it evokes shame and disgust, quite deliberately, as a part of the whole spectacle. In fact, it gives the meaner, lesser emotions a place in its hierarchy of feeling. And when I returned, I felt it might be worthwhile to give these unwonted and ignoble responses their half-hour or so on the stage. Hence *Titus* – an experiment in blending these things with what you rightly call a first sketch for *Lear*. It lasts thirty minutes, and ranges, with a sort of grim lightness, through giggles and yelps, horror and nausea, to sheer melodramatic narrative, and even, at moments, to something approaching awe. It's our attempt to reintroduce to the theatre, if only for a few minutes, the smell of the bearpit which helped to cradle it. I don't say we shall repeat the attempt; anyway, that is why we made it.

More specifically: Peter Myers[3] and I tried, as part of the plan, to retain the best of the clean, classic, unfelt poetry of the play, and I think we've succeeded – I don't think you can fault us for omitting any of the really good stuff. And you're on curious ground, aren't you, when you trounce us for concentrating on the physical horrors, and then go on to trounce us again for cutting the worst of them? I agree with you that the play holds the stage; and I expect you'll be surprised to find that I agree with you about its quality. We like it, too.

About the presence of the St. John's ambulance men: they're not, I assure you, superfluous. An average of two people, in an audience of just over a hundred, have fainted at each performance. And last Sunday, to everyone's astonishment, one of the Ambulance men fainted himself.

Ken Tynan

[1] Published under the headline 'Guignol'.
[2] Near Leicester Square, another of London's club theatres.
[3] Peter Myers (1923–78), English author and lyricist who co-wrote the *Irving Revue* to which KPT contributed an idea for a sketch, 'The Critic on the Hearth'.

To Peter Wildeblood[1]

Written on board 'LIBERTÉ'[2]
Tuesday [11 December 1951]

Dear Peter:

This large, lean twofunneled thing is exactly like the Cumberland,[3] except that I don't think it trembles quite so much: it does, however, dip and sway in a quite reckless manner, and loosens the bowels horrifyingly. I am not liking it very much: the bar, a strip-lit expanse of waxed linoleum and chained chairs, is situated in the most unquiet section of the ship, and heaves like a matron's bosom every three seconds. The Library has little but Bromfield[4] and Sayers[5] and month-old copies of Collier's.[6] The cinema, right on top of the promenade deck, has a flat floor which means either that you can't see over the heads of those in front of you, or that you must take a front seat and become horribly distressed by the movements of the camera, which are always diametrically opposed to the movements of the boat – camera tracks left as boat swings right. There are Get-Together Dances in the Saloon every night, at which a nasal and tinny pair of French saxophonists play 'Smoke Gets in Your Eyes' and 'All of Me'. There are horse races and there is clay pigeon shooting, and the food is plain and excellent, with an occasional soufflé. The sea is all around us, like steel: a desperate grey enemy at which I hardly dare to look, so acute is my sense of our presumption at being there at all in its midst. The whole ship is an elaborate attempt to feign indifference to the sea, and for me at least it doesn't work at all. I am frankly appalled by what I see every time I go on deck. The weather is bleak and stormy and quite unromantic. Our table at dinner is shared by a pair of Indo-Chinese missionaries, husband + wife, on their way home to America. Both are bright yellow and talk quietly but exclusively of mashed potatoes. Elaine is a little trying, + niggles about the lack of amusements. To satisfy her we went last night into First Class, which was deserted and quite splendid, with gilt, padded pillars and shopping arcades. [...] Tonight we see 'Streetcar Named Desire',[7] which may salve the tedium [ ]

Ever
Ken

[1] An Oxford contemporary and best man at KPT's wedding; he was the co-adaptor of Stella Gibbons' *Cold Comfort Farm* planned for the Watergate Theatre, but never performed. Wildeblood was arrested on 9 January 1954 for homosexual offences, along with Lord Montagu of Beaulieu and Michael Pitt-Rivers. KPT proudly stood bail for Wildeblood.
[2] French-owned transatlantic liner.
[3] Cumberland Hotel, Marble Arch, London.
[4] Louis Bromfield (1896–1956) won the Pulitzer Prize for his novels *Early Autumn* (1926) and *Mr Smith* (1951).
[5] Dorothy L. Sayers (1893–1957), English detective-story writer, creator of Lord Peter Wimsey.
[6] American weekly magazine which closed in 1957.
[7] *A Streetcar Named Desire* (US, 1951), film of Tennessee Williams's play, directed by Elia Kazan, starring Vivien Leigh and Marlon Brando.

To Cecil Beaton[1]

29 Hyde Park Gardens,
London. W.2.[2]
Saturday [22 March 1952]

Dear Cecil;

We had your letter ages ago, but the time in which to answer it has been flying. I've been working so hard for Carmel Snow,[3] thanks initially to you, that writing for fun has been pushed into the background. I do captions and profiles every month for her – Alec Guinness, Carol Reed,[4] John Gielgud, and, quite soon, yourself – and I'm covering the Feria of San Fermin at Pamplona[5] for her in July – with Cartier-Bresson[6] doing the pictures, and <u>what</u> do you think of <u>that</u>? When are we going to publish a private little book, with lots of pictures you've never published and lots of captions by me and a dialogue commentary in the text and all fiendishly expensive, bound in wool and done into a book by the Rye Croft Press, Hants?[7] I'd enjoy that, sometime.

We have moved into a smart, warm, huge new flat, overlooking the park from the toppest of top floors in a block of Regency conversions, and the entire thing is pure House and Gardens and mobiles and statics and pitchpine and pile. You must come and give benison to it immediately you return.

What news? Kay Thompson[8] came back to the Cafe de Paris, the youngest 176-year-old Iroquois squaw in captivity, and the livest, wittiest, fireman-save-my-childest lady on earth: do you love her, too, as I do? Kay Thompson is my youth: I used to carry on like that at the Oxford Union, and I'm pleased as Punch to find it's still chic..

'Call Me Madam'[9] opened to delightful roars of recognition – the old ambassadress story that Cicely Courtneidge[10] made such a noise in at the Saville a couple of years ago. Alec Clunes[11] played Moses in Kit Fry's play,[12] and ruined all by striding down to the footlights at the end, heavy under the immemorial beard of the prophet, and blowing kisses at the audience. He is now doing a rather clumsy Peg Woffington in 'The Constant Couple'.[13]

John G., whom I'd never met, asked me suddenly to supper, and we talked until three, I coaxed into silence by his beauty, he garrulous and fluttering as a dove. What a possession for any theatre! It is irrelevant to say that he was fair in this part, good in that, brilliant in that: Gielgud is more important than the sum of his parts, and any theatre that has him securely lashed to its mast will not steer dreadfully wrongly.

A brilliant piece on Graham Greene turned up in, of all places, 'Picture Post', unsigned. It talked about his style as 'emotion recollected in hostility'; and summed up his attitude towards life as: 'Time not wasted is time mis-spent, an opportunity for remorse needlessly foregone.' What a good sentence! I think Douglas Jerrold[14] wrote it, and who would have thought it?

The new Terry Rattigan[15] has the best first two acts I have ever seen in a new play anywhere (world copyright) – I strutted out into the second interval bursting with pride and anticipation. The third act bogs down in morality and lines like: 'There is something beyond life. Beyond life there is hope.' Kenneth More[16] (new to me) is our best answer to Marlon Brando so far, and Peggy Ash.[17] is shockingly plangent as the suicide girl.

Carmel came over, as you will know, and took me to supper with Rebecca West,[18] who reminds me of the remark Fred Emney makes in 'Blue for a Boy'[19] when, entering a Riviera villa, he finds a square old woman dressed formidably in black sitting on a divan. 'What a place to leave a gas-stove!' he mutters, and passes on: so I feel about R. West at the Dorchester. She bristled and barked staccato orders at me, and threw gauntlets in all directions. How can a woman contrive to be a non-smoker and yet look all the time as if she were chewing a cheroot? She seems to me to be Kensington's reply to Colonel Blimp· and yet the best journalist of our time.

The Old Vic did 'Lear', played by Stephen Murray[20] as a cross between Daniel Boone and Old Moore[21] – all fur hats and gloomy prophecies. Disaster.

I am working for television until July, scripting an adaptation of 'Young Man with a Horn',[22] the novel about Bix Beiderbecke, which I shall produce in June. Then in July to Biarritz, Pamplona, Barcelona, San [sic] Tropez – will you be touching any of these airstrips? We both dearly hope so.

We will be parents in early May: will you be a godfather? We may call the child Tracy, male or female. Is this wise? [...]

Ever,
Ken

[1] Sir Cecil Beaton (1904–80), English photographer and designer for stage and film (*My Fair Lady*, US, 1964); diarist and dandy.

[2] The Tynans moved to 29 Hyde Park Gardens early in 1952.

[3] Carmel Snow (1890–1961), legendary editor of *Harper's Bazaar* (1932–57).

[4] Sir Carol Reed (1906–76), British film director best known for *The Third Man* (UK, 1949) and the Oscar-winning *Oliver!* (UK, 1968).

[5] Annual bullfight festival, which starts on the seventh day of the seventh month and lasts for seven days.

[6] Henri Cartier-Bresson (b.1908), French photographer; his pictures illustrate KPT's *Bull Fever* (1955).

[7] *Persona Grata*, a book of one hundred pen portraits and photographs of people they admired, was published in 1953.

[8] Kay Thompson (b. 1913), elegant American nightclub singer, composer and arranger for MGM musicals and inventor of the character 'Eloise'. She played the magazine editor in *Funny Face* (US, 1956).

[9] *Call Me Madam*, by Howard Lindsay and Russel Crouse, with music and lyrics by Irving Berlin, opened at the Coliseum on 15 March 1952.

[10] Dame Cicely Courtneidge (1883–1980), English actress in plays, pantomime and revue.

[11] See letter of 19 March 1946.

[12] Christopher Fry's play *The Firstborn* (1946).

[13] Restoration comedy by George Farquhar (1700).

[14] Douglas Jerrold (1803–57), English novelist, playwright and wit, who was one of the original contributors to *Punch*.

[15] *The Deep Blue Sea* was the latest in a string of West End successes that included *The Winslow Boy* (1946) and *The Browning Version* (1948).

[16] Kenneth More (1914–82), popular English actor whose films include *Doctor in the House* (UK, 1954) and *Reach for the Sky* (UK, 1956).

[17] Dame Peggy Ashcroft (1907–91), English actress who played Desdemona to Paul Robeson's Othello in 1930, Juliet to Gielgud's Romeo in 1935, and many leading Shakespearean roles.

[18] Dame Rebecca West (1892–1983), English novelist, journalist and critic whose early journalism for the *Freewoman* and the socialist newspaper the *Clarion* was collected in *The Young Rebecca* (1982) and whose later work included *Black Lamb and Grey Falcon* (1941), a study of the origins of World War II, and an account of the Nuremberg Trials for the *New Yorker*.

[19] *Blue for a Boy* (1950) by Austin Melford; Fred Emney (b. 1900) played Fred Piper.

[20] Stephen Murray (1912–83), English classical actor.

[21] Daniel Boone (1735–1820), the American pioneer; *Old Moore's Almanac*, an annual booklet of tide times, the phases of the moon and predictions.

[22] KPT and his co-adaptor George Kerr had retitled Dorothy Baker's novel *Young Man with a Horn* (1938) *Tribute to Nick*. It was not performed.

To Christopher Fry[1]

29 Hyde Park Gardens
October 11th [1952]

Dear Christopher;

Reports of your book[2] have begun to seep through. I disbelieved them at first, being a charitable and love-loving fellow. They have since been confirmed, and I stand appalled and sighing. It is a case of shock, I suppose. That explanatory note about ineligible critics[3] strikes a note of Benjamin Robert Haydonism,[4] of Athenaeumism,[5] of Holier-Than-Thouishness which I hadn't imagined you capable of. Something between naiveté and presumption – I am not foolish enough to accuse you of spite. But must you <u>insulate</u> yourself so? God knows I hope not.

And must you be so clumsily inaccurate? The answer is that you mustn't. I have been the official dramatic critic of the 'Evening Standard' since July, and Harold Conway has remained what he always was, the overnight reporter and columnist. This will have to be corrected, please, in any subsequent edition.

A playwright's idea of how a critic works is, I now see, almost as uninformed as the public's, and infinitely more uninformed than a critic's idea of a playwright. You are our raw materials, and we sculpt you as best we can; but we are merely your scapegoats. I am astonished that you should imagine that any word of mine has been censored, inspired, or in any way amended by the chieftains of the Beaverbrook press. As a matter of course I avoid obscenities and outré allusions, both of which are thankfully reprintable later, but otherwise what I write is uninterruptedly mine.

In all this you do yourself so much less than justice that mere regret is out of the question. Something more like horrified dismay is in order, and that is roughly what I am feeling at the moment. When you choose to reenter touchable theatrical society we must have this out. At present I should not lift an eyebrow at the news that you were writing your next play in Javanese for an audience of six.

Meanwhile –
Ken Tynan

P.S. Be happy to learn that you remain eligible for inclusion in any anthology of playwrights of the 1940s which I may compile.

---

[1] Christopher Fry (b.1907), English playwright whose verse plays, such as *The Lady's not for Burning* (1949), were popular in the 1950s.
[2] *An Experience of Critics: The Approach to Dramatic Criticism* (1952), eight short essays by leading theatre critics edited by Christopher Fry.
[3] 'The eight critics invited to complete this book were chosen because of merit and the amount of space at their disposal. There are others among those listed on p. 63 [including KPT] who have strong claims to be included on the first count, but their judgements are often subjected to sub-editors with a passion for headlines, or managements who have a Policy.'

[4]Benjamin Robert Haydon (1786–1846), English painter of historical subjects. Contrary to KPT's accusation, Haydon became a critic of establishment art.
[5]The Athenaeum: a gentleman's club founded in 1824 by Decimus Burton. KPT was attacking establishment exclusivity.

To Christopher Fry

29 Hyde Park Gardens
15th October [1952]

Dear Christopher;

It takes very little to make me a controversialist. Most of my letter to you was dizzy and boozed with self-justification. I must have looked appalling at the time – blood-blotched, possibly.

What happened was that, like you, I didn't see the book until after I wrote the letter – a too-solicitous friend read the relevant bits over the phone to me, and I assumed that Kaye Searle's note was by you.[1] I don't want to blow my top again, so why don't you forward my letter to you on to them?

I've since read the book, and I can't help feeling it's going to stimulate the worst enthusiasms and emphasises the wrongest antitheses. So many definitions of the critic and the artist, so little common ground ... I wish someone had said, early on, that the real distinction is that the playwright writes words that are speakable, the critic words that are readable. The inference which may unhappily be drawn from the outline of the book is that there are only one or two critics whom you think fit to criticise you. I know that isn't how you feel: but ...

To take you to task on a specific point – the acorn and the oak.[2] When an acorn trots up to me, shakes its fist and yells: 'I am an oak!', I think it my duty to indicate the error, and replant the imp.

But the hell with ink. Yes, we have a daughter, called Tracy, five months, slim and mysterious. Yes, K. Hepburn[3] of film fame is her god-momma. And yes, yes, when you rehit town next month we must arrange for you to meet her.

Meanwhile –
Ever –
Ken

[1] Kaye Webb was the editor of *An Experience of Critics*; her husband, Ronald Searle, had done the illustrations for the book.

[2] Fry had written that 'The newly sprouting acorn is dug up several times a week and told that whatever it may think to the contrary, it is not an oak tree', referring to the damage done by constant criticism to the growth and self-confidence of the playwright.

[3] KPT had first met Katharine Hepburn (b. 1909) on the set of *The African Queen* and after seeing her in Shaw's *The Millionairess* he engineered a meeting at the house of the novelist Rosamond Lehmann. It was there that he asked her to be godmother to his daughter Tracy, named after the Hepburn heroine of *The Philadelphia Story* (US, 1940).

To Paul Rotha[1]

29 Hyde Park Gardens
November 5th [1952]

Dear Paul;

A few weeks ago I had a long chat with Michael Barry[2] on the theme of my scripting and (possibly) co-directing a series of famous trials for TV. He was very keen on the idea and told me to go ahead. I had previously discussed the scheme with Royston Morley,[3] who is also very interested in it from the angle of direction. The three trials I had in mind to begin with are (1) The Constance Kent case,[4] about which I enclose a new book, (2) the Lacenaire case,[5] which took place in Paris a hundred years ago; Royston has the book on this subject, which he'll be returning to me shortly, and (3) The Sacco-Vanzetti case.[6]

I'm writing to you in consequence of a letter from Royston in which he says that he feels the idea comes under documentary rather than drama, and advises me to have a word with you about it. If you're interested, and think it's a documentary pigeon, could you (a) let Michael Barry know and (b) glance at the enclosed book. If not, perhaps you could let me have it back. [...]

This is a hell of a burden to spring on you so suddenly. Do let me know your reactions.

Regards,
Ken[7]

[1] Head of BBC Television Documentaries. See also letter of 9 October 1943.

[2] Head of BBC Television Drama, he had produced the TV version of Jean Jacques Bernard's *Martine* (11 May 1952) directed by KPT, who thus became one of the first freelance directors in television drama.

[3] A BBC producer who ran a trainee directing course of 4–6 weeks, which KPT took early in 1952.

[4] Constance Kent, a twenty-one-year-old girl who confessed in 1864 to the murder of her half-brother.

[5] Pierre François Lacenaire, executed in 1836 for a series of murders in late 1834.

[6] Sacco and Vanzetti: two Italian–Americans executed in 1927 for a double murder in 1920.

[7] Nothing came of this proposal.

To Cecil Beaton

29 Hyde Park Gardens
1st January [1953]

Dear Cecil –

Such a happy New Year; and thanks for the letter and for the Thurber enclosure, which is very funny and raises hopes. The new pictures sound gay; other names that have been running around my head include Piaf, Dietrich, Ernest Milton[1] and Eddie Marsh.[2] Try running them round yours and tell me what you think. We arrive en pleine caravan on January 10th and leave February 6th – staying at Essex House.[3] I hope to put together most of the book while I'm there. So sprees will be few.

I can't think where Dick Watts[4] got the notion about being your foe – I doubt if he has cropped up in our conversations more than a couple of times, and never derogatorily. Certainly I don't remember telling him anything of the sort, and I'll write him pertly and tell him so.

I'm fascinated about your new voice: you must tell me what it's like to have one's voice dropped. There's a man who announces in 'The Stage' that he lifts or lowers voices, according to preference, and claims credit for the summer season success of Hal Fairless, 'Scarborough's Beatrice Lillie'[5] – who sings falsetto. Can you sing bass? Kensington's Boris Christoff[6] – what larks!

Maud Nelson[7] sent me your [Maurice] Chevalier and [Peggy] Ashcroft pictures, which I like enormously, especially the former.

The theatre here had a blow between the eyes with John G's production of 'Richard II'[8] – all very stylised, kept under glass, and prettily gilded by that intricate Loudon Sainthill,[9] but as cold and clammy as the estuary of the Ob. Everyone seemed to be sleep-walking, even Scofield; and what [with] the doll's-house miniaturism of the sets, it was rather like listening to an oratorio on the theme

'Larry the Lamb, King of Toytown'. The oddest Christmas show (which lasted only three performances) was a magical thing put on by a Clapham [character] called Count Le Foe,[10] who not only terrified the children he invited on to the stage by breathing huge blasts of brandy into their faces, but forgot where the staircase leading back to the stalls was, and escorted the boys and girls straight into the bass drum. The audience of 11 journalists was swelled by the stage staff, who shot through the pass door after every scene-change, applauded like maniacs and shot back.

In fact, the nicest theatrical event happened at Peter Brook's Christmas party, where Binkie[11] sat slowly and squarely down on to (or rather into) a chocolate trifle which he mistook for a tablecloth. In a delightful tableau, as the papers say, he was sponged off by Alec Guinness.

If you chance to run into Sam or Bella Spewack,[12] I hope you'll bring up the subject of their translation of 'La Cuisine des Anges',[13] which I hear Ferrer[14] will direct for them. It's a play I very nearly worship (we went to Paris two weeks ago to see it), and I pray that it's in good hands.

Meanwhile, our love.
Ever,
Ken T.

---

[1] Ernest Milton (1890–1974), American born actor who played Shakespearean leading roles for the Old Vic Company from 1918 until the 1930s.
[2] Sir Edward Marsh (1872–1953), private secretary to Winston Churchill, and patron and friend of artists and poets; he compiled a 'Little Book' into which most great writers of his day, including Hardy, Lawrence, Yeats and Wharton, copied one of their poems.
[3] Hotel in midtown New York.
[4] Richard Watts Jr (1898–1981), benign theatre critic for the *New York Herald* (1936–42) and the *New York Post* (1946–74); godparent to Tracy Tynan.
[5] Beatrice Lillie (1898–1989), Canadian revue singer who made famous Noël Coward's song 'Mad Dogs and Englishmen'.
[6] Boris Christoff (b. 1914), Bulgarian bass-baritone who had sung at Covent Garden in 1949.
[7] Beaton's secretary.
[8] Gielgud's production of *Richard II* at the Lyric, Hammersmith.
[9] Loudon Sainthill (1919–69), Tasmanian-born theatre designer.
[10] Dominic 'Count' Le Foe, conjurer and theatre performer.
[11] Hugh 'Binkie' Beaumont (1908–73), West End theatre producer and managing director (1937–73) of H.M. Tennent, Ltd, London's leading theatrical management company.
[12] Samuel (1899–1971) and Bella (1899–1990) Spewack, husband and wife playwriting team who wrote the book for Cole Porter's *Kiss Me, Kate* (1948).
[13] By Albert Husson (1952).
[14] José Ferrer (1912–92), Puerto Rican-born actor and director who won an Academy Award

for his performance in *Cyrano de Bergerac* (US, 1950). He directed *My Three Angels* in New York in 1953.

To Christopher Fry

5th Avenue Hotel
5th Ave. (at 9th Street)
New York City
January 29th [1953]

Dear Christopher;

We are returning to London on February 7th. I still haven't thought of a single fight to pick with you.[1] Somebody to whom I mentioned my quandary said: 'Why not argue the metropolitan case against the countryside?' If you feel like playing Thoreau to my Boswell, I'm game. Or perhaps we should conduct a controversy on having a controversy; and publish a series of letters in each of which we suggest a subject for commotion and find that it won't do? The first letter would thus be from me to you, planting the idea that we should fight in print. You would reply with an idea; I would reply scotching it, and suggesting another, which you would likewise scotch . . . And so forth. Would this be worth while? It might illustrate, in the end, that no matter how far apart they may seem, true friends of the true theatre are always etcetera.

We have now been in the close and thankfully unfuliginous embrace of the 20th century for two weeks: in New York I can never escape that embrace. Every neon sign, every Brooks Brothers suit shouts its century and its success; and I sometimes long to hold it away at arm's length and contemplate something Sung or Ming for a moment. But you can't do that even in the Museum of Modern Art, where the interior decoration is constantly congratulating itself on its 20th century unobtrusiveness and you on being privileged to enjoy its air-conditioning. The ring of a telephone rarely means a conversation; it means a summons, a hectic business parley, a date cancelled or a date made. I have been coming out in spots as a sort of physiological protest.

The English colony is prospering, though it doesn't often eat at the Colony.[2] Binkie has been and gone, irritating the New York press by not revealing to them how much he paid for 'The Seven Years Itch'[3] [*sic*]; Peter Ashmore[4] and Frith Banbury[5] are in town, licking each other's wounds; Esmond Knight is here, appearing in 'The Emperor's Clothes',[6] which Harold Clurman[7] is directing; and Beatrice Lillie's one-woman show is by far the best show on Broadway.[8] I had never liked her till now; she reminded me of a comic aunt or two; but she has matured, grown subtler, using almost no gestures and no facial contortions. Where other comedians land an uppercut on a gag, Bea shadow-boxes round it, leading a life quite independent of her material (written with God knows what pain and struggle on the part of somebody or other): when an obvious, natural belly-laugh presents itself, she chooses just that moment to hide her face in an ostrich-feather fan and mumble inaudibly. She is superbly wintry in her scorn; as when somebody enquires whether her maid has 'unimpeachable credentials', and she pauses, affects terrible boredom and shock, and says: 'That I couldn't say – but I'm sure she has two of everything.' She ignores her audience completely; no intimacy permitted; I felt, whenever her eye lit on me, that I was part of a frightfully badly decorated room. She imitates, at one point, a trained bear on roller-skates. If she turns the theatre into a drawing-room (as she does), it is a drawing-room furnished in a manner she rather resents. I don't know whether you remember my old theory about comedy depending on the female aspect of the man, or the male aspect of the woman. If you do, then think back to Bea Lillie's Eton crop. Thus another piece of evidence slips into place.

Last week I saw 'Queen Lear', presented by the Bown Adams Dramatic Professional Actors' Studio Workshop Theatre,[9] I think. Mr. Adams' wife, a rock-like creature called Virginia, played Lear, announcing before the performance that she and her company had tried to 'regender Mr. Shakespeare's character framework'. And by God they had: the Fool was played by a dumpy girl who addressed Lear as 'auntie', and when Mrs. Adams came to:

'I am a very foolish fond old man
Fourscore and upwards ...'

her vanity won the day, and, with resounding brevity, she announced: 'I am a very foolish woman', and left it at that.

Then we saw Bette Davis' revue,[10] and I christened her 'Miss Monumental Mischief of 1953' (this was a terrible experience, best described as 'An Evening Without Beatrice Lillie'). In 'New Faces'[11] there is the serval-like Eartha Kitt,[12] a coloured singer with the daintiness of a wax figurine and the arrogance of an Arab pony; but nothing else. 'The Children's Hour'[13] is standing up very well in revival, and there won't be a better play about Lesbians until somebody decides that they don't have to shoot themselves offstage in the third act. Arthur Miller's[14] new play, 'The Crucible', is surprisingly like 'The Children's Hour' in shape – a little girl spreads a rumour, and wrecks the lives of those around her. But it is a failure dramatically, because Miller (unlike Hellman) doesn't give the other side its due. His play is about the Salem witch-hunt, and he has written it in a fit of white-hot bad temper about McCarthy's witch-hunt: it's as if you were to put your pen down and take up an axe. You'd probably lash out and hurt someone, but it wouldn't be pretty to watch: and it isn't pretty to consider the state of turbulence and fear which provoked Miller to lash out. I could have wished a much less subtle playwright had done it. Elia Kazan[15] is all for it, and says that Miller had to get it out of his system; which is ironic, because ever since Kazan squealed to the Un-American Activities Tribunal, Miller has refused to speak to him. With such political bickerings do our authors waste their time.

'The Male Animal'[16] presents the liberal case much more patiently and wisely: the present revival is a good thing, and beautifully acted. Elsewhere: Mary Chase's[17] 'Bernardine' is a nasty and complacent little play about teen-age boys (the sex-starved little loves); Margaret Sullavan[18] has ruined 'The Deep Blue Sea' by sheer, simple over-playing, making it tense and artificially taut where it should be deliberately slack; Melvyn Douglas[19] is starring in a comedy called 'Time Out for Ginger', with what George Jean Nathan calls a 'variety of facial mime sufficient to sustain the entire Barrault company through a double bill of "Baptiste" and "Occupe-Toi d'Amelie" ';[20] and Josh Logan,[21] with the insolent vulgarity which is all he retains of his childhood, has staged 'Wish You Were Here', the musical version of 'Having Wonderful Time'[22] – all hips and hustle.

This Time-style survey completed, I must run off to Boston, for more delicious theatre-going and clams. Tracy flourishes, and is the toast of the hotel; I blind her almost every minute by flashing pictures of her with a camera somebody has given me. Incidentally, outside the theatre at which 'New Faces' is playing, there is an enormous picture of Eartha Kitt, legs astride, beckoning sensuously, and beneath it a large card reads: 'JUST MY CUP OF TEA: JOHN GIELGUD.' I am photographing every English actor I can find, reacting to it.

I'll be back before you can reply to this. The point is whether or not you think my idea (see p.1) is a good one. If so, we'll start at once.

Elaine sends good tokens and begs your prayers for our flight back, which terrified her.

Meanwhile –
Love
Ken

[1] KPT had suggested to Fry that while he was in the States they should exchange letters, which an American publisher was prepared to publish.

[2] Club in New York.

[3] *The Seven Year Itch*, comedy by George Axelrod playing at the Fulton and produced in London in May 1953.

[4] Peter Ashmore (b. 1916), Director of the Oxford Playhouse (1941–5). He did not have a play running in New York at this time, but his 1951 production of Anouilh's *Eurydice*, retitled *Legend of Lovers*, had not been given an easy ride.

[5] Frith Banbury (b.1912), actor, manager and director of the London and New York productions of *The Deep Blue Sea*. KPT had written an article in the US *Harper's Bazaar* ('An Inner View of Terence Rattigan', November 1952) as pre-publicity for the play which opened on Broadway in December 1952, but the reviews were not good.

[6] Play by George Tabori (1953) which starred Lee J. Cobb. (For Esmond Knight, see letter 16 May 1946.)

[7] Harold Clurman (1901–88), American theatre director and critic who co-founded the Group Theater with Lee Strasberg in 1931.

[8] Beatrice Lillie's one-woman show *An Evening with Beatrice Lillie*, which had opened at the Booth Theatre in October 1952. In 'The Lady is a Clown' (*Holiday*, September 1956), KPT wrote, 'The theatre is Miss Lillie's hermitage. It is an empty room in which she has two hours to kill, and the audience, like Alice, is "just a thing in her dream" '

[9] Bown Adams Professional Actors' Studio in Manhattan. The *New York Times* (4 June 1952) explained that *Queen Lear* had a circus background and an all-woman cast. Virginia Daly featured in the title role and the show was booked on the college circuit for three years.

[10] *Two's Company*, with music and lyrics by Vernon Duke and Ogden Nash.

[11] *New Faces of 1952*, a revue at the Royale.

[12] Eartha Kitt (b.c.1928), American singer and actress who made her stage debut in Orson Welles' production of *Dr Faustus* in 1951.

[13] Lillian Hellman's first play, written in 1934, and filmed in 1961 with Audrey Hepburn and Shirley MacLaine.

[14] Arthur Miller (b. 1915) had already achieved considerable success with *All My Sons* (1947), and *Death of a Salesman* (1948).

[15] Elia Kazan (b. 1909), leading American stage and film director, co-founder of the Actors' Studio.

[16] Play by James Thurber and Elliott Nugent (1940), revived at the Music Box in May 1952.

[17] Mary Chase (1907–81), American playwright best known for the comedy film *Harvey* (US, 1950).

[18] Margaret Sullavan (1911–60), American actress who abandoned films for the stage after her success in the Broadway production of *The Voice of the Turtle* (1943).

[19] Melvyn Douglas (1901–81), American actor who played Hollywood romantic leads in the 1930s and 1940s and pursued a successful career on Broadway in the 1950s, culminating in a

Tony award for his performance in *The Best Man* (1960). *Time Out for Ginger*, by Ronald
Alexander, was playing at the Lyceum.
[20] The Compagnie Madeleine Renaud–Jean-Louis Barrault had presented a four-week repertory
of plays at the Ziegfeld which included Jacques Prévert's pantomime ballet *Baptiste* and
Feydeau's farce *Occupe-toi d'Amelie*.
[21] Joshua Logan (1908–88), American director and playwright who studied under Stanislavsky
at the Moscow Arts and directed a string of Broadway musical hits.
[22] *Having a Wonderful Time* by Arthur Kober (1937); *Wish You Were Here* (1952), book by
Arthur Kober and Joshua Logan, music and lyrics by Harold Rome.

To A. P. Wadsworth,[1] Editor of the *Manchester Guardian*

29 Hyde Park Gardens
July 8th [1953]

Dear Sir,

Please read the enclosed. Some gesture, I felt, had to be made
against the untenably pompous position you have adopted over
sponsored television. What especially moved me to send it was the
astounding news of your supporting the idea that the greedy,
monopolistic adventurers of the B.B.C. (I am using your own emotive
language) should nepotically control all the available wave-bands. I
should point out to you that many of the producers at present under
contract to the B.B.C. pray, nightly, for the quick introduction of
sponsorship, to jog the corporation out of its apathy.

However, read the appended page from 'The New Yorker'. I could
send many more like it. You may, after looking at it, reach two
important conclusions. First, that if what you refer to as 'the lowest
common denominator of public taste' is represented by Mary Martin
and Ethel Merman[2] (not to mention Groucho Marx, George
Kaufman,[3] Bob Hope and Jack Benny), then the phrase becomes a
recommendation instead of a term of abuse, as it must necessarily
seem in a country whose broadcasting system is unable to pay for
any better popular-entertainment idea than the new parlour game,
'Why?'[4] And second, you may realize the vital, fundamental fact
about good sponsored television – the fact that the sponsor wants
not only to sell his product (the greedy old adventurer!), he also
wants prestige. The 'prestige programmes' I have seen in New York
(operas, Shaw, Shakespeare, Ibsen, etc.) are incomparably better than
anything the B.B.C. has ever given us; and better not only because

they cost more, but because they were better directed, better lit, more imaginatively photographed.

You have really been badly misled. There is no feeling against commercial T.V. in this country except (a) among those who have a political axe to grind and (b) those who have never seen and frankly rather dislike television anyway. Unfortunately those who are automatically and naturally in favour of it, the artists, writers, composers, dancers, singers, directors and actors, dare not make themselves heard for fear of being accused of self-interest. You do yourselves, them and – yes – art a great injustice by not recognising this surely obvious fact. Just as the politicians are making an enforced din about the subject so the artists are preserving an enforced silence. A pity, you may think; and rightly.

Yours sincerely,
Kenneth Tynan

P.S. Even the Puritans gave the English theatre seventy years in which to prove itself a hotbed of vice and frivolity before they closed it down in 1642. Why condemn sponsorship <u>unseen</u>? [...]

[1] Alfred Powell Wadsworth (1891–1956), editor of the *Manchester Guardian* 1944–56.
[2] Mary Martin (1913–90) and Ethel Merman (1909–84), American Broadway musical stars. In the *New Yorker* (30 May 1959) KPT described Merman's voice in *Gypsy* as 'the most relaxed brass section on earth'.
[3] George S. Kaufman (1889–1961), American playwright, co-author with Moss Hart of *You Can't Take It With You* (1939) as well as *The Man Who Came to Dinner* (1939).
[4] A BBC television programme broadcast in 1953.

To The Hon. David Astor[1]

29 Hyde Park Gardens
July 30th [1953]

Dear Mr. Astor;

We have never met: but my daughter's god-mother, Lady Barry,[2] has so often been on the brink of introducing me to you that I feel emboldened to make a rather unexpected enquiry.

For over a year I have been the dramatic critic of the Evening Standard, a hazardous post from which I have lately decided to resign, and which I finally relinquish on August 8th.[3] Thereafter I have no fixed plans; but I have been wondering whether there might be any possibility of my acting as second or third string critic to Ivor Brown.[4] At all events, I should be very grateful if we could talk the idea over.

I shall be on holiday in Spain from August 8th to September 4th. May I ring you when I return?

I have, incidentally, written to Mr. Brown on the same subject.

Yours sincerely,
Kenneth Tynan

[1] David Astor (b. 1912), owner and editor of the *Observer* 1948–75; second son of the American-born Nancy (Lady) Astor, the first woman to take her seat in the House of Commons.

[2] Lady Barry, *née* Poliakoff (1912–82), stage name Vera Lindsay, was the wife of Sir Gerald Barry, Director of the Festival of Britain.

[3] In July 1953, KPT threatened to sue the London *Evening Standard* for libel if they published a proposed page of letters headlined, 'Should Actors Be Critics?' Several days later, he was fired.

[4] KPT would in fact replace Ivor Brown, with whose work Astor had become increasingly dissatisfied. Astor called KPT's appointment 'the bravest thing I did, and one of the most important'.

To Tennessee Williams[1]

Hyde Park Gardens
[October 1953]

Dear Ten;

<u>So</u> sorry: I could not put it down.[2]

I know the Byron scene almost by heart. You have written nothing much lovelier than this.

Many thanks:
In haste:
Ken Tynan

[1] KPT became friends with the American playwright Tennessee Williams (1911–83) in London in 1951. His first major homage to Williams was published in *Encounter* in May 1954, and he wrote a 'Valentine to Tennessee Williams' in *Mademoiselle* (February 1956).

[2] The play *Camino Real*, directed on Broadway in March 1953 by Elia Kazan.

To The Hon. David Astor

29 Hyde Park Gardens
19th December [1953]

Dear Mr. Astor –

Many thanks for your letter. The terms of the appointment[1] are exactly as you stated them in our discussion, and I accept them with enormous pleasure and gratitude.

I'm looking forward immensely, with a decent amount of professional rapture, to the prospect of working for you. It will, I expect, be not unlike moving from a brewery into a vineyard. Meanwhile, I should tell you that I have resigned from the 'Daily Sketch',[2] whose pages I shall be quitting in early March.

Thank you again, and a joyous noël.

Yours sincerely,
Kenneth Tynan

[1] He would be paid £1,500 for a weekly theatre column and occasional special articles for a term of three years.
[2] KPT had joined the *Sketch* as drama critic in 1953.

To Cecil McGivern[1]

29 Hyde Park Gardens
May 1st [1954]

Dear Cecil McGivern;

I've just got back from a month in America, where I became quite fascinated with the show called 'This Is Your Life'.[2] I'm sure you know it: the programme which introduces an unsuspecting celebrity to the people who helped to form him – his first girl-friend, his schoolteacher, his first boss, and so forth. This seemed to me pure T.V. and endlessly gripping. I wondered whether it had ever been contemplated for Lime Grove?

Second thing is: after seeing the use of close-up made by Jack Webb in 'Dragnet',[3] I began to ask myself whether Dylan Thomas' 'Under Milk Wood'[4] couldn't be done in just that way. If it could, I'd love to have a hand in it. I'm joining the 'Observer' in a month or so, but I'll have plenty of time for other activities: and this is one I'd hate to miss.

Yours sincerely,
Kenneth Tynan

[1] Controller of BBC Television 1949–60.
[2] The original American series had been devised by Ralph Edwards and was first presented in Britain by Eamonn Andrews in 1956.
[3] Jack Webb (1920–82), American actor, director and producer who conceived and launched the radio police drama series *Dragnet* in 1949, which transferred to television in 1955.
[4] Originally a BBC radio play made in 1954 with Richard Burton; it was staged in 1956, and filmed in 1971 by Andrew Sinclair.

To the Editor, *Truth*[1]

29 Hyde Park Gardens
[Published 8 October 1954]

Sir.—Your Profile[2] of me last week revived a genial technique of inaccuracy and innuendo formerly employed (as your older readers may recall) by provincial editors to provoke a free contribution from the subject. I am sorry to be unable to help you out.

I must, however, congratulate you on the detailed physiological description of my stammer, which delighted my young daughter:[3] and I would appreciate a clarification of the inference that I am effeminate, which I was cowardly enough to withhold from her.

KENNETH TYNAN

[1] General weekly magazine established in 1877, closed in 1957.
[2] In 'Kenneth Tynan: The Boy Wonder' (*Truth*, 1 October 1954) Alan Brien wrote: 'The skin is merely a flesh tint sprayed on the bone ... the stutter starts as a nervous spasm in the solar plexus and leaps to the jaw muscles ... then he will make four or five snapping sounds like a man taking quick bites from an apple and produce a long balanced sentence in which pun cannons into pun in a verbal break at billiards.' Brien went on to insinuate effeminacy in a clever piece that was both flattering and critical.
[3] Tracy was two and a half years old.

To Jocelyn Baines[1]

29 Hyde Park Gardens
29th November [1954]

Dear Jocelyn;
    The quotation I'd like to use as an epigraph after the title[2] is:
        'Chase brave employment with a naked sword
            Throughout the world.'
        (George Herbert: 'The Church Porch')
    I should be grateful if you could insert it for me.
    I enclose some peculiar pictures of myself wielding the cape. Are they of any use?
    As far as other publicity goes, I can't be very helpful. Apart from participating in scrambles with young cows at Pamplona, along with several hundred other people, I've never set foot on bull-ring sand. I only started going to bullfights in 1950, since when I've spent about six weeks of every year in Spain. My ultimate ambition is to buy a half-interest in a bull-ranch and retire there, but at present I don't know nearly enough about strains and breeding to contemplate that.
    Thanks again for luncheon.*

Yours,
Ken

* and for your suggestions about the book

[1] An editor at Longman's; he published an acclaimed biography of Joseph Conrad in 1966.
[2] *Bull Fever*, KPT's idiosyncratic and personal account of Spain and the corrida, was published by Longman's in May 1955, with a revised version in 1966. It was published in the US by Harper & Brothers in October 1955.

To S. J. Perelman[1]

29 Hyde Park Gardens
April 9th [1955]

Dear Mr. Perelman;
    I've been thinking about the slight froideur that has arisen between us over the 'All-Girl Elephant Hunt', and concluded that it might be a good idea to recapitulate. The idea for a musical based on the Hunt came to Betsy Holland[2] and myself when we were sent a

circular last summer advertising a safari for American matrons; we spent several days working out a synopsis of the plot.[3] In the autumn, your series of pieces on Africa began to appear in the New Yorker, and the mention in one of them of the All-Girls[4] gave us confirmation of what we had already suspected – that you would be the right person to approach to adapt our story into a musical.

When Betsy brought you to the hotel for drinks (Sunday, March 27th), we asked you if you were working on anything at the moment, and when you said no, we sat down and I gave you an outline of our story. You expressed interest, said that you and Ogden Nash[5] had been looking for a musical idea for some time, and added: 'This looks as if it might be it.'

Next day you had a telephone conversation with Betsy, telling her that Nash liked the idea, and also mentioning that you thought Groucho Marx a good idea for the White Hunter; we agreed, but felt that Phil Silvers[6] was more likely to be available for the stage. It was only after all this that you 'phoned Betsy to say that you recalled having had the idea of a safari musical yourself; and you declined thereafter to discuss the project with us. Now please understand that I don't question your having had a plan for a musical somewhere along the line; but that you did not have the plan <u>for this musical</u> seems to be pretty clearly indicated by your spontaneous reaction to and comment on the outline story Betsy and I told you. Several people who were present in the hotel room at the time and heard the conversation have since confirmed our recollection of what took place. [...]

What we had in mind when we brought the idea to you was a small royalty of some kind; and we still hope some such arrangement might be made. We're not greedy; but we do feel, now, that we're justified in trying to protect our rights. I have given full authority to my attorney (L. Arnold Weissberger, 509 Madison Avenue, New York) to come to any agreement with you that you both think fair. He also has a copy of the synopsis of our story, in case you should wish to see it and decide once and for all whether or not you want to use it.

I hope, by the way, that the tone of all this hasn't disguised my genuine and boyish delight at having met you and Mrs. Perelman after so many near misses.

Yours sincerely,
Kenneth Tynan[7]

---

[1] S. J. Perelman (1904–79), American humorist and *New Yorker* writer.

[2] An intelligent, pretty girl with Broadway connections, with whom KPT had an affair.

[3] The characters in KPT's script included 'Mictor Vature', a slow-witted crack shot; John Huston, a 'Hemingwayish film director'; 'Helen Hokinson girls' (Hokinson was a *New Yorker* cartoonist famous for her gentle caricatures of middle-aged club women); and 'a bunch of tribesmen'.

[4] 'Dr Perelman I Presume, or Small Bore in Africa: The Artemisses' (*New Yorker*, 6 November 1954).

[5] Ogden Nash (1902–71), American writer of comic verse.

[6] Phil Silvers (1912–85), American comic best known as Sergeant Bilko in the hit TV series *The Phil Silvers Show*.

[7] 'Sounds terrific, what the hell do I need you two for?' Perelman later told Betsy Holland. He followed with a lawyer's letter warning the pair off, and they abandoned the project.

To Terence Kilmartin[1]

29 Hyde Park Gardens
May 15th [1955]

Dear Terry;

This is just to confirm our talk about my covering the Paris Festival.[2] I shall go under my own steam on May 28th to see Eduardo de Filippo[3] and his troupe: this would be a Saturday-to-Monday trip. The subsidised trip would be from Tuesday June 14th to Tuesday June 21st, about which I should hope to write one general piece on the Festival and one piece specifically on the Brecht contribution[4] (if it's as interesting as it should be).

That was a curious party on Saturday. After you left the vibraphone player turned out to be some kind of genius, leaping and singing and shouting took place, and the dawn was of a fantastic purity. I doubt whether it will all do Annie Ross[5] much good publicity-wise; I invited too many columnists, each will think the others are going to mention her, and in the end nobody will. One characteristic encounter lingers in my mind. Venetia Murray[6] found herself facing Sandy Mackendrick,[7] who directs films at Ealing. 'Haven't we met before?' she said. 'As a matter of fact, we have,' he said. 'You interviewed me.' 'So I did,' she said. 'What's your name?'

Love,
Ken

[1] Terence Kilmartin (1922–91), literary editor of the *Observer* 1952–86. In 1981 he revised C. K. Scott Moncrieff's translation of Proust's *A la Recherche du temps perdu*.

[2] On this visit to the second Paris Drama Festival in June, KPT met Bertolt Brecht for the first

and only time. He described him as being 'ovally built, and blinking behind iron-rimmed glasses', conversing in 'wry, smiling obliquities, puffing on a damp little cigar'.

[3] Eduardo de Filippo (1900–84), Italian playwright and actor appearing in Paris in his own play *Questi Fantasmi!* (These Ghosts!).

[4] *The Caucasian Chalk Circle*.

[5] Annie Ross (b. 1930), Scottish jazz singer who sang with Duke Ellington in Harlem and Lionel Hampton in Stockholm. KPT helped to introduce her to London and wrote the sleeve notes for her album *Annie By Candlelight* (1965): 'There is a meditative quality about her voice, a detachment, a refusal to get flurried. At her best, she sings the way Françoise Sagan writes, in a fallen and angelic manner which is at once her trademark and her secret.' She later appeared in Robert Altman's *Short Cuts* (US, 1993).

[6] Venetia Murray (b. 1932), journalist granddaughter of the classical scholar Gilbert Murray.

[7] Alexander Mackendrick (1912–93), Scots film director of *Whisky Galore* (UK, 1948) and *The Ladykillers* (UK, 1955).

To Cyril Connolly

29 Hyde Park Gardens
May 22nd [1955]

Dear Cyril Connolly –

I'm really stricken with apology about our unforgivable failure to turn up for luncheon. I was suddenly beset by a vile intestinal upheaval which kept me in bed and foodless. Out of cowardice, I asked my wife to telephone you, but even she, normally a fairly froward character, shrank from telling you the basic reason for my condition, which was a night spent mostly in the open air with Miss Ava Gardner,[1] six enthusiastic flamenco singers and several bottles of vodka. My hangovers always inhabit my stomach, and this was a lulu. Miss Gardner, whom I hardly know, is a convivial girl and not easily discouraged when she gets the smell of riot in her nostrils, and I allowed myself to be swept in an open car twice across London with her engaging entourage, which was joined at odd times by a policeman and a rich swimmer named Esther Williams,[2] on whose presence Miss Gardner insisted, saying that a party wasn't a party without a drunken bitch lying in a pool of tears. As it happened, nobody wept, but time passed and the air chilled and a condition from which I could ordinarily have recovered in a flash degenerated into internal chaos. I pictured myself slumped and sickly at your table, winced and begged my wife to cry us off. I have been reproaching myself ever since. Please convey my self-disgust to your wife. When you are next in town, I insist on an elaborate penance* for myself. Will you lunch with us at the Ritz on any day of your choice?

Sincerely,
Ken Tynan

* wrong word. I mean reward.

P.S. I send this <u>via</u> the S. T. because my notes on how to get to your cottage don't include the address of it.

---

[1] Ava Gardner (1922–90), American film actress who had recently starred in *The Barefoot Contessa* (US, 1954).
[2] Esther Williams (b.1923), American champion swimmer who became an unlikely Hollywood star in synchronized swimming movies such as *Bathing Beauty* (US, 1944).

To Simon Michael Bessie[1]

29 Hyde Park Gardens
[?4 August 1955]

Dear Mike –

Just back from France, Spain, Ava Gardner, Tennessee Williams and assorted bulls.

I honestly don't think Shaw's for me; I don't really respond to his plays [2] The genius-watching[3] idea will reach you in capsule form within a few weeks. Roughly, it would begin with a study of the meanings genius has had since the word was coined, with examples and quotations. The second part would be semi-autobiographical: my own contact with genius, how to distinguish it from talent, and a statement of my theory that there is too much genius around and too little talent. This I'll elaborate later.

Love,
Ken

---

[1] Simon Michael Bessie (b. 1916), New York publisher at Harper & Brothers whom KPT first met in 1954. He left to work at Atheneum in 1959 and rejoined Harper & Row in 1975.
[2] On 1 July Bessie had written to KPT suggesting that he do a biography of George Bernard Shaw, calling it 'a wonderful subject for you'. On 3 July KPT replied, 'I fear St John Ervine has beaten us to the punch. His authorised biography appears in a month's time, and that would seem to be that.'
[3] In a letter dated 3 July 1955 KPT had suggested to John Guest of Longman's (his London

publisher) 'a book on genius-watching as a life work – hints on how to distinguish genius from talent, how to approach it and talk to it'. The book was never delivered.

To Robert Downing[1]

29 Hyde Park Gardens
October 29th [1955]

Dear Mr Downing –

Thanks very much both for your kind review[2] and your trouble in sending it to me. Also for what you say about my work on 'The Observer'. I must say I envy you Miller and Williams. Being a drama critic here is rather like being a farmer in a desert. It's also like sitting in Pompeii while the volcano is erupting across the bay, which is the Atlantic. It's nice to know that one's screams from the graveyard are sometimes heard even three thousand miles away.

Yours
Kenneth Tynan

[1] Robert Downing (1914–75), American actor, director and playwright who contributed articles on theatre to the *New York Times*.
[2] Of *Bull Fever*.

To John Appleton[1]

29 Hyde Park Gardens
October 29th [1955]

Dear John –

I don't know whether you've yet seen this crazy blood and sand writing-paper.[2] Whether you have or haven't, thanks for your letter and the enclosure. I have been spending much time here making bullfight films for television for Orson Welles, who has been making a series called 'Around the World with Orson Welles',[3] got as far as Vienna and then disappeared, leaving me to clean up for him. A large number of people have started to send me bullfight posters and souvenirs, enough to paper Versailles. If your bathroom needs brightening, let me know and I will send colourful and bloody stuff to paper it with.

Frankly, I don't care if I never see a bleeding bull again. Enough is enough. Love to whoever it is.

Ever,
Ken

[1] An editor at Harper & Brothers.
[2] Yellow with the letterhead in red.
[3] Welles never completed the series, though several shows were broadcast, among them 'Spain: The Bullfight' (Associated Rediffusion, 1955). In 1961 ABC broadcast 'Orson Welles and the Art of the Bullfight', using some of the same material.

To The Hon. David Astor

120 Mount Street
London, W.1.[1]
January 16th [1956]

Dear David Astor –
 I have just received a proposition from Sir Michael Balcon[2] which I feel I must discuss with you before answering. He wants to employ me for twelve months as a script editor at Ealing Studios, whence I have just returned from a talk with him. I first made it quite clear that the job I wanted was the job I already had on 'The Observer', to which he replied that he had no wish at all to interfere with my 'Observer' work or with the trips abroad I might take for the paper. At present I write my column on Friday and go down to Tudor Street on Saturday to see it through the printers, and Balcon emphasised that this time (and of course every evening) would continue to be my own, reserved for what he called 'the very important work' I was doing. The job of script editor would, I gather, involve vetting scripts, giving advice, and having ideas; and it seems nebulous enough to suit me splendidly.
 I have thought about it carefully, and I cannot see any way in which it would cut across or conflict with my work for you. At the moment I spend most of my free days doing outside journalism, chiefly for America, and I have been feeling for some time that I was dissipating my writing energies. If I accepted the Ealing post I should naturally do much less outside work, and I have an idea that this would be a good thing for my writing.
 I told Balcon that the plan interested me but that of course I could not give him an answer before consulting you. This I am accordingly

doing. As far as I am concerned 'The Observer' has first priority on my services, but I am sure that a not-too-arduous outside job in another field would stimulate me considerably. I should be most grateful if you could think about the idea and let me know your reactions.[3]

Yours sincerely,
Ken Tynan

[1] The Tynans had moved to an Edwardian flat in Mount Street, Mayfair, across from the Connaught Hotel.
[2] Sir Michael Balcon (1896–1977), English film producer who founded Gainsborough Pictures in 1928 and was Director of Ealing Studios, 1937–59. Balcon had read an article by KPT called 'Tight Little Studio' in *Harper's* magazine in August 1955 and in the spring of 1956 would take him on as script advisor for £2,000 a year.
[3] Astor agreed to KPT's plan.

To Simon Michael Bessie

120 Mount Street
16th February, 1956

Dear Michael,
    In answer to your questions on the theatre book:[1]
    1. Length. I imagine around 60,000 + words.
    2. I would deal with each theatre contemporaneously, with a round-up chapter at the end – venturing some predictions about what the ideal theatre of the future ought to be.
    3. I should restrict myself to writing about the drama in each country's theatrical metropolis – London, Paris, New York, Moscow. But you're quite right: Berlin ought to be in there somewhere. I have therefore written to Longmans asking them whether they would subsidize me on a fortnight's trip to Berling [*sic*] in the Autumn. This happens to be the earliest I can make it.
    4. Assuming that I went to Berlin in October I could have the book finished by Christmas.
    5. I should aim it at the general reader who occasionally goes to the theatre.
    6. I don't know that I'm very keen on the idea of illustrations. They might make the book look like a complete study of contemporary world theatre. This would be very misleading. What it's meant to be is a series of personal impressions, not an authoritative survey.

Let me know how you react to this. I'm desolated to conclude by saying that we shall be crossing in mid-Atlantic – I'm due to arrive in New York half-way through April, staying for a fortnight. But I will see you on my return to London.

Meanwhile, love.

Yours,
Ken

[1] KPT had proposed to Longman's and to Harper's a book on the four theatres (England, America, Russia, France). Bessie wrote to KPT on 14 February 1956: 'I gather it's your thought to have a chapter on each and that the basic idea of the book would be to set forth the individual characteristics of the theatre in each of the four countries. This sounds like a very interesting idea and something I am confident you could do superbly.' He proposed that KPT include the German theatre and agreed to pay $1,000 advance.

To Eric Bentley[1]

120 Mount Street
12th November, 1956

Dear Eric,

Thanks for your letter.[2]

1. I didn't know that the epilogue was your idea. It still seems a good one.

2. I did read the German original but am of course no judge of its literary merits. In translation, however, I got an impression of heavy-handedness that I'd not got from the original. It's perfectly possible, of course, to make a clumsy translation of Racine or Marivaux.

3. Americanisms. You may be right; I haven't your text to hand. Though why the flier should be Americanized I don't quite understand.

4. I believe in the inviolable text no more than Brecht. Adaptation is something that should befall all good plays – perhaps, for English audiences, yours doesn't go quite far enough. They resent – and to my mind rightly – the length of the first (and weakest) act. They find many of the asides superfluous. Perhaps I mean 'excision' rather than revision.

In spite of all this I hope you gathered from my review that I thought the play very, very well worth doing.

Yours,
Ken T.

[1] Eric Bentley, who had worked with Bertolt Brecht, claimed to have been the first person to have interested KPT in the German playwright and his company; he translated several of Brecht's plays, including *Mother Courage and Her Children*, *Baal* and *The Caucasian Chalk Circle*.
[2] In response to KPT's review of George Devine's production of *The Good Woman of Setzuan* in the *Observer*, 4 November 1956, which referred to Bentley's 'clumsy translation'.

To J.P. Donleavy[1]

Ealing Films Limited,
M.G.M. British Studios,
Boreham Wood,
Herts.[2]
3rd January, 1957

Dear Mr. Donleavy,

That's a marvellous book. Do you really hate films as much as the Mary–Dangerfield[3] stuff at the end suggests? If not, do you think we could meet some day and see if you have any ideas that might be put on celluloid? Dialogue like yours would be something of a godsend to British films.

Ring me any afternoon at ELStree 2000 or any morning at GRO. 4934.

Yours sincerely,
KENNETH TYNAN
SCRIPT EDITOR

[1] J.P. Donleavy (b. 1926), American-born Irish writer whose first novel was *The Ginger Man* (1955), which KPT refers to here.
[2] Ealing Films had moved to Borehamwood when the Ealing studio was sold to the BBC.
[3] The character Sebastian Dangerfield says to Mary: 'Leave the stage and forget the films and we'll live in some quiet place.'

To J.P. Donleavy

Ealing Films Limited
12th February 1957

Dear Mike,[1]

Before you embark on your story for us,[2] I thought I ought to pass on to you a very minor qualm that someone here has raised. Did you ever see a film called 'THE QUIET MAN', directed by John Ford?[3] It was a story about a rich American who goes to an Irish village to live in the cottage where his mother was born. She has just died and he has inherited it. He falls in love with an Irish girl and has a tremendous fight with her brother, a village bully. I think it would be as well if your story avoided any obvious parallels with Ford's.

Otherwise, go ahead and ad lib.

I'm looking forward to the result with enormous gusto.

Love,
[KENNETH TYNAN][4]

[1] Donleavy's nickname.
[2] Entitled 'The Rich Goat', it was never made.
[3] From the story by Maurice Walsh, it starred John Wayne and Maureen O'Hara (US, 1952); John Ford (1895–1973), eminent American director of (mainly) westerns.
[4] Donleavy replied on 14 February 1957 that he was 'delighted with qualm'. He did remember 'vague roses, sunny curtains and shouts round a cottage in emerald fields. My assurance there will be no parallels, not even in the colour of the grass.'

To The Hon. David Astor

120 Mount Street
28th August 1957

Dear David,

I am delighted that my association with 'The Observer' is to be extended.[1] I can't tell you how much your letter cheered me. In the past three years I have often felt as if I were walking on egg-shells. It's wonderfully encouraging to discover that in spite of my fears none got broken. Thank you again for giving me the opportunity.

Yours,
Ken

[1] Astor had written on 24 August offering to renew KPT's contract, adding that he had lent 'a great brilliance and integrity to the paper'.

To Simon Michael Bessie

120 Mount Street
22nd October 1957

Dear Mike,

I read your letter with a pang. I find myself in a mixed-up state about

'The Five Theatres'. As I have told you before, this film job of mine occupies four days of my week completely, and the fifth is reserved for the Observer. Evenings I'm at theatres, and on Saturday night I'm afraid I drink. I never imagined working for Ealing would be like this, but I've made the mistake of getting slightly wrapped up in the job.

Together with my new interest in films has gone a passionate new attachment to Zen Buddhism,[1] which says that the very worst things in the world are those phoney abstract symbols, words. As you will appreciate, this has not exactly had the effect of making me fly to my typewriter. A further deterrent has been the fact that Longmans have expressed interest in publishing a collection of my drama reviews from the Observer and other sources. This has thrown me out completely, since I was intending to use many of them as raw material for 'The Five Theatres'. I know you would not be interested in a straight collection of Tynan reprints: on the other hand, the tempting ease with which such a collection could be put together has combined with the other reasons I've given to keep me idle during the two or three hours every week when I might be working on your book.

Next March my contract with Ealing expires, and I seriously doubt whether I shall be renewing it. From then on my time will be my own, or, if you want to put it that way, yours. Until then several courses of action are open:

(a) I can repay your advance and go ahead with the collected reviews for Longmans.

(b) I can settle down in the Spring to 'The Five Theatres', and forget all about the collection.

or

(c) I can hang on to the advance, go ahead with the collection, and write a book on some quite different subject for you.

I am abjectly sorry about all this, but I've procrastinated long enough and I thought it was time to get things clear. Do let me know which suggestion appeals to you most, if any.[2] I myself have no preference.

Meanwhile all my love,
Yours ever,
Ken

[1] KPT had read and was much influenced by *The Way of Zen* by Alan Watts (1957).
[2] Bessie replied in the first of two letters dated 4 November that his preference among the three proposed courses was an original book on the theatre. If, however, KPT decided to publish the collection, 'we should be happy to carry the advance ahead against another book as suggested in your alternative (c)'.

While Ken was debating whether to write The Five Theatres, *or to put together a collection of his reviews, or to do both, he dined, on 26 October 1957, with Robert Knittel, an American who was chief editor of the publishers Jonathan Cape. Knittel argued that he should do his autobiography, and three days later followed up with a written proposal: 'Quite frankly, I cannot think of anyone else of your age in England to-day to whom I would or could make such a suggestion.' Could he not borrow Tynan from Longman's for this one book, and pay him an advance of £500?*

Ken liked the idea but wrote in return to say he couldn't commit himself until he had heard from Harper's; and that he would want first to have Longman's publish his collected reviews.

To Simon Michael Bessie

120 Mount Street
31st October 1957

Dear Mike,
Before you reply to my letter, I should like to slip you another thought. Jonathan Cape has come up with the idea that he would like me to write an autobiography. This would not be based on any spectacular achievements of mine, but would be an attempt to do for my generation what Robert Graves did for his in 'Good-bye to All That'[1] i.e. make it symbolic as well as personal. This attracts me enormously because it would get me off the beaten track of theatre for a while and allow me to say what I think about human beings. I am telling you this because it wildly occurs to me this book might replace 'The Five Theatres' in my agreement with Harpers.

Although the suggestion came from Cape, my agent feels it would be politic to let Longmans do the book if they are interested, but that of course would not affect the American publication.

Sorry to have to bombard you like this.

Best wishes,
Ken

[1] Robert Graves (1895–1985), English poet and novelist whose works include the historical novel *I, Claudius* (1934). *Goodbye to All That* (1929) is an autobiographical account of his life until the age of thirty, including his experiences as a soldier in France in World War I.

Bessie wrote back on 4 November – his second letter to Ken of that date –
telling him that if he decided to go ahead with the autobiography 'à la Goodbye to All That', *that would be fine and it could substitute for* The Five
Theatres. *(Ken's agent in London, James MacGibbon, and his boss Spencer*
Curtis Brown, agreed privately that the personal book might turn out to be
embarrassing. They thought that their young star was more interesting on
theatre than he was on 'Social and Political Problems'.)

To Robert Knittel

120 Mount Street
20th November 1957

Dear Bob,
I hope you will forgive me some day for the interminable hoverings
and hesitations that have ended in my deciding not to do a formal
autobiography after all. It would be too easy for me to put the blame
on Curtis Brown: easy but not quite accurate. What happened began
with my own qualms about a promise, nearly two years old and long
since signed and sealed, to write a book for Longmans on world theatre.
I'd been growning [*sic*] painfully aware that although I knew a good
deal about London, Paris and New York, my knowledge of theatre in
Berlin and Moscow was pretty thin. For this reason I have been delaying
over the book. It seemed a happy inspiration to turn it into a semi-
autobiographical account of the twelve post-war years in which I have
been getting to know the theatre face to face. This would still come
under the Longmans heading of 'Book by Tynan on World Theatre',
but its more personal form would enable me to admit ignorance instead
of trying to conceal it, as I would had [*sic*] had to do in a more impersonal
form.
This has removed my blockage with Longmans. At the same time it
has unfortunately, and to my great regret, ruled out any immediate
possibilities of an autobiography – if only because the Longmans book
will inevitably cover most of the experiences I have had in and around
theatres during the last twelve years. You would probably be justified
in refusing to converse with me in the future except in the presence of
a lawyer. I hope it won't come to this! Our love to Luise,[1] and let's get
together soon.

Yours ever
Ken T.

¹ Luise Rainer (b.1910), Austrian actress and wife of Robert Knittel, who won Academy Awards for *The Great Ziegfeld* (US, 1936) and *The Good Earth* (US, 1937); her first husband was the playwright Clifford Odets.

The theatre reviews eventually supplanted The Five Theatres: *under the title* Curtains *they were published first by Bessie (who had moved to Atheneum) in 1961, then by Longman's the same year. Since the collection was first mooted, Ken had extensively covered American and European theatre, so that he was able to arrange the reviews under the headings: British, American, French, Russian and German theatres.*

In 1962 he was once again talking with Bessie about a semi-auto-biographical book; and this idea, in different forms, was explored in their correspondence throughout the 1960s.

To the Editor, *Tribune*¹

[120 Mount Street]
[Published February 1958]

The inaugural meeting in London of the Campaign for Nuclear Disarmament² included some thought-provoking analyses, notably by Bertrand Russell³ and Sir Stephen King-Hall,⁴ of our defence position as outlined by Mr. Sandys.⁵

Nuclear weapons are the basis of our defence: our possession of them makes us an automatic target for nuclear attack: we have no defence against nuclear attack.

This seems to be the situation in which the Government has placed us. What nobody has yet pointed out is the unique moral splendour of it all.

We are committed, if war breaks out, to a gesture of self-sacrifice unparalleled in human history. We have volunteered for annihilation.

Some may scoff at us: some may even call us suicidal maniacs. But we British have been called names before. We shall go to our graves in quiet heart, secure in the knowledge that by our sacrifice we shall have made our island uninhabitable to the invading hordes, or for that matter anybody else.

I do not wish to be accused of mealy-mouthed sentimentality: but is there not one family that should be spared? I am sure I speak for every member of it when I say that they would vastly prefer to stay with their people in the event of war and be wiped out alongside them.

All the same, I feel it my humble duty to suggest that the Royal family should be evacuated from these islands without a moment's delay.

We would all, I feel sure, rest easier in our graves if we knew that somewhere in the world a British family survived to carry on the British tradition of civilised decency and respect for human life. And not only survived, but survived intact.

To expose the Royal family to radiation would be to risk the most fearful dynastic consequences. Both patriotism and commonsense lead inescapably to the conclusion I have respectfully suggested.

The royal family should take up residence, with all convenient speed, in some distant British dependency. Let cowards flinch and traitors glare: we'll keep the old flag flying there.

KENNETH TYNAN

[1] A socialist weekly newspaper.
[2] On 17 February at the Central Hall, Westminster.
[3] Bertrand Russell (1872–1970), Welsh-born philosopher and mathematician, he was awarded the Nobel Prize for Literature in 1950. In the 1950s he became a spokesman for the disarmament movement and was imprisoned in 1961 for his part in a demonstration at Whitehall.
[4] Sir Stephen King-Hall (1893–1966), ex-naval officer, founder of the Hansard Society and author of *Defence in the Nuclear Age* (1958).
[5] Duncan Edward Sandys (1908–87), Conservative Minister of Defence 1957–9.

To the Editor, *Encounter*[1]

[120 Mount Street]
[Published March 1958]

The 'Angry Young Man' label,[2] I begin to realise, has its advantages. People who attack one in print take so much care not to be angry themselves that all the edge goes out of their prose, and what started out as a vituperation ends up very like flattery. Look at Randolph Churchill,[3] writing in your January issue about what he calls 'Angry Young Gentlemen': really, he sounds less like a polemicist than a waggish butler. However, my purpose in writing is to answer the one rather desperate point he makes against me, which is that I have accused Evelyn Waugh of anti-Semitism without producing evidence. I should have thought it was clear from the context that, in asking where the Jews stood in the 'Great Chain of Being,' I was merely wondering how a race so utterly classless could be fitted into Mr. Waugh's stratified, hierarchical picture of English society.

Whether or not Mr. Waugh is anti-Semitic I have no idea, although certain passages in his avowedly autobiographical *Ordeal of Gilbert Pinfold* suggest that, whatever his conscious position may be, his sub-conscious has some slightly ambiguous views on the subject. You may remember that Pinfold-Waugh is assailed by persecuting voices, making allegations that horrify him. One of these is that he is a Fascist; another that he is a Communist; a third that he is a homosexual; a fourth that he is an alcoholic; and a fifth that he is a Jew. Now one of these allegations is very much the odd man out. If I falsely accuse a man of being a Fascist, Communist, homosexual, or alcoholic, I would expect him to be nettled and, indeed, would not be surprised if he sued me. But why should anyone be horrified at being called Jewish? The suggestion is not, by any stretch of the imagination, slanderous. Who, one wonders, could possibly be outraged by the imputation of Jewish origin but a man who was, at some deep subconscious level, allergic to Jews?

KENNETH TYNAN

[1] Stephen Spender and Irving Kristol were co-editors. The letter was published under the headline 'Angry Young Gentlemen'.
[2] First used as the title for Leslie Paul's autobiography *Angry Young Man* (1951), and picked up by George Fearon, the press officer at the Royal Court, after the opening of John Osborne's play *Look Back in Anger* on 8 May 1956.
[3] Randolph Churchill (1911-68), journalist son of Sir Winston Churchill who was also Conservative MP for Preston 1940-45.

To the Editor, the *New Statesman*

120 Mount Street
[Published 19 April 1958]

Sir,–

I am baffled by T. C. Worsley's[1] suggestion that judges of the *Observer* competition[2] had a strong leaning towards Abstractionism. The first prize in that competition was awarded to Errol John's *Moon on a Rainbow Shawl*,[3] which is a realistic play. The second-prize winner, *Set on the Earth*,[4] is a realistic play. The third prize was shared between *The Shifting Heart*,[5] a realistic play, and two works by Ann Jellicoe[6] and N.F. Simpson[7] which are non-realistic but happen, by sheer chance, to have reached the stage before the others. 'Abstractionist bias'? If anything, the opposite.

The three 'neo-realist' (T.C.W.'s word, not mine) winners are all due for production in the fairly near future, by H. M. Tennent Ltd, the new Shakespeare Theatre in Liverpool, and Laurence Olivier Productions respectively. I hope Mr Worsley enjoys them.

KENNETH TYNAN

[1] Drama critic of the *New Statesman* 1948–60.
[2] For full-length contemporary plays by new or non-established playwrights; the judges were KPT, Alec Guinness, Peter Ustinov, Peter Hall and Michael Barry. There were 2000 submissions and prizes totalled £800.
[3] A West Indian playwright.
[4] By Gurney Campbell and Daphne Athas.
[5] By Richard Beynon.
[6] Ann Jellicoe (b.1927), playwright and director associated with the English Stage Company; author of *The Knack* (1962). She had submitted *The Sport of My Mad Mother*.
[7] N. F. Simpson (b.1919), English absurdist playwright, author of *One Way Pendulum* (1959). He had submitted *A Resounding Tinkle*.

Rumours that the New Yorker's *Wolcott Gibbs was retiring from his post as theatre critic had reached Ken, and on 22 December 1956 he cabled Edith Haggard at Curtis Brown, his New York agent, to ask: 'Any chance for me?' (See cable below.) Haggard wrote back on 27 March 1957 confirming the rumour, and telling him that she had written on his behalf to the Vice-President of the New Yorker Corporation. In the meantime Mike Bessie had spoken to William Shawn, the magazine's editor. He did not respond to questions about the Gibbs rumour, but showed 'considerable interest in you'. Bessie sent Shawn* Bull Fever, *telling Ken: 'If he thinks that this amounts to a campaign on my part, so be it.'*

In February, Ken wrote to Bessie thanking him for his machinations, but adding, 'This Gibbs rumour has figured fairly consistently in my life for the past four years and it is almost bound to be untrue.'

In August 1958 Gibbs died unexpectedly, and William Shawn telephoned Ken, who was at the Edinburgh Festival, to invite him to New York to discuss the job. He accepted. Shawn subsequently insisted that his choice was entirely independent of outside pressure.

To The Hon. David Astor

120 Mount Street
September 11th [1958]

Dear David –

My thirty-six hours in New York are just over and before collapsing I thought I'd tell you what happened.

William Shawn[1] was most cooperative and agreed to everything we agreed I should suggest. He is perfectly happy for me to contribute a monthly culture-piece to The Observer, and he agrees that after I have been in New York for two or three months he and I should decide whether or not the arrangement should continue for two years – whereupon of course I would instantly let you know.

At present it seems to me most unlikely that I should want to stay longer than one season, the principal reason being that Shawn wants me only as a guest critic for a maximum of two years. After two years I should presumably be jobless, and hence I am much more attracted by the idea of staying for one and then returning to The Observer.

My agreement with him is for thirty-nine weeks (don't ask me why!) starting on Monday November 10th and ending some time next August, so that unless I stayed on I should be available for the 1959–60 London theatre season. The early starting date – in two months' time – is the only drawback, but I see Shawn's point: the Broadway season starts next week and whoever stands in for me on the magazine would be placed in an embarrassing position if his name suddenly disappeared from the drama pages after too long a stint. Shawn also said, quite rightly, that if I delayed longer the season there would be half over. Starting to work there on the 10th really means that I would have to leave England the week before to get settled in to the new apartment, etc., so that (if you agree) my last Observer review would appear on November 2nd.

I can't tell you how grateful I am for your generosity and tolerance over this highly unethical affair. Do let me know if Shawn's proposals are acceptable to you: as you said, he's a most helpful man and I'm sure would play along with any emendations you might suggest.

By the way, I told Terry [Kilmartin] that I thought Wayland Young[2] might be a good replacement for me. What do you think?

Yours,
[Ken][3]

[1] William Shawn (1907–92), legendary editor of the *New Yorker* 1952–87, described by KPT as

'a small dormouse-like man in his early 50s'. KPT admired Shawn's devotion to good writing and his literary taste.

[2] Lord Kennet (Wayland Young) (b. 1923), politician and author of *The Italian Left* (1949) and *Eros Denied* (1965).

[3] Astor replied agreeing to the proposal and hoping KPT would return. He concluded, 'There is no one working for this paper who adds more to its character and credit than you do.'

To Dr Thomas Tennent[1]

120 Mount Street
28th October 1958

Dear Dr Tennent,

Thank you for your letter of October 27th. I am leaving for New York on Saturday and propose to pay a final visit to my Mother on Thursday 30th, probably just before or just after lunch. It would be nice to see you for a few minutes if possible.

Will you have moved her into the main hospital by then? If so, will there be space in her new room for extra furniture? I ask this because, acting on the assumption that she would be moving into the villa, I have arranged for a couple of chairs to be sent to her from Birmingham. These will probably arrive at Northampton on Friday. I hope there will be room to fit them in.

Meanwhile, thank you for your help.

Yours sincerely,
Kenneth Tynan

[1] Dr Thomas Tennent was the medical superintendent of St Andrew's psychiatric hospital, Northampton, to which KPT's mother Rose was admitted on 7 October, accompanied by KPT. She was suffering from what was then called organic dementia and would now be termed senile dementia of an Alzheimer type. On the medical enquiry form, KPT described his mother as 'docile, helpful, pious, and of simple tastes . . . She was unable to marry my father since his wife refused a divorce and lived with him as his wife for about 25 years.' To the question about the possible cause of her illness, he replied, 'loneliness'.

To Sir Michael Balcon

[?Mount Street]
[?December 1958]

Dear Sir Michael,

I owe you £4000.

Morally, that is: for technically I performed the services for which you paid me that sum, plus expenses, over a period of two years. In the spring of 1956 I joined Ealing Films, at your invitation, to act as Script Editor, which meant that I was to recommend to you and the Ealing directors writers, subjects and stories for feature films. In the spring of 1958 I left on six months' leave to concentrate on my own writing, but in the autumn I accepted another job that would take me out of England, and I accordingly resigned my Ealing post. During my two years with you, two years in which I was your adviser and consultant, Ealing made the following films: 'Barnacle Bill',[1] 'Davy',[2] 'Dunkirk',[3] and 'Nowhere to Go'.[4] 'The Scapegoat',[5] adapted from the Daphne du Maurier best-selling romance, was about to go on the floor. Surveying that list, I cannot help feeling that I let you down rather heavily. You may seek to reassure me by pointing out that 'The Shiralee',[6] a simple and honest picture, was made in the summer of 1956; but you know quite well that it was already fully scripted before I joined you. And 'Dunkirk', another honest if dullish piece of work, was also in an advanced stage of planning. 'Barnacle Bill' was an idea of T. E. B. Clarke's, for whom some work had to be found since he was under contract to Ealing. 'Davy' was the brainchild of William Rose:[7] here I can defend myself a little by saying that I never thought it better than mediocre. But my only positive contribution to the company's output was to collaborate on the script of 'Nowhere to Go'; and since I now hear (though I have not seen the finished version) that forty minutes of that picture have been cut, I doubt if I can claim much credit, or discredit, for what remains. Moreover, the novel on which it was based came to Ealing not through me but through Harry Watt.[8] So, if wages are in any sense based on visible output, I owe you £4000.

If there is any justice, I should owe you a great deal more; for at my suggestion, backed up at various times by various directors, you spent large sums of money on writers whose work you never used and books you never turned into films. And I am not counting the many hours of valuable time you spent, at my instigation, meeting writers you never employed and reading books you never bought. If Ealing should collapse, let not my name be absent from the list of those who brought it to its knees. But it occurs to me that many readers[9] may now be thinking you slightly mad to have engaged me at all. I do not myself think you were mad; and to explain why I had better give some account of the way in which Ealing is run and of how I functioned within it.

All Ealing films are 'produced by Michael Balcon', and they are directed by Ealing directors; that is to say, by men under contract to and invariably trained by Ealing, first in the cutting rooms and then as associate producers. This gives them a feeling of corporate loyalty rather greater than one finds in most studios; it also tends to impart to them a sort of corporate docility, since their relationship to the boss often remains what it was at the start of their careers – i.e. that of new boy to headmaster. (Many of them, perhaps for this reason, stammer.) Ealing grows its own plants, and mature alien shoots are seldom if ever grafted on to the organism. There is another handicap: the schooling provided by Ealing includes nothing relating to the handling of actors – a comment applicable to English films at large. Apart from Alec Guinness, Ealing has 'made' no actors of any significance: performances in the company's films vary from the tentative to the workaday, and seldom beyond it.

This proud, and somewhat jealous, insistence on using only Ealing directors makes for certain limitations when it comes to selecting stories. Your principle, Sir Michael, has always been to refrain from imposing subjects on your directors, and it is a generous one, even if it does restrict your programme to the mental and emotional horizons of half a dozen men. My job was to find subjects that appealed to these men and then, accompanied by the director in question, to sell the idea to you. Sometimes a subject I thought superb would appeal to none of them: this would have to be written off, since your code forbade the importation of outside directors. (Robert Hamer,[10] who directed 'The Scapegoat', is not under contract to Ealing, but he counts as an alumnus.) When I joined you, the directors available to you were Charles Frend,[11] Michael Truman,[12] Basil Dearden,[13] Michael Relph[14] and Leslie Norman;[15] later Harry Watt returned from television, and Seth Holt[16] rose from associate-producing to direction. Dearden and Relph departed after 'Davy' and struck out, like Alexander Mackendrick and Charles Crichton[17] before them, on their own. Most of my time was spent with Messrs. Frend, Truman, Norman, Watt and Holt. It looks, in retrospect, as [?if] I wasted most of it, and at your expense.

Possibly my approach to the job was based on a misapprehension. I doubt very much if I would have taken a similar post with any other British company, even in the eccentric event of it being offered. In the spring of 1956 Ealing had just begun to be financed by M-G-M and to live at Borehamwood, where its employees were housed in a sort of outsize Anderson shelter[18] in a corner of the Metro lot; but the terms of the contract seemed to allow Ealing extraordinary freedom. Metro would guarantee either general or art-house distribution in the U.S., and the choice of stories was, subject to Breen Office[19] gripes, up to you. I had just written an article about Ealing[20] in which I complained at the studio's reluctance, shared by British films in toto, to deal at all seriously with sex, social problems or politics. At that time Ealing still seemed to me the only British company capable of filling these gaps. It was run by a man (yourself) of enthusiastically liberal convictions and independent spirit. I imagined that you had brought me in to act as a pipeline for that sort of blood transfusion I thought the British cinema needed. I couldn't (and still can't) think why else you should have employed a drama critic known to be arty and rather more than suspected of being socially 'committed'. I knew, of course, that there would be problems. I had no dreams of turning Ealing inside out. Moreover, I knew from experience my inability to out-argue high executives face to face. In films I was new and nervous, often much too nervous. But I felt sure that I had been engaged as something more than a conscience-salve, and I hoped to push through a few subjects from which controversy would not be wholly absent. My error, as Lindsay Anderson[21] pointed out in a conversation to which I'll return later, was to suppose that the British film industry could be changed from within. But I clung to it, and that is what cost you all that money and time. My only solace is that at least you got some of it back by reselling the scripts.

Your argument against making controversial pictures sounded, at first, extremely convincing. 'I can't gamble', you would say (and I don't think I'm breaking a confidence) 'with other people's money.' But later I decided that, as an argument, it did you less than justice. After all, the whole business of an impresario, unless he is a multi millionaire in his own right, is to gamble with other people's money. There is no other way of making films. You yourself gambled more than half a million pounds on 'Dunkirk'. For about a third of that you might, if you had chosen to, have made a British equivalent to 'The Bachelor Party':[22] but that is another matter. The point is that all art, even bad art, is a gamble. What I think you really felt, when deciding, often after the third or fourth rewrite, against filming an explosive subject, was that something in your temperament shuddered at the thought of handling awkward, naked ideas that might 'in some quarters' give offence. I think you also felt that this something, this kind of ideological <u>pudeur</u>, was reflected in the mind of the cinemagoing public. You may have been right: the attitude is defensible. On the other hand, at that stage in your career and at that nadir in the international repute of British films, it might have been worth while to gamble. More worth while, anyway, than making 'Davy'.

I feel that at this point I had better document my guilt and list some of the subjects I proposed to you. Many, as happens in any company, never got beyond the discussion stage. There was 'The Reason Why',[23] Cecil Woodham-Smith's devastating anatomy of the military Crimean mind, which was subsequently bought by Douglas Fairbanks; there was Joyce Carey's [*sic*] 'The Horse's Mouth',[24] now a prize-winning vehicle for Alec Guinness – that was Leslie Norman's pet. And William Rose's idea for a film that should totally cover a strike, from genesis to settlement: that never looked like getting under weigh. Nor, in 1956, did I really believe that you would ever engage Carl Foreman[25] as a writer, even under a pseudonym; there were problems of American distribution, and also of Mr. Foreman's fees. But what about the writers whose work you bought, and abandoned? Already, in 1956, you owned 'Lucky Jim'[26] and disliked it: and it went elsewhere. For Michael Truman you bought H.E. Bates' 'The Jacaranda Tree',[27] that tough, unsparing account of a group of English residents escaping from wartime Burma; that went through many scripts and a long Oriental reconnaissance before it was dropped; too expensive. Gerald Hanley's 'The Consul at Sunset',[28] about the decline of British rule in East Africa, was an old idea long before I arrived: it was momentarily revived and instantly rejected, because it was too timely. Had it not been timely, that too would have been a serviceable reason for abandoning it. I think, too, of 'Look Back in Anger',[29] which was offered to Ealing; though here the dissuading factor, for you, was the presence in the package of Tony Richardson, an imported director. John Osborne himself, as a screenwriter, you always wanted to use, though you never met him or made him an offer.

Outside the half-dozen efficient, undisturbing, sleek-edged scenarists who write most British scripts, there is a void, which I conceived it part of my job to fill. I recall a plan to hire writers on short-term contracts, the first beneficiary of which was J.P. Donleavy, the uproarious author of 'The Ginger Man'. Mr. Donleavy turned out a wild, biting Irish comedy called 'The Rich Goat',[30] which Orson Welles borrowed from me and called the most brilliant original screenplay he had read for years. I recall that it bewildered you; and I recall betting that you would never make it. Then there was James Kennaway, brought to Ealing by Basil Dearden with a script of his own novel 'Tunes of Glory': you liked it, but another company is making it.[31] At my suggestion Kennaway went on to write a superb, free-ranging study of an itinerant English Dixieland band, sardonic strolling players cutting through the class barriers like processed cheese, behaving with an anarchic wit which, coupled with the jazz ambience, might easily have drawn back to the cinemas the younger audience that is ignoring them. 'The Saints',[32] it was called; but I gather that it needed more plot, in your view; will you really, do you think, make it? It has no simple hero, nor yet a bad chap converted, nor even a good girl wronged: just people, scoffing and confused and worried and sexing around. And do you remember Maurice Richardson's[33] story about crime in a Midland town during a hot summer, the story about a professional informer who is finally crushed by the interpenetration, in our society, of the law and the criminals; and the wife who, by performing a moral act and telling the police about an impending crime, is responsible for her husband's rejection by both sides? Whatever happened to that admirable, documented piece of story-telling? And so many more. Harry Watt's impassioned indictment of our mental homes, and a girl wrongfully confined in one of them, moved me when I read it to tears. He called it, rather too stridently, 'We Are the Friendless':[34] but there was a marvellous film in it. A Polish film, perhaps; all right for a State-run industry, too ticklish for democracy to stomach. And again, there was Colin MacInnes's novel, 'City of Spades',[35] about the African immigrants in London. You bought that, but since it contained references to prostitution and drug-taking, not to mention a black man kissing a white girl, I never seriously expected to see it on the year's schedule, in spite of the fact that it was also very funny. I hear that you have since resold it, or let the option lapse.

For Lindsay Anderson you bought a book called 'Casualty',[36] about life in the casualty ward of a London hospital. To hire Mr. Anderson was a good idea, but it did not work out. His first outline was vague and discursive, as you and I agreed; he began work on a second, then said he felt unable to finish it, since it ran against his idea of the kind of semi-documentary the film should be; his delays having already cost you option money, you indicated that he was out; whereupon he suddenly produced, almost overnight, a much better treatment. By then it was too late. You could not withdraw from your position, and Mr. Anderson knew that he was not wanted. It was during this protracted business that I had the conversation with Mr. Anderson to which I referred earlier. It was after he had submitted the vague outline. I took the line that the film was a narrative medium, he that it was a human medium. What to me was plot was to him compromise. He felt, quite genially, that the film had little chance of being made even if he strengthened the plot. Such was his mistrust of the industry. So he was dilatory over strengthening it. You, I imagine, doubted his ability to make it even if he strengthened it. Such was your mistrust of 'intellectuals'. There was never a meeting of minds; indeed, apart from an initial lunch before a word was written, there was never a meeting. The no-man's-land between Establishment and Outsider never began to be trodden. Yet a lot of time and money was spent on this non-fraternisation.

Of 'Lord of the Flies',[37] what can I say? William Golding's novel about the castaway schoolboys whose primitive society, on a desert island, degenerates into savagery and almost to cannibalism, is an admitted postwar masterpiece. You bought it, Leslie Norman was to direct it (despite strong bids from Peter Brook and Luis Bunuel[38]), and Nigel Kneale[39] wrote a stunning script which, faithfully shot, would have been a sleeping prize-winner at any festival. But, the idea being to shoot it on an island off Australia, you were horrified to hear that certain conservative groups in that continent were objecting to the production of a film so violent and disruptive in their environs. Furthermore, since the whole cast was made up of schoolchildren, there could be no marquee attraction. When I left Ealing last spring, Kneale's latest script had just arrived. When I next heard of it, the book and scripts had been sold to Sam Spiegel.[40] Mr. Spiegel is also an independent, also dependent on box-office and distribution. He is going to make it with Peter Brook directing. He made that other 'British' prize-winner, you will recall, 'The Bridge on the River Kwai'. It was not a masterpiece, but it was an attempt at one, made by an opportunist, but an unfrightened opportunist.

We won't talk of other things, the ideas for musicals, the other chimeras I pursued through two years of Ealing. Nor will we accuse anybody of moral cowardice, since we both suffer from it: I, in plugging ideas, and you, in carrying them out. I want simply to say that I apologise for taking up so much of your time, when I should have known that we both, from the beginning, had different ideas about the function of the cinema. I should have quit; or you should have fired me. On both sides, good taste intervened to prevent action. You still owe the British public a first-rate film. And I still owe you £4000.

Yours sincerely,
[unsigned][41]

---

[1] Seaside comedy directed by Charles Frend, starring Alec Guinness and Irene Brown (UK, 1957).

[2] Comic vehicle for Harry Secombe, directed by Michael Relph (UK, 1957).

[3] World War II drama directed by Leslie Norman, starring John Mills and Richard Attenborough (UK, 1958).

[4]Thriller adapted by KPT and Seth Holt (who directed) from the novel by Donald Mackenzie Smith, starring George Nader and Maggie Smith (UK, 1958).

[5]Produced by MGM, adapted by Gore Vidal and Robert Hamer (who directed), starring Alec Guinness and Bette Davis (UK, 1959).

[6]Comedy set in Australia, directed by Leslie Norman and starring Peter Finch (UK, 1957).

[7]William Rose (1918–87), American screenwriter who entered British films in 1947 and wrote *Genevieve* (UK, 1953) and *The Ladykillers* (UK, 1955). He won an Academy Award for *Guess Who's Coming to Dinner* (US, 1967).

[8]Harry Watt (1906–87), English documentary director (*Night Mail*, UK, 1936) who came to Ealing during the war, where he made five feature films.

[9]This letter was possibly intended for publication.

[10]Robert Hamer (1911–63), English director whose films include *Kind Hearts and Coronets* (UK, 1949).

[11]Charles Frend (1909–77), English director who began as a film editor; his films include *Scott of the Antarctic* (UK, 1948).

[12]Michael Truman (1916–74), English director who came to Ealing as an editor in 1944; his first film was *Touch and Go* (UK, 1955).

[13]Basil Dearden (1911–71), English director, producer and screenwriter whose films include several Will Hay movies in the early 1940s, and *Khartoum* (UK, 1966).

[14]Michael Relph (b. 1915), son of the actor George Relph, first an art director then a director: *Davy* (UK, 1957) and *Rockets Galore* (UK, 1957).

[15]Leslie Norman (1911–93), English editor and producer of films such as *The Cruel Sea* (UK, 1953) who became a director in 1955 with *The Night My Number Came Up*. He went on to direct *Dunkirk* (UK, 1958) and *The Long and the Short and the Tall* (UK, 1961). His son is the film critic Barry Norman.

[16]Seth Holt (1923–71), English director who began as an editor; his films include *The Nanny* (UK, 1965) and *Blood From the Mummy's Tomb* (UK, 1971).

[17]Charles Crichton (b.1910), English director of films including *Hue and Cry* (UK, 1947), *The Lavender Hill Mob* (UK, 1951) and *The Titfield Thunderbolt* (UK, 1953). He later directed *A Fish Called Wanda* (UK, 1989).

[18]Small underground shelters protected by curved, corrugated steel roofs, used by families in World War II.

[19]The American film censorship organization run by Joseph I. Breen, set up as a voluntary measure by the Hollywood studios in 1930; films were to avoid depicting brutality or any kind of sexual promiscuity, and words like 'sex' and 'hell' were forbidden.

[20]'Tight Little Studio', *Harper's* magazine (US, August 1955).

[21]Lindsay Anderson (b.1923), English theatre and film director whose first feature would be *This Sporting Life* (UK, 1963).

[22]Adapted by Paddy Chayevsky from his television play, directed by Delbert Mann, and starring Don Murray and Jack Warden (US, 1957).

[23]C. Woodham-Smith's history of the British military disaster in the Crimea (1953). Though Fairbanks negotiated to buy the rights, Balcon in fact sold them to the actor Laurence Harvey. The story was finally filmed in 1968 by Tony Richardson under the title *The Charge of the Light Brigade* after a legal battle with Harvey over alleged plagiarization of the book in John Osborne's preliminary screenplay.

[24]Joyce Cary's novel (1944) was adapted by Alec Guinness and directed by Ronald Neame (US, 1958) with Guinness as the artist Gulley Jimson.

[25]Carl Foreman (1914–84), blacklisted American screenwriter of *High Noon* (US, 1952) who came to Britain in the early 1950s and wrote *The Bridge on the River Kwai* (UK, 1957) and *Young Winston* (UK, 1972).

[26]Novel by Kingsley Amis (1954); the film was begun outside Ealing by Charles Crichton but

taken over by the Boulting Brothers and made in 1957.

[27] Published 1949; never filmed.

[28] Published 1951; never filmed.

[29] *Look Back in Anger*, based on John Osborne's 1956 play, directed by Tony Richardson and starring Richard Burton (UK, 1959), was produced by Woodfall Films.

[30] To have been directed by Seth Holt, but never made due to the sale of Ealing Films.

[31] *Tunes of Glory* (1956) was filmed by Ronald Neame for United Artists (UK, 1960) with Alec Guinness and John Mills.

[32] Never made.

[33] Later television critic for the *Observer*, 1966–78.

[34] Never made.

[35] Published 1957; never filmed. MacInnes (1914–76) was also the author of *Absolute Beginners* (1957), filmed in 1986.

[36] The story of a young doctor; Balcon refused to appoint anyone to work with Anderson.

[37] 1954 novel by Sir William Golding (1911–93), who was awarded the Nobel Prize for Literature in 1983. The film was finally made by Peter Brook (UK, 1963), and again by Harry Hook (US, 1990).

[38] Luis Buñuel (1900–83), Spanish filmmaker whose early collaboration with Salvador Dali resulted in the surrealist films *Un Chien andalou* (France, 1928) and *L'Age d'or* (France, 1930). He had recently directed *El* and *Nazarin* and was living in Mexico.

[39] Nigel Kneale (b. 1922), scriptwriter responsible for the science-fiction series *Quatermass* and co-adaptor with John Osborne of Osborne's *Look Back in Anger* (UK, 1959) and *The Entertainer* (UK, 1960).

[40] Sam Spiegel (1903–85), Hollywood producer of *On the Waterfront* (US, 1954), *The Bridge on the River Kwai* (UK, 1957) and *Lawrence of Arabia* (UK, 1962), all of which won Academy Awards for Best Picture.

[41] The letter, which exists in draft, may never have been sent.

CHAPTER FOUR

Crest of the Wave

'Jazz, beat, Mort Sahl, "Mad", Salinger, H'wood 10, Dissent, Zen': those were the notes Ken made in his engagement book as he crossed the Atlantic to take up his post at the New Yorker. And those were some of the subjects he explored during two exuberant years in America during which the bland performance of Broadway played second fiddle to the richer stage of politics, travel, and experiments in living and art.

The New Yorker did not permit their main critic to cover off-Broadway, where Genet and Beckett flourished alongside new playwrights like Edward Albee, Jack Gelber, Arthur Kopit and Jack Richardson. So Ken had to make do with the uninspiring mainstream, the 'strolls down memory lane', lit occasionally by an incandescent musical like Gypsy. Handicapped, he yet performed with aplomb. Fellow writers at the magazine, including J. D. Salinger and John Steinbeck, welcomed him warmly; and James Thurber wrote to say he had brought 'a new and special brilliance, style, wit and learning to the theater page'.

Ken respected the New Yorker's passion for clarity, syntax and accuracy and permitted its courtly though puritanical editor, William Shawn, to censor his copy. Mr Shawn in turn thought very highly of his new critic, 'comparable to Max Beerbohm and Shaw yet quite different', but wished he would experiment with other forms. Why not a play?

Ken made notes to 'Write play', 'Write biography' and 'Write pornographic book'. But instead he submitted to a crowded social life, often in the company of Norman Mailer, Allen Ginsberg, James Baldwin, Terry Southern, George Plimpton and Jules Feiffer. According to the critic Richard Watts Jr, 'All you had to do at a New York party to attract attention was to say loudly "Kenneth Tynan", and excited men and women would start arguing violently.'

For the Observer or Holiday magazine, Ken was able to write about the Beat poets, the satirist Lenny Bruce, jazz, the cinema, and the need for an American subsidized national theatre. The Observer published these reports and critiques while trying to persuade him to return. But because of his own and his wife Elaine's tax situation, Ken was advised that he would have to stay out of Britain until April 1960; even two weeks at an English hotel in *the summer might put his financial position in jeopardy. He asked for a second year in New York – suggesting the American critic and theatre director Harold Clurman as a temporary replacement. The* Observer *agreed to hold the post open until his return.*

In May 1959, Ken set out alone for Europe to write about the French, German and English theatre for the New Yorker. *Elaine took their seven-year-old daughter Tracy to Martha's Vineyard that summer, and New York was for a while free of the warring couple. Observers reported that they both seemed to work out of their own individual fortresses. Norman Mailer recalled that 'they'd hit each other shots that you'd just sit there and applaud like you would at a prize fight.'*

While in Europe Ken met and started an affair with an attractive American painter called Addie Herder, a woman with short-cropped hair and a curvaceous figure. She accompanied him to Germany with the novelist James Jones and his wife Gloria. In his New Yorker *report he wrote that he could find no theatre in Europe to match the 'versatility, consistency and extensiveness' of the 121 subsidized theatres in West Germany and the eighty-six in the East. Tennessee Williams read his long piece and wrote to Ken singling out his writing on Brecht: 'It's a piece of literature.'*

Back on Broadway he headed his review of Rodgers' and Hammerstein's The Sound of Music, *'The Case for Trappism'. Since off-Broadway was off-limits, he wrote to Shawn to suggest he list in the magazine a startlingly original first play about the drug culture called* The Connection. *He went to San Francisco to explore the Beats, to admire the 'precise and wittily sepulchral' prose of William Burroughs; and to consort with the Zen philosopher Alan Watts and the alto sax player Paul Desmond.*

On 22 May, at the end of his second year, Ken bade a grand farewell to New York at a party in the restaurant the Forum of the Twelve Caesars. The cast of two hundred guests included Gore Vidal, Lauren Bacall, Richard Avedon, Lillian Hellman and James Thurber – more uptown than downtown. Ken was photographed in a pale blue dinner jacket happily embracing Vivien Leigh. Two days later he flew home to London.

To Terence Kilmartin

56 East 89th St.[1]
N.Y.
Dec 16 [1958]

Dear Terry –
    I hope to send you another piece some time next week – though God

knows what it will be about – and I'll follow it up with some thoughts about J. Littlewood.[2]

Too bad about the Shawl:[3] I must say I had premonitions of disaster when I heard Froth Binbury was on to it. Life here is fine, the theatre so far grim. The New Yorker is madly hospitable but has a sort of Fowler[4] Fixation that makes it jump on the tiniest vagaries of grammar, syntax and punctuation. It's also a bit anti-sex. Once out of the office I curse and mutter obscenities and say 'ain't,' just to let off steam.

I'll send the piece air freight as you suggest.

Love,
Ken

[1] KPT's New York apartment during his year and a half with the *New Yorker*.
[2] Joan Littlewood (b.1914), English theatre director, founder of Theatre Workshop in 1945, which was later based at the Theatre Royal, Stratford East. Her productions there included *A Taste of Honey* (1958) and *Oh, What a Lovely War!* (1963).
[3] Frith Banbury (see letter of 29 January 1953) had directed Errol John's *Moon on a Rainbow Shawl*, winner of the 1957 *Observer* play competition (see letter 19 April 1958), at the Royal Court.
[4] A reference to Fowler's *Dictionary of Modern English Usage*.

To Terence Kilmartin

[56 East 89th Street]
[11 April 1959]

Dear Terry;

Herewith the Broadway piece; I'll send the Mary McCarthy one within a week.[1]

Do you think you could ask David [Astor] – or Tristan[2] – whether it would be possible for me to be paid for this piece and subsequent ones in America rather than in England? My tax chap says that if I'm paid in England it means that I'm employed there and hence subject to full English tax. If on the other hand I could be paid in New York, the problem would vanish. It isn't a very important point, but I'd like to know how Tristan feels.

I spent my time in Havana[3] with Hemingway (venerable), Tennessee Williams (disturbing) and Castro (excellent, ebullient, and a real radical). Alas, I desperately fear that the rich Americans who supported him, thinking he'd never really stick to the programme he promised, are now about to pull out, which may mean both the collapse of his régime and his imminent assassination. This is to be worried about.

I've sent pictures under separate cover.

Love –

Ken

[1] A review of Mary McCarthy's collection of theatre reviews, *Sights and Spectacles* (*Observer*, 10 May 1959).

[2] Tristan Jones, the *Observer*'s General Manager 1953–75.

[3] Written up as 'A Visit to Havana' (*Holiday*, February 1960).

To Bill and Annie Davis[1]

56 East 89th Street

April 30, 1959

Dear Bill and Annie:

Recent conversations with Ernest and Mary [Hemingway] started all kinds of trails of thought, leading to you.

I went down to Havana to do a piece on the town for 'Holiday', and there saw a lot of Poppa,[2] who is in terrific form and spoke much of you. He also made extensive enquiries about the possibilities of privacy at the Cónsula, which I told him were limitless.

By a fluke, Tennessee Williams happened to be in Cuba at the time, and I had the unnerving experience of introducing him to Hemingway and Castro on the same day. The interview with Hemingway was hilarious, though I didn't feel that much real contact was made. Tennessee arrived slightly tanked up in preparation for what he thought was going to be a terrifying ordeal. (He had earlier expressed fears that Hemingway might kick or cuff him). He began by paying fulsome tribute to Poppa's first wife,[3] and asked, rather too persistently, for details of her death. Poppa thought for a minute and then said, 'She died, like everybody else, and after that she was dead.' That ended that subject.

Tennessee then tried bullfighting and started to praise Chamaco;[4] seeing that this wasn't a very good idea, he launched into a eulogy of Antonio.[5] Poppa listened gravely for a while and then asked; 'Do you think we would like him?' Tennessee assured him that we would.

Tennessee's next gambit was William Faulkner,[6] but I am afraid even this didn't bridge the gap between him and Poppa. They temporarily found common ground, however, when discussing the relative longevity of the liver and kidneys.

During the conversation, Tennessee turned to me and remarked raptly, if a bit too loudly, 'Isn't he a beautiful man. I think Mr. Hemingway is such a beautiful man! What I like about his work is the way he is concerned about honor among men. There's no more desperate quest than that.' I mentioned this observation to Poppa afterwards. He said, 'People who have honor don't talk about it. You and me, we don't use the word – what we do is confer immortality on each other.'

All in all, it was a real wild encounter. I'll tell you about Castro when I see you, but I think Poppa is quite right: his is a good revolution.

I am enjoying the 'New Yorker' and have decided to stay on for the next season, returning to England in the Spring of 1960. I am leaving New York next month to spend six weeks writing pieces for the magazine about the theatre in France, Germany and Poland.[7] Then, in mid-July, I am going to meet Elaine and Tracy in Spain, where we'll spend a month. Naturally, we are coming to Málaga, probably about a week before the Feria, which I see begins on August 2nd. Poppa's last word to me in New York, where we spent an evening together the day before he sailed, was that Antonio and Luis Miguel[8] would be fighting together this season; he said he would stay for the whole summer if the bulls looked good and untouched and worthy of Antonio.

Now, be frank: Would it bug, harass, disturb or otherwise inconvenience you if we sought a bit of your incomparable shelter? I mentioned to Ernest that I'd probably write this kind of begging letter and he said he would be very pleased if we were there, but this may have been just politeness and I wish you would check with him before replying. Whatever happens, we can always get into the Miramar,[9] where we would be perfectly happy; I'm writing as early as this so as to be sure that I can make reservations, if necessary.

Antonio was in New York for a few days with an entourage including Cayetano,[10] Camara hijo,[11] Landete,[12] Carmencita[13] and several others. We had lunch with him and Peter Buckley;[14] it turned out to be the usual bullfighters' reunion, with lots of bread thrown about and even a few ice cubes. The odd thing was that it all happened on the top floor of 666 5th Avenue.[15] I think some of the silver-foxed matrons were pretty bewildered.

Let me know how you are and where you'll be. Meanwhile, Elaine sends love, as indeed do I.

Ever,
Ken (Tynan)

The envelope is genuine – I stole it from a producing office, thinking it appropriate for a Broadway Critic.

[1] An American couple with private means who entertained writers such as Hemingway and Cyril Connolly in the manner of the Gerald Murphys. Their house, La Cónsula, in Churriana outside Málaga, was decorated by local craftsmen and had an impressive library.

[2] Hemingway's nickname, more usually 'Papa'.

[3] Almost certainly a reference to Hemingway's second wife Pauline Pfeiffer, who died on 1 October 1951.

[4] The 'ring name' of Antonio Borrero (b. 1935), a highly successful torero who retired in 1967.

[5] Antonio Ordóñez (b. 1932), legendary exponent of classical bullfighting whose fan club included Hemingway; KPT described him in his journal as 'the courteous young maestro of Ronda' and wrote a homage, 'The Testing of Antonio Ordóñez' (*Atlantic Monthly*, May 1973; reprinted in *The Sound of Two Hands Clapping*).

[6] William Faulkner (1897–1962), Nobel Prize-winning American novelist whose works include *The Sound and the Fury* (1929), *Sanctuary* (1931) and *As I Lay Dying* (1935).

[7] KPT wrote *New Yorker* pieces on the theatre in France (1 August 1959), Germany (12 September 1959) and England (26 September 1959).

[8] Luis Miguel González Lucas ('Dominguín') (b. 1944), equally renowned matador with a great knowledge of the bulls; brother-in-law of Ordóñez. He fought his last corrida on 1 December 1973 in Quito.

[9] Edwardian hotel in Málaga, now demolished; KPT would stay there.

[10] Cayetano Ordóñez (b. 1928), elder brother of Antonio, who took his Alternativa (graduation to fully-fledged matador) in 1946 but never reached the level of his father or brother; he retired in 1963.

[11] Camará hijo (literally 'son'), the son of the famous ex-matador José Flores Gonzalez 'Camará', who was also a successful manager (Manolete's) and promoter.

[12] Probably Bernardino Landete, a *rejoneador*, or bullfighter on horseback, active in the late 1950s.

[13] Carmen Ordóñez, first wife of Antonio Ordóñez; she was the daughter of Domingo Dominguín and sister of Luis Miguel Dominguín.

[14] Peter Buckley (b. 1925), American photographer and author of books on bullfighting and on Hemingway.

[15] A restaurant called Top of the Sixes with a panoramic view of New York; it opened in 1958.

To Elaine Tynan

Hotel am Steinplatz
West Berlin
13th [June 1959]

Dear Skip;[1]

At last a relatively free moment to write – which is what, by the way, I've discovered I absolutely can't do without you. It's now three days since I left Paris, and the desire to put it on paper is nil. It's as if it happened only to half of me, to half a machine that can't run without the other half. However: Paris.

Heat and Henry Hewes.[2] An evening with Gene Kelly[3] when we went to a Montparnasse place called the Epiclub which is the centre of the Sagan[4] set. Met the pensive little creature and told her the Dietrich story about her,[5] which she denied outright and was much amused by. Couldn't see her again because she left for St. Tropez next day. Took Janet Flanner[6] out several times, once to see Josephine Baker at the Olympia – who is marvellous, Judy Garland plus Lena Horne and a personality (and figure) as stunning as her voice. Janet stood up and applauded, hands over head; she had been at Baker's Paris opening thirty-odd years ago when she appeared upside down doing the splits wearing a banana-peel. No Mulligan,[7] but Bud Powell[8] the pianist was playing at the Blue Note,[9] a weighty coloured zombie who strums like a robot (dope). [...] Janet fixed for me to interview Malraux[10] at the new Ministry for Cultural Affairs, which I did, with a stenotypist, for two hours. He is dapper, crackling with energy, has a sinus snort and an eye tick [*sic*]; but he was terrifically intelligent – said the reason why all French plays were either stylised tragedy or stylised comedy was because all the French writers had an unconscious desire to 'retrouver le palais'; i.e. become part of the court again. Dined twice with Barrault, who overwhelmed me with charm and talked about his plans for the Odéon, which he takes over in the autumn. (They include Claudel,[11] the new Anouilh[12] – which I saw in Bordeaux with Tom Curtiss;[13] it's a film script about the life of Moliere that Anouilh's producers turned down, so Barrault staged it with no changes, using a dropped-in gilt frame for closeups and tiny puppets for long-shots – and the new Ionesco,[14] a three-acter. I suggested he ought to direct – and play – 'Peer Gynt'.) Incidentally, Barrault's production of 'La Vie Parisienne'[15] is the most satisfying thing – on its level – in Paris; the whole company singing and dancing, and Jean Parédès[16] hysterically funny in three parts. Curtiss introduced me to William Saroyan[17] – quite unlike what I'd expected; looks like a moustached cinema commissionaire off-duty in blue serge suit; talks robustly, and is trying to sell a script to Zanuck.[18] (He is up to here in debt.) Camus'[19] adaptation of 'The Possessed' is four hours long and immensely complicated and gets wildly melodramatic (because of compression) towards the end, but there are some lovely scenes and a lot of explosive writing (Do you remember the mad moment when Stavrogin smilingly advances on some old bourgeois waffler, beckons, and, when the man leans forward, bites his ear?) The Anouilh – 'L'Hurluberlu' – I didn't like a bit; it caters to all the bourgeois prejudices of his audience, quite consciously – anti-democratic tirades, references to 'L'honneur' of France, now alas tarnished, and a twinge of anti-Semitism here and there. (I see Rex H. [Harrison] is doing it in America. It will need a lot of fixing.)[20] [...] Gar and Ruth Kanin[21] spent an evening with me – he was going every night to 'La Bonne Soupe',[22] which is brilliantly staged and acted but tawdry writing most of the way. (It's a cocotte's life told in flashback to a croupier at a casino) [...] Saw the Greniers[23] briefly, thank God. He's finished his novel, which is called 'Yes and back Again'. They went to a Ionesco with me, another full-length item called 'Tueur sans Gages'[24]– two terrible acts and one fine one, the last, in which the Chaplinesque hero pleads with a mysterious, cretinous, immobile, snickering Death-figure not to kill anyone else ever again. Sounds dreadful, but honestly isn't; for one thing the Death-figure wears blue-jeans and looks like a Mongol idiot. [...] Oh yes, and I met Adamov,[25] who is pure Dostoevsky – haggard, chain-smoking, swarthy, early forties, passionately Left, burning eyes, great innocence, great avarice. He took me to a production of Henry IV Part Two by a young man called Roger Planchon[26] who is quite a director – a Brecht student, he's reshuffled Henry IV as a Brecht play, with captions between scenes, speeches paraphrased or precis-ed, and programme notes about the decline of the feudal system. Finally: the only good new playwright, François Billetdoux[27] (yes), who's written a twohanded piece called 'Tchin-Tchin', about a husband whose wife has left him, and the wife of the man's she's left him for. The deserted pair drink through the play and try to have an affair themselves and it doesn't work. Style: realistic-poetic. Very touching. Surprising in Montparnasse.

I saw a good deal of Jim and Gloria Jones;[28] best meal was with them and their German publisher (Fischer), who took us to the Grand Véfour[29] – toast au crevettes followed by ortolans. I said I was going to Germany and Fischer suggested Jim should go. ('The Pistol'[30] has just been published there). He said he would arrange everything, provide car and guide, etc. Jim and Gloria said yes, so here they both are, and it's getting mildly unbearable. The car is nice to have, of course, but those bulldozing conversations, and the way Jim tracks down every casual, lighthearted remark to its lair ... It gets fatiguing, e.g.

Gloria: Everybody here seems to be living in the past.

Me: Well, as Noël Coward said, there's nothing as contemporary as the past. Incidentally, Martin Held[31] – the actor I was talking about – plays all the Coward parts as well as Molière and ...

Jim: What?

Gloria: He says the actor we saw tonight plays ...

Jim: No. I mean what Ken said about Noël Coward. Is he here now?

Me: I don't think so.

Gloria: Ken just quoted a remark he made. Kind of funny. About the past.

Jim: Now we're getting somewhere.

Me: He said there was nothing as contemporary as the past. That's all. I was just telling ...

Jim: Nothing as contemptible as the past, huh? I thought he was very big for the queen and all that horse-shit.

Me: No – nothing as <u>contemporary</u>.

Jim: He said that to this actor?

Me: No – to me.

Jim: Is this actor an old guy or something?

Gloria: Let's all drop the whole thing.

Jim: Don't say that, honey, it makes me look so fucking stupid.

Gloria: Awww.

> (They nuzzle and kiss for three minutes.)

Gloria: Go on about the actor, Ken. What's his name?

Me: Martin Held. He ...

Jim: Who ordered these goddamned dumplings? Go ahead, Ken.

Me: Anyway, Held is the best actor in West Berlin, and ...

Jim: How the fuck do you spell that?

Me: H. E. L. D.

Jim: Says here on the menu it's schnumpelfroodles or some goddamn thing. I know one thing, I never ordered them. Hey, <u>garçon</u> ...

Gloria: Don't yell at the man, honey.

Me: And if you must yell at him, don't yell at him in French.

Jim: I'm not making any trouble. I haven't had a fistfight in fifteen years. It's just this horse-shit we're eating ...

Gloria (quickly): Well, I think it's a perfectly lovely place and I'm damn glad Ken brought us.

Jim (atoning): Sure, it's great. Go right ahead about Noël Coward, Ken. He's a homosexual, isn't he? ... [...]

In my solitudes I've been going over the moments – during this trip – when, had you been here, we might have had rows. They all turn out to be wildly trivial, and to fall under three headings:

1) My edginess on arriving in foreign cities, even when I've been there before. This makes me scared to use the language, and therefore reluctant to ask for directions and get into discussions. This edginess communicates itself to you – hence rows.

2) My chronic indecision, over such matters as: where to eat? shall we meet X before or after the show? shall we see Y at all? This has remained as chronic as ever during this trip, but again it might have led us into rows, as it has often in the past. Honestly, these things are

so peripheral and unimportant, beside the big fact of your absence. Let's never let them divert us again.

3) Haste and hurry rows – including taxis (lack of.) These seemed unnecessary. One day in Paris when there was a Metro strike, I had to walk from the Etoile to Tom Curtiss's apartment underneath the Tour d'Argent. I managed it without too much stress. Yet it might have provoked us to a fight. Madness, my darling, madness.

The trouble is that all the time we're unconsciously saying to each other: 'Why aren't you perfect? Be perfect, damn you. Be decisive and unruffled and unafraid. Or: be patient and tender and understanding.' I've had time lately to realise that I don't want you perfect. I just want you. You are the only proof I have that I exist. I am in love with you in the same way that the earth revolves around the sun. If I don't see you within a few weeks I shall take to my bed and have one of those wasting diseases people died of in Victorian novels.

So far I've had very few late nights (I mean after-two-a.m. nights) and hardly any serious drinking. Yet I can't work. What this proves is that work depends on your proximity. Please be proximitous soon. I die when I think you may be utterly happy without me, with shock-headed Len,[32] the Philharmonic Fool, and saturnine Styron,[33] and that lean, pipesmoking, urbane, thirty-five year old genius you are sleeping with and whose name I'll never know until I get that terrible letter beginning: 'Dear Ken, We always said we'd tell each [other] if either of us fell in love with anyone else, and – well – I think it's happened to me . . .'

I'd better stop before I get maudlin. Writing this is like a drug; it gives me a temporary hallucination that you're here. Give my dearest love to Tracy, and as many hugs as she can count up to, and tell her I've got lots of pictures of the unicorn in the Cluny Tapestry to give her when I get back.

Meanwhile, all my solitary love to you:

K.

[1] Elaine's nickname was 'Skipper'.

[2] Henry Hewes (b. 1917), drama critic for the *Saturday Review* 1954–77.

[3] Gene Kelly (b. 1912), American dancer and screen actor whose films include *Singin' in the Rain* (US, 1952). On his first visit to Los Angeles in 1954, KPT stayed with Kelly, with whom he had become friends in London.

[4] Françoise Sagan (b. 1935), French novelist and playwright, whose works include *Bonjour tristesse* (1954), and *Aimez-vous Brahms?* (1959).

[5] A lesbian saga concocted by Dietrich.

[6] Janet Flanner (d. 1978), distinguished American journalist, Paris correspondent of the *New Yorker* under the pseudonym 'Genêt'.

[7] Gerry Mulligan (b. 1927), American baritone saxophone player and arranger.

[8] Bud Powell (1924–66), American jazz pianist who became a major exponent of bebop and worked with Charlie Parker, Dizzy Gillespie and Max Roach.

[9] A Paris jazz club.

[10] André Malraux (1901–76), French novelist and Minister of Cultural Affairs in de Gaulle's Government 1960–9. KPT's interview with Malraux features in his *New Yorker* article on the French theatre (1 August 1959).

[11] *Tête d'or* by Paul Claudel (1868–1955), had never been publicly performed before Barrault's production.

[12] *La Petite Molière*, by Jean Anouilh (1910–87), whose other works include *Antigone* (1946) and *Becket* (1961).

[13] Thomas Quinn Curtiss, cultural reporter for the *Herald Tribune*.

[14] Eugène Ionesco (1912–94), Romanian-born French absurdist playwright. The new play was *Le Rhinocéros* (1958).

[15] Operetta by Offenbach, playing at the Théâtre du Palais Royal in 1959.

[16] Jean Parédès, French comic actor.

[17] William Saroyan (1908–81), American playwright and novelist, whose works include *The Daring Young Man on the Flying Trapeze* (1934) and *My Name is Aram* (1940). He was married to Carol Marcus, now Carol Matthau, a one-time lover of KPT's.

[18] Daryl F. Zanuck (1902–79), Hollywood mogul, co-founder and head of 20th Century Fox.

[19] Albert Camus (1913–60), French novelist (*L'Etranger*, 1942) and playwright (*Caligula*, 1945), directed his own adaptation of Dostoevsky's novel.

[20] Translated as *The Fighting Cock*, it opened in New York on 8 December 1959.

[21] Garson Kanin (b.1912), American director, screenwriter and playwright who collaborated with his wife, Ruth Gordon (1896–1985) on the screenplays for *Adam's Rib* (US, 1949) and *The Marrying Kind* (US, 1952).

[22] *La Bonne Soupe* by Félicien Marceau. It opened in London under the title *Bonne Soupe* in October 1961, with Coral Browne in the lead.

[23] Richard and Cynthia Grenier, cultural journalists.

[24] *Tueur sans gages* was playing at the Récamier.

[25] Arthur Adamov (1908–70), Russian-born French absurdist playwright whose works include *La Parodie* (1947) and *Ping-Pong* (1954).

[26] Roger Planchon (b. 1931), French director, actor and playwright, founder of a small theatre in Lyon where two of Adamov's early works were first performed. The company moved to the larger Théâtre de la Cité in 1959 and opened with *Henry IV* Parts I and II (with Planchon playing Hal) and was invited to Paris in 1959 by Jean-Louis Barrault.

[27] François Billetdoux (b. 1927), French playwright whose first work was *A la nuit la nuit* (1955). *Chin-Chin* (spelled thus) opened in London in November 1960, with Celia Johnson and Anthony Quayle.

[28] James Jones (1921–77), American novelist whose work includes *From Here to Eternity* (1951).

[29] A pre-Revolutionary restaurant in the Palais Royal.

[30] Novel by Jones (1959).

[31] Martin Held (b. 1908), leading German actor who played Claudius in *Hamlet* and made films including *Der Hauptmann von Köpenick* (Germany, 1956).

[32] Leonard Bernstein (1918–90), American symphonic conductor and composer whose works include *West Side Story* (1958) and *Candide* (1956/88).

[33] William Styron (b. 1925), American novelist whose works include *Sophie's Choice* (1979).

To Elaine Tynan

Connaught [Hotel, London]
Friday [26 June 1959]

Dear Skip –

The fact that it's eight fifteen and I'm sitting in a hotel room writing should tell you a little about the state of things. I got your letter two hours ago as I was leaving to have drinks with Irene Selznick[1] and read it concurrently with the Salinger piece,[2] which has just arrived in England. I came back to the hotel and had two martinis, one of them with the phantom Harry Kurnitz,[3] decided against going out, re-read your letter, looking between the lines for hints that we weren't entirely insulated against each other's blandishments, and then came up to poke at the clattering machine that now seems of no use except to help me talk to you. I'm not writing. It's hot, for one reason, and damp, for another, but that isn't all. Shawn cabled today, tactfully asking how I was, but really meaning where's the stuff. Nowhere; inside but not wanting to come out, to be said to anybody. David Astor took me and the Kilmartins and the reptile Lucian Freud[4] to Bernard Miles' theatre[5] last night; the show is a musical revamp of a tart little play by Fielding, done all clever-coy and whoops-dear, but the theatre is beautiful, wide-staged and equipped with revolve, ideal for Brecht.

And that's part of the trouble. I spent most of Berlin with the Ensemble and nearly defected. In fact they said if I wanted to join them as a dramaturg (play-chooser and semi-director) I'd be welcome, and they weren't actually laughing. They're rehearsing the Drei-groschenoper[6] and the nostalgia was enormous, because it's the same theatre that housed the original production, and Engel[7] the director directed it then; to stroll in from the street and hear the Mackie Messer song was incredibly touching. Then to see 'Galileo'[8] again, so formal and elegant, followed by the Gorki adaptation, 'Die Mutter',[9] in which Weigel[10] gives one of the great performances as a quietly nagging old lady who hates her son to be a revolutionary and then slowly becomes a revolutionary herself, putting her nagging to constructive use – this would have been enough to remind me that this is the best theatre on earth, even if the production hadn't been Brecht's own – the last in their repertoire to bear his name alone – and the sets made with that grey, brown, used-looking, functional-poetic look you get nowhere else. But the next night topped even that – a late Brecht play called 'The Resistible Rise of Arturo Ui';[11] the one that tells the story of Hitler's rise to power in cod-blank verse, set in Chicago at the time of

Capone. Two of the younger directors did this together, with whirling revolves, jazz, tact, and savage speed; Wolf Kaiser[12] plays Goering BUT Ekkehard Schall[13] – the elder son in 'Courage'[14] – plays Hitler, with a ginger moustache and forelock, and a mixture of demonism à la Brando and puppet-farce à la Chaplin, switching from magnificent precise balletic comedy to really terrifying self-hypnotised rages. A perfect, model Brechtian performance – one, I think, of the ten best I've ever seen anywhere. Weigel gave me a present for you – a scarf designed by Picasso to celebrate the tenth anniversary of her 'Courage' – and one for Tracy, or indeed for any child. 'Are you a child, Tynan?' she said, in a mad purple dress, and gave me this thing; a game invented by Mozart and played with dice, whereby you make up your own Mozart waltz or rondo with cardboard squares on which notes of music are inscribed. Tell L. Bernstein this, it would be a great TV bit, damn it. I also saw 'The Entertainer'[15] – odd in German, because they have no music-hall and never had; but a production fifty times as good as Richardson's,[16] tight and cogent and incredibly proving that the central character is of all people the daughter – who's always on stage and who's been made up to stare at Archie throughout with a sort of petrified disgust at each new manifestation of his interior collapse. And there was Ezra Pound's version of Sophocles' 'Women of Trachis'[17] in West Berlin – abstract sets but strong powerful playing, despite a Hitler-Jugend chorus of madchen in gym uniform. One night – a horror: thirty thousand West German college students holding up traffic for hours as they marched under orders carrying torches, flaming torches, as a tribute to the visiting German president. All so docile, no ragging, no laughs, very sinister. What else? Martin Held superb in 'Madwoman of Chaillot'[18] – playing two parts, the Rag-Picker and the head of the oil-company – superb idea. And then Hamburg. They've been kidding us; I expected Liverpool with brothels, but no – this is all lakes and canals and greenery, civic pride and stately homes, stately rivers too – and impressive if stodgy theatre (Brecht again – 'Holy Joan of the Slaughterhouses'[19] – last year Brecht became the first contemporary playwright to be acted on German stages as often as Goethe, Schiller and Shakespeare are). The low-life street – Reeperbahn – is broad, airy, and pretty provincial; night-clubs with chaste stripping (the girl on 49th street would be run out of town) intermingled with showings of nudist-type Swedish films. The mud-wrestling is done by Lesbians in bathing-caps and black swimming costumes and is infinitely nasty and dull. I spent three days only there, because the big theatre was closing for the summer; the last night I went to see something called 'Mississippi-Melody' by Tennessee Williams. It turned out to be four of the one-acters, grotesquely played by a fifty-year-old obese actress-manageress.

Now in London, having seen, apart from Astor, Kilmartin, and other Observer people, nothing and no one. I went into the flat on the pretext of borrowing a book. Melvin Lasky[20] was in Berlin but his wife was there, a strained thin German girl in black, over-made-up and full of horrid condescension and malice about the Berliner Ensemble. Didn't like her at all. The place is clean and well, apart from my study, which Melvin has turned into a morass of manuscript. The bull pictures have been taken down and replaced by rather chichi Chinese prints. My whole feeling is of unreality – sitting in a hotbox hotel room a hundred yards from where we lived. In two days I go to Stratford, and I pray I may have written something by then. My schedule of plays here ends on July 12th. I shall probably stay on for four or five days writing about England and finishing Havana. (How long ago that seems.) After July 20th I just don't know. Your saying that you couldn't manage Málaga plunged me into a sadness. Into the two martinis, in fact – I'm beginning to sit alone in bars and drink, which I've never done before. No sex, except occasional melancholy sessions of self-help to induce sleep. The Joneses went from Berlin to Portofino, where Kurnitz tells me Rex Harrison and Kay[21] are; I forget if I told you the terrible prevalent rumour that she has leukemia; if I didn't, please tell nobody – it may not be true, though Gene Kelly, Clurman and Irene S. all say it is. Irene S. also said that purple rain fell on cars in an English village yesterday. These are hilarious times. Did you see what Dr. Newell of the Naval Radiological Laboratory said to the Atomic Energy sub-committee the other day? His opinion is that an H-war might be a good thing for the race. We can draw, he said, 'an ideal picture of the survivors of world-wide radiation emerging as a bigger, stronger, wiser, gentler, healthier race than would otherwise have developed.' There might not be many of them but by God they'd be gentle.

I notice you didn't say anything about my comments on us. That saddened me too. If I could do anything to replenish your faith I would do it in print and now, but it can only happen by seeing you and holding you (try not to gag at the thought) and talking to you. Please come to Spain. No social game, no Big Personalities, I swear: just us quietly proving we're alive and not mad by quietly and sanely living with each other, and through and for and by each other. I don't want to go Hemingway-hunting; in fact I want to go Davis-dodging.[22] Three weeks – surely Tracy could be lodged with the Bernsteins or your parents, and surely your book[23] could stand twenty days neglect? – to walk about in the sun – slowly, receptively, in pursuit of nothing except ourselves. I didn't vastly like the Salinger story, by the way – seemed to me self-conscious, self-indulgent on the whole, and I got nothing like a clear picture of Seymour. It read like an interminable gushing telephone monologue with one or two moments of excitement relieving a cascade of sheer philosophical gossip. I mention it because it made me want to be with you, to look at you and to say: 'Whatever he's getting at and roaming round, whatever this quality of uncompeting contact between souls is – we had it, and we have it, if we want it.' And I do, my love. Salinger would want to apologise for a sentence like that, and he'd go off into a frenzy of parentheses to explain that he didn't really mean to be sentimental, except, of course, that he did, and it doesn't matter, anyway, because Seymour would have apprehended (not understood – that's square) and his teeth would have glimmered ochre as he dropped them, let them lovingly submerge in, the mug he kept for them, the mug that was never more beautiful than in the moment of drab (not in <u>their</u> sense, but as opposed to garish) enlightenment when he dropped it from the window on 176th Street and hit the lady taxi-driver on the head with it, not trying to or willing to, yet it hit her, and it would need Zooey's kind of ill<u>umin</u>ating memory to explore why, when Seymour smiled (if you can forgive, or even partially condone, the expression) as they stuck six inches of bandaid on the beautiful, hideous Irish lady's scalp, she let him have it square in the chops with a left-arm jab. He still smiled, and she hit him again, this time however with a sort of regretful accuracy, and if it were not four o'clock in the afternoon and I were not writing flat on my back in the cellar I might remember whether or not he had combed his hair that week. (Is this still, as I hubristically tell myself it up to now has been, and may be again, interesting to anyone? The hell with if it isn't, because Seymour had hair that was plain godlike, stiff short warrior hairs, all of which were counted, and all of which, one by one, at a dollar a word, we'll sure as Nirvana count.)

It's 9.38, actually, and I think I'm hungry enough to go out and eat. Please cable me that you'll come to Spain;[24] as you know, the New Yorker will pay (I'll make arrangements there when I hear from you.) We won't regret it.

Ever
K.

[1] Irene Selznick (1910–90), Broadway theatre producer, daughter of MGM chief Louis B. Mayer and first wife of the producer David O. Selznick.

[2] J. D. Salinger (b. 1919), American novelist, author of *Catcher in the Rye* (1951); his story 'Seymour: An Introduction' appeared in the *New Yorker* of 6 June 1959.

[3] Harry Kurnitz (1908–68), novelist, playwright, screenwriter and wit, whose screenplays include *Witness for the Prosecution* (US, 1957) and *A Shot in the Dark* (US, 1964).

[4] Lucian Freud (b. 1922), German-born British painter, grandson of Sigmund Freud.

[5] Sir Bernard Miles (1907–91), English actor and founder of the Mermaid Theatre, which opened in May 1959 with the musical play *Lock Up Your Daughters* (adapted by Miles from Henry Fielding's *Rape Upon Rape*).

[6] The Threepenny Opera (1928), Brecht's adaptation of John Gay's *The Beggar's Opera* (1728). KPT wrote about the rehearsal in the *New Yorker*, 12 September 1959.

[7] Erich Engel (1891–1966), German theatre and film producer.

[8] Brecht's *Galileo* (1937–9), first performed in 1943 at the Zurich Schauspielhaus.

[9] *The Mother* (1930–1), adapted from the novel by Maxim Gorki (1906), first performed in 1932 in Berlin.

[10] Helene Weigel (1900–72), Austrian-born actress and wife of Bertolt Brecht, who played the title roles in *The Mother* and *Mother Courage and Her Children* and ran the Berliner Ensemble after Brecht's death in 1956. KPT wrote of her, 'Her warmth is adventurous, her honesty contagious, and her sophistication extreme.'

[11] *The Resistible Rise of Arturo Ui* (1941), first performed in 1958 in Stuttgart.

[12] Wolf Kaiser (b. 1916), lead actor with the Berliner Ensemble 1950–67, and with the Volksbühne 1967–69.

[13] Ekkehard Schall (b. 1930), lead actor with the Berliner Ensemble from 1952.

[14] *Mother Courage and Her Children* (1938–9), first performed in 1941 at the Zurich Schauspielhaus. KPT first saw the play on 1 January 1955 in Paris and declared, 'I have seen "Mother Courage" and I am a Marxist.'

[15] A production of John Osborne's 1957 play directed by Hans Lietzan at the Schlosspark with Martin Held playing the role made famous by Olivier.

[16] The theatre and film director Tony Richardson (1928–91) had overlapped with KPT at Oxford. KPT was often critical of his work and wrote a savage parody of Richardson's production of William Faulkner's *Requiem for a Nun* at the Royal Court in 1957 (*Observer*, 1 December 1957).

[17] Ezra Pound (1885–1972), American poet whose *Cantos* first appeared in 1917. *Women of Trachis*, his colloquial translation of Sophocles' *Trachiniae*, was playing at the Schiller Theatre. KPT wrote in the *New Yorker*: 'The choral bits were intoned by a group of young women in green gym tunics, who carried out, from time to time, little choreographic stunts reminiscent of a eurythmics class celebrating the opening of the new playing field.' Here he is punning on the famous German film *Mädchen in Uniform* (1931).

[18] Play by Jean Giraudoux (1945), at the Schiller Theatre.

[19] *Saint Joan of the Stockyards* (1929–31), first performed in April 1959 at the Deutsches Schauspielhaus, Hamburg.

[20] Melvin Lasky (b. 1920), American co-editor of the British magazine *Encounter* 1958–90, who was renting the Tynans' Mount Street flat.

[21] Kay Kendall (1926–59), English actress whose films include *Genevieve* (UK, 1953) and *The Reluctant Debutante* (US, 1958); she married the English actor (Sir) Rex Harrison (1908–90) in 1957, and for the two years until she died he kept the nature of her illness a secret from her.

[22] That summer Hemingway, who was covering the *mano-a-mano* between Domínguín and Ordóñez, was staying with Bill and Annie Davis.

[23] Elaine was working on her second novel, *The Old Man and Me* (published 1964).

[24] Elaine and Tracy joined KPT in the south of Spain.

To William Shawn

23 Acacia Road
London N.W.8[1]
July 14 [1959]

Dear Mr. Shawn –

A brief note to explain the delay of the German piece. I was halfway through a last draft when a publisher sent me a proof of a new book on Bertolt Brecht – with whose theatre in Berlin I am dealing at length. The book – 'Brecht: A Choice of Evils', by Martin Esslin[2] – contained so much that was new to me that I decided to revise the article in the light of what I'd learned. I hope to post it off to you by the weekend. The English piece will be much simpler, since it covers people and places that are much more familiar to American readers: I expect to have it finished by July 26.

Another emendation to the French piece:[3] on p.3 of the typescript I'd like to alter the phrase: '... people of Leftist sympathies such as M. Vilar and M. Julien'[4] to read: ' ... people of Leftist sympathies such as MM. Vilar, Camus and Julien.'

Let me know if the delay over the German report is inconvenient for you.

I continue well, blotchily bronzed, and in good appetite. Incidentally, Olivier's Coriolanus[5] was worth being double-taxed for.

Yours
Ken Tynan

[1] KPT was staying with Mrs John Russell (previously Lady Barry; Tracy Tynan's godmother).
[2] Helene Weigel, in a letter dated 30 March 1960 complimenting KPT on his *New Yorker* article on German theatre, was surprised by KPT's positive reaction to Esslin's book, which, she claimed, was permeated by a queer mixture of love (for the work) and hatred (against the man).
[3] On 8 July KPT received a cable from Shawn: 'YOUR FRENCH PIECE ARRIVED AND IS JUST AS REMARKABLE AS EXPECTED STOP SOME WONDERFUL WRITING STOP ALSO A COMPLETE EDUCATION STOP REGARDS.'
[4] Jean Vilar (1912–71), French actor and director, founder of the Avignon Festival, 1947, and head of the Théâtre National Populaire in Paris 1951–63. A.-M. Julien (b. 1903), Director General of the Paris Drama Festival from 1954 to the present day.
[5] The July 1959 production at Stratford, directed by Peter Hall.

To William Shawn

Algonquin Hotel[1]
[New York]
Tuesday [18 August 1959]

Dear Mr. Shawn;

If it isn't piling Pelion on Ossa, I'd like to propose inserting the enclosed paragraph into the German piece.

I'm at the Algonquin as and when required. I don't know if you've been reading the newspaper bits about the bullring rivalry between Luis Miguel Dominguín and Antonio Ordóñez, but having just sped home from Spain I'd like to tell you about it and perhaps to suggest a piece about it. Certainly neither I nor Ernest Hemingstein (as he still calls himself, God knows why) have seen anything so exciting and pure and majestic. The periphery of the combat is pretty funny; I've never seen so many weird aficionados of all nationalities in Spain at any one time. They include an English bankclerk who has given up Britain to follow Ordóñez and become a bullfighter; Betty Ford,[2] the American lady bullfighter; and a strange plump bearded man, known as the False Hemingway,[3] who came to Spain to write a book on Venezuelan Christian names, saw Ordóñez and Dominguín, threw over his project and has since pursued the two matadors across Spain, signing Hemingway's autograph at every bullfighters' bar. Also a fifty-seven year old American snob named Randy Burke[4] (on whom 'The New Yorker', I believe, wrote a short profile in 1940), who has bought himself a cape and a sword and plans to make his debut as a torero in the Málaga ring next month, before which he is to be received into the true church under the name of José-Maria Burke. He is an ex-alcoholic and shakes all over. And of course there is Ernest H. himself. In all, a rough and ready lot.

I hope to see you soon. Thanks again for those cables.

Yours,
Ken Tynan[5]

---

[1] KPT had sublet his New York apartment for the summer.
[2] Bette Ford, an ex-model and actress who became a bullfighter in Mexico in 1955.
[3] Kenneth H. Vanderford, a former executive of an oil company who retired to Spain in 1959. Nine years younger than the novelist, he bore such a striking resemblance to Hemingway that he was often asked for his autograph.
[4] Randy Burke, an American who convinced himself that he could become a matador and drowned in a swimming pool in Málaga in 1961.

[5] KPT did not write about this season until his May 1973 *Atlantic Monthly* article on Ordóñez, but it was the subject of Hemingway's series of articles in *Life* magazine, later reprinted as *A Dangerous Summer* (1985).

To the Editor, the *Reporter*[1]

56 East 89th Street
October 13, 1959

Dear Sir,

I thoroughly enjoyed Gore Vidal's[2] diverting review of the Gielgud 'Much Ado About Nothing'.[3] It contains, however, one or two references that English theatregoers may find baffling. Mr. Vidal mentions a performance of the play he saw at Stratford-on-Avon in 1948, adding that it was 'considerably better than the one now on Broadway.' He continues, 'The sets were elegant; the music apposite; and, as I recall, the couples were first introduced in silhouette, perceived through arches: a fine effect. The late Mr. Godfrey Tearle[4] was Benedick and Miss Diana Wynyard[5] was Beatrice. Mr. Tearle was charmingly stuffy as Benedick, his performance enhanced for me by his astonishing resemblance to the late President Roosevelt.'

To have compressed so many confusions into so few statements is pretty awe-inspiring. Let me explain:

a) there was no production of 'Much Ado' at Stratford in 1948

b) the play *was* presented there in 1949, but Godfrey Tearle did not appear in it. (It would have been astounding if he had; I doubt whether a modern audience would take to a 63-year old Benedick.) It was Anthony Quayle[6] who played opposite Miss Wynyard.

c) Mr. Tearle certainly looked like F. D. R. Mr. Quayle, however, bears a slight resemblance to Theodore Roosevelt. This leaves me in doubt whether Mr. Vidal saw Quayle playing Benedick and thought it was Tearle, or saw Tearle playing something else and thought it was Benedick.

d) Whatever the answer to that one, it is difficult to see how the Stratford production could have been so much better than the Broadway one, since they are the same production. The sets are the same and so is the director, Sir John, who took over the role of Benedick during the 1950 season.

e) It would in any case have been impossible for the lovers to be introduced together, as Benedick enters in the first act only after Beatrice has been on stage talking for some considerable time.

When Mr. Vidal wanders into error, we are in the Hampton Court maze in no time. Later in the same piece, for example, he manages within one sentence to refer to Claudius, King of Denmark, as Claudio, and to his stepson Hamlet as his son. There's nothing like a checking department, I always say.[7]

Yours sincerely,
Kenneth Tynan

[1] An American intellectual periodical.

[2] Gore Vidal (b. 1925), distinguished American novelist, playwright and essayist; his novel *Julian*, purporting to be the memoir of the Roman emperor, was published in 1964. Other works include *Washington DC* (1967) and *Lincoln* (1984).

[3] In September 1959 at the Lunt–Fontanne in New York, with Gielgud directing and playing Benedick.

[4] Sir Godfrey Tearle (1884–1953), English stage and screen actor.

[5] Diana Wynyard (1906–64), English stage and screen actress, star of *Cavalcade* (US, 1933) and *Gaslight* (UK, 1940).

[6] Sir Anthony Quayle (1913–89), leading English actor and director of the Shakespeare Memorial Theatre, Stratford, 1948–56.

[7] The editor Robert Bingham, in his reply dated 19 October 1959, defended Vidal's review on the grounds 'that I have been a changed editor since the evening at Mr Vidal's apartment shortly after your arrival in this country when I heard your eloquent defense of any literate writer's right not to have his copy tampered with by a lot of ink-stained wretches, even when he was in error.' His letter finishes: 'On a more cheerful note ... I consider your own work in the *New Yorker* the best drama criticism that has ever appeared in this country.'

During 1959 Ken travelled extensively in the United States in search of people and pockets of nonconformity. He felt that the standard image – of an affluent country bursting with abundance and self-approval – gave by no means the whole picture.

The result of his research was a programme called 'We Dissent', which Associated Television put out in Britain on 27 January 1960. Put together by Ken, and directed by Robert Heller, it gave the views of twenty-five dissenters, among them Alger Hiss (a former State Department official who twice stood trial accused of being a Communist spy), and the socialist Norman Thomas. The black satirist Nipsey Russell spoke on desegregation, the sociologist C. Wright Mills confirmed that there was no organized dissent. David Wesley, a journalist, complained that the affluent society produced 'freedom of speech with nothing very meaningful to say', and the economist John Kenneth

Galbraith argued for a large public sector to build acceptable capitalism. Most contributors were worried about a nuclear holocaust.

The fallout was impressive. The right-wing press in the States demanded to know why those particular Americans were allowed a shop window in England. Norman Cousins, spokesman for the Committee for a Sane Nuclear Policy, wrote to Ken claiming that he had been misrepresented. He would not have appeared on a programme aimed at exposing what was wrong with America.

That was not the end of it. The FBI woke up to the small furore, looked in their files and discovered that they had already monitored Ken's preparations for the show, which intended to 'discredit the American way of life'. Their sleuthing revealed that Tynan had been known at Oxford for his 'eccentric behavior'.

Meanwhile Senator Thomas J. Dodd, a conservative Democrat from Connecticut and Vice-Chairman of the Senate Internal Security Subcommittee, formed in 1951, and companion to the House Un-American Activities Committee, reported to his subcommittee about 'We Dissent'. He announced that it was 'a sacred duty to combat divisive influences within the Western alliance'.

On 27 April Ken was handed a subpoena commanding him to appear before the Subcommittee in Washington DC. He was the first foreign journalist (and the first Englishman) to be summoned. He did not take advantage of the Fifth Amendment right to silence, as did many of those grilled by the House Un-American Activities Committee, but answered the questions of the inquisitor, J.G. Sourvine.

What particularly interested the Committee was a Fair Play for Cuba Committee advertisement which had appeared in the New York Times on 6 April, signed by – among others – James Baldwin, Jean-Paul Sartre, Norman Mailer and Kenneth Tynan. Ken told the Committee that he was neither a member of the Communist Party, nor of the Fair Play for Cuba Committee. 'How did it happen,' Sourvine asked, 'that you took the action of signing a statement in support of Castro in defiance of the views of President Eisenhower?' Now openly contemptuous of his questioner, Ken defended himself boldly. He wondered whether government grilling of foreign newspapermen was a practice that should be associated with the workings of Western democracy. The Committee then returned to the dire matter of 'We Dissent'. At the end of the hearings Ken insisted that the subcommittee enter his statement in the record. He returned to New York considerably shaken, paid his lawyer Leonard Boudin $1500, and later that month left for London.

To Norman Cousins

The New Yorker
No. 25 West 43rd Street
New York, 36, N. Y.
February 3rd, 1960

Dear Mr. Cousins,

I'm awfully sorry to hear that you feel I misrepresented to you the nature and purpose of my TV show. In fact, if you remember, I didn't; I distinctly recall explaining to you that our aim was to show as wide a spectrum as possible of American non-conformist thought, and that there would be a large number of people on the program apart from yourself, all of them holding dissenting views in politics, philosophy, sociology or the arts.[1] Your contribution was a powerful and timely one, and I am told it had great impact.

At no point was it ever stated by me or any of my colleagues that the aim of the show was to demonstrate 'What's Wrong with America'. That was the invention of a journalist in the South. Rather, the idea was to show the vitality of American democracy, and to demolish the common European misconception that America is the land of conformists, organization men, men in Brooks Brothers suits, etc. Whether we have succeeded I do not know; reports from England indicate that some critics found the dissenting opinions expressed on the program curiously mild in tone; but I feel faintly proud, nonetheless, at having provided a television platform on which America could demonstrate to Europe that her ancient tradition of rational protest was very far from dead.[2]

Yours sincerely,
[Kenneth Tynan]

[1] The following took part: C. Wright Mills, Professor of Sociology at Columbia University; Alexander King, author; Jules Feiffer, cartoonist; Alger Hiss, formerly with the State Department; Norman Thomas, head of the American Socialist Party; Mort Sahl, comedian; Nipsey Russell, Harlem comedian; Norman Mailer, novelist; Allen Ginsberg, Peter Orlofsky, Lawrence Ferlinghetti, Bob Kaufman, Philip Lamantia, Beat poets; Pierre de Lattre, Congregationalist minister working in the Beat zone of San Francisco; Arnold Johnson, member of the American Communist Party; Revd Maurice McCrackin, Cincinnati clergyman imprisoned for refusal to pay taxes for defence purposes; Dalton Trumbo, screenwriter and one of the 'Hollywood Ten'; Trevor Thomas, member of the legislative committee of the Society of Friends; David Wesley, editor of a hardhitting independent newspaper in York, Pennsylvania; J. Kenneth Galbraith, Harvard economist; Clinton Jencks, militant union leader; Revd Stephen Fritchman, outspoken Unitarian minister; Harold Call, director of publications of the Mattachine Society, dedicated to the reform of laws

against homosexuality; Norman Cousins, national chairman of the Committee for a Sane Nuclear Policy; Robert M. Hutchins, President of the Fund for the Republic.

[2] The programme was discussed on the BBC's *Right to Reply* on 29 January. One of the speakers, Professor Eugene Rostow of Yale, found the programme 'a hopeful and healthy sign that American democracy was still vital and alive'.

To Robert Heller

The New Yorker
February 8th, 1960

Dear Bob,

I have received a letter from Benjamin Mandel, the Research Director of the Internal Security Sub-committee of the Senate, asking me to send 'for his files' a transcript of WE DISSENT. With your agreement, I propose to reply (a) that I have no transcript of the show as transmitted, and (b) that the transcript is in any case not my property but that of Associated Television. Do you think this is the wisest course? The point is that after so many people were so splendidly cooperative, it would be unthinkable for us to provide an investigating committee with words that could later be used against them. It is possible, of course, that Mr. Mandel will address his next communication to the directors of ATV. Could you persuade them to take the same line as I do? Let me know as quickly as you can; I'll do nothing until I hear from you.

Love,
[pp. Kenneth Tynan]

P.S.: I've asked my secretary to sign this as I have to leave immediately.

To Robert Heller

[56 East 89th Street]
February 15th 1960

Dear Bob,

I'm enclosing a copy of my reply to Mandel, which I hope is vague enough to keep the ball in the air for a few weeks at least. The first reaction to the show came in the form of a short editorial in <u>The Daily News</u> called 'Here Are Your Hats, Gentlemen'. It listed some of the people who'd taken part (including Hutchins, Cousins, Galbraith and Hiss), said that they'd fouled their own nests, and advised them to 'move the hell out' to somewhere like Russia, China or England. This line was also taken by a number of Southern newspapers, each of which editorialized quite heavily on the assumption that the purpose of the programme was to knock America. Some of these clippings must have reached Cousins, who instantly despatched a telegram of protest demanding that he should be allowed to produce a 90 minute program of rebuttal. I wrote back in a conciliatory vein, explaining that our aim had been to show the variety and vitality of American democracy, etc. etc. In his reply, he took my word for it that our intentions had been good, but reiterated that he had been misrepresented and defamed, and accordingly demanded equal time to reply. I told him briefly and concisely that this was of course out of the question. Last Friday I got a letter from Hutchins associating himself completely with the stand taken by Cousins – he too was relying for his information on the editorials I've mentioned. I must say that this dismayed and rather shocked me; however, I wrote to him at great length explaining that he was mistaken and that the reports he had read gave a completely false picture of the show – how could they do otherwise considering that they were written by people who had not seen it. On Saturday I received a semi-hysterical letter from Cousins, saying that unless I went ahead with his proposal for a rebuttal program, he'd instruct his lawyers to bring action for defamation against me and ATV. He said that Hutchins wished to be associated with him on this, and added that other participants in the program (whom he did not name) might also be involved. I have made some careful inquiries among journalist chums about Cousins' temperament; with no exceptions, they assure me that he is jumpy to the point of paranoia, and is always litigating, protesting and writing threatening letters. It is pretty obvious, I think, that he has no grounds for any legal action; as I pointed out in my first letter to him, I told him in great detail the purpose of the show, and made it quite clear that he would only be one of thirty people taking part. I therefore replied to his last note with a rather bored and deliberately impertinent telegram, the exact wording of which I have forgotten but whose general tone was meant to be that of a man brushing off a gadfly. I'll let you know how he responds to this.

There is no point in exaggerating the importance of these reactions. Apart from Cousins and Hutchins, nobody has made any complaints to me, nor do I anticipate any. You have probably seen the Variety review, which thought the show an interesting failure, but expressed no objections to any of the contents. Insofar as there is a general reaction here, that would probably be it. [...]

Yours,
[Kenneth Tynan]

To Trevor Thomas

[56 East 89th Street]
February 24th 1960

Dear Mr. Thomas,

Thank you for your letter. I cannot tell you how apologetic I am that your time should have been taken up by inquiries about the TV show in which you so generously participated. As you may know, I too have had my troubles over it; the Senate Internal Security Subcommittee has displayed interest in it, and there have been some crude and hopelessly ill-informed newspaper comments in this country, written of course by people who could not have seen the show. A couple of things you say in your letter to Senator Dodd slightly perturb me. The program included only one card-carrying member of the Communist Party and (excluding Alger Hiss, whose political affiliations are unknown) only two other extreme Leftists, Clinton Jencks and Dalton Trumbo. This makes three statements out of a total of twenty-eight – not an enormously high proportion when you consider that in a capitalist society the main source of dissent must naturally be the Left. As to the Beats: less than fifteen minutes was devoted to them in a program of ninety minutes. Without them, by the way, we should have had no youthful dissenters at all.

I omitted the extreme Right, such as Buckley,[1] the KKK, etc., for a very simple reason: charity. The aim of the program was not, as you know, to be anti-American. Had we included the extreme Right, that is how it would certainly have appeared.

Thank you again for writing, and also for your good wishes.

Yours sincerely,
[Kenneth Tynan]

[1] William F. Buckley (b. 1925), conservative writer and journalist, author of *McCarthy and his Enemies* (1954); in 1955 he founded the journal *National Review*.

To Dwight Macdonald[1]

The New Yorker
March 3rd 1960

Dear Dwight,

I'd noticed you'd been using words like 'montage' lately. You want to be careful; those who live by montage perish by montage. I thought you might be interested in THE CRY OF JAZZ[2] as an historian of ideas, not as a film critic. It's the first black supremacist movie. This doesn't mean that it's a good movie, merely that it's an historic one.

See you in Bronxville.

Yours,
Ken.

[1] Dwight Macdonald (1906–82), American writer and film critic who wrote for *Partisan Review*, the *New Yorker* and *Esquire*. His books include *The Memoirs of a Revolutionist* (1957) and *Discriminations: Essays and Afterthoughts* (1974).
[2] 35-minute black-and-white documentary-style film directed by Edward Bland and reviewed by KPT in the *Observer*, 20 March 1960.

To Terence Kilmartin

The New Yorker
7 April 1960

Dear Terry,

I have talked over the question of my return with Mr Shawn, and he says it's perfectly all right for me to skip the last show of the season. This means that I can theoretically leave any time after May 16th, which will be the deadline for my last New Yorker piece. There's one complicating factor: I've been helping to organize a big Sane Nuclear Policy rally[1] to be held in Madison Square Garden on May 19th. The cast includes Mrs. [Eleanor] Roosevelt, Harry Belafonte,[2] Walter Reuther,[3] Mike Nichols[4] and Elaine May,[5] Martin Luther King, etc. etc., and I'm very anxious not to miss it ... in fact, I thought there might even be a piece in it for The Observer. If I stay for the rally, I could fly back on the 20th or the 21st and start reviewing for you the following week. But here another complicating factor comes in: luggage. I've looked up the sailings to Europe in May, and the first decent crossing after May 19th is the Queen Elizabeth, which leaves

New York on May 25th and arrives in Southampton May 31st. (I'd be perfectly happy to start work for you immediately on disembarking.) Is this impossibly late Pryce-Jones-wise?[6] If it is, I could at a pinch take a smaller ship that would get me into England on the 27th; or at an even greater pinch I could fly back and ship the luggage across. I'd rather not do the latter if it is at all possible, because the idea of five or six days rest afloat is pretty appealing. Do let me know what you think about all this.

I had drinks yesterday with Marilyn Monroe. Her bottom has gone to pot and her pot has gone to bottom.

Love,
Ken

[1] Eleanor Roosevelt and Dr Harry Taylor, former president of Sarah Lawrence College, were co-chairmen; Norman Cousins was co-chairman of the Sponsorship Committee. On 19 May 1960 there was a rally at Madison Square Garden attended by 17,000 people, of whom 5,000 then walked to the United Nations building.

[2] Harry Belafonte (b.1927), American actor and singer, star of *Carmen Jones* (US, 1955).

[3] Walter Reuther (1907–70), American trade union leader.

[4] Mike Nichols (b.1931), German-born American director of successful Broadway plays (*The Odd Couple*, 1965) and films (*The Graduate*, US, 1967; *Catch 22*, US, 1970; *Silkwood*, US, 1983).

[5] Elaine May (b.1932) was Nichols's cabaret partner 1957–61.

[6] Alan Pryce-Jones (b.1908), writer and editor of the *Times Literary Supplement* 1946–59, was acting as the *Observer*'s drama critic in KPT's absence.

To Dwight Macdonald

The New Yorker
April 13th 1960

Dear Dwight,

Many thanks for the immense help you've given me with the Lardner biography[1] (which I've just finished and found excellent), the Portable Lardner[2] (which introduced me for the first time to those marvellous plays), and the article by Schwartz,[3] which I thought hilariously weird in some respects – particularly the following sentence: 'The present-day reader will surely realize that "Walter Winchell, a nun" is something more than nonsense.'[4] Your own interpretation of Lardner I thought quite the best short comment I had ever read on the man. Incidentally, the long retrospective letters he wrote towards the end of his life remind me enormously, in style as well as subject-matter, of the long, rambling letters that Jim Thurber is writing today. I hope this isn't a portent of anything.

About my TV show: If Communism is not an extreme form of dissent against capitalism, I'd like to know what is. [...] let's continue the debate over lunch sometime soon.

Thanks again, and also for the party –
Ken

[1] Ring Lardner (1885–1933), American sports writer and humorist whose short plays (among them *Quadroon*, *Dinner Bridge* and *Cora, or Fun at a Spa*) KPT later planned to adapt for the National Theatre. The biography was *Ring Lardner* by Donald Elder (1956).
[2] Published by The Viking Press in 1946.
[3] Delmore Schwartz (1913–66), American poet, short-story writer and critic. His verse collections include *In Dreams Begin Responsibilities* (1938).
[4] From Schwartz's review of Elder's *Ring Lardner*, 'Ring Lardner: Highbrow in Hiding', *The Reporter* (9 August 1956), reprinted in Delmore Schwartz, *Selected Essays* (1978). 'Walter Winchell, a nun' is a character in one of Lardner's nonsense plays.

To William Shawn

120 Mount Street
September 13th [1960]

Dear Mr Shawn,

I remember telling you that I'd be immensely tickled at the idea of covering a trial or a crime for 'The New Yorker'. A possible subject has just come up, and I'd love to have your reactions.

As you may know, a recent change in the English law relating to Obscene Publications[1] has made it possible for the defence to call witnesses testifying to the literary merit of the allegedly obscene work or works. (Formerly, such testimony was not permitted.) The new law is going to receive its first test next month, in the case of the Crown vs. Penguin Books – the book in question being 'Lady Chatterley's Lover', which the Penguin people have lately issued in their paperback series. The action has been brought by the Director of Public Prosecutions himself, presumably with the purpose of finding out (a) exactly what the law now means, and (b) how it feels about 'pornographic' books made widely accessible in cheap editions. The defence has already contacted more than a hundred eminent literary people, asking them to testify to the book's virtues; how many of them have agreed I do not know, but I am assured by the editor of 'The New Statesman'[2] (who was among those contacted) that the trial will be 'the most marvellous circus for ages'. At all events, I should love to do a reporting job on it.

You may very well feel that this lies in Molly P.-D.'s[3] province, and if so I shall understand perfectly. If not, do let me know; I have a slight acquaintanceship with the defence counsel,[4] as well as the publishers, and it would [be] a good idea for me to start swotting up the background as soon as possible.

My best wishes –
Kenneth Tynan[5]

[1] The Obscene Publications Act of 1959 allowed that a book deemed likely to 'deprave and corrupt' its readers could not be condemned if it could be shown that the work was 'for the public good on the grounds that it is in the interests of science, literature, art or learning'.
[2] Kingsley Martin.
[3] Mollie Panter-Downes, London correspondent of the *New Yorker*.
[4] Lord (Gerald) Gardiner (1900–90); later Lord Chancellor in Harold Wilson's Labour government 1964–70.
[5] Shawn replied (21 September) that he had other plans for covering the trial. Penguin Books won the case, and the unexpurgated edition of D.H. Lawrence's *Lady Chatterley's Lover* (first published in Florence in 1928) remained on sale.

To Lawrence Ferlinghetti[1]

120 Mount Street
5th October, 1960

Dear Lawrence,
How right you are about that Third Party[2] – did you read Rexroth's[3] recent piece in 'The Nation', laconically called 'I'll sit this one out'?

I've heard nothing about any writers' conference in Cuba. I suggest you write to the Fair Play for Cuba Committee, at 60 East 42nd Street, New York 17, New York. If I think of anybody in Cuba for you to contact, I'll let you know – of my two former sources there, Castro probably doesn't remember me and I don't think Hemingway's speaking to me.[4]

Love,
Ken

[1] Lawrence Ferlinghetti (b.1920), American poet, publisher and founder of the City Lights Bookshop in San Francisco in 1954.

[2] According to Ferlinghetti, a proposal for a third party to the left of the Democrats and the Republicans.

[3] Kenneth Rexroth (1906–82), American poet and self-described 'philosophical anarchist'. He was paterfamilias to the younger generation of Beat poets.

[4] The contretemps between KPT and Hemingway had occurred during KPT's visit to Málaga in August 1959. The writer A. E. Hotchner recalls that at dinner one night KPT had given an account of a particular kill by Jaime Ostos and had been challenged by Hemingway:

EH: You know, just because you wrote one skinny book doesn't make you an authority. On what authority do you make those statements?

KPT: On the authority of my eyes.

EH: Fuck your eyes. You need glasses.

KPT: (rising) There's no point to my staying at this table any longer.

EH: Maybe you'll stay long enough to pick up the check.

KPT: I'll make arrangements for that.

On his way out KPT passed Bill Davis, who said, 'Why Ken, you look disturbed.'

KPT: I have just been insulted by a man with a white beard who doesn't have the wisdom to go with it.

Hemingway apologized the next morning, but the incident was not forgotten.

To William Shawn

Grand Hotel Orbis
Warszawa Krucia 28
January 8th [1961]

Dear Mr. Shawn,

Taking two weeks off to look at theatre in Stockholm and Warsaw,[1] I suddenly realise that I have not kept my compact with you – I didn't write to you before Christmas about next season. Frankly I long for New York; yesterday I saw a Cary Grant movie and though I think it was set in San Diego it made me miss Manhattan even more. (Answer to checkers: 'more than San Diego.')

But I don't think I can come back in the fall – partly for the reasons you know, partly for an additional one that has come up since I last wrote. My groggy old newspaper is faced next week with a serious Sunday competitor, new and powerful, called 'The Sunday Telegraph'. It will inevitably eat into 'The Observer's' circulation, and I feel I want to be aboard when we hit this iceberg. Hence I've given David Astor a verbal undertaking that I'll stay with him at least until the end of 1961. After that, chaos returns. I hope you'll understand, and excuse my tardiness.

Incidentally, I should love to do a casual[2] on the Warsaw cultural

scene, which is fantastic. Iron Curtain, censorship, etc.; yet a flourishing <u>nouvelle vague</u> film industry (considered by many English critics
the best in Europe), abstract painters, Dada-ist poets, playwrights à
la Beckett and Ionesco, and plays in the theatres by Osborne,
Tennessee Williams, Ionesco, Beckett, Dürrenmatt,[3] Harold Pinter,
Anouilh, Brecht, Shelagh Delaney,[4] Miller, etc., plus the usual
international classics and three student cabaret theatres, all spikily
critical of the régime. The band in this hotel plays pirated arrangements from Dizzy Gillespie's 'Have Trumpet, Will Excite'. Brendan
Behan's 'The Hostage'[5] is temporarily banned because the Church
objects to plays about bordelloes. I leave here Friday after only a
six-day stay – not long enough to write a piece for you – but if 'The
Observer' permits I could return for two or three weeks in June and
gather material for a decent article. I should love to know your
reaction. I don't mean, of course, to suggest that Warsaw is the
cultural hub or anything like that – merely that it's a bizarre and
unique bridge between East and West. Once the living accommodation is as luxurious as the theatrical accommodation I shall feel
happier about the place. There are nine razorblades just out of reach
in the bowl of my bathroom toilet, which when flushed roars like
the Victoria Falls (note Anglophile image) for six minutes nonstop.
But I'm glad to say that the trains don't run on time.

I hope to hear from you. Meanwhile, a gay New Year.

Yours sincerely
Ken Tynan

[1] KPT wrote two *Observer* articles, 'Stars in Hibernation' (8 January 1961) and 'The Opposite
Poles' (15 January 1961).
[2] I.e. a short piece about three or four columns long (usually, but not always, humorous fiction).
The piece was not written.
[3] Friedrich Dürrenmatt (1921–90), Swiss novelist and writer of plays including *Ein Engel kommt
nach Babylon* (1953).
[4] Shelagh Delaney (b.1939), English playwright best known for her first play, *A Taste of Honey*
(London, 1959; New York, 1960). It was filmed by Tony Richardson (UK, 1961).
[5] Brendan Behan (1923–64), Irish playwright and novelist, whose plays include *The Quare Fellow*
(1956) and *The Hostage* (1958).

To Dr Thomas Tennent

120 Mount Street
13th February, 1961

Dear Sir,

I visited the hospital last Saturday and spent some time with my mother. I am sending a parcel of fruit and confectionery off to her today; it is obvious from her condition that she will be unable to consume the contents unaided,[1] and I should like to feel sure that somebody would be assisting her. If you could let me know the name of the nurse who looks after her, I would be most grateful.

Yours sincerely,
Kenneth Tynan

[1] Medical records show that by May 1960 Rose Tynan was 'profoundly demented and no conversational coherent contact can be made with her'.

To Anthony Wedgwood Benn[1]

120 Mount Street
15th March, 1961

Dear Tony,

Of course I support your decision to stand again. God knows what sort of a message I'd be capable of sending – probably something about the past standing in the way of the future and the necessity of preventing good men from suffocating beneath the weight of ermine and purple. I will think about it more precisely when you know what the House intends to do.

Meanwhile, love and best wishes. Let's meet sometime.

Ken

[1] Anthony Wedgwood Benn (b.1925), English Labour politician debarred from the House of Commons in 1960 when he succeeded to the title of Viscount Stansgate upon his father's death. The first MP to renounce his title (and now known simply as Tony Benn), he was re-elected in 1963 and later became Minister of Technology under Harold Wilson, 1966–70.

To the Editor, the *New Statesman*[1]

120 Mount Street
[Published 14 April 1961]

Sir,—In Guatemala American officers are training large numbers of anti-Castro rebels for an attack on Cuba. In Florida and Louisiana thousands more are being mobilised and armed with the full knowledge and presumably the approval of the US government.[2] An alternative Cuban administration, with a programme based on the restoration of expropriated Cuban property to its original owners (many of them large American corporations), has been set up on American soil where it issues daily bulletins announcing its plans for invasion. CIA funds, it is credibly reported, are being poured in to what constitutes an organised attempt to overthrow the government of a neighbouring country by force.

I confess myself astonished that there have been so few protests, even in the liberal press, against these gross violations of the principle of non-interference, all of which are being committed in defiance of the inter-American treaties against foreign interference. Suppose, for example, that Mr Krushchev were to set up, arm and finance an alternative Turkish government on Russian soil. Suppose he were to allow it to plan and execute raids across the Turkish border and to announce its intention of invading Turkey at the earliest opportunity. The outcry in every western newspaper would be enormous.

I choose Turkey as a random example, there is of course, a more obvious parallel. As I. F. Stone,[3] the Washington journalist, has put it: 'the rationale for the attack on Cuba is exactly the same rationale with which the Russians excused their attack on Hungary ... The fate of Nagy[4] is the fate we are preparing for Castro and if one was an immoral crime, so will be the other'. We all have high hopes of the Kennedy administration, but how can we reconcile its talk of bringing new civility to Cold War diplomacy with these undisguised preparations for armed aggression on a neighbour? The time to protest is now, before the invasion and/or civil war have begun. Otherwise Cuba could easily become this generation's Spain.

KENNETH TYNAN

---

[1] Published under the headline 'Preparations Against Cuba'.
[2] 1500 US-sponsored Cuban exiles invaded the Bay of Pigs on 17 April 1961.
[3] I. F. Stone (1907–89), American journalist, author and publisher, who resigned as Washington

editor of the *Nation* in 1953 to launch *I. F. Stone Weekly*, which ran until 1971.

[4] Imre Nagy (1895–1958), Hungarian premier deposed by the Russians after the 1956 uprising and later executed.

To the Editor, *The Times*[1]

120 Mount Street
[Published 29 April 1961]

Sir,—Michael Astor's[2] letter on April 22 about the Cuban situation invites a reply: I write as one of the sixteen people whose protest against American intervention you published last week.[3] Mr. Astor wonders how we can be so sure that the Castro regime enjoys 'solid majority support'; I can only answer that, if the recent invasion attempt proves anything, it is that our estimate of Cuban support for Castro was considerably sounder than that of the American Government.

Our statement that the Cuban revolution has 'wholeheartedly tackled the problems of poverty, ignorance and backwardness' is taken by Mr. Astor to imply 'early aspiration' rather than 'solid achievement'. False inference: within six months of gaining power, the Castro regime had carried out a full and much-needed programme of land redistribution, and within a year unemployment and rents had been halved. In Havana alone, 37 schools had been built, as against one in the preceding 60 years. Houses have shot up at a rate of 20,000 units a year; and the state subsidies have stimulated the Cuban theatre and cinema almost to the point of dizziness. Segregation has been abolished: in sharp contrast to the Southern states of America, who profess themselves threatened by Castro's infection, Cuba today practises complete racial equality.

So much by way of information. It is no part of my brief to pretend that Castro's Cuba is a paradise. (Must a country be a paradise to be immune from foreign invasion?) It is hard to build Utopia when you are in a state of siege. Mr. Astor refers to Castro's use of censorship and arbitrary arrest; and both, I agree, are detestable. Yet both flourished under Batista:[4] was Mr. Astor's voice raised against them then? That there has been suppression I admit and deplore; but in a state of emergency, of declared economic war and impending military conflict, a Government may be forgiven if it has recourse to censorship. (That the emergency was real can hardly be contested: the invasion has taken place.)

Unlike most Latin-American revolutionaries before him, Castro did not change his course as soon as he gathered power. Socially and economically, he did precisely what he had sworn to do: to prevent Cuban profits from flowing to America, he nationalized, and he expropriated. American companies suffered; and America at once shrieked communist, as if any movement towards a centrally planned economy, however great the need for it, were *prima facie* evidence of communist subversion. What followed was relentless hostility from the State Department, and further proof of an ancient truth: that the best way to foster communism is to condemn socialism. It was not ideology, but national survival, that forced Castro to trade with the Soviet block.

To deny America's right to intervene in Cuba is no doubt to incur the full blast of transatlantic obloquy; not to do so, however, is to condone the Russian intervention in Hungary. If the Kennedy–Monroe doctrine is valid, the Peking Government deserves a Nobel Peace Prize for having neglected to annex Formosa.[5] My hope is that public opinion in Western Europe, the neutral countries, and America itself can be mobilized to persuade the Kennedy Administration to reverse its Cuban policy. If another invasion of Cuba takes place a full-scale collision of arms between Russia and America may not easily be avoidable. It would be a disastrous irony if the cause of Western freedom should come to be identified with the inalienable right of the American Government to depose Fidel Castro by force of arms.

Yours faithfully,
KENNETH TYNAN

[1] Published under the headline 'Conflict in Cuba'.
[2] The Hon. Michael Astor (1916–80), MP, novelist and brother of David Astor.
[3] Printed on 19 April 1961, the letter's signatories also included the Labour politicians Anthony Wedgwood Benn and Michael Foot, and the novelist Doris Lessing.
[4] Fulgencio Batista y Zalvidar (1901–73), Cuban dictator overthrown by Fidel Castro in January 1959.
[5] The Monroe Doctrine (1823) stated that the United States would resist foreign (i.e. European) interference in its sphere of influence (i.e. the entire western hemisphere); Kennedy's resistance to Soviet missiles being stationed in Cuba was partly based on this. By analogy, no non-Asian government would have been entitled to interfere in China's sphere of influence should the Communist mainland government have invaded the island of Formosa (Taiwan), the only remaining territory under Chiang Kai-shek's rule which was still recognized by the US as the legitimate government of all China.

To The Hon. David Astor

120 Mount Street
1st May, 1961

Dear David,

I thought yesterday's leader was first-rate: felicitations. I am writing because, as you may or may not have heard, I was partly instrumental in the inauguration, last week, of something called the British Cuba Committee.[1] The members include Manuela Sykes,[2] Michael Foot,[3] Penelope Gilliatt,[4] Basil Davidson,[5] R. Briginshaw[6] of NATSOPA, and half a dozen others; the Chairman is Clive Jenkins,[7] I am the Hon. Vice-Chairman, Eric Hobsbawm[8] is the Treasurer, and Clive Goodwin[9] the Secretary. The aim is to collect and disseminate information about Cuba. At our first meeting last week we discussed ways and means of doing this. We made plans for publishing pamphlets, holding meetings, etc.; but we all agreed that the ideal thing to do would be to send an independent delegation on a short trip to Cuba, and then publish their reactions in full. Names that were suggested include C.P. Snow,[10] James Cameron,[11] John Osborne, and Graham Greene. Three people would be enough, the only proviso being that they should be distinguished and not committed to the Left of the Labour Party. Of course our Committee can't afford to sponsor such a delegation. It occurred to me that The Observer might like to do so; the result would be a tripartite report on Cuba which the paper could print and which our Committee could publish in pamphlet form. If you think there is any point in our talking this over I can be available almost any time.

Yours,
Ken Tynan[12]

---

[1] Instigated by KPT in response to the Bay of Pigs invasion. According to the historian Eric Hobsbawm, there were several meetings in the ten days following the invasion which resulted in a march on Sunday, 23 April, as a gesture of solidarity with the Cuban people; 'I remember the occasion of the Demo ... for the largest concentration of stunning-looking girls.'

[2] A Liberal parliamentary candidate.

[3] Michael Foot (b. 1913), English politician, Leader of the Labour Party 1980–3.

[4] Penelope Gilliatt (1932–93), English novelist, short-story writer and critic for the *Observer* and the *New Yorker*.

[5] Journalist and author of many books on Africa.

[6] General Secretary of NATSOPA, one of two printing unions.

[7] (David) Clive Jenkins (b. 1926), British trade union activist, later chairman of the General Council of the TUC (1987–8); his books include *The Collapse of Work* (1979) and *The Leisure Shock* (1981).

[8] E. J. Hobsbawm (b. 1917), distinguished Marxist historian and Emeritus Professor of Economic and Social History at the University of London since 1982. His books include *The Age of Revolution* (1962) and *The Age of Capital* (1975).

[9] Clive Goodwin (1932–77), actor, editor of *Encore*, founder of the left-wing publication *The Black Dwarf*, and literary agent to playwrights such as Simon Gray and Trevor Griffiths.

[10] C. P. Snow (1905–80), English novelist and physicist whose work includes the *Strangers and Brothers* series, started in 1940, and the Rede lecture 'Two Cultures' (1959). He was knighted in 1957 and created a life peer in 1964.

[11] James Cameron (1911–85), Scots journalist, foreign correspondent for papers including the *News Chronicle*, and later columnist on the *Guardian*.

[12] Astor's response was negative, but ended, 'May we congratulate you on having been right about the importance of American-Cuban relations?'

To the Medical Superintendent, St Andrew's Hospital

[120 Mount Street]
[26 June 1961]

[Dear Sir ...]

I should be grateful if you could give me a confidential reply to a question re my mother, Mrs Rose Tynan, who has been in St Andrew's for some years now. Would it be possible to find out from the nurses who look after her roughly how often her sister Mrs [May] Wooldridge has been coming to visit her? I ask because for some time I have been making funds available to meet her expenses on these visits; and as I have not seen Mrs Wooldridge for some years I am very anxious to be reassured that she has in fact been able to visit my mother with reasonable frequency. As you will be aware, I am unhappily unable to obtain information from my mother in her present condition. I need hardly tell you that I shall treat any information you can provide with the strictest confidence.

[Kenneth Tynan]

To the Medical Superintendent, St Andrew's Hospital

[Telegram]

[London]
11 November 1961

PLEASE TELEPHONE ME GROS 4934 IF THERE IS ANY DETERIORATION

IN MY MOTHER'S CONDITION. WILL TRY TO VISIT HER MONDAY.[1]
KENNETH TYNAN

[1] KPT was telephoned on Monday 13 November, and his mother died 'peacefully and uneventfully' at 12.15 a.m. the next day.

To Edith Haggard

120 Mount Street
March 27th, 1962

Dear Edith,

Sorry I haven't written – am still submerged in television,[1] with which my contract ends on April 15. After that date I'll be able to settle down to finishing off Soho[2] and Miles Davis[3] for Holiday, and to preparing my other piece for Harry[4] on the cast of 'Beyond the Fringe'[5] – the English revue that opens on Broadway in the Fall. On the whole, I don't think I could manage a piece on the Irish Theatre as well. Not only am I pretty unfamiliar with it at first hand, I also haven't the time to find out more. For the first two weeks of May I'll probably be in New York; second two in Spain; two weeks of June in Athens;[6] and for most of July and the whole of August in China and Japan. Incidentally, if Harry would like anything on Greece or the Far East, I may be his man. I'll be doing three long articles for The Observer on China and Japan, and in these the paper wants world copyright; but I'm sure I could easily enough find material for a fourth piece. In The Observer I'll be dealing mainly with the arts and entertainment in the two countries.[7] Can Harry think of another angle?

In answer to your question, I'm not really all right. Combination of overwork and domestic upheaval.[8]

Hope to see you in New York in a month's time.

Love,
Ken

[1] *Tempo*, a fortnightly arts programme devised by KPT, first shown in October 1961. The first of the fifteen-programme series featured an interview with Laurence Olivier by the Earl of Harewood about the new Chichester Festival and later editions included an interview with the ninety-year-old Edward Gordon Craig and the first performance in England of Isaac Stern's Trio.
[2] 'The Soho Synthesis', *Holiday*, February 1965.

[3] 'Miles Apart', *Holiday*, February 1963.

[4] Harry Sions, editor of *Holiday*.

[5] A satirical revue starring Alan Bennett, Jonathan Miller, Peter Cook and Dudley Moore, first presented at the Edinburgh Festival in 1960. It played in the West End for over a year before transferring to the John Golden Theatre on Broadway in October 1962. KPT wrote about *Beyond the Fringe* in the regular column 'The Antic Arts', *Holiday*, November 1962.

[6] KPT was one of a group of playwrights, designers, directors and critics invited by the Greek Tourist office to take part in a UNESCO Conference on 'Mass Spectacles'; others were Tyrone Guthrie, Michel Saint-Denis and François Billetdoux. KPT reported on the trip in an *Observer* article entitled 'Journey to the Cradle', 1 July 1962.

[7] KPT never went to China or Japan, and these articles were never written.

[8] KPT's relationship with Elaine, which for some years had been stormy, now almost completely collapsed. KPT suffered a short breakdown after the death of his mother in November 1961 and enlisted the help of the analyst Paul Senft in order to leave his marriage.

To Tsai Chin[1]

[Telegram]

[London]
22nd September 1962

DEAREST CHIN ESSENTIAL YOU CALL ME SOONEST STOP AM JOINING YOU IN MADRID NEXT WEEKEND STOP CANCEL ALL OTHER ENGAGE-MENTS ALL MY LOVE KEN

[1] Chinese actress (*The World of Suzie Wong*, UK, 1960) with whom KPT was having an affair.

To Tsai Chin

[Telegram]

[London]
[undated]

ARRIVING MADRID AIRPORT 11.15 AM SATURDAY TALL AND DIV-INELY HANDSOME IN BLUE STOP BE THERE STOP STAYING TILL TUESDAY ALL LOVE KEN

To Tsai Chin

[Telegram]

[London]
[undated]

DEAR BRAT UNDERSTAND YOUR QUALMS BUT FULLY INTEND TO
MARRY YOU STOP PLEASE TELEPHONE ME SATURDAY MORNING
BELGRAVIA 4709 STOP THE GOING MAY BE GOOD BUT THE COMING
BACK WILL BE BETTER STOP LOVE KEN

CHAPTER FIVE

Celebrating the Sixties

In 1945 the schoolboy Tynan had seen Laurence Olivier in Richard III, and wrote that 'his performance eats into the memory like acid into metal, but the total impression is one of lightness and deftness'. Thereafter no one admired this actor more lavishly; nor stood guard over his talent so ferociously.

On Olivier's appointment, in August 1962, as artistic director of the newly formed National Theatre, Ken, a vociferous campaigner for such a state-subsidized institution, wrote to offer his services as dramaturg. His letter was delivered in the wake of an astringent attack he had made on Olivier's stewardship of the Chichester Festival Theatre. On receiving the request for a job the great actor was enraged. 'How shall we slaughter the little bastard?' he asked his wife, Joan Plowright, who told him to reconsider. Young audiences, she suggested, would be 'thrilled with the mixture of you and Ken'.

So Olivier wrote to the critic to tell him his suggestion was an admirable one, 'one that I'd thought of myself'. He added, 'Anything to get you off that Observer.' In response Ken gave up weekly theatre criticism for good, and went into service to the National. He earned an average of £46 a week over the decade he worked at the theatre. When abroad on other work, he insisted on going off salary.

He became architect of the repertory and public spokesman. He declared that the theatre would deliver a 'spectrum of world drama': the widest possible selection of good plays from all periods and places. This was what the critic William Archer and the actor/director/author Harley Granville-Barker had proposed in 1907 when they had drawn up a scheme for a 'national theatre'.

On 22 October 1963, the curtain went up for the first time at the Old Vic, the National's temporary home while a new complex on the South Bank was being designed and built. No other British theatre established itself so speedily or so effectively, nor offered such a multifarious and constellated repertory. No other theatre was so international in scope. Of the seventy-nine plays staged between October 1963 and December 1973, more than half were undisputed critical and box office hits. Thirty-two of these were Ken's ideas; twenty were chosen with his collaboration.

He would have liked to expand his brief, to try his hand at directing, but

Olivier did not encourage him; he did however defend his provocative employee against an Establishment that wanted him hanged, drawn and quartered. In defence of freedom for the artistic directorate, Ken frequently locked horns with the Board Chairman, Lord Chandos; and with the Lord Chamberlain, the official censor. Away from the public rows, he worked quietly and diligently.

My romance with Ken coincided with his new life at the National Theatre. In December of 1962 he had swanned into the Observer on a Friday night to deliver his copy, and noticed a new girl working on the arts news column. 'And who are you?' he asked. The following week he took this fledgling journalist to drinks and impressed her with his wit, confidence and charm. He learned that I was the London-born daughter of a Canadian foreign correspondent, and that I had married Oliver Gates, a man I met at Oxford. On 25 January, my birthday, he took me to a restaurant in Soho where he asked me to marry him. He made notes in his engagement book to introduce me to Orson Welles and to start his autobiography.

The wooing continued for eight months, until in August 1963 I went to Edinburgh to stay with Ken, smuggled myself into the annexe of the George Hotel, and fell in love with him. He was there to front a drama conference attended by Olivier, Joan Littlewood, Peter Brook, George Devine, Marguerite Duras, Edward Albee, Lillian Hellman, Eugene Ionesco, Andrzej Wajda, Harold Pinter, and others. He announced at the conference that he liked plays that taught him how to survive with a certain amount of grace and dignity, plays that did not indulge in 'privileged despair'. As for the staged Happening at the conference, involving a nude woman (an event which enlivened the already sprightly proceedings), Ken condemned it. He said that art should impose order on chaos, and that the event was 'totalitarian and apocalyptic'.

The new romance continued until I felt guiltily obliged to cut it off and return to my husband. Meanwhile Elaine came and went, her place filled by theatre companions, sexual partners and confidantes. By mid-May of 1964, under pressure from Ken, Elaine went to Mexico to obtain a divorce on the grounds of incompatibility. At the same time I decided to leave my husband.

The plan was to meet in Spain, where Ken would go first to prepare an article on El Cordobés, the meteoric star of the corrida. On 24 July I arrived at the old Valencia airport: 'You've done it!' Ken said. And from then on we were together.

I moved into 120 Mount Street on our return and discovered that work and play were as one, or so it felt, since we were rarely out of each other's company. Ken was performing as the Observer's film critic, praising Godard at play, the Czech cinema and new work by Fellini, Bergman, Truffaut and Visconti. He did not excel as such, partly because he could have no impact on *the outcome of a movie. Nor could he participate, as he felt he was able to in the theatre. In addition to film criticism,* ex officio *work for the National Theatre, and research required for his journalism, Ken took an active part in various causes and committees. In a spare moment he would polish up a satirical sketch for the BBC's* Not So Much a Programme More a Way of Life. *Friends like Norman Mailer or Duke Ellington or Peter Brook would come to Mount Street and talk into the early hours. On their departure Ken would begin to write.*

By the mid-sixties the celebrated decade was dancing. Poets had already commandeered the Albert Hall with hash and flowers. Skirts were up, princesses were 'mod', and the accents of the working class were fashionable. At the centre of most things was Ken. To a huge party at Mount Street came the Italian director Michelangelo Antonioni, where he lurked around darkly, and later announced that from this celebration came his image of 'swinging London' – which he hoped to capture in Blow-Up. *On reflection the party was hardly decadent: no orgies, and no drugs that I was aware of. I remember sitting on Ken's knee, in his little study in the early hours of the morning, the flat still bulging with noisy guests, and wishing they would all go home so that we could be alone – together.*

During this period Ken began to put together his second major collection of theatre writings, which would be titled Tynan Right and Left *and published in* 1967. *In the introduction he analysed his literary accomplishment: 'Regarded by many fellow journalists as a snob, and by many academic critics as a charlatan ... Probably best summed up as a student of craftsmanship, with a special passion for imaginative craftsmen who put their skills to the service of human ideas. Conclusion: Still unreached.'*

To Alice Glaser[1]

120 Mount Street
20 February 1963

Dear Miss Glaser:

I don't know what I can add to the Atheneum release except to say that my hobbies are eating curries and watching bullfights; and that I am obsessed with word games. In fact, anything to do with words is sure to make me prick up my mind: I discovered only yesterday, for example, in the course of a reverie, that 'hm' is the only English word in the pronunciation of which air is expelled through the nose. I find that research of this nature takes up most of my time nowadays, with the result that I don't get out of bed as often as I used to. Among my phobias: fork lunches, Tories, striped suits, Greek food and proud virgins.

I hope this reaches you in time.

Yours sincerely,
Kenneth Tynan

[1] Of *Esquire* magazine.

To James Hanley[1]

The National Theatre
The Archway
10a Aquinas Street
London SE1[2]
March 11th [1963]

Dear Mr Hanley –
I'm sorry I missed 'Say Nothing'[3] when it was first done. I'd like to see it on stage, though I doubt whether the Old Vic is the right place. This kind of claustrophobic closet-drama seems to me to cry out either for an intimate theatre or (perhaps better still) t.v. or movie cameras. I think you've imagined something very powerful and haunting: what worries me is whether the language isn't a bit too elliptical and even evasive, so that in the end the teasing style becomes a little maddening: you seem to withhold rather too many simple and basic facts for rather too long. But I'm sure Sam Beckett could point to dozens of letters like this in his sottisier file. If you don't object, I'd like to hang on to the play and get a second opinion before finally committing myself.

Yours sincerely
Kenneth Tynan

[1] James Hanley (1901–85), English novelist, short-story writer and playwright whose first book was *Men in Darkness* (1930).
[2] The National Theatre Company was based at the Old Vic Theatre in Waterloo Road from 1963 to 1976, while the new theatre on the South Bank was being designed and built. Its offices were located in temporary Nissen huts near the theatre, first in Duchy Street, then in Aquinas Street.
[3] Hanley's first play was produced at the Royal Court in 1962 and off-Broadway in 1965.

To John P. Marquand Jr[1]

120 Mount St. W.1.
Wednesday [?13 March 1963]

Dear John –
Herewith details of Sevilla.[2]
April 20: Novillada[3] with 'El Cordobés'[4] – he's the <u>blouson noir</u> of the bullring – v. sensational and terrible.
April 21: Another novillada with Cordobés.
22: Free day.
23: Curro Romero, Jaime Ostos, El Viti[5] (Urquijo bulls[6]).
Excellent day. Romero did a faena[7] two years ago at the Sevilla fair that made old men weep and got him contracts all over Spain and Latin America. He's been awful ever since but on his day, when he forgets he's a terrified gypsy, he's the best in the world now that Antonio O. [Ordóñez] has retired. Bulls excellent.
24: Mondeño, Curro Romero, Carlos Corbacho.[8] Mondeño is like a hatstand in his effortless plastic grace. Third guy unknown to me (Do you care about all this? I suspect not.) Good Andalusian bulls.[9]
25: Jaime Ostos, Victoriano Valencia, Palmeño.[10] Ostos was the top man at last year's Sevilla fair and will obviously be trying.
26: The Miura corrida,[11] always a laugh riot. Swords: Jose Julio (brave little chap from the land of port), Chacarte and Pedrosa[12] (two nothings who fight Miuras because nobody else will).
27: Jaime Ostos, Valencia, El Viti. (Viti is very serious and respected and can kill finely) – Salamancan bulls.[13]
28: Mondeño, Corbacho, Palmeño – Andalusian bulls, the hatstand, and two more nothings.
The sad thing is that Paco Camino,[14] who with Ostos is the only possible contender for Antonio's enormous vacant throne, almost certainly won't come (he's asking too much money); and nor will Diego Puerta,[15] the most consistent of the Sevillian school. <u>If</u> the money thing is ironed out, there'd be two extra corridas on the 29th and 30th.
My position is that I'll go if you're going. I saw Rick Sicré[16] at the Savoy the other day and he said he would organize Luis Miguel [Dominguín] and other famed cynosures. He looked particularly thuggish at the Savoy, having just launched a yacht.
Let me know the score.

Love
Ken

[1] John P. Marquand Jr (b. 1924), American novelist (under the pseudonym John Phillips) and *Paris Review* editor. A gentlemanly Yankee wit and a good friend of KPT's since 1953, he married Sue Coward in 1957.

[2] Seville holds the second most important taurine festival in the Spanish season, the Feria de Abríl. The foremost is Madrid's Feria de San Isidro.

[3] A corrida for novice matadors with three- rather than four-year-old bulls.

[4] Manuel Benitez 'El Cordobés' (b. 1936), took the Alternativa in 1963. Known for his spectacular, crowd-pleasing style, he retired in 1971 but staged a comeback 1979–81.

[5] Francisco 'Curro' Romero Lopez (b. 1933), who took the Alternativa in 1959, is still active; he is famous for his craven performances as well as for his artistry. Jaime Ostos (b. 1933) active 1956–74, was noted for his courage and skill with the sword. Santiago Martin 'El Viti' (b. 1938), active 1961–79, was noted for his simple, severe style.

[6] An important breeding ranch of the time with bulls of the Murabe bloodline.

[7] The *faena de muleta* is the penultimate stage in a bullfight. Prior to the kill, the matador attempts to make sixteen linked passes with the red cloth draped over a stick.

[8] Juan Garcia Jimenez Mondeño (b. 1934), active 1959–70, with the exception of 1964–66, during which he retired and entered a monastery; he was a courageous torero and a declared homosexual. Carlos Corbacho (b. 1942), took his Alternativa in 1961, but lost a leg as a result of an infection; he is currently a bullfight promoter.

[9] Considered by some aficionados to be the best.

[10] Victoriano Cuevas Roger Valencia (b. 1933), took his Alternativa in 1958 and finally retired in 1971; a minor torero, today he is a successful manager and promoter. Manuel Fuillerat Nieto Palmeño (b. 1938), a relatively minor figure, was active 1962–75.

[11] Probably the most famous bulls, notorious for their difficulty. The bull ranch was the property of the Miura family for over 150 years.

[12] Jose Julio Venancio (b. 1937), a Portuguese matador active 1959–89. Rafael Echevarria 'Chacarte' (b. 1941), active 1962–8, a brave matador popular in his Basque homeland. Rafael Pedrosa (b. 1931), active 1957–64; he never fulfilled his early promise.

[13] Salamanca is one of the most important bullfighting regions outside Andalusia.

[14] Francisco Camino (b. 1940), active 1960–82, was one of the finest matadors of the 1960s and 1970s, noted for his instinctive knowledge of bulls.

[15] Diego Puerta (b. 1941), took his Alternativa in 1958 and retired in 1974. A close friend and rival of Paco Camino, known as Diego Valor for his courage.

[16] Ricardo Sicré, Spanish businessman and adventurer who kept a yacht in Spain.

Memo to Sir Laurence Olivier, John Dexter,[1] William Gaskill[2]

[The National Theatre]
May 21st [1963]

A Possible Repertoire – 64/65

1. 'Hay Fever'[3] – directed L. O.

2. 'The Crucible'[4] with Scofield[5] (directed W. G.) <u>OR</u>
   'Serjeant Musgrave'[6] with Scofield (directed W. G.) <u>OR</u>
   'Serjeant Musgrave' with L. O. (directed W. G.)

3. 'Much Ado' – directed Zeffirelli.[7]

4. Triple bill. This seems to me an ideal way of combining box-office with experiment.

   As follows:
   (a) 'Swan Song'[8] with L. O.
   (b) 'Dutchman'[9] by LeRoi Jones, with Billie Whitelaw.[10]
   (c) Something festive, preferably with a largish cast. E.g. Fielding's 'Tom Thumb',[11] Jarry's 'Ubu Roi'[12] (in Cyril Connolly's translation), 'The Critic',[13] a Feydeau or Labiche. (alternatively: a double bill consisting of 'La Ronde'[14] – with L. O. – and 'Dutchman'? The latter, after all, deals with one of the few heterosexual pairings that Schnitzler forgot: white and Negro.)[15]

5. 'Edward II'[16] with Scofield (directed J. D.) (and/or the Charles Wood play,[17] directed by J. D. The idea would be to try it out privately on a Sunday night, and then, if it worked, put it into the repertoire for a few trial performances. (One warning: it mightn't be wise to pick a repertoire that included 'Musgrave' and 'Dutchman' as well as Charles Wood.)

6. 'Love for Love'[18] – directed L. O. when his film is finished.[19] Could Scofield be fitted in here?

This would leave the Osborne[20] and 'Three Sisters'[21] for Chichester.[22]

K T

---

[1] John Dexter (1935–90), English theatre director who began his career at the Royal Court in 1957 and was appointed an Associate Director of the National Theatre in 1963. The National Theatre opened officially on 27 October 1963 with the uncut second quarto *Hamlet* starring Peter O'Toole.

[2] William Gaskill (b. 1930), English theatre director, one of the Associate Directors of the National Theatre 1963–5.

[3] *Hay Fever*, Noël Coward (1925), directed by Coward in October 1964.

[4] *The Crucible*, Arthur Miller (1952), directed by Olivier in January 1965.

[5] Paul Scofield had recently played King Lear with the RSC (1962).

[6] *Sergeant Musgrave's Dance*, John Arden (1959), produced originally at the Royal Court in October 1959.

[7] Franco Zeffirelli (b. 1923), Italian stage, opera and film director. KPT had praised his realistic production of *Romeo and Juliet* at the Old Vic in 1960, describing it as 'a revelation, even perhaps a revolution' (*Observer*, 9 October 1960).

[8] Early one-act play by Anton Chekhov (1889).

[9] Radical one-act play produced by the Playwrights' Unit in New York in the early 1960s.

[10] Billie Whitelaw (b. 1932), English actress noted for her performances in the plays of Samuel Beckett, in whose *Play* she made her National Theatre debut in 1964.

[11] *Tom Thumb the Great*, Henry Fielding, first performed in 1730.

[12] *Ubu Roi*, Alfred Jarry (1873–1907), wrote this play when he was fifteen years old and it was first produced in 1896.

[13] *The Critic*, Richard Brinsley Sheridan (1779).

[14] Arthur Schnitzler's study of sexual relationships, written in 1896 and not performed in Vienna until 1920.

[15] Neither *La Ronde* nor *Dutchman* was performed at the National.

[16] Brecht's version of Christopher Marlowe's play (*c.*1590) was eventually directed by Frank Dunlop (opened 30 April 1968).

[17] *Dingo*. See letter of 11 February 1965.

[18] Restoration comedy by William Congreve (1695), directed by Peter Wood in October 1965.

[19] Olivier played the part of Inspector Newhouse in Otto Preminger's *Bunny Lake is Missing* (UK, 1965), a psychodrama adapted by John and Penelope Mortimer from Evelyn Piper's novel.

[20] An adaptation of Lope de Vega's *La Fianza Satisfecha* (*c.* 1614), directed by John Dexter in June 1966.

[21] By Anton Chekhov (1901), directed by Olivier in July 1967.

[22] The National played summer seasons at the Chichester Festival Theatre in 1963, 1964 and 1965. Neither *The Three Sisters* nor Osborne's *A Bond Honoured* was produced there.

To Helene Weigel

120 Mount Street
6 June 1963

Dear Helli:

All goes well with 'Courage'[1] and unless something unforeseen happens the agreement will be made within a week.

Joss Ackland[2] is an experienced classical actor, young middle-aged, who has mostly specialised in Shakespearean comedy – for instance, he was an excellent Toby Belch in 'Twelfth Night' at the Old Vic. He is a very reliable performer and certainly would not disgrace you: my only query is whether he has the intellectual authority for the part. In other words, he might be a bit of a lightweight.

Yours,
Ken Tynan

[1] KPT was negotiating with Stefan Brecht, the playwright's son, on behalf of the National, for the rights of Brecht's *Mother Courage and Her Children*. It opened on 12 May 1965, with William Gaskill directing.

[2] Joss Ackland (b. 1928), English stage and screen actor who had played Shakespearean roles with the Old Vic Company from 1958 and was made an associate director of the Mermaid Theatre in 1962, where he played the title role in Brecht's *Galileo*.

To Emilie Jacobson[1]

120 Mount Street
29 July 1963

Dear Emilie:

1) Is the 'Playboy' offer exclusive? If it isn't, I think I should like to accept it. There's also, of course, the problem of 'Holiday'. I can't see them agreeing to the 'Playboy' arrangement. This is too bad, since they have been very good to me in the past; and I would bc willing to promise not to write for another monthly except 'Holiday' and 'Playboy'; but if this is still unacceptable, I think the 'Playboy' bid is too tempting to resist. I would, however, like to fulfil my obligations to 'Holiday' before the 'Playboy' agreement comes into force. As you know, I owe Harry Sions pieces on Soho, Oxford and the German theatre.[2] I think I should get at least two of these done before starting with 'Playboy'. To sum up, what I propose is that we first sound out Harry Sions; if he objects, we explain regretfully, but firmly, that we need the 'Playboy' money; but we add that we will let him have a couple of pieces before we start working with 'Playboy'.

2) I'd like to expand the Hemingway-Williams meeting,[3] but I doubt if I can do it by September 10. I'm running a drama conference, working for the National Theatre and writing for the 'Observer' simultaneously until the first week of September, and I really have no spare time. Would Murray Fisher[4] consider putting the piece into a later issue?

3) Of course I authorise you to deduct the Burton commission[5] from the next payment you receive.

Yours ever,
[pp. Kenneth Tynan]

[1] KPT's agent at Curtis Brown, New York, who had replaced Edith Haggard in March 1964. KPT signed with *Playboy* to write three pieces a year for an annual fee of $7,000.
[2] The German theatre piece was published in the column 'The Antic Arts' in *Holiday*, October 1964.
[3] The original article had appeared in *Holiday*, February 1960, entitled 'A Visit to Havana'. KPT's update of the encounter 'Papa and the Playwright', appeared in *Playboy* in May 1964.
[4] An editor at *Playboy*.
[5] KPT's *Playboy* interview with the actor Richard Burton appeared in the September 1963 issue.

To Emilie Jacobson

George Hotel
George Street
Edinburgh. 2
Aug 28 [1963]

Dear Emilie –
I have just seen the Burton 'Playboy' interview and am HORRIFIED. They have rewritten all my questions in their own idiot jargon, attributing to me opinions I don't hold, so that hardly a word remains of what I wrote. [...] I have not been as angry as this in 13 years as a journalist. [...]

Yours in outrage,
Ken Tynan
[...]

To Emilie Jacobson

120 Mount Street
9 September 1963

Dear Emilie:
I enclose a carbon copy of the Richard Burton interview as I sent it to 'Playboy'. I also enclose the interview as it appeared. I've underlined, as far as possible, the things attributed to me which I did not say. I could not even begin to list the way in which they have chopped up and re-shuffled everything Burton said, creating totally misleading answers to their own dreamed-up questions. If you read the two pieces one after the other you will see what I mean. The fact that they call me 'Playboy' instead of Tynan seems to me no excuse at all: the cover announces 'an interview with Richard Burton by Kenneth Tynan' and the editorial says that I 'conducted this interview for "Playboy"'.

After I sent my typescript, 'Playboy' asked me for a few small points of clarification, mostly connected with the Burton-Taylor relationship:[1] these I provided, but they were very minor alterations. There are traces of them in the semi-legible scribbles you will notice in the latter pages of my script. They don't affect my principal complaint, which is that about 80% of the words attributed to me are words that I never uttered, written in a style that is vulgar, coy and extremely likely to damage my professional reputation. On the strength of what 'Playboy' published, I wouldn't blame any celebrity if he refused to be interviewed by me. My reputation as a journalist depends on my reputation for truthful reporting. The Burton interview has undermined it, and I feel entitled to claim damages, as well as the right to demand that they should print a letter in which I disclaim responsibility for the questions and for the tendentiously re-arranged answers (I'm particularly annoyed – and so, I imagine, is Burton, by the fact that the exposition of his socialist ideals on pp 17–19 has been entirely cut).

I'd like you to do two things. First, consult Alan Collins[2] about the legal situation, and ask him to contact me as soon as he has considered what steps we can take. Second, could you possibly return my typescript (or a copy or a photostat of it) within a day or two? The reason is that I want to send it to the 'Sunday Mirror' in London, who have made a bid to reprint excerpts from the interview; and I am anxious that they should use the real thing and not the 'Playboy' mess.

I've received a gigantic cable from 'Playboy' apologising for their meddling. I shan't reply to it until I've heard from you or Alan. I might add that if American law makes it difficult for me to proceed against 'Playboy', I intend to write an account of the whole affair and get it printed in some other American magazine. [. . .]

Yours ever,
Ken T.

P.S. One of our strongest legal arguments against 'Playboy', I should have thought, is the fact that they make me ask Burton questions about two events – the premiere of 'Cleopatra' and the announcement of his intention to marry Taylor – that had not taken place when I recorded the interview.

[1] The affair began in 1962 during the filming of *Cleopatra* (US, 1963).
[2] President of Curtis Brown Ltd.

To Kathleen Halton[1]

The National Theatre
[16 September 1963]

Dearest K –

I'm sorry about today. But the weekends are always the worst times.
Every weekend is a weekend stolen from us.

I think I know what solitary confinement must be like.

Ever
K

[1] My maiden name.

To Kathleen Halton

Mount Street
Monday [?23 September 1963]

Dearest Katchen

This is after calling you, and sadness isn't the word. I can't stop
talking to you. With you I have that rarest feeling – a sort of passionate
peace – and sitting here looking forward to a row of empty evenings
and mornings, I realise that I can't do without it. Believe it or not, as
you like, but I cannot imagine the future without you. It's just a hole,
a gap, a mess of irrelevant events which I contemplate with absolutely
no curiosity. I can doubtless survive, and even put on a show of sporadic
energy, but I shall have no sense of where I am going, because where I
am going is you.

Let's list problems.[1] First, yours:

1) You don't trust me. I.e. you think I'll tire of you. The answer here
is that never in my life have I spent so long or taken such pains
over wooing anyone; never have I trod so carefully, never worried so
exquisitely over every step of the way. Now I am certain. We fit; we
mix; we blend. You are air and water, I am earth and fire. That's how
you create the universe.

2) You worry about leaving your 'world'. Believe me, it will outlive
you and all of us. And we have our own world to make – not so
sequestered, not so rich, but travelled and raffish and fairly affluent; an
international network of nice unguarded people who live by their

wits in the arts, and wouldn't exchange their way of life for a dozen Petworths.[2] Occasionally we allow the inhabitants of your present world to entertain us, but we keep our distance, because we prize our independence; also because we suffocate in private gardens, and are too polite to show that we are stifling. We can stand a spell in the hothouse; but not in the conservatory. The air we like to breathe is ambitious and exhilarating, and it gives us a delighted flush that is the wonder and envy of those who have never sniffed it; hence, except now and then, we gently avoid them. This is kindness on our part, not aloofness.

3) You have qualms about living with a man you cannot marry for a year and a half. One possibility: change your name and take mine until you can quietly divorce. If we had a child late next year the hubbub of your bolting would have died down and nobody would raise an eyebrow. By then, anyway, we would be so established that a million raised eyebrows couldn't shake us.

4) You worry, perhaps, about my divorce. Let me reassure you. With or without you, I intend to go through with it, and the petition will be served on me a discreet few weeks after the National Theatre opens in October. Even if we are living together by then, you will not be named; I can swear to that.

5) You worry about money. In an average year I earn around six thousand pounds, and there's little capital to fall back on. After the divorce I shall pay for my daughter's upbringing, but my wife has money in America and has promised to ask for no support. I think, to put it mildly, that we can scrape along.

6) You hate to hurt Oliver. This is a real problem and I cannot solve it for you. All I know is that the longer you postpone leaving him, the greater the injury will be when you finally do so; and if you don't leave him at all, the injury to yourself will be irreparable. Not to mention me.

Now my problems:

1) I want to live with and ultimately marry you. The solution is for you to live with and ultimately marry me. It is in your hands.

I know that nobody ever changed history with a letter. But I had to try. And the illusion of talking to you is better than talking to anyone else.

Love
K.

[1] Problems KPT proposed, rather than ones I had voiced.
[2] Seat of Lord Egremont, its gardens were designed by Capability Brown in 1793.

To Harry Buchanan[1]

120 Mount Street
4 October 1963

Dear Mr Buchanan:

Many thanks for your very informative letter. There seems to be some misunderstanding about the letter I propose to send to 'Playboy'. My intention was that it should be published in their correspondence column. If they were willing to agree to this, I would then consider dropping the action.

As you may know, 'Playboy' have offered me a very lucrative contract whereby they would pay me a large annual sum in return for three articles. If I engage in legal action against them, they will unquestionably withdraw the offer. It is naturally vital for me to balance what I might gain from the action against what I would lose by bringing it. The contract would bring me in 7,000 dollars a year. Do you feel it impossible to give even a vague opinion – to which I certainly wouldn't hold you – as to the sort of sum you think might be awarded me in damages? As an Englishman I haven't the remotest idea what sort of figure to ask for or expect. Before I decide whether to go ahead, this gap in my knowledge will have to be filled. [...]

I will await your advice before taking any further steps.

Yours sincerely,
Kenneth Tynan

[1] Partner in the New York law firm Stern & Reubens.

To Kathleen Halton

Mt. St.
Friday threnody
[4 October 1963]

Dearest K

It's midnight of a bad night. You promised you would only see me once last week; by a mighty effort you saw me twice; but it was a close thing. In fact you kept your bargain, forgetting that the whole point of my life is to cause you to break it forever. I have a weekend of ironclad solitude ahead, broken by tomorrow evening with my mother-in-law[1] and one of her middle-aged friends. Tonight Clive Goodwin and his wife[2] took me out to dinner at a Chelsea club, leaving me so embarrassed that I leapt up in the middle of coffee and ran out to get a cab. I believe in the future, but I can't <u>live</u> in it for much longer. Long honey-coloured limbs flash through my mind, and a flushed face with a prehensile upper lip, and a total presence of you, as precise and fleshy as a peach, and furry like peaches. Thoughts took shape in my loneliness of sending mad cables to Manningham Bullas,[3] requiring your presence in Tangier at tea-time on Sunday to interview a well-known <u>ghavati</u> player from Marrakesh. There are only seventeen <u>ghavati</u> players alive today, and they are all intensively training for the annual finger-plucking championship in Eastbourne. Finger-plucking is a dying art, they tell me, and the Musicians' Union condemns it as a restrictive practice. My desire to pluck and finger you is overwhelming. So is my need to hear you chuckling, and feel you snuggling, and refute you arguing, and love you loving. Please recall our pact: that when I am divorced, you will live with me. And consider rephrasing it: why not start to live with me as soon as the petition, naming Lucia,[4] is served, which it will be in early November? If not then, my hopes dwindle. Meanwhile, goodnight for this sad Friday.

* * * * * * *

Midday Saturday. Morning of devastating introspection and reluctance to get up; spirits not notably raised by morning mail including (a) letter from American magazine[5] indicating polite disappointment with article I wrote a fortnight ago and (b) letter from Tracy passing on news that Elaine has sold the screen rights of her forthcoming novel to Hollywood for a gigantic sum. Charming. Guess that's how the see-saw tilts, etc. I am not overwhelmingly fond of myself at this moment; petty envy and self-pity make a sour mixture. And where are you in my hour of need? Eating kedgeree, I'll warrant, or shelling oysters, or bloody gardening. I took lunch alone at that Chinese restaurant off Leicester Square and masochistically read the new 'Playboy' through eyes still bugged with Welldorm. Excerpt from Lenny Bruce's autobiography[6] very funny; he says all Negroes and all dwellers in large industrial cities are Jews. Colour shot of Elsa

Martinelli's[7] bottom induces brief stab of voyeurism, followed by longer spasm of wanting you. I toy with the idea of watching the racing at Windsor on television. Beryl the lecherous lodgerette puts her head round the door to say that Professor Potts called from Leeds University wanting to discuss his new translation of Rumbo. (Rimbaud, presumably. But why me?) Almost call him up to discuss it; anything would be better than aimless scab-picking like this, and melancholy speculation about what you are doing <u>and who with</u>. I shall try to work now, if I can sweep the erotic images out of my mind. Soya sauce must be aphrodisiac.

* * * * * * * * *

Sunday afternoon. I wrote, rather badly, until two a.m. this morning, with time off for nips of vodka and boring dinner at the Connaught with mother-in-law and friend. TW3[8] tedious beyond belief. THIS CANNOT GO ON MY DARLING: I CAN'T BEAR THE SILENCES: I SHALL SETTLE FOR ANYTHING, ROWS AND VIOLENCE AND BROKEN GLASS, RATHER THAN SOLITUDE. I lunched today with the Ogden Stewarts[9] (you met them at the Coq d'Or) in Hampstead; their son, who works for the New Yorker, was there with his beautiful new wife and newer son, all fun and plans and family. Unbearable. The son asked me whether you and I could dine with them this week (I'd talked about you endlessly): foolishly, stupidly, shamefully, blushingly, I had to say that we didn't dine together, we just lunched. But you're in love with her? they said. Yes, I said. And she's in love with you? She says so, I said. Well then, let's say Tuesday for dinner, they said. I'll talk to her, I said, feeling sillier than I have felt for a long time. Please try to see that I cannot go on getting the worst of both worlds – a marriage without love and <u>in absentia</u>, and love without contact and <u>in absentia</u>. More and more, with Sunday evening looming ahead like the belly of a whale, I feel you must decide soon, and move. I promise that Elaine will not cite you: why should she, since she already has evidence? Unless we are together soon, brainwashing will begin to change us both; the Chinese were not the first to discover that solitary confinement makes people infinitely malleable and susceptible to any outside suggestion. Now for more work: my deadline is tonight. I'm tempted to add: so is ours.

* * * * * * * * *

It's one thirty-one. I've finished my Playboy piece on Hemingway and how I introduced him to Tennessee Williams. It's gossipy but not bad. I am about to go to bed in commonplace misery. I hope this finds you as it leaves me.

Alone,
K.

[1] Elaine Dundy's mother, Florence Rosenberg Brimberg.
[2] Clive Goodwin was married to the actress and pop artist Pauline Boty, who died of glandular cancer, aged 28, in 1966.
[3] Oliver Gates' parents had a country house near Pewsey, Wiltshire, called Manningford Abbas.
[4] A young Bohemian friend of KPT's.
[5] Probably the *New York Times* magazine, though no article can be traced.
[6] Lenny Bruce (1925–66), controversial American satirical comedian. KPT wrote the foreword to the English edition of *How to Talk Dirty and Influence People* (1966).
[7] Elsa Martinelli (b. 1932), Italian film actress.
[8] *That Was The Week That Was*, a weekly BBC TV satire programme.
[9] The screenwriter Donald Ogden Stewart was married to Ella Wintour. His son by a former marriage, Donald Ogden Stewart Jr, was married to an Italian model.

To the Editor, *Playboy*[1]

120 Mount Street
14 November 1963

Dear Sir,

At your invitation I interviewed Richard Burton. When the manuscript left me the questions were written in English. Your staff, or some machine in your office, then rewrote them in a form of chromium-plated Swahili, injecting opinions that were not mine, adding new questions of their own, and chopping up Mr Burton's answers to fit questions he was never asked. May I emphatically deny any connection between what I actually said to Mr Burton and the jargon you attribute to me? And may I also clear myself of any responsibility for the fact that two of the questions I am made to ask Mr Burton refer to events that took place long after the interview – namely, the premiere of 'Cleopatra' and the announcement of his intention to marry Miss Taylor?

Yours,
K. Tynan

[1] The letter was not published.

To Willis Barnstone[1]

[The National Theatre]
22 November 1963

Dear Professor Barnstone:

Sir Laurence has passed your letter to me. As it happens, I read your translation of Lope de Vega in the 'Tulane Drama Review', and it was one of the factors that reawakened my interest in a play I had often heard my Spanish friends discussing with bated breath. It isn't, however, possible to consider using your translation, since we have already commissioned John Osborne to adapt the play for us. It will, I imagine, turn out to be a John Osborne play based on Lope's, rather than a translation!

Yours sincerely,
[Kenneth Tynan]

[1] Willis Barnstone (b. 1927), American professor of literature, author and editor.

To Helene Weigel

[The National Theatre]
26 November 1963

Dear Helli:

I have something rather urgent and important to ask you. The Drama Committee[1] of the National Theatre have decided, during the summer of 1964, to invite a number of visiting theatrical companies to bring productions of Shakespeare's plays to the Old Vic Theatre. The theatre will be available for this purpose between August 3 and October 3, during which time our own company will be on holiday. Our first visiting company will be Joan Littlewood's Theatre Workshop, who will perform 'Henry 1v' Parts 1 & 2 between August 3rd and the 15th. Our Drama Committee has asked me to enquire whether the Berliner Ensemble would be able to bring its new production of 'Coriolan'[2] at any time between August 15 and October 3 – to run at the Old Vic for a period of one or two weeks. Among the other companies we are inviting are the Piccolo Teatro[3] in 'Antony & Cleopatra', and the Nottingham Playhouse's[4] production of 'Coriolanus', directed by

Tyrone Guthrie, which we feel would make a fascinating contrast with yours.

The details can be worked out later between our administrative director and yourself. What I would like to know at this stage is whether the Ensemble would be willing and able to come.

The question of entry permits[5] would of course have to be solved; but our committee feels that the government would not lightly refuse entry to a company officially invited by the National Theatre. (There is also a strong possibility that there may be a change of government next spring.) If you could let me know as soon as possible whether the Ensemble would be free to come, we shall be in a strong position to bring official pressure to bear on the Foreign Office.

Do let me know if you are interested. I might add that we have installed a large revolving stage[6] at the Old Vic, and also enlarged the backstage area. Finally, let me say that we shall make no final arrangements for the period between August 17 and October 3 until we have heard from you – you can pick your own date.

Love to yourself and the company,
[Ken]

---

[1] On his appointment Laurence Olivier had asked the National Theatre Board for a subcommittee to help choose 'a balanced repertory'; chaired by Sir Kenneth Clark, it met for the first time on 11 December 1962. KPT strongly disapproved of this arrangement.
[2] Adapted by Brecht.
[3] Founded in 1947 in Milan by the actor Paolo Grassi.
[4] The Nottingham Playhouse, which had opened earlier that year, was run by John Neville.
[5] The German Democratic Republic (East Germany) was not formally recognized by Great Britain until 1972.
[6] When KPT took Olivier to Berlin on 13–14 April 1963, the Berliner Ensemble had eagerly awaited his verdict on their performance. Olivier stood up and said, 'I've had a marvellous experience this evening. And I was particularly amazed by how you can make your revolving stage move and make no sound. And the second thing is that you must use some spirit gum to stick on your wigs which is better than ours because one cannot see the wig joint.' He then sat down.

To Kathleen Halton

[Telegram][1]

Hyde Park T. S.
9 December 1963

DARLING WHAT HAVE THEY DONE TO YOU[2] STOP DO NOT LET THEM

BRAIN WASH YOU STOP DO NOT DESTROY US STOP I LOVE YOU
IRREVOCABLY MUST SEE YOU IMMEDIATELY = KEN +

[1] Sent to my mother's house in Hampstead.
[2] I had told KPT that I felt I owed it to Oliver Gates to give our marriage a chance.

To Kathleen Halton

[Telegram][1]

Grosvenor T. S.
9 December 1963

DARLING CANNOT BELIEVE THE WORLD CAN END IN TWENTYFOUR
HOURS IMPLORE YOU SEE ME CALL ME SOMETHING ANYTHING =
KEN +

[1] Sent to the *Sunday Times*, where I worked as a reporter on the colour magazine.

To Kathleen Halton

[Telegram][1]

Hyde Park T. S.
9 December 1963

WHY WHY WHY PLEASE TELL ME BEFORE I GO MAD LOVE = KEN +

[1] Sent to Hampstead.

To Emilie Jacobson

120 Mount Street
11 December 1963

Dear Emilie:
   [...] I hope to be sending off my Joan Littlewood profile to 'Holiday'
early next week. Meanwhile I've been reading Spectorsky's letter[1] about
the 'Playboy' situation. What can I say? The bastards have won and I

owe your lawyers 200 dollars. This is what is known as the economic basis of art. See Engels' letter <u>passim</u>.[2] Please tell Spectorsky that I've capitulated and he can start rubbing his hands.

Love,
Ken

[1] The charming and erudite editor of *Playboy* A. C. Spectorsky (1910–72) had written to KPT on 29 October 1963: 'I'm sure you realize the curious inconsistency which would face us both if *Playboy* were to publish the Hemingway-Williams piece with one hand while we were busy with the other defending a suit which you had brought against us for another submission.'
[2] Friedrich Engels (1820–95), German socialist and co-author with Marx of the *Communist Manifesto* (1848); he wrote letters on the economic basis of society, and its relation to super-structure, arts, ideology, etc., in the early 1890s.

To Kathleen Halton

[Telegram]

[St Moritz][1]
24 December 1963

DEAREST CHUM YOUR ADVICE ABOUT DRESS DISASTROUS BLACK TIE OBLIGATORY AT DINNER AND DECORATIONS ARE WORN IN THE STEAMHEATED BOWLING ALLEY KINDLY FLY OUT AT ONCE WITH TAIL SUIT OR CONTRITELY TELEPHONE ST MORITZ 33812 LOVE YOU KEN

[1] KPT and Tracy were on a skiing holiday with the Earl of Harewood and Patricia Tuckwell (later the second Lady Harewood).

To Helene Weigel

[The National Theatre]
26 January 1964

Dear Helli:

Just an interim note. Larry is delighted with the news that the Ensemble could come and visit us, and the financial arrangements you suggest seem perfectly acceptable to us. All that now remains is for the National Theatre Committee to start bringing pressure to bear on the

Foreign Office. For this purpose we are calling a meeting of the Committee on February 1, and when it's over we shall be writing to you in more detail.

It looks, by the way, as if the best weeks for us would be August 17–29. There's a point you might like to consider about bringing 'Ui':[1] a Polish company are performing it in May at the Aldwych Theatre for two weeks. Do you think this would be harmful to our plan? And if so, couldn't you be a brute and stop them from doing it? Let me know what you think.

Yours ever,
[Kenneth Tynan]

[1] *The Resistible Rise of Arturo Ui* by Bertolt Brecht (1941).

Memo to William Gaskill

[The National Theatre]
29 January 1964

I have now read Keith Johnstone's[1] translation of PHILOCTETES twice. I think lots of it first-rate – bony, powerful and compressed. I'm a bit worried, however, that the compression may have gone too far. Some of the speeches read as if he has tried to force a page of Sophocles into half a dozen lines merely in order to produce a few startling images. Allowing two minutes playing time for each page, all we have is 50 minutes – which isn't enough. Also, I feel that Johnstone's compression means that the audience will have to keep their ears pricked up a little too intently all the way through – a little more exposition in simple language would be a very good idea. Do you think we could meet and talk about this?

There's one point that disturbs me about the plot – and it's in Sophocles as well as Johnstone. The basic action of the plot is: to obtain the bow from Philoctetes in order to conquer Troy. Now the terms of this problem are not clearly stated. There is one unanswered question: does the bow only work when operated by its owner? On page 16 Neoptolemus says: 'I believe that the man is inseparable from the bow. The bow is useless without the archer!' Yet at the end Hercules says that Philoctetes and Neoptolemus must use the bow together. I think it's vital to clarify this – otherwise the audience doesn't know precisely what problem the play is trying to solve. If Neoptolemus can operate the bow alone, then all that is necessary is to disarm Philoctetes and steal it. In which case the play would end as soon as Neoptolemus has laid hands on it. If <u>dual</u> control of the bow is the necessary condition for using it against Troy, this must be made crystal clear from the beginning, so that we know exactly what Odysseus is trying to achieve.

One or two verbal quibbles – some of them no doubt due to misprints.

Page 2   'Don't bridle' – isn't the verb unnecessarily quaint? It sounds as if Neoptolemus might be about to stamp his foot like a petulant schoolgirl.

Page 4   '... I'm a poor man uninhabited ...'. What does this mean?

Page 7   'He went all quiet ...' Sounds a bit suburban.

'The man who shares my hatred is my friend.' Too ambiguous – he means 'The man who hates what I hate'. Johnstone's version could mean the opposite.
[...]

Page 17   'I'm up to my neck'. Surely the wrong sort of colloquialism and bound to get a laugh.

'I heal you that together we annihilate Troy.' Too compressed; sounds like a telegram.

Page 18   'I will be destroyed by such unexpectedness'. Meaningless: could be a literal translation from the German.

Page 19   'Don't let them limpet me away from you.' Pseudo-poetic: worthy of Fry.

Why not 'prise'?

'This cliff loves me'. Meaningless: again the result of over-compression.
[...]

Page 20   'Enjoy your habitat'. Sounds comic; one associates the word with nature talks.
(Incidentally, in the previous sentence Odysseus says: 'I draw this bow as easily as you'. This is a further complication I hadn't noticed. If Odysseus can make the bow work, why doesn't he just bugger off with it? This really needs clearing up, rather like the question of whose finger is on the NATO trigger.)

<u>Page 22</u>   'My foot, my foot, when will I be rid of you?' Dangerously
          funny.

<u>Page 24</u>   'Words, words'. Could this be re-phrased so as not to antici-
          pate Hamlet?
          [...]

Am I being too pedantic? I don't think so.

P. S. If you don't want Johnstone to expand the play, we shall have to
find a third item. Yolande Bird[2] has just rather cleverly suggested
'Sweeney Agonistes'. Thus you could have a triptych of classical styl-
ists – Sophocles, Eliot and Beckett.[3] What do you think?

---

[1] British playwright and director associated mainly with the Royal Court.
[2] National Theatre Board Assistant Secretary, then Secretary until 1993.
[3] In the event Beckett's *Play* (1963) opened on 7 April 1964 in a double bill with *Philoctetes*. Eliot's
Sweeney Agonistes was never performed at the National.

To George Devine[1]
(copies to Laurence Olivier and William Gaskill)

[The National Theatre]
31 March 1964

Dear George:
   Forgive me for writing, but I feel I must try to explain more
clearly to you and Larry what is worrying me about 'Play'.[2] I wouldn't
do so if I didn't feel that many of my qualms were shared by others.
   To recap: before Sam B. arrived at rehearsals, 'Play' was recog-
nisably the work we all liked and were eager to do. The delivery of
the lines was (rightly) puppet-like and mechanical, but not wholly
dehumanised and stripped of all emphasis and inflections. On the
strength of last weekend, it seems that Beckett's advice on the
production has changed all that – the lines are chanted in a breakneck
monotone with no inflections, and I'm not alone in fearing that
many of them will be simply inaudible. I suspect that Beckett is
trying to treat English as if it were French – where that kind of
rapid-fire monotony is customary.
   The point is that we are not putting on 'Play' to satisfy Beckett
alone. It may not matter to him that lines are lost in laughs; or that

essential bits of exposition are blurred; but it surely matters to us. As we know, Beckett has never sat through any of his plays in the presence of an audience: but we have to live with that audience night after night!

I wouldn't dream of writing in this way if it were just a question of difference of opinion between us: you're the director and it's your production. But rather more than that is at stake. 'Play' is the second new play the National Theatre has done. The first, 'Andorra',[3] wasn't an unqualified success. Originally we intended to follow it with 'The Master Builder',[4] which we then decided to postpone. This means that 'Play' – our first experimental work – follows straight on 'Andorra's' heels. If it fails to get over with maximum impact, it may jeopardise our future plans for experiment and put a weapon into the hands of those people (already quite numerous) who think the National Theatre, like the Proms, should stick to the popular classics and not cater for minority tastes. It may even provoke the more conservative members of the N.T. Board to start interfering in the choice of plays – which would be disastrous!

Please understand me: I trust the play completely, and I trust your production of it, – up to the advent of the author. What I don't especially trust is Beckett as co-director. If you could see your way to re-humanising the text a little, I'll bet that the actors and the audience will thank you – even if Beckett doesn't!

Yours,
[Kenneth Tynan][5]

[1] George Devine (1910–65), English actor and theatre director appointed Director of the English Stage Company at the Royal Court in 1955. He came to the National specifically to direct *Play*.

[2] Samuel Beckett (1906–89), Irish playwright living in Paris; *Waiting for Godot* had been first performed in London in 1955. In his review (*Observer*, 7 August 1955) KPT wrote: 'A play, it asserts and proves, is basically a means of spending two hours in the dark without being bored.'

[3] By Max Frisch (1961); directed by Lindsay Anderson, it had opened on 28 January 1964.

[4] By Henrik Ibsen (1892), it opened on 9 June 1964.

[5] Devine replied in a letter dated 9 April 1964 that he considered KPT's letter 'impertinent and ignorant', that Beckett's presence at rehearsals was of great help to him and that he would ignore KPT's 'snide' comment about him. He concluded by saying, 'The simple truth appears to be that you got into a panic about *Play*, in case it did not "come off". I'm afraid you'll have to have a bit more guts if you really want to do experimental works, which, nine times out of ten, only come off for a "minority" to begin with.'

Olivier intervened in the dispute on 12 April with a long memo to KPT: 'This is a detonation with an alarming sound-off, but if we just wait till our ears stop tingling, I think we may not see much wreckage about. I don't know if you were conscious of the first V2 arriving in London. I remember shooting up in my bed thinking the whole of London had had it; what had happened was that it hit a gasometer, and that's really what has happened in this case.' He then admonished KPT: 'I like you, I like having you with me, apart from it rather tickling me to have you with me, but you can be too fucking tactless for words.' He then advised KPT to 'be a little quicker in letting me have your thoughts and a little slower in imparting them to others'.

To George Devine

[The National Theatre]
10 April 1964

CONFIDENTIAL

Dear George:

You call me 'impertinent': there speaks the advocate of a director's theatre. (And 'presumptuous' – another word you apply to me – confirms this.)

You profess yourself 'shocked' by the idea that one's obligation to an author need not extend beyond a general loyalty to his script: there speaks the advocate of a <u>writer's</u> theatre. Like you, I would hate the NT to become a museum: but the best way to build theatrical museums is to regard every syllable of every stage direction as holy writ.

I believe in neither a director's nor a writer's theatre, but a theatre of intelligent <u>audiences</u>. I count myself a member of an intelligent audience, and I wrote to you as such. That you should disagree with me I can understand, but that you should resent my expressing my opinions is something that frankly amazes me. I thought we had outgrown the idea of theatre as a mystic rite born of secret communion between author, director, actors and an empty auditorium. The 'dramatic purpose' you mention involves, for me, communication and contact with a live audience: and a live audience is something of which Beckett, by his own honest admission, has little personal knowledge. So far from wanting to 'turn the play into literature', I was proposing that we should liberate it from the author's (to me) rather confined view of its dramatic possibilities.

And of course I want the play to 'come off' – for the <u>whole</u> of the minority to whom it is addressed. If you recall, my main worry was that it would reach only <u>part</u> of that minority. Perhaps I was wrong, but I don't regret having worried.

Yours,
[Kenneth Tynan]

To Helene Weigel

[The National Theatre]
8 May 1964

Dear Helli:

Our telephone conversation saddened me. As you know, we had
hoped to build a whole summer season around your appearance at the
Old Vic, and this has now collapsed. Sir Laurence asks me to express
his great regret.

I reported what you said to the National Theatre Committee yesterday. Despite their disappointment, they have asked me to invite the
Ensemble to come to the Old Vic during the summer of 1965.[1] If you
are able to accept, we can arrange the dates and repertoire later. The
idea is that you should come for two or three weeks bringing two or
three productions. It will not be possible for us to invite you earlier,
since we already have a full programme of our own productions until
next summer. I do hope you are able to give us an affirmative answer.

As I told you, I'd love to come to the run-through of CORIOLANUS in
June. Do let me know the exact date.

Yours,
[Kenneth Tynan]

[1] Weigel's withdrawal was possibly due to visa problems.

To Emilie Jacobson

The National Theatre
May 26 [1964]

Dear Emilie –

I'm writing away from home and haven't got Mr. Spectorsky's
address – so could you possibly forward this letter to him? (Copy
attached)

I like several of his ideas and I have a few of my own, and in what
follows I'll amalgamate both:

1) Interviews. I'd like to do Chou En Lai, Mao Tse Tung or Khrush-
chev, but I have no contacts with any of them: has 'Playboy'? Chaplin
I know is out: I've tried this before with the best possible introductions,
and it won't work. How about Marlon Brando, Dietrich, or a joint

interview with Peter O'Toole[1] and Albert Finney[2] – with all of whom I have strong contacts? (A full profile of O'Toole doesn't wildly appeal to me; I don't honestly think he's <u>that</u> good yet.)

2) Film Festivals. This has been done a good bit, but I wouldn't mind trying a Lillian Ross[3] at Venice in September.

3) The American psychiatrist Dr. Bergler[4] once wrote that artists – so far from being prophets and leaders of the human spirit – were <u>without exception</u> exhibitionists, voyeurs, homosexuals, sadists, masochists, alcoholics or a combination of two or more of these. Would this be worth exploring in a piece? Trouble is that one couldn't name names. But as a theory it seems to me pretty tenable.

4) The Bull Scene '64. Bullfights are pretty old <u>montera</u>[5] – but I shall be in Spain in July and I know the picture pretty well – Orson Welles is probably coming with me to the Valencia Feria. There's a terrible young sensationalist called El Cordobés – the Beatle of bullfighting – who'll be there and who is having a thing with Geraldine Chaplin.[6] How about a piece on him, Welles and the summer Spanish scene?[7]

That's all for now. Incidentally I just mailed off my German theatre piece to Harry Sions.

Love,
Ken

[1] Peter O'Toole (b. 1932), actor of Irish descent who became an international star in *Lawrence of Arabia* (UK, 1962). He joined the National Theatre in 1963 to play Hamlet in the company's inaugural production at the Old Vic.

[2] Albert Finney (b. 1936), English actor who played the title roles in *Billy Liar* (1960) and *Luther* (1961) before joining the National Theatre Company in 1965. He had recently starred in the film *Tom Jones* (UK, 1963).

[3] Lillian Ross (b. 1927), *New Yorker* writer famous for her book *Picture* (1951), an account of the making of John Huston's film *The Red Badge of Courage* (US, 1951).

[4] Dr Edmund Bergler, author of *The Writer and Psycho-Analysis* (1950) and considered to be a leading authority on the psychoanalysis of homosexuality.

[5] In fact, 1964 was a boom year, with three times as many corridas as in 1951 when KPT had first gone to Spain. Bullfights were clearly not 'old hat'.

[6] Geraldine Chaplin (b. 1944), film actress daughter of Charlie Chaplin. The craze for the controversial matador was at its height; it is unlikely that the two had an affair.

[7] 'Beatle in the Bullring' appeared in *Playboy*, January 1965.

To Eric Bentley[1]

[The National Theatre]
[5 June 1964]

Dear Eric:

There's been a slight flurry of letters between Stefan and the National Theatre lately. At one point it looked as if he was categorically going to hold up the production indefinitely. Things look better now but there are still a couple of conditions that will probably irk you. However, it now seems inescapable that we either accept them or abandon the production altogether. So here they are:

1. Stefan doesn't want to collaborate with you on a revised version; he says he would like to offer help 'not with the English, but with the German – with its multiplicity of meanings.' What this means, I take it, is that he would send you a list of verbal quibbles that he has with your rendering, on the basis of which you would propose modifications. We at the National Theatre would all be most grateful if you would consent to this plan – always remembering that once the contract is signed and the play is in rehearsal, you and Bill Gaskill[2] would be able to make further textual revisions to your own mutual satisfaction. The vital thing is to satisfy Stefan now. His idea is that the amended Bentley version would be ready by October (though I would prefer an earlier date – say September); and assuming that Stefan found it acceptable we would then go ahead with a spring production. Naturally, we shall do all we can to see to it that he accepts your revisions without too much quibbling; but legally he has us over the barrel and the final decision will have to be his. [...]

2. Stefan also insists that we should commission a poet to re-translate the songs. This is a point on which he will not budge. His proposal is that whether the poet receives a flat fee or a small royalty, the payment should be shared proportionately by you and the Brecht estate – i.e. 35% of it would come from your share and 65% from Brecht's. I really see no way out of this one and I hope you will feel able to agree to it. Auden, I suppose, remains the number one choice.[3]

So there you have it – a pretty messy situation but the best compromise we could get out of him. Please let us know your reactions. I don't expect them to be joyful; at the same time I hope they won't be too bleak. I suppose the next step would be for him to send you a list of his textual points and for us to start poet-hunting. Then at last we can actually get the show on the road.

Yours,
[Kenneth Tynan][4]

[1] Eric Bentley had already translated several plays by Brecht, including *Mother Courage and Her Children*, which had had its English premiere directed by Joan Littlewood at Theatre Workshop in July 1955.

[2] Gaskill directed the National Theatre's first production of *Mother Courage and Her Children*, which opened in May 1965.

[3] Bentley's contract with Stefan Brecht for his English adaptation of *Mother Courage* stipulated that he would get thirty-five per cent of author's royalties for any production in Britain or the US until 1970. Brecht, who claimed he did not like Bentley's version, was looking for a way out of paying this royalty. On 14 May KPT cabled Weigel to ask her to use her influence with her son to let the National use the Bentley translation. (KPT had reservations about the Bentley version, but the National needed a swift answer if they were to put on the play according to plan.)

W. H. Auden had already written lyrics to a Milhaud score, and KPT thought Bentley could quite easily adapt them to Paul Dessau's score. Auden agreed to work further on the lyrics, and was billed in the National Theatre programme as their translator.

[4] Eventually Bentley agreed to 'take care of' the points in the translation which worried Brecht. On 27 July he wrote to KPT: 'It now looks as if you have found the formula for negotiated peace between east and west.'

To the Editor, *Transatlantic Review*[1]

[120 Mount Street]
July 2 [1964]

Dear Sir,

I've just read Charles Marowitz's[2] interview with himself in 'Transatlantic Review 16.' It's a remarkable piece of narcissistic bravura (one pictures Marowitz, the fastest gun in the West End, practising his draw in front of a mirror), but it contains a few comments on the National Theatre that really ought to be tempered or corrected.

Marowitz derides the N.T. because its company 'lacks any semblance of style'. As I write, the company is just eight months old. If it had evolved a 'style' as rapidly as that I would be ashamed of it, although trend-seeking journalists might well have been impressed. Later in the article Marowitz triumphantly declares that the theatre of the future will have 'no patience with stylistic consistency.' So where does this get us? For lacking 'style', the N.T. is condemned and the theatre of the future applauded. I long to hear this contradiction resolved.

Nor is it the only one. Having singled out Jack Richardson[3] as the most promising off-Broadway playwright precisely because he is a 'language-man and a true parodist,' Marowitz goes on to acclaim improvised 'happenings' and the anti-literary theatre of Artaud[4] as the brightest hopes for the future. Citing the Theatre of Cruelty season at LAMDA[5] to prove his point, Marowitz says that the Royal Shakespeare Company is 'more important' than the National Theatre. He might have added that he is employed by the Royal Shakespeare Company and that he co-directed the LAMDA season. [. . .]

What Marowitz ignores is that the National Theatre works from a wider brief. It is called on to cover the whole theatrical waterfront from Sophocles and Shakespeare to Coward and Brecht. I can't offhand think of a production style that would be equally appropriate to 'Philoctetes' and 'Hay Fever'. Perhaps Marowitz can.

Perhaps, on the other hand, he wouldn't want to. I detect in his prophecies, with their enthusiasm for action painting, 'happenings' and 'booting Ibsen and his whole school solidly up the ass,' the familiar provocations of the professional outcast who loves to be hated, who needs an audience to reject him, who wants experimental theatre to get back to the minority cellars where it began, who resents the idea that minority theatre should ever become popular, and who fails to realise (and this is the crucial, deplorable failure) that the purpose of a true *avant-garde* is not to be an end in itself but a beach-head from which to conquer the majority. For Marowitz, theatre ceases to be art as soon as people like it. I don't think majority theatre, *however good*, would ever have much appeal for him. It's significant that he should have chosen to interview himself. The kind of theatre he prefers could easily end up talking to itself.

Yours sincerely,
Kenneth Tynan

[1] Published under the headline 'Replying to Charles Marowitz'.
[2] Charles Marowitz (b. 1934), American director who co-directed the Theatre of Cruelty season with Peter Brook in 1964 and founded the Open Space Theatre in London in 1968.
[3] Jack Richardson (b. 1935), off-Broadway playwright who established his reputation in the early 1960s with *The Prodigal* (1960) and *Gallows Humor* (1961).
[4] Antonin Artaud (1896–1948), French poet, actor, director and dramatist who invented the Theatre of Cruelty, the principles of which are outlined in *La Théâtre et son Double* (1938). Artaud believed that theatre, like plague, should free the audience from the constraints of reason and morality and force it by a series of psychological shocks to a violent self-examination. His first and only experiment with this theory was his play *Les Cenci* in 1935, which ran for only two weeks.

[5] Brook and Marowitz used the Macowan Theatre at the London Academy of Music and Dramatic Art in Earls Court.

To Terence Kilmartin

120 Mount Street
20 July 1964

Dear Terry:

Here are summaries of the ideas for the colour mag[1] that we discussed on Saturday:

1) A piece by me on THEATRE AS SPECTACLE (i.e. can theatrical spectaculars still compete with wide-screen ones?) – based on THE ROYAL HUNT OF THE SUN[2] which opens at the Old Vic in the week of December 7. As I told you, I think there are two moments in THE ROYAL HUNT which for sheer visual impact beat the wide screen at its own game.[3] I haven't yet found out whether the SUNDAY TIMES or SUNDAY TELEGRAPH have approached the NT for colour coverage of the production. If they haven't already I'll make sure that the OBSERVER gets it exclusively. I'll get my secretary to find out and let you know.

2) October 22 will be the first anniversary of the NT. What I suggest (for the previous Sunday) would be a taped discussion on the year's achievement or lack of it. Possible participants myself, Peter Brook, Tyrone Guthrie, Penelope G[illiatt], possibly even Larry himself.

3) People as disparate as Peter Brook and Arnold Wesker[4] assure me that the most exciting director in Europe today is the man who runs the National Theatre in Prague. His name is Krejca[5] and he always works with a designer of equal brilliance, Svoboda.[6] THE TIMES recently raved about their production of ROMEO AND JULIET, and I know that Peter Hall[7] has invited his company to the Aldwych for the next World Theatre Season[8] in the spring. No doubt the SUNDAY TELEGRAPH (sponsors of the World Theatre lark) will plan to do something on Krejca just before the season opens. It would be nice to pip them by getting in earlier. I could go to Prague for a week and do research.

I will be in Spain till August 10. If I have any other ideas I'll pass them on to you and Michael.[9]

Love,
K.

[1] The *Observer* followed the *Sunday Times* with a circulation-boosting colour magazine in September 1964.

[2] By Peter Shaffer (1964), directed by John Dexter. The National Theatre had successfully tried out the play at Chichester that summer.

[3] Most probably the explosion of the sun, a large metal disk made up of crossed swords which open up into a giant gold sunflower before the invading Spanish, to reveal the Inca king Atahualpa; and the dawn gathering of masked Inca priests awaiting the resurrection of their slaughtered king – a shaft of sunlight illuminates the body but the martyred Atahualpa does not rise. KPT could also be referring to the mimed sequence representing the climbing of the Andes.

[4] Arnold Wesker (b. 1932), English playwright whose early plays, including *Roots* and *The Kitchen* (1959), were first performed at the Royal Court.

[5] Otomar Krejca (b. 1921), Czech theatre director; Director of the National Theatre in Prague, 1956–61; founder of Divadlo za Branoie in 1965 and of a second theatre with the same name in 1990.

[6] Josef Svoboda (b. 1920), Czech designer whose first production for the National Theatre would be Ostrovsky's *The Storm* in 1966.

[7] Sir Peter Hall (b. 1930), English theatre, opera and film director, Director of the RSC 1960–8 and successor to Olivier as Director of the National Theatre 1973–88, where his productions included *No Man's Land* (1975), *Amadeus* (1979) and *The Oresteia* (1981). He was Artistic Director of Glyndebourne Opera 1984–90.

[8] Under the aegis of the *Sunday Telegraph* and the RSC, the impresario Sir Peter Daubeny annually brought important international theatre and ballet companies to London's Aldwych Theatre (1964–70).

[9] Michael Davie (b. 1924), reporter and columnist on the *Observer*, who edited the *Diaries of Evelyn Waugh* (1976).

To Jean Halton[1]

120 Mount Street
August 11th [1964]

PRIVATE AND CONFIDENTIAL

Dear Mrs Halton –

Quite unprompted by Kathleen, I felt I ought to write to you, partly to explain how the present situation between us came about, but mostly to pave the way for a meeting at which we can talk at greater length. I met your daughter early in 1963. At that time my own marriage was already nearing its end; apart from brief reunions in the interest of my daughter Tracy, my wife and I had been separated for nearly two years. I took great care not to rush into anything with Kathleen, although I knew from the beginning that I was in love with her. She was clearly unhappy with her marriage, and had been for a long time before I met her. But it isn't my practice to break up marriages, and although we lunched together quite often, I made no attempt to carry the relationship further until I was sure that she loved me as much as I loved her. It was clear between us that if she asked me to retire in favour of Oliver I would do so without complaint, no matter how painful it might be. She tried hard to make the marriage work, and failed; and when she told me so, I could no more have refrained from seeing her than I could have chopped off my right hand. I sympathise desperately with Oliver, because I know how shattered I would feel if Kathleen preferred someone else to me; but I have to balance his distress against the deep and permanent pain that Kathleen and I would feel if we had to give each other up. I do not know Oliver's parents; if they feel badly about the situation, I am sorry; but I must regard their feelings as less important than Oliver's, my own, Kathleen's and yours. If you knew the heart-searching that has preceded her decision to break with Oliver and his family – the pangs of regret and the moral questionings – you would, I think, be immensely proud of Kathleen. Hers is not a decision taken on impulse, in the throes of infatuation. Nor, I hope you will believe, is mine. I want to marry her if Oliver will give her a divorce next year;[2] but I should tell you frankly that it will take more than his refusal to prevent us from being together. We are more important to each other than that; and the holiday we have just spent together[3] was for both of us the happiest and most constructive of our lives. I think we have laid a good foundation.

I gather that you have formed a rather dim impression of me. I can't quarrel with that; but I do wish that you would verify it at first hand. Would you lunch or dine with me some time in the near future – with or without Kathleen, as you prefer? Almost any day would do, weekends included. Please let me know a suitable date.[4]

Yours sincerely,
Kenneth Tynan

[1] My widowed mother, a Canadian living in London.
[2] Oliver Gates would not instigate divorce proceedings until November 1965.
[3] I met KPT in Valencia on 24 July for the Feria of San Jaime, and we then flew to Palma de Majorca, followed by a brief sojourn in Madrid.
[4] My mother and KPT met for a friendly lunch shortly after the delivery of this letter.

To Robert Graves[1]

The National Theatre
August 25, 1964

Dear Robert –

You remember the idea I broached about revising the text of 'Much Ado' for the National Theatre – replacing dead similes, archaisms and words of changed meaning with <u>living</u> Elizabethan words and images? I've now discussed this at length with Olivier. He likes the notion – though he wishes the play were one of the less intelligible Shakespeares so that you could rewrite the whole thing! Before signing a contract he wonders if you would consider revamping a specimen act for him to look at. In the hope that you will, I'm enclosing a script in which I've marked the bits that I personally find dead and/or unclear. You may not agree with my choice, and certainly you're in no way bound to it; but I thought you might like some idea of the sort of thing I had in mind. What we want is to sweep away the dry cobwebs of text so that full understanding of the words isn't confined to academics. We look to you to inject the needed juice into the dead passages. Would you consider doing a draft of the first act or so? It would take you all of forty-five minutes.

I saw Mike Nichols here last week. He's not divorced yet, merely separated;[2] meanwhile he sends you his best. So does Kathleen, whom you effortlessly bowled over.

Love to Beryl[3]
Ken

[1] Currently Professor of Poetry at Oxford (1961–6), though spending most of his time in Mallorca, Spain.
[2] From Patricia Scott.
[3] Beryl Hodge had married Graves in 1949.

To Robert Graves

The National Theatre
16 September [1964]

Dear Robert

Obviously I'm bursting with gratitude for the speed and thoroughness of your response. What a play-doctor you would make! If anyone objects to your tampering, I have prepared a crafty analogy with the cleaning of old masters.

This is to tell you that as soon as Larry returns from holiday (next Monday) I'll show him your splendid emendations, from which I'm sure a draft contract will follow. Meanwhile I'm surprised you haven't run into him yourself, since he's been splashing about at Formentor.[1] My love to Mag Smith[2] if she's still around.

Yours,
Ken

[1] A town in the north of Mallorca.
[2] Maggie Smith (b. 1934), English actress who had recently played Desdemona opposite Olivier in *Othello*, and went on to play many other leading parts at the National. Her first film part was in *Nowhere to Go*, an adaptation by KPT and Seth Holt (UK, 1958). She would win an Academy Award for *The Prime of Miss Jean Brodie* (UK, 1969).

To Robert Graves

The National Theatre
22 September 1964

Dear Robert:

Larry has now read your MUCH ADO and I'm glad to say that he agrees with me. We'd both like you to go ahead and finish it. If I may, I'll hang on to your text for a day or two, because Franco Zeffirelli – who's directing the play – wants to look at it. When he has done so, I'll let you have it back immediately. (I'm assuming that you have no copy of the emendations.)

Two other things: (a) Larry asks me to warn you that in the course of rehearsals this or that amended phrase may turn out, for some unpredictable reason, not to work theatrically: in which case we may shoot a few of them back at you for further revision. He hopes you won't mind this. (b) Money. We find it very hard to think of an appropriate fee for re-writing Shakespeare. Rather desperately, Larry has asked me to ask you to suggest one. While I await your reply, I'll have a word with your agent.

Maggie Smith saddened me by telling me you were having an operation.[1] I trust it's happily over by now.

Love,
Ken

[1] On his gall bladder.

To the Earl of Harewood[1]

[The National Theatre]
29 September 1964

Dear George:

As Mr Whewell[2] may have told you, the Berliner Ensemble is yours for the asking. Helene Weigel was really very keen on the idea. The plan at the moment is that they should open at the Vic on August 9 and play for three weeks.[3] The only problem arose over the time it takes to transport their very bulky scenery to Edinburgh and set it up. Weigel insists on three clear days to do this, not counting the opening night. Thus, in order to open in Edinburgh on Tuesday, August 31, they would have to leave London after two performances on Friday, the 27th – thus depriving us of the two Saturday shows. Naturally we don't like this prospect at all, so Mr Whewell suggested that they should play the 28th in London and open in Edinburgh on Wednesday, September 1st, possibly playing there for ten days. I'm sure they would agree to do an extra matinee during the last week to compensate for the loss of the Tuesday performance.

Financially their terms are simple. You transport them and their scenery from London to Edinburgh and back to London. You also pay their living expenses in Edinburgh. The entire box-office receipts you keep for yourself. I ought to mention in passing that the total strength of the company (including technicians and musicians) is 140, so it isn't quite such a snip as it looks. [...]

Yours,
[Kenneth Tynan]
[...]

---

[1] George Henry Herbert Lascelles, 7th Earl of Harewood (b. 1923), Artistic Director of the Edinburgh International Festival 1960–5.
[2] Michael Whewell, Lord Harewood's deputy at the Edinburgh Festival.
[3] They played in Brecht's *The Resistible Rise of Arturo Ui*, *Days of the Commune*, and *Coriolanus*.

To Robert Graves

The National Theatre
Sept. 30 [1964]

Dear Robert –

I've talked over your suggested fee with our financial chiefs, and they've asked me to put in a plea for leniency. We aren't as rich as rumour reports us: last year we lost about £70,000 on top of our £130,000 subsidy, and the Treasury is getting a bit restive.

For purposes of comparison: we paid a well-known novelist[1] £300 for a complete adaptation of a foreign play – of which he did two versions. Not to weary you with more figures: would you consider £250?

I hope this doesn't aggravate your convalescence. Please get and stay well. SHE sends love, as does

Yours ever
Ken

[1] KPT had commissioned Alan Sillitoe to adapt Lope de Vega's *Fuente Ovejuna* (*c.* 1614), which was eventually performed as *This Foreign Field* at the Roundhouse in March 1970.

National Theatre Memorandum

[The National Theatre]
[22 October, 1964]

Reflections on Year One

1. Problems of building a company. One thing the season has proved is the immense difficulty of creating a permanent ensemble when the terms of reference are so wide. Most permanent companies are specialists – e.g. the Royal Shakespeare specialise in Shakespeare, the Moscow Art in 19th century plays, the Berliner Ensemble in Brecht. The Schiller[1] (our nearest parallel) has a very small permanent nucleus of actors and recruits outsiders by the season for small parts and as required for big ones that can't be cast within the nucleus. It took P. Hall several years to build his company[2] – and even now he has to cast outside it when he ventures outside Shakespeare. I think it possible that the 'guest performer' principle may have to be a permanent part of our policy.

2. Contact with the Moscow Art actors convinces me that we ought to recruit people on the basis of character as well as talent. We need actors who passionately believe in the repertory idea, who feel evangelical and idealistic about it. Talent alone is not enough to build a company.

3. We need more money and staff for a Publications Department. (Cf. B. Ensemble, the Piccolo Teatro, which publishes books on theatre, new plays, a monthly magazine, etc.) The new Royal Shakespeare magazine, 'Flourish', is something we ought to be able to produce. Needed: larger allocation of cash for this purpose and at least one more full-time member of staff.

4. It would be worth considering reducing the seat prices for productions that are obviously non-commercial. (Cf. the Aldwych [Royal Shakespeare Company] reductions for 'Expeditions One'[3] next month.) If 'Play/Philoctetes' had had this advantage, it would have played to many more people and lost no more money – probably it would have lost much less.

5. Errors of the season (my personal list):
   (a) direction of 'Play'
   (b) casting of Colin in 'Philoctetes'[4]
   (c) casting of Maggie in 'Builder'[5]
   (d) direction and major casting of 'Andorra'.[6]
   (e) direction and casting of 'Dutch'.[7]

I think our guest directors should be tactfully made to realise that every time we open a production, national prestige (not just our prestige) is at stake. I believe we would be more than justified in keeping an eye on all guest productions and if necessary insisting on changes when things are obviously going astray.

As to my casting quibbles: it's surely absurd to expect any but the most exceptional actors to be able to play everything from Coward to Sophocles as well as N.T. standards demand. We expose them to needless humiliation by making excessive demands on them.

6. The season has revealed the following gaps in the company's strength:
   (a) a really strong jeune premier.
   (b) a good ingenue.
   (c) a leading man between 35–50.
   (d) one or two solid character men.

Also: none of the guest directors really came up to expectations. We ought to choose them more carefully in future.

7. The relentless dullness of the supporting players [...]

[KT]

[1] The Schiller Theatre in what was West Berlin. It closed in 1993.
[2] The Royal Shakespeare Company.
[3] A compilation of five short plays by James Saunders, Jean Tardieu, Fernando Arrabal, John Whiting and Samuel Beckett.
[4] Colin Blakely (1930–87), leading member of the National Theatre company 1963–8; he played Pizarro in *The Royal Hunt of the Sun*.
[5] Peter Wood's production of *The Master Builder* with Maggie Smith opened on 9 June 1964.
[6] *Andorra* opened on 28 January 1964, directed by Lindsay Anderson.
[7] *The Dutch Courtesan*, directed by William Gaskill and Piers Haggard, opened on 13 October 1964.

To Robert Graves

The National Theatre
[26 October 1964]

Dear Robert:

We did enjoy seeing you and E(mile? milia?)[1] on Saturday. The quotation I mentioned from Coleridge's Table Talk runs as follows: 'Poetry is certainly something more than good sense, but it must be good sense, at all events; just as a palace is more than a house; but it must be a house, at least.'

I thought I'd jot down the remaining queries I have about 'Much Ado'. The page references are to the script I gave you. [...]

p.20: Beatrice: 'marry within the forbidden degrees' (Graves.) Would 'marry my kinfolk' make the point?

p.25: Ben.: 'Twas the boy that stole your meat, and you'll beat the post.'
The typist has made a mistake at the foot of the page: your emendation actually read: 'that makes the whole world of herself alone and so drives me out.' I've restored the first half of this, but 'and so drives me out' worries me: surely 'gives me out' means 'reputes me thus'? (i.e. the phrase as a whole means: 'she assumes that everyone sees through her eyes, and thus spreads her false opinion of me.')

p.27: I changed 'terminations' to 'terminology' – is this OK?

'the infernal Fate in good apparel.' Do you think 'Fate' is clear

enough? What about 'an infernal fury' or 'the goddess of vengeance'??

p.48: I slipped in 'contrary' instead of 'from all fashions.' If you can
suggest a better replacement, I'd be glad to have it.

p.63: I think you misunderstand my proposed modification of the
stables-folio line. What I suggested was: 'If your husband look
not to the key of his stables, you'll see that his barns are well
stocked with bairns' – or something equivalent, possibly: '. . .
you'll make sure there are bairns in his barns.' I doubt whether
an audience will get the folio-foalio joke.

p.70: I've changed 'an approved wanton' to 'a proven wanton': do you
approve?[2]

p.71: 'a common stale.'

p.80: 'What, let the matter of Hero rest . . .': can this really do service
for: 'What, bear her in hand . . .'? Doesn't it mean something like
'lead her up the garden-path', whatever the Elizabethan for that
is?

Don't hurry over replying: there's no urgency. See you, anyway, in
Oxford.

Yours,
Ken

[1] Graves wrote, in an undated letter from St John's College, of his friend: ' "Aemile" is the name,
alias "Cindy", alias a lot of other by-names: born as: Emilia Maria-Teresa Laraçuen.'
[2] Graves took issue with this suggestion among others: '70: I don't like <u>proven wanton</u> (the <u>en</u>
and <u>on</u>). Manifest.' 'Remember,' he added, 'I don't <u>insist</u> on any of these emendations; if they
offend, keep Shakespeare's own words however difficult.'

To Lord Cobbold[1]

[The National Theatre]
29 October 1964

Dear Lord Cobbold:

SPRING AWAKENING[2]

Mr O'Donovan[3] and I had a very friendly conversation on October 28
with Colonel Johnston,[4] during which we went over the objections

raised by your office to the above play. On the two points raised in Act 1 Scene 5, and two others referring to the beginning of Act 1 Scene 2 and the end of Act 1 Scene 9, we were in full agreement with your recommendations, and in due course I shall be sending stage directions that clarify the action in these instances.

Rather than take up the other points at this juncture, however, I should like to set down a few more general considerations which I briefly outlined to Colonel Johnston, connected with the status of the National Theatre and its special relationship with the Lord Chamberlain's office. [...]

SPRING AWAKENING, to take the case in point, is an accepted classic of German drama which is constantly performed in its own country and elsewhere in Europe. Written around the turn of the century, its general theme is the danger of employing Victorian severity to prevent adolescents from discovering the facts of normal sexual life. It contains two short scenes which illustrate the damage that can be done when brutal repression forces healthy instincts into unhealthy channels. (In one of these scenes two lonely boys tentatively and nervously kiss: in the other a group of boys in a reformatory engage in a game that can be interpreted as symbolising masturbation, though this is not made explicit.) The play has the highest critical reputation both here and abroad as a sensitive and profoundly moral work, as one can see from the unanimously approving reviews it received when it was presented last year for two Sunday-night performances at the Royal Court Theatre. Clearly, it comes well within the category of plays that the National Theatre is expected as a duty to perform. [...]

Yours sincerely,
[Kenneth Tynan]

[1] Cameron Fromanteel, First Baron Cobbold (1904–87), Governor of the Bank of England 1949–61, Lord Chamberlain 1963–71. The Lord Chamberlain's role as legal censor of plays dated back to 1737. His authority was extended by the Theatres Act of 1843, which allowed him to trim or ban 'whenever he shall be of the opinion that it is fitting for the Preservation of Good Manners, Decorum, or the Public Peace'. Cobbold functioned with two Comptrollers.

[2] KPT wanted the National to mount *Spring Awakening* by the German dramatist Frank Wedekind (1891). In July 1964 the play's English agent sent it in translation to the Lord Chamberlain. KPT followed up with this letter, which in turn was followed by a letter (5 November 1964) from Olivier to Viscount Chandos, Chairman of the National Theatre Board. In it, the Artistic Director made a strong plea for *Spring Awakening*. He argued that with *Hay Fever*, *The Crucible* and *Much Ado About Nothing* in the repertory, the theatre needed something provocative, adding that he hoped to make a brief appearance in the play himself.

[3] Desmond O'Donovan (b. 1933), English director of the 'club' Sunday night production of *Spring Awakening* in April 1963 at the Royal Court.
[4] Lieutenant Colonel Sir John Johnston, Assistant Comptroller, later Comptroller in the Lord Chamberlain's Office (1964–87).

To John Dexter

[Telegram]

[?11 November 1964]

BY UNANIMOUS DECISION OF BOARD[1] AND WITHOUT CONSULTATION WITH LARRY PRODUCTION OF SPRING AWAKENING HAS BEEN BANNED OUTRIGHT STOP BOARD FURTHER SAID IT INTENDED HENCEFORTH TO SUPERVISE ALL REPERTOIRE DECISIONS STOP LARRY BILL AND I FEEL THAT AS LONG AS THEATRE HAS CONFIDENCE OF PUBLIC WE MUST INSIST ON ARTISTIC CONTROL AS MINIMUM REQUIREMENT FOR SELF RESPECT STOP PLEASE CABLE REACTIONS AND SUGGESTIONS KEN[2]

[1] The Board of the National Theatre, led by Lord Chandos. Its nine other members, including Henry Moore and Sir Kenneth Clark, unanimously decided to ban the play even with cuts already demanded by the Lord Chamberlain.
[2] Dexter cabled: 'BOARD CENSORSHIP INTOLERABLE AND INSULTING MY RESIGNATION IS FOR LARRY TO USE AS AND WHEN HE SEES FIT'.

To John Dexter

[Telegram]

12 November 1964

DEAR JOHN LARRY SAYS KEEP SITUATION QUITE DARK ALL HOPE LOST IF FACTS DIVULGED AT THIS MOMENT KEN

To Aaron R. Frosch[1]

120 Mount Street
26 November 1964

Dear Aaron:
   I'm delighted about the holiday arrangements, with which of course I agree. The summer vacation begins on July 23rd and ends around

the middle of September (the school hasn't yet fixed the exact date).[2]

I'm not returning the signed letter because my lawyer here advises against it. The point is that I don't regard Tracy's air fares as necessary expenses, since at the time the agreement[3] was drawn up Elaine was resident in London. I shall shortly be writing to Elaine about this and other related subjects, including the desirability of our obtaining an English divorce as well as the Mexican one.[4]

Yours,
[pp. Kenneth Tynan]

[1] Aaron R. Frosch (1924–89), Manhattan lawyer specializing in theatre, film, tax and domestic relations.
[2] In 1963 Tracy Tynan had entered the progressive school Dartington Hall in Devon, founded in 1926.
[3] KPT and Elaine Dundy's separation agreement was drawn up in 1962 and executed in 1964.
[4] Elaine Dundy obtained a Mexican divorce from KPT in May 1964. KPT wanted an English divorce in order to marry me.

Memo to Laurence Olivier and others

[The National Theatre]
1 December 1964

I am afraid that the literary department is simply not equipped to cope with the volume of work that is being funnelled through it. At present we (i.e. Rozina[1] and myself) are handling:

a)   Collection, distribution and return of plays required for reading by the directors and assistant directors (at the moment 90 books are in circulation and every day brings requests for several more).

b)   Acknowledgement, distribution and return of scripts submitted for consideration (up to 20 a week).

c)   Research for programmes, involving the tracking down, collecting and return of prints, photographs, background books, etc; also compilation of programme texts and supervision of reprints.

d)   Travelling to see plays, meet authors and directors, deliver speeches, take part in debates, in London and abroad.

e)   Acting T V and radio interviews for national and international consumption; also giving interviews to critics and journalists, both local and foreign (average: about five interviews a week).

f)   Acting as spokesman for the N T in answering appeals addressed to the Director, and sending messages on its behalf to other theatrical organisations.

g)   Working with playwrights and translators on scripts.

h)   Editing and part-writing N T publications (i.e. books of RECRUIT-ING OFFICER and OTHELLO).

i)   Reading and reporting on plays old and new. Commissioning new plays.

j)   Attending Board, Drama and Building Committee[2] meetings, and representing the N T on the Commonwealth Arts Festival Committee,[3] the Arts Council Drama Panel[4] and the Arts Council Theatre Enquiry.[5]

k)   Writing articles on the N T for publication in foreign magazines and newspapers.

l)   Collating cast list material and supervising reprints.

m) Preventing the <u>Wrong</u> plays from being chosen – as far as possible.

This is frankly too much for myself and one secretary to handle. We badly need extra help, in the form of a shorthand-typist who can also run errands. Unless this is forthcoming, we are going to get swamped.

K.T.

---

[1] Rozina Adler, KPT's assistant at the National Theatre. She worked in a little box of a room next to KPT's and they would shout instructions and gossip to each other through the paper-thin walls.

[2] Set up in 1962 as part of the South Bank Theatre Board to plan the new National Theatre building, eventually designed by Sir Denys Lasdun. KPT was an ex officio member. He argued for a proscenium theatre in addition to the planned open-stage main auditorium, and an experimental space. These became the Lyttelton, the Olivier and the Cottesloe theatres.

[3] To prepare for the Commonwealth Arts Festival held at the Royal Academy of Arts Sept.–Nov. 1965. KPT's involvement was limited to the early stages; he was not on the final committee.

[4] Established in early 1940 to assist drama through 'non-profit-distributing' theatre companies in London and the provinces.

[5] An advisory panel with new powers to recommend grants and bursaries to the Arts Council under Lord Goodman's chairmanship.

To Terence Rattigan

120 Mount Street
January 27 [1965]

Dear Terry –

I didn't reply to your telegram and first letter[1] because it's rather <u>mal vu</u> for critics to reply to abusive mail from authors – and really, they were pretty hot stuff, what with those accusations of personal spleen, etc. I didn't mind, understood how you felt, and was content to let it go at that, feeling that you'd be happier convinced that I wrote a bad notice for personal reasons than if I told you (as you must inwardly have known perfectly well) that I've never in my critical career written a line that was consciously motivated by personal animus. I do, however, feel personally involved in the British cinema (I'm not all that new to films, by the way: I was head of the Ealing script department for two years), and I do tend to get angry when the British film industry spends a pile of money proving once again that it's about twenty years behind the times. I agree that my review was both charmless and graceless.[2] Alas, as I get more silvery around the temples I find myself setting less and less store by charm and grace 'when honour's at stake.'

I can't imagine why you should think me envious of you. Some of the people I most admire are loaded with money, so the envy can't be financial; and there are lots of poor writers whose work I can't stand. What else should I envy you? The fact that the film is successful? Hardly: because when I wrote the review I didn't know that it was going to be; and in any case I could name hundreds of successful films that I've adored. (<u>Vide</u> 'My Fair Lady',[3] last Sunday.) On a purely personal level I'm mildly pleased that you're earning a lot; but I would judge the results by exactly the same standards if you were working for peanuts.

To get down to specifics:

(a) Shirley MacLaine's silences.[4] Obviously I meant her reaction shots – reactions to Scott and Delon.

(b) I didn't say that [Katharine] Hepburn had rejected the script. I said that if it had been offered to her, she would have been right to turn it down.

(c) 'The Browning Version':[5] the only time I ever wrote about it was in my first book, in a section devoted to 'heroic acting'. Most of the piece was concerned with E. Portman's[6] performances in the double bill. I wasn't mad about 'Harlequinade', but I said that in 'The B. V.' Mr. Portman had Mr. Rattigan 'right behind him' – i.e. supporting his talents to the hilt.

(d) 'The Deep Blue Sea'. Let me just quote from my review, reprinted in a collection called 'Curtains'. ' "The Deep Blue Sea", for its first two acts, is a masterly piece of work, and I went out exulting into the second interval, persuaded that I was seeing the most striking new play I could remember.' I firmly reproved those critics who had dismissed the play as 'brilliant theatre' – as if that were somehow shameful. Next, I quarrelled with the last act (the reasons for the heroine's decision to live), but I continued: ' "The Deep Blue Sea" remains the most absorbing new English play for many seasons. And it contains something which no English playwright (save Shaw in "Saint Joan") has provided since Pinero[7] – a long, straight, emotional part for a young woman.' This, you'll perhaps admit, is rather more than 'polite, at least' (your words).

(e) Your suggestion that I committed the cardinal sin of 'blaming a work for not being what it has not tried to be.' I don't understand what you're getting at here. There's no reason why a film about a Rolls-Royce shouldn't be first-rate; and presumably you were bent on writing a first-rate film about a Rolls-Royce. I just didn't think you'd succeeded. I love 'entertainments' at their best: have you ever read my raves about the Tracy-Hepburn films, Cagney's thrillers, the MGM Garbos, etc., etc?

(f) George Scott's 'under-playing'.[8] I meant that where possible he spoke in a controlled undertone lines that a lesser actor would have bellowed. The 'over-playing' was in the conception of the character, not in the performance; and the conception was yours.

(g) I never stated, implied or supposed that the cast was gathered 'by the lure of money.' What conceivable relevance could that have had?

I could continue; but what relevance would it have to our main problem, which is that you wrote something that I didn't like? Without hypocrisy, I wish I could make you happier, without being a hypocrite.

All my (personal) best –
Ken

P.S. Incidentally, my original heading for the review was 'The Model T. Rattigan'. It was changed by a sub.[9]

---

[1] On 3 January 1965 Terence Rattigan sent KPT a telegram attacking critics as 'bilious' and envious. He was responding to KPT's *Observer* review (3 January 1965) of *The Yellow Rolls-Royce*, starring George C. Scott, Alain Delon and Shirley MacLaine, for which Rattigan had written the script. In the absence of a response from KPT, Rattigan sent two further hysterical communications with veiled hints of litigation: 'But, oh the pity of it, Iago – when just a couple of

articulate words from a junior critic to a senior writer would have mended all. No more good wishes.'

[2] KPT wrote of the film: 'There is a smiling, gracious staleness about *The Yellow Rolls-Royce* that gives it the air of some long-forgotten ceremonial occasion – the investiture of Dornford Yates, perhaps, as a Knight of the Garter. The stately blandness of its manner is quite at odds with the fusty triviality of what it has to offer: it condescends from a great depth.'

[3] *My Fair Lady* (US, 1964), a musical version of Shaw's *Pygmalion*, written by Alan J. Lerner, directed by George Cukor, starring Rex Harrison and Audrey Hepburn, and designed by Cecil Beaton.

[4] Shirley MacLaine (b. 1934), dancer, singer, actress and writer who had recently starred in *Irma la Douce* (US, 1963); she later won an Academy Award for *Terms of Endearment* (US, 1983). In his review KPT wrote that MacLaine was 'often touching, especially in moments of silence'.

[5] Written in 1948 and produced at the Phoenix Theatre, London, in September of that year in a double bill with *Harlequinade*. It tells the story of a schoolmaster at the end of his career.

[6] Eric Portman (1903–69), English actor who had played Andrew Crocker-Harris (the schoolmaster in *The Browning Version*) and Arthur Gosport in *Harlequinade* in the original productions in 1948.

[7] Sir Arthur Wing Pinero (1855–1934), English playwright, author of *The Second Mrs Tanqueray* (1893).

[8] George C. Scott (b. 1927), American actor who had recently starred with Peter Sellers in Stanley Kubrick's black comedy *Dr Strangelove* (UK, 1964); he would go on to win an Academy Award for *Patton* (US, 1970).

[9] To 'The Rattigan Rolls-Royce'.

Memo to Laurence Olivier and others

[The National Theatre]
11 February 1965

DINGO[1]

I had a long talk on Tuesday with Colonel Johnson [*sic*] at the Lord Chamberlain's office. The position is that he will not grant a licence to the play in its present form. What he wants us to do is to submit a revised script. The changes he would require fall into the following categories:

1) Deletion or substitution of all the obvious four-letter words. The same applies to the passage in Act 1 p.17: the sexual image about grease in the breech block.

2) More explicit stage directions to clarify the action in passages he considers needlessly horrific. These include Chalky's screaming (which mustn't be continuous), the charred corpse (which mustn't be realistic), the bayonettings in Act 2 and the blood pouring out of the Scot's mouth.

3) The blasphemy: the L.C. objects to the frequent use of 'Jesus'.

4) Lèse-Majesté: the L.C. doesn't like the reference (2.2. p.18) to George II not wanting to be king. Under the same general heading, he feels that the medal pinned to the blonde's knickers in 2.2. p.34 should not be the DSO.[2]

5) Impersonations of living persons: a composite general is okay but he mustn't be identifiable as Viscount Montgomery.[3]

I told Colonel Johnson that we had postponed any further action until John Dexter had returned to London and discussed the position with myself and Charles Wood.

Incidentally, the script we submitted was the original version. The new one, which Charles Wood hasn't yet completed, contains a good deal of additional material, while retaining virtually all of the first version.

K.T.

[1] *Dingo*, by Charles Wood, set in the desert during World War II before El Alamein, and then in a prisoner-of-war camp, was not performed at the National but at the Royal Court in November 1967.
[2] The Distinguished Service Order, awarded to commissioned officers, the only military honour that is an Order of Chivalry.
[3] Field Marshal Viscount Montgomery (1887–1976), Commander of the British 21st Army Group in World War II.

To H.A.T. and L.A. Child[1]

120 Mount Street
1 March 1965

Dear Mr and Mrs Child:

Your letter of February 22nd came as a complete surprise to me. I have since made enquiries and discovered that Tracy's mother, who is now living in New York, wants her to go to school there and has been talking to the people at Brearley. I am not at all keen on this idea and it would in fact be impossible for my ex-wife to carry it out without my consent, since our divorce agreement stipulates that Tracy shall continue to be educated at Dartington Hall. However, it would help me if you could give me a frank opinion of the progress she is making at Dartington. She seems tremendously happy at the school and I would hate to uproot her; but her mother may conceivably try to cause legal trouble over this matter of schooling, and I want to be very sure that – in your opinion as well as hers – Tracy is in the right place. Although she sees Tracy in the holidays, my ex-wife is a very lonely woman and I have no doubt that separation from Tracy during term-time is causing her some pain. Hence my need to be sure that I am justified in continuing to inflict it. I naturally would not wish to get you deeply involved in the situation, but I would appreciate your general impressions of Tracy's present state of development. I shall be coming to Dartington next Saturday, March 6th: if it was possible, we might have a chat then. Do let me know.

Yours sincerely,
Kenneth Tynan[2]

[1] Hubert A. T. Child and his wife Lois A. Child, who ran Dartington Hall. They had written to KPT saying that they had received a letter from the Brearley School (an academic all-girl private institution in Manhattan) saying that Tracy had applied for admission.
[2] Tracy remained at Dartington Hall.

To Sir Cecil Parrott[1]

120 Mount Street
March 2nd 1965

Dear Sir Cecil:

I'm terribly sorry that pressure of people, plays and films made it impossible for me either to thank you properly for a splendid lunch or to have that promised chat about my impressions of the Czechs. What hits one of course all the time is the virtual impossibility of uttering a word, either on stage or screen, that can't be interpreted politically. Even 'Ubu Roi' becomes in Prague a political play, and very nearly a realistic one, too: and Kafka, in this context, becomes almost a political pamphleteer. The theatre seems entirely controlled by directors, designers and writers (in roughly that order) and I saw very little in individual acting that would compare to the standard English article. But I should think the film industry must be – apart from the Italians and possibly the French – the most exciting in Europe. Films like 'The Shop on Main Street'[2] and 'Courage for Everyday'[3] just aren't being made anywhere else; you really feel that the artist is a spokesman for the people in a way that doesn't apply anywhere else in Europe. I think above all you get the feeling that in Prague the artist really counts: what he says – or doesn't say – is of crucial importance to the country's whole future. This bright focus of attention is no doubt a dangerous position for the artist; but it's also enviable.

I hope John and Penelope[4] enjoy themselves half as much as I did. Please give my best regards to The Lady Parrott.

Yours sincerely,
[pp. Kenneth Tynan]

[1] Sir Cecil Parrott (1909–84), British Ambassador to Czechoslovakia 1960–66. KPT had recently returned from his first visit to Prague; his 'view of the cultural landscape', entitled 'Czech Discoveries', appeared in the *Observer*, 7 March 1965.
[2] *The Shop on Main Street* (Czech, 1965), Academy award-winning film directed by Jan Kadar and Einar Klos, set during the German invasion of Czechoslovakia.
[3] *Courage for Everyday* (Czech, 1964), co-written and directed by Evald Schorm. Demonstrates how a devotion to Marxism alienates the protagonist from his fellow human beings.
[4] John Osborne and Penelope Gilliatt had married in 1963.

Memo to George Rowbottom[1]

[The National Theatre]
10 March 1965

I've had a strong note from George Devine complaining that the NT programmes are running an ad from the South African Government. He says that Vanessa Redgrave,[2] who went to the Vic with him, was absolutely outraged.

I must say that the ad in question looks especially offensive in the OTHELLO programme, and, of course, to any Negro in any programme. How much longer are we committed to running this thing? And could it be discreetly discontinued when the contract expires – if necessary on the simple and accurate grounds that it is giving offence to some of our customers? Let me know what you think.

[1] General Manager of the theatre. He left in 1968 to work at the Nottingham Playhouse.
[2] Vanessa Redgrave (b. 1937), English actress, daughter of Sir Michael Redgrave, noted for her support of left-wing and humanitarian causes. She joined the RSC in July 1961, and would win an Academy Award for *Julia* (US, 1977).

To Lord Cobbold

The National Theatre
22 April 1965

Dear Lord Cobbold:

MOTHER COURAGE

I append our comments on the deletions you recommend:

<u>Scene 2.13: '... at both ends!'</u>[1]
This seems to us a characteristic piece of heavy military jocularity –
certainly not to be taken literally! In the context of the play, it expresses
the Army's contemptuous attitude towards the Church – which is, after
all, a fairly vital aspect of The Thirty Years War.

<u>Scene 2.18: 'Balls!'</u>
The song in which this occurs is translated by the poet W. H. Auden.
His translation has to follow the music note for note, and he finds it
difficult to suggest an alternative monosyllable which conveys the same
sense of carefree bawdiness. Since Mr Auden is probably the greatest
living English poet, you will see that we are placed in a somewhat tricky
situation.

<u>Scene 3.31: 'They would even like to find a Protestant by smelling his,
um, excrement.'</u>
The Chaplain is in a state of panic and this line seems to us to express
it with justifiable vividness. On another level, it reflects the sort of
absurd propaganda which was spread by both sides during The Thirty
Years War, and this, of course, is central to the author's theme.

<u>Scene 3.35: 'I am reminded of the Passion of our Lord and Saviour.'</u>
The heroine's son is being led off to execution though he is technically
innocent. The comparison between him and Christ is certainly bitter
but we can't see how it can be held to be blasphemous.

<u>Scene 3.38: '... like Jesus in Gethsemane.'</u>
It is by using similes like this that Brecht reminds us how little religion
meant to people who were involved in a supposedly religious war. This
is the ironic point he is making; he is not trying to be blasphemous.

<u>Scene 4.42: 'Bugger...'</u>[2]
We accept the deletion and will find an alternative which I will submit
to your office.[2]

<u>Scene 4.43: 'You're all shitting in your pants'</u>

Would you accept 'You're all wetting your pants'?

<u>Scene 4.43: 'Bugger...'</u>
As for Scene 4.42 above.

<u>Scene 6.53: '... you can take a crap ...'</u>
The effect of the war on the Chaplain has been to rob him of all dignity
and reduce him to animal level. This collapse is carefully reflected in
his speech, and the use of a coarse idiom at this point seems to us
necessary to the development of his character.

<u>Scene 8.62: 'Jesus ...'</u>
I would defend this with the argument cited above in relation to Scene
3.38.

I should be grateful for your comments on these proposals.

Before concluding, I should like to set down a few more general
considerations which I briefly outlined to Colonel Johnson [*sic*], connected with the status of the National Theatre and its special relationship with the Lord Chamberlain's office.

The National Theatre is the first theatre in this country to have
been set up by express government edict. It is run by government
nominees and it is supported by a Treasury grant. It thus has a political
as well as an artistic significance. In this respect it is unique, and this
uniqueness puts it on a different footing from other theatre companies
such as, for example, the Royal Shakespeare Company, which is a
private organisation with no governmental responsibilities.

Now the National Theatre Board was created with a specific briefing
and a specific task to fulfil: namely, to make available to the public a
repertoire drawn from the best in world drama, ancient and modern,
native and foreign. In this respect its public function is analogous to
that of an institution like the British Museum – a repository where <u>any</u>
book can be obtained, even works not normally accessible on the public
shelves of other libraries. The National Theatre Board was presumably
chosen on the assumption that its members were men and women of
trustworthy taste and judgment: obviously, their decisions are unaffected by commercial considerations – indeed, by <u>any</u> considerations
other than carrying out their mandate. There seems to be an anomaly
inherent in a situation where one government body – the National
Theatre – might find itself deadlocked by another – i.e. the Lord
Chamberlain's office; and it is this general problem (quite apart from
the specific play we are discussing) on which we are anxious to have
your opinion.

Another point may be worthy of reflection. By virtue of its title, the National Theatre attracts an enormous amount of attention in the foreign press, especially when it presents foreign plays. Rightly, I think, it is taken to be a symbol of this country's attitude towards dramatic art. Ambassadors are prominent in the audience whenever foreign works are performed. Here again the political aspect of our work intrudes: is it seemly for us to present a masterpiece from another country in a mutilated form? For any other theatre to do so would be unforgivable: for the National Theatre to do so is to give needless offence.

In the foregoing, let me make it clear that I am referring only to plays of established merit, not to new and untested works. In the latter case, although we may dispute some of your opinions, we recognise that you have a statutory duty to perform and that we must submit our scripts to your customary jurisdiction. But when the National Theatre Board, conscious of its responsibilities, carries them out by proposing to revive an established work of high critical reputation, such as MOTHER COURAGE, it seems logical to suppose that the situation should be more elastic.

With the future in mind, I look forward to hearing your thoughts on this general question, as well as on MOTHER COURAGE in particular.

Yours sincerely
[Kenneth Tynan][3]

[1] 'Drive their cattle away from *us*, while they stuff their priests at both ends!'
[2] The expletive was deleted entirely from the printed version.
[3] On 5 May the Assistant Comptroller replied that the Lord Chamberlain 'has no authority to give preferential treatment to one management, whether state-appointed or not, over another'.

To Emilie Jacobson

The National Theatre
April 30 [1965]

Dear Emilie –
I'm spending ten days motoring around Morocco next month[1] – Fez, Marrakech, Mogador, Casablanca. Do you think anybody would like a fairly light-hearted piece on the subject – perhaps 'Holiday'? It would

have to be pretty subjective, since you can't be authoritative on only ten days' experience. At least I can't.

Love
Ken

[1] KPT and I, with George Harewood and Patricia Tuckwell, left for a Moroccan holiday on 14 May; he never wrote about the trip.

To the Editor, the *Guardian*[1]

120 Mount Street
[Published 14 June 1965]

Sir,—In his review (June 11) of Wayland Young's 'Eros Denied'[2] Maurice Cranston[3] tells us, as if it were something self-evident, that 'the sublimation of sexual energy is the motor of most art and progress.' This is of course a hypothesis with no scientific basis of any kind, yet one is constantly finding it on the lips of people (such as Mr Cranston, for example) who would normally shrink from arguments founded on unproven assumptions.

In certain Eastern religions the sexual act is believed to drain away one's vital capacities and we all know about General Ripper in 'Dr Strangelove'[4] and his 'precious bodily fluids.' But can any of our readers tell me the origins of the fantastic theory that art and progress are contingent on continence? It seems rather like saying that if you hoard enough milk you will produce better wine. –

Yours sincerely,
Kenneth Tynan

[1] Published under the headline 'Sex, art ...'
[2] A historical exploration of the taboos associated with sex and sexuality, ending in a plea for the acceptance of a wide range of sexual activity (1965). It was the first volume in a projected series to be called 'Studies in Exclusion'.
[3] Professor of Political Science at the London School of Economics 1969–85.
[4] *Dr Strangelove (or, How I Learned to Stop Worrying and Love the Bomb)* (US, 1963), a black comedy about global destruction written and directed by Stanley Kubrick. Sterling Hayden played the deranged General Ripper.

To Bill and Annie Davis

120 Mount Street
Saturday [26 June 1965]

Dear Bill and Annie –

In Arctic Wimbledon weather Kathleen and I have been planning ahead a little, and I thought I'd keep you abreast. How would it be if we descended on you by the same plane you left on – i.e. arriving sort of dawnish on the morning of Saturday July 31st?[1] And could you bear us until Monday August 9th, when I have to get back to London for the opening of the Berliner Ensemble at the Old Vic? [...]

Rick Sicré came to drinks yesterday and brought Betty,[2] with whom I haven't seen him for eight years. Also in town: Steve Sondheim[3] ('West Side Story' and 'Gypsy' lyricist), who has invented a murder game that takes four days to play. I am obtaining full details and will bring them with me to the Consula. A final flash, dead secret but (an unscrambled source assures me) dead true! Mike Nichols is having an affair with Jackie Kennedy. This has apparently made him quite insufferable and he preens about all day in dressing-gown like Noel Coward in 'Present Laughter' and knows all the secret service men by their Christian names. More later, as it reaches me. Can the tinsel and glitter of Broadway banish the grief that lingers in the eyes of the mysterious Woman in Black? Will she sacrifice her Wealth and Position to his Wealth and Position? What will become of Dan, the humble Secret Service man who loves her? .... etc.

Love from us both –
Ken

---

[1] The Málaga Feria began on 31 July and lasted one week. The toreros included El Cordobés, Camino, Ordóñez, Ostos and Antonio Bienvenida.
[2] His wife.
[3] Stephen Sondheim (b. 1930), American composer and lyricist whose later work includes *Follies* (1971), *Sweeney Todd* (1979) and *Into the Woods* (1986).

To Jacques Charon[1]

[The National Theatre]
21 September 1965

Dear Mr Charon:

I enclose John Mortimer's[2] English translation of LA PUCE A L'OR-EILLE.[3] You will notice that he has changed the Englishman, Rugby, into a Japanese. I find this a very funny idea, but if you think a Russian, a Swede or a Turk would be funnier, it could easily be revised. Mr Mortimer will provide dialogue for the character later.

Please understand that the translation is subject to any revisions we may think necessary. Several of the expressions Mr Mortimer uses are too modern to suit the play, and he has also anglicised a number of phrases that don't need it – for instance, changing 'le Minet Galant' to 'the Pussycat Inn'. I am carefully going through the translation with Mr Mortimer and before long I hope to have an improved script. The question of cutting will naturally be left to you.

Because Sir Laurence will be directing another play while Feydeau is in rehearsal, he will not be able to play Chandebise/Poche.[4] But we have secured instead an actor we think ideally suited for the double role: Albert Finney, whom you have probably seen in such films as SATURDAY NIGHT AND SUNDAY MORNING[5] and TOM JONES.[6] He joined our company in January and has already proved himself a brilliant and inventive <u>farceur</u>. He is perhaps a little too young for the parts; but he has in abundance the glowing energy which you rightly defined as prerequisites for playing Feydeau.

I look forward to hearing your reactions to the translation. Sir Laurence is at present on a European tour for the National Theatre, but he will return to London on September 30, and I know he would like to arrange another meeting with you soon after that date to discuss your production plans (including decor) and to introduce you to Mr Finney.

Kind regards,
Yours sincerely,
[Kenneth Tynan]

[1] Jacques Charon (1920–75), French theatre director.
[2] John Mortimer (b. 1923), English dramatist, novelist and barrister. His work includes the play *A Voyage Round My Father* (1971) and the Rumpole novels, later adapted for television as *Rumpole of the Bailey*.
[3] *A Flea in Her Ear* by Georges Feydeau (1907), a classic farce.
[4] Albert Finney doubled as Chandebise and Poche in the Old Vic production in February 1966. Olivier played the cameo part of the butler, Etienne Pulcheux, in the National Theatre tour of Canada in 1967.
[5] Adapted by Alan Sillitoe from his novel and directed by Karel Reisz (UK, 1960), it established Finney as an international star.
[6] Adapted by John Osborne from Henry Fielding's novel and directed by Tony Richardson (UK, 1963).

Memo to Laurence Olivier

[The National Theatre]
15 October 1965

Dear Larry:

[...] Now that you are directing JUNO,[1] I have a marvellous idea. People keep telling me that John G. [Gielgud] is dying to work with us. Why not ask him to play Robespierre with you as Danton[2] with somebody else directing? I have a further suggestion. Why don't you alternate Lear and Gloucester with him? This would have enormous historical impact because of the ROMEO AND JULIET interchange,[3] and I needn't tell you what the box-office impact would be. I haven't spoken to John about this but pressures from many quarters suggest that he would be sympathetic to some such plan. In any case, who in A Company[4] would you cast as Robespierre?

[1] *Juno and the Paycock* by Sean O'Casey (1924).
[2] In *Danton's Death*.
[3] Olivier had alternated Romeo and Mercutio with John Gielgud in the production at the New Theatre in October/November 1935.
[4] The company was divided into 'A' and 'B' streams, to serve the repertory.

To Emilie Jacobson

[Telegram]

[London]
18 October 1965

ORSON WELLES DYING FOR ME TO INTERVIEW HIM ON ANY SUBJECT UNDER SUN STOP IS PLAYBOY INTERESTED TYNAN[1]

[1] KPT's interview with Welles appeared in the March 1967 issue of *Playboy*.

Memo to Laurence Olivier and John Dexter

[The National Theatre]
20 October 1965

1) There's no doubt that the Royal Shakespeare are on to a good thing with the idea of midnight readings. The Aldwych was packed and hundreds were turned away. No costume or lighting or sound effects: just actors in lounge suits seated in a semi-circle. The play itself was just an edited transcript of the Auschwitz trial[1] and had nothing new to offer that one didn't already know. But the audience was just the kind that we need to attract to the Vic: a mixture of students and Royal Court supporters. I think we should plan a similar event ourselves, frankly admitting that we are glad to profit by the Royal Shakespeare's experience. The kind of play to choose would obviously be something (a) experimental, and (b) mainly verbal in its appeal. If possible, it should be an English-speaking premiere. There would be little point in reading a play that was already available in print. There's a new play by the brilliant young Czech, Vaclav Havel,[2] called THE MEMORANDUM, which might fit the bill.

2) Now that DANTON is fixed for next August, oughtn't we to negotiate a contract with Svoboda?

3) Any conclusions yet on my idea that L.O. should play Danton to Gielgud's Robespierre?

[1] *The Investigation* (1965), a play by Peter Weiss based on a Nazi war crimes trial in Frankfurt first performed by the RSC in a rehearsed reading at the Aldwych under the direction of Peter Brook on 19 October 1965 and simultaneously at East German theatres.
[2] Václav Havel (b. 1936), Czech playwright and one of the founders of Charter 77; elected President of Czechoslovakia in December 1989 after the fall of the Communist government. *Vyrozumění* (1966) was not translated into English until 1980 (by Vera Blackwell).

To Kathleen Halton[1]

The National Theatre
31 October [1965]

Darling –
If there was ever a fleck of doubt that I love you completely and irrevocably, it vanished a few minutes ago when I hung up the phone.

When you are troubled, I feel it from heart to fingertips; I ache to help and comfort, and everything else turns grey and ashen until you light up again. I have never felt at peace except with you, never understood all the happy meanings of loving-kindness except through you, never known such a constant desire and a constant tenderness as I feel with you. Please be sure of me always. The simple knowledge that you exist, are sitting somewhere, or walking, or smiling, is pure soul-food for me. I feed on it. I know this is silly rhapsody, but when you worry a great knot is tied inside me, and I agonise, wondering whether I am giving you all the nourishing, healing pleasures that you give me, and hating myself for every sad second I have ever caused you. We are so beautifully enlaced and entwined: we continue and complement each other like alternate lines of a marvellously unpredictable book. And to think we have hardly finished the first chapter! It is all such a privilege.

Every day of it – and always, and especially, tomorrow.

In love,
K.

[1] Though I had been living with KPT at 120 Mount Street since the summer of 1964, he often wrote me notes.

To William Shawn

120 Mount Street
10 November [1965]

Dear Mr. Shawn,

I'm glad we had that clarifying talk last week. I've now definitely turned down The Times,[1] and the scheme we discussed would suit my plans perfectly. The idea (if I got it right) is that I would write four pieces a year for 'The New Yorker' – one of extra length (c.9000 words) and three of normal length (c.5000 words) – on theatre in various countries. For these you propose paying around 10,000 dollars plus 2,000 dollars expenses. I would continue to live in London, and would agree not to write for other American magazines (except my three pieces a year for 'Playboy'; and I'd undertake that these wouldn't include anything on theatre.)

There are a couple of points on which I'd appreciate your opinion:
1) I have one outstanding commitment to an American magazine – a

piece for 'Venture' on the city of Bath,[2] which I'm working on now. Is this OK with you?

2) Would you consider letting me do a piece for you on American theatre outside New York – i.e. on developments in Minneapolis, San Francisco, Dallas, etc.? This is just an idea and I wouldn't press it if you weren't keen.[3]

3) Rejoining 'The New Yorker' would mean giving up my job as film critic on 'The Observer', if only because I'd have to spend so much time out of the country researching the theatre pieces. ('The Observer' pays me £3,000 a year, plus expenses and additional payments for long pieces: about £4,000 in all.) I'm not unhappy about abandoning the movies;[4] but this, coupled with the loss of income from other U.S. magazines, might* land me in a slight financial morass. You will probably have guessed my drift: are the figures you quoted absolutely final, or is there any chance of a slight adjustment in my favour?[5]

4) Other things being equal, could we start the new arrangement next summer?

I hope we can work things out satisfactorily. Meanwhile, I'll stay close to the phone.

Yours sincerely,
Kenneth Tynan

* in fact, would.

[1] *The New York Times* had offered KPT the position of drama critic.
[2] KPT researched this piece but never wrote it.
[3] Not written.
[4] KPT gave up being film critic for the *Observer* at the end of May 1966, to be replaced by Penelope Gilliatt.
[5] The *New Yorker* agreed to advance expenses.

On 13 November 1965, on a late-night programme called BBC-3, Ken said 'fuck'. It was the first time the word had been used on television. The subject of the discussion, with the writer Mary McCarthy, was censorship, which they both wished to abolish. The moderator asked Ken whether, were censorship in the theatre abolished, he would allow a play to be done at the National in which sexual intercourse took place. He answered, 'Oh I think so, certainly. I doubt if there are very many rational people in this world to whom the word "fuck" is particularly diabolical or revolting or totally forbidden.'

He had slipped in the word slightly out of context, rather suggesting that he had planned to use it. He went on to argue that the censor should not distinguish between high and low art; once the censor was abolished, a play should be subject to the law of the land. He added that he wanted to see abolished the 'damaging and horrendous things [the Lord Chamberlain] does to free speech and politics and the church'.

During the next few weeks Ken's press service delivered well over a thousand newspaper cuttings. And for a few days, the scandal eclipsed all other news. Headlines read: 'Insult to womanhood', 'Sack 4-letter Tynan'; and cartoons, limericks and philological discussions filled the columns. In the House of Commons four motions were set down attacking Ken and the BBC, while amendments in support were tabled by Tom Driberg, Michael Foot and Hugh Jenkins.

The top brass of the BBC issued not an apology, but an 'expression of regret', recognizing that Ken had used the word in a serious discussion. Huw Wheldon, then in charge of programmes, took a dissenting view, and defended Ken. He was not appalled, and told the press he found the subject had been handled 'responsibly, intelligently and reasonably'.

To Huw Wheldon[1]

[Telegram]

[London]
17 November 1965

MANY THANKS FOR SUPPORT STOP SINCERELY HOPE INCIDENT DOES NOT CAUSE YOU EMBARRASSMENT + KEN TYNAN

[1] Sir Huw Weldon (1916–86), Welsh broadcaster who joined the BBC in 1952, became Controller of Programmes in 1965 and was Managing Director Television 1968–75.

To A. C. Spectorsky

120 Mount Street
December 4th [1965]

Dear Mr Spectorsky –

I'm sorry to hear that you find 'Basic Baroque'[1] an irredeemable failure. I'd understood from our agreement that turndowns would take place only after 'reasonable revisions'; whereas in this case you've stated quite categorically that revisions could do no good. I did an enormous amount of research on the piece, and I'm a bit worried that if you were to reject a couple more in the same way, I just wouldn't be able to turn out my stipulated three pieces by next summer.

Of course I respect your opinion;[2] but it does seem to me to contravene the spirit of our agreement. As a sort of <u>quid pro quo</u>, would you mind if I gave the piece its chance in the open market – including even your competitors? I know our contract precludes my writing for the latter; but it can make no logical, moral or commercial sense for you to sit on a piece you consider unusable. Naturally if it were accepted by a competitive magazine I would waive the $400 turndown fee.[3]

This situation wouldn't arise if it were a travel article or a profile, the kind of thing I could sell to 'Holiday' or 'Harper's'. The trouble with 'Basic Baroque' is that its appeal (if any) is obviously confined to your competitors. It's thus a unique case, and I'd like to make it clear that I wouldn't regard it as a precedent. It's simply the first quasi-erotic piece I've ever tried, and I'd hate it to be sunk without trace or even a second opinion.

Meanwhile, I have the Orson Welles interview, the first 'Fiesta Route' piece and the Film Festivals survey lined up for the future. Welles is in Bucharest, but expects to be accessible in a few weeks time. I'll be writing next week with a suggested itinerary of European fiestas; and the Filmfest deadline, as we've already agreed, will be early summer. Incidentally I've written twice to Castro, so far with no reply.

Do let me know about releasing 'Basic Baroque'. Please understand that I'm not offended by your rejection: that's every editor's right. I'm having a very happy relationship with 'Playboy', and there's no reason why it should be soured by an incident like this, which neither of us could have predicted when the agreement was drawn up.

Yours sincerely,
Kenneth Tynan

[1] KPT's homage to the female bottom. On 22 November KPT had written to Emilie Jacobson: 'My suspicion is that it was too erotic for them. Which is a pity. I'd just begun to believe that *Playboy* really approved of sex and wasn't the titillating fraud that everyone says it is.'
[2] Spectorsky had written to Emilie Jacobson (23 November) that the article suffered from several faults 'that seem to us to be the antithesis of the sort of thing that Tynan would write. To be brutally frank, it seems to have an archness which is middle-aged.'
[3] The article was eventually published in *Cavalier*, a *Playboy*-style magazine, in August 1966.

Memo to Laurence Olivier, John Dexter

[The National Theatre]
31 December 1965

Looking in on TV the other day I saw the ideal replacement for FLEA
IN HER EAR: Tony Hancock.[1] And I'm sure he'd be interested.

K.T.

[1]Tony Hancock (1924–68), English comic actor, star of *Hancock's Half Hour* (1956–61) and the
film *The Rebel* (UK, 1960).

To Lord Annan[1]

[The National Theatre]
3rd Jan. 1966

Dear Noël,
    I am delighted to hear that you are going to bring up censorship in the
Lords, though I think you are being unduly limited in your objective.[2] I
suspect that the climate is riper for a radical change than you imagine.
The Arts Council has a Committee on censorship that has been listening to evidence for some months now and is drafting a Private
Members' Bill for submission to the Commons. At present, the Bill is
being vetted for loopholes by two Q.C.'s. In essence, it provides for
the abolition of the Chamberlain's theatre censorship, the abolition of
the power of local authorities to impose censorship, and a proviso that
no legal action (even under the existing laws of libel and obscenity)
may be taken against plays without the consent of the D.P.P.[3] after
consulting a judge in chambers. On a free vote, I would expect this to
do rather better than Wolfenden.[4]
    The best book on the subject is still – 'Censorship in England' by
Howell and Palmer – published about fifty years ago. This contains a
full account of the findings of the 1909 Select Committee, which
proposed optional censorship. For your amusement, I am enclosing a
copy of a piece I have just written for Playboy magazine,[5] which
contains some hitherto unpublished extracts from John Osborne's correspondence with St. James' Palace.[6]

Yours sincerely,
[Kenneth Tynan]

[1] Noël Annan (b. 1916, created a life peer in 1965), historian, Provost of King's College, Cambridge (1956–66) and Vice-Chancellor of the University of London (1978–81).
[2] Annan proposed that a Select Committee of both Houses be formed, which was approved by the Labour government; its recommendations led to the legislation which ended theatre censorship.
[3] Director of Public Prosecutions.
[4] The Wolfenden Report's recommendations led to the legalization of homosexual activities between consenting men aged 21 and over.
[5] 'The Royal Smut-Hound', *Playboy*, January 1966.
[6] Correspondence with the Lord Chamberlain in reply to the censor's treatment of passages in Osborne's 1959 musical, *The World of Paul Slickey*.

Memo to Laurence Olivier

[The National Theatre]
4 January 1966

I had a long lunch with Tyrone Guthrie. He's tied up until March 1967 but would love to do a production for us opening at the end of May 1967. As you know, he doesn't approve of long rehearsal periods. I mentioned BARTHOLOMEW FAIR[1] and he said that it was one of his favourite plays but that he didn't think we had the right company to do it. (He feels very strongly that we're weak in solid character performers – he particularly named Leo McKern,[2] Paul Rogers[3] and Michael Hordern.[4]) He then mentioned TRILBY[5] – with you as Svengali – and a Regency melodrama called THE ROAD TO RUIN.[6] I hadn't read either of these but am getting copies.

But Tony kept on saying that he was a hack director who needed to be told what to do. I mentioned THE DANCE OF DEATH[7] and he said: 'Great play, but not for me. Why don't you get Maggie Leighton to do it with Larry? She's the kind of guest performer you need.' I then said: 'VOLPONE'.[8] 'That's it!' he said. 'I'll do that anywhere, any time. Could it be Larry as Volpone and Albert [Finney] as Mosca? If Larry doesn't like the part, is there any chance of McKern?'

He also said he adored Firbank, so I gave him my long-beloved PRINCESS ZOUBAROFF.[9] But VOLPONE is clearly the best bet; you and Albert would be perfect for it, but there wouldn't be much wrong with McKern and Finlay.[10] And it would be a splendid contribution to the American tour. I think we should clinch this as soon as possible.

K.T.

[1] By Ben Jonson (1614).

[2] Leo McKern (b. 1920), English actor well known as Rumpole in the popular television series. He began his career in London with the Old Vic Company in 1949 and joined the Shakespeare Memorial Theatre, Stratford, in 1953, where his roles included Touchstone in *As You Like It* and Friar Lawrence in *Romeo and Juliet*. He would play Volpone in the West End in 1967.

[3] Paul Rogers (b. 1917), English actor who joined the Old Vic Company in 1949, where he played Shakespearean leading roles and character parts such as Bottom and Sir John Falstaff.

[4] Sir Michael Hordern (b. 1911), English actor who joined the Old Vic in 1953, where his roles included Polonius, Prospero and Malvolio.

[5] By Paul Potter (1895), adapted from the George du Maurier novel (1894).

[6] By Thomas Holcroft (1792).

[7] By August Strindberg (1901).

[8] By Ben Jonson (1606).

[9] Arch, witty and outrageous play (1920) by the English novelist Ronald Firbank (1886–1926), set in Florence, about the battle of the sexes.

[10] Frank Finlay (b. 1926), English actor who joined the National Theatre Company in 1963, playing Willie Mossop in *Hobson's Choice* and Iago in Olivier's *Othello*.

To A. C. Spectorsky

[120 Mount Street]
4 January 1966

Dear Mr Spectorsky,

Many thanks, in turn, for <u>your</u> understanding and thoughtful letter.[1] As you say, there probably is not much point in a revision at this stage, so I am asking Emilie to peddle the piece elsewhere.

I will be doing the Welles' interview any day now. Meanwhile I thought I would jot down a list of the European Fiestas I am contemplating covering this year. Perhaps you could let me know if you think any of them rather too peripheral or irrelevant:

Fasching:[2]	Cologne and Munich Feb. 19–21 (the annual pre-lenten outburst)
The Easter Feria:	Seville Mid-April
Walpurgisnacht:[3]	Hannenklee in the Harz mountains April 20

May Day:	Moscow
	May 1

Midsummer Eve in	June 25
Sweden	

If I am to cover Midsummer Eve (which I probably should; it is naked virgins dancing round open fires, isn't it?), I would not be able to deliver the piece until mid-July, would this bother you? On the list as it stands, I wonder if Moscow is not more of a political than a popular occasion. My own feeling is that we could do without it.

Incidentally, I am hoping to make these pieces not only impressionistic but helpful – i.e. including a fair amount of touristic information about the best hotels, restaurants, etc.

Once again, thanks for your letter and I will look forward to hearing your reaction to mine.

Yours sincerely,
Kenneth Tynan

[1] In his letter of 29 December 1965 Spectorsky agreed to let KPT place 'Basic Baroque' elsewhere as a one-off exception to their agreement.
[2] Ancient Lenten festival in Munich.
[3] KPT attended neither Walpurgisnacht (All Hallows Eve) nor May Day.

In 1960 Perry Smith and Eugene Hickock were sentenced to death for the murder of a prosperous Kansas farmer, Herbert Clutter, his wife and two teenage children. They killed without apparent motive, though both had a history of crime and character disorder. The writer Truman Capote had got to know the two young men before and after their trial, and their story and his acquaintance with them was the basis of his non-fiction novel In Cold Blood.

At the time of the original sentencing, Ken found himself at a party in New York with Capote. He asked his old friend if he were not exploiting the two murderers, having sought their friendship and trust. If they were insane, as it appeared (and as Capote agreed), should not Capote have provided them with the best psychiatric and legal aid in an effort to save their lives?

The argument between the two continued on other occasions. When the killers were finally hanged in April 1965, Capote, according to Ken's story, jumped up and down and declared, 'I'm beside myself, beside myself, beside myself with joy!' He could now publish without fear of libel. When the book came out in England Ken decided to do a long review (13 March 1966) for the Observer. *He wrote: 'We are talking ... about responsibility ... For the first time, an influential writer of the front rank has been placed in a position of privileged intimacy with criminals about to die, and – in my view – done less than he might have to save them ... An attempt to help by supplying new psychiatric testimony might have easily failed; what one misses is any sign that it was even contemplated ... Where lives are threatened, observers and recorders who shrink from participation may be said to betray their species: no piece of prose, however deathless, is worth a human life.'*

Before writing this review, Tynan conducted some legal research:

To Terence Kilmartin

120 Mount Street
19 January 1966

Dear Terry,

You remember we talked about the Observer helping me to do a little research on the Capote piece? There are two things I particularly need to know – one easy and the other one tricky.

The easy one is: could somebody give me a list of all the Governors of Kansas who held office between 1958 and 1965?[1] The second one you know about: I really need to establish that Columbia Pictures[2] did draw up two contracts with Capote – one for signing if the murderers were reprieved, and the other if they were hanged. Have you got any intrepid news-hound not known in the film industry, who can do a bit of sniffing around Columbia's British office? We really need to use Bond tactics for an operation like this.

I would be tremendously grateful for any help you can provide.

Love,
K.

---

[1] George Docking (1957–61), John A. Anderson Jr (1961–5), William H. Avery (1965–6).
[2] Columbia eventually made a film of Capote's book (US, 1967).

To Emilie Jacobson

[Telegram]

[London]
[22 January 1966]

DELIGHTED TO DO IMPRESSIONIST PIECE ON BOGART[1] WHOM I DIS-
COVERED IN 1937 BUT PLEASE WITHOUT GOING INTO BIOGRAPHICAL
DETAILS STOP IF THIS IS OKAY GET SPECTORSKY TO SEND ME
BOGART BOOKS STOP MUST KNOW SOON ABOUT FESTIVALS AS HAVE
BOOKED GERMAN TRIP IN FEBRUARY LOVE KEN

[1] 'The Man and the Myth' (*Playboy*, June 1966).

To Aaron Frosch

[120 Mount Street]
February 1 1966

Dear Aaron,

May I ask you for a brief professional opinion? I am writing a long article about Truman Capote and his book 'In Cold Blood', which you have probably read. One of the aspects that worries me about it is the legal one. It raises a lot of fascinating questions and if you have a moment, I would love to hear your answers. Naturally, I won't quote you.

1. The book, as you know, contains detailed descriptions not only of the killing of the Clutter family, but of the sexual habits of the two murderers (one of them had a passion for small children) and of another attempted murder of a hitch-hiker. The only evidence that the sexual allegations and the attempted murder allegation are true is Capote's unsupported hearsay testimony. The question is: Do you think he could have published these allegations during the two murderers' lifetime without fear of prosecution for libel, defamation, invasion of privacy, etc?

2. If the boys had not been hanged (as they were, last April), would it have been necessary for them to provide signed releases authorizing Capote to print this and other items of information that might be damaging to them?

3. In the absence of such releases, do you think it would be possible

for the surviving relatives of the two murderers to bring any legal action against Capote?

The point I am trying to establish is that the book could probably not have been published – at least in its present form – if the boys had not been hanged. If I'm right, Capote behaved in a rather ghoulish way, sitting around waiting for the nooses to tighten. Of course, I will treat your replies in the strictest confidence and I shall naturally expect to pay for such expert advice.

The only problem is a certain urgency – I have to deliver the piece within the next ten days.

All my very best,
Ken Tynan[1]

[1] Frosch replied (7 February 1966): 'The broad principle is that there is no right to privacy on the part of the deceased or his estate.' Though he had not read the book, 'I would doubt whether the book would have been released prior to the decease of the accused.'

To Peter Shaffer[1]

[The National Theatre]
16 February 1966

Dear Peter:

It's a pity we weren't able to talk before I left. We journalists are a funny lot, and I must say I was startled to be told that your piece on BLACK COMEDY[2] was going into the programme and mine was to come out. What irked me a bit was that this had been done without consulting me at any stage. So I got slightly worried, and frankly still am.

What I wanted to do was to give a fairly objective account – on behalf of the National Theatre – of the curious events leading up to your great success last summer. It seemed to me (and still seems) that this sort of thing comes better from someone less immediately involved than from the author himself. I wanted this account to be a small contribution to the National Theatre's archives. Since writing it, I have discovered the detailed notes I kept of the early days of BLACK COMEDY and there are several inaccuracies that I now want to correct. I also made it clear to John Dexter that I would be quite happy to make any factual changes you or he thought necessary, and that I was glad to be reminded of the oversight by which I'd omitted to mention the contribution of the company. I had decided to make these alterations when I got back from Germany next Wednesday. But just as I am about to leave for the airport – wham! I'm confronted with a totally new situation – a totally new piece has been written, and I am rather brusquely informed that my further services won't be needed. All this, you will agree, is just a little unorthodox.

I don't want to bore you by dwelling on this problem, but there is one more thing I might add. One of my jobs, when I joined the NT, was to be that of company historian. It's a job I'd still like to carry out. Will you help me? When I return from Germany, could we get together and get the facts straight? If you want to call me while I am in Germany, Rozina will tell you where I am.

Yours ever,
[pp. Kenneth Tynan]

[1] Peter Shaffer (b. 1926), English playwright, brother of Anthony Shaffer, also a playwright; his plays include *The Royal Hunt of the Sun* (1964), *Equus* (1973) and *Amadeus* (1979).
[2] The National needed a new one-act play, and in March 1965 Peter Shaffer proposed an idea: he had been thinking of a Peking Opera performance in which two men fight a duel, supposedly in the dark, but with the stage lights on. With KPT and John Dexter (who would eventually direct), he set about inventing a comic contemporary plot ensuring that the laughs would be directly connected with the light–darkness convention. The play opened (with Strindberg's *Miss Julie*) on 27 July 1965: 'A home-grown addition to the play catalogues,' KPT wrote in the programme 'and the kind of risk only a permanent company could have taken.' On 6 June 1966 it played alongside the opening of John Osborne's *A Bond Honoured*.

Memo to Laurence Olivier

[The National Theatre]
28 February 1966

Dear L:

The enclosed edition of Büchner has a historical note on DANTON that may be helpful to you.

Büchner was 21 when he wrote the play. For some time he had been in fear of arrest by the authorities for his revolutionary activities as a student.[1] A few years earlier he had said in a letter:[2]

'I have been studying the history of the French Revolution. I feel annihilated by the terrible fatalism of history. I see in human nature a horrible uniformity, in human relations an unavoidable violence

... the individual is only foam on the waves, greatness a mere accident, the strength of genius a puppet play, an absurd struggle against an iron law. The greatest of us can only recognise it; to control it is impossible. The word 'must' is the curse under which all men are born. There's a horrible saying: it must needs be that offences come, but woe to the man by whom the offence cometh. What is it in us that lies, murders, steals?'

At first he had intended to write a propaganda play about the early period of the Revolution. He soon abandoned this idea and concentrated instead on the Reign of Terror. After finishing the play, he escaped to France and gave up all interest in politics. He wrote:

'The whole Revolution has now split into Monarchists and Absolutists, and is forced down the throats of the poor and uneducated. Only hunger will ever be the goddess of liberty. Only a Moses, who sends us the plagues of Egypt, has the chance of becoming our Messiah.'

He seems to have reached the state of despair that you sometimes find in people who say that we need a nuclear war in order to start all over again. He died in Zurich in 1837 at the age of 23.

Love,
K.

[1] While at the University of Giessen in 1834 Büchner had joined a revolutionary group led by F. L. Weidig, a Protestant clergyman, with whom he published a pamphlet, 'Der hessische Landbote', which advocated armed insurrection by the peasants. Büchner was forced to flee to his home near Darmstadt, where he was kept under surveillance, before fleeing the Grand Duchy of Hesse-Darmstadt altogether.
[2] To his fiancée Wilhelmina Jaegle, written in the spring of 1834.

To Irving Wardle[1]

[120 Mount Street]
22 March [1966]

Dear Irving,
    If you think I would leave a letter like that unanswered you must be mad.[2] Let me just say that I have never read anything like it and it has given me a glow I have not felt since I got 10 out of 10 in a History

Test at George Dixon's Elementary School in Birmingham in the Spring of 1936.

Love,
Ken

[1] Irving Wardle (b. 1929), assistant drama critic at the *Observer* (1960–3); drama critic of *The Times* (1963–89); drama critic of the *Independent on Sunday* since 1990.
[2] Wardle had written what he describes as a 'piece of fulsome fan mail' after reading KPT's review of Capote's *In Cold Blood*.

To the Editor, the *Observer*

[120 Mount Street]
[Published 3 April 1966]

Sir,—On the strength of his article last Sunday,[1] Truman Capote seems to have invented yet another new art form: after the Non-Fiction Novel, the Semi-Documentary Tantrum. Ignoring the tone of the piece, let's look at the points he raises.

First, the minor ones. I wasn't suggesting that Dick Hickock never tried to rape pubescent girls; merely that Capote's allegations could not have been substantiated in court. A confidential statement to a psychiatrist is not evidence in the legal sense; and Nancy Clutter, aged nineteen, can hardly be called pubescent.

As to Capote's disclosure that Hickock and Smith had told the cops as well as himself about other murders they had contemplated: I took it for granted that if the police had possessed such damning information, the fact would somewhere be mentioned in the book. Here, as elsewhere, it's impossible to deduce from the text which statements are corroborated and which are not.

A couple of months ago I asked my friend Aaron Frosch, partner in the well-known Manhattan law firm of Weissberger and Frosch (120 East 56th Street, New York City), whether Capote's allegations – if based solely on unsupported hearsay – would have been actionable, had the killers lived to deny them. Founding his answer on this assumption, he said: 'I would doubt whether the book would have been released prior to the decease of the accused.' He continued: 'References in the book to the personal habits of the deceased, unless these were part of the charges against him or were true or were reported in newspapers, would be a basis for action if the accused were still alive.'

Mr Frosch, of course, is the 'prominent Manhattan lawyer' whose existence Capote insultingly denies. His letter is on my desk, in lieu of 'a sworn affidavit'; but unless Capote still believes that I am concocting fictitious quotes from a fictitious source, I shall expect his cheque for $500 within a few days. It should be made out to the Howard League for Penal Reform.[2]

To get to more serious matters: the fact that Perry and Dick signed legal releases is quite irrelevant to my central point, which was (and is) that Capote could have done more than he did to save his friends by means of psychiatric evidence.

The day before the trial began, they were examined by Dr Mitchell Jones,[3] a psychiatrist who volunteered his services to the defence lawyers. When asked in court whether Perry knew right from wrong at the time of the offence, he said he had no opinion. According to Dr Joseph Satten[4] of the Menninger Clinic in Kansas, a psychiatrist highly esteemed by Capote: 'This possibly was a tactical error or a mis-understanding on Mitchell Jones's part in the heat of testifying.' (I must pause here to nail a wild misstatement on Capote's part – viz: 'Dr Satten specifically told Tynan that he could not quote from any of his (Dr Satten's) letters without my expressed permission.' I have never been told anything of the sort, nor have I ever written to Dr Satten or received a letter from him.)

Capote maintains that there were '*two* psychiatrists' who knew the case 'at firsthand', the other being Dr Satten. But the truth is that Dr Satten never met either Perry or Dick. He merely discussed them with Mitchell Jones, *who was the only psychiatrist ever to interview the murderers*. I won't bother to refute Capote's naïve assumption that they must have been sane because they had high I.Q.s; but I must challenge his blithe assertion that neither was a paranoid schizophrenic. On page 245 we read of Perry: 'His present personality structure is very nearly that of a paranoid schizophrenic.' This opinion is expressed by Mitchell Jones and endorsed by Satten.

Capote speaks of my 'entirely ludicrous claims to acquaintance with a third psychiatric expert on the Clutter case ... another anonymous person who doesn't exist ...' The psychiatrist's name is Dr Estela D'Accurzio; a friend of Dr Satten's. She worked with criminal patients at the Topeka State Hospital and the Kansas Reception and Diagnostic Centre in 1963–64, and believes that the Clutter murderers could have won their appeal if psychiatric testimony had shown them to be paranoid schizophrenics. Capote, on the other hand, contends that 'fifty world-famous psychiatrists ... would not have done a damn bit of good', because Kansas abides by the McNaghten Rule.[5]

He protests too much; and his plea is demonstrably frail. The McNaghten Rule can be overthrown (and often has been) by any psychiatrist prepared to state that the accused did not know the nature of his act. A typical McNaghten case was that of Ronald True, who was sentenced to death for murder at the Old Bailey in 1922, after two defence psychiatrists had pronounced him insane: he was later reprieved on the evidence of three more medical men who simply reinforced their colleagues' findings.

There are many such borderline cases in British law. American examples are just as numerous: consider the trial of Kenneth Chapin (Massachusetts, 1955), who murdered a fourteen-year-old girl, pleaded insanity and got the death penalty. It was commuted to life imprisonment after the intervention of a celebrated psychiatrist, who declared the condemned man a schizophrenic.

Where Capote is concerned, I see no reason to modify my original judgment: 'An attempt to help (by supplying new psychiatric testimony) might easily have failed: what one misses is any sign that it was even contemplated.' The three Federal judges who turned down the appeal rightly said that no evidence had been produced to substantiate a defence of insanity. But it might have been: in which case it is not inconceivable that one or both of Capote's confidants might now be alive.

In his preface to the book, Capote expresses his thanks to the people who helped him – such as the citizens of Finney County, the staff of the Kansas Bureau of Investigation, and many others. From this roll of honour there are two notable absentees. I hope Capote will not object if I repair the omission by paying tribute, on his behalf, to Perry Smith and Dick Hickock, without whose cooperation, garrulity and trust *In Cold Blood* would never have been written.

Kenneth Tynan[6]

---

[1] *Observer*, 27 March 1966. Capote wrote that he did not believe that KPT had consulted 'a foremost Manhattan attorney' (see letter 7 February 1966). 'If the name and address of this person can be produced, along with a sworn affidavit that he expressed such an opinion to Tynan, I will hand over a cheque for $500 to Tynan's favourite charity.' Capote accused KPT of having 'the morals of a baboon and the guts of a butterfly'.

[2] The Howard League for Penal Reform (founded 1866), based in London, an independent voluntary pressure group.

[3] Dr Mitchell Jones's examination lasted only two hours.

[4] Dr Joseph Satten, reknowned psychiatrist, was contacted by Dr Estela D'Accurzio (of the Henderson Hospital, Sutton, Surrey) on KPT's behalf.
[5] Whereby a man is held to be sane and legally responsible for his actions if he knows that what he is doing is wrong.
[6] Capote, apparently still sceptical, declined to settle his bet until he had seen an affidavit from Frosch. This was eventually provided, and the Howard League for Penal Reform received Capote's cheque for $500, a photostat of which KPT framed and hung on his study wall.

To Thornton Wilder

The National Theatre
5 April 1966

Dear Thornton;

Just a thought: we're doing the first English production of Lope de Vega's LA FIANZA SATISFECHA in an adaptation by John Osborne, entitled A BOND HONOURED. We go in for rather elaborate programme brochures (as you will see from the enclosed) and it would be wonderful to have a note by you on Lope.[1] Have you ever written anything about him that I could reprint? If not, would you consider jotting down a few words to tell our audiences why he is important? The end of April is our deadline.

How are you?

All my love,
Kenneth Tynan

[1] Wilder was an expert on Lope de Vega.

Memo to Laurence Olivier

[The National Theatre]
14 April 1966

I'll be away next week on a journalistic chore in Spain,[1] returning April 25. Here are a few interim notes

1) The Arrabal.[2] I've had an idea for a director: Roman Polanski[3] – the brilliant young Pole who directed KNIFE IN THE WATER and REPULSION. He's also worked in the Polish theatre and Peter Hall is after him to direct a play at the Aldwych. He has exactly the

right combination of fantasy and violence for the Arrabal. Without committing us I have sent him the script to see if it interests him.

2) <u>The Missile Crisis.</u>[4] What we need is a writer who is (a) experienced in documentaries, and (b) a superb showman. This probably means <u>two</u> writers. I tried hard to get Troy Kennedy Martin[5] (of Z Cars) interested, but he decided at the last moment to go off and write a film. Other names suggested have been James Cameron,[6] Clancy Sigal,[7] John Hopkins,[8] John McGrath[9] and Roger Smith[10] – in various combinations. All of these are TV writers and/or journalists. I'll continue the search on my return. John Dexter suggests that Mark Cullingham[11] should direct in collaboration with himself. [. . .]

K.T.

[1] We went to Seville 16–25 April for the Spring Feria with Tracy.
[2] Fernando Arrabal (b. 1932), Spanish playwright and novelist. *The Architect and the Emperor of Assyria* (1967) was produced by the National Theatre in 1971, directed by Victor Garcia.
[3] Roman Polanski (b. 1933), Polish film director; his later work includes *Rosemary's Baby* (US, 1968) and *Chinatown* (US, 1974).
[4] A projected documentary drama on the Cuban Missile Crisis of 1962.
[5] Troy Kennedy Martin (b. 1932); in 1962 he originated *Z Cars*, a realistic police television series, writing the first episode and others during its run.
[6] The journalist James Cameron (1911–85).
[7] Clancy Sigal (b. 1926), American screenwriter and author of novels including *Weekend in Dinlock* (1960) and *Zone of the Interior* (1976).
[8] John Hopkins (b. 1931), English television dramatist whose works include *Talking to a Stranger: Four Television Plays* (1967).
[9] John McGrath (b. 1935), Scottish writer for stage and television, film director, and founder of the radical theatre company 7:84.
[10] He had recently adapted Nell Dunn's *Up the Junction* for the screen (UK, 1967).
[11] An assistant director at the National Theatre.

To Elaine Dundy

[Telegram]

[London]
?26 April [1966]

ENGLISH LAWYERS SAY YOU UNWILLING TO MAKE DISCRETION STATEMENT OR GIVE ACCOUNT OF MARRIAGE.[1] WOULD IT NOT BE SIMPLER IF I DIVORCED YOU SITING [*sic*] MACBETH.[2] IN THAT CASE NO STATEMENT FROM YOU WOULD BE NECESSARY. LOVE KEN

[1] Until the introduction of no-fault divorce, a discretionary statement was required from the 'innocent' party, listing everyone with whom he or she had had sexual relations during the marriage.

[2] The English poet George MacBeth (1932–92), with whom KPT had caught Elaine *in flagrante delicto* at 120 Mount Street.

To David Lean[1]

The National Theatre
26 April 1966

Dear David Lean –

I'm told you referred on TV last night to my late arrival at 'Dr Zhivago'.[2] Perhaps the management of the Empire hadn't told you that I'd driven straight from the airport, where my plane had arrived an hour and a half late. Also that I am seeing the film again on Thursday. I didn't see you on TV and therefore I don't know the exact form of words you used, but nothing could be more calculated to damage a critic's professional standing than the suggestion that he would review a film without having seen it from the beginning.[3]

Yours
Kenneth Tynan

[1] Sir David Lean (1908–91), English film director who won Academy Awards for *Bridge on the River Kwai* (UK, 1957) and *Lawrence of Arabia* (UK, 1962).

[2] *Dr Zhivago* (US, 1965), directed by Lean, adapted by Robert Bolt from the novel by Boris Pasternak, it starred Omar Sharif and Julie Christie.

[3] Lean replied in a letter dated 30 April that it was 'maddening to have a critic of your [KPT's] importance arrive so deep into a first performance', and that 'the very least any film maker can ask is for a critic to see his work from start to finish, in that order!' In reply to KPT's claim of damage to his professional standing, Lean argued that he was merely dealing KPT the treatment he was used, as a critic, to dealing out to others.

To Thornton Wilder

The National Theatre
29 April 1966

Dear Thornton –

I was in Spain when your piece arrived and have only just got back to the office. All I can say is that you're wonderful. Bless you for taking the trouble, for being so speedy, and for writing such a splendid piece.[1] I've just one request: May I cut the phrase about 'exquisite vignettes of family life'? Since 'La Fianza Satisfecha' is full of incest and matricide, I fear some unscrupulous critic might lift the phrase out of context and use it to beat us with.

Once more: our thanks. Larry sends his love.

Yours ever
Ken Tynan

[1] In his accompanying letter of 16 April Wilder wrote that he had an inflammation of the eye, could only read and write at intervals, had no books of reference, but was proud to have been asked for his thoughts on Lope. He ended the letter with 'a four letter word: Love'.

To the Editor, the *Observer*

[120 Mount Street]
[Published 1 May 1966]

Sir,—Before answering the questions raised last Sunday by Joseph P. Jenkins,[1] I'd like to deplore the false and flashy heading that *The Observer* ran above his letter. 'Tynan attacked by lawyers,' it said across four columns, thus conveying the impression that I had been ambushed by a mob, whereas in fact Jenkins was my sole assailant.

Readers of 'In Cold Blood' will recall that Jenkins's association with the Clutter case began in 1962 – two years after the killers had been tried and convicted – when a Federal judge appointed him as unpaid attorney to the condemned men. I have no doubt at all that he and his colleagues fought for the lives of Perry Smith and Dick Hickock as hard as they knew how.

A longer version of Jenkins's letter appeared last week in the American Press, lashing me with phrases like 'utter balderdash' and 'God help journalism!', which I patiently accept as part of the shrill and formalised ritual of American court-room rhetoric. But since I am accused of neglecting the facts, I might as well start by pointing out a couple of peripheral blunders on Jenkins's part. He triumphantly claims that I 'never mentioned' the letter written by Dr Joseph Satten of the Menninger Foundation to my psychiatrist friend, Dr D'Accurzio: in fact, there are quotations from it both in my original article and in my reply to Truman Capote. And it's a pity, considering Jenkins's concern for the defendants, that he manages to misspell Hickock's name throughout.

But to move to matters of importance: Jenkins reveals a sadly tenuous knowledge of (and faith in) psychiatry when he scoffs at the value of evidence tending to prove that Hickock and Smith were 'some sort of "paranoid schizophrenics."' He says that among the legal points he brought up, 'the insanity issue was only one.' In the American text he adds, 'and a minor one at that.' But it was not minor; it was crucial; and this is where I part company with him and Capote, his clients' chronicler.

Let's look first at the pre-trial period, between January 7, 1959, when lawyers were assigned to the accused, and March 22, when court proceedings began. During those 10 weeks Capote could certainly have helped to provide the two men with more adequate psychiatric examination than the hasty two-hour session with Dr Mitchell Jones which they received the day before the trial opened. It's true, as Jenkins says, that the original lawyers failed to obtain a court order directing psychiatric examination in a State hospital; but there is no reason (except lack of funds) why the defendants should not have been examined at length inside the county jail.

Parenthetically, Jenkins remarks that 'even if such testimony were presented at the original trial, a jury would not have to believe it.' Of course; but does that mean that it should not have been proffered? As for the McNaghten Rule: I said that it could be overthrown by 'any psychiatrist prepared to state that the accused did not know the nature of his act.' By this I naturally meant an honest psychiatrist. Jenkins seems to imply that I was advocating perjury. I won't comment on this astonishing assumption.

Now for the post-trial period and the appeals. Jenkins initiated a habeas corpus hearing in the Federal court, at which an unpaid neuro-psychiatrist named Dr Herbert Modlin[2] (who never met either Smith or Hickock from first to last, Mitchell Jones was the only psychiatrist to have that privilege) testified that the accused had not been given adequate psychiatric examination. His evidence cut no ice. 'There is no provision,' says Jenkins, 'in our Federal Rules of Criminal Procedure permitting us to hire top psychiatrists for the purpose of conducting a lengthy psycho-analysis of Hickok [*sic*] and Smith and then eliciting such testimony from the witness stand.' But if other psychiatrists had known what Capote knew about the private fantasies and psychotic drives of the two killers, and had taken the stand to support Dr Modlin, the judge could have ordered a full psychiatric examination.

According to Jenkins: 'The Federal judge is bound by what did or did not take place in the State court. He is not permitted to open new avenues.' This is simply untrue. To determine whether a constitutional error has been made, a Federal judge can (and frequently does) admit testimony adducing facts that were not raised at the trial. The Supreme Court ruled in 1963 (case of Townsend versus Sain) that where a constitutional point was involved in a habeas corpus hearing, a Federal judge might decide 'to hold evidentiary hearings – that is, to try issues of fact anew.' In other words, the question of sanity could have been reopened. And in any case, irrespective of whether Hickock and Smith were insane at the time of the murders or the trial, psychiatrists could have been hired to interview them in prison, in order to establish whether they were fit for execution. The hanging of insane men is clearly 'a cruel and unusual punishment,' and as such forbidden by the Constitution.

So much for the legal quibbles. We touch on the nerve of my complaint when Jenkins says, of my case in general, that: 'it was no concern of Mr Capote's. A writer has no business interfering with the orderly procedure and processes in a court of law.' Really? Had Zola no business interfering in the Dreyfus case?[3] Was it wrong for the late Felix Frankfurter[4] – then a law professor at Harvard – to influence public and legal opinion by writing a famous article in the *Atlantic Monthly* about the Sacco-Vanzetti case? Must we rebuke the many authors and polemicists who tried to prevent the execution of the Rosenbergs[5] and Caryl Chessman?[6] In matters of life and death, there are no interlopers.

One would feel less uneasy about Mr Capote's role in this sorry affair if he had said – even once, even in an interview – that he did not think his friends deserved to hang. 'I personally know,' says Jenkins, 'that Mr Capote did not want Hickok [*sic*] and Smith to die.' No doubt: but it was an opinion that Mr Capote never saw fit, in the course of five years, to make public.

Kenneth Tynan

[1] A lawyer sympathetic to Capote.
[2] Dr Herbert Modlin, a Menninger Foundation neuropsychiatrist.
[3] Emile Zola (1840–1902), French novelist who attacked the French government in an open letter, *J'accuse* (1898), over the case of Alfred Dreyfus, a Jewish French army officer falsely imprisoned for betraying state secrets.
[4] Justice Felix Frankfurter (1892–1965), a Roosevelt appointee to the US Supreme Court 1939–62.

[5] Julius and Ethel Rosenberg, American husband and wife executed in 1953 for passing atomic secrets to the Russians.

[6] Caryl Chessman (1922–60), American author of three best-selling books against capital punishment, spent twelve years on death row before his execution in 1960.

CHAPTER SIX

Soldiers and *Oh! Calcutta!*

Ken did not believe, during this period of revolutionary ferment, that the Western world would crumble, or that the class structure was seriously threatened. Yet he continued to fight for his own brand of romantic socialism. In the English antinomian tradition, he questioned the existing rules and proselytized for the liberation of the instinct. In defence of libertarianism he could be positively bigoted: he liked to transgress, as if to test the barriers that, paradoxically, he seemed to need.

During the last years of the decade, he was engaged in mounting two theatrical events: Soldiers by Rolf Hochhuth, a play about the morality of civilian bombing, set during World War II, and Oh! Calcutta!, a groundbreaking erotic revue of his own invention. A boisterous theatrical changeling, sporting full nudity, Oh! Calcutta! would be described by Newsweek as 'not only revolutionary, but salutary'.

Part of the huge unwieldy play of Soldiers arrived on Ken's desk in December 1966. It was eventually to consist of a prologue and epilogue, set in the bombed ruins of Coventry Cathedral in 1964 where a former bomber pilot is mounting a play. The play within a play is in three acts, representing the afterdeck of HMS The Duke of York in 1943 on its way to Scapa Flow; Sir Winston Churchill's bedroom, in which the bed becomes an image of the battlefield; and the garden at Chequers. In the third act – in the tradition of Schiller – Churchill engages in vigorous debate with an opponent of saturation bombing. While the play is concerned with Churchill's capacity as a war leader, and the quality of his political principles, he emerges as a figure of stature, humour and charm, capable of pettiness yet generously aware of his and our futility.

Ken felt Soldiers addressed the kind of important subject the National Theatre should be tackling. He had seen and liked Hochhuth's The Representative, in which the playwright arraigned Pope Pius XII for not intervening with Hitler on behalf of the Jews. And he was deeply affected by Hochhuth's dictum that 'our own deaths, or those of our grandchildren, may possibly be brought about because the large-scale bombardment of population centres, the specific invention of the years 1940–45, was never condemned by any court.'

Hochhuth felt sympathy for Churchill's sanction of a large number of indiscriminate deaths, because it seemed necessary at the time (though not in retrospect); just as he was prepared to accept the morality of Churchill's assassination of an individual. To illustrate this he took as the secondary theme for his play the death of the Polish leader-in-exile, General Wladyslaw Sikorski. The play implies that Sikorski may have been assassinated by the British Secret Service.

Hochhuth's argument was as follows: the British had gone to war to safeguard the independence of Poland; yet to win the war and to protect the vital alliance with Stalin, Churchill knew well that he would have to break faith with the Poles and hand over half their territory to the Soviets. He had in addition to turn a blind eye to the mass murder of Polish officers at Katyn, for which the Poles blamed the Russians. Sikorski, an international figure, was a constant reminder that victory would have to be achieved at the cost of dishonour.

The problem that dogged the play – and Ken – was the sabotage theme: neither the reasons for it nor the evidence produced in its favour were sufficiently authoritative. Moreover, from the political viewpoint, Sikorski was dependent on the British for everything, including the pay of his troops. His complaints might have embarrassed Churchill but they could never have threatened him. As for the circumstantial evidence of foul play, none of it stands up in the light of hindsight. While maintaining it was the playwright's prerogative to interpret history, and that he was under no obligation to be historically accurate, Ken felt obliged to prove that the playwright's conjectures were within the bounds of possibility.

Ranged against him were the Lord Chamberlain and Viscount Chandos, a one-time member of Churchill's War Cabinet. Already the Board had banned Frank Wedekind's Spring Awakening, *and other plays were threatened. Olivier had his doubts about* Soldiers, *although he told his wife that the portrait of Churchill was marvellous, but he supported its production. Behind the scenes he grew more and more hostile to his arrogant Chairman.*

It was left to Ken to fight the real fight more or less on his own. At huge cost to himself and his career he fought inside the theatre and out – lobbying at the Arts Council, in government circles and vociferously in the press. The Lord Chamberlain's theatre duties were finally abolished in September 1968; as for the National Theatre Board, no play was ever again vetoed under that or subsequent artistic administrations.

No less scandalous and draining was the production of Oh! Calcutta! *Having devised an 'Evening of Erotica' which he hoped to mount in the West End, Ken invited Peter Brook to direct. Brook said no, claiming that the only erotic show he would be interested in directing was a brothel. The show would open in New York (because of the restrictions of the Lord Chamberlain), tour the world and make a fortune for its producers and backers, though not for Ken, through a combination of mismanagement on his part and ill-advised arrangements with the money-men.*

Soldiers *and* Oh! Calcutta! *demonstrated his increasing need to be engaged inside the theatre. In each case he wanted to change existing attitudes. 'With what result?' he wondered years later. 'More sustained and virulent abuse than anyone in the theatre has received in the press for a decade, and probably they changed nothing.'*

To William Donaldson[1]

Mount Street
June 28 [1966]

Dear W.D. –

Just returned from Paris and Sweden, where I thought a lot about our talk.[2] Here are some tentative conclusions:

1. The idea is to use artistic means to achieve erotic stimulation. Nothing that is merely funny or merely beautiful should be admitted: it must also be sexy. A certain intimacy is therefore necessary – i.e. a theatre seating not more than about 900, such as the St Martin's or the Criterion. It should preferably have (or obtain) a variety licence,[3] so that wordless items would not have to be submitted to the Lord Chamberlain. The show would be devised (or produced) by me, directed by some like-minded person (Jonathan Miller?[4]), and choreographed by a non-queer.

2. Title. I made a long list of possibilities, including such outside chances as THE CONSENTING ADULTS SHOW, LET ME COUNT THE WAYS, HOW COME, etc, etc; but I've since found a beauty. I showed you a painting by the ancient French surrealist Clovis Trouille[5] of a reclining girl displaying her bottom, with the caption: 'Oh Calcutta!'[6] While in Paris I discovered that this is a pun – 'Quel cul t'as!', meaning 'What an arse you have!' I therefore suggest calling the show 'Oh Calcutta!', subtitled 'An International Erotic Revue' and using the Trouille painting as a poster. Those who get the joke

will get it, and those who don't will be intrigued. Anyway, it's unforgettable.

3. Component parts. The cast should consist of 8–10 girls, all vivacious dancers and about half of them reasonable singers; plus around 4 men, all expert comics. None of the company need be English: foreigners speaking broken English, whether male or female, can get away with far more outrageous things than home-bred performers (<u>vide</u> 'La Plume de Ma Tante'[7]). Also English comics tend to be coy and domesticated in matters of sex, unlike their French and American-burlesque equivalents.

4. Possible items:
(a) As an opener, I would suggest a pseudo-drag stripper – i.e. a male-looking girl singer dressed up to look like a female impersonator. She would need a baritone voice. At the climax of her strip, she would reveal her breasts – thereby baffling the smart-alecs in the audience who had decided that she was a man. To drive the point home, one might make this a double act, of which the other member was a <u>real</u> female impersonator – who would disclose his masculinity at the same moment that his partner disclosed her femininity.
(b) Later, there should be a pseudo-Lesbian singer in a dark serge suit, wearing no make-up and singing (in a Dietrich-like voice) a ballad about love betrayed. As the song ends, the singer should strip to the waist and reveal that, despite what we guessed, he is a male.
(c) A serial film – directed by Polanski?[8] This should be specially commissioned and used to cover scene-changes – a sort of sexy <u>Batman</u>, preferably in colour. About six episodes should be used in the course of the show, each of which leaves the audience cliff-hanging. The film should be silent, with a dubbed commentary: I can't think offhand of a British director who could make it, but there are many continentals who would be interested, from Jean-Luc Godard[9] to Roger Vadim[10] and the sensational Swede, Vigo [*sic*] Sjoman[11] (director of 'My Sister, My Love').
(d) Vaudeville routines. These, at their best, are always very sexy – I'm speaking, of course, of American burlesque and Parisian music-hall. One could, if money allowed, import a trio of American burlesque comics – the kind of people who work in the Ann Corio show, 'This Was Burlesque'.[12] Alternatively, Robert Dhéry[13] could be engaged to devise three or four routines for French

comics such as Jacques Legras[14] and Christian Duvaleix.[15]

(e) Dance numbers. These might include:

   (1) A ballet based on the paintings (and the world) of Clovis Trouille. He is the Douanier Rousseau of surrealism – in fact, a French poet once described him as Rousseau with balls. His fantastic visions of begartered nuns, girls with bats on their cunts and <u>fleur-de-lys</u> on their behinds, novices doing the splits, circus performers who are half-girl and half-horse, would make the ideal erotic ballet. We'd have to get his permission, because he hates being exploited by people who aren't seriously erotic.

   (2) A Beardsley[16] ballet, based on Aubrey's erotic drawings.

   (3) A French 18th-century ballet, based on the erotic paintings of Boucher and Fragonard.

   (4) A Homage to the Crazy Horse Saloon.[17] Alain Bernardin, who runs this Paris strip-club, is without doubt the greatest and most imaginative innovator in the history of striptease. With his permission, I would borrow several of his best numbers – e.g. 'Hurray for Mr. Touchdown', in which the girls are dressed as American football players; 'Tracy Tiffany', the life-story of a stripper, in which op-art slides are projected on to the dancer's nearly-nude body while she recounts her history in recorded broken English ('My name is Tracy Tiffany. I'm an Aries.'); the classic bath number in which a stripper is first seen in silhouette, projected on a downstage screen, and later perched on a black marble bath, meditatively soaping herself; and of course Bernardin's famous 'La Veuve',[18] in which a widow, sitting in a pew at her husband's funeral, devoutly strips as the organ plays. For all of these numbers we would have to get Bernardin's O.K., and although it would be hard for him to prove violation of copyright, I think it would be wise to offer him some kind of payment. Also he might be useful in recruiting girls – the Crazy Horse employs the glowingest, prettiest, most animated strippers on earth.

(f) Semi-documentary items. These might include:

   (1) Tableaux representing national erotic obsessions – such as a nun being raped by her confessor (Italy), a middle-aged bank manager bound hand and foot by a Superwoman (U.S.A.), and a St. Trinian's sixth-former being birched by John Gordon[19] (Great Britain).

(2) The history of knickers.[20] Unknown until the late 19th century, knickers began to be manufactured by crafty textile tycoons. When they first appeared, the church reviled them, since they were constructed like trousers and the Bible forbade women to wear men's attire. Knickers were condemned in every pulpit, and girls who wore them were considered dangerously fast. Later, sensualists like Frank Harris[21] led a crusade for open as opposed to closed knickers – for Free Trade (as he put it) as opposed to Protective Tariffs.

(g) Straightforward solo strip numbers. Such as:

(1) Gypsy del Rio,[22] the uninhibited acrobat now appearing at the Sunset Strip in Soho.

(2) Dailly Holiday,[23] a fantastic stripper from Guadalupe [*sic*] whom I saw last week in Paris. She is a buxom Negress, built for wrestling, who performs the first and only Black power strip I have ever seen. Instead of attempting (like most coloured strippers) to be more sophisticated and elegant than the whites, she doesn't even try to be charming. She comes on pure black and brutally militant, snarling at the audience and shoving her arse and tits straight into the onlookers' faces. She is Black Supremacy incarnate, and we might have to build a shallow runway down the centre aisle in order for her to operate.

(h) Erotic sketches by wellknown writers. The authors' names would be announced, but not attached to the sketches they had written – which would allow the critics to indulge in a fascinating guessing-game. I would approach people like Harold Pinter,[24] Terry Southern,[25] J. P. Donleavy, Henry Livings,[26] Jean Genet,[27] James Jones, John Mortimer, and of course John Osborne. (In fact, I would even use an excerpt from Osborne's 'Under Plain Cover'[28] if he didn't feel like writing something new.) And there should also be an extract from de Sade's 'Philosophy in the Boudoir'.[29] The writers should be told that if they wished to remain anonymous, their names would not even be mentioned.

(i) Erotic Songs – not folksongs (The Fanny Hill 'Whip' song?[30])

All these items would be shuffled and interspersed, so that a strip would be followed by a sketch, a sketch by a ballet, a ballet by a film excerpt, etc, etc.

Rereading what I've written, I see that I've omitted under section (e), dance numbers – a pop art ballet designed by Pauline Boty, based on paintings that focus on the principal erogenous zones.[31]

When you've pondered the foregoing, let's meet again and make plans.

Love,

Ken Tynan

[1] In early June 1966 KPT met William Donaldson (b. 1935), the impresario who had presented *Beyond the Fringe*, to discuss the idea of mounting an evening of erotica in the West End in spring 1967, which KPT would devise. Donaldson was enormously excited and wrote to Tynan on 13 June that he had 'opened such a large can of beans I thought I would write to you in case you are fearful of seeing some of your better ideas in quite another show under a different name...'

[2] The carbon copy of this letter was heavily annotated by KPT. The bulk of these notes has been left out as they were evidently not sent with the original.

[3] Variety performances did not come under the jurisdiction of the Lord Chamberlain.

[4] Dr Jonathan Miller (b. 1934), doctor, author and director who performed in and co-wrote *Beyond the Fringe* in 1960 and directed his first London production, Osborne's *Under Plain Cover*, at the Royal Court in July 1962.

[5] Clovis Trouille (1889–1975), French 'Sunday' painter of surrealist and erotic subjects.

[6] The title of the painting is *Oh! Calcutta! Calcutta!* and the subtitle *La Conquête de la lune*.

[7] Highly successful revue (1955) by Robert Dhéry.

[8] Never made.

[9] Jean-Luc Godard (b. 1930), French director whose first film *A Bout de souffle* (Breathless) (France, 1959) established him as a leader of the Nouvelle Vague movement.

[10] Roger Vadim (b. 1928), French director whose first film *Et Dieu ... créa la Femme* (And God Created Woman) (France, 1956) made his young wife, Brigitte Bardot, an international star.

[11] Vilgot Sjöman (b. 1924), Swedish director whose films explore the darker side of sexuality. *491*, made in 1964, had run into censorship trouble in Sweden and abroad. *My Sister, My Love* (Sweden, 1966) was about incest. *I Am Curious–Yellow* (Sweden, 1967), which was explicitly sexual, ran into censorship trouble in Sweden and abroad.

[12] Ann Corio (b. 1914), stripper and actress in films including *Swamp Woman*, *Jungle Siren* and *Sarong Girl*. 'This Was Burlesque' toured from the mid-1960s to the mid-1970s.

[13] Robert Dhéry (b. 1921), actor, director, screenwriter, playwright, who started as a circus performer; he specialized in burlesque comedy roles, notably in *La Belle Américaine*, which he also directed (1961).

[14] Jacques Legras appeared in *The Robert Dhéry Show* 1957–8.

[15] Christian Duvaleix (1923–79), French actor and comic, leader of the troupe Les Branquignols.

[16] The writer and artist Aubrey Beardsley (1872–98) illustrated Wilde's *Salomé*, Pope's *The Rape of the Lock* and the *Lysistrata* of Aristophanes.

[17] A Paris nightclub on the Avenue George V.

[18] Shortly after Dodo d'Hambourg had made her reputation in this sketch, her (real-life) husband committed suicide.

[19] St Trinian's: a mythical girls' boarding school invented by the cartoonist Ronald Searle in the late 1940s; John Gordon (1890–1974), a dour, puritanical Scotsman, editor of the *Sunday Express* (1928–54) and columnist.

[20] 'The Empress's New Clothes', a sketch written by KPT and designed by the English painter Allen Jones (b. 1937), presented in the London production of 1970.

[21] Frank Harris (1856–1931), writer and journalist, biographer of Oscar Wilde and George Bernard Shaw. His sexually explicit memoirs, *My Life and Loves* (1923–7), created a scandal.

[22] A Spanish stripper whose 'tiger act' was very popular: wearing a tiger skin, she would crawl across the stage brandishing long fingernails.

[23] KPT saw Dailly Holliday at the Dolce Vita in Montparnasse and wrote about her in 'The Theatre Abroad: France', *New Yorker*, 15 October 1966.

[24] Harold Pinter (b. 1930), English playwright. His first major success was with *The Caretaker* (1960). He had recently written screenplays for *The Servant* (UK, 1963) and *The Pumpkin Eater* (UK, 1964).

[25] Terry Southern (b. 1924), American novelist (*The Magic Christian*, 1960) and screenwriter of films including *Candy* (US, 1959) and *Doctor Strangelove* (UK, 1963).

[26] Henry Livings (b. 1929), playwright and actor; his first play, *Stop It, Whoever You Are*, was produced at the Arts Theatre in 1961.

[27] Jean Genet (1910–86), French playwright and novelist whose works include *Le Journal du voleur* (1949) and *Querelle de Brest* (1947). Though KPT wanted a heterosexual cast, he approached several homosexuals to write sketches. Genet did not in fact contribute.

[28] One of John Osborne's 'Plays for England' (1962).

[29] *La Philosophie dans le boudoir* (1793).

[30] 'Thrash Me, Laddie, Thrice To The Bar', lyrics by Charles Sydney, music by Gerald Coates, from *The Ballad of Fanny Hill, an Original Music Monodrama* (1963), produced and directed by Bill Door, based on *Fanny Hill, or, Memoirs of a Woman of Pleasure* by John Cleland (1748–9).

[31] Pauline Boty had already painted 'Bum' at KPT's request, the first of a planned series. She died later that year.

Memo to Laurence Olivier

The National Theatre
1st July, 1966

Jerome Robbins[1] has been in town and I discussed THE BACCHAE[2] with him yesterday. As you know, since agreeing to doing it for us, he has accepted an invitation from Washington to form a company known as the American Lyric Theatre (with a $300,000 Government grant). He intends to start work on training his singers and dancers in the autumn, and he hopes to have something to show for his efforts by the Autumn of 1967. There is, as he admits, a chance that this new company will dominate his life so completely that he won't be able to come to England. But he has already told the Government of his commitment to us; the idea still fascinates him; and he's promised to let us know by March of next year whether he will be free to go into rehearsal with THE BACCHAE in January, 1968. My own impression is that he genuinely wants to, and that there is a 70–30 chance that he will.

Some other notes on THE BACCHAE:

1. Translation. My own favourite is the one by Kenneth Cavander, which Jerry has read once and is going to read again. If he doesn't

respond to it, he would like us to consider later Shaffer – with whom he has already discussed the idea.

2. For the music he would like Marc Wilkinson.[3]

3. He pointed out something I'd overlooked: that Pentheus is only sixteen or seventeen years old (he goes to his death 'a beardless boy'). Jerry is very anxious to find somebody really young for the part. I suppose our nearest approach would be Ron Pickup.[4]

4. Agave. Jerry is thinking of Peggy Ashcroft, Eileen Herlie,[5] or possibly a younger actress wearing a mask. If we went for either Herlie or Ashcroft we would have to start thinking of other parts with which to entice them. Certainly we have nothing for either of them before THE BACCHAE.

5. Jerry feels that some of the chorus will have to be recruited from outside the Company. We will obviously need a nucleus of trained dancers.

K.T.

[1] Jerome Robbins (b. 1918), American director and distinguished choreographer. His Broadway musicals include *On the Town* (1944), *The King and I* (1951) and *West Side Story* (1957).
[2] Tragedy depicting the death of Pentheus, King of Thebes, at the hands of the god Dionysus, by the fourth-century tragedian Euripides.
[3] Marc Wilkinson (b. 1929), resident composer at the National Theatre until 1974. His film music includes *If* (UK, 1968) and *The Royal Hunt of the Sun* (UK, 1969).
[4] Ronald Pickup (b. 1940) made his stage debut in 1964 and played leading parts at the Royal Court (1964–6) and the National Theatre (1965–73).
[5] Eileen Herlie (b. 1920), Scottish stage actress long resident in the US; she played Gertrude in Sir John Gielgud's 1964 New York production of *Hamlet*.

To Julian Blaustein[1]

[120 Mount Street]
4th July, 1966

Dear Julian,
    The more 'the idea' takes shape, the more I realise that it's basically a theatrical project. In fact, it's a documentary dramatization of the fifteen days of the Cuba missile crisis. Sticking entirely to the historical record, we are going to try to explain to the audience how close they came to the nuclear abyss and what happened to keep them alive today.

We shall use film and closed-circuit TV, as well as live action. It's going to be written by a TV writer named Roger Smith and Clancy Sigal, an American novelist and critic.

Originally the idea was much more nebulous: now that it's hardened into a documentary form, you will realise that its movie potentials have evaporated.

Ever,
Ken T.[2]

[1] Julian Blaustein (b. 1913), film producer, most notably of *Khartoum* (UK, 1966).
[2] Blaustein wrote back (7 July 1966) that the idea might very well find an interested market in the US.

To Patricia Burke[1]

[The National Theatre]
6 July 1966

Dear Patricia:

I thought it would be helpful to put in writing my reactions to what you and David Macdonald[2] told me yesterday afternoon about Rolf Hochhuth's new play. On the basis of the outline Mr Macdonald gave me, I have no hesitation in saying that I am extremely enthusiastic and excited. This is the kind of play that a company like ours exists to present: it's also the kind of play that can help the theatre in general to fulfil its role as a public forum where history, art and morality are brought into one focus.

Please reassure Herr Hochhuth that there are no political problems involved in the staging of such a play at the National Theatre. We are subject to no political pressures of any kind. From what Mr Macdonald said, it would obviously be prudent to have the finished text vetted for libel by a lawyer, but beyond that I can see no obstacles.

The next step, clearly, is for Herr Hochhuth to complete the play. If Mr Macdonald is able to give us a translation of a fairly substantial part of it, I am sure that Sir Laurence and I will very quickly be able to give you a definite decision. But please be in no doubt that I am tremendously interested, and when Sir Laurence gets back from his holiday this will be the first thing I shall discuss with him.

Yours sincerely,
[Kenneth Tynan]
Literary Manager

[1] Hochhuth's English agent at Hope Leresche and Steele.

[2] (Robert) David Macdonald (b. 1929), playwright, director and translator closely associated with The Citizens' Theatre, Glasgow, since 1969. He translated *Soldiers* and acted as intermediary between KPT and Hochhuth.

To Desmond Cooke[1]

[The National Theatre]
August 18th, 1966

Dear Mr. Cooke,

Having just spent a bewildered hour entertaining your lady visitor from Mexico, I am moved to wonder exactly why the F.O.[2] and the C.O.I. thought it would be a good idea for her to talk to me. I gathered from her conversation that she is a gossip columnist and social reporter, and her interest in Richard Burton, Elizabeth Taylor, Stewart Granger and David Niven was unbounded. Not that she asked me any prying questions about them: indeed, apart from enquiring who I was and how I spelled my name, she asked very few questions of any kind. I learned about her abortive career as a song writer and her opinion of the Mexican actress Dolores del Rio – so much, in fact, that I came to the conclusion that she thought I was interviewing her. Possibly she was merely talking to cover her embarrassment, since it was readily apparent that she had no idea that the National Theatre existed or that I was connected with it. I expect I am crying for the moon, but it might have helped if someone from your department had given her a little advance briefing.

Looking back on this baffling encounter, I think I can pinpoint the precise moment when I lost heart. It occurred immediately after Señora Guillen arrived. Perhaps in an effort to break the ice, the charming young woman who accompanied her said that Señora Guillen had enquired whether Sir Laurence Olivier was still working in the English theatre. 'I'm afraid I didn't know,' the young woman went on. 'Have you any idea what he's doing nowadays?' At this point my mind froze over, and I cannot recall exactly what I said, except that it was something to the effect that he was the director of the National Theatre.....

Much as I love the c. o. 1., I shall think twice before welcoming another of its guests.

Yours etc.
[Kenneth Tynan]

¹ Of the Central Office of Information.
² The Foreign Office.

To Laurence Olivier

The National Theatre
August 23rd [1966]

Dear Larry –

After the abortive discussion on Cuba¹ today I'm confused and dismayed. There seems to be nothing I can tell the authors except that we can't talk to them until we have more copies made of the script. Candidly, I don't propose to embarrass myself until I can give them a firm date for a discussion. Part of the reason for my presence in this organisation is to look after our writers – to persuade them that we are interested in new work, that we care about experiment; this is a hard pretence to make when one looks at our record. In three years we haven't had a single top-level (your level) discussion with a single new author. We have dealt only with established names. Unless we treat writers with genuine seriousness and respect, they are simply going to lose interest in us. We may then have to face the unpalatable fact that modern theatre can very well do without us, but it can't do without them.

It's no use saying that we are too busy to see Smith and Sigal. They are busy too: writers often are. At the moment they are keeping themselves workless in order to await our pleasure: in other words, they are losing money and we are not. We are treating them as poor relations – the theatre's classic way of discouraging people from writing for it. And how terribly wrong we are! Grub Street is a thing of the past: nowadays we should be grateful that established writers care about the theatre enough to give it a priority over films and television. We are paving the way for a dismal future if we keep writers in the waiting-room like Victorian hacks. When you specifically invite a good actor to audition for you, you don't keep him waiting three weeks before telling him your reaction: you're pleased that he did the audition at all, and you give him a prompt answer. Smith and Sigal have done their audition – but where is our response?

I think I know more or less how you feel about their draft, and in part (as I explained) I agree. What I'd like to do is talk to them this week, put your point of view across (together with some other comments of my own), and – if they agree with our suggestions – urge them to go ahead with a full script. This will cost us £350. The alternative   in view of the other jobs they've been offered and will otherwise have to take – is to drop the whole project now. This would be a desperately sad decision; and one that would confirm not only their worst doubts but mine about the seriousness of our intentions to make the theatre a place of contemporary excitement.

Do let me know how you feel about this. I'm really troubled.

Love,
Ken

[1] The Clancy Sigal–Roger Smith treatment for a drama documentary on the Cuban Missile Crisis. KPT argued at this time that a theatre – or cinema – without a point of view on world affairs was likely to be 'doomed to sterility'.

To Ned Sherrin[1]

[The National Theatre]
14 September 1966

[Dear Ned]

Here's the draft treatment of the Cuba script. As I told you on the phone, Larry and I have had long talks to the boys, emphasising the need to restrict expenditure and avoid libel. As a result, they have already agreed to abandon some of their extravagant ideas – such as the use of a VTR machine, for example. It's also clear that although we can use library material for film inserts, we can't really go in for specially filmed sequences (like the one involving the Congressman from Louisiana[2]). Nor can we hire chorus girls for the entrance of Dean Acheson:[3] if they want girls they will have to use resident talent.

After you have had a look at the treatment, we must get together. One thing that slightly worries Larry and me is that, in the midst of all the gaiety on stage, the basic thing about the crisis may get lost: i.e.

the fact that for two weeks we were all in terror of being annihilated. I think any stage treatment of the subject that failed to convey that sense of impending doom would be a pointless exercise. I am all for the utmost theatrical inventiveness but not if it distracts attention from the background of approaching catastrophe. We want the audience to go out feeling sobered as well as entertained. The boys think their treatment will do this; at present, I am not so sure. It was different for Joan Littlewood in o what a lovely war:[4] when you're dealing with disaster that killed millions of people you don't need to strengthen the horror. Cuba was a near-disaster that killed no one, and that many people are already beginning to forget.

To recap again: we've now told the boys to go ahead into a full script for delivery in December. That will be the deadline for decisions: if we go ahead from that point, we do so under your direction. But clearly the next step is for you to tell me your reaction to the draft – probably before we all get together with the boys.

I forgot to mention that I am highly excited about all this. One so often overlooks that kind of thing when writing on official notepaper.

Love,
[Kenneth Tynan]

[1] Ned Sherrin (b. 1931), theatre director, television and radio personality who produced the films *The Virgin Soldiers* (UK, 1969) and *Up Pompeii* (UK, 1971) and the television satire programmes *That Was The Week That Was* and *Not So Much a Programme, More a Way of Life*. He was KPT's choice to direct the Cuban play.
[2] Probably either Hale Boggs, a close friend of President Kennedy, or Otto Passman, an extreme isolationist. Neither had a specific role the Cuban Missile Crisis, but were prominent figures in Congress.
[3] Dean Acheson (1893–1971), US Secretary of State 1949–53, then adviser on foreign policy to the Democratic National Committee.
[4] Highly successful documentary musical about the First World War, written and originally produced by Joan Littlewood in 1963 and filmed (UK, 1969) by Richard Attenborough.

To Paul McCartney[1]

[The National Theatre]
28 September 1966

Dear Mr McCartney,

Playing 'Eleanor Rigby' last night for about the 500th time, I decided to write and tell you how terribly sad I was to hear that you had decided not to do As You Like It for us.[2] There are four or five tracks on 'Revolver'[3] that are as memorable as any English songs of this century – <u>and the maddening thing is that they are all in exactly the right mood for As You Like It</u>. Apart from 'E. Rigby' I am thinking particularly of 'For No One' and 'Here, There and Everywhere'. (Incidentally, 'Tomorrow Never Knows' is the best musical evocation of l.s.d. I have ever heard.)

To come to the point: won't you re-consider? John Dexter doesn't know I'm writing this – it's pure impulse on the part of a fan. We don't need you as a gimmick because we don't need publicity: we need you simply because you are the best composer of that kind of song in England. If Purcell[4] were alive, we would probably ask him, but it would be a close thing. Anyway, forgive me for being a pest, but do please think it over.

Yours sincerely,
[Kenneth Tynan][5]

[1] Paul McCartney (b. 1942); the Beatles had been awarded MBEs by the Queen the previous year.
[2] John Dexter's all-male version; the production was for the moment cancelled by Olivier and replaced by Stoppard's *Rosencrantz and Guildenstern are Dead*.
[3] Released in 1966.
[4] Henry Purcell (1659–95), English composer of sacred music and opera, he also wrote incidental music for Dryden's *King Arthur* and *The Faerie Queene*.
[5] McCartney replied (in an undated letter) that the reason he could not do the music was because 'I don't really like words by Shakespeare.' He sat around waiting for a 'clear light' but nothing happened. He ended, 'Maybe I could write the National Theatre stomp sometime! Or the ballad of Larry O.'

To Kathleen Halton

[Telegram]

[Prague][1]
22 October 1966

DARLING LONGING TO SEE YOU PLEASE BRING HOCHHUTH PLAY IF ARRIVED AND PLEASE DONT BE CIVIL WHEN STRANGE MEN CALL STOP CIVILITY KILLED THE CAT STOP TRANSPORTS OF LOVE KEN

[1] KPT was writing about Czech theatre for the *New Yorker*.

To Robert David Macdonald

[The National Theatre]
2 November, 1966

Dear Mr. Macdonald,

I have just read the prologue and first act of 'The Soldiers', and I feel I must write and tell you, that if it goes on as it's begun, I think it's going to be absolutely marvellous. There are all sorts of tiny points I could raise and tiny questions I could ask; but the time for quibbling will come much later. The important thing is that 'The Soldiers' is all that Peter Brook's US[1] isn't – it is precise and specific instead of vague and general, it's informed and impassioned instead of ignorant and tepid and it's a blessedly fearless point of view.

Now for the crunch: is it humanly possible for Rolf Hochhuth and yourself to let us have a completed first draft by Christmas? I ask this for a very important reason. Our production schedule next year is pretty tightly packed except for a vacant opening date at the end of May or early in June. If we could have the full version of 'The Soldiers' by December, that would give us time to get it prepared and cast and ready to open in the vacant slot. Otherwise we might have to postpone it indefinitely – perhaps for a year or even more. The point is that we have announced that we are going to do a 'documentary' play next season. We have already commissioned a play on the Cuba Missile Crisis, which is due to be delivered in December. We couldn't consider doing two 'documentaries' in the same year, and December as I have said is the latest date on which we can decide which to do. I am overwhelmingly in favour of 'The Soldiers', but I absolutely can't push it through unless there is a fairly full text to go on. I would be so grateful if you could explain our situation to Herr Hochhuth and offer him my sincere apologies for seeming to pressure him in this way. I would not do it if I weren't so tremendously convinced of the play's power and stature.

Do let me know your and Herr Hochhuth's reactions as soon as you conveniently can. Meanwhile, please convey to him my deepest congratulations.

[Kenneth Tynan]

---

[1] A group-written play about Vietnam, staged at the RSC's Aldwych Theatre in 1966. It culminated in the release of live butterflies into the auditorium.

To Emilie Jacobson

[120 Mount Street]
7th November 1966

Dear Emilie,

Please thank Mr. Spectorsky for the list of suggestions. They are all worth more than a passing thought, but the ones that appeal to me most are:-

1. The War Crimes Tribunal.[1] I have done a little checking on this, and it's due to start in Paris in March. (The rumours that the French Government were objecting turned out to be false.) It's clearly going to be a fascinating event, and I would love to cover it.

2. The 'Talent Snob' idea. This might get a bit invidious and irritate one or two chums who were omitted: all the same, I'm pretty sure I would like to do it. (Give me a month or so to think it over and see if it is working out.)

3. Interview with Dietrich: this isn't on Spectorsky's list but I wrote to you about it last week. I would like a fairly quick decision on this, because she is only in England for the next four weeks. (Although of course I could always do it in Paris, where she mostly lives.)

4. Interview with Paul McCartney – to me, by far the most interesting of the Beatles and certainly the musical genius of the group.

Do let me know which of these four appeal to Spectorsky most, and in which order he would like them. I could go into the reasons why I'm not so keen on his other proposals, but it will save time if I don't. Hope to hear from you soon.

Love
Ken[2]

[1] The Bertrand Russell International War Crimes Tribunal was set up by Russell to determine whether the activities of the US in Vietnam could be classified as criminal under the laws by which the Nazis were tried at Nuremberg in 1945. It was privately sponsored. Sartre was the executive president. KPT attended in Stockholm in May 1967 and wrote about it for *Playboy* ('Open Letter to an American Liberal', March 1968).
[2] 2, 3 and 4 were never written.

Memo to Laurence Olivier

[The National Theatre]
9 November 1966

Further to the Hochhuth situation: after our talk, I learned from

Patricia Burke (the English agent) that the Aldwych are also in the field. Both Peter Brook and Peter Hall have made direct approaches to Hochhuth about the play. As I told you, he, Hochhuth, hated THE REPRESENTATIVE[1] at the Aldwych and was very much opposed to the idea of letting the Royal Shakespeare get their hands on the new piece. Patricia B is sure that he still feels that way, and of course we still have the right of first refusal. Even so, if we decide against it, it seems virtually certain that they would be next on the list. What may have encouraged them is the fact that 'US' is an absolute sell-out.

K.T.

[1] Rolf Hochhuth's first play (*Der Stellvertreter: Ein christliches Tranerspiel*), first performed in Britain by the RSC at the Aldwych, September 1963.

Memo to Laurence Olivier

[The National Theatre]
23 November 1966

There was an item in the papers the other day that didn't get the prominence it deserved. The Lord Chamberlain has withdrawn his ban on the Oppenheimer play,[1] which is now going to transfer to the West End.

I've talked to Peter Coe,[2] who directed it, and he quite rightly thinks this is a major breakthrough. It's the first time the Chamberlain has permitted the stage representation of living citizens of a friendly power. Here, obviously, is a cast-iron precedent that we can use in the case of Cuba.

K.T.

[1] R. Spiers' play about the investigation into the past Communist affiliations of Julius Robert Oppenheimer was first staged at the Hampstead Theatre Club and granted a licence to transfer on the grounds that, having played for some weeks at Hampstead without any legal complaints being made, it was not offensive to a living person.
[2] Peter Coe (1929–88), stage director whose first London success was with *The World of Suzie Wong* in 1959, followed by *Oliver!* in 1960.

To Emilie Jacobson

[Telegram]

[London]
2 December 1966

ALAS BRANDO REGRETFULLY REFUSES HOWEVER I WOULD LOVE TO
INTERVIEW JOHN HUSTON WHO IS DIRECTING BRANDO MOVIE[1] STOP
GATHER HEFNER[2] IS GREAT ADMIRER OF HIS STOP PLEASE ASK SPEC-
TORSKY IF PLAYBOY INTERESTED STOP HAVE KNOWN HUSTON FOR
YEARS AND AM VERY KEEN ON THIS PROJECT LOVE KENNETH TYNAN

[1] They were filming the screen adaptation of Carson McCullers' novel *Reflections in a Golden Eye* (US, 1967), in which Brando plays a sexually repressed army officer.
[2] Hugh Hefner (b. 1926), American publisher who started *Playboy* magazine in 1953.

To Rolf Hochhuth

[The National Theatre]
8 December 1966

Dear Herr Hochhuth,

Many thanks for your letter. As you probably know, David Mac-Donald will have finished his translation of the play within a week from now, and Sir Laurence and I will present it to our Committee as soon as possible afterwards. By the end of December we hope to have a definite decision – which I confidently expect will be affirmative.

The situation with the Lord Chamberlain is as follows: all plays in this country must be submitted to him for approval. He reads them in private and doesn't discuss them with politicians. (I should explain that the Lord Chamberlain is not a political appointment[1] nor is he a member of any political party.) Usually he has no objections to plays about historical characters, so long as they are dead. In the case of living characters (i.e. Harris[2]) he may require us to obtain the consent of the person involved. This is the only problem that I can foresee. Let me assure you that (a) the Lord Chamberlain is not entitled to forbid plays because of their political content, and (b) any discussions between the Lord Chamberlain, Sir Laurence and myself will be strictly private with no publicity attached.

The question of opening dates has become a little clearer in the past few days. As I am sure you will understand, we have to plan our programme considerably in advance, and it now looks as if the ideal date from our point of view would be late June or early July. The company is on holiday throughout August, and the next date when it will be possible to open your play would be at the very end of October – after the proposed Berlin première.[3] Sir Laurence and I would very much prefer the earlier date, if it can be agreed with the Volksbühne. Do you think this is possible?

On behalf of Sir Laurence, I send you my best wishes. We shall contact you again as soon as the script is delivered by David.

Yours sincerely,
[Kenneth Tynan]

[1] The Queen appoints the Lord Chamberlain.
[2] Sir Arthur Travers Harris (1892–1984), Commander-in-Chief Bomber Command, 1942–5; nicknamed 'Bomber Harris'.
[3] *Soldiers* would have its world première in Berlin at the Volkesbühne on 9 October 1967, directed by Hans Schweikart.

To Mary McCarthy[1]

[120 Mount Street]
December 12, 1966

Dear Mary,

May I intrude on your Vietnam thoughts with an invitation to self-indulgence?

Harold Pinter and I are co-devising (and Harold is directing) an erotic revue for West End presentation in the fall. Its primary aim will be to titillate,[2] and to this end we shall use film, mime, dance, song and words. The title of the show will be 'Oh Calcutta' – which is the title of a celebrated surrealist painting of a girl's bottom. (The painter is French, and the title a rather attractive pun.)

We are inviting about a dozen people to contribute sketches,[3] and we would love you to be one of them – especially in view of what you said on television about having been aroused by pornography.[4] Here are the terms of reference:

(1) Sketches can be of any length from a few seconds to about ten minutes.

(2) Since the show will be an essentially intimate affair, the cast will

not be large, and contributors are advised to confine themselves to about 5 or 6 speaking parts.

(3) Sketches can either be (a) stage reproductions of a pet erotic fantasy or (b) comments – ironic, satirical or what you will – on eroticism. Needless to say, they don't have to be funny. The tone can be as dark as you wish.

(4) Because of the Lord Chamberlain, genital exposure and 4-letter words are out. Almost anything else is in, however, including fetiches [*sic*] of all kinds.

(5) In order to exclude the rather boring area of theatrical camp, we have decided to rule out male homosexuality as a theme.

(6) Payment will be according to the usual scale for revues – ie. in proportion to the length of the sketch.

I do hope you are interested. If so, we would like the material fairly soon – if possible, within a month. If this isn't possible, perhaps you could dash off a postcard-length outline for us to look at. At all events, do let me know whether the idea attracts you.

Love,
Ken

P.S. Other contributors include John Arden, Edna O'Brien, Joe Orton, Penelope Mortimer, Gore Vidal, Brigid Brophy, John Mortimer, David Mercer, Pinter and myself. In order to confuse the critics, we are thinking of suggesting that the authors should be listed alphabetically at the top of the programme, thus leaving it to the audience to decide who wrote what. But we shan't do this unless the authors want it.[5]

[1] Mary McCarthy (1912–89), American novelist and critic whose work includes *Memories of a Catholic Girlhood* (1957) and *The Group* (1963).
[2] KPT added in his similar letter to Terry Southern, 'no crap about art or redeeming literary merit'.
[3] A similar letter was sent to other possible contributors, including Norman Mailer and Tennessee Williams.
[4] On *BBC-3*, 13 November 1965, the same programme in which KPT said 'fuck'. In fact, McCarthy had said, 'I really don't enjoy pornography', but that someone had accused her of loving it.
[5] McCarthy did not reply.

On 4 July 1943 General Wladyslaw Sikorski, Prime Minister of the Polish government in exile, boarded a Liberator in Gibraltar for the UK. His plane crashed shortly after take off, killing everyone except the pilot. The RAF enquiry of the time declared that the controls of the airplane had jammed, though no evidence was produced, and that 'sabotage could be ruled out'.

Those who believed foul play had occurred based their view on the gaps in the official story; the eyewitness report of an unidentified man cited walking along the wing shortly after the crash, clearly not the pilot who had suffered leg injuries; the report that the Governor of Gibraltar, General Mason-Macfarlane, had tried to persuade Sikorski to take another plane; the diary entry of Bickham Sweet Escott, a senior official in the SOE, the secret service organization, of a meeting with Mason-Macfarlane the very day of the crash; two other attempts, at Prestwick and Montreal, reputed to have been made on Sikorski's life; and Madame Sikorski's belief that it was sabotage. She told Hochhuth that after her husband's death Churchill was 'free to deal with Stalin without consulting the Poles'.

To Rolf Hochhuth

The National Theatre
16 December 1966

Dear Rolf Hochhuth,
   In haste: I have just finished reading Act Three and am overwhelmed. Many, many congratulations. I have two queries which David may already have metioned to you on the telephone:
   (a) Could you provide me with any historical references to support the contention that Churchill was responsible for the murder of Sicorski [*sic*]? It would supply me with invaluable help when the play is dicussed by our Committee.[1]
   (b) I am a little worried by the fact that Kocjan[2] makes his accusation so near to the end of the play – and that Churchill[3] is given no opportunity to reply to it. There are people on my Committee who may easily say that the play is smearing Churchill behind his back. I assure you that it would help me considerably if Helen[4] were to put a stronger case for Churchill's <u>personal</u> innocence: so that at least the matter is left open to conjecture – rather than being an open-and-shut case with no defence. For example: could she not develop the possibility that the assassin might have been Stalin? Or, for that matter, some of Sicorski's own colleagues? (The English historian, A. J. P. Taylor,[5] is convinced that Sicorski's death

was planned by the Polish right wing, who suspected that he would sell them out to Stalin.)

Please don't think that I'm trying to re-write your play. I am simply asking the questions that my Committee will ask – and (in the case of the second query) the question that I would have to ask myself as a critic.

Once again, all my admiration,

Yours sincerely,
[Kenneth Tynan]

[1] The Drama Committee of the National Theatre Board.
[2] Fictional Polish captain suspicious of the British.
[3] I.e. the character in the play.
[4] The fictional Helen Macdonald, second officer in the WRNS, Churchill's private secretary in the play.
[5] His works include *The Origins of the Second World War* (1961).

To Sir Isaiah Berlin[1]

The National Theatre
16 December 1966

Dear Sir Isaiah:

I am writing to ask your assistance on a matter of some urgency. The National Theatre has received for consideration a new play by Rolf Hochhuth, whom you may remember as the author of THE REP-RESENTATIVE (the play which arraigned Pius XII for his failure to speak out against the horror camps). His new play is a monumental and devoutly researched study of Sir Winston Churchill during the critical months of 1943 when Stalin was pressing ever more insistently for a second front and Cherwell's[2] policy of civilian saturation-bombing was to be put into effect.

One of the matters it raises is the question of British complicity in the death of Sikorski, whose plane (as you will doubtless recall) mysteriously crashed after take-off at Gibraltar. Hochhuth clearly implies that this was engineered by British Intelligence, who saw in Sikorski a potential threat to Anglo-Soviet relations at that time.

Naturally, a play of such magnitude, dealing with a subject so vast, will have to be fully discussed by the National Theatre Board before we can go ahead into production. Equally naturally, we expect some opposition from certain members of the Board, and one of their key objections is certain to be the author's interpretation of the Sikorski affair – although in fact this plays a comparatively minor part in the play as a whole.

The Board meeting at which the decision will be taken is to be held on January 9, when I shall have to muster all the arguments I can in favour of our producing the play. May I therefore ask you, in confidence, whether this version of Sikorski's death is new to you, and whether you think there's any truth in it? In other words, does it seem to you that an author would be justified in putting it forward as a reasonable conjecture?

If this whole matter were not of such great importance, I wouldn't have troubled you in this way. If you can find time to send me a brief opinion in time for the January 9 meeting, I shall be infinitely grateful.

Yours sincerely,
[Kenneth Tynan][3]

[1] Sir Isaiah Berlin (b. 1909), political philosopher and historian of ideas who expounded his defence of liberalism in *Four Essays on Liberty* (1969). He was one of a dozen historians and experts whom KPT would consult about *Soldiers*.
[2] Frederick Alexander Lindemann, Viscount Cherwell (1886–1957), physicist who was a close friend and personal adviser to Winston Churchill during the War.
[3] Berlin replied that he thought the hypothesis highly improbable and intrinsically too unlikely.

Memo to Laurence Olivier

[The National Theatre]
23 December 1966

Herewith Hochhuth. He has happily agreed to revise the last 20 pages so that (a) Helen puts a much stronger case for British innocence and suggests alternative culprits, and (b) the accusation is not pointed directly at Churchill but at 'the British' in general. He hopes to have the revised version delivered before the Board meeting.

In addition to the Board, copies have gone to the lawyer, the Lord Chamberlain and John Dexter. I am also sending one to Sir Robert Saundby, Harris' No 2 at Bomber Command and a friend of Hochhuth's. Before the Board meeting, I will go and see Saundby (who understands the workings of Harris' mind): Saundby will then take me to see Harris, with whom I'll talk the whole thing over.

Love,
K.

P. S. I don't know whether this is a great <u>play</u>: but I think it's one of the most extraordinary things that has happened to the British theatre in my lifetime. For once, the theatre will occupy its true place – at the very heart of public life.

To John Dexter

[The National Theatre]
28 December 1966

Dear John:

SOLDIERS – THE LITTLE LONDON MYSTERY CYCLE
by Rolf Hochhuth

Herewith Hochhuth minus prologue and epilogue. He's re-writing the final pages of Act III in such a way that (a) Helen puts a much stronger case for British innocence and suggests alternative assassins, and (b) the finger is not pointed directly at Winston but at the Secret Service.

Hochhuth tells me that he has locked up the sworn statements of his secret informants in three bank deposit boxes witnessed by three eminent Swiss scholars with the proviso that they are not to be opened for 50 years. This is to safeguard the families and the pensions of the people who gave him the dope on Sikorski. He was quite happy to make the changes at the end in order to get the play on in England, but he says unequivocally: 'Of course, Churchill knew all about it. He knew from the beginning.'

The decisive board meeting is January 9. Could you possibly send a letter of support which I can read out at the meeting?

Love,
[Kenneth Tynan]

Memo to Laurence Olivier

[The National Theatre]
3 Jan 1967

Dear Larry:

What follows is probably an attack of stage fright in anticipation of the Board meeting on Monday. Anyway, here goes.

I'm worried. Nothing really specific: just a general feeling that we're losing our lead, that we are no longer making the running, that what the NT does has become a matter of public acceptance rather than public excitement. At a time when – as I Cassandra-like keep saying – audiences even for <u>good</u> theatre are dwindling all over Europe, we are doing nothing to remind them that the theatre is an independent force at the heart of a country's life – a sleeping tiger that can and should be roused whenever the national (or international) conscience needs nudging.

We have had no MARAT-SADE;[1] we have no US. Meanwhile, Barrault has gained the respect of Gaullist France by staging LES PARAVENTS,[2] in which the French army is reviled for its Algerian atrocities; the Royal Dramatic Theatre in Stockholm is playing to full house with O WHAT A LOVELY PEACE!,[3] a show that bitterly arraigns its country's politicians for their cowardly neutrality in World War II; and a millennium or so ago a Greek playwright derided his own country's heroes for their wanton devastation of Troy.

Hochhuth may not be Euripides and SOLDIERS may not be THE TROJAN WOMEN, but it is in the same tradition and in this country that tradition is in our hands. Subsidy[4] gives us the chance – denied to movies and TV – of taking a line of our own, with no commercial pressures and without the neutralising necessity of being 'impartial'. In a way, I think Hochhuth is the test of our maturity – the test of our willingness to take a central position in the limelight of public affairs. If the play goes on under our banner, we shall be a genuinely national theatre, and, even as the stink-bombs fly, I shall be very proud of us.

Love,
K.T.

[1] Peter Brook's 1964 RSC production of Peter Weiss's *The Persecution and Assassination of Marat as performed by the Inmates of the Asylum of Charenton under the Direction of the Marquis de Sade*.
[2] By Jean Genet (1961).
[3] Play by Hans Alfredson and Tage Danielsson (1966).
[4] In the financial year 1966–7 the National Theatre received £300,000 from the Arts Council

towards a total budget of approximately £660,000. Ticket sales numbered approximately 230,000.

Memo to the National Theatre Board

[The National Theatre]
7 Jan 1967

Soldiers by Rolf Hochhuth

Some thoughts for the consideration of the Drama Committee and the Board of the National Theatre:

1. It seems likely that if the play is presented by the National Theatre, Lord Chandos will resign as Chairman of the Board. As a former colleague of Sir Winston Churchill's, he feels that he cannot associate himself with Hochhuth's views. It is impossible not to sympathise with this sentiment.

2. Lord Chandos further feels that if the National Theatre puts the play on, it may be difficult to obtain an unopposed vote in the House when the National Theatre Act is amended to increase the amount needed to build the National Theatre from £1,000,000 to £3,750,000.

3. Finally, Lord Chandos denies two of the play's premisses – namely (a) that Sir Winston was responsible for the promulgation of the saturation-bombing policy, and (b) that the British Secret Service might have arranged the death of General Sikorski.

Both the Drama Committee and the Board will no doubt give these points due weight. It may, however, be in order to draw to their attention certain other considerations:

1. It is very understandable that the Chairman should be distressed by the idea of seeming to sponsor a play that criticised the policies of a man to whom he and his country owe so much. On the other hand, there seems no reason why the National Theatre should not behave like 'The Times' or any other reputable newspaper when presented with an article by a respectable writer that runs counter to their editorial beliefs – i.e. print the piece, with a note to the effect that the opinions it expresses are not necessarily those of the editor. (I would go further and suggest that the entire programme-

brochure of the play should be devoted to arguments opposing those advanced in the text.)

To suppress a serious work on a subject of national (and international) concern is an act that the Board should not lightly undertake. In totalitarian countries, such suppression in the arts is easy and frequent; this is, in fact, the argument traditionally used to discredit state-subsidised theatre. The Voltairean cliché – about disliking what a man says but defending to the death his right to say it – should surely be what distinguishes the conduct of affairs at the Old Vic from 'state theatre' in the bad sense. [...]

A theatre can survive without even a first-rate chairman; but it cannot survive without playwrights. (Footnote: if embarrassment at a high level is the problem, it may be relevant to outline the alternative. Assuming that the Hochhuth play is turned down by the National Theatre, it will very likely be staged by the Royal Shakespeare Company, whose patron is the Queen.)

2. The parliamentary question. The National Theatre Act will certainly have to be amended to allow for the increased expenditure that Miss Jenny Lee[1] has promised. It is Lord Chandos' view that, unless the amendment is carried unopposed, a subsequent government might repudiate it. [...]

3. The premises of the play. As regards (a), the responsibility of Sir Winston for the policy of saturation-bombing, Hochhuth has sent me a list of more than a hundred source-books, which I will gladly supply (the list, not the books) to members of the Board. (Only one of the authors, incidentally, is German.) Sir Robert Saundby, Deputy Chief of Bomber Command under Sir Arthur Harris, has thoroughly vetted the text: I spent an afternoon with him last week going over it word by word. He was most helpful in suggesting minor technical improvements (all of which will be incorporated), and although he disagreed with Hochhuth's thesis about the effectiveness of saturation-bombing, he saw no reason why the play should not be staged.

As regards (b), the question of British involvement in the death of Sikorski: I have consulted a large number of historians and military experts, and the result is very much an open verdict.[2] [...] In [another] letter to me,[3] Hochhuth says: 'I have put every conceivable argument into the Prime Minister's mouth to show that he could not have acted otherwise at that decisive moment in world history. What would have happened – to take one isolated instance – if the Poles, in their hatred of Russia, had actually split up the coalition between the Kremlin and Downing Street and caused Stalin to make a separate peace with Hitler? It would have been the end of civilisation ...'

Hochhuth very much regrets that the Board will have read the play without the prologue, which deals at length with the German bombing of Coventry and Rotterdam. It should be borne in mind that the background of the entire action is the shattered interior of Coventry Cathedral. [...]

---

[1] Jennie Lee, Baroness Lee of Ashridge (1904–88), Scots Labour politician and the enlightened Minister for the Arts in Harold Wilson's Government 1964–6.

[2] KPT had asked a number of experts whether the assassination of General Sikorski was 'a hypothesis that a rational man could entertain'. In a memo to Laurence Olivier of 5 January 1967 he listed his evidence. It included the following: 'A. J. P. Taylor believes Sikorski's death was plotted by right-wing Poles.' 'Alan Bullock thinks the crash was an accident.' 'David Irving believes Hochhuth's theory to be correct, on grounds similar to those presented in the play.' 'Malcolm Muggeridge: familiar with the theory, has no evidence, but regards it as an acceptable conjecture.' 'Colin Gubbins (head of SOE [Special Operations Europe] during the war). Strongly denies that SOE was involved in any such plot.' 'M. R. D. Foot ... author of *SOE*, published by H. M. Stationery Office. Thinks it highly improbable SOE was involved, but says: "But I wouldn't put it past British Intelligence or the Secret Service."' 'John Ehrman (author of two volumes of the Official History of the War): Made some "top-level enquiries" on my behalf and consulted the Cabinet Office Historical Section. He then telephoned to say: "The answer is that there is nothing whatsoever to rule this theory out."'

[3] Dated 2 January 1967.

Memo to Members of the National Theatre Board

[The National Theatre]
9 January 1967

NOTE

SOLDIERS
by
Rolf Hochhuth

I have naturally corresponded with Hochhuth at some length about the factual basis of the play. On Saturday I sent him a final cable, asking whether the evidence he gathered to support his interpretation of the events at Gibraltar was quite incontrovertible. His cabled reply[1] is as follows:

'I give you once again absolute assurance that I stand by every word that I wrote in my letter about my sources of information for the tragedy at Gibraltar.'

(He is referring, of course, to the sworn statements now in three western European banks.)²

K. T.³

¹ 9 January 1967.
² In fact only one statement by 'a British secret service man' (according to Hochhuth), of which copies were deposited in three banks.
³ The Board met on 9 January and decided to defer a decision until the final script had been delivered. Personally, Lord Chandos was against any attempt to rewrite when the author 'had been guilty of so grotesque and grievous a libel'.

To Emilie Jacobson

120 Mount Street
January 10th [1967]

Dear Emilie,
    A thought for that 'Speaking Out' feature in the Post:¹ would they be interested in a defence of hard-core pornography?² Naturally, no four-letter words would be involved: I'd simply maintain that it performs a vital social function, can be most enjoyable, and is far less hypocritical than the stuff that claims 'redeeming literary merit'. Could you let me know their reaction?

Love,
Ken

P. S. Can we clear this with Playboy??

¹ *The Saturday Evening Post.*
² 'In Praise of Hard Core' was published in *Esquire*, October 1958.

To Rolf Hochhuth

The National Theatre
January 11th, 1967

Dear Herr Hochhuth,
    Thank you very much for your telegrams. As you will have heard, the National Theatre Board decided to postpone a decision on the play until they had seen the revised text, the prologue and the epilogue. I

am glad to hear from David that you are sending the prologue and epilogue to him shortly.

May I pass on to you one or two points that were raised at the Board meeting?

(1) Lord Chandos (our major enemy) said: 'Of course the Cabinet were worried about the Katyn question in 1943. But it is quite ridiculous to suppose that it would have been necessary to assassinate a dozen people in order to solve the problem. If the government had said to the Poles: 'Don't raise the Katyn question now', they would have agreed at once.'

(2) One member of the Board (Mr. Hugh Beaumont)[1] was in Gibraltar the day after the crash. One of his closest friends – the English actor Anthony Quayle – was Aide-de-Camp to Mason-Macfarlane, and was with him throughout Sikorski's visit. Quayle (whom I have since questioned myself) makes the following statements:

  (i) There was no means of telephoning from Gibraltar to London. I realise that you have introduced a telephone call for theatrical reasons, but it is obviously implausible, and it would be a pity to expose yourself to such easy criticism.

  (ii) Quayle escorted Macfarlane and Sikorski to the aircraft, and he positively states that Macfarlane made no attempt at all to dissuade Sikorski from getting aboard.

  (iii) Maisky[2] did not stay at the governor's house, because the governor personally disliked him. He stayed at the hotel.

  (iv) Maisky's plane took off at lunch-time; Sikorski's plane took off late that night.

  (v) Sikorski's plane did not explode: Quayle was on the airfield and saw it crash. It simply dived into the sea. (All the evidence at the enquiries confirms that no explosion took place.)[3]

  (vi) The plane was massively overloaded when it took off. Although this was not revealed at the enquiries, everyone aboard had been buying huge amounts of whisky and brandy in Cairo (since spirits were almost unobtainable in London), and Quayle says that the amount of cargo on board was enormously overweight.[4]

I thought I should mention these points to you, since they had a marked effect on the Board.

I think it would be an excellent idea if, when David has finished translating the prologue and epilogue, you could come to London and spend an evening or two with Sir Laurence and myself. He is very eager to meet you, as I am myself. Meanwhile, as far as the play is concerned, we have survived our Dunkirk!

Yours sincerely,
Kenneth Tynan

P. S. Mr Quayle is not, incidentally, a pious supporter of Churchill – like many actors, he is almost non-political. Mr. Beaumont did not tell him that the play held Britain responsible for the crash: he simply asked him to describe what he saw and heard.

[1] 'Binkie' Beaumont remained managing director of H. M. Tennent while he was on the National Theatre Board.
[2] Ivan Maisky (1884–1975), Russian Ambassador to London 1932–43. He was returning to Moscow.
[3] The plane reached a height of about fifty feet, levelled off, and began to lose height towards the sea, which it struck after a flight of about 1200 yards. Hochhuth later removed the suggestion that the plane exploded.
[4] There is no evidence to support this.

Memo to Laurence Olivier

[The National Theatre]
12 January 1967

A DELICATE BALANCE[1]

This is beautifully written, an exquisite fandango of despair. English actors could do it easily with mid-Atlantic accents. Casting problem is that all but one of the six characters are in their 50's. Tobias' big speech (pp 159–162) sums up what the play is about – the fact that although we all hate each other, we are stuck with each other. Directed like the best productions of Pinter, it would certainly hold an audience – especially an intelligent and fairly jaded middle-class audience. BUT: Albee's people are so listless, so despondent, so cut off – not only from each other but from the outside world. You're not surprised that they drink, and tremble, and contemplate killing each other: the wonder is that they haven't committed suicide before the curtain rises. If we weren't doing ROSENCRANTZ[2] (another fatalistic play), I think the Albee would be a definite contender for this year. I'd recommend postponing it until 1968.

To John Osborne

[The National Theatre]
13 January 1967

Dear John:

Larry and I can't understand where you saw 'in the national press' that A BOND HONOURED was being withdrawn.[1] As far as we know there has been nothing in the papers about it.

In our booking leaflets, we always put an L alongside a play that is being given its last performance, and you'll notice that we haven't done that with BOND.

The point is that pulling a play out of the repertory doesn't necess-arily mean banishing it for good. The Double Bill[2] has been forced on to the shelf by the impending departure of Maggie [Smith]. Bob [Stephens] is deep in rehearsal for THE DANCE OF DEATH,[3] after which he goes straight into re-rehearsal for MUCH ADO:[4] there's simply no time for him to rehearse with a new Marcela. (Incidentally, MUCH ADO was rested for similar reasons and so was HOBSON'S CHOICE.[5] And there was a time when we had to take BLACK COMEDY and MISS JULIE[6] out of the rep for six months because Maggie was making a film) If Larry had taken a final decision to drop the Double Bill for good, you'd certainly have been the first to know. As it is, it hasn't, which is why we haven't been in touch. O.K?

Love,
[Ken]

P.S. To answer your P.S.: we have already given 51 performances of BOND, as against the 40 stipulated in the contract.

[1] Osborne felt 'this sort of thing is not far removed from rotten old Shaftesbury Avenue' (letter of 12 January 1967).
[2] *A Bond Honoured* and *Black Comedy*, which had entered the repertory on 6 June 1966.
[3] This production of Strindberg's play, with Laurence Olivier in the lead, was directed by Glen Byam Shaw and opened on 21 February 1967.
[4] A production directed by Franco Zeffirelli, starring Maggie Smith and Robert Stephens, which opened on 16 February 1965.
[5] *Hobson's Choice*, by Harold Brighouse, directed by John Dexter, opened on 7 January 1964.

[6] A double-bill which opened in Chichester in July 1965.

To Lord Chandos

[The National Theatre]
13 January 1967

Dear Lord Chandos:

I'm sorry if I stated your position incorrectly;[1] it was probably due to the fact that we were talking on a very indistinct line.

I hear at second hand that the Government may well introduce the Bill[2] fairly soon. Obviously, a great deal would depend on when the Second Reading took place. It seems extremely unlikely that we could put the play on before November: do you think it is reasonable to hope that the Second Reading would have happened by then? While I agree with you that a rancorous debate would not be desirable, a debate of some kind might not be altogether harmful if it enabled the Minister to lay it down as a principle that the artistic direction of the National Theatre is wholly autonomous and not subject to political pressure from the Government (or any other source).[3]

I had not, as you rightly say, considered the position of the GLC.[4] It does, however, seem fairly obvious that the Conservatives would look rather foolish if one of their first acts on gaining control of the Council were to curtail the activities of one of London's principal cultural amenities.

On the general question of whether we should give critics sticks to beat us with, I feel that from time to time this may be a very healthy thing to do. On the whole, I would rather be attacked by would-be censors than patted on the head.

It will obviously be necessary to submit the script to Sir Arthur Harris. I thought it wise, however, to consult Sir Robert Saundby first. He thought that it would be a sensible precaution to correct any technical details relating to RAF procedure, nomenclature, etc, before sending the script to Harris. These corrections are now being made. A further point is that Harris also makes a brief appearance in the prologue, on which the translator is now at work. And within two – or at most three weeks – the entire text (complete with revisions relating to Harris) should be available. I should have thought – and I hope you agree – that it would be pointless to ask Sir Arthur to read it before then – since if he does, he will only have to plough through it again immediately afterwards. Please let me know if you think I am interpreting the wishes of the Board too loosely.

There is, of course, Hochhuth's own position to be considered. I am sure he would be opposed to our submitting an incomplete and unrevised script which might needlessly prejudice Sir Arthur when he came to read the revised version.

Yours sincerely
[Kenneth Tynan]

[1] The Chairman had told his Board that KPT (in his memorandum of 7 January 1967) had misrepresented his views on the effect that staging *Soldiers* might have on the building of the National Theatre. The Government, he said, were already committed to this. What the play would jeopardize was the amount of future subsidies.
[2] The amendment to the National Theatre Act 1949 was not introduced until October 1968, and passed in March 1969; it authorized the Secretary of State to make contributions 'not exceeding £3,750,000' to the cost of building and equipping the National Theatre.
[3] Chandos replied (17 January 1967) that such a position was 'untenable'. 'No public authority can vote money to any institution and then disclaim all responsibility for the way in which it is spent.'
[4] The Greater London Council also contributed £3,750,000 to the building.

To Lord Chandos

[The National Theatre]
19 January 1967

Dear Lord Chandos:
Just two points:

1. About artistic autonomy: the Arts Council grants this to all the theatres and companies it supports. Do you think the National Theatre should be an exception?

2. Nobody in the Cabinet – indeed, no politician except yourself – has read the script. Sir Robert Saundby has not been 'lobbied': the translator and I merely consulted him on the accuracy of the text in relation to Air Force matters.

Yours
[Kenneth Tynan]

To Rolf Hochhuth

[The National Theatre]
20 January 1967

Dear Herr Hochhuth,

Very many thanks for your admirable replies to my questions. I do apologise for seeming to cross-examine you, but I am becoming as fascinated by this subject as you are. May I comment on two points you raise:

1. Maisky in Gibraltar. Anthony Quayle definitely states (and this is confirmed by the Sikorski Institute's booklet on the Gibraltar crash) that Maisky arrived in Gibraltar very early in the morning of July 4 and left a few hours later, at 9.30 am. So the fact is that he stayed neither at the hotel nor with the Governor. Mr Quayle was in fact instructed to take him on a sight-seeing tour of Gibraltar in the car, which he did.

2. The question of the explosion. Lieutenant Lubienski, the Polish liaison officer in Gibraltar, witnessed the crash and said in his report: 'It started to fall as if gliding down towards the sea. We hoped the pilot would have time to lift the nose of the aircraft. Unfortunately, dead silence followed. The pilot had cut off the engines in order to avoid an explosion.'
   This is confirmed by Quayle, who was also at the airport.
   Major Dudzinski, an officer in the Polish Air Force, was sent from London to investigate the circumstances of the crash. On August 10 he said in a report that the plane 'turned over and sank within five or six minutes after impact.' The first rescue boats arrived a few minutes later and saved the pilot who was floating in his life-jacket. There is no mention of an explosion in Dudzinski's report.
   If I understand you correctly, you say that only a few of the bodies were recovered. Surely this isn't the case? All the official enquiries showed that eleven bodies were recovered out of the sixteen who were killed. Also, I am not quite clear what you mean when you refer to the condition of the corpses. Do you mean that they were mutilated? If so, they were not disfigured beyond all recognition. Lieutenant Lubienski (whom I mention above) was present when the first corpses were brought to the shore. He says: 'I recognised the bodies of the Commander-in-Chief (Sikorski) and his Chief-of-Staff, General Klimecki.'
   Incidentally, do you think that the frogman¹ was in any way

connected with the plot? It might be significant that although there was a search for the elevator control equipment (which was supposed to have jammed), this vital piece of evidence was never found.

3. One final question. Do you really think there is great significance in the nationality of the pilot?[2] He was, after all, quite badly injured, and there could have been no guarantee that he would not be killed.

To conclude, I think you have refuted Lord Chandos' arguments decisively. I am looking forward to asking him when he last saw Sikorski alive.

Yours sincerely,
Kenneth Tynan

[1] British airman Derek Qualtrough, one of the first to reach the scene of the crash, was surprised to find a man in a canoe already there, no doubt the mysterious 'frogman' referred to.
[2] Edward Prchal, a Czech Flight Lieutenant. He was in no way responsible for the crash.

To Lord Chandos

[The National Theatre]
23 January 1967

Dear Lord Chandos:
Just three more points:

1. On the subject of artistic autonomy, we are in a semantic tangle. It is obvious, as you say, that 'autonomous bodies are subject to political pressures', in the sense that they are subject to legislation that is enacted by Parliament. What I meant – to phrase it more precisely – is that the artistic policy of the National Theatre should not be subject to interference <u>on political grounds</u>.

2. I don't recall having said that I had 'talked to' two Cabinet ministers. All I did was to put out feelers through a third party, to find out approximately when we may expect the new National Theatre Bill to be placed before the House, and whether they felt that the future prospects of the NT might be endangered if the Bill were not unopposed.

3. About Harris: you misunderstood me if you thought I said that Harris was complaisant. All I said was that in Sir Robert Saundby's opinion Harris would certainly not sue and might not even bother to read the script.

Yours,
[Kenneth Tynan]

To Emilie Jacobson

20 Thurloe Square
London, S.W.7[1]
February 27, 1967

Dear Emilie,

(1) Delighted to hear that Playboy will accept 2,000 words on hard-core pornography.

(2) Last Wednesday a suitcase of mine was stolen from a train: it contained fifty selected letters from people like Hemingway, Thurber, Dietrich, Brando, Welles, Katie Hepburn, etc., which I was going to use as the basis of my 'Talent Snob' piece. I have offered a reward for their return but the chances are minute. The point is that these letters were to have been the raw material for the piece, and I have no copies. What I would like to do is write the pornography piece next, followed by War Crimes, and make these my last two pieces under the present Playboy contract. (I could get around to 'Talent Snobism' later, but I'd have to approach it from a radically different angle.) I hope this reshuffle is OK with Playboy.

(3) Could we postpone a decision about my future with Playboy until Spectorsky brings it up? Frankly, I'm not sure that I can afford to forego the monthly cheque.

(4) Could you confirm with Don Erickson that I will do the Radziwill piece under a pseudonym to be agreed?[2] The terms sound excellent. As you say, the best plan would be for Esquire simply to send me the air fare in advance in the form of a cheque.

(5) About the Playboy round-trip offer: you might tell them that the Montreal World Fair[3] are flying me over to America anyway, and so I won't need another sponsor. The main thing, I suppose,

will be to avoid bumping into Playboy people while I'm in Chicago.

Love,
Ken.

[1] We had just bought and moved into this corner house in South Kensington.
[2] Lee Radziwill, sister of Jacqueline Kennedy, was preparing to play Tracy Lord in *The Philadelphia Story* in Chicago. Don Erikson of *Esquire* asked KPT to fly over and review it; the pseudonym was in order to get around *Playboy*'s exclusive contract. The piece was never written.
[3] KPT was in Montreal for EXPO 18–22 June and spoke on the National Theatre on 19 June.

To Alan Dent[1]

[The National Theatre]
9 March 1967

Dear Jock:
    Not only do I know the Agate review of THE DANCE OF DEATH, I actually had it set up in type to go in the programme. But then Larry and I re-read it and decided that it didn't fit into the way we were approaching the piece. James Agate says the leading characters are insane monsters who could only exist in Strindberg's demented brain (Iago marries Medea, etc.). But Larry and I regard the play as a wholly realistic study of marriage red in tooth and claw. In fact, there are whole passages that take me back to dear old Notley.[2] In view of all this, we decided to drop the piece rather than confuse the audience.

All love,
[Kenneth Tynan]

[1] Alan Dent (b. 1905), drama critic for a number of publications and author of books on Vivien Leigh and Laurence Olivier. See letter of Monday [September 1948].
[2] Notley Abbey, near Bicester, the country house of Olivier and Vivien Leigh whose marital rows were witnessed by KPT, a weekend visitor in 1958.

To Air Marshal Sir Robert Saundby

[The National Theatre]
15 March 1967

Dear Sir Robert,

At long last, Rolf Hochhuth has revised and completed his play. Copies are now being made, one of which should be in your hands immediately after Easter. Sir Laurence and I would be enormously grateful if you could find time to have a look at it. I think (and hope) you will find that the errors you pointed out to us have been satisfactorily corrected. There's one major exception – the attribution to Sir Arthur Harris of your own interest in lepidoptery. You will see from the Epilogue that the author has rather ingeniously admitted that this is a deliberate mistake, and provided a dramatic justification for making it.

I would be particularly glad to hear your comments on the passages relating to Harris, since our next step must obviously be to ask him to read the play. My own view is that there is now nothing offensive in Hochhuth's treatment of Harris; I am especially pleased to see that he has removed that unfortunate joke about monkeys climbing trees![1] You have already been so helpful to us that I hate to be importunate, but the National Theatre Board is meeting on April 24 to reach a decision on the play, and I have been asked to ascertain Sir Arthur's reaction by that date if possible. As we agreed, I don't propose to submit the play to him until I have heard your reactions. I should therefore be extremely grateful if we could arrange a meeting as soon as possible. I shall be available to come and see you whenever you wish.

Meanwhile, may I thank you in advance, on behalf of Sir Laurence and myself, for your time and trouble.

Yours sincerely,
[Kenneth Tynan]

[1] A proverb: 'The higher the monkey climbs, the more he showeth his arse.'

To Rolf Hochhuth

[The National Theatre]
15 March 1967

Dear Herr Hochhuth:

Many thanks for the enormous trouble you have taken to get the script completed for us. It is now being typed for distribution to our

Committee. Incidentally, the meeting of the Committee has been postponed until April 24, since Sir Laurence will be on tour outside London in the early part of the month.

May I ask you one or two questions about the epilogue?

1. Are you quite sure that it is theatrically a good idea for all the military men to be drunk? Doesn't it turn them into rather obvious caricatures? To my mind the most horrific thing about militarists is their superficial reasonableness. Having seen a play like the Mystery Cycle,[1] they would probably react with calm benevolence, and explain to Dorland[2] (as if he were an idiot child) that although they respect his sincerity, he must understand that his proposals are quite out of touch with political reality, etc., etc. This is how Saundby reacted to the first draft of the play – and his calm inhumanity frightened me far more than drunken belligerence would have done! If the American, for instance, were a suave, deceptively genial Pentagon type, wouldn't you be able to make your point more effectively?

2. Isn't it strange that nobody refers to Sikorski in the Epilogue? To omit all mention of the Sikorski incident might look as if you were evading the issue. Is it possible that Dorland's son could bring it up?

3. When Harris accuses Dorland of historical inaccuracy, Dorland compares the relationship between playwright and historian to that between a business man and the Income Tax officials:
   'If he doesn't give them one or two little
      things to worry over,
   They get really inquisitive.'
   But this implies that the business man has much more to hide than he is admitting. And that the playwright confesses to small errors in order to conceal big ones! Surely this is not what you are trying to say?[3]

Forgive these queries –
And, once again, my heartfelt thanks.

Yours,
[Kenneth Tynan]

---

[1] The 'play within a play' in *Soldiers*.
[2] A character in the Prologue directing the play within a play.

[3] As the Epilogue was dropped in the London version of the play, these lines are not in the published English version (1968).

To Emilie Jacobson

20 Thurloe Square
March 17, 1967

Dear Emilie,

Suppose I wanted to drop everything and take a few months off to write a book. Are there any Foundations in the States that offer fellowships to which Englishmen can apply? If so, could you possibly let me have some information about them. And I promise you that Curtis Brown will handle the book!

[pp Ken][1]

[1] Emilie Jacobson promised (20 March 1967) to do some research and asked what kind of book KPT had in mind. KPT replied (29 March 1967) that he wished to research a book on the Mediterranean coastline; alternatively an autobiography 'not only of myself, but of my generation at Oxford'. On 7 April Jacobson reminded KPT he already had a contract with Atheneum for an autobiographical project with an advance of $1500 payable on demand. These plans did not materialize.

To Rolf Hochhuth

[The National Theatre]
29 March 1967

Dear Herr Hochhuth:

Before our Board meeting on April 24, I should like to offer a suggestion.

You will, I hope, be aware how very personally I have become involved in DIE SOLDATEN; I cannot recall when I have ever been more impressed by a new play. At present I think there is a good chance that the Board will allow the National Theatre to do the play; but lately I have been wondering what will happen if the Board turns it down.

It would obviously be disastrous if the play were to be presented in London by a management that was not wholly in sympathy with its content. And from your point of view it would be tedious to begin all over again with a new group of people, going over the text line by line, answering familiar questions, producing your evidence, etc, etc. Perhaps (I do not know) you may want to offer the play to the Royal Shakespeare Company. But before you make any decisions, I should like you to consider another possibility.

It is as follows: if the Board says no, John Dexter and I would like to present the play in London ourselves – either under our own management or as a co-production with a management we both trust. Dexter (who directed the Olivier OTHELLO, Peter Shaffer's ROYAL HUNT OF THE SUN, and BLACK COMEDY, HOBSON'S CHOICE, Osborne's A BOND HONOURED, etc, for the National Theatre) has just resigned his job as Associate Director of the National Theatre.[1] From the very beginning he has been a passionate supporter of DIE SOLDATEN and he has always wanted to direct it. [...]

Naturally, I hope this whole plan will be superfluous, and that the Board behaves sensibly. Nevertheless, I would be glad to know whether it appeals to you. I have not mentioned it to anyone else, and it would perhaps be best if you regarded it as confidential until the April 24 meeting has taken place. Meanwhile, I look forward to hearing from you.

With Best Wishes,
Yours sincerely,
[Kenneth Tynan][2]

[1] Dexter's resignation came after a falling out with Olivier unconnected with *Soldiers*.
[2] Hochhuth replied giving KPT rights to mount the play in English.

To Air Marshal Sir Arthur Harris

[The National Theatre]
30 March 1967

Dear Sir Arthur:

On behalf of Sir Laurence Olivier, I'm sending you the text of Rolf Hochhuth's new play, 'Soldiers', which we are considering for presentation at the National Theatre.

As you will see, you appear as a character in the play and it is for this reason that I am writing to you. We have naturally submitted the text to the Lord Chamberlain's office: and although we haven't yet received his comments, he normally requires – when living people are represented on stage – that permission should be sought from the person concerned. Failing such permission, he generally rules that the production should not take place.

Sir Laurence and I would therefore be extremely grateful if you could spare the time to read the play and to let us know whether we have your permission to proceed. I should like to emphasise that we are more than willing to consider any cuts or alterations which you may think necessary or desirable in the passages relating to yourself. (In any case – as you will appreciate from the sheer bulk of the text – a good deal of cutting will have to take place if the audience is to get home before dawn.) The author is similarly open to suggestions. He has already corrected several factual errors that were pointed out by Sir Robert Saundby, who was kind enough to vet the first drafts of the script for us. [...]

Yours sincerely,
[Kenneth Tynan][1]

---

[1] Sir Arthur Harris wrote to Lord Chandos (18 April 1967) that he found 'the whole thing thoroughly objectionable with references to me', and thought it an insult to the bomber crews who 'at such bitter cost in casualties, we know saved this country from being the first recipient of the atom bomb and, therefore, from inevitable defeat'. He had no intention of giving permission.

To the Assistant Comptroller, the Lord Chamberlain's Office[1]

[The National Theatre]
10 April 1967

Dear Sir,

SOLDIERS by Rolf Hochhuth

I am at a loss to understand your communication of April 6. Nothing in the Theatres Act (1843) stipulates that a theatre manager must guarantee production of a play before the Lord Chamberlain expresses an opinion on it. I am therefore compelled to repeat my request, which is made to you on behalf of Sir Laurence Olivier and the Board of the National Theatre: will you kindly fulfil the function laid down for your office in law – namely, that of informing us whether or not you will grant a licence for the public performance of the play in question?

To drive the point home still more clearly: whether or not the

National Theatre subsequently decides to present the play is – quite obviously – none of the Lord Chamberlain's business.

The reasons for your procrastination are, of course, perfectly obvious. The implication is that you propose to judge the play by one standard if it is presented at the National Theatre, and by another standard if the National Theatre decides against it and some other management undertakes the production. This is quite clearly an indefensible attitude for your office to take. I need hardly tell you that there would be considerable outcry in the press and in the theatre as a whole if it became known that the Lord Chamberlain's office was granting favours to the subsidised theatres which it withheld from commercial theatre.

Yours faithfully
[Kenneth Tynan][2]

[1] Sir John Johnston. The Lord Chamberlain had written to Lord Chandos (12 January 1967) asking to have 'a private and informal word' about the play. The Assistant Comptroller had written to KPT (19 January 1967) that he had read the manuscript of *Soldiers* but was not prepared to make any comment until a final script was formally submitted by the Board of the National Theatre. On 5 April Chandos wrote to Cobbold saying that KPT was authorized to submit plays to the Lord Chamberlain's Office. Chandos said it was his view, however, that on a controversial matter the Chamberlain was 'entitled to ask that the play should be submitted to the Board before you give an opinion'.
[2] On 14 April Johnston replied that it was only obligatory to give a decision when the play was submitted by 'the Master or Manager of the theatre'.

To William Shawn

20 Thurloe Square
April 14, 1967

Dear Mr. Shawn,

A small problem has arisen on which I would like your opinion. It concerns my piece on the English theatre, which is due for delivery before May 31st.

Naturally I'll be talking at length in the piece about the National Theatre, for whom I work. But between now and the end of May my whole relationship with the company may have changed. For nearly a year now, I have been working with a translator on the script of a new play by Rolf Hochhuth, who wrote 'The Representative'. His new piece deals with a controversial wartime episode in the life of Winston Churchill, and frankly I think it's a masterpiece.

The problem is that the Chairman of the Board of the National Theatre is Lord Chandos, who was a member of the War Cabinet at the time of the events that Hochhuth is discussing. He and the other members of the Board have now read the play and are meeting at the end of April to decide whether Olivier and I will be allowed to present it. If they decide against it, I shall very probably resign.

As you will realize, the piece I might write as an employee of the National Theatre would be very different from the piece I'd want to write after resigning from it. And the difference would not be minor; the two most important features of English theatre life today are the National Theatre and the Royal Shakespeare Company and whatever I write about these two will be the lion's share of the piece. And I shan't know until the beginning of May whether I shall be writing as an outsider or an insider.

I am wondering, therefore, whether you would consider giving me an extra 2 or 3 weeks to finish the piece, without sacrificing the quantity bonus? It is, after all, a double length piece, and until I know where I stand vis-à-vis the National Theatre it's difficult even to start it with much assurance.

Do let me know how you feel about all this. I'll be letting you have the Italian piece[1] within a few weeks.

Yours sincerely,
Kenneth Tynan

[1] 'The Theatre Abroad: Italy' (*New Yorker*, 21 October 1967).

To Mr Ivor Lewis[1]

[The National Theatre]
17 April 1967

Dear Mr Lewis:

Forgive me for taking you back rather a long way, but I have just been reading your church issue of the Sunday Times Magazine, and I noticed your statement to the effect that Bishop Bell of Chichester 'would have succeeded to Canterbury if he hadn't spoken out against saturation bombing when he did'.[2] I wonder if you could tell me what your authority was for saying this? I'm particularly interested because Bell is a character in a new play on saturation bombing which the National Theatre is considering at the moment. I'd be most grateful for any help you can give me.

Yours sincerely,
[Kenneth Tynan][3]

[1] Assistant Editor, *Sunday Times* Magazine.

[2] In the *Diocesan Gazette* (September 1943) Bishop Bell had written: 'To bomb cities as cities, deliberately to attack civilians, quite irrespective of whether or not they are actively contributing to the war effort, is a wrong deed, whether done by the Nazis or by ourselves.'

[3] Lewis replied (21 April 1967) that he had written from several sources but that what he wrote about Bell was correct.

The weekend before the crucial board meeting on 24 April which would decide the fate of Soldiers *(now completed, with prologue and epilogue), Ken and Rolf Hochhuth went to stay with the Oliviers in Brighton. The thirty-seven-year-old playwright, modest in manner, scholarly, and somewhat paranoiac, explained that he had chosen to live with his family in Basel, rather than in Germany, after the strong reaction to his play about the Pope. He said that the idea of* Soldiers *was suggested to him by an article by the historian David Irving, author of* The Destruction of Dresden. *Carlos Thompson (the Argentinian actor husband of the German actress Lilli Palmer), a friend of the Oliviers, was there as translator.*

On the train to London on Monday morning, Olivier chose passages from Aristotle's Poetics, *which he later read at the Board meeting: 'The poet's function is to describe not the thing that has happened but a kind of thing that might happen, i.e. what is possible as being probable or necessary.'*

That afternoon the Board ignored both Aristotle and Olivier's request to be granted more time to work on the play. At one point the Chairman brought up the matter of Ken's memorandum of 7 January in which he stated that he had consulted a number of contemporary historians, and that their view of the Sikorski plot was 'very much an open verdict'. At the 9 January meeting, when asked if Professor Hugh Trevor-Roper had been consulted, Ken had replied, 'Yes.' Chandos now wanted to know why he had failed to inform the Board that Trevor-Roper had dismissed any possibility of Sikorski being murdered for political reasons. The Literary Manager said that he had deliberately postponed going into detail about the views expressed by individual historians until the play should be discussed again. He said that according to his notes, which he had in his hand, Trevor-Roper's comment was that the theory was 'bizarre'.

By the end of a long afternoon the eight-member Board – already canvassed by Lord Chandos – unanimously decided that the play was unsuitable for production at the National Theatre, and a press release to this effect was dictated. 'Some of the characters,' Chandos had written into the statement, 'in particular Sir Winston Churchill and Lord Cherwell, were grossly maligned.' Olivier said he would like to add a comment. Chandos replied, 'I don't think that's necessary.' 'I'd like to say that I'm unhappy about the decision,' Olivier said. Here a member of the Board, Sir Kenneth Clark, cut in with, 'Oh let him be unhappy if he wants to.' Thus Olivier was allowed to add his dissent to the bulletin.

The press were critical; not even The Times *offered support to Lord Chandos, who in turn commented that 'there are matters of judgment which the artistic directors are not completely fit to decide.' Olivier announced that he deplored the Board's decision. What he really deplored, more than the loss of the play, was his Chairman's arrogant stance.*

From the Royal Shakespeare Theatre, Peter Hall declared that it was a 'black and miserable day for the English theatre'. Ken wondered whether to resign and decided not. He made a note to himself: 'If one's country is held by an occupying army, that is no reason to desert it. That is what they would like.' He and Olivier now decided that they would mount Soldiers *in the West End, outside the National.*

To Rolf Hochhuth

[The National Theatre]
28 April 1967

Dear Rolf:

You will have heard all the news by now, and I needn't tell you how sickened I was by the behaviour of Chandos and his henchmen. The result has been a nasty defeat for the National Theatre, but Larry and I are determined to turn it into a victory for your play.

I expect you will have heard what we have in mind, but in case you haven't, let me tell you what we propose. The idea is to put the play on under the auspices of a company[1] that Larry set up many years ago and which has been inactive since he joined the National Theatre. The new directors of the company will be Larry, myself, Peter Hall (of the Royal Shakespeare Company) and William Gaskill (of the Royal Court

Theatre). Thus the play will be presented with the full and explicit backing of England's three leading state theatres. It is the least we can do to demonstrate that, whatever the reactionaries may do or say, our theatre as a whole is behind you.

Larry has gone to Canada for the weekend to take part in the opening ceremonies of the Montreal Exhibition, but as soon as he gets back his lawyers will get to work re-constituting the company and preparing contracts for you and David.

The aim, naturally, will be to get the play on as soon as possible after the Berlin opening, bearing in mind that Larry will be touring Canada with the National Theatre Company until the middle of November. Although he will not be directing SOLDIERS himself, I expect he will want to keep his eye on the last few weeks of rehearsals, and this will mean that the earliest opening date would be early December. Do you think it would be at all possible for the Volksbühne to postpone the première for a week or two, so as to bring it nearer our opening date?

I have, incidentally, made it clear to the English press that any revisions you make will not in any way affect or modify the arguments of the play.

I immensely enjoyed meeting you last weekend at Brighton, and it will be nice to renew the experience in more relaxed circumstances. The sooner, the better.

Very sincerely
[Kenneth Tynan]

---

[1] The St James's Players.

To the Editor, *The Times*

20 Thurloe Square
[Published 4 May, 1967]

Sir,—Lord Chandos asks (May 2) why 'absolute and complete power' should be vested in one man to run a National Theatre.[1] In asking this question he begs another. The director's power can never be 'absolute and complete', since it is limited by the subsidy given to him by the state and the local authorities, and by the function that the theatre he directs was created to perform.

Within these limits, however, he should have full authority, for the simple reason that – as history amply demonstrates – there is no other way to run a theatre effectively. Ships are not captained by committees. Navies, of course, may well benefit from committee rule: but this is an argument in favour of an Arts Council, not of a National Theatre Board.

What is needed, if any state-subsidized theatre is to operate without friction, is a clear separation of powers – between the public element in the enterprise, which should keep an eye on expenditure and the broad outlines of stated policy (in the National Theatre's case, a policy of presenting the best plays of all periods), and the artistic directorate, in whose realm all specific decisions on repertoire and casting should lie. (Unlike Lord Chandos, I do not subscribe to the patronizing myth that men of the theatre are unqualified to make responsible judgments on matters of serious consequence.) In course of time the director may lose the confidence of the public and the critics. If so, the state can always give him the sack. But it must first give him the freedom to be proved wrong.

While we are discussing the director's function in a state-subsidized theatre, it may be relevant to open another question: what, precisely, is the function of the board? The usual argument is that an independent board is a safeguard against state interference. But the National Theatre Board is not independent: its members are appointed by the Department of Education and Science. If a bulwark is required between the National Theatre and the party in power, that bulwark is surely the Arts Council.

No paternalistic boards sit in judgment on the activities of the Comédie Française, the Théâtre de France or the Théâtre National Populaire. In this country, likewise, *je n'en vois pas la nécessité*. A rational solution might be for the director of the National Theatre to be appointed by the Arts Council, in consultation with the D.E.S. He and his staff would then hold regular meetings with representatives of these two bodies and of the G.L.C. They would make sure that he justified his budgetary demands, and otherwise leave him alone to get on with the job.

I need hardly add that these are my personal opinions, and not necessarily those of the National Theatre authorities.

Yours sincerely,
KENNETH TYNAN[2]

---

[1] Chandos continued: 'Those who advocate this form of authoritarianism or dictatorship in the arts would be the first to condemn it elsewhere.'

[2] In another letter to *The Times*, written on 5 May, Laurence Olivier criticized the Board on two points: '(a) I think they should have respected my request for more time to work on [*Soldiers*] ... and (b) the Chairman expounded what amounted to a forcefully one-sided view of my ambivalent contract in his letter (May 2)'.

To the Editor, the *Sunday Times*

[20 Thurloe Square]
[Published 7 May 1967]

Sir,—I'd just like to comment on two points raised by Lord Chandos in his interview with Francis Wyndham about Rolf Hochhuth's play:

(1) *'It's perfectly absurd, but all the documents relevant to the Sikorski incident are deposited in a Swiss bank, not to be opened for 50 years.'*

This is wrong. Nearly all of the vast pile of relevant documents will be published by Hochhuth when the play is presented later in the year. The only exceptions are one or two cases where publication might jeopardise living informants. (Hochhuth followed the same procedure with his first play, 'The Representative'.)

(2) *'... I think it's very odd that Mr Tynan should conduct a campaign against his chairman and board while retaining his salary.'*

It would indeed be odd if the National Theatre were an industrial concern in which the chairman and board were majority share-holders. Happily, it is nothing of the sort. My first loyalty is to the National Theatre, not to its board.[1] *Pace* the chairman, the two are not necessarily identical.

Kenneth Tynan

[1] This remark infuriated Lord Chandos.

Memo to Laurence Olivier

[The National Theatre]
1 June 1967

1. Peter Weiss writes to say his new play[1] will be finished and available for inspection in mid-June. It has 15 characters, including two women.

2. Nigel Dennis[2] has read the Goldoni[3] and would very much like to adapt it.

3. I'm going to make a speech about the theatre at Expo on June 19. After that Kathleen and I thought we'd go to New York and get married,[4] have two weeks' honeymoon and get back to London July 16. Is this OK with you?

[K. T.]

[1] Peter Weiss (1916–82), German playwright, novelist, painter and filmmaker, author of *Marat/Sade*; *Song of the Lusitanian Bogey* (1966) was a surrealist allegory about Angola.
[2] Nigel Dennis (b. 1912), English novelist and playwright of works including *Cards of Identity* (novel 1955, play 1958).
[3] Three plays by Carlo Goldoni (1709–93) which KPT hoped Giorgio Strehler, co-founder of the Piccolo Teatro in Milan, would direct.
[4] We were married on 30 June in Englewood, New Jersey. Marlene Dietrich was matron of honour. Penelope Gilliatt took the photographs and the songwriter Steve Vinaver made the jokes.

To Ingmar Bergman[1]

[The National Theatre]
12 June 1967

Dear Mr Bergman:

Sir Laurence Olivier has asked me to approach you with a suggestion. In February 1968, the National Theatre is going to present a production of Ibsen's THE PRETENDERS, with Sir Laurence as Skule and Sir John Gielgud as Bishop Nicholas. Sir Laurence and I would be delighted if you would consider coming to London to direct it. Please let me know if the idea appeals to you. It excites us enormously: and our company would, I know, be thrilled by the prospect of working with you.

Apart from Sir Laurence and Sir John, no decisions on casting have been taken: these would be matters for discussion between yourself and Sir Laurence. The choice of a designer, of course, would be entirely up to you.

As far as the translation is concerned, we have commissioned an English version of the play from Tom Stoppard,[2] the young English author whose first play, ROSENCRANTZ AND GUILDENSTERN ARE DEAD, has just entered our repertoire with tremendous success.

I look forward to hearing whether you will be able to accept our invitation.[3]

Yours sincerely,
[Kenneth Tynan]

[1] Ingmar Berman (b. 1918), Swedish film director who gained international recognition in the mid-1950s for *The Seventh Seal* and *Wild Strawberries*; he has also directed theatre and opera in Sweden and abroad.
[2] Tom Stoppard (b. 1937), Czech born English playwright whose later works include *Travesties* (1974) and *Arcadia* (1993).
[3] *The Pretenders* was never done. Bergman would direct *Hedda Gabler* for the National Theatre, with Maggie Smith, which opened 29 June 1970.

Memo to Laurence Olivier

[The National Theatre]
13 June 1967

Dear L:
  It's going to be marvellous.[1]

Act 1 Bob's entrance:[2] too confident, assured, smug? Wouldn't he be a little less assertive in a strange house?

Paul:[3] now and then I feel Chebutikin should be more of a buffoon, more bear-like, perhaps more extrovert. 'Look how small I am!': isn't this, for example, meant to be a boisterous joke?

Kenneth's first entrance:[4] I think he's overplaying the fussy pedant too farcically. (He gets much better later on.) Also, I'm sorry his line about the carpets and curtains has gone. Moura's[5] idea about replacing it with 'covers on the furniture' seems a good one.

Joan and Bob: perhaps this is deliberate, but I didn't feel anything starting between them in Act 1.

Act 2 Paul: 'Balzac was married in Berdichev' – more sudden and emphatic, cutting more strongly across the previous dialogue. (In fact, I hardly heard him say it.)

Is it clear that Natasha has broken up the party? As staged, it's hard to tell.

When Anfisa tells Irina that the carnival people have arrived, oughtn't we to hear a guitar and some singing offstage – to get a sense of gaiety going on <u>somewhere</u>? (Moura agrees with me on this.)

Act 3 (Just an observation but watching this scene I realised what the fire symbolises. It's all the banked-down, unexpressed, unfulfilled emotion in these people's lives bursting suddenly into destr[uct]ive flames.)

Paul: his speech after breaking the clock ('Maybe I didn't break it – it only seems as though I had!') – surely the lines are meant to be funny – a big boorish drunken joke?

Act 4 Louise:[6] might she do a sudden little shiver to lead into the line: 'Everything frightens me today'?

Andrey:[7] how about 'prickly' instead of 'bristly-coated'?

The Irina–Tusenbach farewell: this somehow wasn't as moving as I expected. Is it because Louise is playing it <u>as if she knows the ending is going to be tragic</u>? For the first half of the scene she must surely be quite composed and matter-of-fact – so that we almost want to shout out and tell her that Tusenbach's going to be killed. The more normal she is, the more we feel for him. Even <u>after</u> the piano and key bit, I feel her line: 'What should I say to you? What?' should be gentle not pitying.

Vershinin's farewell to Olga: I know he's nervously waiting for Masha, but at present Bob behaves rather as if he's taking his leave after a pleasant weekend rather than a three year stay. In other words, he's too formal and polite: oughtn't he to be more serious and meditative and caring? 'I've become a part of you', etc. – this is a goodbye to an old friend and he means it.

I do hope you'll keep Paul on to the end: he's the old, unregenerate, idle Russia that the sisters will never escape.

I realise you want the girls drifting off like ghosts at the end to echo their entrance, but I think it's a bit dangerous. After all, the point is that others come and go: they stay. Life moves on: they don't. They are static: we can see the future, but they can't. (If they're going to move, could they perhaps do it after the last line rather than before?)

K. T.

---

[1] Olivier's production of Anton Chekhov's *The Three Sisters*, starring Joan Plowright as Masha, which opened on 4 July 1967.

² Robert Stephens as Vershinin.
³ Paul Curran as Chebutikin.
⁴ Kenneth Mackintosh as Kullighin.
⁵ Moura Budberg (1892–1974) translated *The Three Sisters*. A Russian baroness and intellectual, she was the mistress of Maxim Gorki and H.G. Wells.
⁶ Louise Purnell as Irina.
⁷ Anthony Hopkins as Andrey Sergeyevich Prosorov.

To Peter Hall

20 Thurloe Square
London, S. W.7
16 June 1967

Dear Peter:

I've just talked to Peter Brook, from whom I gather you aren't altogether happy about the Hochhuth situation.

First of all, I'm astonished and apologetic to hear that you never got the script. Larry certainly meant to send it to you, and must have forgotten; as you may have guessed from the weekend's news,[1] he's been a bit preoccupied lately. Anyway, I apologise on his behalf.

Before the board meeting at which the play was rejected, Larry and I had obviously considered alternative courses of action. Clearly, a production under Larry's auspices was the best face-saver, since it would leave no doubt that he hadn't lost faith in the play. Rolf welcomed the idea, and said that at all costs he wanted Larry to continue to be associated with the play. He also wrote in a letter to me: 'I leave the English and American rights in your hands.' So naturally we went ahead and drew up a contract. It was Larry who suggested inviting you and Bill to join himself and me as directors of St James's Players.

I'm sorry we contacted Peter Brook without first talking to you, but I'd heard from David MacDonald that Lars Schmidt[2] was approaching Peter to do the Paris production, and it seemed only logical to jump in as soon as possible with an invitation to do the London one instead – especially as you had given your blessing to the venture. I accordingly phoned Peter earlier this week to explore the ground, and found that he was already reading the script that MacDonald had given him for Lars Schmidt.

I do hope you'll forgive our faulty communication system, especially in recent weeks; and I hope that it will be possible for

Peter to do the play with your approval under our joint auspices.

Love,
[Ken]

[1] It was announced in the press that Laurence Olivier was being treated with radiotherapy for cancer of the prostate.
[2] Swedish film producer and third husband of Ingrid Bergman.

To A.C. Spectorsky

Hotel Algonquin
59 West 44th Street
New York NY 10036
June 27 [1967]

Dear Spec –

Both afloat and ashore (where I was more than once slightly afloat) you and Theo[1] gave us a wonderful time in Chicago, and we're terribly grateful. Manhattan seems fetid by comparison, and much less efficient, too – everything (and nearly everybody) seems rusty and polluted. The old theory is true: civilisation really does move westward – Athens to Rome to Paris to London to N.Y. to Chicago.

Marriage preparations are preoccupying us here to the exclusion of almost everything else, but I thought I'd jot down a list of the ideas we (i.e. you and Jim Goode[2] and I) discussed for Playboy pieces:

(1) Open letter to an American Liberal (about Vietnam). I'll get down to this as soon as I'm back in London. Jim suggested that an American liberal might be invited to reply. How about Norman Podhoretz?[3]

(2) The Social History of Underwear[4] – from Queen Victoria to the miniskirt. This would be moderately documented and wholly deadpan. I told Jim that I'd be grateful for any help your researchers could give me in establishing when American womanhood first encased itself in drawers. Most of the books on the subject are confined to European underwear.

(3) Either (a) The Homosexual Mafia[5] – a study of the faggot influence on the arts, with historical evidence tending to assure the American public that there is no cause for panic, since the arts have always been natural havens for sexual misfits. One query (if that is the right

word): do you think I should concentrate on the performing arts, or take in painting, sculpture and fiction as well? I incline to the former, with passing glances at the latter.

Or (b): Politics and the Sexual Revolution. Can you change society without first changing sexual mores? Does the paternalistic, authoritarian state depend on the survival of its microcosm – the paternalistic family hierarchy? This is an idea based on Wilhelm Reich.[6]

Both of these subjects appeal to me. I'd be grateful if you could tell me which you prefer.

(4) Interview. My suggestion was Katharine Hepburn, despite your antipathy. As I told you, Kate to me is the keeper of the flame, the woman of the year, Adam's rib, and the star-spangled girl. If she would play, I'm confident that I could get some luminous chatter out of her on almost any subject. Alternatively: a panel on the dismal state of American theatre, featuring Miller, Williams, Albee and some of the off- and off-off-Broadway dissidents. Again, both of these ideas excite me. There isn't time to do either of them on this trip, since we have to go home next Wednesday, but I could come back almost any time to tape them.

A third interview notion that I may have mentioned before: Stanley Kubrick?[7]

I'll await your reaction to all these projects. The idea you mooted on the boat – about my coming to Chicago for a few months as editorial assistant – is highly attractive: its practicability depends mostly on the state of Olivier's health, about which I shall know more later in the year.

Finally: could you tell Jim Goode that I've been unable to trace the NYCAYA gallery in New York, which shows the paintings of Charles Stark (a man possessed by visions of female bottoms), and I'd be glad and grateful if he could supply the address of the place.[8]

And thanks again. Kathleen sends love.

Yours,
Ken T.

[1] Theo Feigenspan, Spectorsky's third wife.

[2] A *Playboy* editor.

[3] Editor of the American right-wing periodical *Commentary*.

[4] The research was used for the *Oh! Calcutta!* sketch, 'The Empress's New Clothes'.

[5] Spectorsky replied (7 July 1967) that the magazine had decided to turn the idea into a panel discussion. It was his view that culture hounds were paying homage to 'faggotismo as they have never done before'. KPT contributed to this 'panel', April 1971.

[6] Wilhelm Reich (1897–1957), Austrian psychoanalyst expelled from the German Communist Party in 1933 and the International Psychoanalytical Association in 1934. He emigrated to the US in 1939. KPT had read Reich's *The Sexual Revolution* (1927) a decade before and had been deeply impressed by his view that you could not change society without first changing sexual mores.

[7] KPT did not write pieces on Reich, Hepburn, the American Theatre or Kubrick.

[8] KPT found the gallery and bought two drawings.

To John Gielgud

[The National Theatre]
14 July 1967

Dear John:

What with Larry's illness, Vivien's death and now Cecil Tennent's fatal accident,[1] we're beginning to feel like the House of Atreus.[2] This is by way of apology that it's been so long since you last heard from us. It's also to assure you that we haven't been idle. We've been through dozens of plays looking for a companion piece for OEDIPUS. Our list has now reduced itself to three possibilities which we'd like you to consider. At the same time we'd like to hear of any thoughts you may have had. We shall have to come to a decision pretty soon, because it now looks as if the best time for the double bill to open would be February. Anyway, here are our contenders.

1. THE REHEARSAL[3] – which I like and Larry has doubts about. If you were really keen, however, I'm sure his doubts could be allayed.

2. ALL THAT FALL[4] – a radio play by Sam Beckett. It's never been done on stage, but we think it would respond beautifully to imaginative direction. You would be Mr Rooney – rather unusual casting, you may think, but I'd love you to consider it seriously. There's one argument against the play: the rather downbeat ending might make it a less than ideal partner for Seneca.

3. Three short plays by John Maddison Morton.[5] (To me, this is the most exciting prospect.) Morton is the founding father of English farce: he wrote literally hundreds of one-actors in the mid-nineteenth century, and I think re-discovery is long overdue. He's mainly remembered nowadays for BOX AND COX. Gordon Craig told me about ten years ago that Maddison Morton was the funniest playwright that England had ever had; I remembered this a couple of months ago and got hold of a batch of his work. Frankly, I think

he's better than Feydeau. The idea would be to take three of his plays, cut them a little and present them one after the other (with lightning scene changes) under some such title as 'The World of Maddison Morton'.

A possible grouping would be:

a) TICKLISH TIMES (with yourself as Griggs)
   or
   WHITEBAIT AT GREENWICH (with yourself as Buzzard)

b) SLASHER AND CRASHER (without you)

c) AN UNWARRANTABLE INTRUSION (with you as Snoozle).[6]

I hope you will agree with me that the latter is a little masterpiece.

Incidentally, pay no attention to the estimated times of performances at the beginning of each text: the Victorians must have played them at snail's pace. According to my timing, they work out as follows: TICKLISH TIMES – 38 minutes; WHITEBAIT AT GREENWICH – 38 minutes; SLASHER AND CRASHER – 37 minutes; AN UNWARRANTABLE INTRUSION – 25 minutes. The aim would be to cut the chosen three down to a total of 90 minutes maximum.

Do let us know if any of these ideas appeal to you. Meanwhile, good luck to you and the other 599,[7] and love from Larry.

Yours,
[Kenneth Tynan]

---

[1] Vivien Leigh died on 8 July. Olivier left his hospital bed to say his farewell. Olivier's friend and agent Cecil Tennent was killed in a car accident on his way home from Vivien Leigh's funeral.
[2] Euripides, the *Oresteia*
[3] By Jean Anouilh (1951).
[4] Written in 1957.
[5] John Maddison Morton (1811–91).
[6] *An Unwarrantable Intrusion*, directed by Robert Stephens, opened on 18 June 1968 as part of a triple bill without Gielgud.
[7] The 'Six Hundred', a group campaigning to save BBC Radio's Third Programme. Though the BBC had announced its intention of renaming it and changing its character, the change did not take place until 1970.

To Laurence Olivier

[The National Theatre]
17 July 1967

Dear Larry:

Here's Rolf's revised script. The play-within-a-play would last about three hours, I estimate; the prologue about forty minutes, and the epilogue five. I've also sent a copy to Peter Brook. My own feeling after reading it is that some kind of prologue is absolutely essential – you may remember that Peter wanted to cut it altogether.

Even if you don't get around to reading it for a day or two, could we have a small chat about the casting of Churchill? As I told you, Peter's first thought was Orson [Welles]; but when I saw him at a party last night he started to talk about Eric Porter[1] as a possibility. Peter points out that Porter is going to play Lear at Stratford next year, and he figures that anyone who can play Lear can play Churchill. As for me, I retain my loyalty to Albert [Finney] and Leo McKern. But I think we ought to approach somebody with a definite offer pretty soon.

I saw the Sisters on Saturday and loved it – especially Joan [Plowright], Tony Hopkins, Frank Wylie and Derek [Jacobi].[2]

All my love,
[Ken]

[1] Eric Porter (b. 1928), English actor best known at the time for his performance as Soames Forsyte in the television series *The Forsyte Saga*.
[2] Frank Wylie as Captain Solloni; Derek Jacobi as Baron Tusenbach.

To Emilie Jacobson

The National Theatre
18 August 1967

Dear Emilie,

A few weeks ago (probably about four) there was an article in either ESQUIRE, LOOK or THE SATURDAY EVENING POST about a beauty contest for men in drag. It had some fantastic pictures of the winning transvestites. I need a copy of this article urgently since I want to use some of the pictures in the National Theatre's programme for AS YOU LIKE IT, which we are presenting with an all-male cast. Could I beg you to be a darling and see if you can trace it for me? I can't think of anybody else to write to, since if I approach the magazines themselves, I may pick the wrong ones. All I need is the article itself, not the whole magazine. If you track it down, could you airmail it, as our deadline is very soon?

Love,
[pp. Kenneth Tynan]

To Joseph Heller[1]

[The National Theatre]
21 August 1967

Dear Joe:

I have now read the revised version twice. I think all your changes are improvements, and the passages leading up to the two curtains are absolute knock-outs.

But, as I told you when we lunched, I still don't think that the Pirandello convention – how real are actors? how real are characters? – quite comes off. I still find something uncomfortable and a bit self-conscious in the references to the length of parts, parts they would rather be playing, parts they already have played, etc. And I remain convinced that the killing of Henderson may not have as much impact as you intend. I may be hopelessly wrong about this, I am not renowned for my visual imagination, but I think there will be a terrible risk that the essential seriousness of what you are saying might get lost in a plethora of gags and trimmings. And the trouble is that these gags and trimmings are inherent in the convention you have chosen.

So with every kind of regret, I think the National Theatre had better bow out of the situation. In any case, I think the play cries out for American actors to make it work properly. Although you say the cast can be of any nationality, the timing and the rhythms are tremendously American, and this is a style that English actors have never really mastered. I needn't tell you that I hope my cavils are unjustified, and that you find a director who is able to prove that I am out of my mind.

My love to Bob Brustein[2] and yourself.

And good luck with the count-down on December 4.

Love,
[Kenneth Tynan]

[1] Joseph Heller (b. 1923), author of *Catch-22* (1961); his first play, *We Bombed in New Haven*, was first produced at the Yale School of Drama in December 1967.
[2] Robert Brustein (b. 1927), director and critic who founded the Yale Repertory Theatre (1966); later drama critic of the *Observer* (1972–3).

To Peter Brook

[The National Theatre]
29 August 1967

Dear Peter:

Here's the second draft of the Seneca.[1] I spent two days doing revisions with the translator, and he is perfectly willing to make any more changes we may feel necessary.

As you suggested, I told Larry not to contact Peter H.

About the Hochhuth: At last, things seem to be moving. Larry has taken the necessary legal steps to change the directorship of St James's Players, and you will shortly be getting a letter from his lawyer inviting you to join the board. We have also approached the Court to ask them whether we can use their club[2] to open the play in the West End. They will be giving us a decision within a few days and I'm fairly sure it will be yes.

See you soon

Love,
[Kenneth Tynan]

[1] *Oedipus*, adapted by Ted Hughes and directed by Peter Brook, was produced at the National Theatre in March 1968, with John Gielgud and Irene Worth.
[2] 'Club' theatres were not subject to the Lord Chamberlain's censorship.

To Jacques Levy[1]

[The National Theatre]
19 October 1967

Dear Jacques:

Congratulations on your notices.

New from here: Peter Weiss' agent writes to say that he is revising the whole of the Vietnam script,[2] and that in any case it can't be done in English until after the German première, which is tentatively scheduled for the late spring. The first half of the present script (Vietnam from 500 BC to 1945) was fresh and exciting – a sort of balletic documentary. Part II is just a string of quotes from Dulles,[3] Eisenhower, JFK, LBJ, etc, which gets very dry and pedantic. I hope this is the part he's re-working. But if he sticks to the quotation technique, I expect our censor will ban it – remember the LBJ quote in AMERICA HURRAH.[4] So the whole Weiss situation is pretty cloudy at the moment.[...]

About the sex show:[5] have you read the material yet? What do you think of it? Michael[6] and I feel more and more that we'd be mad to put it on while the Lord Chamberlain is still operating – he would never pass the script, and if we tried to make it a club performance, I'm sure he'd intervene as he did with AMERICA HURRAH. But we have reason to believe that he will be abolished during the next parliamentary session which ends in June, so we could open in July.[7] How would this suit you? It would, of course, be ideal if you were to do a production at the National in May and follow it up with Sex in July. Let me know your thoughts.

Love,
[Kenneth Tynan]

[1] Jacques Levy (b. 1935), American director whose production of 'Motel', one of the three short plays in *America Hurrah* by Jean-Claude van Itallie (1966), had opened at the Royal Court on 2 August 1967.
[2] *Vietnam Discourse* (1968).
[3] John Foster Dulles (1888–1959), US Secretary of State 1953–8.
[4] In 'TV', another of the short plays, President Johnson appears as a character inside the television set; some of his lines were adjudged by the censor to be offensive to a living person.
[5] KPT liked the non-orgiastic, extremely cool, style of *Motel*, and invited Levy to direct *Oh! Calcutta!*
[6] Michael White (b. 1936), theatrical impresario who had produced Joe Orton's *Loot* (1966) and would later produce Anthony Shaffer's *Sleuth* (1970) and *The Rocky Horror Show* (1973).
[7] The Lord Chamberlain's censorship powers were abolished in the 1968 Theatres Act.

To The Hon. David Astor

20 Thurloe Square
October 24, 1967

Dear David,
    A little problem has come up on which I'd like your advice and (if possible) your help.
    A literary magazine in Milan called <u>Fiera Literaria</u> wants to reprint

some of the columns I shall be writing for <u>The Observer</u> next year. They are offering me a surprisingly large sum of money per piece.[1] Is this going to create a problem? I'm desperately anxious to accept, because this has been a wildly expensive year for me (buying a heavily mortgaged house, facing four lots of lawyers' fees for a double divorce, etc.) and frankly this extra income might well be all that stands between me and semi-bankruptcy. At least it would mean that I'd be able to concentrate more on the <u>Observer</u> job and not have to accept every American commission that comes along in order to keep my head above water.

When <u>The Sunday Times</u> first approached me earlier this year to write a column for them, Harold Evans[2] made it clear that foreign rights would remain in my hands. As things worked out, I was delighted that <u>The Ob</u> was interested enough to make a counter-offer; but I'd feel much happier if the foreign-rights clause in our agreement could be made flexible enough to accommodate this new and quite unexpected development. It wouldn't be the thin end of any wedge: it would simply be a single exception to what I'm otherwise prepared to accept as the rule. I'm told (though you may correct me on this) that you have a similar arrangement over syndication with John Crosby.[3]

The fact is that, if I'm unable to accept the Italian offer, I shall be losing almost as much as I'm earning by working for <u>The Observer</u> – not, you may agree, the happiest frame of mind in which to start an exciting new job.

Sorry to bother you like this, but I'm very much troubled.

Yours ever,
Ken T.

[1] KPT wrote a weekly arts and general column called 'Shouts and Murmurs' for the *Observer* between 28 January 1968 and 30 March 1969. He was paid £4,000 for 40 articles a year. The Italian offer to which the *Observer* reluctantly agreed was for a further £4,000.
[2] Harold Evans (b. 1928), editor of the *Sunday Times* (1967–81) and *The Times* (1981–2).
[3] John Crosby (1912–91), American journalist who wrote 'Crime Beat' for the *New York Herald Tribune* in the mid-1930s; a syndicated columnist on the *Observer* 1965–75.

On 14 August 1967 Ken heard from the Lord Chamberlain that before Soldiers *could be put on he would require written approval from the surviving members of the families of the historical characters. Ken commented:*

> *'After Chandos had banned us*
> *We were nobbled by Cobbold.'*

By the autumn, Olivier had withdrawn because of illness, and with him went the idea of a co-production with Peter Hall and Peter Brook. The producer Michael White stepped in. On 9 October the play had its noisy world première in Berlin. The author was booed and the play was condemned. Berlin was followed more successfully by productions all over Europe. In Britain the Lord Chamberlain, in his last few months in power, would still not grant permission for the play's production. Against the odds, Ken began to look for actors to play Churchill. Orson Welles had shown interest ('I've got the cigar'); Richard Burton wanted to do the part until his wife, Elizabeth Taylor, warned him, 'Over my dead body.'

To William Shawn

The National Theatre
November 2 1967

Dear Mr Shawn –

I feel I owe you an explanation of the delay in delivering my British theatre piece. Partly the reason is <u>force majeure</u> – Sir Laurence's illness (and present absence on tour in Canada) has meant that I've been saddled with lots of unsought responsibilities here; and the arrival of a baby daughter[1] six weeks ago was another, more pleasant interruption. A bigger setback, however, has been the recent history of Rolf Hochhuth's play about Churchill. I intended, as I told you, to use this play – and the various bans, objections and scandals connected with it – as one of the foundation stones of the piece. I wanted to end the story with the play overcoming all obstacles and finally being presented in London. Recently, alas, the situation has taken a new turn. The government announced in the summer that it was going to abolish the Lord Chamberlain's theatre censorship (he had already banned the play): but this plan has now been postponed, and the Lord Chamberlain will continue in power. This means that the play cannot be presented in England in the forseeable future: and that I am left with a complicated story that has no resolution. Frankly, I would rather postpone telling it until there is an end in view.

Meanwhile I am recasting the piece in a form that excludes the Hochhuth episode (except perhaps for a passing mention). I can promise delivery during December – until then I hope you will be indulgent.

Yours sincerely,
Kenneth Tynan

[1] Roxana Nell Tynan was born on 14 September 1967.

To Irene Worth[1]

[The National Theatre]
27 November 1967

Dear Irene:

I've arranged two seats for you for the Lennon play.[2] It starts at 7.30 on Sunday and the tickets will be in your name at the stage door.

We're busily investigating HEDDA, ANTONY AND CLEOPATRA, APPLE CART,[3] and ACHE.[4] A further thought: how about giving us your DUCHESS OF MALFI? Peggy [Ashcroft] did it at the Aldwych, but that was seven years ago.

I'll be writing again before the end of the week.

Love,
[Kenneth Tynan]

P.S. Peter Brook was auditioning members of our company for the Chorus in OEDIPUS yesterday. It was absolutely riveting. When he's really engrossed in a project as he is now, Peter makes every other director in England look fraudulent and trivial.

[1] Irene Worth (b. 1916), American actress. She played Lady Macbeth and Goneril in *King Lear* at the RSC in 1962; Irina Arkadina in *The Seagull* at Chichester in 1973.
[2] *In His Own Write*, co-written by John Lennon, Adrienne Kennedy and Victor Spinetti, opened on 18 June 1968.
[3] *The Apple Cart* by George Bernard Shaw (1930).
[4] *A Slight Ache*, a one-act play by Harold Pinter (1960).

To Mary McCarthy

[20 Thurloe Square]
19th December 1967

Dear Mary,

Thank you so much for the gorgeous fish slice.[1] I'm at a loss, however, to understand why you think I resemble it. It has a high polish, a dulled edge and a highly specialised function; and it's 167 years old.

On second thoughts, I see what you mean.

Love from us both – it's a beautiful thing.

Merry Christmas,

Ken

---

[1] An eighteenth-century fish slice, sent as a wedding present.

To Richard Findlater[1]

[20 Thurloe Square]
22nd January 1968

Dear Richard,

There's nothing like a bit of controversy. How charming of you to welcome me back to The Observer by printing four letters attacking my first column[2] and not one supporting it. I notice that contributors attacked in other letters were given an opportunity to reply. I was neither told that the letters were to be printed, nor invited to answer them. To say that I find this shabby treatment would be putting it very mildly indeed. I can sum up my feelings by saying that if the Sunday Times offer was still open, I would be tempted to accept it.

Yours,
Ken[3]

---

[1] KPT's editor at the *Observer*.

[2] On 14 January he attacked both the government and the Queen over the delay in abolishing theatre censorship, and defended a French propaganda film attacking the war in Vietnam.

[3] Michael Davie wrote to Astor on 24 January that KPT was 'understandably' very upset. 'I expect he will be flattered and mollified by a note from you.' Astor apologized (25 January) but expressed concern about KPT's next column, on pornography (28 January), which he felt was likely 'to provoke the disagreement of most readers'. He asked KPT to agree to the deletion of one sentence: 'Language can be employed in many delicate and complex ways to enliven the penis.' 'It will be said that this phrase is published so as to shock, rather than to advance the argument.' KPT modified the sentence.

Memo to Michael Hallifax[1]

[The National Theatre]
5 February 1968

One or two points on which I need your help: [...]

2. Victor Spinetti[2] and John Lennon will need the services of George Martin, the Beatles A & R man, to prepare the sound tape to accompany the Lennon play. Martin did this tape as a favour for the Sunday night production, but something more elaborate will be required when the show enters the rep, and I feel he should be approached on a professional basis as Sound Consultant, or some similar title. I have written to him to find out if he is willing to help and will let you know as soon as he replies.

3. Victor Spinetti is now working out what his casting requirements will be for the supporting parts in the Lennon play. He would very much appreciate it if he could have a list of the A Company actors who would be available to take part in it. Do you think you could possibly supply him with this?

4. John Lennon says that as far as his own contract is concerned, we should deal directly with him at NEMS[3] rather than his publisher.

I have discussed the question of billing with Lennon, Spinetti and Miss Kennedy.[4] They suggest either:
'Script by Adrienne Kennedy, John Lennon and Victor Spinetti
(based on IN HIS OWN WRITE and A SPANIARD IN THE WORKS
by John Lennon)'
or
'Script by Adrienne Kenndy, with a little help from her friends,
John Lennon and Victor Spinetti
(based on IN HIS OWN WRITE and A SPANIARD IN THE WORKS
by John Lennon)'
I would happily settle for the former. Incidentally, they would like the show to be called IN HIS OWN WRITE instead of SCENE THREE ACT ONE.

K.T.

---

[1] Executive Company Manager for the National Theatre 1966–74; later Company Administrator.
[2] Victor Spinetti (b. 1933), actor whose work with Joan Littlewood included *Oh, What A Lovely*

War!, for which he won a Tony award when it transferred to Broadway. He was director as well as co-author of *In His Own Write*.
[3] The management company run by Brian Epstein.
[4] Adrienne Kennedy (b. 1931), Afro-American playwright.

To Paul Scofield

[The National Theatre]
22 February 1968

Dear Paul:

I needn't say how much I'm hoping that you will be able to join us.

In the meantime, I wonder if you would like to look at the enclosed script. It's Charles Wood's new play about the Indian Mutiny.[1] He unleashed it on us about a month ago. We know (and he knows) that it's far too long, that it's highly repetitive, and that it doesn't explain the historical origins of the mutiny. But somewhere inside this vast hunk of marble an extraordinary play is waiting to be chipped out; and Wood is shortly going to embark on the job of reducing it to shape and clarity. If he succeeds in doing so, would you like to play Havelock?[2] He was an ascetic, even saintly man, who committed huge barbarities with the noblest motives. Some of the long speeches Charles has given him are, I think, classics of their kind.

I long to know your reactions.

Yours,
[Kenneth Tynan][3]

[1] *H, or Monologues at Front of Burning Cities*, directed at the National in February 1969 by Geoffrey Reeves, with Robert Lang rather than Scofield.
[2] Brigadier General Henry Havelock, commander of the first relief column to reach the besieged city of Lucknow.
[3] Scofield's first production at the National Theatre, *The Captain of Kopenick*, opened 9 March 1971.

To Emilie Jacobson

[20 Thurloe Square]
15 March 1968

Dear Emilie,

For the last month or so I've been so ill with bronchitis[1] that I've fallen behind in all my work. Tomorrow I go into hospital for a check on lungs and sinuses. Could you suggest to 'Playboy' that they should stop all payments to me from this date onwards until I have caught up with what I owe them? I can send the Underwear piece by the end of April, and the Talent Snob piece (hopefully) by the end of May, but I'd rather not be paid any more until I have delivered some goods.

Yours,
[pp. K. Tynan]

[1] KPT learned in 1965 that he had a mild degree of emphysema. From early 1968 he suffered a series of asthma and bronchial attacks, culminating in a bout of pneumonia in New York (23 February – 8 March).

To John Lennon

[20 Thurloe Square]
16 April 1968

Dear John L,

Welcome back. You know that idea of yours for my erotic revue – the masturbation contest? Could you possibly be bothered to jot it down on paper? I am trying to get the whole script in written form as soon as possible.

Yours,
Ken Tynan[1]

[1] Lennon replied (n.d.): 'you know the idea, four fellows wanking – giving each other images – descriptions – it should be ad-libbed anyway – they should even really wank which would be great ...'

To Noël Coward

[The National Theatre]
3 July 1968

Dear Noël:

As you may have read, we're going to revive Maugham's HOME AND BEAUTY[1] in the autumn. Naturally, we're all hoping it will have the same kind of success that you gave us with HAY FEVER.[2] And this hope has prompted me to ask you a favour. Could you spare a moment to write me a little letter about Willie Maugham's plays and what you think of them, which I could then reprint in the HOME AND BEAUTY programme? However brief, it would [be] a lovely gesture and very well seen. If you decide to do it, I would need the letter by August 12.

Please don't worry if the idea fails to appeal.

Meanwhile, love from Larry and

Your devoted
[Kenneth Tynan][3]

[1] Farce by W. Somerset Maugham, written and produced in 1919.

[2] Coward's production of his 1925 play in October 1964 at the National Theatre, starring Edith Evans, followed by Maggie Smith.

[3] Coward wrote in a programme note: 'When I began my career as a playwright W. Somerset Maugham was one of my immediate gods of the theatre and now, when I am rapidly approaching the cherished position he described for himself in his later years – "an elderly party on the shelf" – I find with pleasure that my early idolatry has in no way diminished.'

Memo to Laurence Olivier

[The National Theatre]
16 July 1968

PROSPECTS FOR 1969

When we are planning for the post-Christmas period, please let us bear in mind that, as far as new plays are concerned, our situation at the moment is healthier than it's ever been. We have:

a) The Plowright Project[1] – assuming that Shena Mackay's play can be made to work and we find the right framework for the evening.

b) The Conor Cruise O'Brien[2] – subject to counsel's assurance that there's no substantial risk of libel.

c) The Charles Wood – newly revised out of the blue.

d) The Dennis Potter[3] – which, as I told you, he finished last November. However, he refuses to show it to us in its present form because 'it isn't a play, it's a scream of pain'. He promises that by October 31 he'll show us either (i) a revised version, or (ii) the original scream.

e) <u>The Peter Shaffer</u> – Peter now plans to arrive in September with
the completed version of his new play.[4]

f) <u>Que Ferez-vous en Novembre?</u>[5] – the new French play which our
readers have gone wild about and part of which I'm having translated
for us.

My own feeling is that if we feel enthusiastic about any of these, they
should take precedence over everything else except Lear.

K.T.

---

[1] Joan Plowright commissioned a play from each of four women novelists (Shena Mackay,
Margaret Drabble, Gillian Freeman and Maureen Duffy) for an experimental season at the
Jeanetta Cochrane Theatre.
[2] *Murderous Angels*, an examination of the 1961 Congo crisis, first performed at the Playhouse,
New York, in December 1971.
[3] *Son of Man*, which showed Christ as a rough-tongued, wild-haired desert prophet, uncertain of
his Messianic identity. Eventually a BBC television play (1969).
[4] *The Battle of Shrivings*.
[5] René Ehni's play about the 1968 Paris student revolt.

To Kathleen Tynan[1]

[20 Thurloe Square]
[?July 1968]

Darling –
    There were many people in the thirties who went to lunch at Clive-
den[2] with von Ribbentrop.[3] They were not necessarily pro-Hitler;
many of them were liberals who knew the Astors, liked their other
friends, and saw no harm in taking the opportunity of urging Ribbentrop to turn his master's mind against war. Whatever their motives,
they are not remembered with honour, and they do not thank those
diarists who recorded their names as guests at Cliveden.
    I suppose there are people who would turn up at a lunch in honour
of Marshal Ky's[4] son. It would be interesting to argue whether it is
more desirable to pay indirect tribute to a puppet than to pay it to his
pay-master. Myself, I think there is an element of farce in the former
tribute that almost excuses it; but to attend the latter without feeling
slightly soiled and compromised seems to me almost impossible.

Opponents of capital punishment do not, I hope, raise their glasses to the executioner's daughter.

Unless, of course, they are going to tax the girl with her father's idiotic savagery. And that would only be worth doing if it was likely to have even the smallest effect on her father's behaviour. Which, I think you will agree, it will not. So the choices open to any decent person attending the lunch are two in number – either to provoke a scene by means of political argument (which will be ineffective), or to acquiesce in the idea that homage to brutality is not wicked as long as it is private. And if they take the second course, I am not sure that they continue to be decent people. Helene Weigel was once asked to a dinner in West Berlin at which one of the guests was the son of a Nazi judge who had just become a judge himself. She sent a polite refusal, to which she attached the death certificate of her sister, who died in Auschwitz. If your parents had been born a few hundred miles further south,[5] you might have sent Lynda Bird your brother's draft card.

It isn't a big thing, but it isn't so small that we shan't sometimes remember it. Please think of what we would like to stand for, and find some quiet way out of that silly lunch tomorrow.[6]

K.

[1] I had been asked to a lunch in honour of Lynda Bird Johnson, President Johnson's daughter, at the American Embassy.
[2] The Astors' country house outside London; Nancy Astor and her friends supported Neville Chamberlain's policy of appeasement of Nazi Germany.
[3] Hitler's ambassador to Britain, then Foreign Minister 1938–45.
[4] Air Marshal Nguyen Cao Ky led a short-lived coup in Vietnam in 1965, and was closely involved with the Americans during the war. He was evacuated to America during the fall of Saigon.
[5] My parents were born in Canada.
[6] I cannot remember whether I attended this lunch or not.

To Tennessee Williams

[The National Theatre]
20 August 1968

Dear Ten,

Bless you for sending that piece[1] – I wish it was four times as long. I have sent a copy off to Jacques Levy, the Director, and I will write again when I hear from him.

I hope, by the way, that I did not give you a false impression. The show is not meant to satirize sex: in fact most of the material is serious to the point of obsession. It will, I hope, be a sort of playground for private fantasies.

All love,
[Ken]

[1] Sketch for *Oh! Calcutta!* about an unhappily married couple who can only make love after fighting. It was filmed for the show but not used.

To William Shawn

20 Thurloe Square
3 September 1968

Dear Mr Shawn,

My present contract with The Observer ends on December 31st, and the editor has started to talk to me about renewing it. Before doing so, I wondered if there were any plans I could make with the New Yorker for 1969. Weekly sprinting is no substitute for the occasional long-distance-run.

In addition to pieces on theatre, I'd love to try my hand at a profile (I remember long ago we vaguely discussed Paul McCartney; though John Lennon is rather more accessible); and I'm enormously attracted by the longer critical pieces you've lately taken to publishing, such as the ones on Bonnie and Clyde and The Graduate. If we could agree on – say – a quartet of such subjects, I would be able to pull out of The Observer; but naturally they want me to give them an answer fairly soon.

I'm expecting to be in New York for a day or two at the end of September. Perhaps we could meet for a drink?

Yours sincerely,
Kenneth Tynan[3]

With the rights in his possession, Ken gave permission to the English director Clifford Williams (who had directed the all-male As You Like It *in lieu of*

John Dexter at the National in 1967) to direct the first English-speaking version of Soldiers. *It opened at the Royal Alexandra Theatre in Toronto on 28 February 1968, to spectacular reviews. One critic wrote that 'Hochhuth makes Churchill guilty of greatness.' The play was mounted in May in New York, was well reviewed but ran for only three weeks.*

By September 1968, the Lord Chamberlain's powers of theatre censorship had been abolished. Michael White and Ken now had the London production, also to be directed by Williams, in hand. In the run-up to the opening night on 12 December, the press had a field day.

To Robert David Macdonald

20, Thurloe Square
September 15 [1968]

Dear David –

I've sent Kathleen's piece[1] off to Mrs. Rolf[2] and hope it arrives in time.

Michael [White] and I wish desperately that Rolf could be dissuaded from getting publicly embroiled with Trevor-Roper.[3] If it comes to court it could do enormous harm to the play which the British press will be quick to exploit. Trevor-Roper is a skilled and acid polemicist who will probably sound better in his native language than Rolf will in a courtroom translation. Also, I can't think where Rolf got the idea that T.-R. supported the Sikorski theory. When I consulted him, all he said was: 'Bizarre.' (I've checked with my original notes, and that's all they say.) Is there any means of quashing the quarrel?

I don't think it will be like the Lenin film,[4] which was an essay in hagiography: 'Soldiers' isn't. But much depends on the way the play opens. We talked glibly of starting with Cherwell and Alanbrooke[5] and removing the romantic element from Kocjan and the girl: but <u>has this been done?</u> Time is getting short and it is becoming urgent to see a final draft of the first few minutes.

Quite agree about a strong Sikorski – Michael is seeing two Bismarckian German actors in the next few days. Stepanek[6] one feels is too large and lumbering: we need more of a ramrod-backed martinet. [...]

Love,
Ken

[1] An article on the background to *Soldiers*, 'Sabotage in High Places' (*New York* magazine, 29 April 1968).
[2] Hochhuth's wife, Marianne Heinemann, spoke English.
[3] Professor Hugh Trevor-Roper, Baron Dacre (b. 1914), Regius Professor of Modern History at Oxford 1957–80, author of *The Last Days of Hitler* (1947).
[4] Macdonald had referred KPT to the 1942 Soviet play (not a film) *Kremlin Chimes* by Nikolai Pogodin as an example of how not to present recent history.
[5] Sir Alan Francis Brooke, First Viscount Alanbrooke (1883–1963), Commander-in-Chief of the Home Forces 1940–1, appointed Chief of the Imperial General Staff in 1941.
[6] Karel Stepanek, Czech actor who came to Britain in 1940. The part of Sikorski was eventually played by George Coulouris.

To Jacques Levy

20 Thurloe Square
September 17 [1968]

Dear Jacques:

Here's a quick rewrite of Knickers.[1] At least all the information is there – and obviously a lot of it can be cut. The commentary can be divided between the commentators in any way that's convenient. They should both be crisp blue-stocking intellectual types, their manner contrasting with what they're talking about. Whether they should <u>participate</u> or merely <u>describe</u> I'm not quite sure.

I've received a sketch from Ann Jellicoe[2] and will pass it on when read.

Love,
Ken

[1] 'Theatre of Knickers', an *Oh! Calcutta!* sketch by KPT, eventually titled 'The Empress's New Clothes'.
[2] Not performed.

To Hillard Elkins[1]

20 Thurloe Square
1st October 1968

Dear Hilly,

I lunched with Mike Nichols yesterday, and talked about the show. His absolutely firm opinion is that we should go for a <u>fringe</u> Broadway house such as the place off Washington Square where they did <u>Man of La Mancha</u>,[2] or somewhere like the Henry Miller (if that's the place where the A.P.A.[3] used to be). I'd hate to be the one that said Mike was wrong on a thing like this.

Love,
Ken

---

[1] Hillard Elkins (b. 1929), a fast-talking showbiz entrepreneur from Brooklyn (soon to marry Claire Bloom), had heard about *Oh! Calcutta!* from Jacques Levy (whom he represented), and approached KPT in a New York restaurant, announcing that he was the only man to produce it.
[2] *Man of La Mancha*, a musical based on *Don Quixote*, was first performed at the American National Theater and Academy in November 1965.
[3] Agents for Performing Arts.

To William Shawn

20 Thurloe Square
14th October 1968

Dear Mr Shawn,

It was good to see you at the Algonquin, also good to know that you were interested in the idea of my doing some more work for you. As I explained, I shall be pretty fully occupied until the end of April 1969, but I could embark then on a plan to contribute four pieces in the following twelve months. (Twelve months would anyway be the target: it's possible that I might overshoot it, as happened last time, because of sudden flare-ups of time-consuming activity at the National Theatre.)

The pieces we discussed were:

1) Valencia – a profile of the city.[1]
2) Harold Pinter. (My wife wrote a piece on him last year for Vogue, and I'd have to make sure that he could stand another Tynan invasion.)
3) Oxford University and what it did to my generation of undergraduates.
4) A few days in the life of Paul McCartney (which we agreed should come at the end of the series of articles, because of the current over-exposure of the Beatles).

Since talking to you I've had an idea which interests me enormously – an informal profile of the brave Yugoslav maverick, Milovan Djilas.[2] He has fascinated me for years, and now seems to be the true prophet of the Dubcek liberalisation in Prague. If there's one man who can act as interpreter to the West of what is happening to the culture and politics of Eastern Europe, I should think it would be Djilas. As far as I'm concerned, he could replace either Valencia or Oxford. Do let me know if he interests you.

Yours sincerely,
Kenneth Tynan[3]

[1] 'The Judicious Observer will be Disgusted' (*New Yorker*, July 1970).
[2] Milovan Djilas (b. 1911), Yugoslav politician imprisoned for outspoken criticism of the communist regime; released in 1966. His books include *The New Order* (1957) and *Land Without Justice* (1958).
[3] The pieces on Pinter, Oxford University, Paul McCartney and Djilas were never written.

To The Hon. David Astor

[Telegram]

[London]
27 October 1968

SIKORSKI MURDER THEORY IS BASIC TO HOCHHUTH PLAY. ASTON-
ISHED THAT YOU SHOULD DISMISS IT AS PREPOSTEROUS.[1] THIS ILL-
MANNERED AND BOORISH TREATMENT OF AN AUTHOR WHO HAS
GRANTED YOU EXCLUSIVE SERIAL RIGHTS IS CONTEMPTIBLE =
KENNETH TYNAN +

[1] David Astor replied (30 October 1968), 'I should have thought that many who admire the play, as I do, would agree that the Sikorski Theory was "preposterous" ... I cannot quite see how "The Observer" could be accused of "boorish" treatment of an author to whom we have given up a page and a half of the paper ... as we said in the introduction on Sunday [to the excerpt from *Soldiers*], the play should not be judged as history, but as drama.'

To Emilie Jacobson

[20 Thurloe Square]
28th October 1968

Dear Emilie,
    Frankly I'm not surprised by Playboy's decision about <u>The Empress's</u>

New Clothes¹ – they are scared stiff of anything that might go against their healthy open-air attitude towards sex. Why don't we try it with the women's magazines you mention – and then go on to Vogue, Harper's Bazaar, Mademoiselle, etc. You're right that I concentrate mainly on English examples – this is because the American pattern simply followed the British one, usually a few years later. I could always add a few words explaining this.

Before you send the piece around, I wonder if you could have the first page (p 15) retyped? The first four lines would remain the same, but from there onward, I'd like it to read:

> 'Nowadays they wear impenetrable body stockings and read "Myra Breckinridge".²
> 'Is this progress? Why don't women return to the knickers of the old regime, ostensibly chaste but in fact profoundly lascivious?
> 'As John Osborne says in one of his most moving lyrics:³
> Knickers, knickers,
> Those are the things to wear;
> For if you buy a pair of knickers,
> Then you won't have your bum all bare.'

Let me know how things go. Meanwhile, I have written to Murray Fisher [of *Playboy*] suggesting two possible subjects for interview – Jean-Luc Godard and Mick Jagger.

Love
[pp Ken Tynan]

¹ The article was eventually published, after several further rejections, in *Evergreen* (December 1969).
² Gore Vidal's satirical novel (1968) whose central character undergoes a sex-change.
³ From *Under Plain Cover* (1962).

To Sir Hugh Carleton Greene¹

20 Thurloe Square
30th November 1968

Dear Sir Hugh,

As you may know, I am involved in the presentation of the English premiere of Rolf Hochhuth's play Soldiers, which opens at the New

Theatre on December 12th. On behalf of the author, the director, the company and my partners in the management I should like to protest in the most emphatic terms against the way the play was treated in the November 29th edition of the BBC 1 programme called How It Is.

About ten days ago, I was telephoned by a representative of the show, who asked me whether I would be willing to appear on November 29th to discuss the play. I agreed to do so. Late on the evening of November 28th, however, I was telephoned again and asked whether I would mind cancelling my appearance. The speaker said that the producer had decided to postpone dealing with the play until a date nearer to the London opening. Once again, I agreed.

You can imagine my amazement when, switching on the programme next day, I saw a historian – described as Winston Churchill's biographer[2] – delivering a venomous five-minute diatribe against the play direct to camera. There was no interview, no discussion, no statement of the opposite point of view: merely an uninterrupted blast of hostility, full of inaccuracies and distortions. (According to the speaker, the play presents Churchill as 'lustful and despicable', and 'compares him to a sex murderer', which is a malicious lie.) At the end of the speech, Angela Huth[3] announced that next week's issue of the programme would include further discussion of the play by Winston Churchill Jr.[4] and Rolf Hochhuth. It is fairly easy to predict what Mr Churchill's attitude will be; and Herr Hochhuth will be in no position to answer Mr Churchill's charges very effectively, since he speaks no English. [...]

In all my knowledge of television, I cannot recall a parallel to what took place last night – the deliberate sabotaging of a play before it has been seen by either the English critics or the English audience. There is no way in which the harm can be undone. But I cannot help protesting at such a wanton betrayal of the BBC's honourable traditions of impartiality and fair play.

Yours sincerely,
[Kenneth Tynan][5]

---

[1] Sir Hugh Carleton Greene (1910–87), Director-General of the BBC 1960–9.
[2] Martin Gilbert, author of the final six volumes in the eight-volume biography of Churchill begun by Randolph Churchill, and editor of ten volumes of Churchill documents.
[3] Novelist, journalist and playwright, the presenter of the programme.
[4] Journalist, author and Member of Parliament, the son of Randolph Churchill.
[5] Carleton Greene wrote back (9 December 1968), 'When one considers the total exposure

Hochhuth's play has had so far, it would seem to exaggerate the stature of "How It Is" to ascribe to it the effect of "destroying two years' work".'

To Laurence Olivier

[The National Theatre]
8 December 1968

Urgent Memo

Dear Larry:

Okay, I understand about the first night.[1] But there's one thing that you or Joan could do. I've been told over the week-end that Carlos Thompson[2] intends to disrupt the premiere by calling a press conference in the interval to denounce Hochhuth to the world press and television. This would be the last bloody straw after two years of slogging. If we try to chuck him out it will make matters worse – 'punch-up at Hochhuth opening', etc, etc.

Could you PLEASE call him and beg him to leave us in peace for this one night? I shan't try to prevent the publication of his book – why should he prevent the play from being heard? If he does what he threatens to do, we have no way of stopping him and all our work will go down the drain because of his appetite for publicity. I know you're busy rehearsing for an opening next week, but I've been mentally rehearsing for this opening for 26 months.

Love,
Ken

[1] Olivier had told KPT he did not want to attend the first night because of the press.
[2] Though he had acted as interpreter for Olivier and Hochhuth, he wrote an attack on Hochhuth, *The Assassination of Winston Churchill* (1969).

Soldiers *opened at the New Theatre on 12 December 1968 (its twenty-first presentation) in a shortened version of Clifford Williams' original Toronto production, and with a fine cast led by John Colicos, Alec Clunes and Raymond Huntley. The producer Michael White, who had received bomb threats and hate mail against the 'Churchill smear play', had placed guards at every door. But all passed smoothly (Carlos Thompson was ill and did not turn up), and the actors were greeted with an ovation at the curtain call. With the successful conclusion of his two-year campaign, Ken wept with relief.*

To the Editor, *The Times*

20 Thurloe Square
[Published 14 January 1969]

Sir,—My belief that, if anything, Soldiers enhances Sir Winston Churchill's reputation is no mere eccentricity: it is shared by many more objective judges who have had the advantage, denied to your correspondent Winston S. Churchill, of having seen the play.

Lord Harlech told a reporter after the premiere: 'It is a very good play, and allegations that Sir Winston has been smeared are totally unfounded.'[1] The critic of the Sunday Express wrote: 'It is clear that Hochhuth has the greatest admiration for Churchill ... Churchill's greatness ... inundates the fabric of the play from the moment the curtain rises.' The Daily Mail said: 'In Churchill [Hochhuth] has created one of the few real heroes of modern drama': The Sun felt that 'the overall effect of the play is of Churchill's nobility, utter dedication and tremendous gift of leadership'; your own critic thought it an 'addition to the Churchill legend'; and the Evening News aptly concluded that 'it will offend only those with very literal minds'.

On the matter of libel: what I told Mr Churchill was what I have told hundreds of people whenever this question is raised – albeit in a somewhat truncated form, since he would keep interrupting.[2] If his grandfather had been alive when the play was written, I would have sent him the script in the hope that he would allow it to be performed. If he had refused, a jury might have been unwise enough to find it libellous. Or again, they might not. But it does not, of course, follow from this that I think it libellous.

Suppose a man had the opportunity (in Hochhuth's phrase) 'to save the alliance that saved the world' by ordering the death of a single individual: is it vilification to suggest that he may have (and ought to have) taken it? After all, we know that Winston Churchill was responsible for the murder of 1,200 French sailors, allies less than two weeks before, when he ordered the bombardment of the French fleet at Oran – a ruthless action, but one that was justified by the overriding necessity of defeating Hitler.[3]

The historical basis for Hochhuth's interpretation of Sikorski's air crash is something on which, being no research expert, I cannot pronounce: but I notice that Hochhuth has recently suggested the formation of a committee to investigate Sikorski's death, consisting of Bernard Levin, David Irving, John Barry of The Sunday Times, General Sikorski's son-in-law and Winston S. Churchill himself. He further proposes that the Government might consider waiving the Official Secrets Act for the committee's secret hearings, so that informants might speak freely without fear of prosecution. Whether or not this latter proposal is realistic, the idea of a committee seems to me admirable, and I hope Mr Churchill will embrace it.

Meanwhile, I would recommend him to be less personally abusive. Hochhuth's play, whatever its faults, was written in good faith by a man whose principal weaknesses, I should say, are an exaggerated mistrust of his fellow-Germans, and a perhaps excessive hero-worship of Sir Winston Churchill.

I leave it to others to decide whether it was desire for 'money and notoriety' that drove me, two years ago, to press for the presentation of Soldiers at the National Theatre. Such notoriety as attaches to the play has been created by its detractors, not its supporters: and if it finally had its premiere in the commercial theatre, that is because my original plans for it were frustrated.

Shortly before Randolph Churchill's death, I gave him the script to read, and discussed it with him on television. He fiercely disagreed with what the play said, both about Sikorski's death and the bombing of civilians; but when we continued our talk after the programme, he told me he saw no reason why it should not be performed. Perhaps the grandson should learn from the magnanimity of the son.

Yours faithfully
KENNETH TYNAN

[1] Harlech was misquoted. He wrote to *The Times* (18 January 1969) that he had been asked whether Churchill was implicated in the death of Sikorski and had answered, 'I do not think there is one shred of evidence', but had added that he thought it was 'a very good play'.
[2] *The Frost Programme*, December 1968.
[3] The French fleet was sunk by the Royal Navy on 3 July 1940 to prevent it from falling into German hands after the capitulation of France.

To Emilie Jacobson

[20 Thurloe Square]
20 January 1969

Dear Emilie,

Would Playboy like a gutsy sexy interview with famed Polish lenser Roman Polanski?

I would love to do one.[1]

Love,
[pp. Ken Tynan]

[1] The article was eventually published by *Esquire* (September 1971) under the title 'The Polish Imposition'.

To the Editor, *The Times*[1]

20 Thurloe Square
[Published 21 January 1969]

Sir,—As a journalist, I am dependent on people's faith in my trustworthiness and veracity. These have been challenged in your columns by Professor Trevor-Roper (January 17),[2] and I must trespass on your space to refute his charges.

When 'Soldiers' was under consideration at the National Theatre, I sounded out a number of historians, journalists, editors, Polish émigrés and people connected with the wartime intelligence services to obtain their reactions to the plausibility of Hochhuth's hypothesis about the death of Sikorski. I asked Hochhuth if he minded my doing this, and he raised no objection; he said he hoped Professor Trevor-Roper was on my list. I replied that he was; and indeed, as a historian and former intelligence officer, he was an obvious candidate.

When I telephoned him, I said I was speaking on behalf of the National Theatre, and explained that his opinion would be treated in confidence – meaning, of course, that it was not for publication and would not be repeated outside the confines of those directly concerned with the play. This undertaking was strictly respected. (My own recollection of what Professor Trevor-Roper said is that he called the Hochhuth theory 'bizarre' rather than 'absurd', but no matter.)

At the January, 1967, board meeting of the National Theatre, I reported in a written memorandum: 'I have consulted a large number of historians and military experts, and the result is very much an open verdict.' In other words, many shades of opinion were represented, pro, contra and neutral. I added that I could provide a detailed breakdown on request, but I was never called upon to do so. When asked whether Professor Trevor-Roper himself had been consulted I replied that he had. But neither then nor at any time did I say or write to anyone that

Professor Trevor-Roper himself had returned an open verdict, or that he thought the matter an open question. If Lord Chandos claims otherwise, I can only refer him to the memorandum quoted above.

Even if I were such an untrustworthy reporter as Professor Trevor-Roper imputes, I would have had to be certifiable to lie about his opinions in front of a board any one of whose members could have proved me wrong by means of a simple telephone call to Oxford.

As for Hochhuth's letter in Der Spiegel: I asked the playwright's English translator to tell him that Professor Trevor-Roper's reaction was firmly negative. Presumably aware of the professor's background in the Intelligence Service, Hochhuth seems to have drawn some rather melodramatic conclusions (sealed lips, &c.) that certainly did not emanate from me, and for which I cannot be held responsible.[3]

Yours sincerely,
KENNETH TYNAN

[1] Published under the headline 'Winston Churchill and the Death of Sikorski'.
[2] Trevor-Roper claimed that KPT had misrepresented to the National Theatre Board his reply when asked about the likelihood of Churchill's complicity in the death of Sikorski.
[3] On the same day as this letter was published *The Times* reported that Trevor-Roper had issued proceedings for libel against Rolf Hochhuth. Neither this suit, nor KPT's suit against Trevor-Roper (filed 18 March) for libelling him in *The Times*, reached court.

To Laurence Olivier

[The National Theatre]
21 January 1969

Dear L,
    Many thanks for your <u>Times</u> letter.[1]
    Let's hope this is the end of the matter. It would be so nice to pick up the <u>Times</u> and not see that dread word Sikorski.
    I quite understand why you felt it necessary to mention the definition of 'open verdict' – and I assume that my private memo to you will remain with its privacy uninvaded.

Love from both –
Ken

[1] Written on 17 January 1969, defending KPT's version of events.

To Hillard Elkins

20 Thurloe Square
February 10th 1969

Dear Hilly:

This is just to confirm our talk on Saturday. We go ahead with 'Oh Calcutta' off-Broadway – my terms being those agreed with Harold Stern[1] last fall – on condition that the items I think integral to the show are rehearsed and performed in previews. (They can only be dropped in rehearsal by mutual consent of yourself, Jacques, Michael and myself.) Similarly, the items Jacques thinks essential are also rehearsed and previewed. I think it's vital that the show should retain its exotic British ingredients. Here, therefore, is my list of the numbers without which it would lose the flavour I wanted it to have:

> The Beckett mime[2]
> Polanski films[3] (if financially possible)
> Who: Whom[4] (if necessary, I'll rehearse it myself to prove to Jacques that it works)
> Knickers[5] (in any form – using the basic idea but not necessarily the words)
> London Life[6]
> I'll Shoot Your Dog ... [7]
> You and I[8]
> Will Answer all Sincere Replies[9]
> St. Dominic's[10] (and it would be attractively camp to have one of the girls black)

Okay? And the same conditions (rehearsal and preview) would apply to any new material that either of us may supply and think essential – so long as it isn't legally or financially prohibitive. (For example, I've just ascertained that David Mercer will have written two new sketches before we go into rehearsal.)

Finally: you agree to fly me over for the last three weeks of rehearsals and for all the previews, and to give me food and shelter during that period. Also, I'd naturally get my proportionate share of the authors' royalties.

Love to Jacques and yourself. Incidentally, I owe you $91 for Harold Stern's champagne.[11] I hereby empower you to deduct it from my advance. Since we haven't discussed an advance, better deduct it from the first royalty cheque.

All my best,
Ken

P. S. Afterthought: the suspended girl in 'Who: Whom' could be in a cage or tied to a chair if suspension proves a scenic problem.

[1] Harold H. Stern, KPT's lawyer, partner of the New York firm Stern, Wincor and Burns.
[2] Samuel Beckett's one-minute wordless sketch, called 'Breath', was used as the Prologue to the show.
[3] An idea for two three-minute films called 'The Railway Compartment' and 'The Train', which Roman Polanski devised but never directed.
[4] A cerebral sketch about sado-masochism, written by KPT and included in the show.
[5] KPT's sketch 'The Empress's New Clothes', performed in London, not New York.
[6] A sketch eventually titled 'Suite for Five Letters', by KPT and Stanley Walden, inspired by the sexually perverse letter column of a defunct and otherwise ordinary magazine called *London Life*. The sketch was performed in New York and London.
[7] Sketch by Edna O'Brien; performed only in previews.
[8] Sketch by David Mercer; performed only in previews.
[9] Sketch by David Newman and Robert Benton.
[10] Sketch by KPT, a humorous homage to girls' schools in the manner of Angela Brazil; performed only in previews.
[11] A thank-you present to KPT's lawyer.

To Emilie Jacobson

[20 Thurloe Square]
19th February 1969

Dear Emilie,

In the next two months, I'm afraid I've got too many theatre commitments to do a full profile of Cohn-Bendit[1] (also I shall be writing a New Yorker piece on the Spanish city of Valencia).

But how would Playboy react to my doing a really exhaustive interview with him? In the course of questioning, I could go into his background as well as his present activities and convictions; and it's not difficult to imply criticisms in the way the questions are phrased. Assuming Cohn-Bendit was willing and could be tracked down, I could undertake to deliver a pretty definitive interview inside six weeks. I met him during the student revolts last May; but since then he's become so opposed to the cult of personality that he may refuse even to be interviewed.

About payment: may I make a new suggestion? I realise I'm in debt to Playboy, but working for nothing is a luxury I can't afford with the tax man yapping at my heels. Would Playboy pay me half the proposed fee, and credit the remainder to my account? In this event, of course, there would be no return to monthly payments.

I'm not too eager to take on Murray's second idea.[2] I don't think many serious critics have been taken in by the kind of solipsistic movies he's talking about; in fact, I'd say that nowadays the problem was a precisely opposite tendency to rave about the movies of people like Howard Hawks and George Cukor, as if they were irreplaceable masterpieces.

Do let me know Murray's reactions to my Cohn-Bendit plan.

Love,
Ken

[1] French leader of the Paris student revolt in May 1968.
[2] A proposed article on the trend toward private, plotless, stream-of-consciousness filmmaking.

To John P. Marquand Jr

Hotel Astoria Palace
Valencia – 2
March 17 [1969]

Dear John –

In this fetid city I think of you. I am going to write a sort of anti-profile of the place for 'The New Yorker', pointing out that for all its hideousness it's about the only remaining chic resort on the Mediterranean, since only one's most handpicked friends go there.[1]

Could you possibly jot down any images or reactions you recall from the days spent here so very long ago? I would quote you with great gravity: 'Mr. John P's response to the celebrated pest-hole was ...'

Anything you can recall would be invaluable. Sue too. [...]

All love
Ken

[1] From time to time KPT invited his friends to join him in this unfashionable, ugly town. He wrote of it: 'Some people go on vacation in order to meet strangers. Others go to meet themselves. For this group, Valencia, world hub of anti-tourism, is the predestined haven and hiding place' (*New Yorker*, 25 July 1970).

Memo to Laurence Olivier

[The National Theatre]
31 March 1969

I'd love you to see Part II of IVAN THE TERRIBLE,[1] which has several remarkable colour sequences. Of course it takes place in 16th century Russia; but Russia in the 16th century equals almost anywhere else BC. The atmosphere, of an overwhelmingly authoritarian court, is tremendous. And there are several useful hints in the costumes and décor. The film is available on 16mm and I can arrange a showing at my place any time.

Love,
Ken.

[1] KPT and Olivier had discussed co-directing *King Lear*. KPT suggested that they do it in the scenic style of Eisenstein's *Ivan the Terrible*, Part II.

To Tom Stoppard

The National Theatre
April 1, 1969

Dear Tom –
   Sorry I was out when you dropped in yesterday. It reminded me that I hadn't written to tell you, once more, how much I appreciated your readiness to invest in 'Soldiers' and how terribly sorry I am that it's been for nothing. Or rather, not quite for nothing: we <u>did</u> get the play on, and squeezed 130-odd performances out of it – although, with the notices we got, we ought to have clocked up 300. One of the hundreds of things that I've learned from the whole experience is that Establishment opinion can so penetrate the public mind that people feel ashamed to go against it. Another is that British audiences aren't ready for serious plays about modern politics, probably because the Lord Chamberlain

has prevented people from writing them for more than two centuries.

Anyway: bless you for helping us at such a crucial moment, and so generously.

Yours,
Ken

To Hillard Elkins

[Telegram]

[London]
26 April 1969

AMERICAN FRIENDS RETURNING FROM NEWYORK ALL FEEL SHOW IS BEING GROSSLY LUDICROUSLY OVER PUBLICISED[1] STOP TENNESSEE WILLIAMS WITHDRAWAL ENTIRELY DUE TO SENSATIONAL PUBLICITY STOP BEG YOU TO SOFT PEDDLE ALL PUBLICITY UNTIL OPENING WEEK STOP ADVANCE NOT WORTH A DAMN IF REVIEWS NO GOOD KEN

[1] An example of Elkins' publicity: he had set up a movie screen outside the Eden Theatre which flashed nude pictures of the cast. This provoked a number of car accidents, and a demonstration by Catholics who paraded with placards which read 'Down With Nudity' and 'Ban Lust'.

It seemed that most of New York was going down to the Eden Theatre on Second Avenue and Twelfth Street to attend one of the forty-one previews of Oh! Calcutta! *Meanwhile, Norman Mailer was running for mayor, and the magazine stalls were full of explicit images of the body's most hidden regions. Senator Javits thought the show was 'very interesting', Rudolf Nureyev declared that the bodies were beautiful, and Jerome Robbins described the show as 'joyous, healthy and alive, a celebration'. By now* Calcutta *was no longer simply a series of sketches, but – a precursor of* A Chorus Line *– a show in which the actors had a stage presence outside the sketches. The cast, liberated beyond recall, told stories of the dramatic change in their private lives. As the revue was made ready for the first night on 17 June, sketches by Samuel Beckett, the cartoonist Jules Feiffer, Robert Benton and David Newman, Leonard Melfi, Dan Greenburg, the playwright Sam Shepard, John Lennon, Ken and assorted musicians and painters remained in.*

To Hillard Elkins

[19½ East 62nd Street
New York, New York 10021][1]
[?14 May 1969]

Production Notes for Oh! Calcutta!

For Hilly:

Thoughts after Preview One:[2]

With such a huge coordinating burden falling on Jacques, would it help to engage an assistant director who could run through numbers with members of the cast not needed by Jacques? That way much time could be saved and polish acquired.

1) Opening. Calcutta song needs a slightly faster tempo – at present it's a little dirge-like and overlong. I'd like to see two minutes cut from this number, preferably towards the end (perhaps it should end with the frieze of frozen nudes as the white light comes up).

2) Dick and Jane.[3] Nancy's[4] bedlight shines directly at audience and prevents our seeing her face. (Fans[5] were particularly deafening in this item.) Suggest that laughs are being lost because of timing and inflexions. I.e. 'better than the clean-cut pornography I get around here' – Alan[6] stresses pornography instead of clean-cut, and loses the laugh. Nancy: 'You don't use me in your fantasies? – this is a question, but she does it as a statement, thus losing the laugh. 'This is a very tense bed' would be funnier if he pointed to the bed instead of kicking it.
      Suggest cutting the headstand (dead time) and going straight from '... like a steel column' to 'You make me want to hit you.'
      There should be some light left after the lightshow, otherwise audience will think the number is over (as they have so far).

3) Jack and Jill.[7] George's[8] pauses are interminable: could he be speeded up?
      The way he pulls the ruler out of Jill is too rough: couldn't he extract it more gently and leave the rough stuff until the fuck?
      Boni's[9] running around the stage on 'I won! I won!' seems to me excessive – wouldn't twice be enough?
      And doesn't she shriek too much during the fuck? Must she drown all George's lines?

George's pauses get even more noticeable after the fuck. And: could we cut 'flies and moths and butterflies'? It's very arch.

4) Shoot Your Dog. We really can't start with three downbeat sexual duets. If this number is to stay, could we make it crisper by (a) eliminating the stockings and the line about liking 'a fat leg'? Let her be discovered already wearing her dress. (b) cutting her unbuttoning of his shirt, which wastes time and isn't sexy, and (c) quickening his packing-up afterwards – all he needs to do is pack his gown and wig, he needn't change into jacket and bowler. That way there would be no pause after her line about: 'This one stinks!' and his reply. Pauses are weakening this whole piece. [...]

8) Empress [...] Margo[10] must either wear just the flower in her cunt, or we should cut the Can-can altogether. 'Chase Me, Charlie': let's leave it at just the single chorus sung by Katie at the top of the steps (showing her one-legged drawers) unless we can think of a really witty way of ending it. [...]

The gusset: Fred[11] should be advised that the gusset must fit snugly into the crotch. Nancy's dangles about four or five inches from her cunt. This isn't sexy.

I can't hear Mark's[12] line about 'Plastic lunar bloomers' – can the Window[13] help?

The drawn-out cavorting before Raina's[14] entrance is terribly tedious. What is she going to be wearing? U.V. paint? Unless it's something really spectacular, I think we must work out a completely different way of ending the item. For example: it could end on 'Edible Panties' with the whole cast rushing towards the unrolling paper and munching a handful of it as the Open Window sing the coda. The lights would fade on everyone grimly chewing.

9) Anybody Out There?[15] We couldn't hear the lines coming from upstage – 'religious fuck show', 'come into the audience'. [...]

(General note: Nancy stroking Raina is by far the sexiest thing in the show so far. At least it is for me and the men I've talked to. Please bear in mind the harem syndrome – men like girls on stage with no male competition, and girls also like to see girls making love to each other because it removes their fear of men. If we need an extra number, it should be a female love-making dance designed by Margo for three girls or more.) [...]

Love
Ken

[1] KPT was staying at Elkins's apartment in Manhattan.
[2] On 13 May 1969.
[3] This sketch, by Jules Feiffer, provided the inspiration for the film *Carnal Knowledge* (US, 1971).
[4] Nancy Tribush.
[5] The air conditioning had broken down.
[6] Alan Rachins.
[7] Sketch by Leonard Malfi.
[8] George Welbes.
[9] Boni Enten.
[10] Margo Sappington. Previously a member of the Joffrey Ballet, she had appeared in *Sweet Charity* and *Promises, Promises*. Her association with the choreographer Michael Bennett led to her choreographing and appearing in *Oh! Calcutta!*
[11] Fred Voepel, costume designer.
[12] Mark Dempsey.
[13] 'The Open Window', a group who wrote music and lyrics for the entire show: Peter Schickele, Stanley Walden and Robert Dennis.
[14] Raina Barrett. She wrote *First Your Money, Then Your Clothes* (1973), a book about *Oh! Calcutta!*
[15] A group number.

To Hillard Elkins and Jacques Levy

[19½ East 62nd Street]
[17 May 1969]

Saturday pm: To Hilly and Jacques
Production notes

I think you'll agree that I haven't tried to cast the show or direct the actors or pick the designer or musicians or interfere in the business set-up; but in the matter of material I do claim some expertise and responsibility, and I think recent events have indicated that my instincts haven't been very wide of the mark. I believe we can start to build a first-rate show if we cut our losses and drop the following four items: 'EMPRESS', 'SPECIAL GIRL',[1] 'GREEN PANTS',[2] and 'BATH'.[3]

[...] Some notes based on the Friday marathon:

1. Beckett. Surely it's fatal to <u>start</u> the show with a pause as the slipstage comes in. Could we somehow preset the garbage and hide it with drapes that could fly up with the screen?

2. Robe.[4] The tempo seems to be getting dangerously slow. And I'm surer every time that the logical end is where the audience applauds – just after the frieze of nudes.

3. Dog. Let's put in the cuts, plus an additional one: Leon's 'to me and to you'. ('To you and to me' is enough.) Also I think Katie[5] gags too much and too loud on the dirty torch.

4. Dick and Jane. Alan is getting very slow. Nancy still seems too coarse-grained. And why can't she sit further downstage on the bed at the beginning? 'You don't use me in your fantasies?' must surely be a question: his smile tells her the answer and she explodes: 'You bastard!' The ending is still unclear: I think he should start to talk immediately the lightshow ends, before the audience has had time to applaud. Also let's cut: 'Jane – weren't you there?'

5. Suite.[6] Let's put in the cuts. The words start to get lost about halfway through: could the music be much much quieter? And couldn't we consider freezing the masturbation fantasies whenever anybody comes up with one that's authentically personal and really bizarre? Otherwise won't they tend to get less authentic as the actors run out of genuine fantasies and start to improvise phony ones to get easy laughs? If a thing is true, why shouldn't it be repeated?

5. [*sic*] Sincere Replies. Could they restore the lines about how Bill[7] hurt his arm? Otherwise it looks like some sexual kink. I wish the pause to get drinks could be eliminated; also the lines about the kids ('little princess', etc.) Also I feel we're missing a laugh when Leon[8] notices Margo's tits. I don't think it's clear from 'See somethin' you like?' that she means her tits. Could Bill say 'Some set of boobs, huh?' Also: 'I don't mean folks where you just come in and lay your pecker on the table' – surely the stress should be on 'table' rather than 'pecker' to get the right laugh? The noises off on the sofa are again getting out of hand. It sounds like mass diarrhoea. [...]

12. Who: Whom. I couldn't see Katie's gag. It is important for the sense of the item that she should be obviously tied up while Nancy is physically free. A black patent leather gag might do it, and black patent leather straps round wrists and ankles.

Could we please cut the line about 'happily married' and the one about her hobby being the Times crossword – and just leave in her age and favourite food?

I thought Nancy was a little too reticent last night in the rectal spread department – a touch more disclosure would be appropriate.

13. Was it Good?[9] I thought Mark overdid the paper-dropping – or didn't time it properly. Nancy's 'I need a nipple' was tragically lost – too many of her lines have to be directed upstage, which is a pity. (The same thing happened to 'inter-uterine camera'.)

I feel it's a mistake to have Alan use the same vicious jab to turn her on as he uses to react to: ' ... one of the two best sexual experiences I've had in my entire life.' Shouldn't the latter be savage, and the other ('did he do this?') quite different, perhaps involving not only a manual gesture but a fantastic squirm of the whole pelvic area?

Bill jumping over the wires, by the way, is gorgeous. But later on our attention gets distracted all over the stage. Let's build to a chaotic climax, but always with Perlmutter[10] and the girl at the height of it. And if we're keeping in the opening soliloquy, then we need the one at the end. We can cut both, but only if the climax of the bed scene is a real firework display. [. . .]

[1] Sketch by Bruce Jay Friedman, tried out but not used.
[2] Sketch by Marie Irene Fornes, used only in the New York previews.
[3] Sketch by Jacques Levy, used only in previews.
[4] The opening group number, 'Taking Off the Robe'.
[5] Katie Drew-Wilkinson.
[6] KPT's sketch 'Suite for Five Letters'.
[7] Bill Macy.
[8] Leon Russom.
[9] 'Was It Good For You Too?', sketch by Dan Greenburg.
[10] Character in Greenburg's sketch who answers an ad for an experiment in a sex clinic.

To Hillard Elkins

The National Theatre
May 20 [1969]

Dear Hilly –

I came back to a pile of press clippings about 'Calcutta' including two viciously contemptuous reviews of the sketches at the press con-ference – and (which is much more damaging) a full-length review of the Thursday preview, headlined: 'Mr Tynan! Your sex show is a total bore!' This was in the 'Evening News', with 2 million readers. If any other English journalists sneak in, there must surely be feedback in the

American press. Is there anything we can do to keep them out? Could the box office be instructed to check on ticket buyers with English accents by asking them if they are press?

The effect all this is having in Britain is <u>devastating</u>. Two people called within an hour of my arrival to say how sorry they were that the show was such a disaster. And I've just been shown a nasty item today in the 'Evening Standard' hinting that we have postponed because of the poor quality of the material...

Lock those doors to Limeys! Don't forget that C. Barnes[1] is an assiduous reader of the English press.

Love
Ken

[1] Clive Barnes, drama critic for the *New York Times* 1967–78.

If Lord Chandos and his Board had wanted to rid themselves of their unruly employee two years before, they now had in hand the right weapon: Ken's request for four months' leave of absence to write a book.

Ken had gone to see Chandos on 30 April seeking a sabbatical. Chandos warned him that he was under fire due to the Soldiers *controversy, and recent interviews on 'nudity and sexual intercourse'. The public might be misled into thinking that what Tynan wrote represented the Board's views. There would be a risk in taking the leave of absence. A new approach, a new mind, was needed on the job. Ken replied that he hoped to retain his job (always a part-time one, which permitted his freelance activities) until the new theatre opened on the South Bank.*

Chandos discussed this meeting with his Board members on 12 May. They would grant Ken six months' leave of absence, and a further year's employment before terminating his contract. On 22 May Chandos reported to the Board that Ken had once again come to see him: to say that he might withdraw his request for a leave of absence. Chandos said that nonetheless the post of Literary Manager would be abolished. Ken argued volubly in his own defence.

At this point Olivier stepped in behind the scenes. He later reported that the bitterest battles he had with Chandos were on Ken's behalf. 'The Board knew that if they did fire him, they'd have fired me too, and there wouldn't be a National. It made them hate Ken more and finally made Chandos hate me.'

To Lord Chandos

[The National Theatre]
28 May 1969

Dear Lord Chandos:

Thank you for passing on to me the Board's decision, which is that if my application for six months' leave is granted, I shall be dismissed at the end of 1970 and my job abolished.

Since my work for the National Theatre is my main professional interest in life, and since I know that Sir Laurence is anxious for me to remain in the organisation, I have decided to withdraw my application in its present form. Instead, I should like to ask for three months' leave, bearing in mind that my contract with the National Theatre provides for free time to pursue 'authorship activities'.

Perhaps I should have mentioned another reason why I should be grateful for an opportunity to spend a reasonable period of time away from London and its climate. Last year, an X-ray revealed that I was suffering from an incurable but not incapacitating lung disease called emphysema. The specialists who examined me have since urged me to take the first opportunity to spend some time in a better climate and a relatively unpolluted atmosphere. I can of course produce medical certificates if they should be required.

Finally, I hope the Board will not hold against me certain statements I made over two years ago, for which (incidentally) I have been neither carpeted nor reprimanded. I understand that exception was taken to my saying that my principal loyalty was to the National Theatre rather than to its Board. In my own defence, I can only say that this seems to me analagous to a Labour M.P. declaring complete loyalty to the Party while disagreeing with a specific Cabinet decision. I should imagine that even the Board might feel that its main loyalty was to the National Theatre rather than to itself: in any case, the incident in question took place a long time ago, and in the absence of any indication to the contrary, I had assumed that it had passed into oblivion. I am extremely sorry if this remark of mine should have given offence to yourself and the Board.

I shall be grateful if you would let me know the Board's response to my new application.

Yours sincerely,
[Kenneth Tynan]

To John Mortimer[1]

20 Thurloe Square
May 28, 1969

Dear John –

I hate to bother you with the enclosed, but I am very troubled by the situation and would be enormously grateful for any help you can give.

Larry will be calling you, too. The problem is that neither he nor I will be allowed to raise the question of my employment at the June 9th Board Meeting. And it really must be settled then – because I've signed publishers' contracts, rented our London house and am on the brink of paying a deposit on an Italian apartment ...

Love from us both –
Ken.

Notes for attention of John M.

The situation came about as follows: I wanted 4 months off to write a book. (My contract provides for free time to pursue 'authorship activities.') Kenneth Rae[2] told Larry I would need the Board's permission, since I was 'a Board appointment.' (This isn't strictly accurate, except in the sense that <u>everyone</u> in a top job at the N.T. is a Board appointment. Larry proposed me to the Board six years ago, just as he proposed John Dexter and Bill Gaskill, and they agreed. I now become a 'Board appointment' so that Larry is excluded from the meeting at which I am dismissed.)

Anyway, I went to see Chandos and explained my request – pointing out that Bob Stephens had just been granted a similar application for leave of absence to star in a movie. He said that (a) I might as well make it 6 months, and (b) that I was running a great risk. I asked why. He said that the Board was hostile to me because of certain statements I had made when they rejected the Hochhuth play, principally a remark about my main loyalty being to the National Theatre rather than to its Board. [...] Chandos' statement that 'the Board' was hostile could hardly withstand much scrutiny – apart from himself, only two members of the present Board (Victor Mishcon[3] and Nancy Burman[4]) were members then.

As you know, the Board went into secret session before the May meeting (i.e. Larry, Frank Dunlop[5] and the Arts Council and Dept. of Education people were not admitted). A few days later I went to see Chandos to find out the results. At our previous meeting he had told me that the Board might suggest a terminal date for my appointment if the leave of absence were granted; I replied that I had no wish to leave the N.T. until the new theatre opened its doors on the South Bank, and that if the Board suggested an earlier termination I reserved the right to withdraw my application. He now told me that the Board had decided on what he described as 'the following package': I get six months' leave, at the end of 1970 I am dismissed, the office of Literary Manager is abolished, and replaced (if the Board sees fit) by that of Literary Consultant.

I have since written to Chandos saying that I must now consider whether or not to withdraw my application. He told me at our last meeting, however, that even if I did so, he felt that the Board would still want to dispense with my services, though of course he could not speak for them in advance etc., etc. [...]

A list of productions that I pushed for (and which probably wouldn't have been done if I hadn't) would include: 'Othello', 'Mother Courage', 'Dance of Death', 'Edward II', the all-male 'As You', 'Black Comedy', 'Flea in her Ear', the Zeffirelli 'Much Ado', 'Rosencrantz and Guildenstern', 'A Bond Honoured', 'Andorra', 'Oedipus', 'H' and the forthcoming 'Back to Methuselah'.[6] In fact, I doubt if any of them – except 'Courage' – would have entered the rep without my plugging.

A change of title from 'Literary Manager' to 'Literary Consultant' doesn't worry me. But in abolishing the former job, the Board ought to know that it is going against the wishes of Granville Barker in his specifications for the National Theatre. Barker felt that there should be only two permanent employees on the artistic executive – the director and the Lit. Man. (He didn't want permanent associate directors, since he felt they might fill the repertoire with plays that just happened to suit their directorial talents.) I don't agree with this, but perhaps the Board should be aware of it. In most other respects we have modelled the organization and its programmes on Barker's principles.

So: what to do? I have absolutely no wish to get involved in the kind of public row-cum-debate that would follow the announcement that I have been fired. Nor do I want a big showdown with Lord Chandos. I am quite content with peaceful co-existence. Larry certainly does not want me fired, but feels (though check this with him) that between now and the end of 1970 the Board – i.e. Chandos – may be persuaded to change its mind. Knowing Chandos, I do not believe he would allow this to happen: if I go off on my leave in June, he will consider me fired, and with my own consent. This will be a pretty big triumph for him, and a poor prospect for me. I gave up being 'The Observer's' drama critic to join the N.T.; the major critical posts are now all filled, and no other subsidised theatre needs a Literary Manager. [...]

How about adopting a middle course, which K.T. would accept without demur? Namely, that he should continue in his present job until December 1970 (as suggested), after which his contract should be renegotiated and the title of his job reconsidered.

You can probably tell from this outpouring how much this post has meant to me. I think the emphysema point is quite powerful and will carry weight. The renegotiation of the contract would let them offer me five quid a week, but I'll take that risk. Larry will consult with you about his letter.[7] If you want to raise the subject, it would probably be better to do it under 'Any Other Business', since otherwise Chandos can anticipate it and rule it out of order.

I needn't add that if you think I haven't a leg to stand on, I won't hold it against you.

Ever,
Ken
[...]

[1] A member of the National Theatre Board.
[2] Secretary to the National Theatre Board.
[3] Lord Mishcon (b. 1915), solicitor and partner in the law firm Mishcon de Reya. A member of the GLC 1964–7, he sat on the National Theatre Board 1965–7 and on the South Bank Board 1977–82.
[4] Also Administrator of the Birmingham Repertory Theatre.
[5] Frank Dunlop (b. 1927), English director who joined the National Theatre in 1967 as an Associate Director; was founder director of the Young Vic in 1969 and director of the Edinburgh Festival 1984–91.
[6] Play by George Bernard Shaw (1921); directed by Clifford Williams and Donald MacKechnie, the National Theatre production opened 31 July (Part 1) and 1 August (Part 2) 1969.
[7] Presumably a letter to the Board arguing that he wished to retain KPT.

To Lord Chandos

19½ East 62nd Street
June 18, 1969

Dear Lord Chandos:

Many thanks for your letter of June 10. I am very sorry to hear that I misconstrued the import of the Board's original proposal.

On the whole, however, I think I should like to accept the new offer which you outline – namely, that I should take six months' leave (of which three would be salaried), after which I would return to the National Theatre on the same contractual basis as at present, except that my title would be changed to that of Consultant.

I should be glad if you would convey to the Board my thanks for their generous provision in the matter of my salary, and also for their sympathy in the matter of my health.

Yours sincerely,
[Kenneth Tynan]

To Laurence Olivier

[19½ East 62nd Street]
18 June 1969

Dear Larry,

By now you will have received and probably read the Shaffer play. It reminds me of a vast Baroque church – full of decorative fantasies and operatic gestures – and although I think a lot of it is tinsel rather than gold leaf, I think we ought to do it. After all, it will have to be cut quite heavily and a good director could make sure that the tinsel went first. It is perfectly obvious that the play will not work without two enormous star performances. Both of them have to carry off some tremendous feats of bravura without slipping off the tightrope. My own list for Gideon would be:

1. Scofield
2. Guiness [*sic*]
3. Hordern

And for Mark:

1. You
2. Nicol Williamson
3. Scofield (who might play it rather interestingly in a cold, spikey, satanic style.)

I need hardly tell you where I think the tinsel is – the watercress on the head, the habit of addressing people as birds, etc., etc. Also, I doubt whether Mark's Jewishness is really necessary to the plot, and I don't think he should say so dramatically that he killed his wife when we learn in the end that in fact he didn't. But these things are all curable.

Let's frankly approach the play as a vehicle for two soloists and cut the parts to suit their talents.

Shaffer would like Peter Hall or Anthony Page[1] to direct, in that order, and I entirely agree with him.

I gather we have to make up our minds quite soon about the play or Peter will feel obliged to offer it to Binkie [Beaumont]. If you decide to go ahead with it, it might be an inducement to suggest playing it in repertoire from January until the end of the season and then detaching it to play in the West End for a run.[2]

Hope you're happily recovered.[3]

Love to Joan and yourself from both of us.
[Kenneth Tynan]

[1] Anthony Page (b. 1935), English director who worked as an assistant at the Royal Court and then at the RSC before being appointed Artistic Director of the Royal Court in 1964, where he directed *Inadmissible Evidence* and *Waiting for Godot*.
[2] *The Battle of Shrivings* would have its first performance at the Lyric, Hammersmith in 1970, directed by Peter Hall.
[3] In April Olivier had had to be flown back from New York for an emergency operation.

To Tracy Tynan[1]

Hotel de l'Abbaye
Talloires
Lac d'Annecy
July 2 [1969]

Dearest T –

We are both stricken with liver attacks, having spent four days motoring across France and eating at 3-star restaurants. We are now at the tiny village of Talloires, which is a unique gastronomique miracle – one 3-star place, two 2-stars, two 1-star – unable to eat anything except consommé. Also it is raining. In two days we cross the Alps for Milan and then Porto Ercole. If we are strong enough, that is. Hannibal did not cross the Alps on consommé.

I thought I'd tell you a bit about 'Oh! Calcutta!' in New York. Don't be depressed by what you read in the English papers. At least 2/3 of the show is just as I would have wanted it – elegant, funny, at times disturbing, and pleasantly sexy. But sympathise with the problems

facing the critics. We were confronting them, for the first time, with
private areas of experience – sexual realities – in a public place – a
theatre. I think they were stunned. And as most of them are middle
aged men accompanied by their wives, they had to say that they found
the show 'boring'. (That's what early critics said about 'Lady Chatterley', Henry Miller[2] and Joyce's 'Ulysses'.) There we were, acting out
their fantasies before their eyes: they must have been dumbfounded.
One of them – a bachelor who writes for 'Newsweek'[3] – saw the point
of what we were trying to do and said that I had brought the sexual
revolution to the middle classes for the first time!

What pleased me more than anything was a note from Jerome
Robbins (who directed 'West Side Story', 'Fiddler on the Roof', etc,
etc). He said the show was 'a triumph, joyous, beautiful, a true celebration – full of High Definition Performance.[4] You can't say fairer
than that.

In any case, we are playing to capacity. This may not last when the
really hot weather comes, but it's encouraging.

I'm sorry I was asleep the other night when you called us back. I just
wanted to make sure that you were going to join us in Italy in September. We haven't had a holiday together for centuries, and I would
enjoy it enormously. The villa is big enough for us all to have privacy.
You can bring a girl or boy friend, as you wish, and lead your own life
as much as you want to. The villa is near Pisa and Florence and only a
short drive to the sea. [. . .]

[last page missing]

[1] Tracy was still at Dartington Hall.
[2] Henry Miller (1891–1980), American author whose works include the sexually explicit novels
Tropic of Cancer (1934; published 1961) and *Tropic of Capricorn* (1938; published 1962).
[3] Jack Kroll.
[4] KPT had defined his concept of high definition performance as 'supreme professional polish,
hard-edged technical skill, the effortless precision without which no artistic enterprise – however
strongly we may sympathise with its aims or ideas – can inscribe itself on our memory [. . .] the
hypnotic saving grace of high and low art alike, the common denominator that unites tragedy,
ballroom dancing, conversation and cricket.' ('Shouts and Murmurs', the *Observer*, 7 April 1968).

To William Shawn

Fattoria Mansi-Bernardini[1]
Segromigno Monte
Lucca
September 17th 1969

Dear Mr Shawn,

Your cable was tremendous.[2] I can't tell you how grateful I am, nor how unlikely I am ever to forget the exact spot on the terrace of this villa where I was standing when I read it. I'll now await your detailed comments on the proofs.

When this piece has been nudged into its final form, I'd like to go on to either Mr. Pinter or Paul McCartney. I shall be here in Italy until November (possibly through November), so I can't start work on either gentleman until then: but I'd appreciate your thoughts on which of them seems at present the likelier subject. I incline towards McCartney, who has isolated himself more and more in the past from the other Beatles and indeed from the public: he seems to have reached an impasse that might be worth exploring. On the other hand Pinter is a much closer friend and would be more accessible to intimate scrutiny. Do let me know what you think.

More squalidly: would it be premature to ask you whether I could have a cheque for Valencia? It would be very welcome.

Meanwhile, thank you again for the cable.

Yours sincerely,
Kenneth Tynan

[1] A rented seventeenth-century villa.
[2] 15 September: 'YOUR VALENCIA PROFILE IS THE PIECE EYE DREAM ABOUT BUT RARELY SEE PERIOD TRUE HIGH SPIRITS AND HUMOR AND WRITING COMMA WRITING PERIOD [...]'

To John P. Marquand Jr

Fattoria Mansi-Bernardini
Sept. 29, 1969

Dear John –

Happy to get your note. It now seems almost certain that we shall be here throughout November, so why not aim to come for a week or so in late October or early Nov.? The weather at present is blue and hot by day but chilly at night: winter, we're told, isn't perceptible by day until November at the earliest, though sudden slashing storms occasionally hit the area. Kathleen and I tend to work mornings and play in the afternoons and evenings. An excellent idea would be for you to rent a car so that you aren't trapped in our fastness during the mornings. As I told you (didn't I?) we're about eight miles out of Lucca, with Florence, Fiesole, Pisa, Volterra, Sam Gimignano* and the sea all within a 20–60 mile radius. Bologna, Porto Ercole and Siena are a bit further away but not much.

Incidentally, Shawn of the New Yorker seems quite thrilled by my Valencia piece, in which you were quoted. He sent me a memorably enthusiastic telegram.

Let us know when to expect you. No one else is here except small daughter, nanny, a dog, two goldfish and conceivably a cat.

Love to both:
Ken

*You remember Sam. Used to be a big wheel in Cosa Nostra until Hoover had him deported. Cousin of Shrimps Marinera.

To Laurence Olivier

Fattoria Mansi-Bernardini
October 21, 1969

Dear L:

Your letter of October 13 has obviously crossed with two of mine. I'm terribly sorry about the Shaffer: I knew nothing of what was happening, but your letter indicates pretty clearly that Peter was playing both ends against the middle. I'm glad that 'The Idiot'[1] has turned out well, and I look forward to reading it. Finally, the reorganization of the press dept. sounds just darling.

The Derek Granger idea[2] worries me, mainly because of the unfortunate timing. I'd always understood that if you decided to appoint another Lit. adviser it would happen during my leave of absence, thus forestalling any tricky queries from the press. I was going away, you needed a stand-in, and it was agreed to keep him on to work with me, etc., etc. But now? If Granger comes in, he'll be starting about the time I get back. My heart sinks as I foresee the questions from the papers:

1) Isn't the National Theatre happy with your advice, Mr. T?
2) Why have you been demoted? Has there been a quarrel with Sir Laurence or Lord Chandos?
3) Why does the National need <u>two</u> literary advisers when other theatres don't need <u>one</u>?
4) Where is the money coming from to pay his salary? Will he be paid the same as Tynan? (You'll remember that Lord Willis attacked the N.T. in the Lords for paying even one Literary Manager's salary.)

Ironically, things would be a little easier if 'The National Health'[3] had been a flop. As it is, I smell trouble, which is something of which we have all had enough to last us for a long time. I was perfectly content to let Lord C. get away with his little plan to downgrade me so long as it didn't look like a deliberate rebuff. If the second consultant had moved in to cover my absence there would have been no problem. Now, however, it can only look (to mix a couple of metaphors) as if I've been reduced to the ranks immediately after picking a winner.

I wonder, therefore, if it wouldn't be wise to wait a bit, at least until you and Derek and I can work out a solution that doesn't expose us to journalistic crossfire.

Do let me know your thoughts.[4] I have to pay a quick visit to the States early in November, and I shall be in London all day November 10th (a Monday). Could we have a chat then?

All love,
Ken

[1] Simon Gray's adaptation of Fyodor Dostoevsky's novel, directed by Anthony Quayle, designed by Josef Svoboda, opened at the National Theatre on 15 July 1970.
[2] Chandos had insisted on appointing a second Literary Consultant; Olivier chose Derek Granger (b. 1921), previously theatre and film critic for the *Financial Times* (1952–8) and drama and current affairs producer at Granada Television and LWT (1958–69). He was Literary Consultant at the National 1969–73.
[3] Peter Nichols' black comedy about the health service was directed by Michael Blakemore and opened on 16 October 1969, starring Jim Dale.
[4] Olivier sent a telegram (31 October) saying that it was too late to go back on Granger and that he truly thought KPT would be delighted with the new arrangement. He added that KPT's guidance was much missed during his absence.

To the Editor, the *Evening Standard*

Villa Bernardini
[Published 28 November 1969]

I've just seen Londoner's Diary for November 14, in which I'm reported as having said that Oh! Calcutta [*sic*] will be 'more decadent and perverse' in London than in New York.

I'm afraid someone has been twisting my words. A journalist in California asked me whether there was any difference between English and American sexual habits. I replied, in what I hoped was a flippant tone, that it was well known that the English were far more decadent and perverse. This little joke is the source of the remark attributed to me. I really must make a note never to be flippant in public again.

Kenneth Tynan

CHAPTER SEVEN

The Troubled Seventies

After his sabbatical in Italy, Ken returned early in 1970 to the National Theatre. He had been demoted to 'Literary Consultant', though in effect it was business as usual.

He sought out more plays: and he got Olivier to bring in Michael Blakemore to direct Peter Nichols's The National Health, and Jonathan Miller, The Merchant of Venice. In 1979 William Gaskill's direction of Maggie Smith in The Beaux' Stratagem and Ingmar Bergman's production of Hedda Gabler were roundly applauded. The next year two of Brecht's directors came from Germany to mount Coriolanus. In July 1971 Adrian Mitchell's Tyger opened, a celebration of the life and work of William Blake. At the end of that year Ken persuaded Olivier to take the lead in Eugene O'Neill's Long Day's Journey Into Night. The next production was Tom Stoppard's philosophical romp, Jumpers, whose text Ken had worked on effectively. In July 1972 Ben Hecht and Charles MacArthur's The Front Page – yet another Tynan choice – had a resounding success.

The theatre was decidedly out of the doldrums it had sunk into during the late 1960s. Ken felt impelled to point out the successes to the press, while privately castigating Olivier (now seriously ill – a thrombosis followed cancer) for his unsteady leadership. He did not demand more status, or money on his own behalf, but asked that his job be recognized for what it was.

In mid-1971 Lord Chandos was relieved of his job as Chairman and replaced by Sir Max Rayne, a property tycoon with a strong interest in the arts. The following April, Olivier was summoned by Rayne and told that the Board had appointed Peter Hall in his place. Neither Ken nor his colleagues, John Dexter, Michael Blakemore and Frank Dunlop, had been consulted. Ken began a counter-offensive. At a Board meeting on 18 April 1972 he presented his arguments in favour of the Olivier regime. He added that in the best of the theatre's productions there was an analytical intelligence and textual clarity, along with 'a flamboyance, a showmanship'. 'We are the Cavaliers, Stratford' (which Peter Hall had run) 'the Roundheads.' Under Peter Hall the country would have two Roundhead theatres. But his (almost) *lone battle was fought too late to change the day: Olivier had done nothing to plan his succession.*

The die was cast, and Ken prepared to leave. 'I feel ... a slight pang now all has been said and the end of the chapter settled,' he confided to his journal. 'But enough of vicarious living. I must go back to taking responsibility for what I do, which is write.'

He continued to work at the National until the end of 1973, closely involving himself with the production of Equus *(by Peter Shaffer), and two further productions which he had proposed: Trevor Griffiths' political study of the left,* The Party, *and Eduardo de Filippo's classic,* Saturday, Sunday, Monday.

Oh! Calcutta! *had opened in London in June 1970 at the Roundhouse in Chalk Farm, north London. Though the Lord Chamberlain's power to censor had been abolished, the vice squad was despatched to keep an eye on the proceedings, and a battalion of Grundys went to work to have the show banned as 'depraving and corrupting'. On opening night, nearly everyone agreed that the revue was a theatrical breakthrough, that the sex barrier had been crashed once and for all.*

However, Ken was disturbed by the show. To his journal he confessed his own sexual preferences: 'The slow revelation of the body, not immediate nudity ... certain voices and the combination and use of words ... I don't like group sex, and, as a matter of fact, I haven't tried any.' He wanted to make amends for the show's shortcomings, and to that end he spent much of the next decade devising other projects with sex as the theme, designed to deliver what Oh! Calcutta! *had failed to achieve.*

After their collaboration on the script of Macbeth, *Roman Polanski suggested that Ken write another film for him, an erotic scenario. 'Two girls and a man,' Ken suggested, 'a Mediterranean villa, an atmosphere of secrecy and slightly decadent sensuality.' When Polanski eventually dropped out, Ken decided to direct the script himself, titled* Our Life with Alex and Sophie.

As his wife, I was not enthusiastic about the project. I tried to understand the puppetmaster who created Alex – himself a puppet pulled by his own compulsions – and the man whose voice came to me so movingly. Ken eventually abandoned the project in favour of a proposed biography of the Austrian analyst Wilhelm Reich, based on research he had begun for a New Yorker *article. Since falling upon a copy of Reich's* The Sexual Revolution *in late 1958, he had admired the young disciple of Freud and Marx. He wanted to find out why this maverick had turned against his mentors, and to explore his view that orgasmic potency was a prerequisite of physical and emotional balance.*

In December 1972 Ken started an affair with a young out-of-work actress.

He wrote in his journal, 'The more K. is convinced that I love her, the more she suffers when I see N.' His public life remained as packed as ever. Tynan the pundit delivered his views in his Observer *column, 'Shouts and Murmurs', while he was endlessly interviewed in the press and for radio and television – activity which filled the gap of meaningful work.*

To his journal he confided his uncertainty, his pain, and a more complex exploration of ideas than he permitted in his journalism. He wrote, 'I disbelieve in art because I no longer believe that there is a secret something inside me which, when properly expressed, will take on a higher reality and deserve the name of "art".' On another occasion he wrote that he could no longer write well without a cogent moral or philosophical stance. But even in his worst moments, a new plan could jolt Ken out of his depression; he nearly bought a Cadillac hearse (having just learnt to drive), and settled for a Jaguar. At one point he contemplated buying a 150-foot Victorian Gothic tower, ignoring the fact that his emphysemic lungs might find the steps daunting. He took me and the two children on jaunts to Wales, to Oxford, to Spain and to France and noted in his journal that Roxana and Matthew were both 'breath-bereaving in their prettiness'. In the marriage, however, complaints were registered by both of us, while I began to work more consistently on my own projects.

In 1975, eager to leave England (he had been hospitalized on several occasions, and advised to seek a warmer climate), Ken proposed himself to William Shawn of the New Yorker *and the editor enthusiastically took on his former critic as a profile writer.*

On 30 September 1976, Carte Blanche, *the sequel to* Oh! Calcutta!, *opened in London to generally poor critical response. But the* New Yorker's *offer and life in America promised new hope. On 30 October Ken flew to California to join me and the children. He never again lived in England.*

To William Shawn

20 Thurloe Square
5th January 1970

Dear Mr Shawn,

I'm saddened to have to tell you that Paul McCartney doesn't want to be written about at the moment – at least, not by me. I gather that for some time now the Beatles have been moving more and more in separate directions. Paul went to a recording session for a new single last Sunday which was apparently the first Beatles activity in which he'd engaged for nearly nine months. He doesn't know quite where his future lies, and above all he doesn't want to be under observation while he decides. I quite understand how he feels, but, coming on top of the Pinter turndown, it's a bit of a blow.

May I propose another idea? I was lunching the other day with an exiled Czech writer[1] who used to edit the literary magazine that was the cultural spearhead of the Dubček reforms. He has the advantage of speaking enough foreign languages to be able to work outside Czechoslovakia; but he told me that most Czech artists were nowadays feeling terribly isolated and abandoned. They are trying in small ways to continue their work under pressure, and nobody outside Czechoslovakia is paying any attention. 'If you get the chance,' my friend said, 'do write something to show them that they're not completely forgotten.' I know these people well, and I too have been guilty of blotting them out of my mind since the new régime imposed itself. Would you consider letting me do a piece, on Prague Revisited,[2] to find out what remains – if anything – of that brutally dismantled artistic renaissance? I don't mean a series of reviews of plays, films, etc., but an attempt to understand the atmosphere in which these men are working. I do not imagine that it could be other than a fairly melancholy piece.

Do let me know if this idea has any appeal for the magazine.

Yours,
Kenneth Tynan

[1] Antonin J. Liehm (b. 1924) served on the editorial board of the Czech Writers' Union journal *Literarni Noviny* in the early 1960s; expelled from the Communist Party in 1967; edited *The Culture of Politics* (1970).
[2] Not written.

To Hillard Elkins

20 Thurloe Square
5th January 1970

Dear Hilly,

As you say, we can postpone the final decisions on the London production of 'Oh! Calcutta!' until you arrive. But could I say a couple of words about the foreign productions?

I think we (by which I mean you) are asking too much. I hear from Michael [White] that you are hoping to get 30 per cent of the gross on the Dutch production. Frankly, I don't think any established and respectable producer would give you anything like as much, with the result that you may end up dealing with people on the theatrical fringe who are neither very knowledgeable nor entirely trustworthy. And I'm rather worried that the same thing may happen in France and elsewhere. I would much rather we made a reasonable deal with a knowledgeable and tasteful producer than make a fantastic, epoch-making deal with a third-rater. For example, one of the leading Dutch impresarios is a buddy of Michael's, and he is sure that no respectable Amsterdam producer would touch the proposal you are making. The result may be that you get the show on all over the world at a record-breaking percentage, but under auspices so uncertain that it collapses after a short run.

There's one step I feel I ought to take to protect what remains of my reputation. We've already discussed the Australian production, in which you agreed to some such form of words: 'based on the New York production devised by K. T.': but as far as European productions are concerned – since they are nearer home and more widely reported in the British press – I feel I must reserve the right to withhold my name altogether if I don't like the production set-up or the contents of the show. In theory, for example, one of the big clip-joint beer-halls in Hamburg might be willing to pay the earth to put on a smudged and sleazy carbon copy of the show, but I certainly wouldn't want my name on it.

Please accept these comments in the spirit in which they are presented. They are mainly prompted by the truly appalling word-of-mouth I am getting on the West Coast productions.[1] Worse than that, there have been several instances lately where old friends have come to dinner and deliberately refrained from mentioning that they've seen the show, in order not to endanger our friendship. I really can't let that happen in Europe.

Can't wait to see you in London. Incidentally, I see in 'Variety' that Jacques is supposed to be doing a Broadway musical this spring. Is this true?

Love,
Ken

---

[1] *Oh! Calcutta!* opened in San Francisco in September 1969 and in Los Angeles in December 1969. On 28 October 1969 the San Francisco Vice Squad arrested one of the actors and accused

him of 'illegal genital contact'. Seven members of the Los Angeles cast were arrested on charges of lewd conduct and indecent exposure.

To Mike Nichols

[Telegram]

[London]
15 January 1970

FURTHER TO PREVIOUS CABLE CAN OFFER YOU LONG DAYS JOURNEY INTO NIGHT[1] WITH OLIVIER AND NICOL WILLIAMSON STOP OPENING AUTUMN 1970 OR REASONABLY SOON AFTERWARDS STOP HOW DOES THAT GRAB YOU LOVE KEN TYNAN

[1] By Eugene O'Neill (1957).

To William Shawn

20 Thurloe Square
23rd February 1970

Dear Mr. Shawn,

Something has fortunately come up which gives me the perfect shape for my piece on Nicol Williamson.[1] He has just been invited by President Nixon[2] to give a solo 75-minute performance at the White House on March 19th.[3] So far as I know, this is a unique honour; nobody else has ever been given such a free hand to assault the President's cultural sensibilities. The story of how Williamson plans and executes the whole operation should be fascinating.

My covering it raises two questions on which I'd like your help:
1) Would the New Yorker pay my travelling expenses to fly with Williamson from London to Washington and back?
2) Could anyone on the magazine help me to obtain a press pass into the White House on March 19th?[4]

I hope you are as excited by this development as I am.

Yours sincerely,
Kenneth Tynan

[1] Nicol Williamson (b. 1938), Scottish-born actor associated with the RSC and the Royal Court, who played Maitland in John Osborne's *Inadmissible Evidence* (1964).

[2] In February 1969 Richard Nixon dined at Chequers with Prime Minister Harold Wilson, who had just seen Nicol Williamson playing Hamlet in a production by Tony Richardson and raved about the actor's performance to his guest.

[3] The official White House invitation announced the appearance of 'Nichol [*sic*] Williamson in "Five Hundred Years of Entertainment in Poetry, Drama and Song".' The programme included speeches from *Hamlet*, John Osborne's *Inadmissible Evidence*, an erotic poem by e e cummings, the final pages of Samuel Beckett's novel *How It Is* and songs such as John Dankworth's 'Dunsinane Blues'. KPT wrote a lengthy account of the event, 'Are You the Entertainment?', *New Yorker*, 15 January 1972.

[4] Shawn cabled (March 1970): 'WASHINGTON HAS AGREED TO SEND YOU AN INVITATION IN YOUR CAPACITY AS WHAT IT CALLS A BRITISH THEATRE NOTABLE.'

To William Shawn

20 Thurloe Square
5th March 1970

Dear Mr. Shawn,

Thank you for your cable about expenses and credentials for Williamson at the White House. The occasion is developing very promisingly. Williamson has slightly alarmed the President by insisting on bringing with him a group of veteran musicians called 'The World's Greatest Jazz Band',[1] and he is coming to New York next Wednesday to rehearse for a week before the big night. I shall be coming with him, and it would be very gracious if the magazine could let me have some money to cover my expenses while I'm there. If I may, I'll telephone you when I arrive on Wednesday. I'll be staying at the Algonquin.

Yours sincerely,
Kenneth Tynan

[1] The group included Bud Freeman and Bob Haggart. Apparently they played 'South Rampart Street Parade' and Kid Ory's 'Savoy Blues' while Williamson was resting between speeches.

Memo to Laurence Olivier

[The National Theatre]
6 March 1970

Dear L:

I gather from various sources that Mike Nichols is taking it for granted that LONG DAY'S JOURNEY is on. I can't tell you how embarrassed – personally and professionally – I shall feel if we abandon the project.

No director in the history of entertainment has been more in demand than Mike is now.[1] He has been offered every assignment in every medium and he can name his own price anywhere on earth. Out of hundreds of possibilities he selected our offer. I say 'our' because it was yours as well as mine. You authorised me to offer him yourself in LONG DAY'S JOURNEY as part of the package. He accepted. It now turns out that the actor he had always wanted to play Jamie also happens to be in our company. Mike's dates, yours and Bob's[2] all happily coincide. The production would reflect enormous prestige on everybody concerned.

I know that the thought of another big part daunts you. I'm writing in the hope of persuading you to look at this from my point of view. On your authorisation I made a firm offer to Mike. If we back out now, my 'credibility' with him will be badly, perhaps irrevocably, damaged. Whenever in the future I approach him with an idea, he will remember this fiasco and watch his step. I value his friendship and trust as much as I value his talent, and I have known all three for a very long time. Please let this bond be honoured.[3]

Yours ever,
[K.T.]

[1] Nichols had directed the films *Who's Afraid of Virginia Woolf?* (US, 1965) and the award-winning *The Graduate* (US, 1968).
[2] Robert Stephens.
[3] Olivier wanted to direct a film the following spring (this never happened) and didn't feel he could learn a long part at the same time: 'For myself,' he wrote to KPT (10 March 1970), 'I must say that I feel a bit incredulous that you should be quite so prepared to land me in for studying a huge part and sweating out performances for possibly many months, having at least one hour and a half sessions on being heard my lines before each one, feeling nothing but cold dislike for the part, the play and the whole occasion simply in order to save you from what turns out to be an entirely imaginary danger' – Nichols had 'assured me he was not at all put out'. *Long Day's Journey Into Night* eventually opened on 21 December 1971 with Olivier playing James Tyrone and Michael Blakemore directing.

To Hillard Elkins

Algonquin Hotel
March 18 [1970]

Dear Hilly –
You will be delighted to hear that the lack of flying facilities at the Roosevelt Grill' will <u>not</u> mean that you will have to drop 'Who/Whom'.

Last year I evolved with Jacques a contingency plan if flying was not feasible at the Eden. Instead of <u>lowering</u> the girl in a net, you <u>wheel</u> her on a trolley, suspended from a crossbar, thus:

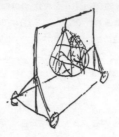

OK?

Love
Ken

<hr>

[1] Elkins was planning to mount *Oh! Calcutta!* at the New York hotel venue; this never happened.

To Michael White

[20 Thurloe Square]
10 April 1970

CONFIDENTIAL

Dear Michael,

While we were all getting het up the other night, there were two points I ought to have made and didn't. They are as follows:

1) Whatever Clifford does or does not do with the show, the press are going to call it what they've always called it – Kenneth Tynan's 'Oh! Calcutta!'. Not Hillard Elkins'; not Jacques Levy's; but mine. Now you and I know perfectly well that this is a wildly misleading description. Nevertheless, there is nothing we can do about it. My point is that, whatever happens, I am going to be held responsible by the public and the critics. This is partly why I reacted so strongly to the bland suggestion – or so it seemed to me – that it would be a fairly simple matter to throw out the existing music and choreography and start all over again.

2) I think Clifford is a first-rate director. I think Jacques is, too. Yet if it had not been for a whole night spent cajoling and pleading with him and Hilly, 'Oh! Calcutta!' would have opened with 'Special Girl', 'Bath' and 'Green Pants' still in it. If that had happened, I wouldn't have been surprised if the show had folded after a couple of months.

love,
Ken

To the Editor, the *Sunday Telegraph*

[20 Thurloe Square]
[Published 12 April 1970]

Last Sunday your reviewer, Frank Marcus, described me as 'reduced, it seems, to propagating titillation by nudity and chemically induced ecstasy'.

While I thoroughly approve of titillation ('titillate – v.t. Tickle, excite pleasantly' – Concise Oxford Dictionary), I have never advocated or recommended 'chemically induced ecstasy' of any kind. A fairly abject retraction would oblige.[1]

KENNETH TYNAN

[1] Frank Marcus replied: 'I was referring to Mr Tynan's advocacy of the legislation of marijuana.'

To Jonathan Miller
(copy to Laurence Olivier)

[The National Theatre]
14th April 1970

Dear Jonathan,
  Just one or two thoughts after last night's runthrough[1] – some of which I mentioned to you, others not:

a) Is there too much incidental music in the opening scene? Newcomers would find the plot hard to follow.

b) I wish Antonio had a stronger whiff of queerness – a hint of mint, as Mel Brooks says. Could he perhaps wear a ring or two, or a more flamboyant necktie?

c) In the borrowing scene, Bassanio's move D.R. is strikingly unreal – people surely don't walk away from café tables while talking to people <u>at</u> café tables.

d) I feel Shylock is too quickly and too early stung to anger. In the 'yes, to smell pork' speech, shouldn't the tone be one of easy, bantering superiority? I think he should be smiling broadly, taking no offence at all. He has turned down such invitations a hundred times before. Much later, in the Tubal scene, he says that he has not felt the curse of Jewishness 'till now'. If so, he should not show it earlier.

e) I think Jim Dale[2] is giving one of his rather familiar Cockney music-hall performances. In particular, we have seen that jaunty shuffling walk rather too often before. Could he perhaps be made a bit more countrified?

f) The scene of Jessica's escape seems rather lack-lustre. You say that Gratiano and the others are meant to be bored and disapproving, but what comes over at present is just listlessness.

g) Could Morocco be brown instead of black? He's too much of a golliwog.

h) It's a pity that you have <u>two</u> blind old men, bent double. Perhaps Harry Lomax[3] could adopt a more upright walk – some blind men walk leaning backwards. Aragon's nose-picking seemed a bit superfluous.

i) I think two intervals are one too many for a play as light in texture as this. Why not have one, at the end of Bassanio's casket scene and the letter from Antonio?

j) I don't understand what Joan [Plowright][4] is playing in this scene. Whatever it is, I feel it could do with more <u>energy</u>. I know you want an anti-romantic interpretation, but I should have thought this could be achieved without such a total loss of warmth. Couldn't Portia be a fulsome Victorian Candida to Bassanio's Marchbanks?[5]

k) We mentioned the fact that the first three lines of 'Tell me where is fancy bred' end in rhymes for 'lead'. I don't know whether it's possible to make this a clue for Bassanio, but it might be worth trying.

l) Audibility is a bit of a problem throughout, the worst offenders being Joan, Jeremy[6] and Tony Nichols[7] [*sic*].

m) 'My people do already know my mind,
    And will acknowledge you and Jessica ...'
It might be nice if Portia had to struggle to remember Jessica's name. As far as I know, this is the first time she mentions it.

n) Shylock: 'You have among you many a purchased slave. ...' – would this not be more pointed if one of the gentiles had a black manservant?

o) I think Portia's tone in the mercy speech should be one of pained bewilderment, as if patiently spelling out the facts of life to a simpleton:
    'The quality of mercy is not <u>strained</u> –
    It <u>droppeth</u> ...'

p) Tony Nichols finds it very hard to be ignoble or unlikeable on stage, but surely there must be more icy smiling relish – more overt malice – when he insists that half of Shylock's goods should go to Lorenzo, and that he should become a Christian. Gratiano could whoop with delight at both proposals.

q) I'm not sure about Shylock's offstage collapse. The fact that nobody makes a move to help him is rather hard to swallow.

r) Would it help with your scene-change problem if Portia and Nerissa came back to the courtroom for a forgotten book or document so that the ring scene could be played there while the chairs are being struck?

s) 'On such a night...' I think it's just possible to mock these speeches, but I think it might work better if Lorenzo and Jessica were sitting side by side leaving longer and longer pauses between each speech as each desperately tries to think of another analogy. But Lorenzo's 'How sweet the moonlight sleeps' speech simply can't be sent up: it defeats mockery. Even oafs may have poetic moments, and this is Lorenzo's. Incidentally, I don't understand Jessica's behaviour in this scene. Is she happy, or not? Also, I feel there's much too much music hereabouts. I don't see why it should start before Lorenzo's line about waking Diana with a hymn.

If these points seem carping, it's merely because I've left out all that I liked, which was a very great deal.

love,
[Ken]

---

[1] Miller's production of *The Merchant of Venice*, with Olivier playing Shylock, would open on 28 April 1970.

[2] Jim Dale (b. 1935), English actor, playing Launcelot Gobbo.
[3] As Old Gobbo.
[4] As Portia.
[5] Characters in George Bernard Shaw's *Candida* (1897).
[6] Jeremy Brett (b. 1935), playing Bassanio; a National Theatre actor 1967–71, he later starred on television as Sherlock Holmes.
[7] Anthony Nicholls (1907–77), playing Antonio.

Memo to Laurence Olivier

[The National Theatre]
23 April 1970

Much of what follows probably belongs in the teach-your-grandmother-to-suck-eggs department. All the same it may be worth while to re-state the obvious from time to time.

I suspect that we may be falling into a trap. We are tending to confuse ends and means in planning the repertoire. Let me explain what I mean.

Of course it's vital to find enticing parts for valuable company members. But we are getting into the habit of placing this aim above that of finding the plays we ought to be doing. We ask ourselves: 'what can we find for X next year? – otherwise he'll leave us.' The implication here is that the purpose of keeping the company together is merely to keep the company together. But of course it isn't. The purpose of keeping the company together is to do first-rate plays, the best plays of all periods, the celebrated spectrum, in fact. Keeping individual actors happy is the means, in which we frequently lose sight of the end.

We can't find a great part that Derek Jacobi[1] can play so we manufacture a part for him. You mustn't tell me that we would have thought of doing THE IDIOT but for the sake of keeping Derek happy. To keep Edward Woodward[2] happy we do Cyrano, another play we none of us have thought of doing. And would we really be longing to revive Patriot[3] if we didn't want to keep Bob [Stephens] happy? I know I'm exaggerating; but it would be nice to worry less about which actors we have to please next year and more about what contribution we're going to make to the art of drama next year.

K.T.

[1] Sir Derek Jacobi (b. 1938), stage, film and television actor who joined the National Theatre in

October 1963. His roles there included Laertes in *Hamlet* (1963), Brinsley Miller in *Black Comedy* (1956) and Myshkin in *The Idiot* (1970).
[2] Edward Woodward (b. 1930), English actor who had joined the National Theatre in 1969 to play Flamineo in *The White Devil*, and the title role in *Cyrano* (October 1970).
[3] *A Patriot for Me* (1965) by John Osborne was first produced in June 1965 at the Royal Court, with George Devine as Baron von Epp.

Memo to Laurence Olivier

[The National Theatre]
23 April 1970

Dear L. O.

I've just been looking at the back page of the latest cast list. It's a mine of information about who does what at the NT. If I like the way a wig has been combed I can drop a mash note to Amanda Ashton. If I'm bowled over by the cutting, I can send a valentine to Edith Carter. If the armour strikes me as having been particularly well-burnished, I can get Reg Amos to autograph my programme. But if I like the choice of play and general shape of the repertoire, the only person I can congratulate is you. Similarly, if I'm an undiscovered Osborne, there's no indication of how and to whom I should submit my script, except presumably to yourself. Would it be too much to ask, however lowly its position may be, that the literary department should get some acknowledgment of its existence as part of the National Theatre Staff. Incidentally, this note might profitably be read in conjunction with my other memo of today's date.

Yours,
[K. T.]

To Laurence Olivier

[20 Thurloe Square]
[April 28, 1970]

Dear Larry,

This is just to thank you not only for giving by far the best performance of Shylock I've ever seen, but also for the privilege of watching some of it take shape.

I think it is one of the most astonishing things you have ever done –
and, as always, you do something with the part so shatteringly and
obviously right that one wonders why nobody has thought of it before.
<u>You show us Shylock turning into a Jew before our eyes</u>.

The man at the beginning of the play is a businessman first and
foremost, only secondarily a Jew. When the Christians steal his daughter, he begins to realise what it means to be Jewish, and by the end of
the trial he knows it through and through – so indelibly that no-one in
the theatre will ever forget it.

You do not need luck or prayers or good wishes tonight. All you
need is an audience.

Love
[Ken]

To Laurence Olivier

20 Thurloe Square
12 May 1970

Dear Larry,
1) Re Chandos's attitude towards <u>Guys and Dolls</u>:[1] it may be necessary
to quote to him the following paragraph from the chapter headed
'Priorities and a Panorama' in the Arts Council Theatre Enquiry's
report,[2] published in March:

IN SUBSIDIZED THEATRES THE CHOICE OF PLAYS SHOULD REST
ENTIRELY WITH THE ARTISTIC DIRECTOR, AND FAILURE ON THE
PART OF THEATRE BOARDS TO IMPLEMENT THIS PRINCIPLE
SHOULD BE A MAJOR FACTOR IN ARTS COUNCIL CONSIDERATIONS
REGARDING FINANCIAL SUPPORT.

2) Re Bob Stephens and his statement to the Board that whenever a
Broadway musical is done with an English cast, the result is always a
'disastrous flop': here's the list you requested of American musicals that
have been produced in London with non-American casts:

1953	Paint Your Wagon	477 performances
1953	Wish You Were Here	281 "
1954	Can-Can	324 "
1955	The Pajama Game	578 "
1955	Wonderful Town	207 "

1957	Damn Yankees	258	"
1958	My Fair Lady	2,281	"
1958	Where's Charley?	380	"
1961	The Sound of Music	1,946	"
1963	A Funny Thing Happened on the Way to the Forum	762	"
1964	Little Me	334	"
1964	Camelot	518	"
1967	Fiddler on the Roof	Still running	
1968	Sweet Charity	484	"
1968	Hair	Still running	

Love,
[Ken]

[1] Book by Abe Burrows and Jo Sherling, music by Frank Loesser based on stories of gamblers by Damon Runyon (1950). In *Confessions of an Actor* (1982), Olivier recalled: 'Tynan hit me with a dazzlingly brilliant idea – to put on *Guys and Dolls* at the National . . . the greatest of all American shows'. Though Chandos thought the play was unsuitable, he came around and 'all looked promising when bang went my leg with that infuriating thrombosis'. The show was cancelled while Olivier was away and he felt betrayed by the Board.
[2] The Enquiry's members included KPT, John Mortimer, Lord Bernstein and Sir Max Rayne.

To William Shawn

20 Thurloe Square
1st July 1970

Dear Mr. Shawn,

My piece for you on Nicol Williamson – which has been delayed by a film script[1] in which I've become briefly involved – seems to be developing into something more than a conventional profile. The bulk of it will be a blow-by-blow, drink-by-drink account of how I steered this moody and unpredictable man to the White House, and almost destroyed my health in the process.[2] I shall be delivering it in the course of the summer. I'm assuming that you don't regard it as a topical item, and that it won't matter if there is a gap of six months or so between the events described and the publication of the piece.

Meanwhile, I'm enclosing a full and final list of the expenses I incurred in preparing it. There is one item at which you may raise your eyebrows – the first class supplementary air fare from London to New York. I had of course booked a tourist ticket, but Mr. Williamson, who was travelling first class, came weaving down into the steerage section and volunteered to tell me the story of his life if I would join him. I felt I had no alternative and I hope you will understand.

Yours sincerely,
Kenneth Tynan

[1] *Macbeth*, a collaboration with Roman Polanski.
[2] In the preparation for Williamson's White House appearance KPT tried to 'drink for Nicol': when he ordered wine, Ken would consume as much of it himself as he discreetly could, in order to keep the actor's energies fresh for rehearsal. 'I do not know whether this unselfishness was of any real use to him. It nearly crippled me!' he wrote in 'Are You the Entertainment?' (*New Yorker*, 15 January 1972).

To the Editor, *The Times*

20 Thurloe Square
[Published 7 August 1970]

Sir,—Lord Salisbury joins several of your other correspondents[1] in ascribing to me the phrase 'tasteful pornography'. Whatever his Lordship may have read, I have never used this expression to describe 'Oh! Calcutta!' or anything else. I have a horror of the word 'tasteful'.

Yours sincerely,
KENNETH TYNAN

[1] *The Times* was running a correspondence on 'Law and Morals: the Problem of Artistic Merit'.

Memo to Roman Polanski

[The National Theatre]
September 15, 1970

We have discussed this already, but I don't think it can be over-stressed:
   Almost anyone you cast as Macbeth[1] will start to play the part <u>already aware that it's a great tragedy</u>. I was looking at the script last night and there is no doubt in my mind that when Macbeth hears the prophecy,

his reaction is one of immense exhilaration. He is like a man who has dreamed all his life of inheriting a million and suddenly hears that he is going to inherit 5 million. I think he should be absolutely thrilled.

'Stay, you imperfect speakers ...'

There should be nothing furtive or sombre about this – he is really dying to know more. When he and Banquo start to laugh in Sequence 10, I think there should be a note of supressed hysteria in Macbeth's laughter. Similarly: 'The Thane of Cawdor lives / And to be King ...' here again he is wide-eyed with expectation; and I am sure that when he says to Banquo: 'Do you not hope your children shall be kings?' there is nothing sly or secretive about it – he is simply congratulating himself and Banquo on the marvellous future that has opened out for them.

Banquo's line about 'the instruments of darkness' injects the first note of doubt into Macbeth's mind; until then he has felt nothing but mounting excitement. And even now he can't believe that the witches are evil. Banquo's words momentarily raise the dark thought of murder, but he soon recovers: 'If chance will have me King, why chance may crown me . . .' With this speech he dispels the shadow thrown by Banquo's suggestion and rides off to the King with his confidence restored.

The longer he can hang on to his innocence, the more sympathetic he becomes and the more fascinated we shall be as he gets sucked into violence.

When he says: 'Stars, hide your fires', this should be the first time that he admits to himself that he is capable of crime. Thus I think it should not be said rhetorically but in tones of shame, even self disgust. He has just caught himself wishing the Prince of Cumberland dead. He stops and for a moment, almost begs the stars to prevent his 'black and deep desires' from ever fulfilling themselves.

All this makes much more sense of the 'milk of human kindness' line, and makes it much more plausible that he should be shocked and appalled when Lady Macbeth suggests that Duncan should be murdered.

I know we have discussed all this before, but I felt it might help to put it on paper. English actors approach this part with so many preconceptions that you have to scrape them off like removing layers of varnish from an old master.

No Christianity except for Banquo 'in the great hand of God' line. There is evil but no organised good in this universe.

Not a tragedy written by a philosopher;
A melodrama written by a great poet.

---

[1] Released in 1971, starring Jon Finch and Francesca Annis.

Memo to Michael White and Clifford Williams

[The National Theatre]
21 September 1970

I saw the show on Friday night. This is Monday morning. It's as well that there were no sleeping pills in the house over the weekend.

Some of it is in good shape. The music in particular is much improved. Domini[1] and Richard[2] are just fine. As for the rest:

Up in Chalk Farm[3] audiences will tolerate sloppiness and rough edges that they would never accept in the West End. We are going to the West End next week and I believe we are in exceptionally bad shape. [...]

In 'One on One' [Jonathan Burn][4] lifts adequately but simply looks ungainly and wooden. Worst of all, I discovered that he has refused to sing the line about the 'limb-deficient woman' in 'Suits'. Instead, he says 'self-sufficient' (apparently with Clifford's consent). This makes the whole verse pointless since the entire number is about deviations and there is nothing deviant about wanting to go to bed with 'self-sufficient' women. I talked to him afterwards about this and he says he found the line offensive and disgusting and reiterated his refusal to sing it. I told him that as far as I was concerned, that meant that he would have to be replaced in the number. I feel very strongly indeed about this and I hope you will back me up. The point of the number is to demonstrate to deviants that they are not alone and anyone who finds deviations disgusting and offensive certainly does not belong in the number and probably not in the show. Can we get Richard to replace Jonathan on that stool? I am quite willing to rehearse with him with Mike[5] if Clifford hasn't the time.

As you may or may not know, the cast is split up into cut-throat cliques, all of whom button-holed me after the performance. [...] (Incidentally, some of the stories I heard were hair-raising – did you know that a male dresser had had to go on in drag to replace Jenny[6] at the end of 'Knickers' one night?) [...] Is this true or is it just the queer Mafia in operation? If there is any chance of it being true, I think we should check.

Another major problem is company discipline. Noel[7] would like to be made responsible for keeping the whole show – and not just the dance numbers – as it was on the opening night. I consulted Domini, who said she thought that some sort of discipline was essential, but wondered whether Noel might not be too 'bossy' for the job. She suggested Nick,[8] but of course he cannot be there every night. In a show like ours, where ad-libbing can easily run amok, I think we must take the plunge of appointing a member of the cast to represent our interests, however invidious this may seem. They simply do not listen to Tom.[9]

Some other points: [...]

5) 'Was it Good': This is a shambles. Tony's[10] latest contribution is to look at Brenda[11] and say 'See nipples and die'. I almost did. Jonathan plays the whole number with his cock hanging out and looked as if he was going to hit me when I suggested he might refrain. At the end he and Tony mime the act of buggery: this is perhaps the lowest point of the whole evening. Brenda has put in a line about being fucked by the Count Basie Band. Could she please go back to the Mormon Tabernacle Choir?

6) 'Four in Hand': [X] now grasps his cock throughout this number and I'm not at all sure that his fly wasn't open. Could this please be stopped.

7) 'Rock Garden': Bill[12] used to freeze throughout Richard's mono-logue, saving everything up for the surprise fall at the end. Tony does two big reactions of shock and incredulity in the course of the monologue. These get two small laughs. When he falls off the chair he gets no laugh at all. Can he be made to realise that the originality of the sketch lies precisely in the fact that Pa does not react until the end? And that the sketch lacks all suspense if he signals his reaction in advance?

[...] Well, I guess that covers some of the ground. [...]

Love
KT

---

[1] Domini Blythe.
[2] Richard Monette.

[3] *Oh! Calcutta!* had its London première on 27 July 1970 at the Roundhouse, a converted railway building in Chalk Farm, north London.

[4] The dancer in the duet 'One on One'.

[5] Mike Allen, musical director.

[6] Jenny Runacre.

[7] Noel Tovey.

[8] Nick Renton, Clifford Williams's assistant.

[9] Tom MacArthur, production and stage manager.

[10] Anthony Booth, who later played Alf Garnett's son-in-law in the long-running television series *Till Death Us Do Part* (adapted in the US as *All in the Family*, where the role was known as 'Meathead'). He is now the father-in-law of the Labour Party leader Tony Blair.

[11] Brenda Arnau, American singer and cabaret performer.

[12] Bill Macy, American actor who had played in *America Hurrah* and in Peter Brook's *The Tempest*; a member of the original New York cast.

Memo to Roman Polanski

20 Thurloe Square
27th October, 1970

Re-reading the first witches' scene with Macbeth and Banquo, I had a thought which I'd like to pass on.

Although the witches should look bizarre, there is no reason for them to be frightening or sinister. <u>They are bringing good news</u>, and neither Banquo nor Macbeth expresses the least fear of them. If they are obviously evil – cackling old crones, leering and rolling their eyes – then Macbeth is clearly a fool to act on their prophecies. I think they should be presented in such a way that any sensible person in the audience might also find them trustworthy. They are more like spiritualist mediums than demons – morally neutral creatures who may inspire us with a faint twinge of unease but certainly should not make us shudder with revulsion. Hindu holy men in loincloths with matted hair, Japanese seers like the one in Rashomon[1] – these are the sort of images that come to mind.

[1] Directed by Akira Kurosawa (Japan, 1951).

Memo to Roman Polanski

Shepperton
[? November 1970]

Re: '<u>MACBETH</u>'

The following are suggested lines for crowd to shout at the meeting of
the English and Scottish armies:-

> 'HAIL THE PRINCE OF CUMBERLAND!'
> 'HAIL THE SON OF DUNCAN!'
> 'HAIL KING OF SCOTLAND HEREAFTER!'
> 'GOD SAVE OLD SEYWARD!'
> 'AYE AND YOUNG SEYWARD TOO'
> 'DEATH TO THE TYRANT!'
> 'WHERE THE FUCK IS DONALBAIN?'

K. T.

To Emilie Jacobson

20 Thurloe Square
23rd November, 1970

Dear Emilie,

The piece[1] I want to write about the Macbeth film is mostly a piece
about Polanski – this extraordinary survivor, a child of the Warsaw
ghetto, losing his mother in Auschwitz, then a boy in Stalin's Poland,
then penniless in Paris, teaching himself French in a few weeks, then
crossing to London with hardly a word of English, finally successful,
suddenly and horribly bereaved,[2] and then starting all over again not
with an easy melodrama or a farce, but one of the greatest tragedies
ever written. I want to write about working with him and what it taught
me about cinema – Roman's passion for concrete detail, his hatred of
anything vague or imprecise, his ability to draw ideas from the most
unlikely sources (some of the sequences in Macbeth were inspired by
comic strips), his genial contempt for actors, whom he calls 'the comics',
and causes to be fed bananas every morning before shooting, his feudal
distaste for Women's Lib, which goes so far that if a girl so much as
volunteers to make a cup of coffee he grumbles: 'What are you – some
kind of militant?'. (Roman's women must either sit down or lie down.

To stand up except when commanded is an act of insurrection).

Like some of the greatest generals, he won't let his actors do anything he wouldn't do himself. One hot afternoon last summer, we both stripped to the waist and rehearsed the brutal murder of King Duncan by Macbeth, in Polanski's bedroom, alternating the roles. For several hours we rolled about on the floor, brandishing daggers, until we discovered that our wrestling was being watched from across the court-yard by a group of middle-aged English party-goers sipping sherry on a balcony. I have no doubt that they thought we were two raving queers engaged in some sado-masochistic ritual.

I shall be following the making of the film from the location work, now being completed in the fogs and near hurricanes of North Wales, to the studio sequences which should be finished in February. By then we shall know what Polanski can do to a masterpiece and what a masterpiece can do to him. Out of this story I think I could fashion a pretty interesting portrait of Super-Pole in action.

Let me know if anybody shows interest.

Love
Ken

[1] 'The Polish Imposition', *Esquire* (September, 1971), reprinted in the *Sunday Times* magazine (7 November 1971).
[2] Sharon Tate, Polanski's first wife, was murdered by the Manson family. *Macbeth* was his first film since the murder.

Memo to Laurence Olivier

[The National Theatre]
4 December 1970

Re: <u>Germaine Greer's[1] piece in the MRS WARREN[2] Programme</u>

I've already cut 200 words of her piece, including two other uses of the word 'fuck', the word 'cunt', a reference to the anal practices of prostitutes and to the amount of semen in a prostitute's vagina. I've blackmailed her into doing this by saying that the printers refused to print the offending passages. At first she saw no reason to agree to any cuts, saying that it would be ludicrous and contemptible for someone like myself, who has always fought against censorship, to insist on censoring others.

I finally wore her down in the course of three long phone calls, but she insisted on retaining one four-letter word simply because she loathes the pedantry of words like 'copulation'.

If we bring any further pressure on her she will either despise me, tell the story to the papers or both. Please bear in mind that she is a highly respected authoress and a university teacher.

K. T.[3]

[1] Germaine Greer (b. 1939), Australian feminist writer and academic, author of *The Female Eunuch* (1970).
[2] *Mrs Warren's Profession* by George Bernard Shaw (1898), opened at the National on 30 December 1970.
[3] KPT wrote in his journal of 9 December 1970 an account of the spat: Olivier called Germaine and got her to change 'fucking' to 'sexual intercourse': 'I blamed myself, Kennie, I told her you had shouted at me. I said it was my fault.'

To Roman Polanski

[20 Thurloe Square]
[21 January 1971]

Dear Roman,

May I buzz you further with what I was saying in the car today? I am sure that the number one Macbeth problem is to see the events of the film from his point of view. Seen from the outside, everything he does is simply and relentlessly shitty and cruel. He may have a few looks of doubt and a few speeches of hesitation, but otherwise he's merely a bastard who's scared of being found out – <u>unless</u> we can get into him and experience all the terrors and guilts that torment him.

And this is all related to the problem of getting inside Jon Finch,[1] who, as I said, resists invasion of his privacy.

Obviously part of the answer is to get him to express and reveal more in the later stages – and this will inevitably happen in the Banquo ghost scene for example, but it may be desirable to help him out by doing more close-ups and (especially) more shots from his view point, than you normally like to use – e.g. in the tent scene, the 'sleep no more' speech, segment 63 the 'come seeling night' speech, of course the Banquo ghost scene and segment 75.

I expect you have thought of all this, but it has been worrying me, and I don't want to leave it unsaid.

Love
[Ken]

[1] Jon Finch (b. 1941); after *Macbeth* he went on to do *Frenzy* for Alfred Hitchcock (UK, 1972) and *Lady Caroline Lamb* (UK, 1972).

To Michael White

20 Thurloe Square
22nd January 1971

Dear Michael,

As you requested, here is a summary of the modified proposition I put to you yesterday, for a lunchtime 'Calcutta':

1. The aim (or aims) would be to attract new actors to the show, to attract new audiences (including summer tourists and people who might be too shy or too poor to come to the evening show), and to try out new material for subsequent inclusion in the evening show.

2. The idea would be to put into rehearsal half a dozen sketches, (Peter Nichols,[1] David Mercer,[2] Leonard Melfi,[3] Sherman Yellen,[4] Mike Weller,[5] Carl Tunberg[6] and my own) with a cast consisting of Tony, Linda, Domini and three newcomers. This material would be boiled down to a programme approximately seventy-five minutes long. It would open at the Royalty[7] in the late Spring (April or May) and would be announced as being for a limited run of – say – twelve performances. This would be at a rate of four performances a week.

3. The new actors would be hired on the condition that they would graduate from the lunch-time show into the evening show, taking some of the new material with them. They would have the option of not appearing in the group numbers, if they did not want to.

4. The critics would be invited to the lunch-time show, but we would explain to each of them personally that it was merely an experimental workshop to provide new challenges for the actors. We did this with the National Theatre when it had its season at the Jeanetta

Cochrane,[8] and it worked enormously well, putting the critics into a friendly frame of mind.

5. This arrangement would give us enormous flexibility for the lunchtime show. If it is a success, we could extend its run indefinitely. (And why not? It would have a potential gross of £2,800 a week). [...]

Love,
Ken

[1] Peter Nichols (b. 1927), English playwright, author of *A Day in the Death of Joe Egg* (1967) and *The National Health* (1969). The sketch, never performed, was called 'Neither Up Nor Down'.
[2] 'You and I'; never performed.
[3] 'Jack and Jill'; performed only in New York.
[4] 'Delicious Indignities'; performed in New York and London.
[5] 'The Vortex'; never performed.
[6] 'Human Sexual Response'; never performed.
[7] *Oh! Calcutta!* transferred to the Royalty Theatre in the West End on 3 October 1970. The lunchtime show, which was to be called 'The Gamut', never happened.
[8] Three national theatre productions on 8, 11 and 17 February 1969. The second was the 'Plowright Project' of four short plays by women writers.

To Clive Jenkins[1]

[The National Theatre]
26th January 1971

Dear Clive,

The stage staff at the National Theatre are represented by N.A.T.K.E.[2] [*sic*], the actor's cause is fought by Equity. But nobody looks after the administrative staff, of whom I am a patient member. Have you thought of moving into the subsidised theatres?

If it would interest you, is there someone at your office – assuming you are too busy yourself – with whom I could have a preliminary chat?

I need hardly add that I am writing unofficially. Lord Chandos would erupt if he thought that yet another Union was about to invade what he has come to think of as a family business which he holds in trust for the Nation.

All my best.
[Kenneth Tynan]

[1] Head of ASTMS (Association of Scientific, Technical and Managerial Staffs). See also letter of
1 May 1964.
[2] The National Association of Theatrical, Television and Kine Employees.

To Charles Marowitz

[The National Theatre]
11 February 1971

Dear Charles:

I liked your TIMON[1] very much indeed, but two problems worry me:
(1) As I told you when you first mentioned the idea to me, we have to
be rather careful – as a national institution – about what liberties we
take with the national poet. After a Victorian MERCHANT, an all-male
AS YOU and a Sicilian MUCH ADO, I don't know whether it would be
politic for us to venture into a jazz-age TIMON. This is a big but not
insuperable objection.

2) I don't see how Alcibiades fits into your historical analogy. Who or
what does he symbolise? It's only here, I feel, that the parallel breaks
down. Or have I missed something? Does he – or could he – stand for
the militant workers whose insurrection FDR is able to diffuse?[2] I'd
like one or two other people here to look at the script, if that's all right
with you.

Yours,
[Kenneth Tynan]

[1] The script for a musical adaptation of *Timon of Athens*; it has never been performed.
[2] The setting for Marowitz's *Timon* was the Depression-era event known as the Bonus March, in
which, in late 1932, while Herbert Hoover was a 'lame duck' President before handing over to
Franklin D. Roosevelt, destitute World War I veterans (not 'workers') marched on Washington
DC to demand bonuses owed to them, and were eventually routed by the US Army. Alcibiades
represented the leader of the march.

To Václav Havel

[The National Theatre]
25th February, 1971

Dear Václav Havel,

You may remember that we met several times in Prague some years
ago when I was writing about the Czechoslovakian theatre.

I am now writing to you on behalf of Sir Laurence Olivier and The

National Theatre of Great Britain. It is our policy to encourage exciting contemporary playwrights of all countries, and we would therefore like to commission a new full length play from you, to be performed by our company at The National Theatre in London.

If you are interested in the idea, we would make an advance payment to you, in return for which you would agree to deliver the manuscript by an agreed date. When the manuscript was delivered, you would receive a further payment; and of course when the play began its run, you would receive the usual royalties.

But these are details which we can discuss later. It is necessary first to establish whether you are interested in our proposal – and to assure you that both Sir Laurence and I would be delighted if you feel able to accept. Needless to say, the theme and subject matter of the play would be left entirely to you.

We send you our most cordial greetings and look forward to hearing from you.

Yours sincerely,
[Kenneth Tynan]

To Simon Michael Bessie

[20 Thurloe Square]
15 March 1971

Dear Mike,

I had lunch with George Weidenfeld' a couple of days ago, so please regard this as a follow-up to my previous letter. The idea of a book on 'The Surviving Plays' is one that I find extremely attractive. It would start with a definition of the qualities that make a play last. Then one would devote a chapter to each of the great periods of theatrical history, isolating the survivors from the non-survivors, (always in a highly personal way) and dwelling at some length on plays that seem to need special attention. I feel equipped to write this book because it is based on exactly the kind of work I have been doing for Olivier for the past decade. By the time it is finished I shall have presumably left the National Theatre and will feel free to move on to the autobiographical book.

The problem seems to be money. To cover myself against having to do ephemeral journalism to pay the household accounts, I need an advance of £10,000 to cover the British and American rights for both books. Out of this I would of course repay the advance from Longmans.[2] George tells me that he thinks this amount should be split up so that approximately sixty-percent comes from the American partner and forty from him. Frankly and candidly and in the beaten way of friendship, can you see your way to accepting this kind of proposition?

If you decide that the deal is not possible for you, the whole situation will have to be re-considered. If we can find another American Publisher who is interested in both books I might ask you to release me from our present contract. Regarding payment of the advance in this case, I would be in the position of repaying you and Longmans which would make quite a hole in £10,000. On the other hand, if I stick to the present contract with you and make a deal elsewhere for the new book, you would have to wait several years before I could fulfill my obligations to you.

There's no doubt in my mind which I would rather do, both books with you and George. With the ball thus squarely placed in your court, I sign myself

Yours ever,
Ken

[1] Arthur George Weidenfeld (b. 1919), created Lord Weidenfeld of Chelsea in 1973; with Nigel Nicolson he founded Weidenfeld and Nicolson in 1949. He wished to handle world rights for the projected book *300 Plays That Stood the Test of Time*, for which he offered £10,000. Doubleday would be the US publisher.
[2] KPT had signed a contract with Longman's for an autobiographical book on *Soldiers* and *Oh! Calcutta!* (31 March 1969). Bessie was to publish it in the US.

To Václav Havel

[The National Theatre]
19 March '71

Dear Václav Havel:
Sir Laurence and I were delighted to receive your letter. He perfectly understands what you say about the contractual problem[1] and we will wait to hear from you before we take any further action.

We are very pleased to hear that you have already begun the final draft of 'The Conspirators'[2] and we look forward eagerly to reading it in July.

Meanwhile, there is a question on which you could help us. We are urgently looking for a new play to put in our repertoire in the autumn, and naturally we would like to consider your play for this date. Unfortunately it's necessary for us to plan a long time in advance, and it would be very useful if you could let us know now approximately how many characters there are in 'The Conspirators' (with some indication of the physical types required)[3] and how many settings are involved.

Once again, please accept our best wishes.

Yours sincerely,
[Kenneth Tynan]

P.S. In answer to a question you raise: yes, it would be a very good idea if your contract with Rowohlt included a clause stipulating that your play should be offered to the National Theatre for its world premiere.

[1] On 15 March 1971, Havel pointed out that 'Nothing that bears my name may be published at present in my country, and the monopoly-state-agency DILIA is forbidden to conclude any contracts for any play with partners abroad.' Nevertheless, as the copyright owner he felt he could lawfully make a deal through Rowohlt Verlag, his German publisher; but he could not accept an advance until matters were resolved.

[2] Five conspirators set out to protect a weak democratic government in a country newly rid of a colonial legacy. The audience gradually learns that, paradoxically, the danger comes from the plotters themselves who become, by the nature of their actions, sympathetic to the former dictator. 'They want to seize the power, in order to save the country from the danger that they might take possession of the government themselves' (rough notes in a letter from Havel to KPT, 2 April 1971).

[3] In the same letter Havel replied that there were four big parts including a police colonel and a rich widow; and six smaller parts, including a chief censor, a prime minister, and a 'permanent prisoner'.

To Simon Michael Bessie

Thurloe Square
25 March 1971

Dear Michael,

I scarcely know how to begin this letter, but to avoid suspense I had better tell you the end at once: the book is not ready.[1] The reasons for this are several, and I should like to lay some of these before you.

As I told you last spring, I did not think that the story told by the book would be complete until Oh! Calcutta! opened in London, which it successfully did, after a long and harassing gestation period, last summer. But by then I had already taken the decision which was to blow me off course more than I could have predicted. Roman Polanski had asked me to work with him on his film of Macbeth – not only on the script, but on the shooting. The script took only six weeks, but I had no idea how deep my involvement in the shooting would become. It began last November and is still continuing. The current prediction is that the cameras will not stop turning until mid-April.

Two other factors conspired against me. In the late summer, when I had hoped to break the back of the book, I had a nasty little bout of emphysema, which kept me in bed on and off for a month. Finally, and most distressingly, my boss Lord Olivier was stricken with a blood clot on the leg which incapacitated him for several months and for a while looked like signalling the end of his career. In the last three months or so, he has made a remarkable recovery, but last autumn things looked very dark indeed. The point is that I had planned to resign from the National Theatre at about that time in order to write about my work there without the constraints of an employee. Larry's illness made resignation impossible; it would have looked like desertion. So the result has been that I have spent nearly all my non-Macbeth moments at the National.

So where does this leave us? Clearly, it leaves me depressed and apologetic as far as you are concerned. Equally clearly, the material for the book is now all there if I can allot myself the time to write it. There is talk of another film which I may script,[2] but it is extremely nebulous, and I have no other major projects of any sort in mind. Olivier's recovery means that I can once more contemplate a phased withdrawal from the National Theatre. Apart from a couple of magazine articles, I have no journalistic commitments at all, and don't intend to incur any. In all, I see no reason why I shouldn't polish the book off this year.

But of course that's what I felt last year. Let me reiterate what I said then: that if you would like me to return the advance, I will willingly do so. On the other hand, I shall obviously have to get the book out of my system some time; and with inflation increasing at its present rate, the advance you paid me may come to seem quite small!

It is for you to decide what course you wish me to take. Meanwhile, all I can do is to offer you once more my deep regret and my even deeper embarrassment.

Yours sincerely,
Ken

[1] The autobiographical book on *Soldiers* and *Oh! Calcutta!*, a few pages of which KPT had written in Lucca in 1969.

² This idea became *Our Life With Alex and Sophie* (see letter of 19 May 1971).

To Dr Colin Woolf¹

20 Thurloe Square
16th April 1971

Dear Dr Woolf,

I suffer from a mild case of emphysema, and would be most grateful for your help. Is there any available published material on the care of emphysema and new developments in the field? If so, I would like to get hold of these and any information on the subject, to present to my own doctors here. I would of course, be willing to pay any expenses incurred.

Yours sincerely,
[Kenneth Tynan]²

¹ Of the Emphysema Care Unit, Toronto General Hospital.
² Dr Woolf suggested a possible lung operation (which was not relevant), that KPT test for hereditary enzyme deficiency (KPT confirmed he had an alpha₁ antitrypsin deficiency) and that he improve 'his exercise tolerance'.

To Vanessa Vreeland¹

[20 Thurloe Square]
19 April 1971

Dearest Vaness –

This is to thank you for some hospitality you are probably not aware of having given me. The little converted-bordello hotel² where I usually stay in Paris closed down a few weeks ago and so having come to Paris for a couple of days, I remembered your super offer of shelter, called Helen H.³ and got her to alert Ho Chi Minh⁴ – the upshot being that I slept under your roof last Wednesday, Thursday and Friday nights with that tragically lonely pussy.⁵ (Not Helen). Purpose of visit was to look at the rehearsals for the French production of 'Oh Calcutta'⁶ – petrified of police intervention, they have cut out about three-quarters of the text and put in lots of little froggy whimsies, like chaps in love with goats or making love to trees and so forth. Very nasty I thought, and said as much; but unluckily I don't control the foreign rights so all I could do was tell the press that it wasn't my show any longer.

Anyway the weather was summer-hot and the Saviour of his Country turned up to cook breakfast every morning. I also paid a laundry bill for him, and why not? A most impressive-looking valet also turned up. He had a strange sense of humour and at first claimed to be Alexander of Yugoslavia,[7] but I told him to iron my trousers and stop trying to be so fucking funny. His face darkened for a moment but you could have sliced bread with the crease he put in my pants. No two ways about it, peasants do make the best servants. I think you should know however, that all is not well among your staff. The big valet told me that Ho Chi Minh was a raging transvestite who swooped around in bra and knickers whenever I was out, using Bangkok more as a catamite than a cat. (Oh look it up.) I told him I never listened to back-stairs gossip and gave him a big kiss, which seemed to mollify him.

But I kept my eyes skinned from then onwards and on one occasion, darting into the kitchen, I caught the Founder of the People's republic putting his lipstick away in the icebox and humming 'Love for Sale' in what he imagined to be a sexy falsetto. When I upbraided him for this filthy carry-on he stuck out his yellow tongue and muttered something about rots of ruck. I think you should take this up with him or at least lock up your knickers.

Kathleen is having her baby on June 9th[8] (by order of her gynaecologist). Come and see us as soon as the lure of the pampas wanes.[9] And thanks again.

Love
[Ken]

[1] Vanessa Somers McConnell (now) Vreeland, artist and good friend.
[2] The Lutèce in the rue Jules-Chaplain.
[3] Helen Hayes, a fashion executive.
[4] Vanessa's Vietnamese servant.
[5] A Burmese cat named Bangkok.
[6] It opened on 15 May 1971.
[7] The first cousin of the last king of Yugoslavia.
[8] Matthew Blake Tynan was born 9 June 1971.
[9] Vanessa was going down the Amazon.

To Archbishop Lord Fisher of Lambeth[1]

[20 Thurloe Square]
May 1, 1971

Dear Lord Fisher,

I am afraid I seem to be less fascinated by the question of genital display than you are. Boredom, not bad manners, explains my tardiness in replying to your latest letter. So let me say, succinctly and (I hope) unequivocally. no, I would not support any legislation to forbid genital exposure on stage or screen – provided, of course, that the persons taking part in such displays do so of their own free will, without coercion. If such spectacles titillate people, I see no reason to interfere with their pleasure. According to my dictionary, 'titillate' means 'tickle pleasantly', which sounds to me both enjoyable and desirable. If a stage or film show causes me to have an erection, my immediate reaction is gratitude for a nice experience: to wish to ban it would seem to me churlish in the extreme.

Yours sincerely,
[Kenneth Tynan]

[1] Lord Fisher of Lambeth (1887–1972), former Archbishop of Canterbury (1945–61) had asked KPT to address himself to the question of 'possible legislation to enforce the common law against the exposure of the genital organs in theatres and elsewhere' as a 'stimulus to sexual interest'. He had written again on 30 April when KPT failed to reply.

To Kathleen Tynan

Château de Meyrargues[1]
19 May 1971

Dear One –

This place is all it promised to be – a great ironbound mediaeval castle on a hill, with a Provençal village curled round the foot of it and a winding road leading up to it along avenues of pines and a small diningroom in the converted refectory with grives and cailles and pintadeaux[2] (pour deux personnes, hélas, hélas) and a nice but slightly cheating patron (he tried to charge me 115 NF for full pension but I beat him down to 100). My room is up dozens of angular stone stairs right at the top, with a tiny work alcove and two tiny windows – a former battlement, I suppose.

When I arrived – at 9 on Monday – a mistral was raging and a tree was being torn up by its roots behind the château. In this haven of peace I did not sleep a wink. Not only because the windows rattled and the shutters rattled and the wind howled and the rain battered but because, inaccessible in a locked attic, there was a mysterious Barn Door that banged open and shut every thirtyfive seconds, about five feet over my head. They say they have traced it: tonight, if the mistral returns, we shall see. Anyway, the result was that I slept most of the day, except during the afternoon, when I tottered down to look at the village (dull) and climbed a near-vertical hillside path back. I doubt if I shall leave the building again (except for the trips to Noves and Avignon which I've promised myself); apart from meals and an aperitif on the windswept terrace, I shall keep to my room and sort of work and very much think of you. Unless I succumb to Tony Mayer.[3] I forget to mention that after I'd staggered sweating from Orly Sud to Orly Ouest (I had to change not only planes but airports) carrying my briefcase and the typewriter, I slumped into my seat on the Marseilles plane only to find myself alongside Tony Mayer. So he may seduce me to Ménerbes for an evening.

Oh one, this is strange. What am I doing here churning out pornography? It is very shaming. I shall try to do it with a will but truly I question whether I should do it at all. I look out over this still and God-bitten countryside and feel very pampered and trivial. Should I not return to Nicol W? Or to you? And forget Andy Pandar?[4]

Advise me my darling, and take and hold all my love for ever –

K.

[1] Near Aix-en-Provence, where KPT had retired to write the first draft of the erotic film script which was eventually titled *Our Life With Alex and Sophie*.
[2] Thrush, quail and partridge.
[3] Ex-French cultural attaché to London who owned a house, with his wife Thérèse, nearby.
[4] Andrew Braunsberg, a film producer interested in KPT's project.

To Kathleen Tynan

Château de Meyrargues
21 May 1971

Dear One –
I believe other people work because they do not have you; or because, knowing you or having heard of you, they want you; or because they have a vision of you; but I do not believe that anyone, having had the

reward of you, could be so vainglorious as to suppose that he deserved any other reward of life. No, I am not encroaching on work time to write this; it is after dinner and the mistral once more rattles my roof; but I think it explains the fits of accidie that beset me so often when I should be working. Nathanael West[1] once wrote: 'I need women and because I can't buy or force them, I have to make poems . . .' But I do not.

I did not leave the castle today, merely worked, read and ate. (A special crêpe soufflée is ruining my diet.) Lonely all the time – and without the comforting thought I'd have in a town, of being able to go for a walk and <u>see people</u> at sunset – I am loneliest now, after dinner at 10.15, with a great gap between me and sleep. I have not spoken a word of English to anyone for over 48 hours. I look yearningly at the phone and realise that you are out at the ballet with God knows whom.

Some gleanings from Auden's commonplace book:[2] the name of the Angel devoted to June is Muriel – would you like that for a daughter? 'A tom will remain playful until he is quite old: but even in play his face never loses the gravity that is stamped on it' (Colette). And:

> Meekly smiling with her mouth,
> And merry in her lookes,
> Ever laughing for love –

from an anonymous mediaeval man who somehow glimpsed you.

I look out over the black valley and have gloomy night-thoughts about the soul. Perhaps those who die unbelieving really <u>do</u> die as atheists imagine it – like the switching off of a light – while only those who have achieved the hard miracle of belief achieve the greater miracle of resurrection? That seems fair to me, but I am just as far from belief. I type this letter however knowing that God may be watching and may give me a mark or two for trying, or at least caring, or at least seeming to care, or at least for being humble enough to confess to mere seeming.

I doubt if I shall sleep much tonight, what with wind-banging and lack of you. Tomorrow I shall have myself shifted to some other attic. And tomorrow evening I shall go into Aix-en-Provence, expecting it to be still 1886 there, and of course it will turn out to be Wolverhampton-sur-Rhône.

Extract from imaginary book review by J.B. Morton:[3] 'Freda Trowte has been called the Anatole France of Herefordshire.'

Don't be surprised or censorious if I suddenly come home. Could we meet perhaps at Teazel Cottage[4] – perhaps on Monday? I'm serious –

call me – working in a total vacuum is airless work, bad for the spiritual lungs, literally uninspiring.

Love to my one always –
K

---

[1] Nathanael West (1903–40), American novelist known for *Miss Lonelyhearts* (1933) and *The Day of the Locust* (1939).
[2] *A Certain World*, an alphabetical collection of other people's writings, first published in 1971.
[3] J. B. Morton (1893–1979), journalist and writer of humorous novels.
[4] Emma Tennant's cottage on the Avon river in Wiltshire, which we rented for weekends.

To John Dexter

[20 Thurloe Square]
[? June 1971]

Dear John –

Adrian's poem, 'The Children of William Blake',[1] is Adrian's property and Adrian's copyright. He conceived and wrote it long before you were involved in the show and indeed had ever heard of it. I do not know by what right you dispose of it as if it were yours.

Next week Kathleen is going to have a baby. She has the show as close to her heart as it has been to mine. I promised her this song as a welcoming present for the child – she has not yet heard the score. It was to have been recorded outside rehearsal hours with a simple piano accompaniment. It would have been heard by nobody except Kathleen and myself. (And the baby.) The recording would have taken, at the most, five minutes. (You will be aware that the poem is all of nine lines long.)

I now hear that you have forbidden the taping to take place.

Forgive me if I am speechless.

K.[2]

---

[1] A song from *Tyger*, Adrian Mitchell's play about William Blake, whose words are: The children of Blake dance in their thousands / over nursery meadows and through sinister forests, / Beyond the spikes of cities, over the breasts of mountains, / The children of Blake dance in their thousands. / They dance beyond logic, they dance beyond science, / They are dancers, they are only dancers, / And every atom of their minds and hearts and their deep skin / And every atom of their bowels and genitals and imagination / Dances to the music of William Blake.' John Dexter's and Michael Blakemore's production of *Tyger* opened at the Old Vic on 20 July 1971.

[2] Dexter replied on 2 June 1971, 'You may be speechless, but you are obviously not wordless, nor am I,' and suggested KPT make his recording outside rehearsal hours. KPT brought the cassette to the hospital and played it to me and Matthew Blake.

To Bernard Levin[1]

20 Thurloe Square
20th June, 1971

Dear Bernard,

Over the years, people on the Left have taken a good deal of fairly contemptuous abuse from you over the conduct of the Americans in Vietnam. Whenever we doubted the sincerity of L.B.J.'s desire for peace, whenever we questioned your faith in his tolerance and compassion, whenever we dared to suggest that the motives behind the bombing pauses were not altogether humanitarian, how loftily you sneered at us! To your readers we were either dim-witted dupes or conscious subversives. On the <u>Daily Mail</u> you had the further advantage of working for a paper that had no Letters Page on which we could reply.

We are waiting with interest to hear your comments on the documents recently printed in the New York Times.[2] Has that newspaper, too, fallen under the sway of the Lefties? Or are the documents Communist forgeries? Surely one of these must be the case; because otherwise you would be in honour bound to admit that you had been terribly wrong for many years and had wantonly insulted a great many decent people who now turn out to have been right.

Yours sincerely,
Ken.[3]

[1] (Henry) Bernard Levin (b. 1928), drama critic for the *Daily Express* (1959–62) and *Daily Mail* (1962–6); author of books including *The Pendulum Years* (1971) and *The Way We Live Now* (1984); a columnist on *The Times* 1971 to date.
[2] From the Pentagon Papers, a massive top-secret history of the US role in Indo-China 1945–68.
[3] Levin replied from *The Times* (24 June): 'Please don't answer this question to me, but to yourself, when you are alone. Have you actually <u>read</u> the NYT material, other than the headlines on it? If you have, it only confirms once again that my opinion of you – which is that I am very fond of you but that you have no ratiocinative faculty whatever – is the right one. Yours ever, Bernard.'

To Václav Havel

[The National Theatre]
6 July 1971

Dear Václav,
   Many thanks for your letter[1] but please don't worry or accuse yourself. We are ready at any time to see your play but only when you think
it's ready for us to see it.

All good wishes,
Yours sincerely,
[Kenneth Tynan]

[1] In a letter dated 30 June 1971 Havel apologized for not being able to meet the 1 July deadline
for his new play but promised to send the final text within a month. He explained that he
'overestimated my strength' and that there were 'external circumstances' such as a head injury
which had delayed him.

To Jerry Zeitman[1]

20 Thurloe Square
7th July, 1971

Dear Mr Zeitman,
   At the request of my friend Edna O'Brien, the novelist, I am sending
you the enclosed script. Her last work for the cinema was the new
Elizabeth Taylor film 'Zee and Co',[2] which (she tells me) has turned
out be a grotesque travesty.
   'Stag'[3] is something else. I[t] would be categorically the most outrageous sexual fantasy ever filmed, and obviously not very costly. Last
month Edna showed it to the very talented Scandinavian director Jörn
Donner,[4] who said he would give his right testicle to direct it. I wouldn't
go quite as far as that, but I would be very pleased to know your
reaction.

[Kenneth Tynan]

[1] A film producer.
[2] A sexual melodrama directed by Brian G. Hutton and co-starring Michael Caine and Susannah
York (UK, 1971).

³ Never made.
⁴Jörn Donner (b. 1933), Finnish writer and director whose first film, *A Sunday in September* (Finland, 1963) won a prize at the Venice Film Festival.

To the Editor, *The Times*[1]

20 Thurloe Square
[Published 27 July 1971]

Sir,—Is it for fear of driving undecided Tories into the pro-Market lobby that the left in this country has thus far soft-pedalled the strongest single argument against our joining the EEC – namely, that entry will do enormous and possibly irreparable harm to the chances of socialism in Britain? (I mean, of course, genuine socialism, and not the sort of coalition-caretaker-capitalism which your editorials have been holding out as bait for hesitant leftists). Sir Tufton Beamish[2] is one of the few Tories who have openly admitted that the tremendous threat it poses to the left is among the Market's most enticing features.

The EEC is a capitalist power block dedicated to the perpetuation of the postwar schism of Europe. Its face is set firmly against the Warsaw Pact countries, so much so that Dubček's Czechoslovakia – the finest flower of European socialism since the war – would have stood no chance at all of being considered for admission to the EEC. The Market is essentially the economic arm of NATO, and it deplores any backsliding towards neutralism, let alone socialism and its dread concomitants, the public ownership of land and the means of production.

One sees why the Labour right are so eager for entry: it would mean that they would never again have to worry over much about placating their left. Yet it is sad that a wing of the party so rich in historians should not have reflected that the Common Market in its fullest state of development will be the most blatant historical vulgarity since the Thousand Year Reich. Hitler's blueprint for the salvation of Europe was a vision in which the western powers – Germany, Britain, France, Italy, Spain and the Low Countries – led the world on a crusade against communism. He failed to realise his dream. The Market could come close to fulfilling it for him.

Not long ago the Swedes, after careful thought, withdrew their application for full membership on the grounds that it would be incompatible with their tradition of political neutrality. They are quite content with associate membership, which has all the economic advantages and none of the political fetters of full membership. Perhaps we should learn from their example. Recent history has spelled out a message we would be foolish to ignore. It is that small countries are flexible and capable of change, while large power groups (the USA, the USSR) are musclebound dinosaurs, inherently conservative and equipped with enough repressive strength to resist any internal pressures for change.

A politically and economically unified western Europe would be a capitalist fortress in which this country would have lost its manoevrability and above all its freedom to choose the socialist path.

Yours sincerely,
KENNETH TYNAN

[1] Contributing to a correspondence about Britain's sovereignty and the EEC.
[2] Rear Admiral Sir Tufton Percy Hamilton Beamish, Conservative MP for Lewes 1924–31 and 1936–45.

To Hillard Elkins

20 Thurloe Square
30th July 1971

Dear Hilly,

Do you remember that Grove Press anthology[1] you master-minded for me two years ago? I have just realised that I have no copy of my contract with them. Do you have one? If so, could you let me have it as soon as possible?

Between ourselves, the problem is that I have had a very disappointing response from the many authors I contacted with a view to contributing the stuff.[2] Many of those who agreed to take part have failed to come through, and most of the few contributions that have actually arrived are lousy. Before I go any further I want to make quite sure what my obligations are. There is no need to talk to Grove Press about this; I will let you know if there are any developments.

Love,
Ken

[1] A collection of masturbatory fantasies by famous writers to be called *For Myself Alone*. It never materialized.

² Over the course of two years some twelve authors contributed items, while a further dozen agreed but did not deliver. A vast number of writers turned KPT down. Nabokov had 'no interest whatever in pornography'; Graham Greene didn't feel like joining 'this children's game'; Auden felt pornography should be written, if at all, 'to amuse one's intimate friends'.

To Penelope Gilliatt

20 Thurloe Square
August 5 [1971]

Dear Pen –

Having some work to do I thought I'd write to you and see what was up. Where are you this hot summer? Is all well or wellish? We saw Andy Warhol's 'Pork'¹ last night and thought of New York which it so crisply captures (I liked it more than I expected and responded to the Warhol cult for the first time). Oh and I am a father again, as maybe you knew, a boy called Matthew Blake: ever fearful of the competing prick, I had hoped for another girl, and had even named her Angelica Tiffany: but when the announcement came from matron, I said farewell to Angelica Tiffany, summoned from the shadows only to recede again, and welcomed Matthew Blake who thank God is no bulletheaded thug but a long-lipped, long-eyelashed charmer of distinctly feminine looks. I have entered him for the Royal Ballet School and am buying him a few nice frocks, so all should be well. Or wellish.

Kathleen is feeding him and when weaning ends (c. August 20) we go to Sardinia for ten days and then to Andalusia for another ten, getting back here in mid-September. What are your moves? 'Macbeth' is still editing and dubbing, and looks good to me in many parts; Roman grows a little bored with it and keeps flying off to St Tropez, leaving me to look after the post-synching, which in a movie like this represents an awful lot of acting. There is talk of another picture together, but only talk as yet. The National is in a bit of a slough, since Adrian Mitchell's outrageous insurgent musical about William Blake 'Tyger' was trampled on by most of the middle-aged critics (and most of them are middle-aged now: average age, I discovered, is over fifty: whereas I was 26 when I took over 'The Observer') and adored by the underground press. I thought it 70 per cent marvellous and agreed with Charlie Marowitz when he called it on radio 'a theatre poem'; but I see that it's too passionate and extreme for modish taste, which is mostly formed these days by critics who prefer the sigh and shrug and the stoically tightened lip. Jonathan Miller followed 'Tyger' (which John Dexter and Michael Blakemore codirected) with a bloodless production of 'Danton's Death'[2] that the critics adored – with the mob cut out and the debate scenes staged without the Assembly's reactions. It was like a high explosive bomb directed by the Bomb Disposal Squad. Ah well, or wellish.

Write soon. Did you read in Ruth Gordon's autobiography about George Kaufman's review of an Italian actor called Guido Nadzo: 'Guido Nadzo is nadzo guido'? I'm sure you did.[3]

Love from us both –
Ken

[1] Play in which the characters were takeoffs on Warhol's Factory associates; a hit in London, it opened at the Roundhouse in July 1971, two months after its unsuccessful New York run.
[2] Opened 3 August 1971.
[3] A well-known witticism from the Algonquin Round Table.

To Herbert Kretzmer[1]

20 Thurloe Square
19th October, 1971

Dear Herbert,
So at last you have penetrated the secret of my double life. At weekends I nip off to Fez and have it away in my harem and stuff hash down my earhole and that, after which I stagger back to London like a dwarf refreshed. Also I charge a nifty royalty for the use of my image on coins, stamps, cigarette cards, ash trays etc. etc. After all, as I told my Ombudsman (Moroccan word for tax consultant), before having him flogged last Sunday, if royalty can't charge a royalty, who can?

Love from all my hairy ladies, and please send more money.

Yours devotedly,
[Ken Tynan]

[1] Herbert Kretzmer (b. 1925), theatre critic and lyricist, had sent KPT on 6 October 'a Moroccan dirham containing a likeness widely held to be your own'.

To Vera Russell

20 Thurloe Square
November 11, 1971

Dear Vera,

You are entitled to your opinions, but I am not obliged to swallow the effrontery that goes with them. If I disgust you so much, you really ought to have made the effort and refused the invitation to my house. [...] But I am amazed that, having been crass enough to accept my hospitality and repay it with vulgar abuse, you should still expect to go on picking Kathleen's brains and relying on her aid in rounding up our friends to support your ludicrous festival of European elitism.[1] I have borne with you through many vicissitudes and have always defended you against those who laughed you off as a pompous name-dropper. I shall do so no longer.

The fact that you disliked 'Oh! Calcutta!' is unimportant. What is not forgiveable is the contempt with which you accuse a friend – before giving him a chance to speak – of selling himself for money-grubbing sensationalism. I am glad to tell you that you will not be called on to spend any more of your time in the company of someone as odious as

Yours sincerely,
Ken[2]

[1] The government-sponsored European arts festival was scrapped shortly after.
[2] Vera Russell replied, 'You are always welcome in my house.'

To Václav Havel

[The National Theatre]
30 November 1971

Dear Václav Havel:

I apologise for the delay in writing. I was in New York when your play arrived, and then it was necessary to obtain a literal translation before I could read it. I asked a young Czech director on the National Theatre staff to prepare this translation – not for use in production but just for myself and Sir Laurence to read. I did this because I had never read any of your work except in Vera Blackwell's versions and I thought it might be useful to see what you sounded like in someone else's translation. If we produced the play, we would ask Vera to translate it – I believe you have written to her indicating this is your desire.

Before commenting on the play, I should like to ask if you would be kind enough to send me the notes you mentioned you have written for it.[1] Probably they will answer some of the questions I want to ask. I enjoyed reading the play very much and liked individual scenes enormously: but I felt that in some ways it had departed from what I thought was the original conception. As I understood it, the idea of the play was to be that a group of conspirators, plotting to overthrow an indecisive government, received information that a second group were planning a similar coup. This drove the first group to take even stronger measures, and so on and so forth. Finally they would discover that the information was in fact about themselves, fed out by a spy and fed back through the secret service.

Now there are elements of this in the play as it now stands but they have been outweighed by the plots and counter-plots <u>within</u> the conspiracy – such as the changes in the balance of power when X allies himself with Y and Y with Z. This – although interesting – seems to me less brilliant and exciting than the original idea, which was at once fantastic and utterly logical, like all your best work. Do you feel this yourself? And may it perhaps be that the play would work better if there were in fact no Olah?

Another (and minor) question: are you quite happy with the pin-pricking? It seems to me a bit too farcical in a fairly orthodox way.

I look forward to your comments on these points. How I wish it were possible for us to talk them over face to face.

One final query: Vera tells me that you are now in a position to sign a contract and to receive money in Czechoslovakia. If so, please let me know and I'll get our finance department to send a contract and an advance payment.

Yours sincerely,
[Kenneth Tynan][2]

---

[1] Havel sent his notes on 13 October, which were translated by Vera Blackwell. He wrote that the play was 'not at all concerned with such problems as those of dictatorship or of democracy, for example; one might rather say that its theme is <u>truth</u> ... Truth is not only what is being said, it also depends on who says it and why. Truth is guaranteed only by the full weight of humanity ... The modern rationalistic age leads to a continually greater automization of the so-called "objective truth", as though it were a freely transferable, fully objectified commodity which could be appropriated by anyone ... this is the main theme of the play ... the man who ceases to be, so to speak "in truth", to <u>be</u> truth, thus loses his own identity.'

[2] *The Conspirators* was not performed at the National, because it was felt that the script needed work and Havel could not come to London. Havel apparently still does not consider it ready for production. His secretary for literary and theatrical matters, Anna Freimanová, says: 'In our country ... the only production of this play has been staged by my husband Andrej Krob in the Divadlo na zábradlí in 1992.'

To Laurence Olivier

20 Thurloe Square
December 9, 1971

Dear Larry

To make no bones about it, I think 'Goodnatured Man'[1] is a dead bore. So much so that I saw no point in talking to John [Dexter] about it. One could suggest a patch here and there, but (a) the play is threadbare beyond salvation and (b) we haven't got the actors to conceal (a).

Recently I seem to have been elected N. T. Spokesman. At Craig's[2] request, I let the press come to interview me about The Crisis at the National; and Tynan Strikes Back, gallantly declaring that there's nothing wrong that a couple of hits won't cure, upholding the theory of Collective Responsibility to discourage journalists from trying to apportion blame, and generally insisting that it's just a question of a little weak casting here, a touch of poor directing there, with a soupçon of bad play-selection to boot. I told 'The Times' all this the other day, and they're printing a piece on the N.T. on Saturday. After 'G.N.M.' opens I have no doubt that I shall be attacked for having chosen a play I consistently opposed.

I'm sure you see why I feel unhappy. I opposed 'Cyrano';[3] it flopped. I opposed 'The Idiot' and 'Mrs Warren' and 'Rules'[4] and (your interpretation of) 'Amphitryon'.[5] I agree that I also supported the Arrabal[6] and 'Tyger'; but if you look at the figures you'll find that the Arrabal averaged between 73% and 77% of seating capacity, which isn't contemptible.

I'm writing this partly just to get it off my chest, but partly because I think the company is at present so weak that it could not succeed in any programme of plays. There isn't anyone at the Vic (except possibly [Ronald] Pickup) to whose next appearance one looks forward with real excitement. Unless the company is rebuilt from the ground upwards (starting with Richard[7] and continuing with the Greeks[8]), it will not much matter what plays it performs, because it will be unable to perform anything more than feebly. What I'm suggesting is a cutback to a figure of about 15 actors (at most) and building from there. We have nothing to lose – by the end of March the rep. will be empty except for 'Goodnatured Man' (if it survives that long) and 'Jumpers'.[9] There may not be another chance like this of rising from the ashes. If the acting choices we make now aren't the right ones, if the changes aren't radical enough, we shan't deserve to survive.

I'm sure your own thoughts must be running along similar lines. And I apologise for reiterating so much that you already know. It's just that I couldn't help sharing with you my deep sense of urgency and distress.

Love,
[Ken]

[1] *The Good Natured Man* by Oliver Goldsmith (1768), directed by John Dexter, opened at the Old Vic on 9 December 1971.

[2] Craig Macdonald, the National Theatre's Publicity Manager.

[3] *Cyrano de Bergerac* by Edmond Rostand (1897), adapted and directed by Patrick Garland, had opened at the Old Vic on 27 October 1970.

[4] *The Rules of the Game* by Luigi Pirandello (1918), directed by Anthony Page, had opened on 15 June 1971.

[5] *Amphitryon 38* by Jean Giraudoux (1929), directed by Olivier, had opened on 23 June 1971.

[6] *The Architect and the Emperor of Assyria* had opened on 3 February 1971.

[7] *Richard II*, directed by David William, opened at the Old Vic on 29 March 1972 with Ronald Pickup in the title role.

[8] Euripides' *The Bacchae*, adapted by Wole Soyinka and directed by Roland Joffé, opened on 2 August 1973.

[9] A philosophical romp by Tom Stoppard, whose main purpose is to affirm the existence of God, it received its première at the Old Vic on 2 February 1972.

To Laurence Olivier

20 Thurloe Square
December 14 [1971]

Dear Larry,

I was just sitting down to write you a note of appreciation when Michael [Blakemore] called. Among other things he mentioned that you'd been upset by my letter.[1] I'm shattered to hear this, and I'd like to explain why I sent it when I did. Firstly, if I'd waited until 'Good Natured Man' opened, it would have looked as if I was merely climbing on the bandwagon of the bad reviews. Secondly, I was under the (mistaken) impression that the major decisions about the reshaping of the company were going to be taken at the end of the week. And with no planning meeting until December 31, there would have been no chance to put my point of view.

It goes without saying that I'm terribly sorry if my timing bothered you. My best excuse must be that if I felt less strongly about the N.T. I probably wouldn't have said anything at all.

'Long Day's Journey', as all four of you are playing it, emerges as a masterpiece of so many kinds that I stopped counting. At various moments it looks like (a) the best American play, (b) the best Irish play, (c) the best <u>Greek</u> play, (d) the best family play, (e) the best Freudian play and (f) the best Marxist play ever written. Thanks forever for doing it.

Love,
Ken.

P.S. What an irony that that poor devastated man spent 30 years writing grandiose pseudo-tragic plays when all the time the great play he had it in him to write was about how his family made him precisely the sort of poor, devastated man who would spend 30 years writing grandiose pseudo-tragic plays! (I <u>think</u> that's what I mean.)[2]

---

[1] Of 9 December 1971.
[2] Olivier acknowledged KPT's 'thoughtful note' in a letter dated 28 December 1971 and apologized for being unable to give him a considered reply due to the demands of rehearsals

To William Shawn

20 Thurloe Square
December 20th, 1971

Dear Mr Shawn,

I have had an idea which I'd like to pass on to you. It has been provoked partly by 'W R – Mysteries of the Organism',[1] the Yugoslav film about Wilhelm Reich, and partly by my own memories of his remarkable early book 'The Sexual Revolution'. The film refers, though not very explicitly, to the problems that afflicted Reich's later years in America, culminating in his trial and imprisonment, and the destruction of his books. I hold no special brief for the man, who was obviously very difficult and probably paranoid; but I found myself longing to know more about his later life, and particularly about his skirmishes with the law. Would a piece by me on this be of any interest to you?[2] If so, I'd be happy to come to the States to do the necessary research.

Let me emphasise that I'd be approaching the subject with an open mind. I am not contemplating yet another addition to the liberal martyrology.

Happy Christmas, Mr. Shawn.

Yours sincerely,
Kenneth Tynan

[1] Directed by Dušan Makavejev (Yugoslavia, 1971).
[2] Shawn said yes to the Reich idea.

Memo to Laurence Olivier, Michael Blakemore, Peter Wood, Tom Stoppard[1]

[The National Theatre]
[January 1972]

A few proposals after the run-through – based on the conviction that even when the technical problems are solved, we shall still be over-length.

Prologue: the audience must realise that the party continues until the shooting – that its all one scene. At present there are no guest reactions through the jumping of Dottys song. [*sic*]

The flat looks too fantastic and futuristic. Would it help to cover the big T.V. screen with curtains, until the T.V. is in use?

George's long speeches are working well: its the murder plot that isn't. On 2.3. when George hears that there is a body and goes into the bedroom to check, why doesn't he react to the absence of a body? Even more important, <u>why doesn't Bones</u>? It's utterly implausible. Instead of following the plot-line they go off into routines about 'softly softly' and 'Bones the Osteopath'. At this point we stopped taking the murder plot seriously, with very bad effects on [what] follows. Why not go straight from their entering the bedroom to 'what's happened to Professor McFee'? Even so Bones should make some comment on the body's disappearance.

'If Duncan's a spirit he'll cut his throat.' Suggest: If Duncan finds out he's a spirit, he'll cut his throat. Or: 'If Duncan turns out to be a spirit. ...'

I know Tom's objection to this, but I still maintain that to set up a whodunit and not reveal whodidit is very confusing. The audience will feel cheated.

[1] Michael Blakemore was now an Associate Director of the National; Peter Wood was scheduled to direct *Jumpers*.

Private Memo to Laurence Olivier

[The National Theatre]
9 March 1972

Dear Larry:

This is in reply to your letter of February 16.[1] You are indeed 'unduly suspicious'. I wasn't interested in getting the record straight – I was <u>overcome</u> by a strong feeling and expressed it as directly as I could.

If getting the record straight, however, is our aim, there are one or two entries in your list that I would question. Although both were commercial failures, ANDORRA and THE DUTCH COURTESAN were both ideas that originated with me. The ladies for the Jeanetta Cochrane season were chosen by Joan in consultation with me. THE ADVERTISEMENT[2] came to Joan via Martin Esslin before I had ever heard of it. THE DANCE OF DEATH is something I had always wanted you to play and I always thought that I had proposed it for the repertoire. This same is true of THE MERCHANT OF VENICE: I can remember pressing Shylock on you at meeting after meeting, only to be told that you didn't want to play it, and Jonathan [Miller] was one of my top suggestions to direct it. Finally, I would have thought that both THE WHITE DEVIL[3] and HEDDA GABLER were generally agreed choices; I certainly never opposed either of them. On the other hand, I was not in favour of THE RULES OF THE GAME and repeatedly said so.

All of which, alas, doesn't really get us any nearer to the subject of my last letter – the one about my title.[4] I didn't, as you seem to have thought, 'require' an answer in two weeks: I simply mentioned that I would be away for that period if you wanted to talk to me. But you are now going to be away for much longer than two weeks and I am thus left in the dark as to precisely what my function is to be during your absence. I knew what I was as Literary Manager; I know what Derek [Granger] is as Literary Consultant. At present I am something betwixt and between which enables my enemies to attack me for holding a sinecure when the NT is doing well and to blame the whole of our artistic policy on me when the NT is doing badly. Would it really be so hard to get the position clarified one way or the other? Could it, for instance, be raised by the Board while you were away? I am not asking for more status or more money – simply for a recognition of the fact that whatever task I am performing at the moment, it is different from that which is being performed by Derek.[5]

[1] A detailed response to KPT's letter of 9 December 1971, in which Olivier sensed, 'I hope without being unduly suspicious ... that there was some wish on your part to put the record straight.' Olivier listed all the National's productions up to *Richard II* and columnized them as follows: 1) 'K.T.'s originals', 2) those 'generally agreed ... between all of us', 3) those 'without blessings of K.T.'s support'. Under 1) he put *The Advertisement*; under 2) *Andorra, The Dance of Death*, and *The Rules of the Game*, and under 3) *The Dutch Courtesan*, the Jeanetta Cochrane season, *The Merchant of Venice, The White Devil* and *Hedda Gabler*. He finished with a P. S.: 'I can't emphasize enough how grateful I am for your care over the Stoppard and for Kathleen's marvellously kind coping.'
[2] By Natalia Ginzburg (1965), directed by Donald MacKechnie and Laurence Olivier, starring Joan Plowright; it opened on 24 September 1968.
[3] By John Webster (1612), directed by Frank Dunlop; it had opened on 13 November 1969.
[4] Literary Consultant.
[5] Olivier replied on 10 March that it was 'the Board who concertedly agreed that you should no longer be called manager' and that it was only by calling KPT a 'consultant' that he had managed to keep him on, 'and then only if I had another one besides yourself'.

To Emilie Jacobson

20 Thurloe Square
13th March, 1972

Dear Emilie,
   I have got your letter of March 9th. I am very sorry if Arthur Kretchmer[1] would be embarrassed, but I assure you that his embarrassment is nothing to the embarrassment I have suffered during the last few years with <u>every</u> journalist in Europe referring to me as 'Kenneth Tynan, the well-known Playboy Editor'. The point about the

description is that it is <u>totally false</u>. I haven't contributed for years, and I have never edited. Please emphasise to Mr. Kretchmer that there is nothing personal in this. The plain fact is that I would be far more likely to contribute if the agreement with Spectorsky were respected and my name removed from the masthead immediately. If it is not respected, I shall consider it evidence of bad faith, and I wouldn't wish my relationship with the magazine to be soured in this way. I am quite immovable on this point and am rapidly becoming angry. Please, Emilie, don't be ambiguous when explaining my feelings to Mr. Kretchmer or Mr. Butler.[2] I want my name taken off <u>NOW</u>.

Yours sincerely,
Ken.

[1] Executive Editor of *Playboy*.
[2] David Butler, also at *Playboy*.

To William Shawn

20 Thurloe Square
March 29, 1972

Dear Mr. Shawn,

My research into Reich goes well: he gets more fascinating by the minute. I don't know anyone into whom more of the complexities of the twentieth century were unhappily crammed.

As I told you, I want to focus on his last, increasingly lunatic years, culminating in his trial, imprisonment and death,[1] and this will involve a trip to the States to talk to his widow, his son and daughter, his legal advisers, and some of the people – analysts and quasi-scientists – who regard themselves as keepers of the Reichian flame. The in-fighting within the latter group is, I am told, exceptionally savage. Thankfully, the research will not entail much travelling in the States – most of the people concerned live in New York, Massachusetts and Connecticut – but it will entail some expenditure.

What I propose is to come to New York in late April or early May, and spend about a month gathering material. Since (apart from my honorific job at the National Theatre, and a dwindling trickle of author's royalties from 'Oh! Calcutta!') I have no regular income, it would be immensely helpful if 'The New Yorker' could let me have some expenses in advance to pay for my air trip, accommodation and travel in the States. Any sum you feel able to provide would be very welcome. I will of course keep a record of how it is spent.

There is one other problem on which I'd like your advice. Reich's trial took place in the Federal Courthouse at Portland, Maine, on May 3, 4, 5 and 7, 1956. Is it possible (and would it be costly) for me to obtain a transcript of the proceedings? If so, is there anyone on your staff who could set about procuring it for me so that I shall have it to hand when I get to New York?[2]

I look forward to hearing from you. I'm sorry to impose on your benevolence, but this piece shows every sign of burgeoning into a small book.

Yours sincerely,
Kenneth Tynan

P. S.: I ran into Nicol Williamson the other day, not having seen him since my piece appeared.[3] I asked him whether he had read it. 'Oh no,' he said (lying I am sure in his teeth), 'but my friends tell me it displays a certain glib facility.' With a wintry leer he passed by.

---

[1] Reich claimed to be able to concentrate natural energies in 'orgone accumulators'. This and other of his experiments incurred, in 1956, the hostility of the American Medical Association and the Federal Food and Drug Administration. He was put on trial for fraud, pronounced guilty and imprisoned. His books were burned, his research and scientific equipment destroyed. He died in 1957.
[2] Shawn had the *New Yorker* obtain the documentation.
[3] Two months previously.

To Peter Hall[1]

The National Theatre
April 20, 1972

Dear Peter –

I trust you suffered no lasting wounds from being caught in that flurry of crossfire[2] between the Board and the executive. I told the Board on Tuesday (and you last week), none of us had anything against you personally. What we deplored about the whole exercise was the total lack of consultation. My own feeling was that within a year or two Michael Blakemore might have emerged as a candidate, and it shook me to learn that Max Rayne had never even met him; but if the appointment was to be made now, then it obviously had to be you.

We also felt upset about the timing. It looked as if the Board had lost all faith in the organization at a moment when it just happened to be having one of its most successful seasons.[3] Michael, John Dexter, Frank Dunlop and I have proposed that we should attend Board meetings from now onwards (I used to do so until Lord Chandos excluded me a year or two ago) to make sure that failures of communication don't happen again. I hope the Board is sagacious enough to agree.

I pointed out to them, by the way, that we weren't asking for the right to vote and fully realised that we weren't ready for self-government – though it would have been nice if Lord Goodman had offered us unimpeded progress towards it, as he did for the Rhodesian blacks![4]

So: congratulations – and I needn't warn as wary a bird as you to keep a sharp eye on the Board and its doings.

Yours,
Ken

[1] Now Artistic Director designate of the National Theatre, he would replace Olivier in 1973.
[2] The theatre's artistic directorate did not welcome an outside appointment and felt Olivier had been usurped.
[3] Including highly praised productions of *Long Day's Journey Into Night* and *Jumpers*.
[4] In a speech in the House of Lords, 21 June 1972.

To Simon Michael Bessie

[20 Thurloe Square]
4 May 1972

Dear Mike,

I would have replied earlier to your letter, but I have had a week of sleepless nights trying to fix a last-minute settlement to this bloody libel action.[1] It seems that if you advance the possibility that General Sikorski's crash was due to sabotage and then mention the undeniable fact that the pilot was the sole survivor, that in itself constitutes a libel under British law. [...] The final settlement has cost me a bomb.[2] I shan't have to sell the house or anything like that, but a sizable percentage of my savings has been wiped out.

Now to our problem, on which the above has a certain bearing. I want to start all over again on the 'autobiographical book'. Some weeks ago Peter Hall was appointed Director Designate of the National

Theatre. He will take over from Larry early in 1974, when the Company moves into its new theatre on the Banks of the Thames. When this announcement was made, I had several feelers from publishers about the possibility of books on Larry and/or the National Theatre, the assumption being that I would be leaving when Peter Hall takes over. This assumption, as I've told you, is pretty well-founded: I <u>do</u> intend to leave as soon as the job of piloting Larry into the new building is finished.[3] And it would be nice if the book were to appear shortly after that happens.

As I know [*sic*] see it, the book will be mainly about Larry and the National, partly about the Hochhuth affair (and its implications) and partly about 'Oh! Calcutta!' (and <u>its</u> implications). I want to start work on it soon (i.e. in the Autumn, after I have written a long <u>New Yorker</u> piece on Wilhelm Reich). <u>BUT</u>: I honestly can't afford to do so on the present terms. One of the British offers I have received (for English-speaking rights) is large enough to make the proposition viable; but it would involve a slightly larger outlay on your part (I don't know precisely how much) than our present contract provides for.

I wouldn't dream of suggesting this if I weren't financially over a barrel. One way of putting it, perhaps, would be to say that the Hochhuth damages were expenses incurred in the course of my researches, for which I need partial compensation! The point is that if you can rustle up a slightly bigger advance, I'll ask the English publisher[4] (who for some weird reason wants to be anonymous) to ring you and outline what he has in mind. If this works out, I will write you a hell of a book. The alternative is that, for purely financial reasons, I shall have to do the Weidenfeld book first.

I really hate to strain our friendship like this; but I am going through a crunch period in my life and if I'm to get out of it the book that is in it, I shall need your help.

Yours sincerely,
[Kenneth Tynan]
[. . .]

---

[1] On 7 January 1970 the pilot of the plane in which Sikorski had died, Edward Maximillian Prchal, sued KPT, Michael White and Clifford Williams for libel. A separate writ went out against Hochhuth and another against the publishers of the play.
[2] In May 1972 KPT had to pay £7,000 in damages and costs, as there was no truth in the implication that the pilot was in any way responsible.
[3] KPT left the National in 1973 (Olivier left in 1974). The new building did not open until 1976.
[4] George Weidenfeld. KPT hoped the advance for the *Surviving Plays* book would allow him to

Ken, 1962

Right Ken's critic's notes on the programme of the Berliner Ensemble's *Coriolan*, 1964

Die Tragödie des Coriolan

Left Party in London for the Berliner Ensemble, 1965 (left to right: Helene Weigel, Ken, Marlene Dietrich, Ekkehard Schall)

Ken and I, Thurloe Square, 1966

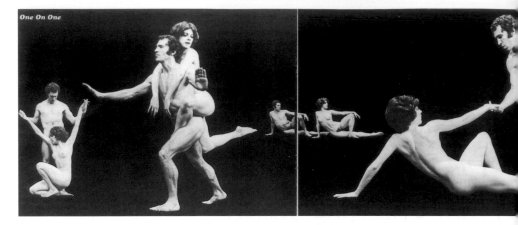

WHITTOCK

OH! CALCUTTA!

"I didn't think much of the costumes."

'I'm afraid, Ponting, the Public Prosecutor has given us the highly distasteful task of reporting on 'Oh! Calcutta!''

Above Oh! Calcutta!, New York, 1969

Left Cartoon in the *Birmingham Evening Mail*, 28 July 1970 *Below left* Cartoon by Marc

Below Costume design by Ken for 'The Empress's New Clothes' in the London production of *Oh! Calcutta!*, 1970

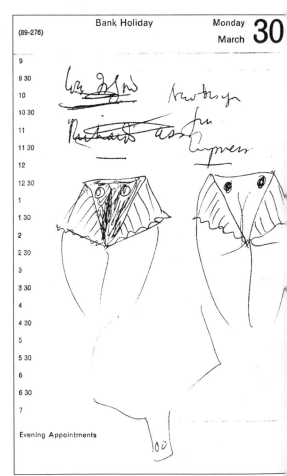

	Bank Holiday	Monday	30
(89-276)		March	
9			
9 30			
10			
10 30			
11			
11 30			
12			
12 30			
1			
1 30			
2			
2 30			
3			
3 30			
4			
4 30			
5			
5 30			
6			
6 30			
7			
Evening Appointments			

om Stoppard, 1968

Peter Shaffer during the National
Theatre production of *Equus*, 1973

Ken and I in Spain, 1970

Ken with Roman Polanski, Thurloe
Square, 1971

Ken in London, c. 1974

The *Carte Blanche* programme amended by Ken, 1976

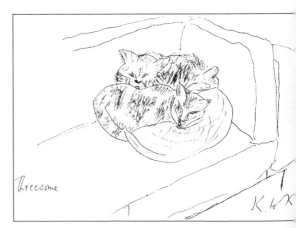

A drawing by Ken, 1974

photograph of Louise Brooks in
ove 'Em and Leave 'Em, 1926,
scribed by her to Ken

*Kenneth—
Louise
Brooks
1978*

postcard from the Paris
staurant La Tour d'Argent,
1979

Le numéro de votre canard **560230**
(depuis 1890)

Frédéric préparant son célèbre Canard

LA TOUR D'ARGENT
CLAUDE TERRAIL

LA TOUR D'ARGENT
le plus ancien restaurant de Paris
(1582)

It is not generally
known that Ibsen stole
the title of his play
'Wild Duck' from the
speciality of the restaurant
run by his twin
brother Fred (*SEE
OVER*)
Gode Schnorkjing!
K.

CARTE POSTALE

Mr. K. Tynan
20 Thurloe Square
London S.W.7.

15 QUAI DE LA TOURNELLE · PARIS-V⁵
033-23-31   *fermé le lundi*

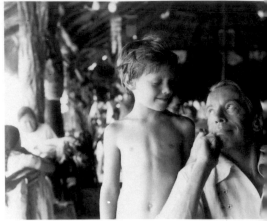

Above Matthew and Ken in Puerto Vallarta, 19

Below Ken in Bel Air, 1979

Above Roxana and Ken in Oxford, 1979

Ken, Matthew and I in Malibu, 1977

pay off Bessie and Longman's for the autobiographical book already under contract. He would then write an autobiographical book of a different order which Weidenfeld would publish in the UK, and (KPT hoped) Bessie in the US.

To Tracy Tynan

[12 May 1972]

May 12
Poem for Tracy's 20th birthday:[1]

> Twenty
> Is plenty
> For most girls, who then
> Cease to be people
> And live through their men.
> You, on the other hand,
> Take the long view –
> Mankind your brother and
> Womankind too.
> Ever a chooser
> And never a beggar
> (Quoting Marcuse[2]
> And even Heidegger),
> Herewith I wish you
> Health, love + gaiety –
> Down with the preachers
> And up with the laity!
> Down with the tyrants,
> The prudes and the owners!
> Arriba the rebels,
> The clowns and the loners!
> Be an empiricist
> In Socialism and sex!
> Read Wilhelm Reich
> And remember the Czechs!
> Weep for the world
> Yet seldom look sad –
> And never kick sand on
> Your much-loving Dad.

To Rose Hecht[1]

20 Thurloe Square
18 May 1972

Dear Mrs Hecht:

I've just read your letter to Laurence Olivier about THE FRONT PAGE. It shattered me because as Larry's literary adviser, I'm responsible for the idea that the play ought to be in the repertoire of the National Theatre. I've admired it for a quarter of a century, ever since I was in high school; and like thousands of other sane young Englishmen, I hated what was being done in our name by the British in Palestine and I fully sympathise with your late husband's feelings on the subject.[2] Now please understand this:

<u>One of my main reasons for wanting our company to do THE FRONT PAGE was to atone for what the idiot chauvinist British press had done to your husband.</u> The production would triumphantly demonstrate that in spite of their scurrilous jibes Ben Hecht lived on in his work.

(And incidentally, we can't be accused of wanting to do the play for profit. We are a non-profit-making organisation.)

In case this sounds like special pleading, I'd like to tell you a couple of things about the National Theatre which you may not know. The chairman of the Board that runs the organisation – the Board that employs Laurence Olivier and me – is Sir Max Rayne,[3] who's not only Jewish but a constant and generous contributor to the Joint Palestine Appeal and the Anglo-Israel Cultural Foundation. The other Board members include Harold Sebag-Montefiore,[4] who is also Jewish and who represents the London municipal authorities on our Board, and a prominent Jewish lawyer, named Victor Mishcon, who is a tireless fund-raiser for the Zionist cause.

In other words, our motives and our background are at least respectable. Please don't let the shadow of the past fall across our attempt to let the name of Ben Hecht triumph over his enemies.

I suppose I should add that I'm writing this letter off my own bat;

nobody asked me to write it. All I hope is that you will read it with urgency and sympathy.

Yours sincerely,
[Kenneth Tynan][5]

[1] Widow of Ben Hecht (1894–1964), the co-author with Charles MacArthur of *The Front Page* (1928).
[2] Hecht was a fervent Zionist and chairman of the American League for a Free Palestine. In 1946–7, during the final phase of the British mandate for Palestine, he had made a number of attacks in the US press, saying that the British armed forces were violent oppressors. One appeal signed by Hecht claimed that every time a bomb or gun went off against the British in Palestine 'the Jews in America made a little holiday in their hearts'. The British press reacted with outrage.
[3] Later Lord Rayne (b. 1918), businessman and philanthropist, chairman of the National Theatre Board 1971–88).
[4] Barrister and Deputy Circuit Judge (b. 1924).
[5] *The Front Page* opened at the National on 6 July 1972.

To Emilie Jacobson

Castillito Mariposa[1]
Cuarton Tarifa
Spain
August 30 1972

Dear Emilie –

I'm here in Spain writing some New Yorker pieces, but something has come up that might interest Sports Illustrated. Hemingway wrote a book called The Dangerous Summer[2] about the rivalry between 2 great bullfighters, Luis Miguel Dominguín and Antonio Ordóñez, brothers-in-law who were the 2 best in the world at their profession. Ordóñez, the younger of the two, emerged triumphant. Luis Miguel retired shortly afterwards: Ordóñez retired a couple of years ago. Last season Luis Miguel, in need of money, made a comeback – quite successfully, because bullfighting is at present in the doldrums,[3] following the retirement of El Cordobés. Now Ordóñez has decided to come out of retirement for one day to fight on the same bill as Luis Migel – in his (Ordóñez's) home town of Ronda in Andalucia. The fight is on September 7, and it will be the first time the two have appeared together for 13 years – since the Hemingway summer, where they gave me (and Papa) the best taurine afternoon of our lives.

(Incidentally, Ordóñez is a rich man, with no financial incentive to return to the ring.)

All seats were sold 40 minutes after they went on sale last week. Luis Miguel is 46; Ordoñez is 40; yet it will unquestionably be the bullfighting event of the year.[4] Would <u>Sports Ill</u>. like a highly-paid account of it? Please advise me quickly.[5]

Love –
Ken (Tynan)

P. S. Part of the point would be to demonstrate how stagnant bull-fighting has become when a contest between two ancients, both long accepted in the hall of fame, can be the sensation of the year. But it would also be necessary to say that Ordóñez is one of the half-dozen greatest performers in <u>any</u> art that I have ever seen.

P. P. S. Please cable.

[1] A villa between Tarifa and Algeciras belonging to Vanessa McConnell.
[2] A fuller version of Hemingway's *Life* magazine articles (1960), edited by James Michener (1985).
[3] 'Totally misleading' according to the bullfight expert Michael Wigram, who writes for *6 Toros 6*: 'On the contrary it was enjoying a boom.'
[4] Wigram continues: 'The "Goyesca" corrida in Ronda was important only to Antonio Ordóñez's personal army of fans. It was very much a sideshow with very small bulls in a third class plaza. In the event, Dominguín was injured and Antonio Bienvenida appeared in a *mano a mano* with Ordóñez. Ordóñez cut eight ears and three tails from four bulls of the Carlos Nuñez ranch.'
[5] 'The Testimony of a Bullfighter: Antonio Ordóñez' was published in the *Atlantic Monthly*, May 1973.

To the Editor, *The Times*

20 Thurloe Square
[Published 11 October 1972]

Sir,—It is really very cheeky – and insultingly hypocritical – of the press to accuse Mr Wedgwood Benn of seeking to impose censorship.[1] Most of our newspapers are owned and run by men who strongly oppose the Left wing of the Labour Party. These men decide on the relative prominence with which news items are presented and the sort of editorial comment with which they are accompanied. (Or, as so often, mixed up. For example, the front-page *news* story in yesterday's *Daily Mail* began: 'Mr Wilson will today repudiate Mr

Wedgwood Benn, whose *ridiculous* comments last week about TV and Press coverage of politics have made the Labour Party look *absurd*.' My italics.)

The 'free' press of this country is in fact an extremely effective machinery for suppressing or distorting news and comment that is favourable to Socialism. (And please let's not bring up the hoary instance of Beaverbrook hiring David Low.[2] To every court its jester.) If I understand him rightly, Mr Benn's view is that news and comment are matters too vital to be exclusively entrusted to the paternal care of a few rich men and their servants. (This view was described in the news columns as 'Benn's astonishing outburst'; had the newspaper proprietors agreed with him, it would have been 'Benn's bold stand'.) His position is surely one with which every journalist of radical leanings should sympathize. To our shame, printed news in this country is still private property. Are we really so besotted with capitalism that we cherish this state of affairs? Would journalists who work for (say) Sir Max Aitken[3] really march with tears in their eyes to protect their employer's sacred right to censor from his papers all editorial opinions that do not mirror his own? Is this their rallying cry: 'We may disagree with what you say, but we will defend to the death your right to prevent us from saying anything else'?

To my mind, the nastiest aspect of the whole episode has been the dutiful eagerness with which journalists themselves have fallen to the task of sneering at Mr Benn for (as he thought) speaking up in defence of their rights. But of course people who boast of their independence and freedom never like to be reminded that they are neither independent nor free.

Yours sincerely,
KENNETH TYNAN

[1] At the Labour Party conference on 6 October Benn had said: 'I sometimes wish that trade unionists who work in the mass media ... would remember that they too are members of our working-class movement and have a responsibility to see that what is said about us is true.'

[2] Sir David Low (1891–1963), British left-wing political cartoonist on the *Evening Standard*, creator of Colonel Blimp.

[3] Sir Max Aitken (1910–85), British newspaper publisher, son of the First Lord Beaverbrook, and owner of Express Newspapers.

To Joan Plowright

[20 Thurloe Square]
13 October 1972

Dear Joan,
What a lovely understanding letter.[1] You put into words exactly what we both felt. Let's meet again soon and be <u>properly</u> determined and <u>properly</u> flippant instead of both at the same time.

Love,
[Ken]

[1] Plowright had written on 11 October 1972: 'There is always such a determined flippancy about we four when we get together again after long absence and it is difficult to break through to a more serious note ...

'For instance your letter in "The Times" [supporting Wedgwood Benn] is one of the most courageous (because truth always hurts) I've seen for a long time [...] The other thing I wanted to say was that I may have seemed disinterested when you rang once or twice during that Revelations chapter of N.T. history (the leak about the director designate) but it was just that I knew it was too late to fight ... Nor was I sure, if I fought against that particular appointment, what I would be fighting FOR ... So, once again, you fought a lone battle without the troops to back you up.'

To Kathleen Tynan

[20 Thurloe Square]
[?24 October 1972]

Darling,
If I had had her number[1] I would have called it off. Not having it, I couldn't have stood her up – because in any case that would have meant another meeting at some other time.

It was a nice lunch. She was very nervous. She said after a while that in return for my getting her an audition at the NT she had expected that I would want her to use her influence with Sam[2] on some project or other. I found this faintly insulting, but no matter. She told me she had done several TVs and a year of rep since leaving RADA, which meant that she qualified for an NT audition. This surprised me, so I began to question her in more detail about her career as a student. She seemed awfully vague and when I pursued the matter she finally broke down and confessed that she had been lying; hadn't even got into RADA; hadn't done any rep; in fact, had only done two TVs not yet shown.

Which would rule her out of the National. I told her if she could tell the same lies convincingly to Anne Robinson[3] that was OK with me, but I couldn't help her myself – if for no other reason, because the lies were so easy to check. She said she quite understood and that was that.

Then I took her home and fucked her.

Or at least that is what I would have tried to do if I had suddenly gone stark staring berserk. But I am not berserk, and I know that non-berserk people do not exchange coral lagoons in the sunshine for tin baths in the back kitchen; nor do they, when they have the key to the secret garden, toss it into the canal in favour of a season ticket to the municipal baths. So, in the full glow of my sanity, and not regretting a split second of it, I wished her the best of luck, and said goodbye on the pavement and set off to walk the half-mile to where I had parked the car. On the way I began to whistle to myself and to think of simple congenial everyday irreplaceable things like caviare and Diamant Bleu champagne and the New Oxford Book of English Verse and you.

K.

[1] The phone number of an actress KPT had met at a party and arranged to meet.
[2] Sam Spiegel, the film producer.
[3] National Theatre casting assistant.

On our return to London in mid-September of 1972, after two healthful months in the sun, Ken caught a severe cold and developed bronchial repercussions that stayed with him well into the autumn. A different kind of chill settled on me. I was so used to Ken's colds that I no longer – as I should have done – took them seriously. I was concerned that no work was being done, that one holiday followed upon the other, that we were running out of money. To try and ground myself, I read, wrote journalism and made notes for a planned novel, and tried to figure out why our beautiful life was in jeopardy.

On 11 November, with the first two chapters of his book on Wilhelm Reich in his luggage, Ken flew to Tunisia, to the sun, to try and cure his latest cold. I declined to go with him.

To Kathleen Tynan

Hotel Amilcar
Sidi Bou-Saïd,[1] le Sphincter Mundi
Tunisie
[Postmark 13 November 1972]
Sunday 7.15

Dear 1–

I have a new moon (have you?) and made the usual wish. For 24 hours now I have been in the usual limbo reserved for new arrivals anywhere. The hotel is a Torremolinoid structure like a vast cribbage peg planted by the beach just outside Sidi B. Said. It is full, but not with the slightly puzzled tourists I had expected; no, as one might have guessed, the off-season function of these places is to house <u>conventions</u>; so there are 200 dark-suited Arabs holding hands everywhere and haranguing each other, lavishly amplified, in a conference hall from 9 am. till 8 pm., with an hour's break for what passes for lunch. (Today: chilled macaroni, semolina encasing scrag-end of lamb – couscous – and damp Swiss roll).

There were 2 children and a sour-looking sunburned matron on the beach today; I attended with circumspect shirt and trousers, because although a rather watery sun manages to climb about 50° up the sky, there's a persistent breeze ruffling the palm trees, and one isn't remotely tempted to swim. From time to time a water-skier flashes by, but the pool is deserted and nobody delivers newspapers to the souvenir shop. Saddest of all, the sun sets at 5pm – a sudden guillotine I hadn't been warned about – and then it's coat and sweater time with a vengeance.

Again following our routine, I changed my room today. The first one adjoined what, judging by the noises and odours, must have been the only loo available to a dormitory-load of convention members; also it overlooked the car park where the same lot came tyre-screamingly, gear-grindingly home between 2 and 4 am, presumably from the brothels of Tunis. (More returned than set out, clearly, because well after midnight the concierge entered my room and removed one of the beds, claiming that there had been a miscount at reception.) The walls are of cardboard, and loos two or three doors away hold no secrets for me. My new room is two floors higher and will serve as soon as I can persuade them to give me a pillow and a plug for the bath. I console myself with reading Graham Greene's film criticism[2] (superb) and Craft's book on Stravinsky,[3] which is full of humiliatingly well-read conversations with Huxley and Auden. (I'll send excerpts in a later letter.)

I test my lungs every few minutes to see whether the rattle is subsiding. So far, not; but it's early days. Tomorrow, if they can produce a promised plug, I shall try to start work. Tonight I go to what I think is the restaurant you recommended: could it have been the DAR ZARROUK? I'll stop now and continue when I get back from dinner.

———

At the Dar Zarrouk: it is a large room (inaccessible by car: you walk the last 200 yards along white alleys) with pillars swathed in rugs (bold red stripes) and multicoloured chandeliers and lots of faience? First course spécialité: something called brik à l'oeuf – a fried egg with shreds of meat folded into a parchment envelope of pastry – delicious? Wrought iron grilles on the windows?

Hardly anyone is here. I miss you lovingly, and wonder for the hundredth worried time why you cried the other night, and whether you will ever tell me. [...]

Acres of loneliness lie ahead. Write truly and also comfortingly. I am in a maze and need your thread to lead me out.

Kiss Roxana and Matthew. Caress yourself where I would.

Love love
K.

[1] An old village on the Tunisian coast.
[2] *The Pleasure Dome* (1972).
[3] *Stravinsky: Chronicle of a Friendship 1948–71* (1972).

To Kathleen Tynan

Sidi Bou-Saïd, le
Monday
[Postmark 14 November 1972]

Dear 1–

Another workless day has drifted by, because the promised plug for the typewriter failed (despite repeated appeals) to appear. The convention is over now and the hotel is sepulchrally empty except for 2 English couples. At first I feel snootily superior to them ('Shall we go up to Siddy-Boo for a doughnut?'); suddenly on the beach the two men reveal themselves to be championship-level water-skiers. I am humbled and feel paunchy and worthless.

Last night was atrocious and ominous. I was in bed by 10 but did not sleep till 2, every fifth breath producing a spasm. I am sure now that the sinuses and antrums are a big factor, and I must have them washed out by Kingdom[1] <u>as soon as I get back</u>. You cannot imagine the yearning with which I look back to Luxor[2] in the spring: it seems ten years ago, I feel ten years older. Are you <u>sure</u> my last attack was last autumn? I can't recall being ill in Cuarton or Fuentebravia or Jeréz.[3] Surely it was the year <u>before</u>, when we stayed with the Axelrods in Sardinia? I seem to remember 2 good years, years when I did not have to take every breath as a conscious experiment that might lead to an explosion. O one, figure-toi how I feel. When well, I can <u>work</u> – in the past year I did after all write the film as well as Nicol [Williamson] – at least a little.

Today, after coughing till 2, I was awakened by the usual intrusive chambermaid at 8. (There are no 'don't disturb' signs) and lay sadly thinking of you. I have dozed through the day, partly on the windy beach, partly on my bed. It's 4 pm. now: soon the sun will set.

A man has just arrived with the long-sought plug. Perhaps tomorrow –

Write, my love. There is no help anywhere else. At least teach me to stop self-dramatising. (I find it a sad proof of my mental decay that I can no longer find exact images in which to express it.)

Kiss your image in the mirror

Your

I

P.S. The electrician has finished fixing the plug. It doesn't work.

P.P.S. INCREDIBLE!! The reason it doesn't work is that Tunisian voltage is 110 and ours is 220. I asked Jill[4] to check this with Cook's and they said it was 220 in Tunisia. Could you please <u>blow them up</u> for me? The hotel says it has no transformer, I will have to go to Tunis tomorrow and BUY one – thus wasting time and money.

P.P.P.S. I've checked the exchange rate, by the way: the hotel costs £80 almost exactly – which means the airfare must be around £98, which I can't believe.

P.P.P.P.S. Love.

---

[1] Leonard Kingdom, an ear, nose and throat specialist at University College Hospital.
[2] We had spent a month's working holiday at the Old Winter Palace in Luxor in February.
[3] We had spent a summer holiday with the children at Castillito Mariposa, then left the children

and moved to an Atlantic beach hotel at Fuentebravia in order to visit the nearby feria of Jeréz de la Frontera.
[4]KPT's secretary Jill Fudakowska.

To Kathleen Tynan

Sidi Bou-Saïd, le
Tuesday p.m.
[Postmark 15 November 1972]

Dear 1 –

Self-evidently the machine now works. Just as I was leaving to buy a transformer in Tunis, the assistant electrician turned up with the brilliant discovery that, although the hotel light-plugs are 110v., the air-conditioning is 220, so he connected me to the latter and all's well. Or will be tomorrow, when Work Begins . . .

Last night was a terrible cheat. Miraculously I fell asleep with no hacking and was dreaming all sorts of delights when, at 2 a.m. I woke up for a two-hour spasm which left me limp. I had been to Tunis for the first time and eaten at a superb restaurant called Le Malouf (strange eggy peppery dish to start with, followed by half a lamb carcass – incidentally I shall need this place now, because the Dar Zarrouk closed yesterday for the winter); on the way back I had one of those medically-minded cabbies, who heard me coughing and said this was the best climate for bronchitis, had I tried 'piqûres chaque quinze jours contre l'asthme',[1] etc – finally he took me to an allnight chemist with the result that I'm now loaded with rhumicides and bronchodilatory suppositories and sinus-expectorants . . . No pîqures yet, though.

Today the same driver took me on a little tour of Sidi Bou and district. The blue-and-white village is beautiful; so, even more, is the La Marse area beyond, with a really splendid sea-side hotel called the Baie des Singes. 'Why don't you live here?' he said. I murmured about work, wife children . . . 'What use are they without health?' he said 'Same use as food to a man without teeth.' It would be nice to come back here WITH YOU. In the village I bought a photomagazine that has some pictures of women by Lartigue[2] – one of them, incredibly sexy, shows his first wife, Bibi, sitting coyly on the loo in 1920 – 'Elle n'était pas très consentante et m'a dit: "Tu exagères un peu . . ."'[3]

One of the two couples in the hotel has left, leaving us a threesome. In the mornings a strange dyky-looking fortyish woman lies on the beach but does not appear to belong to the hotel. It is all faintly spooky. Tonight I shall go back to Le Malouf. Chest seems easier today. I have finished Craft's Stravinsky (much under-rated: I was moved and much amused – he really is near-Goncourt level) and started on C.P. Snow's 'Last Thoughts'[4] [*sic*] – yes, I'm already forced back to local paperbacks. Here are some promised goodies from Greene's movie reviews:

(Of Lloyd's of London,[5] 1936)

The name of England is so frequently on the characters' lips that we recognise at once an American picture.

... It remains a hot-weather picture: human relationships converge with the slowness and inevitability of pawns, though a film should consist of knight's moves only: the oblique jump, the unexpected encounter ...

... We can leave 'characters' to the stage; the film at its finest – in the acting of Garbo and Chaplin or in the direction of Pudovkin – generalises ...

(From a review praising Robert Donat[6] and dispraising Larry): Mr. Olivier's burnt-out features, his breaking voice require the emotional situation all the time; he wants all Blackfriars[7] to rant in; he must have his drowned Ophelia, his skull and swordplay ... Mr Olivier's acting is of the nerves: it demands an audience and a partner ... (Hence Greene prefers Donat as a movie actor because he can be normal.)

... all the ignobility of a besetting pleasure ... (context doesn't matter: what a haunting phrase!)

... As if a plot mattered at all except as a dramatised illustration of a character and a way of life. (He's pointing out how French films leave in the details that British directors cut out because they 'don't advance the story-line')

... One is apt to forget that the literature of escape is literature just because it is a real escape; it contains a recognition of life as much as the action of a deserter contains the recognition of an enemy ...

... The secondrate cinema mind has always been attracted to symbolism – the apple blossom falling in the rain, the broken glass, all the sham poetic ways of avoiding the direct statement which demands some insight into the way men really act ...

(of Bette Davis) ... that precise nervy voice, the pale ashblonde hair, the popping neurotic eyes, a kind of corrupt and phosphorescent prettiness ...

*   *   *   *   *

Sorry to go on so. This is my conversation for the day. I try to imagine and anticipate your comments and get the illusion of contact. I do love you so.

Now I must be ruthlessly unselfpitying and start typing after breakfast.

In saying that I am merely trying to demonstrate how well I understand my faults.

And in saying <u>that</u> I am merely demonstrating my unswerving candour.

And in saying <u>that</u> I am merely showing you that I am capable of cynical self-observation.

And in saying <u>that</u> ...

The aim is always and only to make you love me.

The next letter will be wildly erotic. Full of what G. Greene calls 'charming minor Middle European humiliations.'

I squeeze your bum.

Love –

I

A final word before licking the envelope, <u>please</u>, on receiving this, send me a cable employing the word 'love'.

[1] Injections every fortnight for asthma.
[2] Jacques-Henri Lartigue (1894–1986), French photographer and painter.
[3] 'She wasn't very willing and said, "You're pushing it a bit." '
[4] *Last Things* (1970).
[5] Film biography of the founder of the insurance company, directed by Henry King and starring Tyrone Power (US, 1936).
[6] Robert Donat (1905–58), popular English theatre and film actor who starred in Hitchcock's *The Thirty-Nine Steps* (UK, 1935) and won an Academy Award for *Goodbye Mr Chips* (UK, 1939).
[7] The Blackfriars playhouse was an Elizabethan theatre.

To Kathleen Tynan

Sidi Bou-Saïd, le
Wednesday
[Postmark 16 November 1972]

Dear 1 –

Notes on tourism and health:

(1) Tourism. This morning I went into Tunis for the first time by daylight. I find it infinitely more sympathetic than Cairo simply because it's French. The streets are better-planned (I like the big Boulevard Bourguiba with the central pedestrian pathway full of trees, bookshops

and flower-stalls) and the buildings are prettier. Above all the food strikes my ideal balance between French subtlety and tropical fire. I lunched in a place called the Bagdad with Moorish decor and French clientele eating fiery flamboyant dishes and reading Temps Moderne[1] and Le Monde: perfect. And there's a raffish Boul 'Mich' air about the students' clothes that's also appealing. Weather hot for the first time today: high 70's, I should guess. At noon I went out to the Musée de Bardo (where the Greek and Roman and mosaic stuff is), only to find that it <u>closes</u> at noon: I dashed round in ten minutes but must go back next week. Last night I ate again at Le Malouf (which I now realise is absurdly expensive compared to other places – my meal plus half-bot. of wine cost £3, as against thirty bob at the Bagdad) and then sat through half an hour of the new Truffaut with Kika Markham ('2 Anglaises et le Continent'[2] – pointless period triangle with endless voice-over commentary) – that means the film <u>stars</u> Kika M, not that she accompanied me. Toyed with the idea of venturing into nightclub, then remembered my hatred of bellydancing and antipathy towards cigarette-smoke and came home instead. Trip takes 20 mins by taxi and costs about a pound a time.

Lack of conversational practice has brought on fantastic and impenetrable stammer. I can hardly ask for my key without giving the impression of imminent coronary.

(2) Health. UNDISTURBED NIGHT, first for weeks. And NO SPASM IN MORNING. This afternoon to my great chagrin, slight rattling and coughing returned; but I really think upswing may have started. (Darling, do forgive all this tedious lung talk, but the fucking problem is so omnipresent for me, I can't help it. Anyway you can switch off or skip.)

Query: IF the infection really touch wood goes in the next week or so, should I really come back? Won't it all start again? Half of me wants to return NOW, next plane, to see and touch YOU: the other half says that to return at all would be tempting providence. Please advise.

Query: assuming I come back, I want to have anti-catarrh injections AS SOON AS POSSIBLE – e.g. on Sunday before going into hospital. Could you call Williams[3] and see if this is fixable? I'm not coming back defenceless.

Query: whom are you seeing? what doing? with whom laughing? into whose responsive eyes staring? beside whom sleeping? with whom bemoaning the sad decline of

Your loving

I

P. S. I don't actually feel as gloomy as that, it just seemed a neat way of ending the letter. [...]

---

[1] Review founded in 1945 by Jean-Paul Sartre and Simone de Beauvoir devoted to philosophy and politics.
[2] Directed by François Truffaut (1971).
[3] Dr Ronald Williams, KPT's G P at the time.

To Kathleen Tynan

[Telegram]

[Sidi Bou-Saïd]
16 November 1972

DYING OF LONELINESS PLEASE SEND LOVING CABLE ALSO TELE-PHONE NUMBERS FROM FRECK[1] LOVE LOVE KEN

[1] Frederick Vreeland, diplomat son of Diana Vreeland, later married to Vanessa McConnell.

To Kathleen Tynan

Sidi Bou-Saïd, le
Friday
[17 November 1972]

Dear 1 –

And how are things in your prison of battleship-grey skies, with its bars of rain? The sun here comes blinding off the sea, it is blue from horizon to horizon, no palm tree as much as sways. We live the thickness of one garment – at most, two – away from nature, and think of you as of some vicious banished tribe condemned to live in perpetual torment outside the pale of civilisation. Did you know that the good Lord Byron – whose prose works I am reading with huge pleasure – left England for two years in his late teens (before any scandal shoved him), travelling mainly in Greece and Turkey, from whence he wrote to his mother that he occasionally looked back on England with a pang of total indifference? He was, as in so much, right. You do not live in the real world. <u>We</u> do that, here; we live in society, out in the squares, together in the markets and broad streets, yes, and on the beaches; whereas you live in little personal fortresses, behind weatherproof walls in stony enclaves, dashing from one to the other swathed in furs and woollens and heated vehicles. That is not how the soul flourishes, though it may be the way 'individuality' flourishes. Your cable says you are working on route out of the maze. Well, the route is known, I have taken it. Stick to your damp cellar[1] if you like, to that leaky infested vault, and wonder why you are pricked by so many doubts and qualms and fears; but never wonder why I am suddenly feeling expansive and capable and guiltless for the first time in years. One owes it to the sun, you see; one cannot deny it; it would be sinful not to grow with those reckless extravagant beams pouring all round one. Growth becomes duty.

All I have here is sun, pure air and good food. All I miss is you. I do not need TV, movies, most other people (yes, I do need books, I forgot); and though I know there is an artificial element about my life here, since it is in a hotel full of servants, it would I know be the same – and of course much cheaper – in a villa.

I don't know what it is modish to think about Tunisia. Is it notoriously corrupt or brutal? It seems fine to me: Tunis is full of bookshops, magazines multiply, the streets are relatively clean, beggars are minimal, and the French have left a decent heritage behind them.

I forgot to mention: my lungs are clear again. Yesterday a tickle remained; last night was free of trouble; and so far today nothing but the usual half-dozen morning coughs, none of them spasmodic or épuising.

London is a foreign country to me now. Here – or in places like it – is where I live.

Please keep this letter as a sort of (not to be pompous) manifesto.

Love,

I

I reopen the envelope to add this tag from Byron: 'As a shilling performs the duty of a pound (besides sun and sky and beauty for nothing) in the East – <u>that</u> is the country.'[2]

---

[1] Meaning England.
[2] Journal entry, 22 November 1813.

To Kathleen Tynan

Hotel Amilcar
Sidi Boo-Saïd
Friday
[Postmark 17 November 1972]

Dearest 1,

Well, today is the <u>best</u>. High still heat, the sea so glassy and quiet that the little incoming ripples are up to a hundred yards long and still don't break. Six newcomers disturb my solitary tenancy of the hotel (and the concierge says eighty more arrive tomorrow), among them a tall roving blonde and her squat male mate, who waterskied prettily this morning, she wriggling a good long bum on the turns.

I send you a sketch of the view from my balcony. Do you wonder I ask myself whether I should not go on to Luxor instead of back to Blighty?

If I ever write an autobiography, Byron has found me the title: 'The Summer of a Dormouse'. From the following:

'When one subtracts from life infancy (which is vegetation), – sleep, eating and swilling – buttoning and unbuttoning – how much remains of downright existence? The summer of a dormouse ...'[1]

I will send you some Wit and Wisdom of Lord B. soon. He, Wilde and Shakespeare would be my chosen English writers at a dinner. Odd

how Victorian literature is sealed off at each end by an anal scandal –
Wilde up Bosie's bum, Byron up Annabella's.

I take no wine by day, and in the evening only a demi-boot. You
would think I would have more energy, but it is all within, stored up
for who knows what. Does one lose it by fucking, or does fucking
release it for other uses? My plan here is: a week's convalescence, a
week's work. As health returns, guilt diminishes. I believe I could
corrupt you if you were here. ONE MUST LAUGH MORE. Byron again:
'I remember a Methodist preacher who, on perceiving a profane grin
on the faces of part of his congregation, exclaimed: "No hopes for them
as laughs." '²

I am glad and not ungrateful that you shivering troglodytes have
burrowed so energetically away inventing things to make your beastly
lives liveable. I see where you would need coal and central heating and
colour TV and doubledecker buses and Calvinism and sexual guilt
(wogs are animals) and palais de danse. And in fact we here need
one or two of your minor achievements – refridgeration [sic], air-
conditioning, and motor-cars – but that's all. Alas none of the things
that make us happy here is exportable. The feel of water on open-air
bare flesh, etc.

Two and a half hours of sunlight left. I must hurry or a minute or
two will be missed.

WHY NOT COME HERE NOW? NOW, AS YOU READ THIS. I HAVE A
DOUBLE ROOM ANYWAY, SO THE ONLY COST WOULD BE AIR FARE.
FOOD IS DERISORILY CHEAP. IF I'M RIGHT, YOU SHOULD GET THIS
ON TUESDAY AT THE LATEST. IF YOU ARRIVED WEDNESDAY WE
COULD HAVE THURS, FRI, SAT AND SUN, RETURNING MON. I CD.
POSTPONE THE HOSPITAL FOR A COUPLE OF DAYS. ONE CAN POST-
PONE ANYTHING A COUPLE OF DAYS EXCEPT SEEING EACH OTHER.

But I'll cable this and anticipate myself.

Love,

I

<hr>

¹Journal entry, 7 December 1813.
²Letter to Augusta Leigh, 19 December 1816.

To Kathleen Tynan

Hotel Amilcar
Saturday
[Postmark 20 November 1972]

Dear 1 –

The talk here is all of hurricanes in London – the concierge shakes his head and says streets were blown down – so I worry about your roof, and our children, and my typewriter, and my books? My guilt is doubled by the continued blaze here: 'We did not have such a summer', says a waiter. I wait all day for an affirmative answer to my cable, though I know all the objections: nanny problems, Requiem Canticles, Frecknessa dates – but HOW IRRELEVANT AS YOU WOULD SEE IF YOU WERE HERE ...

A morning toasting by the pool with Byron. His great maiden speech in the Lords defending the Luddites against the severities of the law is the classic English piece of liberal rhetoric and made me weep; and he wrote a letter about his trials as official play-reader for Covent Garden that horribly paralleled my own N.T. experiences. Wit and Wisdom must wait: there's too much of both for a letter. He saw an epitaph in Ferrara that said:

Martini Luigi

Implora pace –

and hoped for the same himself. How he deserved it. My one regret is that, instead of writing the great English comedies for which he was supremely fitted, he wrote tragedies instead[1] – for once acquiescing in received opinion, which held tragedies higher than comedies.

After lunch, to Tunis and its Suqs (Souks is wrong: it's vulgar French phonetic spelling, as if we should call Hammersmith 'Ammersmiff' – I got this snatch of linguistic insight from the guide-book.) The best I've ever seen; compared to Cairo's, what Fortnum's is to Sainsbury's. And vast! Acres of interlocked alleys and mosques, some deafening with the metal-workers, others redolent with parfumiers, many susurrant with stuffs, and always that wellknown azure canopy above ... I passed a doorway and saw large brown eyes out of the corner of my own, and a lissome shape, and a lovely falsetto crooning; I stopped, turned and with elaborate unconcern made my way back, sexually tickled, and at length directed my most insolently lecherous leer straight into the face of this puzzled sixteen-year-old boy.

Then to the zoo, in an emerald park on the outskirts: and very good it is. Stars include a hippo who leaps and grimaces like a dolphin, teasing its keeper playfully letting him sit in its mouth while pretending to bite off his balls. The thing weighs almost a ton and frolics like a kitten. Also, behind chickenwire in a tiny unlabelled cage, a miraculous small creature which please look up for me: a minute fox with huge elfin ears and eyes, the whole thing pale chinchilla coloured. What can this be? I'd like one.

Before dinner, saw Bergman's 'La Honte'[2] and now want to see all the Bergman we've missed. A terrifying fable about how war brutalizes: at one awful point when the leading couple, a husband and wife, are being submitted to some fearful moral humiliation, the wife says: 'I feel we are in someone else's dream, and when they wake up, they will be ashamed.' Very mouvementé dinner at the Bagdad Restaurant. My waiter, strongly resembling James Baldwin, was insouciant and clearly high as a Chinese kite – served my hors d'oeuvre, main dish and pudding <u>simultaneously,</u> while overcharging the couple next to me £5. After one hour he was quietly fired. Meanwhile, four Left-wing students had come in. Annoyed by the lax service, they began to bang the table and call for the manager. When he arrived, they yelled that he was favouring the bourgeoisie and ignoring the students. He demurred, but they all marched out chanting 'Bourgeois! Bourgeois!' First time I ever saw bad service made the excuse for a Left demonstration.

So back here to bed. I see from 'The Times' that [Charles] Marowitz is advertising the Pontac play[3] as a 'ribald comedy for decadent wits'. PLEASE BEG HIM NOT TO USE THIS PHRASE AGAIN, EVEN IF IT'S IN PONTAC'S SCRIPT – IT GIVES THE CRITICS A STICK TO BEAT US WITH, AND AT BEST LOOKS LIKE AN APOLOGY.

Love Love –

I

[1] His plays *Sardanapalus* (1821), *The Two Foscari* (1821) and *Marino Faliero* (1820) are rarely performed.
[2] *The Shame* (Sweden, 1968).
[3] Perry Pontac's *The Old Man's Comforts*, an Orton-esque parody which Marowitz directed at the Open Space (December 1972). KPT had initiated the project.

To Kathleen Tynan

Amilcar
Sunday
[Postmark ?20 November 1972]

Dear 1 –

This will be positively the last medical bulletin, but it must be issued.

I am well. Lungs clear, sleep untroubled, nothing but the usual two or three trivial morning coughs. The day before yesterday I walked a mile – mostly uphill, quite steeply – into Siddy Boo to send your cable, and a mile back. With ease. Not having to stop. Yesterday I walked several miles around the centre of Tunis. No problems. Last night I did wake up, but it was because of excess energy – I awoke glowing with my own restored health, like a child who keeps waking up before dawn on Christmas morning to reassure himself that the Big Present is really there. In fact I was so cheerful that I sang a selection of 40's songs, including 'Accentuate the Positive', 'Blues in the Night' and 'Cow Cow Boogie'.[1] It's 9 a.m. now and here I am at the typewriter.

The reason is shining through the window. King Sol, Phoebus Apollo, bless his many names. I shall rechristen myself and from henceforth be known as Smackh-naten (He who Spanks in the Sunlight), with his queen of the Two Lands, Nefer-Titti (better known as Mosli-Botti) – please giggle – oh love, it is so good to be myself again.

All this produces several reflexions:

1) I really cannot face going back into hospital immediately I get back. I would feel trapped. Please understand. Could you call Drs. Williams and Batten[2] and explain? I could go in instead on Monday, January 1st – not a bad idea after New Year's Eve. No earlier date is workable.

2) Again, please reiterate to Williams that I want the anti-catarrh injections as soon as I land, practically. (God, I hope it <u>was</u> this that kept me well – suppose it was just coincidence??)

3) I notice that here I drink almost no water at night – as against a whole carafe in London. Obviously ductair heating plays a part in weakening the bronchi – so could we make sure the humidifier is working?

4) Finally, I'm sure that one of the big factors making London so mortal to the lungs is its constantly changing temperature – going

from hot to cold and back again is what aggravates things. Obviously nothing can be done about this, but it's as well to be aware of it.

Probably I've said some of these things before. If so, forgive me. No (1) is the most important.

Enough self-preoccupation.

Love from –

and <u>really</u> from, not from just a shadow of –

Your,

K.

P. S.: Before getting up I busied myself thinking of Unlikely Married Couples. The usual example is Barry and Ella Fitzgerald.[3] My suggestions:

Grace and Shipwreck Kelly[4]   Edmund and Patricia Burke[6]

Peter and Annie Lorre[5]   Samuel and Ella Mae Morse[7]

(Don't pretend you got all of those.)

---

[1] 'Accentuate the Positive' by Johnny Mercer (1944); 'Blues in the Night' by Johnny Mercer (1941); 'Cow-Cow Boogie' by Don Raye, Gene de Paul and Benny Carter (1942).

[2] Dr John Batten, a chest specialist at the Brompton Hospital.

[3] Barry Fitzgerald (1888–1961), Irish actor; Ella Fitzgerald (b. 1918), American singer.

[4] Grace Kelly (1929–82), American actress and later Princess of Monaco; John Simms 'Shipwreck' Kelly (1910–86), Kentucky-born sportsman and social figure, so called by sportscasters (he co-owned and played for a football team known as the Brooklyn Dodgers) after a previous Shipwreck Kelly, famous for sitting on flagpoles (an early 20th-century fad).

[5] Peter Lorre (1904–64), Hungarian-born actor; 'Annie Laurie', Scottish folk song by William Douglas (1688).

[6] Edmund Burke (1729–97), Irish statesman and philosopher; Patricia Burke, Rolf Hochhuth's English theatre agent.

[7] Samuel Morse (1791–1872), inventor of Morse Code; Ella Mae Morse (b. 1924), American jazz singer.

To Kathleen Tynan

Amilcar

Tuesday

[21 November 1972]

Dear 1 –

Talking to you reduces the pressure to write: but there are just one or two things ...

Today I recruited the first Tunisian cat. She limps from a nasty sore on a hind leg, is small and thin and black and white. With a bogey all over her nose. She came to befriend while I was having my solitary coffee by the pool today. I gave her the lait and there was no holding her: up onto shoulders, round neck, rubbing face against book and hands and shoes. Then a vast shambling Alsatian dog ambled up – possibly the inflictor of her wound – and stood staring contemptuously. She advanced within a foot of it, arched her back disdainfully and SPAT – so loudly that it echoed round the garden. Alsatian jumped a yard back. She SPAT again. And he ran. I ordered more milk to celebrate.

In Tunis last night for dinner I succumbed and popped into one of the city's half-dozen night-clubs. Empty dance-floor, bar-girls at bar, drinks £1 each. Fat bellydancer from Cairo chatted to me; had worked Omar Khayyam in London; also Mid-Eastern boîtes in Paris; was leaving for Teheran next week. Nice girl: advised me not to sit near dance-floor as bottle of champagne cost £15 and bot. of whisky £25! Thanked her and left for home, clutching my three-day-old 'Guardian' and week-old 'Cinémonde'' for company. The real bore is that I tire too early for these places: the spectacle doesn't start till 12.30 and I'm bushed at 10.30.

I have been thinking about future winters. Here are some of my thoughts:

The months to be away (for me) are November, December, Jan, Feb, March. Best plan is for me to leave in November; and you to join me with children in December when school holidays have started. We all then stay abroad till mid-March or thereabouts. Where? In no particular order, these are my contenders:

(1) Tunisia. Plus: proximity (relative), plenty of villas available (off-season), excellent food, stable and reasonable régime, French language. Minus: doubtful climate in Jan and Feb (could you ask Jill to find out what the average temp. and rainfall here is in Dec, Jan, Feb and March? Also: how does it compare with temp. and rainfall further south at Jerba or inland at Gafsa or in the desert areas? or at Sfax, a bit north of Jerba, which Ronald Firbank called the most beautiful city in the world (it's on the coast)?); school problems.

(2) Bangkok. Plus: ideal climate; lots to see in immediate area and farther afield (incl. Vietnam); English spoken; almost certainly English or American schools (could Jill check with Thai Embassy?); Minus: distance and travel expense (could Jill ask Cook's if there's a cheap way of going there for long periods such as 4–5 months?)

(3) Arizona/New Mexico. Plus: climate (I presume, but could Jill

check on this?); English language; schools; medical care. <u>Minus</u>: food, distance and travel cost (ask Jill to find out cost and how soon cheap transatlantic fares start – the ones where you just turn up and buy a ticket?).

(4) West Indies. <u>Plus</u>: ideal climate; plenty to see (proximity to Mexico, Cuba, etc); English spoken; schools. <u>Minus</u>: distance and travel cost (again, ask Jill to find cheapest way of going for long periods), unpleasant people.

(5) S. Italy. (Jill to find climatic details for Positano.)

Only four days now.

Love,

1

P. S. Weather still superb – mid 70's – despite some high drifting clouds.

---

¹A French film magazine.

At the end of Ken's stay in Sidi Bou Saïd, a long letter from me reached him. In it I gave the best answer I could to the question he had asked in his first letter from Tunis: 'Why you cried the other night, and whether you will ever tell me.' I wrote that I had wept out of a kind of frustration, years of seeing him handle small everyday practicalities like a man from Mars, 'making everything insanely and pointlessly difficult for yourself – letting all these small failures build up to block you and what you are. It seems to me you have become armoured against other people's reaction to you', and I added that he was without pity. I went on to argue that being politic at the National Theatre had been wrong for him: 'Your talent and your need to impose was horribly, brilliantly thwarted and mutilated by Larry. Just as writing a column for the Observer *you were trying to change your readers' views on major subjects, while at the same time required to offer them meaty cultural gossip.' He needed to climb out by writing a book, or making a film, not juggling a lot of different worlds at once.*

This letter had a remarkably hurtful effect on Ken. My refusal to join him, and what he saw as a censorious and no doubt pompous letter, helped to cause a rupture in our relationship and to propel him to start an affair with the woman whom he had turned down before his departure for Tunisia.

To John Dexter and Michael Blakemore

> Blue Lagoon Hotel
> Talahena,
> Negombo,
> Ceylon[1]
> January 29 [1973]

Dear John and Michael –

I hope by now you will have received the Trevor Griffiths play.[2] I think it is superb – just the play that bright people of my generation and younger have been waiting for. It's funny; it's unsentimental <u>and</u> uncynical (rare combination); and it has fantastic passion. To my mind it would be ideal for Spring, 1974. [Colin] Blakely perfect for Sloman; and even a part for one of the blacks in 'The Bacchae', I don't know which of you might want to direct it but please reach an amicable agreement. I hope we can present a fairly united front when it comes up for discussion.

My quibbles are as follows:

1. Trevor doesn't bother to explain what to Socialists is self-evident but may not be to the whole audience: i.e. why there is a need for revolutionary change in Britain. Perhaps Joe could have a short speech about this before the debate starts. (E.g. 'I don't suppose anyone here needs reminding . . .' etc.)

2. At the beginning of Act II I think Joe and the others should express their self-disgust at not being present in Paris; might even make plans to go over and take part. Thus Tagg's speech contemptuously dismissing the students' revolt would come as a greater shock.

3. Tagg's cancer is a plea for sympathy and unnecessary.

And other details, too trivial to explore here. I'm back on February 9.

> Love,
> Ken

---

[1] We were on holiday in Sri Lanka.

[2] Trevor Griffiths (b. 1935), English playwright whose works include *Comedians* (1975). *The Party* was set in England during 1968, and explored variations on the theme of left-wing commitment and the doubtful possibility of revolutionary change in Britain unless the working class creates its own leadership. It opened on 20 December 1973 with John Dexter directing Olivier in the part of John Tagg, an elderly Glaswegian Trotskyite.

Memo to Laurence Olivier
Copy to: Michael Blakemore, John Dexter

[The National Theatre]
21 February 1973

EQUUS[1]

I'm a bit surprised to hear that EQUUS has become a <u>fait accompli</u> without ever being mentioned at a planning meeting. In my view it will need quite a lot of revision to qualify for the repertoire. As I told Peter Shaffer:

1. The subject is so bizarre[2] that it needs the flattest, simplest, most prosaic dialogue to keep it from flying away into the realms of the ludicrous and implausible. Peter's style – admirably restrained in the early scenes – does tend to splash into rhetorical purple patches: 'I am He and He is me.' 'Against the Bowler and the Jodphur! [*sic*] Against all the host of You-There's', etc, etc. Dysart's speech in Act I page 1 is a perfect example of what I mean. The <u>situation</u> is poetic: it doesn't need 'poetry' laid on it with a palette-knife.

2. The Derek–Jill–Alan triangle is very conventional.

3. The climax is confusing just when the play ought to come into sharp focus. Does he stab the horses merely because they are witnesses to his impotence? We expect something grander and more universal than that. Or is he impotent <u>because</u> of them? It isn't clear.

Please understand, I think the play's theme is fascinating and exciting. But – especially when we of the old regime have so few slots left to fill – I wish we could have the chance of discussing it before rushing into production.

KT

---

[1] *Equus*, by Peter Shaffer, was directed by John Dexter, with Alec McCowen and Peter Firth. It opened on 26 July 1973 and was brought back in 1974, when it transferred to Broadway.
[2] The blinding of six horses by a teenage boy.

To Laurence Olivier, Michael Blakemore, John Dexter

5 March 1973

NOTES ON MEETING WITH PETER SHAFFER ON FEBRUARY 28 AND MARCH 4

Equus

Peter has now agreed to my suggestions on the following points:

1. To tone down the rhetoric, purple patches and prose-poetry which are at present over-heating a theme which is already pretty hot.

2. He will re-vamp the psychiatrist's whole attitude towards the boy's fixation on horses. In the old version, boy and girl enter stable; boy forces girl to strip at the point of a weapon; boy finds that he is impotent with her and expresses his rage by blinding the horses whom he holds responsible for his impotence. In my proposed new version, the girl voluntarily strips; the boy fails with her and is crestfallen. She is trying gently to arouse him when one of the horses enters the stable. The boy immediately feels as if he had been caught masturbating in church; the stable for him is a holy place and his real love is for the horses. Stricken with shame, he bundles the girl out. He cannot bear the thought that the horses have seen him betraying them with the girl: hence he attacks them.

3. In the present version it is assumed that the psychiatrist should try to remove the boy's fixation on the animals (which, of course, signifies any fixation which is regarded by straight people as a perversion). In the new version, the psychiatrist will make the point that the boy's real crime – the attack on the horses – was caused by sexual guilt. If he had not felt guilty there would have been no crime. So at the end the psychiatrist's view is that in a wiser world than ours, it would have been more humane to accept the boy's obsession rather than try, against his will, to uproot it. The play thus becomes a study of what happens when a repressive environment drives a boy into psychotic behaviour by inflaming his sense of sexual guilt.

4. Peter agrees to soften the characters who are at present the two obvious villains of the story – the boy's pompous father and Jill's bullying boyfriend.

KT

To Laurence Olivier

The National Theatre
16 April 1973

Dear Larry –

I'm writing a piece about Morecambe and Wise,[1] and while I was dining with them the other night they revealed that one of their life's ambitions is to get you as their guest on their Christmas show. They have a very funny idea for a sketch which I won't spoil by revealing. I don't think it would be <u>infra</u> your <u>dig</u>: anyway Christmas is traditionally the time when the squire puts the false whiskers on. And they handled Glenda Jackson and Dame Flora[2] beautifully. Can I let them know that you'd consider it?[3]

I promised them I'd mention it and I have.

Love
Ken

[1] KPT admired the comic Eric Morecambe and celebrated him and his partner Ernie Wise in 'The Top Joker', *Observer* magazine, 9 September 1973.
[2] Dame Flora Robson (1902–84), English stage and film actress; her films include *Fire Over England* (UK, 1936) and *Black Narcissus* (UK, 1947).
[3] Olivier eventually agreed, but would not go to the studio. Morecambe and Wise settled for a running gag, filmed at Olivier's home, in which Olivier repeatedly answered the phone in a variety of voices (including that of a Chinese laundryman), evading all requests to do the show.

Memo to Peter Hall[1]

April 28, 1973

Many thanks for your memo. I hadn't read your Policy Statement when I suggested doing Lyttelton plays in pairs.[2] You're obviously right.

I'll bring the Lardner plays[3] in next week. The more I think of a Lardner evening, though, the more I suspect it may be a one-shot, too <u>sui generis</u> to be part of a Theme season.

I am, however, quite sure there is a winning and dazzling trio of Mediterraneans[4] in 'These Ghosts',[5] 'Zoubaroff'[6] and 'Play's the Thing'.[7] The Molnár shows a Hungarian's Italy; the Firbank is an Englishman's Italy; and the de Filippo is the place itself. All three are plays about play-acting and pretence; all three have a strain of deep escapism. I really think the de Filippo is an exceptional piece of light theatre – theatrically a superb juggling display, and moving as well as funny. (I would, of course, suggest another translation: the only reason why the play hasn't been done in England is that it's never been properly Englished.) As I said, for an actor to play Molnár's and de Filippo's heroes would be a marvellous double. I shouldn't think anyone could resist.

I take your point about John Schlesinger.[8] But couldn't he do 'The Alchemist' next year, saving the Molnár (may I presumptuously suggest) for the opening Theme season? It's a pure proscenium play, with its eavesdroppings and box-set realism, and would fit the Lyttelton ideally.

(So would the other two: for the Firbank, it would be nice to open up with the whole stage and use all the available space, wings and all, to convey the view over Florence.) Also, to speak crudely of commerce, I would hazard that a Theme season of escapist comedy would probably get the Lyttelton off to a pretty prosperous start.[9]

KT

[1] He had joined the theatre as director designate on 1 April. He would take over fully from Olivier on 1 November.

[2] Of 26 April 1973. KPT had suggested to Hall in a memo of 13 April that he might select two plays requiring approximately the same number of people, rehearse them in tandem and open them in consecutive weeks. They would then run side by side for six to eight weeks, during which time the next two plays would be in rehearsal. Peter Hall in his policy statement of February 1973 envisaged the Lyttelton as the subsidiary theatre of the company, open to visiting companies and the Olivier theatre as the main repertory stage.

[3] See letter of 13 April 1960.

[4] KPT had proposed a season of comedies with a linking theme of 'the Mediterranean as the cradle of escapism'. Hall liked the idea.

[5] By Eduardo de Filippo (1955).

[6] In his memo of 26 April Peter Hall wondered if there wasn't a case for a 1920s programme which would include the Lardner project and Firbank's *Princess Zoubaroff*.

[7] By Ferenc Molnár (1926).

[8] John Schlesinger (b. 1926), English film director who won an Oscar for *Midnight Cowboy* (US, 1969).

[9] Hall was not able to run seasons at the Lyttelton until 1975, and would not be able to involve KPT until 1976. Nothing came of the Mediterranean plan.

To Bernard Oliver[1]

[20 Thurloe Square]
21st May, 1973]

Dear Mr. Oliver,

Many thanks for your very helpful exercise in total recall! Your experience with Reich seems to have been shared by many others. I suggest it is conceivable that Reich's eyes were even more sensitive than your own; he frequently suffered from ocular complaints after very brief spells when working with microscopes. What he claimed, as I understand it, was that the 'sensations' he saw were linked to sexual experiences, but that both were manifestations of the cosmic energy he called orgone.[2]

Once again, thank you for taking so much trouble.

Yours sincerely,
[Kenneth Tynan]

[1] Then Vice-President, Research and Development, of the Hewlett Packard company of California. In 1940, while working at Bell Laboratories, he had visited Reich on Long Island.

[2] In a letter dated 1 May 1973, Oliver described the visit: 'Reich first described to me some of his theories regarding "Orgone", a mystical emanation which he believed to originate from living things as well as from organic substances. . . . [he] stated that it was possible to see this emanation when one's eyes were completely dark adapted and invited me into the basement where I agreed to spend the next hour or two in complete darkness ... In one corner of the basement he had constructed a screened cage in which were placed various objects of organic origin ... I tried very hard to detect any light such as he described but was unable to see a thing. At this time my eyes were so sensitive that normally invisible static electric effects appeared to be quite brilliant ... Even tapping a fingernail on a desk top produced a visible flash of light as the fingernail struck the surface. . . . I think [Reich] really believed in the things he talked about and therefore cannot be classed as a charlatan. Nevertheless, I remain convinced that there is absolutely nothing whatever of merit in any of his work or his hypotheses.'

To Irwin Shaw[1]

as from
20 Thurloe Square
4 June, 1973

Dear Irwin,

'Did I spell Meyraque correctly?' she said.

'It's never been spelled better,' he said.

In that case, neither have Humphrey Bograt or Billy Wyler or Carlos Ponty or Alfred Hotchkick. <u>Evening in Byzantium</u>,[2] forsooth; you might at least have spent a Morning with Michelin. You would then have discovered that the hotel you rightly praise (and which, thanks to your reckless publicity, is now probably overrun with tourists) is situated in the charming village of MEYRARGUES.

'Spell Meyrague,' he said.

'I-r-v-i-n-g S-h-a-w,' she said.

I hate to seem picayune, but Muhammad Ali is twice misspelled on the very same page.

Please don't rewrite anything else in the novel, which I enjoyed enormously.

Love,
Ken

---

[1] Irwin Shaw (1913–84), playwright and novelist, author of *The Young Lions* (1948) and *Rich Man, Poor Man* (1970).
[2] Written by Shaw in 1973.

To John Dexter and Peter Shaffer

[The National Theatre]
16 July [1973]

Production Notes – Equus

1. I take it we are absolutely sure that we want to open with the image of the boy and Nugget actually embracing? We don't feel that it detracts from the later moments when they embrace; or that it reveals too much of the plot too early? It is a powerful physical image: perhaps too powerful to be squandered so soon. Also it tells us that our theme will be the love of boy for horse – when surely we should assume, from Hester's outline of the crime, that he hates them. My advice is to reconsider.

2. Please can Alec[1] address us, the out-front audience, with his opening speech? He must hold us with his glittering eye, lead us, buttonhole us into the story, which we are to see through his eyes. Downstage as he is, facing half up, we get the wrong focus and also miss some vital and difficult phrases. [...]

5. Our audience will be avidly sniffing for clues all the way through, and I think we offer too many relating to eyes. Could we cut Mrs Strang's line about the horse picture: 'it was all eyes'? It's too obviously planted as a clue.

6. 'Forgive' at the act-drop is just wrong. Earlier in the second half there's talk about 'with my body I thee worship': he hasn't <u>abused</u> the god by experiencing sexual ecstasy: sexual ecstasy is the culmination of the Dionysiac ritual. 'Forgive' sounds like a Protestant guilt pang. I much prefer: 'Amen.' [...]

9. As we know, the passage from the abortive fuck to the murders needs restructuring. I think Alan should see in his mind the looming heads of the horses peering in at his attempt to fuck the girl; he should react to them with guilty panic, which prompts Jill to think he must be crazy, and this is what sends her scurrying offstage. He must surely not put on those briefs (they look like a last-minute concession to prudes): he remains naked because he is hypnotised by the horses' accusing eyes, because he expects punishment, because he sees himself as a sacrifice to the horse-god, because single combat in the ancient world was always carried out in the nude – find your own reason, but please keep those knickers off.

[1] Alec McCowen, who played the role of Dysart, the psychiatrist, in the first production of *Equus*.

To John Dexter

[20 Thurloe Square]
[?23 July 1973]

Dear John,

Congratulations. I saw the show with Kathleen on Saturday night, and when I led her round to Alec's dressing-room afterwards she was crying almost too hard to speak. It's the best thing you have done for years and Peter possibly ever.

THERE IS JUST ONE THING HOWEVER ... I've already mentioned this to Peter. Please (this is a real beg) restore the best speech in the play, the clincher, the one that makes it universal and applicable to all of us (not just this particular hippophile boy and this particular worried shrink), the one that every time I've heard it has forced me to realise that the play is about me – I mean the paragraph where Alec talks about all the phenomena of the nursery and how suddenly one of them strikes and a chain is magnetised that shackles us. It is beautfully written and it sums up the permanent meaning of the evening. And it is really not (as I hear you suspect) a lecture, any more than the chorus's final comment on a Greek play is a lecture. It is, rather, an epitome. And it belongs there at the end and nowhere else. If you do not put back this keystone to the great arch I will mentally walk out on Thursday night. You will still have a great success but it will be a success that is a critique of psychoanalysis and a plea for primitivism and an appeal for sympathy with wild psychotics – it will not be the kind of success that forces the audience to find Alan in their own toilet training and in themselves.[1]

Love and blessings –
[Ken]

[1] Peter Shaffer believes the speech was restored, and it appears in the published version (Act II Sc. i). The doctor, Martin Dysart, speculates on the nature of childhood imprinting: 'Why? Moments snap together like magnets forging a chain of shackles. Why?'

To Peter Hall

20 Thurloe Square
September 29, 1973

Dear Peter,

I've just had a very disquieting talk with Trevor Griffiths and, since I commissioned 'The Party' and shepherded him through the writing of it, I can't help writing to you about the ugly situation that seems to have developed. As I understand it, because of the large number of new productions you have planned for 1974, and because Larry and Finlay[1] are leaving in March, it won't be possible to give the play more than 34 performances next year.

This strikes me as simply appalling. To begin with, it is quite unprecedented. The National has never imposed a guillotine on a play's run <u>before it opened</u>. (Unless you count the inaugural 'Hamlet',[2] when – by a mistake he now regrets – Larry engaged O'Toole for only 21 performances.) As I'm sure you did at the Aldwych, we always waited to assess the public and critical response before deciding one production's future. It is terribly damaging to Trevor's reputation, not to mention his purse, that the National should write his play off as a flop (34 performances equals a month's run in the West End) before it is even in rehearsal.

Has Harold Pinter's widely-known dislike of the play got anything to do with this? Or has the play other enemies with other motives? Is the same axe going to fall on 'Saturday, Sunday, Monday'[3] when Frank and Larry leave? Is the new regime wielding a new broom or conducting a purge? Are Frank and Larry irreplaceable (both have been replaced at the National before)? I must urge on you that these are all questions of some public interest, since I cannot see how one can justify spending public money on a <u>predetermined</u> flop. And although the choice and timing of the production was not your responsibility, the decision to close it certainly is.

I hear there has been talk about the possibility of permitting a West End transfer. This sounds to me like what Larry calls chimera-department talk. It would mean finding a management willing to transfer a success (if it's a flop the question wouldn't arise) with a completely new cast. It would also presuppose that John Dexter would be willing and available to direct a completely new cast. And whereas National audiences come to see the company and accept replacements for stars like Larry, West End audiences are a very different matter.

All in all, I cannot recall an occasion on which a greater blow has been dealt to a talented writer at such a crucial stage in his career. Welcome to the big league, we say, and then slap his face and show him the door. Is there no way of repairing at least some of the damage before the repercussions begin to spread?[4]

Yours,
[Ken Tynan]

[1] Frank Finlay played Sloman in *The Party*.
[2] *Hamlet*, directed by Olivier, opened on 22 October 1963.
[3] *Saturday, Sunday, Monday*, by Eduardo de Filippo, directed by Franco Zeffirelli, was to open on 25 October 1973.
[4] Hall replied (3 October 1973) that there was no conspiracy against *The Party*, that he admired the play but had casting problems. A mobile production was done by David Hare in November/December 1974.

To Laurence Olivier

20 Thurloe Square
October 1, 1973

Dear Larry,

I've hesitated a long while before writing this letter, but at last I've decided to take the plunge.

It's about money. As you know, Peter Hall and I had a chat last year in which we agreed that I should leave the N.T. when the company moved into the new building. Peter confirmed this in writing. When it became clear that the move wouldn't happen until the spring of '75, he asked me if I'd mind leaving earlier. I said O.K.

and it was decided that I would move out at Christmas, 1973, and be paid until the end of the financial year (i.e. March 31, 1974).

Soon afterwards an official of the A.S.T.M.S. (the technical and managerial union to which I belong) rang up and asked me how much severance pay I was going to get. I said I was merely getting three months' salary in lieu of notice. Severance pay hadn't been discussed. He was quite incredulous. He told me that after ten years' service I was entitled to at least a year's severance pay, and he explained that he had obtained precisely that for Rozina.

He reminded me that in the whole decade I had not received a single salary rise, and added that, as far as he knew, there was no other salaried worker in the country of whom that could be said. (Incidentally, my present salary[1] is now the official <u>minimum</u> wage for apprentice reporters in the newspaper world.) He told me that in his view the year's severance pay should be adjusted to include the increase in the cost of living since 1963. I said that was up to him to negotiate, but that I would be quite prepared to settle for a year at my current salary. He said he was sure there would be no problem about that.

A little while afterwards he reported that he'd talked to Paddy[2] and Tony Easterbrook.[3] He said he'd noticed a definite note of hostility in their attitude towards me. They told him that, anyway, I didn't need the money. As it happens, they couldn't be more wrong (I share the 'Oh! Calcutta!' royalties with 13 other authors, 2 directors, 2 composers and a choreographer); but even if they were right, it would be perfectly irrelevant to the point at issue. In any case, my Union chum told me not to worry: all would be well.

He now tells me that he has received a letter from Paddy, turning me down flat. After ten years, no severance pay. Hence this letter to you. I would hate my association with the N.T. to end on a note of bitterness. I don't in the least mind being pushed out, but to be pushed out without proper compensation (granted readily to my assistant) leaves the permanent suggestion that I've failed in the job. Apart from K. Rae, you and I are the only survivors of the original team, and you are thus my only effective character witness. A long period of book-writing lies ahead of me, and I could frankly use a lump sum to help tide me over it. If you think I have a case, would it be too much to ask you to drop a word in the ears of P. H. [Hall] or Paddy or both? By all means show them this letter if you think it appropriate.

Sorry to importune, really sorry; but I have no other court of appeal.[4]

Please let's meet soon to talk about jollier things.

Love,
[Ken]

[1] £46 a week.
[2] Patrick Donnell, Administrative Director.
[3] Anthony Easterbrook, General Manager.
[4] Olivier wrote to Sir Max Rayne on KPT's behalf. KPT was eventually awarded £2,500, and with that his career at the National Theatre came to an end.

To Jack Benny

[20 Thurloe Square]
17 October 1973

Dear Jack,

I am tremendously grateful for the exquisite gold money-trap you sent me with the wonderful cartoon of Bela Lugosi on the back.[1] I have set it out in the living room and baited it with old writs and as soon as it catches any money I will let you know. If all else fails I may loan it out to Twiggy as a chastity belt.

Anyway, bless you again and all my love.

Yours,
[Ken]

[1] KPT had renewed his friendship with the comedian (in London performing at the Palladium) at a dinner given by Ava Gardner. Benny was inclined to give out gold money clips with his engraved image.

To the Editor, the *Sunday Times*

[20 Thurloe Square]
[Published 11 November 1973]

I know it is bad form to kick a man when he is down, but what does one do if the man who is down is also the one who is doing the kicking?

I am thinking of John Osborne, whose peevish comments on the National Theatre, Laurence Olivier and myself you published in the Magazine last Sunday.

So far I have been a model of stoical restraint in the face of Mr Osborne's eccentric provocations. Some years have now passed since he first started to behave strangely. In 1970 he attended Olivier's New Year's Eve party at which the host and I took him into a corner and invited him to write a new play for the new National Theatre building. 'Help us to make a little history', we said. 'I've already made history,' he said loftily, and turned his back.

Shortly afterwards he wrote a furious attack on Sir Laurence and the National for the Evening Standard. Next there appeared in Private Eye[1] a letter in which he abused us for mishandling the great gifts of actors like Alec Guinness – a curious charge, since Sir Alec had never appeared at the National. By then it was already clear that the talent which had given us 'Look Back in Anger' (still the best play written in postwar Britain, as the current Young Vic revival demonstrates), had begun to run dry. I told myself that Mr Osborne was going through a bad patch professionally and that it was distorting his judgment.

Well, the patch has since spread to the dimensions of a king-sized quilt and Mr Osborne's reservoir of bile has swelled as his audience has dwindled. Now, offering no evidence to prove his case, he claims that I have had 'a disastrous influence' on Olivier, whom I have 'deluded' and 'sadly misguided' with my 'intellectual spivery'. He declares that I have 'absolutely the wrong attitude toward running a theatre', and that Olivier is 'the least suitable person to run a national theatre.' What can I do but point to the record? And the record of the National reveals a higher percentage of critical *and* popular successes over a ten-year period than any other British theatre company in history has ever achieved. (Except perhaps Shakespeare's Globe, for which I have no attendance figures.)

I do not regret having done all I could, as a critic, to obtain for Mr Osborne in his early days the recognition that his gifts deserved. But nowadays I feel rather like a good Samaritan who has crossed the road to be greeted by a kick in the face. Henceforward Mr Osborne will have to fend for himself. In his present condition, I wish him luck.

Kenneth Tynan

---

[1] The satirical magazine published Osborne's letter, a rambling attack on both the National Theatre and *Private Eye*, in the issue of 9 April 1971.

To the Editor, the *Guardian*

The National Theatre
19 November 1973

Sir,—Two bones to pick with Michael Billington's[1] review of 'Olivier'.[2]

First, he says that the National Theatre has 'signally failed to keep great actors within the company.' Can he name any company in this country that has managed to keep top actors for long periods? With very few exceptions, they simply won't sign up for more than a year or so, and one can hardly blame them: films and TV offer too many rival inducements. In any case, I thought Mr Billington preferred companies without stars? At least, that's what he's always telling us.

Secondly, he claims that Olivier 'never created the house-style needed to underpin such an eclectic repertoire.' Now you can have a house-style, or you can have an eclectic repertoire; but you cannot have both.

One of the things we set out to do at the National – and expected to be congratulated for doing – was precisely to *avoid* creating a house-style. The Comédie Française has one: can you imagine what they would make of 'The Front Page' or 'The National Health'? The Berliner Ensemble has one: but they only do plays by one author. And can Mr Billington tell me what sort of house-style would be simultaneously appropriate for Sophocles and Noël Coward? Our hope was to find for each play its *own* style, not to force every production into the same stylistic mould. A house-style would not have 'underpinned' our repertoire. It would have destroyed it.

Yours sincerely,
Kenneth Tynan[3]

[1] Michael Billington (b. 1939), author and drama critic of the *Guardian*.
[2] By Logan Gourlay (1973).
[3] Billington redefined what he meant by 'house-style' in the *Guardian* (3 December 1973): 'a manner of performance that develops naturally either from a shared attitude to society or from having a permanent team of directors, actors and designers. It is not something you impose: it is something that grows.'

To Tsai Chin

[20 Thurloe Square]
27 March 1974

Dear Tsai,

It was nice to see you looking so chirpy the other night. Here, in condensed form, are my comments on 'Monkey':[1]

1. All good drama should have a plot that can be expressed in the form of an active verb – i.e. the plot of 'Oedipus' is 'to find out who killed Oedipus' father'. You must find an active verb for 'Monkey'.

2. The main character or characters in all good drama must be driven – by a process an audience understands and can identify with – to a state of desperation. For instance, if there are many gigantic obstacles preventing Monkey from achieving his aim he will be driven to the right state of desperation, but if his aim is to find the Secret Jade Hair Lotion of the one-eyed Celestial Goddess Wupi, the audience will neither understand or identify and you will be fucked up.

3. I suggest that Monkey's quest should be for the secret of life rather than the secret of immortality – and that when he finds it, the secret of life should turn out to be something like: 'Live It' – which is precisely what we have watched him doing for the last two hours.

4. Use magic tricks by all means, but not as methods of resolving plot problems. And don't go in for spectacular scenic effects which the cinema and the cartoon film can do better.

5. I think Marc Wilkinson of the National Theatre would be first rate for the music and Julian More[2] is a very experienced and witty lyricist.

All you need now is to sit down and write a synopsis of the action – the longer the better.

Soak up the sun and call me when you get back.

All my love, dear little Tsai. In the words of the late Noël Coward, Tsai no more.[3]

Yours,
Ken

[1] The script for a musical, never staged.
[2] Co-writer of the London production of *Irma La Douce* (1958) and lyricist of *Songbook* (1979).
[3] 'Sigh No More', song (1945). See letter of 13 November 1945.

To Joanna Dunham[1]

20 Thurloe Square
June 11th, 1974.

Dear Joanna,

I thought you were super on the box last night.

Here's the script. As I told you, we shall be shooting in Southern France in September and October. Robert Stephens is playing Alex, and I am directing. The aim is to make an erotic film that looks beautiful and outrageous at the same time.

The part I would like you to look at is Sophie. As I also told you, there will be scenes and lines that will alarm you – do not be alarmed. They are there for bargaining purposes, and I am perfectly open to discussion, especially with an actress as right for the part as yourself.

Everyone working on the film will be engaged in an act of collective audacity. Whatever the results may look like, they will not be squalid.

I will be in Paris until Thursday afternoon.[2] Do call me any time after that.

All my best,
[Kenneth Tynan]

[1] Joanna Dunham (b. 1936), English actress who had played Helen in *Soldiers* (1968) and Mary Magdalen in the film *The Greatest Story Ever Told* (US, 1965).
[2] For casting.

To J. Paul Getty Jr[1]

20, Thurloe Square
September 26 1974

Dear Paul,

What is holding us up? My life these days consists – as it has now for many weeks – of sitting idly by the phone awaiting the call that tells me I can start work on our film and redeem the promises I've made to so many people, not least of them you. A dozen times a day I get calls from agents, cameramen, production managers, film editors, art directors, asking whether we are still going ahead. Once a day it's a newspaper, gloatingly enquiring whether there's any truth in the rumour that the film has been cancelled for want of financial support. And once a day it's Richard Johnson's[2] agent, saying that unless we commit ourselves to a contract by September 30, we lose him to another picture. (I can't think of a comparable alternative: can you?) Of no other project shall I ever be so sure that it will be at once a unique work of pornographic art and an immense financial success. (All other work seems a stupid irrelevance: I cannot set my sights elsewhere.) So: I stagnate, awaiting a word from you.

I know, believe me, that you have lately had private problems to contend with,[3] and I sympathise. In different ways, we are both immobilized. But I won't believe we are defeated. The whole Establishment would rejoice if our film were cancelled: why should we give them this victory? My lawyer and your accountant have apparently worked out a simple way to solve the financial problem – something to do with a Bill of Exchange, to be presented at your bank next March, by which time (I gather) you will once again be financially liquid. On the strength of this document we can raise the cash and forge ahead. All that is needed is your signature.

Your enthusiasm in July, your promise of help, gave me the encouragement I needed to go ahead and put together a hand-picked team of actors and technicians to carry out this delicate and difficult project. They, too, have been marking time ever since. During this period I've increased my own overdraft by $5000 (which I don't want repaid) to pay for the preparatory work being done in Paris. The moment you sign, we are in business and the film I want you to see can be made in the way I want to make it.

When you offered your support, I triumphantly cut off negotiations with the money-men who were trying to screw me. Even if I wanted to, I could not go back to them now. So the ball is in your court – or rather, my balls are in your court. Our deadline is next week, after which we lose our star and, with him, our other investors. A word from you, before then, to Julian Lee,[4] and everything will come up roses and lollipops. Please pick up the phone.

I'm sorry if this sounds like an emotional appeal, but an emotional appeal (based of course on solid budgetting!) is exactly what it is. As a non-believer in stiff upper lips, I see no reason to hide it. And I don't think you would want me to.

Take care.
Ever,
[Ken Tynan][5]

[1] John Paul Getty Jr. (b. 1932), American multimillionaire and philanthropist awarded an honorary

KCBE in 1986. KPT first sent him the script in March 1974 and recorded in his journal (23 July 1974) the subsequent elusiveness of his backer: 'I even sent the lease of my house – the only capital I possess – over to Getty's house as security for his investment . . . unless [Getty] delivers the film is off. The plan in that eventuality is simple. A one-way ticket to some far-off place with a phial of sleeping pills. A few days to settle myself and then suicide.' Getty was asked to invest $150,000 of the $300,000 budget.

[2] Richard Johnson (b. 1927), English classical actor who worked extensively for the RSC. His films include *Captain Horatio Hornblower* (UK, 1951) and *The Pumpkin Eater* (UK, 1964).

[3] Getty had been ill in hospital.

[4] Working on the film.

[5] The 'hermit millionaire', as KPT called him, did not deliver. Instead, Getty went to hospital to endure a painful operation on his private parts. 'God must be very cynical,' Getty commented, 'and very ribald. Otherwise He wouldn't have lasted so long.'

To Kathleen Tynan

[Telegram]
[London]
14 February 1975

HAPPY VALENTINE DARLING SEE SONNET 109[1] KEN

[1] Shakespeare's sonnet No. 109 begins 'Oh never say that I was false of heart, / Though absence seem'd my flame to qualify'. I was spending a fortnight in Los Angeles.

To Gore Vidal[1]

[20 Thurloe Square]
[?20 March 1975]

Dear Gore,

> 'I have never known anyone who was
> not more interested in sex, in one
> manifestation or another, than in
> anything else, whatever social
> pretences he put up, whatever
> sublimation his interest underwent.'
> (The Autobiography of an Englishman by 'Y'[2])

So much by way of stating my theme. I don't know if you saw 'Oh! Calcutta!' or what you thought of it, but it was very much a first attempt at presenting an erotic show for intelligent people. We are now planning a successor, which we hope will be an improvement on the original. Because everybody doubted whether it would be possible to stage a show like 'Oh! Calcutta!' there was a lot of pressure on us to opt for broad comedy in order to gain audience acceptance. This time we can extend our range. We can aim at a show that seriously explores eroticism – that excites people at the same time as entertaining them.

I'd very much like you to be a contributor. What we're looking for are short dramatic items (I don't like the word 'sketches', which has the wrong associations), monologues, poems, songs and ballet scenarios. The prerequisite is this: we want you to write something that you yourself would go to an erotic show to see – i.e. something by which you yourself would be excited. It may be something bizarre, or something very simple. All that matters is that you present or dramatise it in a way that turns you on. The length can be anything from a few lines to around 15 minutes. If the material is a very personal fantasy, your anonymity will be preserved, since we shall not reveal which author wrote which item, unless the author expressly desires it. Nudity is of course fully permissible. Payment would follow the traditional revue formula – the authors' royalties would be shared according to the relative length of their contributions. They would also participate in film, television, radio and other publication rights. There will be no payment before the acceptance of the manuscript. The proposed title, by the way, is 'After Calcutta'.[3] I shall be the devisor of the show, and Clifford Williams will again direct.

One important thing: we need prospective contributions as soon as possible – preferably by the end of May. Let me know if you are interested. And please call me – 589 9223 if you have any queries, or if you'd like to meet to discuss the project in more detail.

Love,
Ken[4]

---

[1] This was more or less a stock letter sent to people including Germaine Greer, Joseph Heller, John Mortimer and Irving Wardle.

[2] Published 1975, the personal narrative of a homosexual.

[3] One of the many titles KPT considered. Others included *The Soft Anvil* and *Second Skin*.

[4] Vidal replied (undated, Rome): 'Last time I put cock to page in your interest, *Myra Breckinridge* came, as it were, into all our lives. I'll try again as summer progresses.'

To Kathleen Tynan

[20 Thurloe Square]
25 June [1975]

Darling,

The Waterside Inn is closed on Mondays, and so is the Juliénas, that new French place at Farnham Common, so I am at a bit of a loss for Monday.[1]

Since I wrote that sentence Clive James[2] has called to say that he can't continue the Donaldson adaptation,[3] doesn't like what he has done and is giving it up. Won't be dissuaded and is coming over to apologise. Just another day in the sun-drenched life of K.T. Whom else shall we get (all hope of an autumn opening and possibly some financial good news now having gone)? Keith Waterhouse?[4] Miguel de Unamuno (now alas dead)? Isaiah Berlin?

While you ponder these pretty tidings, think too of where we might go on Monday. I think it must be Monday, that being the exact day; Tuesday would be a cop-out, like pancakes on Shrove Wednesday, or Christmas prezzies on Boxing Day. Etoile too is out, since my plane doesn't land till 8.20[5] and the place closes its doors at 9.30. Mirabelle? We don't like it. (Nor it us.)

Ernesto Hemingway says that those who have had love are all marked by it, and he goes on: 'All those who have really experienced it are marked by it after it is gone, by a quality of deadness. I say this as a naturalist, not to be romantic.'[6] I think there are other sorts of deadness, and I do pray that the sort (or degree) I am feeling is one of the latter.

I shall introduce Patrick Kernon[7] in Geneva as 'Patrick Kernon' in inverted commas, with heavy emphasis and some nudging, the inference. I hope to convey being that he is in fact (though balding from recent worry and with his formerly luxuriant moustache trimmed pencil-thin) none other than the elusive Lord Lucan.[8]

On second thoughts I don't think Kernon has a moustache, so forget that. I shall still, however, hint that he is the nanny-basher, and shall sprinkle our conversation with references to backgammon, lead piping and the ancestry of Victor Lownes.[9] Thus he will be the beau of the ball and the further fact that he is en route for Australia will strengthen existing rumours about a possible tie-up with Stonehouse.[10]

(Wilton's? In June? Sans bivalves? Don't be silly. What about the Gavroche?[11] Tasty chewing there.)

I hope you enjoyed Wimbledon, where I've no doubt you are. How lucky it is that in my absence you wind up in places where I wouldn't be seen dead. Or even half-alive, which is how I feel.

I keep the part of me which is yours locked up in a deep recess to which I have thrown away the key. Do the same for the part of you that is mine.

K.

[1] Our wedding anniversary was 30 June.
[2] Clive James (b. 1939), author and television critic, he reviewed for the *Observer* 1972–82.
[3] KPT and Clifford Williams had stage and screen rights to *Both the Ladies and the Gentlemen* (1975), William Donaldson's funny autobiographical account of his life as a gentleman ponce. When James left, they commissioned John Wells to do the adaptation, but it was never produced.
[4] Keith Waterhouse (b. 1929), English novelist and dramatist whose second novel, *Billy Liar*, earned critical and popular success.
[5] KPT would be spending the weekend in Geneva.
[6] *Death in the Afternoon* (1932).
[7] KPT's loyal and expert accountant.
[8] Richard John Bingham, 7th Earl of Lucan (1934–?), disappeared on 7 November 1974, fleeing the police who suspected him of battering to death his children's nanny.
[9] Chairman and managing director of the Playboy Club.
[10] John Stonehouse (1925–88), English Labour politician who disappeared in 1974, reappeared in Australia, and was extradited in 1975 to face charges of fraud and embezzlement.
[11] Where we dined.

To John Dexter

26 Thurloe Square
19th November, 1975

Dear John,

Good God. What an unexpected little letter and how nice.[1] I have a book coming out next Thursday (called 'The Sound of Two Hands Clapping') and I'm putting together a rather startling sequel to 'Oh! Calcutta!', which will open next spring. After that I shall very likely be in New York, where nothing could be more stimulating than to see you. Are you <u>all right</u>? Jonathan Miller has been directing a lot of opera lately and he has developed the most ghastly swelling on the right side of his jaw, about the size of a billiard ball. You want to watch out for this kind of thing. Look carefully for tell-tale bulges in the mirror while shaving. Above all, look out for 'Rigoletto'. Jonathan has just done it – as he does everything else – in nineteenth-century costume. It looks like a Trollope novel with an absolutely insane butler at the centre of it. Jonathan says directing opera is a lovely holiday. I'll leave you with that thought and hope you're having a splendid vacation. Write soon, in nineteenth-century costume if you like.

Love,
Ken

P. S. A Sicilian I know tells me that baroque opera is still 'in'. I just thought I'd pass it on.

[1] Dexter was Director of Production at the Metropolitan Opera, New York, 1974–81.

To William Shawn

20 Thurloe Square
December 2, 1975

Dear Mr. Shawn,

I'm thinking of coming back to the States for an indefinite period, beginning next year, and when I mentioned this at a party to Clay Felker,[1] who was in London last month, he asked me whether I'd like to be drama critic of 'New York' magazine.

He's since repeated the offer in a letter. I've told him that, once having performed in that capacity for you, I regard myself as a 'New Yorker' man, and that I'd have to check with you before making any decisions.

Hence this letter. Please understand that I'm not plotting to oust Brendan.[2] It's simply that (a) I wanted to make sure that he would be continuing in the job, and (b) I shouldn't like to turn up as drama critic for any other Manhattan magazine without first consulting you. I plan to arrive in New York during the late summer.

I was relieved, by the way, to see a denial of the 'Observer' story that you were going to retire. And I hope you enjoy the enclosed book,[3] in which the best items were drawn from your pages.

Look forward to hearing from you.

Yours ever,
Kenneth Tynan

[1] Editor of *New York* magazine.
[2] Brendan Gill, drama critic of the *New Yorker*.
[3] KPT's collection *The Sound of Two Hands Clapping* (1975).

To the Editor, *The Times*

20 Thurloe Square
[Published 5 January 1976]

Sir,—I notice that Lord Thomson[1] is quoted in your pages (January 2) as having said in a magazine interview:

'In Canada everyone is looking at me and saying "I want that bastard's job." Well, they are not going to get it. Over here I don't think anyone aims that high. They don't have the ambition and it's wrong.'

He attributes this state of uncompetitive inertia to a 'surfeit of socialism'.

Lord Thomson's remarks betray a certain unfamiliarity with the contemporary political scene, and I believe I am in a position to cheer him up. Let me assure him that, as the unemployment figures continue to rise, there are many thousands of workless people in this country who are looking at their working compatriots and saying, as bitterly and competitively as Lord Thomson could wish: 'I want that bastard's job.' And this admirable state of affairs has been achieved under a Labour Government,[2] which must indicate that Socialism has more to be said for it than Lord Thomson supposes.

Yours sincerely,
KENNETH TYNAN

[1] Lord Thomson (1894–1976), Canadian-born British newspaper and television magnate, owner of *The Times*.
[2] Under Harold Wilson; re-elected in 1974.

To William Shawn

20 Thurloe Square
January 19, 1976

Dear Mr. Shawn,

I'd very much like to accept your generous offer, and I've written to Clay Felker telling him as much. What I particularly like about your proposal is that it allows me a good deal of geographical mobility – I wouldn't be permanently confined to New York.

Please tell me if I've got the terms right – six profiles (subjects to be mutually agreed) of between 4,000 and 10,000 words, over a period of one year. For these you would pay me $44,000 (including $5,000 on signature, though actually I wouldn't want this until the one-year period had actually begun), plus $3,000 expenses to transplant myself and family to New York.

Could you drop me a line to confirm this? And would it fit in with your plans if I arrived in New York at the beginning of September? And finally: oughtn't I to come to New York fairly soon for a day or two to discuss possible subjects for profiles with you? I have a couple of ideas that I'd really need to explain face to face.

I can't tell you how much I'm looking forward to working with and for you again.

Yours sincerely
Kenneth Tynan

To Clifford Williams and Hillard Elkins

[20 Thurloe Square]
[January 1976]

Thoughts on Carte Blanche[1]
These are personal reflexions after reading the latest script. I do not think we have to mount a massive display of energy and exertion in order to make the show what it ought to be. 'Bang Bang'[2] and 'The Lady and the Gent'[3] are the only numbers that deal in broad comic effects. We need to create an inviting atmosphere of sexual ease – which is impossible without complete relaxation on both sides of the footlights. Cool and confidence are the key words. Any sense of strain in the performers will create strain in the audience, and the right sensual mood will be dispelled. (Nobody makes love to clamorous noise.) Easy, civilised camaraderie – friendly equality with the audience – these seem to me the essential notes to strike. We are leading them gently as the man leads his partner in ballroom dancing. We are not trying to overwhelm them.

Anything pushy, over-emotional, driving, insistent, vulgar will dry up the juices that ought (if we have done our work properly) to be flowing. We have to coax rather than command, so that embarrassment vanishes and the audience can get sexually aroused without feeling either ashamed or manipulated. If the juices dry up, then all the applause we may garner from song, dance or comedy will be irrelevant and wasted. It would be easy to make this show run six months. The trick is to make it run six years.

Above all, if we try to stage a repeat of 'Oh! Calcutta!', we shall fail. 'Carte Blanche' is not 'Oh! Calcutta!' and should not resemble it. Whenever we have a choice between a knockout number that will <u>not</u> turn the audience on, and a lightly carressing number that <u>will</u>, we should go for the light caress. This will take courage at times, but it will also pay off at the box office: it will give us a new kind of hit instead of a copy of an old one. Decibels of applause and laughter are not the criteria by which we want to be judged (although I've nothing against either applause or laughter in the right places). The audience should go out feeling freer, more relaxed, more intrigued, more informed, more tolerant and less guilty about sex than when it came in. If we achieve that, the show will be the kind of success I think it ought to be.

[1] The sequel to *Oh! Calcutta!* Clifford Williams directed, Elkins co-produced with Michael White.
[2] 'Bang Bang You're Almost Dead', by Pat McCormick.
[3] 'The Lady and the Gentleman', by Rudy De Luca and Barry Levinson.

To Adrian Mitchell

20 Thurloe Square
February 8, 1976

Dear Adrian,

Many thanks for the disgusting lyrics,[1] which both Clifford and I liked <u>very</u>* much. At present we're preparing a boiled-down script (we have about four hours of possible material), and as soon as we have something worth showing we will send you a copy.

Meanwhile let any ideas about sexual liberty and the purpose and problems thereof run freely in your mind, and transmit the fruits to us at once.

I'm tapering off nicotine at last, not without agony: I find it works out again to the equation sip/puff being replaced by sip/sip, which involves a doubled alcohol conumption. (A conumption is a compressed consumption, leading to instead death, and is possible only on IBM type-writers where you cannot insert letters without retyping the entire paragraph. 'Instead' means 'instant', by the way, if you are using an

IMB – or IBM – typewriter and do not have one of those erasing devices.)
Will be in touch soon.

Love,
Ken

* They're sexy, funny and weird – and who could ask for more?

---

[1] New lyrics to 'Moons Are Balloons', an Astaire–Rogers number.

On 30 January 1976, The Times *ran a fierce editorial in the wake of the
acquittal of Linda Lovelace's autobiography,* Inside Linda Lovelace, *on
charges of obscenity. The leader, titled 'The Pornography of Hatred', declared
that Miss Lovelace's advice on sexual positions was 'physically dangerous' and
warned that its publication would encourage more dangerous pornography,
books which 'illustrate and glorify sadistic practices'. 'Such pornography does
deprave; indeed we can see that pornographers themselves have been depraved
by just such an exposure to the pornography of cruelty. (In last week's* Times
Literary Supplement *Mr D.A.N. Jones analysed the development of Mr
Kenneth Tynan's acceptance of cruelty; the process of corruption in a talented
writer was precisely that of pornography).'*

*The critic D.A.N. Jones had reviewed two of Ken's collections, published
in 1975,* A View of the English Stage *and* The Sound of Two Hands
Clapping. *On 11 February he wrote to* The Times *dissociating himself from
their leader, and there were other letters in Ken's defence. Meanwhile, in
another newspaper, the* Daily Telegraph, *the journalist Richard West recalled
meeting a group of mercenaries in Vietnam 'whose only reading matter was
a magazine containing an article by Kenneth Tynan on the subject, if I
remember right, of masturbation. Who can say that pornography did not
influence some of those troops to the rape that was so frequent in Vietnam?'*

Ken, deeply shocked, began legal proceedings against The Times.

To William Rees-Mogg[1]

20 Thurloe Square
24th February 1976

<u>Without Prejudice</u>

Dear William,
I thought I'd cut a few legal corners by replying to your letter myself.

I can't use your correspondence columns to reply to your attack on me, for the following reasons:

1) What you said about me, quite unequivocally, was that I had been 'depraved and corrupted' by the pornography of cruelty – in which generic term you specifically included Nazi pornography, as practised in the concentration camps, and 'the pornography of rape and the rapist'. This is such a stupefying charge that even to deny it is in part to legitimise it. It is like trying to answer the question: 'When did you stop getting pleasure from seeing Jews gassed?' (except of course that in your case the question would read: 'Is it not true that you get more and more pleasure from seeing Jews gassed?'). I won't refute that kind of charge: it's simply too monstrous. Moreover, since it's an attack on my own character, I can hardly act as character witness in my own defence. That's best left to others. (Incidentally, I gather from Michael Billington and Al Alvarez[2] that they both wrote letters supporting me, and I notice that you haven't printed either of them.)

2) More crucially, you base your case against me entirely on D. A. N. Jones' piece in the T.L.S. To refute it I would therefore have to go over his piece point by point. But how can I do that in the columns of 'The Times', whose readers haven't read the Jones review? If, on the other hand, I reply in the columns of the T.L.S., my letter won't be seen by readers of 'The Times'. So neither of these alternatives fits the bill.

When I read the Jones review, it seemed to me so transparently dotty as to need no comment: it never occurred to me that anyone could take it seriously. At the risk of boring you, I'll run over the points he made:

a) Writing in 1946 about Peter Brook's production of Sartre's 'Huis Clos' [*No Exit*],[3] I said it ended with three people in Hell suffering 'the completest torture that malevolence could prescribe for them'. This is precisely accurate: but the torture involved is not physical: it is simply – each other's company! Realising this, they burst into a 'frightful peal of laughter, exquisitely timed and protracted by Mr. Brook'. So they do: this is the laughter of the damned. Yet from this sentence Jones extracts two words, puts them together to form the phrase 'exquisitely frightful', and later cites this phrase (which I never used) as one of the milestones on my road to perdition!

b) In 1949, I praised Brook for his handling of the last act of 'Measure for Measure'[4] – 'a scene of such coincidences and lengthy impossibilities, such forced reconciliations and incredible cruelties that most producers flog it through at breakneck speed towards the welcome curtain.' Jones quotes only the second half of this phrase, from 'incredible cruelties' onwards – and omits to mention my reason for applauding Brook's treatment, which was that he <u>removed</u> the 'incredible cruelties' and instead made the climax of the scene <u>Isabella's successful plea for Angelo's life</u>. In other words, cruelty was replaced with mercy.

c) In the same production, I talked about the 'ghastly comedy' of the prison scenes (they were and are both ghastly and comic) and mentioned one 'horribly funny piece of invention' (it was both horrid and funny, in keeping with Shakespeare's text: one first smiled, then shuddered, as at the work of many great satirists.)

d) I described (also in 1949) Brook himself as having 'a thuggishly wicked little grin'. This is straight journalistic description, not praise. Yet from it Jones sombrely concludes: ' "Wicked" was beginning to mean "good" in Tynanese.' Is one really to answer such stuff as this?

e) Reviewing the Brook production of 'Titus Andronicus'[5] in 1955, I wrote: '<u>One accepts the ethical code</u> which forces Tamora to avenge herself on Titus, and then Titus to avenge himself on Tamora: <u>it is the casualness of the killing that grows tiresome, as at a bad bullfight.</u> With acknowledgements to Lady Bracknell, to lose one son may be accounted a misfortune; <u>to lose twentyfour, as Titus does, looks like carelessness.</u> Here indeed is "snip and nip, and cut, and slish, and slash", a series of operations which only a surgeon could describe as a memorable evening in the theatre.' I've italicised the phrases Jones took out of context, reshuffled, and printed out of order. Isn't it perfectly clear that the whole passage is meant ironically? It seems the old rule holds good: never attempt irony when thick skulls are around.

f) <u>A propos</u> of Brook's handling of Lear in 1962,[6] I referred to 'Mr. Brook's cruel, unsparing egalitarianism: his production is amoral because it is set in an amoral universe.' Exactly: a fine, brief definition of Brook's approach. But the fact that <u>Brook</u> sees the universe as 'amoral' does not mean that I do. Yet Jones comments: '(Tynan) has resolved the problem about the portrayal of cruelty: blame the universe.' Wilful misrepresentation could go no further.

g) Jones says these steps (and I have omitted none) mark my progression towards 'the Theatre of Cruelty'. This is nonsense: as a critic, I always <u>opposed</u> the 'Theatre of Cruelty'. In fact, I was under fairly constant attack for what some saw as my simplistic belief in the theatre as a positive force for social betterment: my critical persona, in most people's eyes, was that of an almost-too-starry-eyed humanitarian! My book is full of passages expressing this faith. Two will suffice: in a series of articles[7] denying Eugene Ionesco's belief that value judgments had no place in the theatre, I said: 'I shall be looking for something more, something harder: for evidence of the artist who . . . concerns himself, from time to time, with such things as healing. M. Ionesco correctly says that no ideology has yet abolished fear, pain or sadness. Nor has any work of art. But both are in the business of trying. What other business is there?'

Again, there's an interview (from 'Playboy'[8]) in which I praise 'Island' – 'Aldous Huxley's last and to my mind most human novel. In it he envisaged an island set between the spheres of influence of East and West, somewhere in the Indian Ocean, a sort of surrogate Eden . . . it embraced the best of liberal Socialism and the best of Buddhism. It was a very good dream and it attracted me a lot.' There follows this exchange:

Playboy: 'Hasn't a book like "Lord of the Flies"[9] taken your Eden-myth and exposed its inherent flaws?'
Tynan: 'That's a very potent piece of iconoclasm, yes, the very opposite of the Utopian myth, claiming that if people are left alone to develop by instinct, they will plump for evil, and destroy one another. But I do not subscribe to that thesis. The ideal community can be constructed, and Caliban can be pacified. The least we can do is try.'

Is this my 'acceptance of cruelty'? Is this 'the process of corruption'?

h) Jones complains because Roman Polanski and I decided to show the murder of Duncan in our film of 'Macbeth', although Shakespeare (not wishing to offend the Scots king before whom the play was to be staged) kept it in the wings. Well, Laurence Olivier showed the murder of Hamlet's father in his film of 'Hamlet'; does this make him a por-nographer of cruelty? And, because everyone in the Middle Ages slept nude, we showed Lady Macbeth naked in the sleepwalking scene. This may be open to criticism as an artistic decision: but its connexion with concentration-camp pornography escapes me.

i) My book contains a short essay about a bullfighter. According to Jones: '. . . for Mr. Tynan, the idea of a sword is not "merely painful". In the hands of a bullfighter, it becomes an instrument to develop a "deep harmony" of man and beast.' Another cynical misquotation: what I actually wrote was: 'Beneath an apparent contradiction – the

bull's power versus the man's intelligence – we perceive a deeper harmony.' The passage refers to the bullfighter's <u>cape</u> and the bull: it has
nothing to do with swords. It should be pointed out here that my book
about bullfighting – 'Bull Fever' – was published in 1954,[10] and dealt
with the same bullfighter[11] as the essay Jones cites. Apart from the
'Macbeth' film (made in 1971), all the evidence thus far quoted by
Jones to demonstrate my love of cruelty dates back more than twenty
years!

j) My book contains a long, serio-comic account of Nicol Williamson's
one-man show for Richard Nixon in 1970, reprinted from 'The New
Yorker'. Desperately hunting for quotes to bolster his thesis, Jones cites
a brief reference to a novel by Simon Raven[12] which I read 'with my
usual sense of pleasurable loathing'. Pleasure at the style, loathing for
the implicit values: is this so unusual, bizarre or wicked?

m) The book ends with a long travel piece about the city of Valencia,
also reprinted from 'The New Yorker', entitled 'The Judicious
Observer will be Disgusted'. (Jones calls it 'The Judicious Observer
will be Shocked'.) It's a smelly, crowded place, but at least you can get
away from tourists, and that was the point I made in what was intended
to be a funny piece. Jones quotes my reference to its 'noisy and majestic
ugliness . . . Let me stress that it really is something ultimate in pest-
holes.' Really straining himself at this point, he cites this as another
example of my 'sense of pleasurable loathing'. Good God! The Valencia
article is one of the best things I've ever done, containing not a syllable
about violence or pornography or anything remotely controversial.
It's simply extremely amusing. But Jones, as I've hinted before, has
absolutely no sense of humour.

And that (believe it or not) is that. I've mentioned and answered
<u>every point</u> Jones brings against me. Can you honestly maintain that
this justifies the accusations levelled in your editorial? Where is the
evidence of depravity or corruption? Even Jones himself shrank from
being identified with the interpretation you put upon his review, and
hastily disassociated himself from what you said.

May I end by offering two final extracts from 'The Sound of Two
Hands Clapping' – extracts which really have a bearing on your editorial? First: 'The most dangerous book I have ever read was shown to
me at the end of the war: it was a military Small-Arms Manual, which
had a detailed description of how to bayonet people – how to put in
the knife, how to twist it, how to inflict the maximum agony, all that –

and as I read it, I felt sick. I thought: this ought to be banned, it's evil, it's militarist, it's sadistic, it's antisocial to the highest degree. But, on reflexion, I know I couldn't ever be the one to say: ban this book ... The only answer to a rotten book is not a bonfire, but a better book.'

And second: 'I don't accept that good can't be made more attractive than evil – look at C.S. Lewis's novels. People don't automatically side with the villain in a Western; they don't automatically get bored when Everest is climbed; they aren't automatically horrified when a heart transplant succeeds, or a mass murderer is caught. More people went on the freedom march to Washington than ever went to a Nuremberg rally. It's surely not that hard to make good seductive.'

In your letter to my lawyer you say that I would have to show that the facts on which Jones's review was based were mistaken.'³ You then say: 'The facts as opposed to the interpretation that might be put on them are <u>not seriously in dispute</u>.' (My italics.) But, as I've demonstrated, they are very seriously in dispute. Most of them are not facts at all. Now I don't want to take up thousands of words defending my reputation against such nonsense. It would be too self-important and too time-consuming. But whatever our differences of opinion may be, there is no malice between us that I'm aware of, and I would always regard you as an upholder of gentlemanly practices in journalism. Don't you think it would be fair if you were to print a short retraction, to the effect that, upon mature reflection, you feel that the evidence contained in Jones's review did not justify the extreme gravity of the charges your editorial levelled against me, and that you were mistaken in suggesting that I accept or condone the values of the concentration camp or the rapist? Such a statement – we can discuss the phrasing some other time – would not be a victory for me over you: it would be a victory for something both of us value – something as old-fashioned as fair play.

Yours,
[Kenneth Tynan]¹⁴

¹ KPT's Oxford contemporary was now editor of *The Times*.
² A. Alvarez (b. 1929), poet, novelist and literary critic, editor of the anthology *The New Poetry* (1962).
³ At the Arts Theatre, with Alec Guinness.
⁴ At Stratford, with John Gielgud.
⁵ At Stratford.
⁶ *King Lear*, RSC production starring Paul Scofield, later filmed (UK/Denmark, 1970) by Peter Brook.

[7] KPT's article 'Ionesco: Man of Destiny' (*Observer*, 22 June 1958) led to an exchange of published letters with Ionesco and others, including Orson Welles and Lindsay Anderson. See *Notes and Counternotes* (1959).
[8] An unpublished interview with KPT which he included in *The Sound of Two Hands Clapping*.
[9] *Lord of the Flies* (1954), William Golding's first novel, about a group of schoolchildren who, stranded on an island, revert to cannibalism.
[10] It was published in 1955.
[11] Antonio Ordóñez.
[12] *Friends in Low Places* (1965).
[13] Rees Mogg's letter to KPT's lawyers Wright & Webb, Syrett & Sons, 18 February 1976, in which he stated: 'It would be difficult to prove that no reasonable man could form this view about Mr Tynan's development.'
[14] On 18 May 1976 *The Times* printed a 'correction' saying, 'We did not intend to suggest, nor do we, that Mr Tynan condones rape or torture.' Rees Mogg replied (25 May) that he would be 'perfectly happy' to pay KPT's legal costs.

To the Editor, *The Times*

20 Thurloe Square
[Published 8 April 1976]

Sir,—Now that Britain has been so sternly stood in the corner by Alexander Solzhenitsyn,[1] many of your readers may be under the impression that the exiled novelist regards the entire Western world as a lost cause. I am happy to assure them that this is not the case. Mr Solzhenitsyn sees at least one beacon of enlightenment in the surrounding gloom. In the course of a recent 48-minute interview on Spanish TV he enthusiastically described General Franco's victory in the Spanish Civil War as a victory for 'the concept of Christianity'. He went on to congratulate the Spanish people – in whose midst he had spent eight whole days – on possessing what he described as 'absolute freedom'.

We can safely dismiss as Bolshevik extremists those Spanish citizens whose first impulse, on hearing these opinions, was an overwhelming desire to spit squarely in the great moralist's eye.

Yours sincerely,
KENNETH TYNAN

[1] Alexander Solzhenitsyn (b. 1918), Russian novelist whose experiences in a labour camp served as the basis for *The Gulag Archipelago* and other works. He was awarded the Nobel Prize for Literature in 1970. On 1 April 1976 he had made a broadcast on Radio 4, 'Warning to the Western World' (reprinted in *The Times* on 2 April, and as a booklet in May), condemning the decadent materialism of the West, its confusion and 'loss of will'. According to Solzhenitsyn

Britain exemplified this condition, and he drew attention to Britain's responsibility for the forced repatriation of Soviet citizens at the end of World War II.

To David Perry[1]

20 Thurloe Square
7th May 1976

Dear David,

As promised, here is a list of some High Definition Performances:[2]

1) Jazz	BIX BEIDERBECKE ('I am coming, Virginia', 'Way down yonder in New Orleans', 'Sorry', 'Thou Swell', or 'Changes')[3]
	THE COUNT BASIE TRIO (only one LP, issued last year)[4]
	DUKE ELLINGTON ('Dusk', 'Blue Goose', or any of the slow tempo tracks of 'Such Sweet Thunder')[5]
	MILES DAVIS ('Kind of Blue')[6]
	BILLIE HOLIDAY ('Am I Blue', 'I'll Get By')[7]
2) Theatre and Cabaret	JOHN WOOD[8]
	COWARD AND GERTRUDE LAWRENCE (in 'Shadowplay')[9]
	ABE BURROWS ('The Girl with the Three Blue Eyes')[10]
	AL JOLSON ('About a Quarter to Nine')[11]
	SHIRLEY MACLAINE at the Palladium[12]
	CARL REINER and MEL BROOKS ('The 2,000 Year Old Man', 'Reiner and Brooks at the Cannes Festival' – the track called 'The LMNOP Agency')[13]
	KAY THOMPSON ('Quelle Joie')[14]
	IRWIN COREY ('The World's Foremost Authority')[15]

ZERO MOSTEL ('There's a Girl in the Heart of Wheeling, West Virginia, with a Watch that belongs to me')[16]

GROUCHO MARX ('Show Me a Rose')[17]

THE MILLS BROTHERS ('Till Then')[18]

CHARLOTTE RAE ('Everybody Loves You' on 'Rodgers and Hart Revisited')[19]

BERTOLT BRECHT (singing songs from 'The Threepenny Opera')[20]

LOTTE LENYA ('Let's Go to Benares', from 'Mahagonny')[21]

3) Pop singers   THE BEATLES ('Strawberry Fields', 'Here, There and Everywhere', 'Girls')[22]

HARRY NILSSON ('Making Whoopee')[23]

4) Classical music   THE AMADEUS QUARTET[24] (playing any Mozart string quartet)

RICHARD TAUBER[25] (singing Mozart)

BRUNO HOFFMANN[26] (playing the 'Adagio for Glass Harmonica')

5) Television   JOHNNY CARSON[27] (there's an LP 'The Best of Johnny Carson')

6) Movies   GARBO (in 'Grand Hotel' or 'Queen Christina')[28]

7) Cricket   GARY SOBERS[29]

CLIVE LLOYD[30]

JEFF THOMSON[31]

COLIN MILBURN[32]

8) Ice skating   JOHN CURRY[33]

On the whole, I think we would be wise to restrict ourselves to actual performers – that's to say, ignoring poets, novelists, playwrights, painters and composers. Otherwise the field gets too enormous.

As I said, I have copies of most of the recordings mentioned above, many of them on obscure or defunct American labels.

Let's confer again soon. Meanwhile, it would be nice to hear from your contracts department.

Yours,
[Kenneth Tynan]

[1] On the staff of the BBC Radio arts programme *Kaleidoscope*. They would broadcast a 'special edition' of the programme, 'Kenneth Tynan in Conversation with Michael Billington', on 18 June 1976.

[2] See letter of 2 July 1969. He added to his definition in the Preface to *The Sound of Two Hands Clapping*: 'The ability – shared by great athletes, sportsmen, bullfighters and conversationalists as well as stage performers – to communicate the essence of one's talent to an audience with economy, grace, no apparent effort and absolute hard-edged clarity of outline.'

[3] Bix Beiderbecke (1903–31), American cornetist who came to symbolize the Roaring Twenties, though he was largely unknown at the time of his death. 'I am Coming, Virginia', 'Way Down Yonder ...', 'Sorry' and 'Changes' (1927); 'Thou Swell' (1928). All available on *Bixology* (1988). See also letter of 22 March 1952.

[4] William 'Count' Basie (1904–84); the Trio (actually a quartet) were Basie on piano; Freddie Green on guitar, Walter Page on bass and Jo Jones on drums. One record side of the double album *Good Morning Blues* (1975) contains the 78 rpm recordings made by the Trio in 1938–9.

[5] Duke Ellington (1899–1974), American big-band leader. 'Dusk' (1940) on *The Indispensable Duke Ellington Vols 5 & 6* (1940); 'Blue Goose' on *Jumpin' Pinkins* (1965); *Such Sweet Thunder* (1940). See also letter of 13 September 1943.

[6] Miles Davis (b. 1926), American trumpeter; *Kind of Blue* (1959).

[7] Billie Holiday (1915–59), American jazz singer; 'I'll Get By' (1937) and 'Am I Blue' (1941) available on *The Billie Holiday Collection: 20 Golden Greats* (1985).

[8] John Wood (b. 1930), English actor who joined the Royal Shakespeare Company in 1971.

[9] Title song of the play by Noël Coward (1936), in which he starred opposite Gertrude Lawrence; on *Tonight at 8.30* (1936).

[10] Abe Burrows (1910–85), wrote (with Jo Sherling) the book for *Guys and Dolls* (1950) and wrote, produced and directed *Can-Can* (1953, music and lyrics by Cole Porter).

[11] On the film soundtrack *Go Into Your Dance* (1935). See also letter to Elly Horovitz, Wednesday [? June 1948].

[12] Album *Shirley MacLaine at the Palladium* (1976).

[13] Carl Reiner (b. 1922) and Mel Brooks (b. 1926) had turned out sketches for Sid Caesar's comedy television show *Your Show of Shows*, and together created 'the 2000-Year-Old Man'. Both went on to become directors: Reiner's films include *Oh God!* (US, 1977); Brooks's many spoofs include *The Producers* (US, 1968), *Blazing Saddles* (US, 1974) and *Young Frankenstein* (US, 1975). Both sketches are on *The Cannes Film Festival* (1962).

[14] On *Kay Thompson with orchestra conducted by Joe Lipman*. See also letter of 22 March 1952.

[15] Irwin Corey (b. 1912), American actor and comedian famous for his 'Professor' character, developed in 1943 with the writer Abe Mechlowitz: *'Professor' Irwin Corey, 'The World's Foremost Authority'*, at Le Ruban Bleu.

[16] Derived from a 1913 song by Ballard MacDonald, 'There's a Girl in the Heart of Maryland ...' On *Zero Mostel Sings Harry Ruby: Songs My Mother Never Sang* (1966).

[17] His signature song, on *'Hooray for Captain Spaulding' and other songs by Harry Ruby and Bert Kalmar sung by Groucho Marx* (1952).

[18] 1930s male vocal quartet; 'Till Then' on *The Best of the Mills Brothers* (1944).

[19] Charlotte Rae (b. 1926), New York actress and cabaret singer; 'Everybody Loves You' was cut

during previews of *I'd Rather Be Right* (1937), but was included on *Rodgers and Hart Revisited* (1973).

[20] *Bertolt Brecht singt zwei songs aus der Dreigroschenoper* (1928/9).

[21] Lotte Lenya (1898–1981), Austrian actress and singer well known for her recordings of Weill and Brecht. *Mahagonny* was recorded with the North German Radio Chorus (1958).

[22] 'Strawberry Fields Forever' on *Sergeant Pepper's Lonely Hearts Club Band* (1967); 'Here, There and Everywhere' on *Revolver* (1966); 'Girls' on *Rubber Soul* (1965).

[23] Harry Nilsson (1941–94), American singer/songwriter ('Without You') who played the singer in *Midnight Cowboy* (US, 1969). 'Making Whoopee' available on *All the Best of Harry Nilsson* (1993).

[24] British string quartet formed in 1947 (Norbert Brainin and Sigmund Nissel, violins; Peter Schidlof, viola; Martin Lovett, cello); it ceased playing on the death of Schidlof in 1987.

[25] Richard Tauber (1892–1948), Austrian-born operatic tenor. On the album *Mozart Historical Recordings* (1991).

[26] Bruno Hoffmann (b. 1913), German player of and composer for the Glass harmonica; on the album *Mozart and Weber – Miscellaneous Works* (1993).

[27] Johnny Carson (b. 1925), American TV personality, host of *The Tonight Show* on NBC television 1962–92. *Here's Johnny: Magic Moments from The Tonight Show* (double album, 1974).

[28] *Grand Hotel* (US, 1932), directed by Edmund Goulding; *Queen Christina* (US, 1933), directed by Rouben Mamoulian.

[29] Sir Garfield St Aubron (Gary) Sobers (b. 1936), West Indian cricketer, captain from the late 1960s to the early 1970s. Perhaps the greatest all-round cricketer of the century, his record Test score of 365 not out stood for 27 years.

[30] Clive Lloyd (b. 1944), West Indian cricketer, captain for ten years from the mid-1970s. At 6 ft 5 in, he was a magnificent fielder and a formidable left-handed batsman.

[31] Jeffrey Robert Thomson (b. 1950), Australian fast bowler, played Test cricket 1972–85.

[32] Colin Milburn (1941–92), Falstaffian Northamptonshire and England cricketer 1966–9; his career was cut short by the loss of an eye in a car accident.

[33] John Curry (1949–94), English ice skater, Olympic men's champion 1976.

To Richard Pilbrow[1]

[20 Thurloe Square]
20 June 1976

Dear Richard,

A couple of years ago I wrote a film script that never got made – due mainly to the fact that, although I sometimes got the money together and sometimes the right cast, I could never get <u>both</u> together at the same time. It was then budgeted at around £300,000.

My associate producer, Christopher Neame (son of Ronald and a chap with excellent credits) has just come up with a plan for producing the picture for less than half this amount by a private subscription scheme. He's just finished producing a picture directed by Henry Pembroke[2] by this means, and brought it in for £130,000. After talking to him last week, I said I would approach you and see if you'd be interested in investing in my picture along similar lines.

The first thing is for you to look at the script, of which I enclose a slightly tea-stained copy. The aim was and is to make the first elegant erotic movie that could both win the Cannes prize and appeal to lechers everywhere.

If you're interested, let's have a talk.

Ever,
[Kenneth Tynan]

---

[1] Richard Pilbrow (b. 1933), English producer and lighting specialist whose company was responsible for the technical design of the new National Theatre, and who was a producer on *Carte Blanche*.
[2] The 17th Earl of Pembroke (b. 1939), owner of Wilton House; his film *Emily*, with Koo Stark, was released in 1976.

To Hillard Elkins, Michael White, Richard Pilbrow

20 Thurloe Square
6th August 1976

Dear Hilly, Michael and Richard,

Do you want 'Carte Blanche' to fail? Two recent developments make me wonder.

First, a press release about the show – on which Clifford and I have worked for two years – was issued without being read by either of us. It described the show in true Paul Raymond[1] fashion as 'an erotic revue', and it identified me as the devisor, although we had specifically agreed that for legal reasons this was to be avoided at all costs. That release has probably steered us on to a direct collision course with the law. The Festival of Light[2] people must have been overjoyed to get me at last in their telescopic sights, and I don't doubt that they have already started to consult lawyers.

Secondly, I've just heard, with incredulity, the salaries you have been offering. Jean Warren,[3] an actress Clifford wanted very badly, told a friend of mine today that she was offered £65 a week for a minimum period of a year – less than anybody in the original 'Calcutta' cast received six years ago! And the 'Calcutta' people for the last five years haven't been required to sign up for more than six months. Jean W. – and several others – turned the offer down with justified disgust. I gather that Clifford complained to Hilly weeks ago about the low salaries and that Hilly promised something would be done. It wasn't.

Now it's obvious that 'Carte Blanche' is a far more demanding show, in terms of acting and dancing ability, than 'Calcutta'. It is far more dependent on a top-flight company of actors. No wonder – at these derisory figures – that we haven't got one. I gather there are still a couple of gaps in the cast. If you really want to avoid disaster (and last-minute replacements during rehearsals), you will have to spend far more than £65 a week to fill them.

Ken T.

[1] Paul Raymond (b. 1945), owner of Raymond's Revue Bar in Soho, London, and publisher of erotic magazines.
[2] A crusade against pornography and moral pollution led by Malcolm Muggeridge, Mary White-house and the Right Revd Trevor Huddleston, Bishop of Stepney. Two hundred beacons were lit up and down the country, there was a rally in Trafalgar Square and a march in Hyde Park on 25 September 1971.
[3] Jean Warren did appear in *Carte Blanche*.

To Adrian Mitchell

[20 Thurloe Square]
19th August 1976

Dear Adrian,

I enclose a script for your confidential scrutiny.

The opening number has already gone through several meta-morphoses. The points it was intended to make are roughly as follows:

1) a boy and a girl address the audience on terms of friendly equality.

2) They try to find out what makes people come to see erotic enter-tainments.

3) They show the so-called erotic zones of their bodies.

4) They wonder whether the same zones would turn people on if allied with unprepossessing faces.

5) They wonder whether their bodies are more attractive in photo-graphs than in reality.

6) They wonder whether the audience thinks that actors are exploited

and humiliated by having to show their bodies. They reassure the audience that they themselves feel no sense of humiliation or exploitation.

7) They try touching each other to see if it will turn the audience on. They attempt to make love, but fail. However, they explain that it doesn't matter – it may work out the following night.

Now that I've set it out like that, I realise how confused it all is. What we really need is a number (using speech and song) which would – in the most unpretentious way – show the audience those parts of the body that are of unique importance to erotic theatre, demonstrate what makes sex in the theatre different from sex in pictures, explain that nobody involved feels used or humiliated, and demonstrate that – much as we might like to do it – fucking on stage is simply not on.

If you can dream up a way of making these points (or some of them, or any related ones that occur to you), I'd be delighted. Give me a ring if anything bubbles up.[1]

Love,
Ken

[1] This opening number was replaced by 'Masks', which was not written by Mitchell.

To Roxana Tynan

[20 Thurloe Square]
14 September 1976

Roxana's 9th Birthday by Ken

For Roxana at Nine

Lift the glasses! Pour the wine!
Dear Roxana, you are nine!
There was much to celebrate
When you reached the age of eight;
And two years ago, by heaven,
How we cheered when you were seven!
And a man with magic tricks
Made you laugh when you were six.

'May you prosper! May you thrive!'
Was my wish when you were five;
And the same was true at four
(Sorry if I sound a bore);
While the day that you were three
Friends and neighbours roared with glee.
When the candles numbered two,
Mummy cried (and Daddy, too);
And there never was more fun
Than on birthday number one
(Not since that September morn
When stars danced and you were born).
Still, for nine I'll do my best
Joy I wish you, health and rest.
Happy work to useful ends,
And a few beloved friends;
Just the right amount of money
And a sense of what is funny;
Grace and courage when you're pressed,
And each day a good night's rest.
Sunshine and blue skies attend you
All these gifts I'd like to send you,
As befits a girl of nine
Who is pretty, wise and mine
(In return, I ask for this;
Give me, now and then a kiss;
Learn the language used in France:
And – above all – learn to dance.)

On 30 September 1976, Carte Blanche opened in London at the Phoenix Theatre. Several critics found it visually stunning. One reviewer noted that an erotic revue which contained contributions ranging from the work of the seventeenth-century poet Earl of Rochester to the journalist Molly Parkin could not be without interest. (There were also sketches by Joe Orton and Michael Weller.) The work of the choreographers Robert North and Robert Cohan, was applauded. Critics praised the surrealist playlet by Frantz Salieri, based on Tristan and Isolde, which included transvestites miming to Wagner and Mozart; and a dark sketch by Eugene Ionesco (already tried out in the Paris version of Oh! Calcutta!) about the evanescence of youth and beauty.

Yet overall the reviews were poor. The show was described as stylish yet low in wit and high on pretentiousness. It failed above all in delivering sexual intercourse on stage. In retrospect the producer, Michael White, felt that it was staged at the wrong time, with the wrong team. Its reception was a considerable blow to Ken.

To Germaine Greer

[20 Thurloe Square]
Oct 1, '76

Dear Germaine –
    I expect you will have seen the front page of today's 'Evening News'.[1] You are, of course, entitled to your opinion, and you are entitled, if you wish, to share it with a million newspaper readers. Whether you are then entitled to attend a party in celebration of the show you have just knocked, and to seek a heart-felt reconciliation with the person who devised it, I am not certain. But there is one thing to which I know you will never be entitled, and that is my friendship.

Yours,
Ken

[1] Greer told the *Evening News* (1 October 1976) as she left the theatre, 'It simply didn't come off. They couldn't sing well enough and they couldn't dance well enough.'

To William Shawn

42 Lord's View,
St John's Wood Road
London NW8[1]
16th October 1976

Dear Mr. Shawn,
    My London show has now safely opened. Unfortunately I've contracted a bronchial infection which will prevent me from travelling to the States for another week or so. This means that I'll be arriving in Los Angeles during the last week of October. My wife and children are already installed there at the following address: 765 Kingman Avenue, Santa Monica, California 90402.
    All in all, it seems to me that the best plan would be for our agreement

to start when I get to Los Angeles and continue until the end of October 1977. I've started research on Tom Stoppard, and will be writing the piece during November and December. Meanwhile, I can continue work on Ralph Richardson during the month of November, when he opens on Broadway in Harold Pinter's 'No Man's Land'. Richardson would be the subject of my second piece, for delivery early in the New Year. I hope this sounds o.k. to you.

It looks as if the remaining four pieces will be about Carson, Mel Brooks, John Curry and Bob Kaufman,[2] the black poet from San Francisco about whom I told you. I've talked at some length to Swifty Lazar,[3] but I fear he's a rather doubtful starter, since he's writing an autobiography, for which he will unquestionably reserve all his best stories. [...]

Yours ever,
Kenneth Tynan.

[1] 20 Thurloe Square had been rented out.
[2] Bob Kaufman (1925–86), known in the US as 'the Original Be-Bop Man' and in France as 'the black American Rimbaud'; his poetry includes *Solitudes Crowded With Loneliness* (1965). One of the original Beat poets, he founded a poetry magazine, *Beatitude*. When President Kennedy was assassinated, he took a Buddhist vow of silence until the Vietnam War ended, twelve years later.
[3] Irving 'Swifty' Lazar (1907–94), legendary Hollywood agent.

Memo to Clifford Williams and Michael White

[20 Thurloe Square]
October 18 [1976]

We haven't got a backlog of publicity to help us, and we haven't got notices. We are going to live or die on word of mouth. The w.o.m. on 'Oh! Calcutta!' was good because it delivered what it promised, which was explicit nudity. I hate to be wise after the event, but I did warn you that 'Carte Blanche' was not delivering in this area. (And the cutting of my two numbers – 'Flesh and Fantasy' and 'Triangle' – removed two of the most explicit examples, not only of nudity but of <u>touching</u>.) We find ourselves with a show that is not 'artistic' enough for the sophisticates, and not sexy enough for the lechers. The basic requirement of a sex show – the female body exposed and touched – is simply not fulfilled. Therefore I suggest:

A new look at every item in the show, and an attempt to make every item more attractively naked. (Since we must by now have been vetted by the police, we needn't worry about being prosecuted.) [...]

WHAT WE HAVE NOW IS AN ARTISTIC COMPROMISE. We undertook to turn people on – and we failed to deliver the fundamental ingredient without which a show about sex ceases to be sexy: i.e. the female form happily, guiltlessly, totally and intimately revealed. [...]

We can save this show if we work on it – and if we agree that the most damaging reviews were those which said (like Fiona Richmond's[1]) that you can see more flesh elsewhere. We should be offering wit and beauty <u>and flesh</u>. Without flesh, the wit and beauty are pointless. A thought from the past: in the late 50's Josh Logan[2] opened a Broadway musical called 'Wish You Were Here'. It got terrible reviews. Instead of closing it, he announced that he was going to re-rehearse it for a month and then re-open it. He did, and it ran for over two years. I'm not proposing that we should make any announcements. But I am, very strongly, proposing that we should re-rehearse. And that Clifford should be paid for the work involved in re-rehearsal.

K.T.

[1] The blue-movie actress Fiona Richmond had apparently tried to contribute a sketch, which KPT rejected. She wrote in the *Evening Standard* (1 October 1976): 'Mr Tynan reckons this (I hesitate to call it entertainment) is a "guided tour around the wilder shores of love". I reckon that at best it's intellectually pretentious and at worst it's a load of old cobblers.'
[2] See letter of 29 January 1953.

To the Editor, *The Times*[1]

[20 Thurloe Square]
October 29, 1976

Dear Sir,

Whenever the Government pursues policies urged upon it by Trades Union leaders, the press erupts in outrage, complaining that the democratic process is being subverted. The Cabinet has capitulated, we are told, to the brutal economic demands of a small and irresponsible pressure group, not accountable to the electorate at large but concerned merely to further its own interests.

Yet when a much smaller and far more irresponsible pressure group – namely, the foreign holders of sterling, who care nothing for the British electorate and whose self-interest is naked and undisguised – makes even more brutal economic demands (cuts in public spending and welfare, etc), the same newspapers insist that the Government should instantly capitulate to proposals of such transparent sanity and commonsense.

From this a principle emerges. A democratically elected Government must never give in to outside pressure, except when it is exerted by people sympathetic to the basic precepts of Toryism.

Yours sincerely,
KT

[1] Not published.

CHAPTER EIGHT

Exile in Los Angeles

Ken's health as a 'climatic émigré' in Los Angeles rapidly improved. We settled into a sprawling Spanish-style house in Santa Monica, and began to explore the region. Ken was sought out by agents, movie stars, and elderly socialites. More agreeably he found an oasis of friends: among them Tony Richardson, Christopher Isherwood, Gore Vidal, Orson Welles, Joan Didion and John Gregory Dunne. He asked himself what he had done, and, 'more ominously', what he was going to do, to deserve it all. The place confirmed his view that the United States was a country of success for its own sake, and of timing for timing's sake.

He completed his first New Yorker profile, which appeared in February 1977, on the great actor Sir Ralph Richardson. 'Fact, fiction and philosophy is neatly joined together,' Sir Ralph wrote by way of a thank-you. He added, 'An absolutely true portrait would have been damn dull.'

Ken's profile of Tom Stoppard focused on the playwright's work, drawing a parallel with another playwright of Czech origin, the dissident Václav Havel. Havel's plays were 'disturbing mirrors in which one recognised the truth'. 'Stoppard,' he wrote, 'belongs in precisely the same tradition.' Ken's next choice of subject was the talk-show host Johnny Carson, that 'king-sized ventriloquist's dummy' whose Tonight Show he worshipped.

Early in 1977 he went to London to interview Laurence Olivier. There he developed 'flu' which stayed with him on a trip to Madrid (about which he intended to write). On his return to Los Angeles he went to see Dr Elsie Giorgi, who confirmed that he had a rare genetic deficiency by which the elasticity of the lung tissue is destroyed, and life expectancy is inevitably reduced. Dr Giorgi noted two aspects of her new patient: his need to test people – particularly his wife – and his continuing abuse of his lungs with cigarettes. 'He always felt that he was going to live,' she believed, though he complained of and dramatized his condition. After some months of sexual abstinence, he wrote in his journal: 'Bankruptcy, emphysema, paralysis of the will – and now this! I feel that God is making his point with rather vulgar overstatement.'

In May 1977 we sailed from New Orleans to Havana, on a Greek *cruise ship which had been given permission to land briefly in Cuba. In memory of Hemingway Ken took me to visit the writer's finca at San Francisco de Paula, and to the Floridita bar to drink 'Papadobles'.*

By the summer he had begun his third profile, of Mel Brooks, whose manic talent for comedy he had admired since the late 1950s. I returned to England to work on the screenplay of my novel, Agatha, and the marriage became considerably strained, marked by fierce quarrels. Ken wrote to me, 'I am stopped in my tracks, wakeful, trapped at a fork in the road, knowing that if I move forward I shall split on it, as if it were a circular saw ... Counted the faithful pink pills. Only 22 and a half. Not enough. Is this your doing – saving me from myself?'

Early in 1978 he decided to write about the then nearly forgotten silent-screen actress Louise Brooks. At first she refused to see him, but after an exchange of letters in which Ken promised to keep certain information confidential, she gave in: 'What a relief to be able to write to you without the fear of seepage.' She wrote to Ken: 'Deceit enrages me – it destroys the freedom and grace of my mind – and that's all that's in it.' She told him before they met (but after countless telephone conversations) that she was overpowered by feelings of love – 'a sensation I have never experienced with any other man. Are you a variation of Jack the Ripper who finally brings me love which I am prevented from accepting, not by the knife but by old age?' She added that she had never been in love. 'If I had loved a man would I have been faithful to him?' She told Ken that she needed to be alone a great deal, which was why she had made an impossible wife and mistress.

On 2 May 1978, wearing a long leather coat, and bearing a gift of expensive Burgundy, Ken pressed the doorbell of Brooks' apartment, where for three days they talked. So began the friendship of two soulmates. 'I've been killing myself off for twenty years,' she told him, 'and you are going to bring me back to life.'

In February 1979 we moved yet again, from Beverly Hills to a clapboard house deep in Stone Canyon, Bel Air. Olivier, meanwhile, had instructed his friends not to speak to Ken, who had plans to expand his New Yorker profile into a book. Olivier wanted to write his own book, but his manner of refusing an old and admiring friend caused great hurt. Ken had decided to avoid tax on the promised advance by setting up house in Mexico. To this end he and I travelled to Mazatlán and San Blas, ending up at Puerto Vallarta on the Pacific coast, a tourist village surrounded by rich vegetation, with easy access by air to Los Angeles where the children would continue to be schooled.

Installed there, hitched to an oxygen tank, Ken would dictate the odd letter and make half-hearted notes on Olivier. He complained to me that he'd made the wrong decisions: that he should have followed the escape route of Gauguin; that he was only ever happy working as a director; that he'd never had a moment's pleasure from writing. The house he had rented stank of tropical plants, yet it felt as arid as a dustbowl.

In December Ken finalized contracts for his autobiography, payment for which would amount to $250,000. But instead of working on the book he planned Christmas. He went in search of a charro suit for Matthew, and a hat big enough to fit his son's long English head. In January, he abandoned Puerto Vallarta for good.

On 2 March he flew to New York to help publicize a collection of his New Yorker *profiles, called* Show People. *On his last night in New York, an old friend, Jean Stein, asked him to dinner with Norman Mailer, his new wife Norris Church and the film director Milos Forman. Mailer recalled that, despite Ken's emphysema, he was more magnetic that night than he had ever seen him. 'I think he knew that he was near his end. He told a story as well as I've ever heard a story told. He played all the parts. One just had to lay down one's arms and listen. He was incredibly funny.' Less than a fortnight after that dinner Ken was admitted to St John's Hospital in Santa Monica. Thereafter he went from hospital to hospital, while he instructed me to buy the latest Michelin Guide for France, and to book rooms at Talloires on Lake Annecy for mid-July. He told me, 'It's up to you to look after me all the time, and to make me want to live.'*

We unpacked in yet another rented family house, this time in Brentwood. On 26 July Ken was taken unconscious to St John's Hospital in Santa Monica where he died that afternoon. A small funeral service, with his family and friends, was held in Los Angeles, then I took Ken's ashes to England for burial in Oxford, at St Cross Cemetery, behind Magdalen College.

A memorial service was held at St Paul's Church, Covent Garden, in London. At the service Tom Stoppard spoke about Ken's wit, his toughness of mind, his sense that history could be nudged; and of his writing: 'His paragraphs – paragraphs were the units of his prose, not sentences – were written to outlast the witness.' Then he turned to Ken's children and said: 'For those of us ... who shared his time, your father was part of the luck we had.'

To Ralph Richardson

[765 Kingman Avenue
Santa Monica
California 90402]

Sir Ralph at 74: December 19, 1976[1]

Falstaff, Teazle, Bottom, Hirst –
May I be among the first
(Enobarbus, Sheppey, Cherry)
To enfold you in a very
(Richmond, Clitterhouse and Face)
Humble and sincere embrace
(Kent and General Saint-Pé)
As a tribute on this day
(Bluntschli, Sloper and Vershinin)
To the many plays you've been in
(Viscount Pascal, Edward Portal)
Some of which were not immortal
(Collie Stratton, Prospero)
Though you managed to bestow
(Vanya, Brutus and Peer Gynt)
On each one of them a hint
(Gridley, Johnson, Merrygreek)
Of the magic and mystique
(Gaunt, Mercutio, Caliban)
And the oddity of man –
(Bolingbroke and Absolute)
For your birthday, this salute
(Shylock, Captain Hook and Timon)
From yours truly, Kenneth Tynan[2]

With love
from
Ken

[1] KPT's profile in the *New Yorker*, 'At Three Minutes Past Eight You Must Dream', was published in February 1977.
[2] Falstaff: *Henry IV Part 2*; Teazle: Sheridan, *A School for Scandal*; Bottom: *A Midsummer Night's Dream*; Hirst: Pinter, *No Man's Land*; Enobarbus: *Antony and Cleopatra*; Sheppey: Maugham, *Sheppey*; Cherry: Robert Bolt, *Flowering Cherry*; Richmond: *Richard III*; Clitterhouse: Barré Lyndon, *The Amazing Doctor Clitterhouse*; Face: Jonson, *The Alchemist*; Kent: *King Lear*; General

Saint-Pé: Anouilh, *The Waltz of the Toreadors*; Bluntschli: Shaw, *Arms and the Man*; Sloper: Ruth and Augustus Goetz, *The Heiress* (based on Henry James, *Washington Square*); Vershinin: Chekhov, *The Three Sisters*; Viscount Pascal: 'James Bridie', *The Switchback*; Edward Portal: Enid Bagnold, *The Last Joke*; Collie Stratton: Maugham, *For Services Rendered*; Prospero: *The Tempest*; Vanya: Chekhov, *Uncle Vanya*; Brutus: *Julius Caesar*; Peer Gynt: Ibsen, *Peer Gynt*; Sam Gridley: Priestley, *Beer on the Boat Deck*; Johnson: Priestley, *Johnson Over Jordan*; Merrygreek: Udall, *Ralph Roister Doister*; John of Gaunt: *Richard II*; Mercutio: *Romeo and Juliet*; Caliban: *The Tempest*; Bolingbroke: *Richard II*; Sir Anthony Absolute: Sheridan, *The Rivals*; Shylock: *The Merchant of Venice*; Captain Hook: Barrie, *Peter Pan*; Timon: *Timon of Athens*.

To Dr John Henderson[1]

765, Kingman Avenue
January 27, 1977

Dear John,

Kathleen and I have now been here for nearly four months, and the effect on my health has been highly encouraging – infection of chest cleared up, breathing improved, mobility increased, and though the tests I've had done at U.C.L.A.[2] have been VILLAINOUSLY expensive, they've confirmed that I'm not deteriorating, which is nice to know. The temperature today was over 70, if you see what I mean.

There's one problem with which you might be able to help. As you probably know, it's impossible to get Drinamyl[3] in the U.S., and the alternatives available simply don't work with me – they make me jittery, in fact. My mother-in-law, Mrs. Jean Halton (of 14, Oakhill Avenue, London, N.W.3.) is coming to visit us in mid-February, and it would be very helpful if she could bring over some Drinamyl for me. Do you think you could send her a prescription (in my name) for whatever is the maximum permissible amount of the stuff, so that she can bring it with her? I'll be out of England until next year, so I need all I can get; and since I've been taking it now for a quarter of a century without upping the dose, I doubt if I'm likely at this stage to start swallowing handfuls of it. It certainly relaxes me as nothing else does. [...]

We miss English friends, but not English weather. I haven't worn even a raincoat since I arrived in October. If you are ever this way, on some medical junket or other, please let us know and we will show you at least some of this sprawling, astonishing town.

Love from us both –

Yours Ever,
Ken

[1] The late Dr John Henderson was KPT's London general practitioner from 1965, though he deserted Dr Henderson for Dr Ronald Williams 1971–6.
[2] University of California, Los Angeles, which has a renowned Medical Center.
[3] A mixture of sedative and stimulant.

To Laurence Olivier

765 Kingman Avenue
27 January 1977

Dear Larry,

This may not be an altogether welcome piece of information, but I thought I had better warn you that I am going to write an enchanting profile of you for 'The New Yorker'. 'I will not excuse you, sir; you shall not be excused; excuses shall not be admitted; there is no excuse shall serve; you shall not be excused.'[1] The fact is that I'm so pleased with my piece on Ralph [Richardson] – soon to appear – that I couldn't resist going on to do you. It won't, of course, be a full biography or anything like it; chiefly I shall deal with the years at the National.

I'm therefore coming to London at the end of February in the hope of seeing you – not for long, and not with a tape-recorder, but just for memory-refreshing purposes. I'll be in England for the first three weeks of March, and could stay until the end of the month if necessary. After that, however, I have to leave the country and stay out for that all-important income tax year.

What I am asking, therefore, is: will you be in England during March? And, if so, could we meet for a chat?

Do let me know as soon as you have a moment. So many people have asked me to write about you in the past few years that I'm glad, at last, to have decided to do it for the best magazine in the world.

Life is cloudless here in every sense. Your name crops up frequently, as you might expect, especially in dentists' waiting rooms and at Swifty Lazar's parties[2] – which have a great deal in common. The other night the following conversation took place between me and Miss Tatum O'Neal[3] (who cannot be a day over 38):

K T (breaking the ice): Good evening, Tatum.
Tatum: Mnnnh.
K T: I suppose you know everyone in this room, don't you.
Tatum: Yrnnnh.

K T: Is there anyone in the world that you don't know who you'd like to meet? Anybody at all?

Tatum: Nah. (Pause.) Maybe Laurence Olivier? (She ponders deeply for a moment. Long pause. Then she shakes her head.) Nah.

Still, you <u>almost</u> made it.

Kathleen sends love, as does

Yours ever,
Ken

[1] *Henry IV Part 2*, Act V Sc. i.
[2] The agent Irving Lazar, with his wife Mary, gave frequent star-packed parties at their Beverly Hills house.
[3] Tatum O'Neal (b. 1963), child star who won an Academy Award for *Paper Moon* (1973).

To William Shawn

765 Kingman Avenue
February 23, 1977

Dear Mr. Shawn,

I leave tomorrow on my Harvard safari[1] with Johnny Carson. Then on Saturday to London, where I shall (a) see as much of Olivier as I can, hoping to get permission to quote from his many letters and memoranda to me, and (b) establish contact with John Curry, see his 'Theatre of Ice' show and decide whether I think I could make a Profile out of him.

As I told you, I did my research on Madrid about eighteen months ago, and in many ways – especially where the arts and journalism are concerned – the scene has radically changed, so that I shall probably need a week there to bring my facts up to date. Eager, as always, to keep my expenses to a minimum, I've taken a 21-day economy flight to London and back, which means that I can't return to the States before March 20th. Adding a few days in Madrid, I expect to be back here not later than March 27th.

To avoid running up hotel bills in London, I'll be staying in a small rented flat. (My own house of course is rented for a year.) I'll let your secretary know the address as soon as I arrive there.

My Carson research – and, more specifically, the lack of a secretary to help organize my life in California – has impeded the completion of the Tom Stoppard Profile. I've written about 3000 words of it, but – as with the Richardson piece – it will be about two weeks late. I shall mail it to you from London. The recent arrest of the Czech playwright

Václav Havel[2] has given me a new idea for the shape of the piece. Stoppard, as I expect you know, was born in Czechoslovakia. He is Havel's almost exact contemporary; Havel, like Stoppard, is a writer of the dandy type, and many of his plays – absurdist and full of fantastic wordplay – read as if Stoppard could have written them. So I thought I would reconstruct the Profile so that it intercuts between the life of the Czech <u>émigré</u> and the life of the Czech who stayed at home. You may have seen Stoppard's piece in <u>The New York Times</u>[3] a few days ago, protesting against the arrest of Havel and other Czech dissidents.

To sum up: you will receive Stoppard (probably at greater length than you bargained for) in mid-March. Carson will follow at the end of April (shorter, I hope). Then Mel Brooks two months later. Then Madrid. And then Olivier (long, I fear). After that, if they seem to deserve it, Curry and the magician Jimmy Grippo.[4] Incidentally, I talked about Grippo to Orson Welles the other day, and Welles regards him as the best close-up magician alive.

I'll be in touch soon. Meanwhile, thanks again for all your encouragement.

Yours,
Kenneth Tynan

[1] As part of the research for his profile on Johnny Carson, KPT accompanied the talk show host to Boston where, on 24 February 1977, he was being fêted by Harvard's theatre and social club, the Hasty Pudding, as Man of the Year.

[2] On 14 January 1977 Havel was arrested and jailed as one of three designated spokesmen for Charter 77, which urged the Czech government to support the Helsinki Accords of 1975.

[3] 'Dirty Linen in Prague', *New York Times*, 11 February 1977. A letter of protest was also published in the *New York Times* on 17 January, and in *The Times* (London) on 7 February 1977, with Stoppard among the signatories.

[4] Magician and sleight-of-hand virtuoso who performed at Caesar's Palace, Las Vegas.

To Terence Kilmartin

as from
765, Kingman Avenue
March 12 [1977]

Dear Terry,

I'm in London for a couple of weeks (leaving March 19, phone number till then 286-5951), during which time I've chatted to Tom Maschler[1] and have a message for you.

I can't remember if you ever met my Oxford friend Alan Beesley[2] –

a compact, explosive writer whom we all thought, thirty years ago, the nearest thing to a genius in our generation at the university – or whether I mentioned the extraordinary autobiographical book entitled 'Breakdown', which he wrote for Cape, just before committing suicide. I thought it by far the best and most moving account of a total nervous collapse that I'd read, and I wrote an introduction to it for Tom.[3] It was announced in Cape's list a couple of years ago, but the author's brother strongly opposed publication (because he felt it would damage him to be associated with a suicide), and only in the last few months has it become possible to remove the legal obstacles. Cape now intend to bring it out next spring.[4]

Within a few weeks you'll be receiving a proof from Tom. This is to urge you to read it – and to consider devoting one or more review fronts to excerpts. As a study of a pure outsider, a man of enormous energies but no capacity for fitting into any of society's slots, it takes some beating – or equalling. If you wanted to use any of my preface, I wouldn't need any payment.

In some haste and with much affection. (California is marvellous. Every day a large golden disc rises in the sky, exuding heat. People undress and jump into pools of water. It is all very new to me.)

Yours,
Ken

[1] Chairman of Jonathan Cape.
[2] See letters of 19 March 1946 and 5 July 1946.
[3] After Beesley's death in November 1971 KPT added an 'afterword'. Despite his friend's suicide, KPT wrote: 'Buoyancy, verve, and Cagneyish resilience, and a bright, invincible optimism – these were the words that ... summed him up'.
[4] *Breakdown*, though announced for publication under the pseudonym Alane Deane, has never been published.

To Roxana and Matthew Tynan

LONDON
ENGLAND
March, 16, 1977

← ME IN LONDON STANDING IN TYPICAL LONDON PUDDLE.

Dear Roxana and Matthew –

I hope the sun is shining for you and that you are well and bright and merry. The sun in England has disappeared completely. Winds howl all the time like horrible wolves and the rain hits you in the face whenever you go out. I have spent most of my time lurking indoors and missing you both very much. People in England are quite nice but they all look a lot less happy than people in California. I think it is the weather or what they eat that causes the trouble. I am so much looking forward to coming back to America to be with you again.

I have not done anything very interesting except write a bit and talk to a few people, mostly lawyers and businessmen and people like that. (I haven't laughed very much.) The television is better here than it is in America, and the tomatoes taste nicer, but that's about all.

I hope Matthew's ears are o.k. now,[1] and that he is leaping about and playing as happily as ever. I also hope that Roxana is dancing and making music and that you are both being terribly thoughtful and considerate to Hilary and Sheila.[2] Please give them both my love.

I am coming back to Kingman Avenue on Sunday March 27th, probably in the early evening. I can't wait to hug you both and do my silly best to make you laugh. Also give my regards to every one of the fish, not to mention Teddy.

Now – boo-hoo – I have to go out into the TORRENTIAL DOWNPOUR to see ANOTHER DULL LAWYER.

Adios. Au revoir, arrivederci, auf wiedersehen – all of which are foreign ways of saying: SEE YOU SOON.

LOVE FROM
Daddy

---

[1] Matthew suffered from blocked Eustachian tubes.
[2] Hilary Champion was the children's English nanny; Sheila Weeks a Canadian who cooked for the family.

To William Shawn

23A Warrington Crescent
London W.9.
March 18, 1977.

Dear Mr. Shawn,

I thought I'd send you a short progress report. First of all, I'm afraid the sudden move from Californian sunshine to the barbaric English climate had a disheartening effect on my bronchial problems. Within 48 hours of disembarking at London airport I was felled by a bronchial bug, and most of my time since then has been spent in bed and on antibiotics, coughing volcanically. This is maddening if only because it has prevented me from finishing the Stoppard piece, which will now have to wait until I get back to the States. I hope this doesn't disrupt your plans too much.

Meanwhile, I haven't been idle (these bronchial infections fluctuate in their impact from day to day). I've had a couple of excellent sessions with Olivier, who has given me full permission to use all his correspondence with me. I've seen Stoppard several times – enough to give me a new idea for the structure of the piece. John Curry, I fear, is a non-starter, at least as profile material: a nice lad, and his ice-theatre is very pretty, but the personality is pallid, and I can't see any way of writing about him without boring myself.

Tomorrow I go to Madrid for six days to bring my research there up to date. (Address, should you need it: Hotel Victoria, Plaza del Angel

7.) Then back to California on March 27. Stoppard in final form should be with you shortly afterward.¹

Incidentally, the trip to Harvard with J. Carson was very fruitful.

Yours,
Kenneth Tynan

¹ KPT wrote to Shawn on 26 March to explain he'd cut short his stay in Madrid because of a bronchial attack and returned earlier than planned to Santa Monica. A further bulletin on 22 April announced that he was well at last, but did not see how he could deliver six profiles within the year; he also asked for help in extending his visa.

To Marlene Dietrich

[765 Kingman Avenue]
June 28, 1977

Dearest Marlene,

So happy to hear from you. I knew of course about your troubles,¹ and am all the more delighted to note that you now sound as chipper and dauntless as ever. I'm also pleased to see that the Bloody Book² is getting itself written. I remember you mentioned it almost the first time we met, and I shudder to think of the number of publishers' advances you have shamelessly gobbled up since then.³

Titles: none of the ones you suggest seems quite right to me. 'Flashback', as you say, is serviceable but slightly predictable. 'Ghosts I Have Laid' smacks just a <u>leetle</u> of bad taste. Here are one or two others that come to mind – none of them, I fear, anything like the ideal:

'Survivor' (sounds boastful)

'Autograph' (which means an original manuscript as well as a signature)

'The Face I Face' (from that song)

'Mirror Writing'

'Travelling Light'

'All You Need to Know' (sounds churlish: comes from the Keats quotation: 'Beauty is truth, truth beauty: that is all/ You know on earth, and all you need to know.' But it still sounds churlish. How about 'I Enjoy Being a Churl'?)

'Open Secrets'

'Before I Forget'

But I'll go on thinking and the moment anything more promising turns up I'll rush it to you.

Santa Monica is very strange after London. Every morning a large golden disc appears in the sky, exuding heat. People remove their clothes and jump into pools of water. It is all very odd. During the few hours when I am dry, I sit at this typewriter trying to crank out pieces for 'The New Yorker'. We shall probably be here throughout the winter, though I may be passing through Paris in September.[1] If so, I will warn you and we must have dinner.

Love from us both –
[Ken]

[1] Dietrich reported (19 June 1977) from her Avenue Montaigne apartment that she had had an accident in Australia and had been in traction for two months, adding, 'On top of it all my husband died which hit me the hardest.'
[2] She had to write 'this bloody book, because, as usual, I have money-troubles'. She added that she had no one 'to talk, to advise me'. Could KPT help her find a title?
[3] Dietrich wrote back (undated): 'Alas I have had to decide to write instead of sing. How easy singing is (and there is involved, companionship, musicians, lighting-men and all the fun ...) compared with this loneliness which I had never known.'
[4] KPT planned to return to Madrid to finish his research on the city.

To Marlene Dietrich[#]

[765 Kingman Avenue]
August 10, 1977

Dear Marlene,

You're probably right. 'Dietrich by Dietrich' is the best so far.[1]

Did you get my letter about the Notre Dame saga?[2] Reminding you of the imaginary scenario you invented in which your former lovers fly in from all over the world to follow your cortège down the Champs Elysées to Notre Dame? Fairbanks,[3] Gabin,[4] Remarque,[5] etc. And Hemingway pacing up and down outside the door unable to gain admittance to the cathedral. I remember every detail and it could go on for pages.

I think this would be the most elegant and amusing way of referring to your private life without going into the bedroom details.

Incidentally, I have just learned that Swifty Lazar is going to call his biography 'Swifty'. The one thing we must pray is that Dietrich Fisher-Diskau[6] isn't planning an autobiography . . .

Love
[Ken][7]

P. S. Somehow I can't see a book called 'Fisher-Dieskau by Fisher-Dieskau' making the best seller list.

[#] This letter, and others carrying this symbol, have been transcribed from secretarial notebooks, so may not exactly match what was sent.

[1] Dietrich had suggested the title in a letter of 6 August, ' "Dietrich by Dietrich" which is still better than "Marlene", I think. It sounds so conceited to call a book "Marlene" . . . conceit as you know, was never one of my characteristics.' It was eventually published under the title *Thank God I'm a Berliner* in German (1987) and *My Life* in English (1989).

[2] KPT's letter to Dietrich of 18 July had suggested she tell the 'Notre Dame Incident'.

[3] Douglas Fairbanks Jr (b. 1909), American film actor.

[4] Jean Gabin (1904–76), French actor, star of *La Grande illusion* (France, 1937), *Quai des Brumes* (France, 1938), and *Le Jour se lève* (France, 1939).

[5] Erich Maria Remarque (1898–1970), German novelist, known for his war novel *All Quiet on the Western Front* (1929).

[6] Dietrich Fischer-Dieskau (b. 1925), German baritone, one of the foremost interpreters of German Lieder.

[7] Dietrich replied (12 September 1977) with a family story from 'the poor Jews: All the little spermatosones (spelling?) are waiting to be shot off. There is a little one who is running faster than all the others. Suddenly he comes to a screaming stop and yells "Deceipt, Backwards – we are in the ASS . . . that is what your letter spelled out to me. I thought I had a title. But I am "in the ass" once again.'

To Laurence Olivier

765 Kingman Avenue
17 August 1977

Dear Larry –

(1) We have a splendid cook.

(2) We'd love you to see our lush little domain.

(3) I need to have a rambling chat with you for my 'New Yorker' profile, mainly about your frenetic activities since 1973.

(4) Kathleen would love to see you. So would our ornamental carp, not to mention the goldfish.

So please come to dinner – or weekend lunch – as soon as you possibly can. I'm off on a working mission to Spain at the end of September, and I'd like to have finished my research on you by then.

We'll line up another guest to make up four if you like; otherwise just the three of us.

Love,
Ken[1]

[1] Olivier replied (9 September 1977) that he would 'love to have seen your lush little domain' but that he had had to return to England. He provided a 'breakdown outline of my frenetic activities since 1973' for KPT's *New Yorker* profile.

To Bill Davis

765 Kingman Avenue
December 7, 1977

Dear Bill,

I just got back from Madrid where I was amazed to find myself treated as a sort of cultural hero because of the success of 'Oh! Calcutta!',[1] which is the biggest hit in the city. It seems that they read political implications into the nudity. One reporter asked me whether I saw myself as leading a heterosexual revolution in Spain, to which I replied that most of the nightclub shows I had attended were inclined to be homosexual. The result of this was a headline the next day: 'KENNETH TYNAN SAYS ALL SPANISH MEN HOMOSEXUALS'. The concierge at The Suecia was very frosty with me after that and positively threw my keys across the desk at me. Another little journalist kept saying that to him I represented 'might'. I told him I did not believe in might, but he persisted and it took me nearly half an hour to discover that he meant that to him I was a 'myth'.

All in all, though, I find the situation rather lacking in dynamism. It's as if the gates of the Bastille were open, but nobody wanted to storm it. Forty years of Franco and the tourist boom have really anaesthetized the Spanish people. It seems to me that nobody wants a revolution because it would frighten the tourists away and destroy the economy beyond repair. After all, Franco died in his bed: nobody pushed him. My gloomiest prediction is that in five years Madrid will be Düsseldorf with bullfights.

We'll be here until next spring, after which I want to spend the summer in Spain, preferably in the neighbourhood of Mojácar, which I lately visited for the first time. I'm in touch with an estate agent there, but if you have any private contacts in the area, I'd love to know of them. What we need is a villa with roughly two reception rooms, three bedrooms, one study, kitchen, and two bathrooms, either in Mojácar itself or in a secluded position nearby. I'd be prepared to take it for six months.

Love to Annie and G. Brenan[2] if you see him.

Love,
Ken

[1] Playing at the Teatro Principe in Madrid.
[2] Gerald Brenan (1894–1987) English travel writer, Hispanophile and novelist who lived near Bill Davis.

To Marlene Dietrich

765, Kingman Avenue
January 13, 1978

Dearest M –

Much as I'd love to come to Paris,[1] my 'New Yorker' work will keep me here until at least April; and in any case my health won't let me return to Europe before then. But I'm usually awake and functioning by 10 a.m. Californian time, which is 7 p.m. your time, so after that hour you can normally reach me.

A few more notes on what you sent me,[2] some important, some trifling, in no particular order:

A. Insist on your $50,000 immediately. Tell Nizer[3] that if he won't, you will, and shoot off a firm note to Putnam's asking why they have failed to fulfil their obligation. (Has Nizer done anything, by the way?)

B. Page 1 of preface: 'I, personally, am not interested to tell about my life. But as there seems to be a vast interest ...' Dear Marlene, please do not sound so grudging. You really cannot start out a book by saying you have no interest in writing it. The reader's reaction will be: 'So why should I be interested in reading it?' Also, if you'll pardon the expression, it sounds a touch arrogant.

C. AVOID PRINTING WORDS IN CAPITAL LETTERS. It's too melodramatic. If you want to add emphasis, just underline the key words or put them in quotes. (E.g. 'fame', not 'FAME'; no diaries, not NO DIARIES.) This is important.

D. Contrary to what you say, the facts (not FACTS) <u>do</u> matter. Part of your purpose in writing the book is to set the record straight.

E. Page 2 of preface: ' ... the white skin that is the red-head's priority.' I think you mean something like 'birthright'. I mention this because there are hundreds of little wrong notes of this kind in the text, all of which could easily be put right by a good editor. (Same goes for spellings like 'Marocco'.)

F. Try not to have paragraphs that are only one or two sentences long. Run them together into longer blocks of prose. It looks less scrappy. Here again, any competent editor could do this for you with no difficulty.

G. You say you 'hate anecdotes'. Please don't. One's life is an extended anecdote. And you can tell good anecdotes very well, such as the story about the Texan and the crabs.[4]

H. A personal note: I'm sorry you admire Richard Burton's writing so much.[5] I promise you it's really flabby, like Dylan Thomas with all of the alcohol and none of the genius. However ...

I. Childhood section: I liked all this very much. It was new to me and beautifully remembered. But there are certain essential facts we need to know from the beginning – what city we are in, what your father's job was, and (yes) when you were born.

J. Page 43: 'I often think that being revolutionary is just a matter of no opinion at all.' This simply doesn't hold water. Whatever you may think of Lenin or Brecht or Rosa Luxemburg,[6] they certainly had very strong and precise opinions, and not just negative ones, either. This passage makes you sound politically a bit naive, which is a pity. You say: 'Don't just destroy what you don't like.' But surely it would have been worth while to 'just destroy' Hitlerism in 1939? This brings me to a general point. Later on, when you describe how you always did exactly what the dictator von Sternberg[7] told you, and how the actor's job is to obey the supreme commander, people may draw a parallel between your <u>artistic</u> obedience and the <u>political</u> obedience the German nation gave to Hitler. I think you should be careful of this. Perhaps add something to the effect that the German quality of respect for authority has its bad side.

K. When you decide[d] to go on the stage, didn't your socially well-connected family raise any objections?

L. Similar to (C): never use more than one ! or ? at a time. It's over-emphatic.

M. About the matter of 'no trespassing' (on your private life). I know you want to protect your husband and Maria;[8] and I am <u>not</u> suggesting detailed descriptions of erotic wrestling matches, etc. But there are discreet ways of indicating that your relationships with (say) von Sternberg, Remarque and Gabin were different from your relationship with (say) Paustovsky.[9] You tell me: 'Nobody of any stature ever related with whom they slept.' Well, Stendhal did; and so did Boswell and Samuel Pepys and Jean-Jacques Rousseau and Bertrand Russell. It's true that some of these were writing private journals, not intended for publication; all the same, their candour has not injured their reputations. You will help us to understand you if we know the kind of men who attracted you physically as well as intellectually. You will also help us to <u>like</u> you. Otherwise we wonder: why so much space on a writer like Remarque? What is she hiding? And we may start to imagine things much worse than the plain romantic truth. 'He attracted me because' is just as respectable as 'I admired him because ...' So why not say it? I remember one evening you told me the depth of your feeling for Gabin and how much you agonised over his demand that, if you were to stay together, your career must come second to his. It was a very moving story. Your book needs it.

N. I stupidly stopped making notes of page numbers, but somewhere you name Phyllis Haver, Evelyn Brent and Georgia Hale[10] among the 'stars' created by von Sternberg. I've never heard of any of them. Another trivial point: you describe Orson as 'young' when in fact, incredible as it may seem, he is now 62!

O. Elsewhere you launch a tough attack on 'bookworms' and 'professors'. I've forgotten the context; but the attack sounds somehow unpleasant, especially coming from someone like you, who admires intelligence so whole-heartedly. One of the best editors I ever worked for once warned me: 'Never take the anti-intellectual side in an argument. You'll find that most of the people who applaud you will be people you hate.' He was quite right.

P. Tiny point: I didn't understand why you were so scared by dancing with Walter Wanger[11] at the speakeasy. This isn't clear.

Q. The whole portrait of von Sternberg is superb and definitive. Your picture of him is better than the one in his own book.[12]

R. I can't recall whether you mention the Lubitsch film 'Angel'.[13] (I mention this for no other reason than that I'm going to see it again next week. There's a Dietrich movie playing somewhere in L.A. every night of the week.)

S. Putnam's may be worried about what you say <u>à propos</u> of the G.I.'s feeling let down by the country to which they came back after the war. Don't let them influence you on this. It's a powerful argument and well worth stating, even though it may not endear you to the great American public.

*   *   *   *   *

These are scrappy notes, written far too long after reading the script. To sum up: I think you are at your best when recounting factual events in which you were personally involved, whether in pre-Hitler Germany or Hollywood or wartime France. My advice is to devote yourself to this kind of thing, and to spend less time on generalisations (for example, the section on the importance of friendship). Generalisations are anyone's property. What happened specifically to you is uniquely yours, and that is where your strength lies. That is your territory; that is what gives the book its weight. If you are frank with us, we will trust you. If not – if we feel you are holding us at arm's length – we may suspect that you don't trust <u>us</u>. And a reader must feel trusted.

Finally: a little more about people you <u>didn't</u> like or admire would not come amiss! A pantheon of gods is very nice, but there's room for a rogue's gallery as well. (The portrait of Jannings,[14] for instance, is wickedly good.) I know you didn't dislike Garbo, but a word or two about her would be very illuminating: the pair of you reigned side by side, and to leave her out would be like a book by Duse[15] that didn't mention Bernhardt.

No more to say, except that I can't wait to read Part Two.

If I can find a reasonable villa, I hope to spend May-to-October in South-East Spain. Perhaps I could pass through Paris en route.

Meanwhile, continue to hit those keys, avoiding only the capital shift-lock and restraining the temptation to multiply ? into ???

Kathleen joins me in sending megatons of love.

Ever,
Ken

---

[1] Dietrich suggested that her publishers would pay to bring KPT to Paris.
[2] On 6 December 1977 Dietrich had sent the MS that she had delivered to G. P. Putnam's Sons in New York.
[3] Louis Nizer, Dietrich's lawyer at Phillips, Nizer, Benjamin, Krim and Ballon.
[4] Dietrich, *My Life*, pp. 188–90.
[5] Dietrich had read Burton's *Christmas Story* (1965).
[6] Rosa Luxemburg (1871–1919), German Communist, co-founder of the Spartacus League with Karl Liebknecht, she was murdered after an unsuccessful Communist uprising in 1919.
[7] Josef von Sternberg (1894–1969), German film director who first worked with Dietrich on *The Blue Angel* (Germany, 1930). He also directed many of Dietrich's first Hollywood films, including *Shanghai Express* (US, 1932) and *The Scarlet Empress* (US, 1934).

[8] Rudolf Sieber, with whom she had a daughter Maria, later an actress known as Maria Riva. She wrote a biography of her mother, *Marlene* (1992).

[9] Konstantin Paustovsky (1892–1968), Soviet novelist, author of the six-part *Story of a Life* (1945–63); Dietrich greatly admired his story 'The Telegram'.

[10] Phyllis Haver (1899–1960), American silent-screen actress; Evelyn Brent (1899–1975), American film actress who starred in von Sternberg's *Underworld* (US, 1927) and *The Last Command* (US, 1928); Georgia Hale (b. 1906), American film actress, star of von Sternberg's first film, *The Salvation Hunters* (US, 1925).

[11] Walter Wanger (1894–1968), American producer whose films include *Queen Christina* (US, 1934) and *Invasion of the Body Snatchers* (US, 1956). See Dietrich, *My Life*, p. 64.

[12] His autobiography, *Fun in a Chinese Laundry* (1965).

[13] *Angel* (US, 1937), romantic comedy directed by Ernst Lubitsch and co-starring Herbert Marshall and Melvyn Douglas.

[14] Emil Jannings (1885–1950), German actor who played opposite Dietrich in *The Blue Angel*.

[15] Eleonora Duse (1859–1924), Italian actress whose reputation rivalled that of Sarah Bernhardt. Shaw championed her when she and Bernhardt both appeared in Herman Suderman's *Heimat* (retitled *Magda* in English) in London in 1895.

On Sunday morning 8 January 1978, while flipping through the television guide, Ken saw that at 1 p.m., on Channel 28, Louise Brooks would be appearing in a 1929 silent movie by G.W. Pabst called Pandora's Box, *based on the Wedekind play. He had seen it twice before and would eagerly watch it again.*

The film brought back all his infatuation for Miss Brooks, and he wrote in his journal: 'She runs through my life like a magnetic thread, this shameless urchin tomboy, this unbroken, and unbreakable porcelain colt. This Fairie Princess ... creature of impulse, unpretentious temptress capable of dissolving into a fit of giggles at a romantic climax, amoral but selfless, Lesbian and hetero, with that sleek black cloche of hair that rings so many bells in my memory ... the only star actress I can imagine either being enslaved to or wanting to enslave.'

To William Shawn

765 Kingman Avenue
Jan. 16, 1978

Dear Mr. Shawn,

Many thanks for the cheque covering my expenses for the Carson piece.

I'm slightly embarrassed to bring up another money matter so soon, but here goes. While I was in Madrid last November, doing my research on the city, I rented a car from a company called 'Europcar', not only to get around Madrid itself, but to make a tour of the fantastic constellation of towns and villages – e.g., Toledo, Segovia, El Escorial, Avila, Aranjuez, La Granja, Chinchon and the beautifully named Madrigal de las Altas Torres (birthplace of Queen Isabel, 'mother of America') – by which the city is encircled. None of these, except the last, is more than an hour's drive from Madrid, and one of the points I want to make in the piece (which will follow Mel Brooks to your desk) is that no other capital city in the world has such a remarkable necklace of satellites. At all events, car rentals are expensive in Spain, and I enclose the American Express charge [...]

To change the subject: does the name of Louise Brooks[1] mean anything to you? She was a silent movie star, first in the States and later in Germany, where she made a couple of classic films for Pabst ('Pandora's Box' and 'Diary of a Lost Girl'). I've always thought of her as the most beautiful woman – with the possible exception of Garbo – who ever illuminated the screen; and – with no exceptions at all – the most sexually attractive.

Seeing 'Pandora's Box' again the other day prompted me to do a little research. It seems that she is now living alone in Rochester, N. Y., mainly to be near the Eastman Institute of Photography, which has a nearly complete collection of her films. She is in her early 70's, lives in modest circumstances (but not penury) and is prevented from travelling by severe arthritis. She writes occasional articles for specialist movie magazines and seems, by all accounts, to be a woman of strong opinions and total recall. Would the magazine be interested in a casual, dealing with a trip to Rochester to meet this unlikely survivor from the classic era of the European Cinema? (She was born and raised, of course, in the u.s. – Wichita, I believe.)

I look forward to hearing from you.[2] This piece, if you wanted it, would follow Madrid and precede Olivier.

Yours sincerely,
Kenneth Tynan

[1] Louise Brooks (1906–85) started as a dancer with the Denishawn Company and made her Hollywood debut in 1925. Her best work was for the German director G. W. Pabst, for whom she starred in *Pandora's Box* and *Diary of a Lost Girl* (1929). After the French film *Prix de Beauté* (1930), directed by Augusto Genina, she returned to America where her career went into steady decline. She retired in 1938.
[2] Shawn responded enthusiastically to the idea of a Brooks profile rather than a 'casual'.

To Louise Brooks

The *New Yorker*
February 6, 1978

Dear Miss Brooks,

You probably don't know me, but I'm an English writer and author who used to be drama critic for the London 'Observer'. I also worked for ten years as Laurence Olivier's assistant at the National Theatre of Great Britain.

Last year I came to the States to work for 'The New Yorker'. The editor invited me over to write a series of profiles of people whose work I admired. To come to the point as quickly as possible. I have been an admirer of yours ever since I first saw 'Pandora's Box' many years ago: and when I saw it again the other day on TV, my admiration for you was rekindled as strongly as ever. I immediately telephoned the editor of The New Yorker and found that he, too, has long been a Louise Brooks fan. I proposed that I should explore the possibility of writing a piece about you, and he readily agreed.

I am at present working on another profile in California, but I expect to be coming East after the end of March. Would it be possible for me to come and talk to you in Rochester sometime in early April? If we could spend a couple of sessions talking about your life and work, I would be very much gratified.

I would also be glad of a chance to see some of your American movies;[1] as of course you know, prints of them are very hard to obtain. If you agree to let me talk to you, I will write to Mr. Pratt at the International Museum of Photography[2] to find out whether it would be possible to arrange some showings for me. Perhaps you could tell me which are your favourites, so that I can make a special request for these. I would appreciate it if you could let me know fairly soon whether my proposal appeals to you. Unfortunately, I have to leave for Europe on a long trip in late April, and it would be useful to know well in advance whether I am going to have the pleasure of meeting you before I depart.

I look forward very much to hearing from you.

Yours sincerely,
Kenneth Tynan
[...]

---

[1] These include *A Girl in Every Port* (US, 1928), directed by Howard Hawks, and *Beggars of Life* (US, 1928), directed by William A. Wellman.

[2] George Pratt, a curator of the George Eastman House, a museum of cinematography started after World War II in Rochester N.Y. and renamed in 1972 the International Museum of Photography.

To William Shawn

765 Kingman Avenue
February 9, 1978

Dear Mr Shawn,

Now that Carson is finally in the bag, may I bring up a couple of questions – of no special urgency, but perhaps worth raising now so that you can consider them at leisure?

(1) Assuming I can readjust to writing without cigarettes, I expect to send you my first draft of the Mel Brooks profile by the end of March. Early in April, I hope to spend a few days in Rochester, N.Y., talking to Louise Brooks and seeing some of her movies. (Did you know, by the way, that she once appeared in the [Ziegfeld] Follies with W. C. Fields?) After that, it would be nice to come to New York for a week or two. But after that, I'd very much like to go to Europe for a while – partly because I have to cope with some financial matters (e.g. the re-letting of my house in London, which will be tenantless from June onward); partly because I can write the Madrid and Olivier pieces just as easily in Europe as here; and partly because I'd like a holiday. Would you, in short, mind if I spent the summer in Europe? (Completely at my own expense, of course.) The main problem from your point of view, I imagine, would be that this would entail doing the editorial process on Mel (and perhaps Louise) Brooks over the transatlantic telephone. As you may recall, however, we did this with the Nicol Williamson piece, and it seemed to work.

(2) A more premature question, to which I don't expect anything like an immediate response. Do you think it likely that the magazine might want to retain my services for a third year (beginning in September, 1978)?[1] I ask, firstly, because there's nothing that would please me more; secondly, because it's never too early to start applying for visa extensions; and thirdly, because my lease on the Santa Monica house expires in the summer, and (since I suspect the owner plans to raise the rent beyond my means) I shall have to find alternative accommodation before too long.

I'll look forward to hearing from you. Rereading this letter, I discover that there is, in fact, some slight urgency about the first question, because, if you agree to my summer plan, I would need to start looking for a Mediterranean dwelling-place pretty soon.

Yours sincerely,
Kenneth Tynan

[1] Shawn agreed to extend KPT's services.

To Louise Brooks

The *New Yorker*
February 22, 1978

Dear Miss Brooks,
   This is to confirm in print what we discussed on the phone yesterday:[1]

1) It is understood between us that the piece I want to write is a celebration of, and tribute to, your work in movies. It will be relatively short – not more than about five thousand words – and in no sense a full length biographical profile.

2) I undertake not to question anyone about your private life,[2] with which I am not concerned.

3) I will send the manuscript to you for your scrutiny and comments as soon as it is completed. The piece will be published only if it meets with your approval.

4) I will come to Rochester sometime in April to visit you and to see as many of your movies as I can persuade the Eastman people to show me. I leave it to you to decide whether you would prefer our chat to be tape-recorded. If so, I could arrange for a copy of the tape to be sent to you, so that you would have a safeguard against misquotation.

   I hope to hear from you soon. Meanwhile, thank you for talking to me yesterday. For me, at least, it was an exciting experience.

Yours sincerely,
Kenneth Tynan

[1] KPT had discovered Louise Brooks' telephone number via her friend the actor Roddy McDowall.

[2] KPT knew that Louise Brooks received a small monthly stipend of some $700 from the Paley Foundation. She had had an affair with William Paley, the founder of CBS, in the late 1920s and when she fell on hard times he offered to help. Behind the front of his Foundation he had helped to support her since 1954. Ken rightly guessed that Brooks feared Paley might disapprove of publicity.

To Sara Lippincott Spencer[1]

S. Monica
Cal 90402
Feb. 13, 1967 [1978]

Dear Sara –

Thanks for the clip and staff intelligence info. Will withhold latter from S.[2] Your secret is safe with M.* I have deliberately misdated this letter in order to throw dust in the eyes of unauthorised readers. This dust is for their eyes only. In addition, I am writing these lines by hand in order to avoid laying ourselves open to forgery by typewriter. Would-be forgers by hand will also be confounded because certain words (never ask me which) are not in my normal hand-writing. This should pull the wool over their eyes, already smarting from sand.

Eat this letter before burning it.

Vôtre
K.T.

* Me.

[1] *New Yorker* magazine checker.
[2] The editor, William Shawn.

To Louise Brooks

[765 Kingman Avenue]
20 March 1978

Dear Louise,

I can't tell you how blue I've been since our last phone call.[1] Such a sadness. This is just to tell you that I shall be going ahead and writing a piece about your movies, which George Pratt is arranging to show me on May 1, 2, and 3. So I shall be in Rochester for that period.

One thing that makes me especially sad is that you allowed Roddy [McDowall][2] to photograph you and let my old friend, Rickie Leacock[3] film a whole interview with you. Yet I, who only wanted a crust of home-baked bread, am excluded from the presence. Heigh-ho ...

Anyway, such are my plans. One thing is certain: I am not looking forward to not seeing you.

Do call me collect any time you feel like a chat. I miss you.

Yours,
[Kenneth Tynan]

[1] Brooks told KPT, after a number of lively and forthcoming telephone conversations, that she could not agree to be interviewed.
[2] McDowall (b. 1928) has published several volumes of his photographs, including *Double Exposure* (1966).
[3] Richard Leacock (b. 1921), documentary filmmaker.

To Simon Michael Bessie

[765 Kingman Avenue]
March 24, 1978

Dear M,

Bless you for your letter about my Carson piece.[1] At present, The New Yorker have me under indefinite contract to turn out profiles, one of which will be a monster on Laurence Olivier. I hope that this will form the backbone of my book on the National Theatre.[2] California is treating my lungs well, though I am not, and this means that I operate at a fairly low energy level. People tend to find me on all fours rather than the bipedal posture proper to our species. I lie down whenever I work up the energy to climb into bed.

Even this letter, as you will see from the lack of errors, is being typed by a third person.

I am off – the man in the Whirlwind Wheelchair – for a quick trip to Spain next month. In fact, I may not be back till the fall. It would be nice to see you.

Yours ever,
[Ken]

[1] 'Fifteen Years of the Salto Mortale', *New Yorker,* 20 February 1978.
[2] KPT still owed Bessie an autobiographical book on the theatre.

To Peter Vukasin[1][#]

[765 Kingman Avenue]
March 28, 1978

Dear Mr. Vukasin,

I have received a letter from Mr. J.Greenfield,[2] whose book 'Wilhelm Reich vs. The U.S.A.' I read some years ago.

I do not wish to sound intrusive, but I would find it strange indeed if Mr. Greenfield's interest in the work of Reich should in any way militate against his academic advancement. As the years pass, the respect of the intellectual community for Reich's achievements seems to increase rather than diminish. Though many of his findings, especially in the paranoid final decade of his life, do not bear close scientific scrutiny, the questions he asked still seem to me to be central to the problems of the 20th century. I mean, especially his attempts to bridge the gap between Marx and Freud, and his pioneering work in the realm of psychosomatic medicine, which was in itself an attempt to bridge the gap between mind and body. I could imagine few figures of our time better worthy of our study and attention.

Forgive me for taking up your time, and thank you for bearing with me.

Yours sincerely,
[Kenneth Tynan]

[1] Vice-President for Academic Affairs at the State University of New York.
[2] Jerome Greenfield (b. 1923), a professor of English and Creative Writing at the State University of New York, was concerned that his book *Wilhelm Reich versus the USA* (1973) might hinder his chances of promotion, and had asked KPT and others for letters of recommendation. KPT sent him a carbon of this letter with a note saying 'I hope the enclosed may be of some help.'

To William Shawn

765 Kingman Avenue
April 7, 1978

Dear Mr. Shawn,

Two things, one short and simple, the other tangled:

(1) Mel Brooks. I've done 15,000 words and still have to tackle his film career. I'm hoping to get him finished before I go to see Louise Brooks

at the end of April, but after that I go almost immediately to Spain, so it's possible that I may have to polish it off there. (Of course I'll deal with Miss B. far more briefly.) I'll let you know my Spanish address before I leave.

(2) I'm enclosing herewith the first draft of the first half of my study of Wilhelm Reich. As you may recall, it started life as a series for 'The New Yorker' and then snowballed into a book. In 1974 or thereabouts, after writing the first half, which deals mainly with Reich's life before he came to the States in 1939, I shelved the project – partly because I felt overwhelmed by the sheer mass of work that lay ahead, and partly because I needed money and someone invited me to write a film.[1]

I had signed a joint agreement with two publishers[2] – one in England, the other here – whereby they could bring out the finished book after it (or parts of it) had appeared in the magazine, or if the magazine turned it down.

I thought the whole thing had been indefinitely postponed. Now, however, the publishers have read this chunk of MS. (it's about 72,000 words) and – to my amazement – they want to bring it out as it stands, with the addition of a brief final chapter explaining that in the States Reich became paranoid, went to prison and died.

I'm against this, because I don't think the MS. stands up in its uncompleted form, and also because Reich's American years (on which I have a great deal of hitherto unpublished material) were to have formed the climax of the book. I wouldn't mind it appearing as Vol. One of a two-volume biography – part two would be roughly the same length as part one – but the publishers don't like this idea. On the other hand, if I refuse to let them publish I shall have to return my advance of $16,000,[3] which I can't afford to do.

My point in writing, therefore, is to ask whether you would find time to look at the MS. (It's a less than perfect photocopy, I'm afraid, but the original hasn't yet arrived from England.) The latter part of it gets far too minutely involved in scientific details. But I'd be grateful to know whether you think – in a truncated form and with the unwritten American section completed – it would be of interest to the magazine. Bear in mind that it's an unrevised draft, and that the American section, still to come, will probably have a more obvious appeal to your readers.

If you are interested, I could go ahead and finish the book – after doing Mel Brooks, Louise B., Madrid and Olivier. Realistically speaking, I think this would mean delivery of the final MS. to you some time next year. The publishers, however, are impatient and won't wait any longer: either they go ahead and publish now, or they want their money back. So I'm caught in a dilemma.

One possible solution would be for the magazine to advance me the $16,000. I would thus be able to repay their money and sell the book elsewhere, always with the proviso that 'The New Yorker' has the right to prior serialisation. I could then repay your $16,000 out of whatever advance I got from the new publisher.

If you decide that the magazine isn't interested, I don't see how I can prevent the present publishers from forging ahead. In that case, of course, the serial rights would revert to them. I would much prefer any solution that enabled my work to be brought to birth in the pages of 'The New Yorker'. To lay my cards on the table, I have no future plans as a writer in which the magazine does not take priority. If you wanted a written assurance that, for any number of years you care to mention, I would contribute to no other American magazine without your permission, I would not only be flattered to death, I would sign it without any mention of money.

God! Please forgive all these complexities. I only hope I've explained the situation clearly. The immediate necessity is to get your opinion on the stuff I've enclosed. I needn't add that, even if you don't find it acceptable, the statements I've made in the previous paragraph would still hold good.

I'll hold the publishers off until I hear from you. If you can possibly give me a ring before the end of the month, it would be a great boon.

Thanks for bearing with me.

Yours,
Kenneth Tynan

[1] *Our Life With Alex and Sophie.*
[2] Jonathan Cape (UK) and Holt Rinehart and Winston (US), for *A Very Strange Tale of Real Life Adventure.*
[3] The first third of the US advance.

To Arthur Miller

765 Kingman Avenue
April 26, 1978

Dear Arthur,

Sorry to be a pest, but I have a small favour to ask. In order to go on working here for 'The New Yorker', I'm applying for an immigrant visa. The application form has to be accompanied by brief statements from eminent chaps, testifying that I have achieved 'national or international recognition' as a writer and journalist.

I'd be enormously grateful if you could spare a moment to cook up a few lines in support of this grotesque claim. The idea is to make my presence here like an immense boon for the United States ...

I'm leaving the States in a few days to spend three months in Europe, so if you feel able to come up with anything, the best plan would be to send it to my lawyer in Los Angeles, who is handling the application for me. [...]

Apparently these things take time to go through the bureaucratic process, so the sooner [he] can file the papers, the better. If you're too busy, I shall quite understand. Otherwise, many, many thanks.[1]

Yours ever,
Ken

[1] Miller provided the character reference.

To Tom Maschler

[765 Kingman Avenue]
April 27, 1978

Dear Tom,

In reply to your letter of April 11: 'The New Yorker', as I expected, wouldn't want to publish extracts from the Reich book until the American section is completed. Nor, I suspect, would any other magazine or newspaper, since the most obviously dramatic episodes of his life are the events leading up to his trial, imprisonment and death in jail. In other words, to publish what I have now would mean killing off any chance of serialisation. To kiss goodbye to such a source of income – and of publicity for the book – would be plain crazy.

Though Mr. Shawn is eager to see the finished work, he didn't suggest a deadline. As you know, 'The New Yorker' seldom does.

Until we get a reaction from Holt, Rinehart we clearly can't make a final decision. Meanwhile, my feelings are these:

(1) I don't want the manuscript to appear in its present form, for the reasons given above.

(2) As I've already pointed out, I'm under no legal obligation to return the advance.[1]

(3) Since I can't guarantee a delivery date for the finished product, the best plan – on both sides and with many regrets all round – might very well be to let the contract lapse.

Let me know your reflexions on this sad conclusion.

My best,
[Ken Tynan]
[...]

---

[1] Holt, Rinehart and Winston, under their new owner CBS, would eventually sue for repayment of the advance. $5,000 was repaid under a settlement agreement of 14 August 1980.

While Ken was in Spain, I flew to London to rent our London house, and returned to Los Angeles to pack up our house there and look for other accommodation for the autumn. I felt under a good deal of pressure, both emotional and financial. We were separated for two months, the longest – and coolest – spell apart of our married life. Our reconciliation on my arrival in Spain with the children on 1 July was extremely affecting for us both.

To Kathleen Tynan

c/o Roger Bush,
Apartado 71,
Garrucha, Almeria,
Spain
[May 21, 1978]

Dear K,

You will by now have heard of my mishaps. Took off from Rochester (after three prostrating days with Louise B.); plane grounded for mechanical defect, then cancelled, too late to make my JFK connection to Paris. I throw giant wheelchair fit, claiming I have been waiting three months for life-or-death appointment with Paris doctor who is leaving for Karachi following night and has granted me his last date. This has its effect and I am rushed on to plane for Buffalo, thence to Toronto, where it is discovered that my seven pieces of baggage, due to heroic speed of operation, are not aboard. I am wheeled, cornering at 70 m.p.h., on to KLM flight to Amsterdam. (Have omitted to mention that Buffalo–Toronto plane was also a substitution – Allegheny Airlines flight to JFK, on which I had been rebooked, had <u>also</u> been cancelled, due to explosion of port engine. Note that all Allegheny Airline employees have crazed eyes [...], and apologise even when telling you the time of the next cancellation. Announcements, when audible over Tannoy, sound like: 'Allegheny Airlines are pleased to announce the safe cancellation of the Flight 2112A to Cleveland. Free oxygen will be served in the Amelia Earhart Memorial Discotheque.') Flight to Amsterdam arrives too late for me to make connection with Garuda Indonesian Airways (<u>yes</u>) to Paris, and staff informs me that due to confusion between my name and elderly Pole named Szynanski, travelling from Dallas to visit his grandchildren, my luggage has been sent to Warsaw. I reach Paris on another KLM flight, to be told that my bags will be returned from Poland via Air Canada within 48 hours.

You may well titter to hear that Allegheny have made arrangements to fly me on to Karachi free of charge to see the French doctor about whom I made the giant fuss in Rochester. Would I like my luggage sent there? All this has to be disentangled before I reach Paris hotel, where Dacia¹ has been waiting for four and a half hours.

Back at de Gaulle next day. No sign of luggage. Am sent from one bland official to another (unable to smoke because of story about French doctor) and, just as am on verge of real collapse, darling Air Canada girl turns up pushing trolley containing my baggage. Fall to me knees and pray to C. S. Lewis. Rush to American Express to collect cash for summer, arrive with three minutes to spare and find queue forty yards long of similar applicants. Throw another wheelchair fit and get money. Retrieve Jaguar from vast underground car park near Etoile, where Dacia has left it. And discover that power steering has broken down. Car plus luggage is of course undrivable without power steering. Take it to three Jag. depots in Paris for repair. All tell me that because car is right-hand drive, spare part is unobtainable in France and must be sent from England. This will take at least four days. Dacia sets wheels in motion to have missing piece sent over air-freight, after endless cross-Channel phone calls and synchronised watch-settings. Then blessedly proud French Jaguar expert rises to challenge and calls to tell me that he has combed Paris and found genuine righthand-drive Jaguar spare part. I rush out by cab and test his word. By blue, the fellow has reason! The machine marches! I pay through the little grey nose and zoom out of town toward Lyon, only three days late.

Am bowling along autoroute at 100 mph about two days afterwards with no ill effects except screaming migraine from 4 a.m. to 8 a.m. every morning when SCRUNGE-UPPITY-SCRUNGE-UPPITY-CRANG-CRANG-CRANG-PHUT. The car bumps, shudders, rocks, stops and won't start. Some unidentified jagged metal object has torn front left tyre to shreds. Traffic is heavy. Car has to be pushed through hail of oncoming Volkswagens and Juggernauts to accident lane. All luggage must be removed from boot to gain access to spare tyre and repair kit. Temperature is roughly 88 degrees. Spare tyre contains about as much air as my left lung. Change takes approximately ninety minutes. I roll delicately along nearly flat new tyre to next service station, where attendant gallantly accepts tip of fifty francs to pump air into it. He says all other tyres have too much air and before I can stop him he lets half of it out. Only trouble now is that (a) I have no spare tyre (only obtainable in England, etc) and (b) irked by my berserk reaction on seeing him emptying air from tyres, he slams front bonnet down so hard that it CANNOT BE OPENED, thus making it impossible to add water or oil to engine. (This is still the case.)

Some of this has now been put right, but I still have no spare tyre; and for a week after the 1800-mile trip I could not sleep after 4 a.m. because of head-splitting ache – which has taught me never to attempt a journey of such length again without another driver to share the burden.

Which brings me to Mojácar

(1) The villa is fine. Not chic. Too close to other similar villas. But a large living-dining-room with adjoining kitchen, two double bedrooms (each with bathroom), single bedroom (which I've appropriated as study), and a tower room with spiral staircase and two beds which R. and M. could have if they preferred it to the ground-floor one. Garage. Garden of untended scrub (about 100 yards square). Excellent beach at bottom of road (roughly 100 yards away) with good adjoining café complete with umbrellas, beach-beds and food like sausage and bacon, chile con carne. Whole of our roof is sun-bathing area and there's a patio. Dozens of beaches nearby, including a nude one and several topless. Large swimming-pool, to which we have access, about a kilometre away. Butane gas, delivered weekly! Excellent laundry nearby. Roger Bush[2] eagerly helpful and highly mechanical (knows all about cars, transformers, etc.). BUT the price is exactly twice what he quoted. He blames this on the American owner of the house and the fact that Mojácar has suddenly become the smart place for the upper-middle-class <u>Spanish</u> tourist to spend his vacation. (It's about the only place

left – driving down the coast from Barcelona was a nightmare.) Instead of 15,000 pesetas – = 100 pounds a month – in high-season months of July and August, it's 30,000 pesetas, precisely twice as much. Similarly, it's 20,000 pesetas – 133 pounds a month – in May, June and September, as against the promised 66 pounds. I've protested, and I feel slightly put-upon! On the other hand, everywhere else is taken, and this really does seem to be the year in which Mojácar has taken off. Yet the provincial authorities still insist – rather à la Aga Khan[3] – on no buildings taller than two storeys and all designs to conform to local style of architecture, which makes them unique in Spain. There is no large hotel or highrise block for fifty miles in any direction. One is still getting excellent value for money.

(2) More serious: since arriving here, I've bought the 1978 Spanish Michelin. I had worked out the cost of our two-week Northern pilgrimage on the basis of the 1976 Michelin. The price-change since devaluation of the peseta in 1977 has been stratospheric. For example: of the places we'd planned to visit, a double room in Burgos has risen from 2100 pesetas to 3300. In Leon, from 2000 to 3100. In Puzol (the Ivanhoe Hotel near Valencia)[4] from 2500 to 4125. In every case, the prices are up by a minimum of 50%, and in Santiago by almost 175%. This means that on room charges alone (without taking into account the cost of food, drink, and petrol), our fortnight's pilgrimage will cost 250 pounds more than we planned, PLUS the extra 100 pounds rent on the Mojácar villa, PLUS 15% service on hotel rooms, PLUS the cost of my return journey to Mojácar (at least three or four more hotels) – and bear in mind that after my last solo driving effort and the resultant migraine (which by the way has sent me to a doctor here), I'm desperately reluctant to repeat the experience. What I'm building up to is this: oughtn't we to consider abandoning the Northern trip for another year and spend the whole month in Mojácar? How would the children feel? The weather down here would certainly be better and they'd be saved the problems of car-sickness. You and I would certainly be deprived. But perhaps you could make a contribution: I don't know your financial health at the moment.[5] Another point is that I've already paid 19,150 pesetas (=127 pounds) deposit on certain of the Northern hotels, but if I knew quickly that we were going to cancel, I think I could get most of it back.

Do please give this urgent thought and let me know how you feel. If you think the cancellation would shatter the children, then of course we must go ahead as planned. Au contraire, Mojácar has a lot to offer them – added to which there's a spare double room that could shelter a couple of friends (ours or theirs).

Please drop everything and ponder hard and write or cable urgently. I still have no plans after the end of August. Have you?

In haste –
Love
Ken

P.S. N.B. on petrol: at 9 miles to the gallon, the cost of petrol was by far the biggest single element in the cost of getting from Paris to Mojácar. And don't forget I have to get the car back to Paris somehow, somewhen.

[1] Dacia Mills, KPT's London secretary.
[2] Local agent who found the villa.
[3] The Aga Khan's Costa Smeralda development in Sardinia.
[4] A huge, kitsch folly of wrought iron and red velvet called the Monte Picayo where we used to take friends as part of the elaborate joke that was Valencia.
[5] I was receiving monies for a novel and a screenplay.

To William Shawn

Almeria
June 26, 1978

Dear Mr Shawn –

A word to explain my delay in completing Mel Brooks. The idea of isolating myself to work in this remote part of Spain has temporarily backfired. The strain of driving down here from Paris (around 1600 miles, I think) with two punctures and one total breakdown en route was greater than I expected, on me as well as the car. I wrote my way to within 4000 words or so of the end and then emphysema forced me to bed for recuperation. Last week, during the day, as I slept, thieves entered my bedroom and took all my valuables – camera, gold pen, about $800 dollars in cash, and a handbag containing my passport, other personal documents, driver's license, car log-book, a sheaf of credit cards and $11,000 dollars in travellers' cheques. The Spanish police are busily investigating, but my hopes are not high. On the same day my electric typewriter – a model unknown in Spain – suddenly emitted clouds of smoke and ceased to function, owing to an ancient voltage transformer I had borrowed in the neighborhood: hence this hand-written letter. The nearest city that might be able to handle the repair job is over a hundred miles away – and spare tires for my Jaguar are unobtainable any nearer than Madrid. Finally, my wife and children arrive at the end of this week, expecting to find me with work completed and ready to spend four weeks holiday with them . . .

All of which may serve to explain why Mel Brooks is unlikely to be polished off before mid-July. I shall devote August to Louise Brooks (with whom I struck up a life-time friendship when we met in May). My apologies, and hopes that you will understand. I'll be back in the States some time in September.

Meanwhile, there is the question of my visa to re-enter the U. S. I am applying for a new British passport, but this may take a few weeks. I would be very grateful if you could ask Joe Cooper[1] (1) to inform the relevant U.S. authorities (if he thinks it necessary) that my passport has been stolen and that the replacement will not bear the number on the application, and (2) to confirm that the new visa should be issued at the U. S. Embassy in Madrid. Could he also be kind enough to drop me a line reminding me of the number of my old passport, which I have forgotten and for which – since I now have no means of identification – I am constantly being asked (by cops, credit card companies, etc.)?

Sorry to burden you and Mr. C. with all this, but I felt you were entitled to an interim report on the reasons for my long silence.

Yours sincerely,
Kenneth Tynan

P. S. Incidentally, Mr. Cooper might also let me know whether the visa application has been granted.

[1] Of the *New Yorker*.

To Louise Brooks

[Telegram]

[Madrid]
14 August 1978

HAVE BEEN ROBBED AGAIN[1] IN STREETS OF MADRID STOP EVERY-THING HAS GONE PASSPORT TRAVELLERS CHEQUES CREDIT CARDS THOUSAND DOLLARS CASH STOP RETURNING STATES TOMORROW

TEMPORARY ADDRESS C/O AXELROD[2] 8341 SUNSET BOULEVARD
HOLLYWOOD CALIFORNIA 90028 PLEASE LIGHT ALL AVAILABLE
CANDLES STOP DIARY CONTAINING YOUR PHONE NUMBER ALSO
STOLEN LOVE KEN

[1] As KPT left Valentin's restaurant in Madrid, a young Spaniard sprinted past him and snatched his new handbag. He gave chase but tripped over a kerb, badly cutting both knees. Once more he was forced into a bureaucratic nightmare, with the added disadvantage, he noted, that people to whom he applied for refunds were 'reluctant to believe that lightning could have struck twice within such a short time'.

[2] KPT returned to Los Angeles alone while I – on a work project – took the children to Cuba.

To Roxana Tynan

[9454 Lloydcrest Drive
Beverly Hills, Cal. 90210][1]
14 September 1978

TO ROXANA AT ELEVEN

+   +

LIFT YOUR GLASSES HIGH AS HEAVEN –
MISS ROXANA IS ELEVEN!
BRIGHT AS BUTTON, GAY AS BEE,
MOST NICE THINGS A GIRL SHOULD BE:
PRETTY AS A POT OF PAINT,
SHE SAYS 'ISN'T', NEVER 'AIN'T';
WORKS WITH DEDICATED ZEAL,
DIVES AS SLEEKLY AS A SEAL;
YES, I WOULDN'T BE SURPRISED
IF SHE GREW UP CIVILISED.

*   *

NOW, LIKE EVERY OTHER DAUGHTER
OF HER AGE, SHE'S ON THE BORDER –
LEAVING CHILDHOOD'S NURSERY
FOR THE REALMS OF PUBERTY,
WHERE THE SHADOWS SEEM MUCH LONGER
BUT THE SUNLIGHT IS FAR STRONGER.

*   *

ALL I WISH YOU, DARLING ROX,
FROM MY LITTLE MAGIC BOX,
IS THE POISE OF A ROLLS-ROYCE
AND THE WIT OF HEPBURN'S VOICE,
PLUS THE VISION OF KING ARTHUR
AND THE WISDOM OF SIDDHARTHA
(WHICH, YOU'LL FIND, IS JUST ANUDDER
NAME FOR HIM WE CALL THE BUDDHA):
AND THE VALOUR OF SAINT JOAN,
SERVING GODS THAT ARE YOUR OWN
(DON'T STARE ALWAYS AT THE STEEPLE –
LOOK INSIDE AND SERVE THE PEOPLE);
NEXT, THOUGH YOU MAY THINK THIS IS SILLY,
BE AS LOONIE AS BEA LILLIE
(WHICH, AS I'LL EXPLAIN TO YOU,
IS QUITE DIFFICULT TO DO),
AND, UNLESS IT'S TOO MUCH BOTHER,
BE AS LOVING AS YOUR MOTHER
LASTLY: SHOW COMPASSION,
   EVEN TO A BADDIE –
NEVER KICK SAND
   UPON YOUR LOVING DADDY
      X   X   X
      X   X   X
      X   X   X
      X   X

[1] We were now renting the Beverly Hills house of Joan and George Axelrod.

To Louise Brooks

9454 Lloydcrest Drive
October 9 [1978]

Cara Luisa –
   My wife, who is bowled over with delight by your reaction to
'Agatha',[1] has released from her private collection the enclosed two
rather seedy pictures of me. She insists on hanging on to every shot of
which she doesn't have a copy, and these were all I could prise out of

her grasp. Note the stricken, saintly look, emphasised by the beard, acquired in Spain but removed this morning because I felt it made me look too wise. The girl with me in the monochrome pic is my daughter Roxana.

I hope by the time you get this that I shall have received your definite acceptance of our invitation to California.[2]

Still a non-smoker but also, alas, a non-worker, I remain

Your devoted
Ken

[1] A speculative fiction based on the eleven-day disappearance of Agatha Christie in 1926 (1978).
[2] Brooks would not accept our invitation. She wanted 'to talk and laugh and look at Hollywood again', but could not face the journey.

To Patrick Kernon[1]

9454 Lloydcrest Drive
November 2, 1978

Dear Pat:

Thank you for your letter of October 26. At present my tentative plan is to return to England for part of the summer of 1979. I have two reasons for doing so – (a) to visit my daughter, who will be going to school in England, and (b) to receive treatment for my emphysema. Unfortunately, my lung condition has been deteriorating lately (I now wear a mobile oxygen unit) and my doctors here feel that I should be placed under observation by specialists at the Brompton Hospital, where the most advanced work on lung diseases is being done. I can of course support this claim with a letter from my physician.

Articles bearing my name will probably appear in The New Yorker during my stay in England, some of them profiles of English people, but these would have been written prior to my arrival in the country.

Does it seem to you – as it does to me – that the above circumstances would absolve me from U.K. tax liability?

My long-term plan, I think, is to remain in the States and make occasional trips to England. Whether it would be worthwhile to incorporate myself, I am not sure. The impairment of my health has meant a reduction of my working capacity and, consequently, my income.

How much would I have to earn for there to be any advantage in becoming a corporation? [...]

                                                              [Ken]

---

[1] KPT's London accountant.

To Joseph Heller

9454 Lloydcrest Drive
November 14, 1978

Dear Joe –

Thanks for liking my piece on Mel [Brooks] and for depriving me of two working days while I devoured <u>Good as Gold</u>.[1] Talk about savage indignation: Swift was a beginner in this department compared to you. It's a howl of laughter and of despair, often within the same sentence. The Kissinger diatribes[2] are some of the most demolishing invective I've ever read: after that torrent of abuse he will surely have to prove Mel's point that Jews sometimes do commit suicide. It could be argued that your book contains such a repulsive gallery of Jewish characters that it almost makes anti-Semitism seem obligatory. Even so, what an achievement and what virtuosity!

I could carp, and I will, as ornamentally as I can. A few queries remain to bother me:

(1) Why are all these grown people so shit-scared of the old man? This seems barely credible to a European goy like me.

(2) Why do you drop a hint that Gold may be Conover's bastard, and never refer to it again? Or have I misunderstood?

(3) When Gold seriously believes Ralph's hint that he may be offered the State Department, you modulate irrevocably from realism into fantasy, and Gold tends to become a puppet whom we can no longer take quite seriously ourselves. What follows is no less funny or brilliant, but we're less involved.

(4) I don't think you gain anything by the paragraph on p. 302 in which you speak in the first person as the author. It sounds almost apologetic – as if you were saying to the reader: 'In case you think I'm treating my characters as puppets, I admit it – and it's intentional.'

Carping concluded. Congratulations reiterated. You've written one of the most subversive books I've read for ages. The passage on pp.318–319 alone is enough to get you deported.

Bless you for letting me see it.

Yours,
Ken[3]

[1] Published in 1979; Heller had sent KPT a proof copy.
[2] The novel is about a university professor named Gold who plans to write a book on Henry Kissinger (National Security Adviser and Secretary of State to Presidents Nixon and Ford), whom he despises as a Jew who does not allow his Jewishness to affect him in public life: 'Kissinger urged sending B52s against Cambodia, supported dictatorships in Chile, Greece, and the Phillippines, was dedicated to the perpetuation of racist minority rule in Africa, and contributed to the re-election of Richard Nixon. He had been kissed on the face by an Arab who detested Jews and handed a flower by the Chancellor of West Germany. Gold had a title he liked. He would call his book "The Little Prussian".'
[3] Heller replied (10 December 1978), 'Your carping was really so small that it really is carping. There are bigger holes ... that I can point out – but won't.'

To Louise Brooks

[Telegram]

[Beverly Hills]
13 November 1978

LIEBE LOUISE
UPON MY KNEES
WITH LOVE I HAVE COLLAPSED
I WISH YOU HAPPY BIRTHDAY PLEASE
YOURS TRULY GEORGIE PABST
KT

To Laurence Olivier

9454 Lloydcrest Drive
November 30, 1978

Dear Larry:
You may have been wondering (or again, you may not) what happened to the New Yorker profile I was writing about you.

The answer is twofold. Firstly, my bloody chest disease has slowed my work down rather more than I expected. And secondly, the piece itself is turning out to be much longer than I expected. So long, in fact, that I hope to publish it – in expanded form, of course – as a book when 'The New Yorker' have finished with it. There's nothing I'd rather write, and although it won't be the authorized biography or anything as impressive as that, it might be quite a nice little monument.

I'm coming to London for a couple of months in April to do some additional research. If you're going to be there, I'd love the chance of getting together for a chat.

Meanwhile, all my love to Joan and yourself.

Ever,
[Ken]

To Irwin Shaw

9454 Lloydcrest Drive
December 21, 1978

Dear Irwin:

I have just read 'Two Weeks in Another Town' for the first time, and I thought I'd let you know how enormously I enjoyed it. (This is not a Christmas present: the season is a coincidence.) For some reason I missed it when it came out, but I got the impression that some people did not rank it with your best work. Tant pis for some people. If they were right, then it has certainly improved with time. (There are books that do that, have you noticed?) The portrait of Rome is extraordinary and total; the gallery of characters really does represent a whole epoch; and there are very few novelists active today who could handle a crowd scene in the way you handle, for example, the Holts' party.

Critics are always saying of American writers that they are tough on the surface but soft underneath. I find you the opposite. The style is often lyrical (and at times, shall we say, even rhetorical?) but beneath it there's rock.

I was thinking the other day of how long we have known each other. Do you realize we are on the brink of being very old friends?

Happy New Year.

Love
[Ken][1]

[1] Shaw wrote a grateful letter back (29 December 1978), saying that he believed *Two Weeks in Another Town* (1960) 'is the best writing I've done in the novel form', and adding, 'We have been friends for a long time and it has been too bad that we've ... seen each other so little in recent years. I miss the good old days, the Basque Coast, Spain and London.'

To Michael Korda[1]#

[9454 Lloydcrest Drive]
[?early March 1979]

Dear Michael

Thanks for your February 27 letter. I'm not quite sure that I agree with you about removing dates. In fact, I like to go out of my way to anchor my pieces in historical realities, and dates help to do this. Why, for example, conceal the fact that Richardson opened in a Pinter play on December 19, 1976? And my piece on Carson deals with the man as he was in 1977 – he may be very different now. The usual practice, when reprinting essays of this kind, is to put the date of publication in parentheses at the end of each piece; and, if you approve, I'd like to do the same in this collection.

Obviously, to avoid confusion, one would want to replace phrases like 'last year' with the precise year in question.

As for the title: isn't 'Show Biz' a little <u>too</u> ambitious? It sounds as if the book is going to be a survey of the whole show business scene, which will be very misleading. How about 'Show People',[2] with your excellent subtitle 'Profiles in Entertainment'?

All my best,
Yours,
[Kenneth Tynan]

[1] KPT's editor at Simon and Schuster for a collection of his *New Yorker* profiles.
[2] Published in 1980 by Simon and Schuster in the US, Weidenfeld and Nicolson in the UK.

To Michael Korda#

[9454 Lloydcrest Drive]
[? April 1979]

Dear Michael,

I opened 'Charmed Lives'[1] and suddenly lost two days out of my life. It really is fascinating; although even you cannot quite manage to explain how Alex[2] walked the tightrope of bankruptcy with a yacht in one hand and a penthouse at Claridges' in the other, you come much closer than I'd have thought possible. This will be your 'Private Life of Alexander the Great' and will do for you [what] 'The Private Life of Henry VIII'[3] did for Alex. There were odd moments when one tended to gag on the glittering details of conspicuous consumption; and there may be a little too much about your school days and military service; but apart from these small carpings I would not have wished the book a page shorter.

Need I add: congratulations? My only regret is that I can't praise the book publicly, since it would look like an author scratching his publisher's back.

Incidentally, who was the American comedian with whom Larry Olivier was rumoured to have had a queer affair?[4] This was news to me. Isn't it also rather libelous? I remember Larry telling me that the only thing that would drive him to bring a libel action would be any suggestion that he was homosexual.

I leave for London in May to start serious research on our book.[5] Hope to be back in September. Meanwhile, renewed felicitations.

Yours
[Ken]

[1] Michael Korda's autobiographical book (sent to KPT in proof) about his father and his two uncles, *Charmed Lives: A Family Romance* (1980).
[2] Michael Korda's uncle Sir Alexander Korda (1893–1956), Hungarian film director and producer who settled in England in the early 1930s, where he founded 'London Films', the company responsible for classics such as *The Thief of Bagdad* (UK, 1940) and *That Hamilton Woman* (US, 1941).
[3] *The Private Life of Henry VIII* (UK, 1933), directed by Korda, with Charles Laughton in the title role.
[4] Rumour had it that Olivier had an affair with Danny Kaye – a rumour discounted by anyone close to Olivier.
[5] KPT had signed a contract with Simon and Schuster (January, 1979) to write a biography of Laurence Olivier. KPT received $60,000 as an advance and $30,000 for research.

To Laurence Olivier

1500 Stone Canyon Rd
Los Angeles
CA 90024[1]
April 2, 1979

Dear Larry;
I understand from Laurie E.[2] that you were upset by that New

York Times piece.[3] (I didn't see it in the 'Daily Mail', but I can imagine how those malignant idiots handled it.) This is to tell you how much I hope that you won't let this unpleasant experience poison your mind against <u>all</u> attempts to capture you in print. I also hope you are in no doubt about my good intentions. It was seeing you in those Old Vic seasons at the end of the war that convinced me that I wanted nothing more passionately than to write about the theatre. The book I have in mind will be a belated act of thanksgiving.

Moreover, it will make no attempt to be an 'authorized biography'. It will deal almost exclusively with your post-war career – with the years since I sat in the gallery of the New Theatre and first heard you say 'Now is the winter of our discontent ...' A fellow-critic came up to me after the premiere of 'A Little Romance'[4] and said: 'I hear you're writing a book on him. I just wanted to say that you on Olivier sounds like a literary marriage made in heaven.' I would probably have shed a grateful tear if I hadn't been crying already at that outrageously touching movie.

I know you look back with something less than rapture on the ten years at the National. For me, they were a golden time and I shall always be proud of whatever small contribution I may have made to their success. As you know, of course, they did not make me (or any of us) rich. My health has not been exactly radiant in these past few years, and I doubt if I have the stamina left for more than one full-length book. I was thrilled when my publishers agreed that you would be the ideal subject for it. You may have read newspaper reports about the amount of cash involved. They were past [*sic*] about, I suspect, by my agent, and are much exaggerated. In addition, the money is payable over a period of five years, and if I fail to deliver an <u>acceptable</u> manuscript within three years, the entire advance must be repaid. If I die before that time, the contract demands that my wife must repay it.

And that's enough appealing for your sympathy. The point of this letter is to say that I am not in the business of scavenging for gossip, that I'm writing a personal memoir that won't compare with any autobiography you may be planning, and that I want to see you and talk to you in the same spirit as a sculptor meets the man whose head he is modelling.

In short (a) may I phone and hope for a meeting before you go back to London? and (b) I'll be in London myself from May 15 onwards – will you be accessible by then?

Meanwhile, all my <u>hommages</u> and love to Joan.

Yours,
[Ken]

[1] We moved in February 1979 to a clapboard house deep in Stone Canyon, Bel Air.
[2] Laurence Evans, Olivier's agent.
[3] In 'Talking with Olivier' by Curtis Bill Pepper (*New York Times* magazine, 25 March 1979), Olivier spoke about why he left Vivien Leigh: 'I was afraid of killing her. I nearly did once.' He regretted he had given the interview.
[4] *A Little Romance* (US, 1979), directed by George Roy Hill and starring Olivier.

To Joan Plowright

1500 Stone Canyon Road
April 3, 1979

Dear Joan

I'm taking the liberty of enclosing a copy of a letter I sent to Larry yesterday here in Hollywood. He called me about an hour ago with the rather shattering news that he didn't intend to cooperate with me in any way. He added that he would also recommend his friends and associates not to see me.

The consequences of this for Kathleen and me could be highly damaging. Nearly three years ago I had a long meeting with Larry at which I told him I wanted to write a series of long pieces about him for 'The New Yorker'. To my great relief, he gave the project his full blessing. A year or so ago, I interviewed him over lunch at the Bel Air Hotel, and he could not have been more helpful.

He now says that a series of magazine articles are not the same as a book. At 'The New Yorker', in point of fact, they are. A three-part New Yorker profile is a book-length manuscript, and almost every week a book is published that started life in this way. After a lot of legal effort I have managed to extricate myself from other plans I had made for other projects with other publishers. Now, just as I have got decks cleared for the next three years, I am faced with this sudden and chilling change of heart.

I am writing to you, an old friend, for advice. I gave Larry ten years of my life.¹ What else do I have to do to make him trust me? Have you any suggestions?

Yours ever,
[Ken]

P. S. As I told Larry, I'll be back in England on May 15. Are you going back into 'Filumena'?² It would be nice to meet for a drink.

---

¹ KPT was Literary Manager 1963–9, Literary Consultant 1970–3.
² *Filumena Marturano* by Eduardo de Filippo (1946).

To Louise Brooks

1500 Stone Canyon Road
April 5, 1979

Dearest Louise,

Here it is at last, and at great length, and with love.¹

I am praying that you will like it, and that you will try (since I am a sensitive soul) to confine your negative comments to really gross factual errors. (I absolutely hate rewriting – almost as much as I dislike writing.)

Whatever your reactions are,² do please call me as soon as you can. I cannot go around indefinitely with my fingers crossed.

I am convinced there is nothing in the text that could possibly violate the undertaking I gave to the other gentlemen involved,³ but it would be nice to be reassured on that point, too. I know 'The New Yorker' would like to publish the piece as quickly as possible.

Blessings on you. I have not done you full justice, but – who could?

Yours ever,
Ken

---

¹ KPT's portrait of Brooks, 'The Girl in the Black Helmet', was published in the *New Yorker* on 11 June 1979.
² Brooks was very pleased with the profile but wondered whether KPT would cut her off with the end of 'Black Helmet'. KPT continued to write, which made her happy, 'Because a little piece of me and a little piece of you will always belong together'.
³ Of the Paley Foundation.

To William Shawn

1500 Stone Canyon Road
April 5, 1979

Dear Mr Shawn,

Herewith Louise Brooks, together with a summary of my expenses.

The piece is longer than we expected it to be, and there are one or two passages more sexually explicit than the magazine may care for. In their defence, I can only say that Miss B. made her name in erotic roles and that she talks about sex as openly as you or I might talk about the weather. But I await your judgment.

As you may recall, I had to agree to submit the piece to Miss B. for her approval, primarily to convince the gentleman who pays her rent that his name would not be mentioned. I am sending her a copy of the manuscript and will let you know if she has any comments.

Meanwhile I look forward to hearing yours.[1]

Yours sincerely,
Kenneth Tynan

[1] On 12 April Shawn wrote back: 'I am still bowled over.'

To Johnny Carson

[1500 Stone Canyon Road]
April 22, 1979

Dear John,

What follows is sheer impertinence on my part; all I can say in its defence is that it is well-meant. When I read in the paper that you might be quitting 'The Tonight Show' in the fall, I felt a twinge of quite definite grief, and suddenly realized how much it had meant to me, when contemplating a trip to this country, to reflect that whatever else might have dried up or degenerated, one sparkling fountainhead of pleasure would still remain – Carson at 11.30. Here at least was something I couldn't get anywhere else in the world. I cannot tell you how many bad days you have saved, and good days you have improved, by simply being there on Channel 4, doing what nobody else can do anything like as well.

And I now hear talk of Specials. Dear John, all your shows are

Specials. I hear,·too, that you are bored. Was Dickens bored after writing novels for seventeen years? Did Matisse burn his brushes after seventeen years' daubing? Did you never hear the great remark of the painter Delacroix: 'Talent does whatever it wants to do: genius only what it <u>can</u> do'? What other T.V. format would give you the freedom to improvise, to take off and fly, to plunge into the unpredictable? Carson scriptbound would be Carson strait-jacketed. We all know you are like a great dish that combines all your flavours. It resembles the pressed duck at the Tour d'Argent in Paris: the recipe hasn't changed in my lifetime, yet it tastes as inimitably fresh every time I order it.

Was it unadventurous for Astaire to stick to tap-dancing instead of venturing into ballet? On the contrary: it was brave, and it was what made him (and will keep him forever) a classic. Similarly, I honour Cary Grant for never having played 'Macbeth' and Muhammad Ali for staying out of the Wimbledon championships.

I wouldn't insult you by supposing that you haven't thought along these lines yourself. I'm sure you are convinced that there is a new Carson ready to emerge from the old and to stagger us all once again. And your track record is such that you may well be right. But I beseech you – as Oliver Cromwell said on a famous occasion[1] – to consider in the bowels of Christ whether ye may not be wrong. (I may have misquoted Cromwell but I hope ye get my drift.)

No need for a reply. This is an impulse letter that I simply had to get off my chest. In terms of entertainment, to lose Carson would be like erasing a star from the flag.

Yours sincerely
[Kenneth Tynan][2]

---

[1] Cromwell wrote to the General Assembly of the Kirk of Scotland (3 August 1650) as his English armies invaded, 'I beseech you, in the bowels of Christ, think it possible you may be mistaken.'

[2] Carson replied (9 May 1979): 'I have never received a more flattering letter in my life and you may well have helped me give a new direction to my thinking.'

To Laurence Olivier

Brompton Hospital[1]
Fulham Road
Sunday evening
[?24 May 1979]

Dear Larry –

Forgive handwriting – shaky due to illness.

I've just read – for the first time – the 'Evening News' piece on Kathleen that prompted you to cast me into the wilderness.[2]

My dearest L. – didn't you realise that it was all lies? That it was a classic bit of journalistic trouble-making? Did you seriously think that Kathleen would say you had 'chosen' me to write your 'definitive' biography – because you wanted 'the truth' to be revealed about your relationship with Vivien?? Why should she tell blatant untruths of a kind that could only damage my relationship with you?

I've just read the article over the phone to her in L.A. She, too, had never read it before and is outraged and appalled. She was in London at the behest of the company that made 'Agatha' and she talked to the 'News' man to promote the film. All she said about me was that I was working on a book about you. (As I wrote to you myself, if you remember, in a letter dated November 30, 1978.)

We were both on a motoring trip in Mexico when you blew your top, and so had no inkling of what had happened. Nor could any journalist reach us for comment. When we got back to L.A. I spent only one night before leaving for London.

On the plane I had a slight collapse (due to faulty air-compression) and had to go straight to the Brompton Hospital – knowing nothing except an L.A. rumour that you were somehow unhappy. It's only in the last few days that I've discovered what's been going on – and I had no way of contacting you, since the old phone numbers are obviously out of date.

Now I see that things are escalating. The 'Sunday Express' has got into the act, and 'Newsweek' (my American secretary tells me) has sent a man over from New York especially to write a feature on the story. A story that simply doesn't exist. That envious little prick on 'The News' must be cackling on how he fooled you – and the rest of the press.

What's to be done? I can't think of a rational solution. The Press

Council? Too ineffectual. Libel? But nobody's been libelled at any rate. Please find a moment.

Love
[Ken]³

[1] KPT was in London to research the book on Olivier, and required oxygen treatment after fainting in a bank. This was the second hospital visit since he had arrived.

[2] The gossip columnist Richard Compton Miller of the *Evening News* (2 May 1979) inaccurately reported me as saying that Olivier wanted the 'truth' about his relations with Vivien Leigh to be told.

[3] I wrote to Olivier on 29 May 1979 to tell him I had written to the editor asking 'for an immediate retraction and stating that their article was untrue, preposterous, and damaging'. Olivier wrote to KPT on 31 May 1979 admitting my reported quote 'did seem to be most unlike her'. He added: 'I may, in my own mind, have made some excuses for her presumed eccentric conduct by a natural sense of urgency she may have had to back you up in our current differences, which differences may, not unnaturally, have affected or cooled her enthusiasm for our ancient friendship and past happy associations.'

To Laurence Olivier

[Draft]¹

20 Thurloe Square
June 15th [1979]

Dear Larry –

I've postponed replying to your letter because I wanted to see if 'The Evening News' would publish a retraction of their account of what Kathleen said. I enclose a clipping from today's issue.²

Your letter dismayed me because it seemed to violate some quite basic rules about civilised behaviour between friends. E.g.: if a gossip columnist prints a damaging story about a friend of mine, and the friend assures me the story is untrue, I naturally believe him (or her) rather than the columnist. You – amazingly – appear to believe the columnist. You say that you cannot believe that a newspaper would dare to publish reported statements if they were 'all lies'. And you continue, 'I find myself unable to believe that any newspaper would deliberately and knowingly print an outright lie about a colleague. [...]' Some years ago 'Private Eye' said that I had removed my trousers in a restaurant and exposed my genitals to a 12-year-old girl.³ By your own criteria, you must believe that, too. And talking about 'reported sentences', am I asked therefore [to] believe all the remarks Miss Pepper attributed to you in the 'New York Times'?

If, as you telepathically infer, Kathleen made the alleged remarks in a state of momentary seizure or in order to 'back me up', why on earth should she say things that could only exacerbate matters?

Incidentally, the man did not even interview her. I learned from the editor of the 'Evening News' that he merely bumped into her at a discothèque and exchanged no more than a couple of sentences.

The relevant bit of my letter to you, dated November 30, 1978,[4] ran as follows: 'The piece itself (i.e. on you) is turning out to be much larger than I expected. So long, in fact, that I hope to publish it – in expanded form – as a book when 'The New Yorker' have finished with it. There's nothing I'd rather write, and although it won't be the authorised biography or anything as impressive as that, it might be quite a nice little monument.' Receiving no reply, I took your silence for consent. Only then did I enter into negotiations with a publisher. Much later came Pepper's piece, your phone call to us in Los Angeles, the 'Evening News' lies about Kathleen and your consequent statements to the press about me, coupled with your instructions to friends (of mine as well as yours) not to talk to me.

I cannot imagine why you seem so anxious to avoid being perpetuated in print by a colleague who has written about you with greater admiration than any other living critic.[5]

[signature missing]

---

[1] Though the letter that appears here is a handwritten draft, something like it was sent.

[2] In the *Evening News* of 14 June 1979, Compton Miller reported that his previous story 'seems to have provoked much anguish. Kathleen says I misquoted her [...]. Tynan tells me, "It was my idea simply to do a personal memoir: it certainly won't be the definitive biography ... and I told Sir Larry this last year." '

[3] *Private Eye* retracted the charge.

[4] Olivier claimed he never received this letter, though it is in his archive.

[5] Olivier replied (20 June 1979) in apology, saying that old as he was he did not seem yet to have 'learnt my final lesson about the monstrosities of which the press is capable'. He asked 'pardon for allowing my credulity even a short innings. The fact is I have sinned by my fault, my own fault and my own most grievous fault, and humbly ask pardon of God and of you, Father, counsel, penance and absolution. And if Kathleen should know of your first letter, my first offending reply to that and this tame reply to that one, may I ask these three of you, Mother, as well.'

KPT cabled Lazar to stop the deal; he still intended to do a profile for the *New Yorker*, but returned the advance for the biography.

To Michael Korda

1500 Stone Canyon Road
July 25, 1979

Dear Michael,

I enclose corrected proofs.[1] I particularly hope the changes in the Louise Brooks piece don't run me into too much expenditure. The point is that they were made (mainly for legal reasons) by 'The New Yorker' after the version that I sent you.

More important: the matter of the title. Having now read the thing right through, I think it's quite a substantial book, and 'Show People' seems altogether too lightweight to suit it. (It sounds like a gossipy history of vaudeville.) How do you feel about the following:

'Party of Five'
'Five in the Evening'
'Special Faces' –

or – to my mind the best of all –

'Above the Crowd'

In each case, of course, the subtitle would be 'Profiles in Entertainment', OR – and I think this is better still:

ABOVE THE CROWD

Profiles of Show People
by
Kenneth Tynan

Let me know your thoughts. From Sunday (July 29), I'm at: Mina 442, Puerto Vallarta, Jalisco, Mexico.[2] (Tel: Puerta Vallarta 21936).

All my best,
Ken[3]

---

[1] KPT wrote in the preface for his collection of five profiles on Ralph Richardson, Tom Stoppard, Johnny Carson, Mel Brooks and Louise Brooks: 'I have spent much of my life as a literary sprinter, writing thousand-word pieces of plays and movies. But I have also aspired to be a middle-distance man, and the pieces that follow are my latest efforts in this game.'
[2] KPT installed himself in a house in Puerto Vallarta, on the Pacific coast of Mexico. In August, I joined him with the children.
[3] They settled on the title *Show People*.

To Louise Brooks

Calle Mina 442
Puerto Vallarta
Jalisco
Mexico
August 25, 1979

Dear Louise –

I'm writing this at the request of Jean van der Heuvel[1] and Stephen Graham,[2] both of whom are dancing about in their impatience to acquire an option on the screen rights to Your Extraordinary Story. They urge me to urge you to urge Robbie Lantz[3] to conclude some kind of a deal while the time is ripe, and I'm bound to say I think they're right. There is a tide in the affairs of movies as of man, and if you miss the moment things are likely to languish in the doldrums for years and years – a dismal process I've seen all too often in Los Angeles since I arrived there in 1976.

You have the following propitious circumstances:

(a) two genuinely independent producers with access to genuine money, who are both passionately in love with the project and have no other commitments.

(b) the rapturous enthusiasm of a director, Mike Nichols, who would (I believe) be ideal for the job. He would make the film a celebration of you, not a maudlin threnody about the Heartbreaks of Tinseltown. Moreover, he will make you laugh. And, propitious or not, he wants me to work with him on the script. We would go to the studios with a completed package, scripted and cast, that belonged to us and not to them, and over which we would have full control. I.e. we'd be working under ideal conditions for film-making.

But this state of affairs must be caught on the wing before it flies away. Nichols has plenty of other offers, and if he is to be pinned down Stephen G. and Jean v.d.H. will have to give him assurances <u>very soon</u> that they have reached agreement with you. So could you please tell Robbie Lantz to say yes as quickly as possible? When I talked to him in Hollywood last month he said he saw no reason why a film deal shouldn't be made quite separately from a publishing contract.

Incidentally, I'm not writing to you out of self-interest – I have more than enough work already to keep me busy for the next couple of years. And you know how lazy I am.

Someone has sent me a full-length photo of you toying in profile with a rope of pearls[4] long enough to lasso a bronco. It's exquisite and quite enough to make anyone toy with themselves.

Puerto Vallarta in the steam heat of summer has poleaxed me – it's a major effort to write a letter like this. It's a giant step from 80 degrees (L.A.) to 90 (P. Vallarta) and if the humidity doesn't relent a bit I may be forced back north by Christmas.

Call me collect at any reasonable time – I'm two hours earlier than you. Tel. no.: P. Vallarta 2–19–36.

All love,
Ken[5]

[1] Daughter of the MCA founder Jules Stein.
[2] Son of Philip and Katharine Graham of the *Washington Post*.
[3] Brooks's literary agent.
[4] Portrait of Brooks by E. R. Richee, Hollywood 1928.
[5] Brooks angrily turned down KPT's offer. KPT wrote to her (24 September 1979): 'You said on the phone that I wanted to make a sexy exploitation film about you ... If anyone ought to be offended, I should think it would be me. What *does* cause the pain is your intemperate response to a well-meant letter about three well-meaning people. Of course the decision is yours. But need you have expressed it so violently?'

To Roxana Tynan

[Calle Mina 442]

POEM FOR SEPTEMBER 14, 1979

ROXANA'S TWELVE;
SO LET US SHELVE
ALL GLOOM AND TRIBULATION,
AND GREET THE DAY
WITH HIP HURRAY
AND WILDEST CELEBRATION!
MUMMY BAKES A BIRTHDAY CAKE –
MATTHEW'S TUM FORGETS TO ACHE –
AND A PURRING, LOUD AND CLEAR,
ADDING TO THE SONGS OF CHEER,
TELLS US MARSHMALLOW[1] IS NEAR.

*   *   *   *

MEANWHILE, SPARE A THOUGHT FOR ONE
WHO'S EXCLUDED FROM THE FUN,

WHO MISSES YOU AND FEELS SO SAD —
IN OTHER WORDS, YOUR POOR OLD DAD,
KNOWN FAR AND WIDE AS THE CRAZY MARTYR
WHO SITS AND SWEATS IN PUERTO VALLARTA,
WHERE ROOSTERS SERENADE THE MORN
SEVEN HOURS BEFORE IT'S DAWN.

*   *   *   *

HE SENDS YOU LOVE AND HOPES YOU EARN
ALL THE THINGS FOR WHICH YOU YEARN.
MAY YOU MOVE IN PATHS OF GRACE
WITH YOUR FRIENDS, THE HUMAN RACE.
(If you've nothing else to do,
please continue on page 2.)

MAY YOU SMILE, BUT NEVER SNEER;
GROW A MENTAL INCH EACH YEAR;
LEARN THE MIRACLES OF REASON,
AND OF EVERY CHANGING SEASON,
TRAVEL WIDELY, THINKING DEEPLY;
AND, IF POSSIBLE, LIVE CHEAPLY.
MAKE SURE WHAT YOU'RE TAUGHT IS TRUE;
DON'T TOUCH ANY DRINK THAT'S BLUE;
AND ABOVE ALL, DARLING, NEVER
BE ASHAMED OF BEING CLEVER.

*   *   *   *

IN MY MIND, I SEE YOU DANCE
THROUGH THE SUMMERTIME IN FRANCE
SPAIN, AND OXFORD, AND BEL AIR,
NOT FORGETTING THURLOE SQUARE,
WITH THE SUNLIGHT IN YOUR HAIR.

*   *   *   *

BEST BELOVED BALLERINA,
HERE'S A KISS FROM CALLE MINA.
          X
LOVE FROM DADDY

---

[1] Our ginger cat.

To Irving Lazar[1]

Mexico
26 September 1979

Dear Irving:

A word or two about the autobiography. I've always been a talent snob – in other words, I've always wanted to meet and know and analyze the people I admire, whether they are actors, playwrights, directors, politicians, athletes, conversationalists, or what have you. A major theme of the book will be this quest for the best in all fields; and an allied theme will be my attempts – as journalist, propagandist, and impresario – to celebrate talent and make more room in the world for it to flourish. This has involved me in almost continuous controversy since I was in my early 'teens. First as an outrageous exhibitionist at school; then as a spectacular figure in post-war Oxford; then as a fire-breathing drama critic in London and New York; then as Head of the Script Department at Ealing Films; then as a sexual crusader in 'Oh! Calcutta!'; then as grey eminence to Laurence Olivier for ten years with Britain's National Theatre. And always as a tireless pleasure-seeker – through travel, sex, food and drink, as well as the arts.

I shall be writing about many friends, including those who for one reason or another have turned into enemies. The cast-list will include: Marlene Dietrich. Laurence Olivier and Vivien Leigh. Norman Mailer. Gore Vidal. Ernest Hemingway. Roman Polanski. John Huston. Richard Burton and Elizabeth Taylor. Marlon Brando. Mike Nichols. Dick Avedon.[2] Miles Davis. Christopher Isherwood. Gene Kelly. John Lennon. Ava Gardner. Sam Spiegel. C. S. Lewis. Hugh Hefner. John Osborne. James Jones. Bertolt Brecht. Harold Pinter. Irwin Shaw. Peter O'Toole. Elia Kazan. Orson Welles. Princess Margaret and Tony Snowdon. Sue Mengers.[3] Tennessee Williams. Lena Horne.[4] Betty Bacall.[5] James Thurber. Kingsley Amis.[6] Phil Silvers. Jonathan Miller. Alec Guinness. Arthur Schlesinger Jr.[7] Allen Ginsberg.[8] Peter Brook. Jack Benny. Cecil Beaton. Antonio Ordóñez. Groucho Marx. Joshua Logan. Stephen Sondheim. Germaine Greer. Paul Getty Jr. Jessica Mitford.[9] Lord Harlech.[10] Lillian Hellman.[11] Leonard Bernstein. Adolph Green and Betty Comden.[12] Vanessa Redgrave. Laurence Harvey.[13] Paul Newman. Alger Hiss. Mort Sahl.[14] Lenny Bruce. Franco Zeffirelli. Shirley MacLaine. Louise Brooks. Lord Harewood. Joseph Heller. Robert Graves. William Shawn. Terence Rattigan. Fidel Castro. Thornton Wilder. Mary McCarthy. George Plimpton.[15] Maurice Chevalier. John Gielgud. Albert Finney. Peter Hall. Terry Southern.

Peter Shaffer. Jerome Robbins. Coral Browne and Vincent Price.[16]
Beatrice Lillie. Robert Morley. Britt Ekland.[17] James Baldwin.[18]
Kenneth Clark.[19] Rex Harrison. Janet Flanner. Jules Feiffer. Sidney
Lumet.[20] David Merrick.[21] Edna O'Brien. Maggie Smith. S.J. Per-
elman. Stephen Spender. Robert Shaw.[22] Peter Sellers. Tom Stoppard.
Michelangelo Antonioni.[23] Simone Signoret.[24] Peter Ustinov.[25]
    And thousands more.
    Will this do to be going on with?[26]

Love
[Ken]

[1] A letter intended as ammunition in selling the rights to an autobiography.
[2] Richard Avedon (b. 1923), American photographer whose books include *Observations* (text by
Truman Capote, 1959) and *Nothing Personal* (text by James Baldwin, 1964).
[3] Witty and original Hollywood agent.
[4] Lena Horne (b. 1917), American singer and actress, the first black performer to sign a long-
term contract with a major Hollywood studio, star of *Stormy Weather* (US, 1943) and *The Wiz*
(US, 1978).
[5] Lauren Bacall (b. 1924), American film actress and author. She made her debut in *To Have and
To Have Not* (US, 1944) with Humphrey Bogart, whom she married the following year.
[6] Sir Kingsley Amis (b. 1922), English novelist and poet best known for his first novel *Lucky Jim*
(1954).
[7] Arthur Schlesinger Jr. (b. 1917), American historian, special assistant to President Kennedy
1961–3, and Pulitzer Prize-winning author of *The Age of Jackson* (1945), *A Thousand Days* (1965)
and *The Disuniting of America* (1991).
[8] Allen Ginsberg (b. 1926), American 'Beat' poet.
[9] Jessica Mitford (b. 1917), English writer, one of the Mitford sisters, whose work includes *Hons
and Rebels* (1960) and *The American Way of Death* (1963).
[10] William David Ormsby-Gore, 5th Baron Harlech (1918–85), Minister of State for Foreign
Affairs 1957–61, British ambassador in Washington 1961–5, president of the British Board of
Film Censors 1965–85.
[11] Lillian Hellman (1907–84), American playwright whose work includes *The Children's Hour*
(1934), *The Little Foxes* (1939), and *Toys in the Attic* (1960).
[12] Betty Comden (b. 1919), began her career in a cabaret act called *The Revuers* with Adolph
Green and Judy Holliday. In collaboration with Adolph Green, she wrote the book and lyrics for
musicals such as *On The Town* (1944), *Bells are Ringing* (1956), *Applause* (1970); and the screenplay
and lyrics for *Singin' in the Rain* (US, 1952), *The Band Wagon* (US, 1953) and *Auntie Mame* (US,
1958).
[13] Laurence Harvey (1928–73), Lithuanian-born screen actor who starred in the British films
Room at the Top (1958), and *Darling* (1965) and whose Hollywood career began in 1960 with *The
Alamo*.
[14] Mort Sahl (b. 1926), Canadian actor, satirist and comedian.
[15] George Plimpton (b. 1927), American writer (*Out of my League*, 1961; *Shadow Box*, 1977) and
editor of the *Paris Review*.
[16] Coral Browne (1913–91), Australian-born actress, star of *An Englishman Abroad* (BBC, 1983),
wife of the American horror-movie actor Vincent Price (1911–93).
[17] Britt Ekland (b. 1942), Swedish model and actress, one-time wife of Peter Sellers.

[18] James Baldwin (1924–87), black American writer, author of *Go Tell It On the Mountain* (1953), *Another Country* (1963) and *Just Above my Head* (1979).

[19] Lord Clark (1903–83), English art historian and creator of the television series *Civilisation*.

[20] Sidney Lumet (b. 1924), American director whose films include *Twelve Angry Men* (US, 1957), *Serpico* (US, 1973), and *Network* (US, 1976).

[21] David Merrick (b. 1912), American theatre impresario who produced *The Matchmaker* (1955), *The Entertainer* (1958), *Hello, Dolly!* (1964), *Promises, Promises* (1968), *Travesties* (1975).

[22] Robert Shaw (1927–78), Irish actor whose films include *A Man for All Seasons* (UK, 1966), *The Sting* (US, 1973), and *Jaws* (US, 1975).

[23] Michelangelo Antonioni (b. 1912), Italian film director whose films include *L'Avventura* (Italy/France 1959), *La Notte* (Italy/France 1961), and *Blow-Up* (UK, 1967).

[24] Simone Signoret (1921–85), French actress who won an Academy Award for her performance in *Room At the Top* (UK, 1958).

[25] Sir Peter Ustinov (b. 1921), British actor, dramatist and wit, whose plays include *The Love of Four Colonels* (1951) and *Romanoff and Juliet* (1956).

[26] Contracts for the book were signed with Lippincott and Crowell in the US, and in the UK with Weidenfeld and Nicolson.

To Betty Comden

1500 Stone Canyon Road
November 4, 1979.

Dear Betty,

Kathleen just called me with the news about Steve.[1] I'd been away in Mexico for a while and didn't know. It's as if a foundation stone has been removed from all our lives. I never knew a man who combined such rock-like trustworthiness with such gentleness and compassion. Whenever we met, he would be asking about my problems, my excitements, my tribulations, always responding and recording and remembering. And never a word about his. In any situation, he would have had my absolute faith. All sorts of knightly words like honour and tenderness march into my mind when I think of him. He should be buried in a cathedral with his arms folded across his sword. And such courteous, appreciative eyes. I'm proud to have known him, and happy that you spent so many years together. Across the continent I hug you and share your sadness. I don't expect to be in New York in the immediate future, but if you are this way, please stay with us for an evening of shameless reminiscence.

I love you dearly.

Ever,
Ken

[1] Steve Kyle, Comden's husband, had recently died.

To Grant Ujifusa[1#]

[1500, Stone Canyon Road]
[November/December 1979]

Dear [Mr] Ujifusa,

As I told you on the phone, I have now [had] time to read more than half of the collection of suicide notes,[2] and I find them haunting and extremely moving. In an anthology called 'Texts and Pretexts',[3] Aldous Huxley quoted a suicide note left by a young English worker, and said it did not look out of place among the excerpts from the classics that made up most of the book; and I would say the same of many of these letters. They're all messages from the extreme edge of human experience, and as such they cannot fail to be of interest to students of mankind as well as of literature. What is remarkable about many of them is the lack of hysteria or vengefulness; a high proportion of them are benevolent in tone and disturbingly persuasive in argument. If I were editing them, I would cut out some of the religiosity which occupies too much space; but I'm sure that you could not be accused of exploitation or sensationalism. You respect the anonymity of the dead; you give us no grisly details; and, after all, the act of suicide is a central part of stoicism, a highly respectable philosophy which teaches that it is a man's duty to choose the moment and the means of his own death, rather than leaving it to nature or to other men.

It might be a good idea to classify the letters in some way – perhaps according to age groups or something. And it would certainly help to set the right tone if you commissioned an introduction of three thousand words or so from some respected writer. Norman Mailer is a name that suggests itself; so does that of Graham Greene,[4] who experimented with suicide in his early years.

To sum up, the material is fascinating and I promise to order the book as soon as it is announced.[5]

Yours sincerely,
[Kenneth Tynan]

[1] An editor at Random House.
[2] Ujifusa had solicited KPT's opinion as to whether or not such a book should be published.
[3] An anthology of his favourite writing (1932).
[4] In the first volume of his autobiography, *A Sort of Life* (1971), Greene gives an account of his fascination for Russian roulette.
[5] The book was never published.

To Adrian and Celia Mitchell[1]

1500 Stone Canyon Road
February 2, 1980

Dear Adrian and Celia –

I've been living and trying to work in Mexico since last autumn and didn't get your letter till I got back here last week. Life in Puerto Vallarta (where they made 'Night of the Iguana'[2]) is perfect in the winter for my wonky chest – 80 degrees every day, low humidity, low rents – but the drinking water is otter-coloured and it's hard to type in the toilet all day. Yes, the food defeated me: my stomach is still in the intensive care ward of a goat-infested clinic 'south of the border' (remember that old hit of Dame Clara Butt's?[3]), or so at least it feels. Also it's not conducive to work where everyone else is water-skiing, playing backgammon and vomiting. I lost weight and now resemble a bronzed but bloodless vampire. Women flock to me and hang their coats on me.

We shall be here until July, when we return to Thatcherland for a month or two. After that, God knows. Kathleen wants to live in New York with the children, but the winter climate there is too icy for me and I don't altogether relish her idea of banishing me to the Bahamas on my tod from October to March. Maybe we'll come back here and try to find a house where the rent isn't backbreaking: not an easy task with two children plus a nanny. I'm starting to write this autobiography, trying to walk the thin line that separates candour from self-pity, and will fit in the odd 'New Yorker' profile if I can find the energy. The children and I miss England more than Kathleen does (she wants to write more films and there are no British films): but we all miss you like mad. If you get here before mid-July we shall expect you under our roof.

I may go and live among the Calabashi Indians of Ecuador, whom I invented last month to fool a tourist in Puerto Vallarta. They live to be 106 years old in a high mountain valley where nothing grows except forests of Caramba[4] trees. They eat the bark and carve canoes out of the rest. This traditional craft has survived despite the fact that there has been no water in the valley since the neolithic era. This of course accounts for their longevity: nothing keeps you fitter than paddling a canoe on dry land.

The Cromwell Road arrangement[5] sounds ideal – please give our love to Boty[6] – and I envy you the cottage in Suffolk. Your news about the Hoagy-Bix show[7] delights me: I had heard good rumours about it and hope Tennents[8] keep their word. As you probably know, the best showcase for it in L.A. would be the opportunistic but very bright chap called Gordon Davidson.[9] Plays often start there and transplant to Broadway and it thrives on experiment. If I can help to make this connexion, let me know.

Politically things could not be more ominous than they are at the moment. You can't pick up a paper or turn on the TV without hearing some suave pundit predicting war before summer. Even the liberals are hedging their bets for fear of being dubbed unpatriotic: line up behind the President is the current watchword. The feeling is that it's about goddamn time for the World Heavyweight Championship – no more piddling little local wars, let's go for the Big One. (In a haunting editorial 'The New Yorker' pointed out that we shall not on this occasion be <u>going</u> to war: the war will come to <u>us</u>, in our baths, in our kitchens, on our way to work ...) A wildfire madness is at large when people are seriously talking about sacrificing our species in order to defend OPEC oil, which will have run out anyway in twenty or thirty years.

But I needn't tell you all this. What would you say about us all going to Australia, one of the few places on the planet that seems likely to escape fall-out? Sydney sounds awfully tempting these days.

Am pondering your Disneyland idea[10] and will let you know if I come up with any helpful thoughts. Trouble might be that picture books are wildly expensive to produce; also that the Disney people savagely resent the faintest whiff of sour comment.

Last week a book of New Yorker profiles by me called 'Show People' appeared, hailed by the best reviews I've ever had – including <u>two</u> raves in 'The New York Times'. It'll be out in England later in the year. Indeed, it would be out now except that my agent, Irving 'Swifty' Lazar, regards the English market as something on a par with Albania and therefore forgot to sell the English rights. Like most of the people (agents, lawyers, accountants, etc) I pay to work for me, he is eighty-five thousand times as rich as I am.

The children are tops – Matthew enchanting, Roxana a beautiful mind in a beautiful body. Kathleen is blossoming (working on a film script). And we smuggled two kittens in from Mexico. One has a black moustache and constantly bumps into things and therefore had to be named Clouseau. The other leaps out at him from behind doors and cupboards and is known as Keito, after Inspector Clouseau's Oriental servant.[11]

What else? Last year I met Cary Grant. Top that. Oh, and if Britain brings back compulsory military service (which the u.s. may do any day now) and you know anyone who's called up for the Navy, pass on to them the following piece of hygienic advice, which Johnny Carson has just uttered on TV as I type this: 'Refuse to accept as a bunk-mate anyone whose nickname is Fungus.'

Write again soon.

All love,
Ken
(+ Kathleen, who's in New York this week)

[1] The poet, novelist and playwright Adrian Mitchell had met his actress wife Celia when she was working on KPT's television arts programme *Tempo* (1961).
[2] Film adaptation of the Tennessee Williams play directed by John Huston (US, 1964). Huston was also living near Puerto Vallarta at this time.
[3] Dame Clara Butt (1873–1936), English contralto for whom Elgar wrote his *Sea Pictures*.
[4] A Mexican swear word.
[5] The Mitchells had moved into a new flat.
[6] Boty Goodwin (b. 1966), daughter of Clive Goodwin and Pauline Boty.
[7] *Hoagy, Bix and Wolfgang Beethoven Bunkhaus*, about Hoagy Carmichael, Bix Beiderbecke and an obscure dadaist poet they both knew, was toured by the Wakefield Tricycle Company in 1979 and produced at the King's Head Theatre in London the same year.
[8] H.M. Tennent Productions Ltd.
[9] Artistic Director of the Mark Taper Forum, part of the Los Angeles Civic Center, who did agree to stage the play.
[10] An idea, never carried out, to explore the underside of Disneyland with a photographer friend and recount their boozy adventures and revelations in a book.
[11] From *The Pink Panther* (US, 1963).

To Derek Lindsay[1#]

[1500 Stone Canyon Road]
February 5, 1980

Dear Deacon,

I have just re-read 'The Rack' and it seems to me even more impressive than when it first appeared. There were many pages so terrifying that I had to avert my eyes.

Why was it never filmed?[2] In 1958 I could imagine the English-speaking film industry finding it too depressing, but I'm certain it could be made quite uncompromisingly now. (Possibly by Milos Forman, who directed 'One Flew Over the Cuckoo's Nest', but there are others worth considering.) Since I live here at the moment, would you mind if I passed it around?

Do let me know how you feel. Among much else, I'd forgotten how funny the funny bits are.

Yours,
[Ken]

---

[1] See letter of 5 July 1946.
[2] While he was living in Puerto Vallarta KPT talked at length about *The Rack* to John Huston, who worked on the project for two years. It has not yet been filmed.

To Pauline Whittle[1]

1500 Stone Canyon Road
March 14, 1980

Dear Paul,

Received letter and pictures, both wonderful. Where were they taken, by the way?

I was fascinated to hear about your unorthodox married life. I wish I'd known you were in California so recently – why didn't we meet?

I was hoping to lure you away from the BBC to do research for my autobiography, but I am afraid I couldn't match the salary you're currently earning. Perhaps you could give me some part-time help? Anyway, we can discuss this and other things, when I get to London in Mary or early June.

Incidentally, what is your telephone number and can you be called at home? If not, what is your office number?

All love,
Ken

---

[1] KPT had advertised in various literary magazines for information about himself for his auto-biography. Pauline Whittle Siff had written back with her memories of their friendship, and with photographs.

To Elsie Giorgi[#]

[1500 Stone Canyon Road]
[? April 1980]

Dear Elsie,

Following our phone conversation, this is to authorize you to write a description of my physical condition which I will then transmit to my lawyers in England.

I am enclosing the offending item from [the] London Daily Express[1] which is, by the way, the most widely read newspaper in the country. You will note phrases like:

'Dangerously ill', 'Has to rely on oxygen for daily survival', 'terminal', 'has only part of one lung left' etc.

Moreover I have not been spending a 'few days away on holiday', I have been working for six months in Mexico. And my mother-in-law is not flying from London especially to see me; it's part of an annual trip to see relatives in Canada.

Naturally, I don't expect you to paint a portrait of me as Tarzan, but if you could point out that emphysema can be halted, that thousands of people who suffer from it live to an advanced age, and that oxygen, which I use at night, is a quite normal part of the treatment, and that I have more than part of one lung left, it would be enormously helpful. The essential thing is to establish that I am physically capable of functioning as a writer. As I told you my English publisher,[2] after reading this report, refused to sign a contract worth $150,000, and it took me and my agent an hour on the long distance telephone to persuade him that I was not on my last legs. Your letter is crucial if I am to prove to the newspaper that my professional reputation has been damaged.[3]

Yours ever,
and God Bless,
[Ken]

[1] In the 'William Hickey' gossip column.
[2] George Weidenfeld.
[3] KPT's lawyers advised him not to sue the *Daily Express*.

To Nicholas Reed[1#]

[1500 Stone Canyon Road]
6 May 1980

Dear Mr Reed,

I have been working for the past four years in L.A. where I saw your appearance on Phil Donahue's TV show. In the past few years, suicide has claimed the lives of several of my closest friends, and I would be immensely grateful if you could tell me whether it was possible to obtain a copy of the manuscript of 'A Guide to Self-Destruction'. It would be for purely private consumption – that is to say I would not use it for journalistic purposes. I would of course be willing to pay for any postal cost involved in mailing and returning the script.

The most elegant writing I know on the subject of man's right to determine the time of his own death is contained in the philosophical works of Seneca – I am sure you know his letters to Lucillus?

I look forward to hearing from you.[2]

Yours sincerely,
[Kenneth Tynan]

[1] General Secretary of EXIT, the Society for the Right to Die with Dignity.
[2] KPT received a copy of this booklet but never opened it.

To Toody Compatello[1#]

[1500 Stone Canyon Road]
[? 7 May 1980]

Dear Toody,

Forgive me for not writing for the last two months. I've been hopping from one hospital to another[2] like a jumping bear. My last specialist even called in a psychiatrist, who listened to my tale of woe and then said he'd never heard a better argument in favour of suicide. This was not quite the advice I was expecting.

I enclose my current checking account at the Banco Industrial. It covers only dollars; I can't find the peso account. I also enclose a self explanatory letter to the manager. When you're next in the

neighbourhood, do you think you could go in and show him the letter
and the account? And let me know what happens?

Love from both of us to you
Ever
[Ken]

---

[1] KPT's secretary in Puerto Vallarta; she and her actor husband Tom, both American, became
friends and guardians to KPT.
[2] From St John's Hospital in Santa Monica to Cedars-Sinai intensive care unit in West Hollywood
to the Brotman Hospital in Culver City.

To Elaine Dundy[#]

[1500 Stone Canyon Road]
May 20th, 1980

Dear Elaine,

I read the book[1] in hospital in one long munch. It wasn't until I'd
finished that I realized what an enormous amount of research you'd
done, and how lightly you carried it off. I might give you an argument
about Finch being 'a very great actor'; but apart from that, I have
nothing but congratulations.

I liked your letter, too.[2] It was very nice to feel, after so many years,
that something like a normal relationship was being resumed. I know
what you mean about Paris and always will.

Love and thanks for everything.

[Ken]

P. S. I'll write at greater length when I am sprung from my sick bed,
which may not be for a month or more.

---

[1] Elaine Dundy, then living in London, had just finished a biography of the actor Peter Finch,
Finch, Bloody Finch (1980). She asked Tracy to deliver a copy to KPT.
[2] Elaine wrote from London (11 May 1980) reminding him of their good times in Paris 'and the
real beginning of my life'.

To Harold Hobson[1#]

[1500 Stone Canyon Road]
[? May 1980]

Dear Harold,

What a warm and welcome letter![2]

I had hoped that working in the Californian sun would miraculously revive my lungs. Alas, I was too optimistic. But I shall be out of hospital soon; the merry hum of an electric typewriter will once again be heard in the depths of Bel Air.

I was stunned to hear about Elizabeth.[3] I do not get the English newspapers here and had not heard of your loss. It is seldom that one meets a person who radiates such benevolence; to converse with her was like warming one's hands at a fire. It is at moments like this that one envies your religion.

I certainly miss our duelling days[4] – The trouble with our successors is that nothing seems <u>at stake</u> for them.

Once again, thank you for writing.

Yours ever,
[Ken]

[1] Harold Hobson (1904–92) distinguished theatre critic for the *Sunday Times*. From Oxford KPT had written to Hobson asking for his job. Quite soon after this, Hobson met the young upstart in Oxford, thought him very tall, very prescient and 'favourably resembling Jack Buchanan'. Impressed by some of KPT's undergraduate reviews, this generous critic introduced him to Mark Longman, who in turn commissioned his first book.
[2] Hobson had written from London (29 May 1980) to say he was sorry KPT had not been well, telling him that he was tremendously missed.
[3] Hobson's wife, who had died in 1979.
[4] Hobson had written: 'The great days when you and I did weekly battle over the plays – generally, indeed almost always, ending in your victory – now seem a part of some legendary Homeric past.'

To William Shawn

1500 Stone Canyon Road
May 20, 1980

Dear Mr. Shawn,

As you will probably have realized, this has not been my most productive winter. My trip to Mexico last year was not as stimulating as I expected; and since I've returned to Los Angeles at the end of

January, my lungs have been acting up, and I've been under observation at three different hospitals. Much to my relief, the doctors now think they have found a rehabilitation programme that will suit me, and I shall be embarking on it within a week or so.

All this is by the way of explaining why the Olivier profile has been delayed. The research is all there, and the piece is planned; what I need is a long period of peace in which to finish off the writing.[1] I don't know exactly when our current arrangement comes up for renewal, but I would very much like to extend it for another year. When you have a convenient moment, I would be very grateful if you could let me have your thoughts on this.

Yours ever,
Kenneth Tynan

[1] KPT organized the profile but wrote only a page or two of it.

To Matthew Tynan[1]

[1500 Stone Canyon Road]
9 June 1980

> DEAR MATTHEW, DEAR BOY,
> RELAX AND ENJOY
> THE DAY OF YOUR BIRTH.
> START YOUR TENTH YEAR ON EARTH
> WITH A WILD JUNGLE YELL
> AND A KISS FOR MICHELLE[2]
>
> WHEN YOU WERE SEVEN
> YOUR IDEA OF HEAVEN
> WAS BEING A WHIZZ AT KARATE,
> THEN YOU WERE EIGHT,
> AND YOU THOUGHT IT WAS GREAT
> TO STAY OUT ALL NIGHT AT A PARTY.
>
> NOW THAT YOU'RE NINE,
> I'M SURE YOU'LL BE FINE —

FUNNY, AND FINE, AND CLEVER –
AND I SEND YOU MY LOVE FOR EVER.

Daddy –
June, 1980[3]

[1] This was the last letter, set down in a shaky hand, that Ken wrote.
[2] Michelle Winebrenner, Matthew's nanny.
[3] The day of Matthew's birthday, William Shawn sent KPT a letter informing him that his 16 May 1979 agreement with the *New Yorker* had been extended for a year. 'I'm happy you are beginning to recover. The writing will follow.'

Ken died in St John's hospital, Santa Monica, on 26 July 1980.

BOOKS BY KENNETH TYNAN

(excluding contributions to collections)

He That Plays the King
London: Longman's, 1950

Persona Grata
London: Allan Wingate, 1953
New York: G. P. Putnam's Sons, 1954

Alec Guinness
London: Rockliff, 1953, 1961
New York: Macmillan, 1955

Bull Fever
London: Longman's, 1955, 1966
New York: Harper Bros., 1955; Atheneum, 1966

Quest for Corbett (radio play)
London: Gaberbocchus, 1960

Curtains
London: Longman's, 1961; Penguin (paperback, retitled *Tynan on Theatre*), 1964
New York: Atheneum, 1961

Tynan Right and Left
London: Longman's, 1967
New York: Atheneum, 1967

A View of the English Stage
London: Davis-Poynter, 1975; Paladin, 1976

The Sound of Two Hands Clapping
London: Jonathan Cape, 1975
New York: Holt, Rinehart and Winston, 1975; Berkley Books, 1981

Show People
London: Weidenfeld and Nicolson, 1980; Virgin (paperback), 1981

New York: Simon & Schuster, 1980; Da Capo Press, 1981

Profiles
London: Nick Hern Books, 1989
New York: HarperCollins, 1989

INDEX

NOTES: Letters are shown under correspondents' names by a bold-type **L** followed by page numbers, and after all other references except book and play titles. Short notes on individuals appear at the end of each letter, usually on the first occasion of mention, and are not signalled in the index. The suffix *n* following a page number indicates a mention only in the notes and not in the text of the letter.